The Genealogical Register

of the

Descendants of the Signers

of the

Declaration of Independence

Descendants of the Signers

of the

Declaration of Independence

Volume 7

NORTH CAROLINA, SOUTH CAROLINA
and
GEORGIA

by

The Rev. Frederick Wallace Pyne

PICTON PRESS
ROCKPORT, MAINE

First Printing June 2000

This book is available from:

PICTON PRESS
P.O. Box 250
Rockport, ME 04856-0250

Master Card/Visa Orders:
1-207-236-6565
FAX Orders 1-(207) 236-6713
e-mail: sales@pictonpress.com
Visit our Website: www.pictonpress.com

Manufactured in the United States of America
Printed on 60# acid-free paper

DEDICATION

This Volume of the Descendants of the
North Carolina, South Carolina and Georgia Signers
is dedicated to my son

STEPHEN VAN RENSSELAER PYNE

A lover of History and companion in research, life member of
The Descendants of the Signers of the
Declaration of Independence
who as a boy attended two summer "camps" at the Citadel
in Charleston, SC

TABLE of CONTENTS

TABLE of ILLUSTRATIONS

PREFACE

This is the seventh and last of a seven volume work that provides genealogical information on all known descendants of the fifty-six signers of the Declaration of Independence. Volume 7 covers the States of North Carolina, South Carolina, and Georgia, which in 1776, included essentially the bounds of the present states.

It is the intent of the author to make available **genealogical**, but **not** biographical, information on the descendants of the signers. This information is scattered about in various repositories; including libraries, some in the files of Family History Associations, some in hereditary society records (such as Daughters of the American Revolution, Sons of the American Revolution, Descendants of the Signers of the Declaration of Independence), and some in the public vital records of numerous political subdivisions. Additional genealogical data is kept by individual families in Bibles, pedigrees, Family Group Sheets or other forms and not published. But nowhere is this information collected, organized, and available in a single place. That is a major purpose of this work.

Additionally, it is hoped to rescue from oblivion or loss, many vital records of descendants that have never been used for any other genealogical purpose (such as an hereditary society), or are buried in poorly kept record books, subject to decay and destruction.

Another obvious purpose is to make available, in an easy to follow, generational form, all the known and available vital records, along with family records and information, with appropriate references to their location; for all the descendants of the signers. This approach then makes it simple and easy for an individual, believing himself to be a descendant of a Signer, to discover just how that may be so, and what the line of descent is, and references as to where the genealogical records are located that prove the statements of birth, marriage, and death that are the guts of pedigree presentation!

The Introduction discusses the background of interest, the origin of, and the history and progress of this genealogical effort. It is followed by ten (10) Chapters (one for each Signer), organized into three Books, one each for the States of North Carolina, South Carolina, and Georgia.

A work of this nature is never the product of a single individual. I acknowledge my indebtedness to the earlier work of Frank Willing Leach [1855-1943], without whose efforts this work would have no initial basis. All the photographs in this Volume, except that of the Author, were obtained through the National Park Service at the Independence National Park in Philadelphia, PA. Volunteers who helped with review, proof reading, or data gathering for this Volume 7 were: Margie Amelia Wills, Irene Weston Croft, William G. Thompson, David Walker McCullough, Henry S. Heyward, Thomas deSaussure Furman, Thomas Gailliard Heyward, Allan McAlpin Heyward, the Rev. Benjamin B. Smith, and Barbara Doyle.

Below, on this page, you will find guidance and instructions on just how you may be able to add to this body of knowledge, and how you can get yourself and your family line into future editions of this work.

HOW to CONTRIBUTE to THIS GENEALOGICAL REGISTER

Each of us owes something to those who have researched before us. For that matter, genealogically speaking, where would any of us be without all of us? It is the efforts of many that make for the genealogical fruits of all! To add your (and your family) genealogy to this work, to provide missing information, to provide better referenced information, or better vital records for existing information, please send your supported genealogical data either directly to the Author at the address below, or to the Publisher at:

PICTON PRESS
P.O. Box 250
Rockport, ME 04856-0250
1-(207) 236-6565
ATTN: Genealogical Register

3137 Periwinkle Court
Adamstown, MD 21710-3643
2 Feb 2000 (Candlemas)

HISTORICAL NOTE

Most folks are aware that the War of the Revolution first began on the small green of the Village of Lexington in Massachusetts when a Company of Militia was fired upon, spread to Concord as the British troops sought to destroy some supplies there, and American Militia followed them on a linear retreat back to Boston. This was the famous "shot heard 'round the world".

Many people are also aware that we as a nation, have a document declaring ourselves to be free and independent, absolved from all allegiance to the British Crown, and that all political connection between us and Great Britain is totally dissolved. What they are **not** aware of is that these two events (the battle on the village green and the Declaration of Independence) did not happen concurrently, or even within a few weeks of each other. They are separated by a period of more than 15 months!

Following the Battles of Lexington and Concord on 19 April 1775, and the retreat back to Boston, the British forces were loosely confined to the City by the surrounding Americans. In order to more closely contain these British troops, the Americans decided to enter the Charlestown peninsula, to erect breastworks, and to bring their artillery to play upon the City. It was thought, if effective, that this would force the British to abandon their positions as untenable, thus freeing the City from British control.

However, it was not to be. The British reaction was immediate and violent! They came out of their quarters and stormed the poorly supported American positions, ultimately defeating them and taking control of their lines. This we know as the Battle of Bunker Hill.

The Continental Congress was requested to adopt the New England Militia around Boston, to augment it with troops from other colonies, and to support it. Appointed as General of the Armies, Washington thus had to contain the enemy while at the same time he built an army. After the Breed's Hill - Bunker Hill fight on 17 Jun 1775, there was a lengthy siege by the patriot army of the City of Boston. In December 1775, COL Henry Knox loaded 59 pieces of artillery, flints, powder and ball on scows and sledges, and hauled it all over the Berkshires in his famous trek to bring these cannon from Ticonderoga to Boston.

Throughout the summer and fall of 1775 and the winter of 1775-76 this host of Americans, calling themselves an army, but mostly Massachusetts, Connecticut and New Hampshire militia who had been incorporated into the new Continental Army, kept an ever changing noose around the city that finally did result in its evacuation by the British in March of 1776. The British went to Halifax, and were reinforced by many additional troops, including rented soldiers from several of the small German states. We lump these all together as "Hessians". This action of hiring mercenaries, so incensed American sensibilities that it helped arouse in them a determination to be completely rid of the British Parliament and the British throne. With all these troops, the British were able to descend upon New York. In July 1776 General Howe had more than 310 ships in the New York harbor area and more than 30,000 troops on Staten Island.

During this time from April 1775 to July 1776 many Americans hoped for reconciliation, compromise, or peaceful resolution to the issues dividing them. As month succeeded month with no response to pleas for compromise, and as fighting and bitterness and repression continued, minds began to turn toward the heretofore unthinkable. If King and country could not be made to accommodate these colonies within a framework of brotherly understanding and the English Constitution, then perhaps the idea of "Independency" was not so terrible after all.

With the writing of Thomas Paine's *Common Sense*, and the increasing difficulty of attempting a discussion with British authorities, the stage was set for the colonies to agree that the time had come to take action more drastic than mere talk. In early June Virginia proposed a resolution recommending independence. The Congress acted upon this by forming a committee to draft a declaration to that end. The Virginia Resolution was voted upon favorably by the Congress on 2 July. The language of the Committee draft was argued and modified and fully approved on 4 July 1776. This document is the Declaration of Independence!

Thus was the birth document of this nation created! It has survived many vicissitudes and now resides under guard in a sealed glass chamber in the Archives Building in Washington, D.C. There you see the original engrossed parchment. Now badly faded, its noble words have been preserved for us and are readily available in most dictionaries, encyclopedias and American History books, and in facsimile copies.

During our centennial celebration in 1876, the popularity of the period of the Revolution and our earlier colonial period grew immensely. Many persons were interested in finding and documenting the roots of their ancestors who had served the country during these early periods. Hereditary societies by the dozens were formed in the decades following this centennial and through WWI. At the tricentennial of the founding of Jamestown, Virginia, celebrated at the Jamestown Exposition near Norfolk on 4 July 1907, numbers of the attendees found that they were also descendants of a Signer of the Declaration of Independence. There was an immediate reaction toward developing still another hereditary society, one devoted to honoring these Signers.

Following the public exercises of the day, over 150 descendants, who represented a majority of the Signers, assembled in the Pennsylvania State Building on the Exposition grounds, and an organization was effected. This new society styled itself "Descendants of the Signers of the Declaration of Independence". It is now incorporated under the laws of Washington, D.C., with an address headquarters at 1300 Locust Street, Philadelphia, Pennsylvania 19107. Any **direct lineal** descendant of a Signer is eligible to become a member.

Thank you, Dear Reader, for finding, using, contributing to, and being interested in these Descendants of the Signers of the Declaration of Independence.

The First Continental Congress met in Philadelphia at Carpenter's Hall in 1774. The Second Continental Congress met in the Pennsylvania State House. Because of its importance to the founding of the country, and the strong association it has with the Declaration of Independence, this building is now more popularly known as "Independence Hall". It is now owned and cared for by the National Park Service, which is why, when you visit this shrine of American Independence, you see Park Rangers on duty.

On the page opposite is a picture of Independence Hall. It was in this building that the delegates from all the Colonies met, argued, compromised, and finally established the United States of America!

Independence Hall

When the Second Continental Congress assembled in May 1775, we must remember that the fighting had already started in Lexington, Massachusetts the month before. For more than a year this assembly of noted delegates had a very great deal to do. There was the huge problem of creating and maintaining an army. There were multiple problems of supply, commissary, clothing, pay, and organization. They were not all solved by the stroke of a pen. Sometimes techniques would be tried that did not work, and then were approached using a different tack.

This trial and error method was further compounded by the efforts of the States to support their own local needs. The Congress formed many Committees, some for short term (ad hoc) purposes, and some for longer term continuing efforts. It was through the work of these various committees that the real business of conducting the War of the Revolution was done. Most delegates served on many committees, sometimes several at the same time.

When it finally became apparent that the Home Government in England was **not** going to accommodate themselves to any solution other than physical and political coercion, the Congress heard a resolution advocating "Independency". They then appointed a committee to draft a possible statement for use in such an eventuality. The document was presented, argued, approved, emended, and signed in the room in Independence Hall known as the Assembly Room. A picture of this Assembly Room is shown on the page opposite.

Assembly Room

Perhaps the most famous and surely the best known depiction of the Declaration of Independence is the painting by John Trumbull. However, it is **not,** as many people assume, a representation of the act of signing the document. It shows the drafting committee of five (John Adams, Benjamin Franklin, Thomas Jefferson, Robert R. Livingston, and Roger Sherman) presenting their work to the Continental Congress.

Trumbull's original 20" x 30" painting, done between 1786 and 1797, now hangs in the Trumbull Gallery at Yale. It includes 48 men, 43 of whom were signers. Most of these were taken from life portraits or paintings made by himself or others. The copy shown here was done in 1818 and enlarged to 12' x 18'. Another copy was done late in his life and was purchased by the Boston Atheneum. All the copies show the Assembly Room in which the delegates argued the merits of the document, emended it, and finally signed an engrossed copy in August of 1776. The title of the painting is "The Declaration of Independence," even though it shows little of the actual document itself. Mostly we see a grouping of men around a room listening to a presentation of some papers to a Chairman or President of the Assembly.

On the opposite page is a picture of the enlarged copy of this famous painting that belongs to the United States and hangs in the rotunda of the United States Capitol.

A numbered key is furnished to help with identification. It is printed by permission of *Linn's Stamp News* [Copyright; Sidney, OH, 1994]. The five men painted into the scene who were **not** elected Delegates and Signers of the Declaration of Independence are: 8) George Clinton, 18) Thomas Willing, 33) Robert R. Livingston, 42) Charles Thompson, 45) John Dickinson.

1. George Wyeth, 2. William Whipple, 3. Josiah Bartlett, 4. Thomas Lynch, 5. Benjamin Harrison, 6. Richard Henry Lee, 7. Samuel Adams, 8. George Clinton, 9. William Paca, 10. Samuel Chase, 11. Richard Stockton, 12. Lewis Morris, 13. William Floyd, 14. Arthur Middleton, 15. Thomas Heyward Jr., 16. Charles Carroll, 18. Thomas Willing, 19. Benjamin Rush, 20. Elbridge Gerry, 21. Robert Treat Paine, 22. William Hooper, 23. Stephen Hopkins, 24. William Ellery, 25. George Clymer, 26. Joseph Hewes, 27. George Walton, 28. James Wilson, 29. Abraham Clark, 30. Francis Hopkinson, 31. John Adams, 32. Roger Sherman, 33. Robert R. Livingston, 34. Thomas Jefferson, 35. Benjamin Franklin, 36. Thomas Nelson Jr., 37. Francis Lewis, 38. John Witherspoon, 39. Samuel Huntington, 40. William Williams, 41. Oliver Wolcott, 42. Charles Thomson, 43. John Hancock, 44. George Read, 45. John Dickinson, 46. Edward Rutledge, 47. Thomas McKean, 48. Philip Livingston.

"The Declaration of Independence" by John Trumbull

INTRODUCTION

The genesis of this work arose from a Project started twenty years ago by the Descendants of the Signers of the Declaration of Independence (DSDI). This small hereditary society had a previous Project flowing from the Bicentennial in 1976 in which members subscribed to a fund to pay for a large Bas-Relief Plaque placed in the East Entrance of the Rotunda of our Nation's Capitol.

Following the completion and dedication of that Plaque, the DSDI then found that it had no particular "focus" for its purpose in being. The "Object" of the Society, as set forth in its Constitution, includes " . . . to perpetuate the memory of those men . . . ". Since it was felt that there should always be some kind of "Project" drawing our attention to this end, a fund was included in the budget for such an item. A little later it was determined that a particularly good "Project" for our Society would be to rescue the "Leach Paper Manuscript" from oblivion.

Frank Willing Leach, born in 1855, was a gentleman of good education and position. During the centennial celebration of 1876, a very great deal of interest in the Signers of the Declaration of Independence was generated. By 1877 young Leach had been admitted to the Philadelphia Bar. He had also prepared some genealogical work on old Philadelphia families.

Because of his education, position, and genealogical experience, he was approached with a view toward compiling a genealogy of the Descendants of the Signers. He undertook this work beginning in 1885 and pursued it for a period of more than thirty years. He spent a great deal of time writing, contacting, and researching with special assistance from those persons who were second and third generation descendants of the Signers.

By the end of WWI, Leach despaired of ever completing such a huge task. The effort had consisted of much correspondence with relatives, research work, and organization of the genealogical data. **All** of his material: files, letters, papers, notes, and related articles, was stored in his summer seaside home at Tuckerton, New Jersey. He offered all this work to the Library of Congress, but it had no budget item to fund the effort.

It was then that he offered it to a hereditary society, The Descendants of the Signers of the Declaration of Independence (DSDI), formed in 1907. Since neither it, nor a companion hereditary society, The Sons of the American Revolution (SAR), could independently fund the negotiated price, Mr. R. C. Ballard Thruston of the SAR and the Filson Club agreed that he would personally advance the money if the then Secretary-General of the DSDI, John Calvert, would inspect the materials to be purchased and return a favorable report.

The inspection was made, a very favorable report was returned, and the material was purchased for the sum of $2,000 in 1922. All the material was removed to the offices of John Calvert in Philadelphia, PA. For the next six years secretaries, partly supported by funds donated by the DSDI membership, typed, re-ordered, and mounted these papers. Indexing followed, and four typed legal page size copies numbering more than 6,000 pages were produced. They were bound into 20 volumes and are officially known as the **Leach Manuscript** [hereinafter Leach MSS].

There are some gaps and incomplete lines in the Leach MSS. This is a result of his inability to communicate with, or an incomplete communication with, the relatives of the Signers to whom Leach applied for much of the information he was seeking. It is appalling how little information some people seem to have regarding their own immediate family! One still finds, in this day of computers, numbers of people who do not know about their own forebears, do not care to know, or are unwilling (for reasons this author just cannot fathom) to share information with others. Much of the research data Leach was able to get from newspapers and other printed sources of the day. Remember, there was no computer data base in those days to cross check or verify information.

The years of the Depression and WWII left little opportunity for dealing with any update, filling in, adding to, or improving the genealogical work started by Frank Willing Leach. Numerous hereditary societies having interests in the period of the American Revolution, including the Daughters of the American Revolution (DAR), the SAR, and the DSDI, are good repositories of information on the Signers. Where the applicant to one of these Societies used a Signer as the means of entrance, the application may contain very good genealogical data. In many cases, this information has been referenced in this work.

There has been a great increase of interest in genealogical pursuits within the last generation or so. That coincided with our nation's Bicentennial in 1976. That in turn, led the Board of Governors of the Descendants of the Signers of the Declaration of Independence to initiate a project that would "do something" with the Leach MSS, although just what such a project would be was not set forth. The effort did not have much push and dragged on for several years.

A genealogical software program was tried for a while, but was found to be too confining in its numbering system, and much too tedious in user friendliness, and was abandoned. Quality copies of the Leach MSS summary pages for each signer were purchased from the Filson Club, and reviewed for their genealogical, not biographical content.

Genealogical Data extracted from the Leach MSS then became the basis of the work of preparing the narrative text using the Word Perfect program. Thus was the framework created. Adding information from the applications of members of hereditary societies and a considerable amount of independent genealogical research helped to correct, to bring up to date, and to include persons not noted in Leach's work. Many compiled genealogies were consulted, and visits were made to many Genealogical Libraries, including the Family History Library in Salt Lake City, the National Genealogical Society Library, The South Carolina Historical Society in Charleston, and the John D. Rockefeller Library at Colonial Williamsburg. Individual chapters were also reviewed and supplemented by persons noted in the Preface.

The Modified Register System is used throughout this work. The Dictionary of American Biography (DAB), and Local Vital Records (VR), have been used and are noted in the references. The work in this Volume 7 has three "Books", one for each State represented in the Continental Congress. Each of these three "Books" in turn, is divided into chapters, one for each Signer, making a total of ten chapters in this Volume 7.

Additional research in Manuscript and published Genealogies of the Signers and their descendants yielded further information along some lines. Notices of "Genealogies in Progress" have helped to spread the word that data were being sought. Where it is not a duplication, any new information thus generated has been included, and its source referenced.

Frank Willing Leach

Anyone with a pretense to genealogical knowledge, working in the area of the Signers of the Declaration of Independence, cannot have gone very far in their efforts without coming across the name Frank Willing Leach and his work known as the "Leach Manuscript" [Leach MSS]. While the present work is by no means merely just an "update" of the *Leach Manuscript*, it is quite strongly indebted to his original work for its foundation. This then, is a good place to present a brief biographical sketch of Leach, and particularly the work he did for nearly a third of a century on the descendants of the Signers.

Frank Leach was the son of the Rev. Joseph Smallidge Leach and his wife Sophia Ball. He was born in Cape May, NJ on 26 Aug 1855, and died in Philadelphia, PA on 16 Feb 1943.[1][2] After attending schools in Cape May County, at age seventeen he entered into the study of Law with his brother Col. J. Granville Leach and was admitted to the bar in Philadelphia, PA on 31 Mar 1877.

Young Leach was twenty-one years old during the Nation's Centennial celebration of the Declaration of Independence held in Philadelphia in 1876. Laid out in huge sheds were many new or improved devices. Bell's new telephone was displayed, as were machines for electrical generation, and new types of printing presses. Newly printed and reissued limited numbers of recent stamps were available. Wondrous new engines of great size could be viewed. One could marvel at all the grand "progress" mankind seemed to be making. The United States of America was flexing not only it's physical, but it's social muscle. On display was the engrossed and signed copy of the Declaration of Independence.

It was quite an Exposition, including: parades, speeches, displays, fireworks. Leach was enchanted! It caught both his imagination and interest since he was enormously impressed with these signers, men who would put their lives on the line for the liberties of the people and in defense of their country.

---

[1] Autobiography, *Frank Willing Leach, a Partial Portrait*, [Wickersham Press, Lancaster, PA, 1943].
[2] *New York Times*, 17 Feb 1943, p. 21.

The Declaration of Independence is the birth document of this nation. It includes the deathless lines: "When in the course of human events, it becomes necessary for one people to dissolve the political bans which have connected them with another . . . a decent respect to the opinions of mankind requires that they should declare the causes which impel them to the separation. We hold these truths to be self-evident; that all men are created equal, that they are endowed by their creator with certain unalienable rights, that among these are life, liberty, and the pursuit of happiness. That to secure these rights, governments are instituted among men, deriving their just powers from the consent of the governed . . . "

Then there follows a list of twenty-seven "injuries and usurpations", that were a part of the fundamental differences the Colonies were having with the home government. The fifty-six heroic men who were the Signers of this noble document firmly relied upon the protection of Divine Providence, and did, "mutually pledge to each other their lives, their fortunes, and their sacred honor".

Leach was enthralled. Although he had been admitted to the Bar, he really had little interest in the legal profession. He was much more interested in literature and politics and public service.

Because of his great interest in these Signers, Leach was persuaded by Dr. Frederick D. Stone, the eminent Librarian of the Historical Society of Pennsylvania, to gather and produce something by way of genealogical information on the descendants of these famous men. This was a very natural suggestion, since Leach had already been a contributor to the genealogical column of several leading Philadelphia papers. He had also authored a number of biographical and genealogical works.

Since the Signers themselves were all deceased at the time of the Centennial Celebration, Leach looked upon this effort as a true genealogical reporting of information that he hoped to gather directly from second, third, and fourth generation descendants. He wrote to everyone whose name, connected to a signer, came into his purview. He followed up on almost all this massive correspondence. He then organized the collected material by families (not generations). Considering his numerous other activities, the wonder is that he was able to collect as much as he did!

There are four (4) sets of Leach MSS. They are located in the following Genealogical Libraries: the Filson Club, The SAR Library, the DSDI copy in the Historical Society of Pennsylvania, and John Calvert's copy also in that library. Fortunately for all researchers, the LDS Church has microfilmed the best of these copies at the Filson Club. These microfilms (six rolls) are available at the Family History Library (FHL) in Salt Lake City, and the now more than 3,200 Family History Centers (FHC) located around the world. The references for each Signer, include the FHL Film number, and the page numbers of the hard copy bound Volumes for that Signer's Leach MSS information. The Leach MSS for each Signer includes not only the summary of the data Leach had collected, but copies of the letters exchanged that form the bases for the summary.

Numbered references to all statements of birth, marriage, and death are included in each Sketch though the 19th Century. Whenever possible, the first or primary record is referenced. That, however, is not always possible, in which case, the best available source is noted. In spite of diligent searching, references to these data of Vital Records sometimes cannot be found. Because vital records of persons still alive (or presumed to be so) is difficult or legally impossible for a researcher to obtain (but easy for a family member), no references are included for those born **after** the turn into the 20th Century.

How to Find a Descendant

You must know the name of someone you believe to be a descendant. Go first to the every name Index at the back of this volume to find the name of that person. Turn to the page number for that person, and there you will find a listing, looking like this example:

618. THOMAS GAILLARD HEYWARD[7] (Gaillard Stoney Heyward[6], Daniel Hasell Heyward[5], Robert Chisolm Heyward[4], George Cuthbert Heyward[3], Thomas Heyward[2], Thomas Heyward, Jr.[1]) child of Gaillard Stoney Heyward and Lila Griffin was born in Bluffton, SC on 6 Mar 1942. He married (1st) Clare Frances WALKER in Columbia, SC on 11 Aug 1967. She was born in Shenandoah, PA on 31 Dec 1944, and died in 1991. Children:

The person you were seeking is a descendant of Thomas Heyward, Jr., as individual #618, he is the 7th generation removed from the Signer, his parents are given, as is the generational line of descent, and his children.

By looking up each of the listed names in the generational line, the page containing genealogical information is located. As you go to each page, and find the person you seek, you will quickly be able to build a pedigree chart from your ancestor Signer to you, or to build a Family Group Sheet for any generation or person you wish.

Nothing in genealogy is ever "complete". If you have a tidbit of information that helps to fill in gaps, data, persons, dates, places *please* see that it is reported for inclusion in future editions of this Register (See the Preface on "How to Contribute to This Genealogical Register").

It must be remembered that this Volume 7, and every other volume in this seven-volume Register, contains genealogical information about the **Descendants** of the Signers of the Declaration of Independence, **not** information about their ancestors. This work is a genealogical register, not a biographical essay; it contains data, not stories. Readers must recall also that uncles, aunts, brothers, sisters, or cousins are *not* descendants of the body of the Signer, and are not included. However, to make the Register as complete as possible *all* descendants, including [1] those who died either in infancy or youth before age 21 (dy); [2] those who never married (unm); and [3] those who married, but never had issue (dsp, or sp), are listed because it is deemed important to convey such information. Additional marks of child identification are: kia (killed in action), and unk (unknown), meaning nothing is known about the child beyond birth.

The Modified Register Numbering System (in which **every** person is assigned a number), and the generational presentation throughout this work should make it easy to use and easy to understand. Children are numbered and listed under their parents. Where any such child has issue, a + sign will precede the number, indicating that further genealogical information will be found with that number in the next generation. The references to the vital record information on each person, and the complete Index are particularly important aspects of this Register.

A Word about References

Both as foot notes at the bottom of pages in the Introduction, and as sources in each Chapter of this Carolina - Georgia Volume, there are references to material supporting the statements made in the text at the end of each sketch. The first numbered reference in the Sketch for the Signer at the beginning of each Chapter includes support information about that particular Signer. Books or Genealogical Journal Articles concerning the ancestry, a biography, and sometimes the family of that Signer are noted. In that same numbered reference you will find the Family History Library (FHL) film number pages for the Leach MSS microfilm of the Signer. You will also find the location in the Dictionary of American Biography (DAB) for a brief biographical write-up for each Signer. Except when an individual has held high national office (President, VP, MC, Cabinet Office), you will find **no** biographical notes in the sketches for descendants; this is a **Genealogical** Register.

In addition to this first numbered reference, other helps in support of the genealogy of the Descendants of a Signer are found in the remaining numbered References and may include: the Vital Records (VR) of many places for statements of birth, marriage, and death; newspaper notices such as obituaries, social notes of marriage or birth, wills; and Compiled Genealogies, Registers, or Lists of descendants of a Signer or his ancestor, sometimes maintained by Family Associations. Notes may also be found included in these references, more fully explaining the background, caution in use, or limitation of a source.

Some repositories of Vital Records have restrictive rules regarding the availability of their records. This is especially true of birth records for more recent years. If a person is still likely to be alive, obtaining official documentation information about his date and place of birth is difficult, and VR for persons born after 1900 are, for that reason, no longer provided.

Where the reference lists an Hereditary Society application number as a source, that application contains (or the file for that application contains) vital record data documenting statements. These applications frequently have original material that was submitted by the applicant to prove descent. Copies of the DAR and the SAR application may be obtained from their respective HQ for a small fee:

Daughters of the American Revolution
1776 "D" Street
Washington, DC 20006

Sons of the American Revolution
1000 South Fourth Street
Louisville, KY 40203

Applications from the DSDI are more difficult to obtain, because that Society does not yet have a similar system. One must apply to the Registrar-General of the DSDI, Inc. and request a copy of a named member or a numbered application. Bound volumes of the records of the Registrar-General of the Descendants of the Signers of the Declaration of Independence are kept at:

> The Historical Society of Pennsylvania
> 1300 Locust Street
> Philadelphia, PA 19107

NORTH CAROLINA

The Roanoke Voyages of the mid 1580s attempted to create a settlement on the North Carolina Coast, without success. Several incursions into the area of Albemarle Sound were made by settlers from Virginia in the 1650's. But it was not until the Charters of Carolina [1663 & 1665] that a formal setting aside of what would include the future Colony became established by King Charles II. The Province thus created was so large, and distances so great between settlements in the northern and southern parts, that a government was set up for each.

The second Charter of 10 Jul 1665 fixed what became the northern boundary of North Carolina at "the north end of Currituck Inlet" at about 36^0 30' north latitude.[1] Albemarle, known after 1691 as North Carolina and governed by a deputy, was torn by sectionalism and unrest.[2] The Tuscarora War of 1711-12 resulted in the massacre of many settlers, a defeat for the Indians, and their removal to New York where they joined the Iroquois and became the sixth nation. The separate governments of the two Carolinas were finally given full effect by the Crown and Parliament in 1729.

During the period of our Colonial Wars, North Carolina, with local militia, provided assistance in several campaigns, including the Cherokee Expedition of 1761. As difficulties with the home government increased, North Carolina was among the first to resist the encroachments of royal authority, including the Battle of the Alamance in 1771. English rigidities of manner in governing and leading did not sit well with most Americans. Many of the problems that developed were a function of misunderstanding and inflexibility. The Boston Port Bill of 1774 did nothing but stir up the colonies to support the beleaguered citizens, and North Carolina was in the forefront of this movement. She elected the three Delegates to the Second Continental Congress who became the signers from that State.

---

[1] Geological Survey Bulletin 1212, *Boundaries of the United States and the Several States*, (US Government Printing Office, Washington, DC, 1966), p. 152.
[2] Richard B. Morris, *Encyclopedia of American History*, (Harper & Brothers, NY, 1953), p. 54.

Wm Hooper

47: WILLIAM HOOPER

"He who is wrapped in purple robes. "

William Butler Yeats

William Hooper signed the Declaration just to the left of the large signature of John Hancock, at the top of the signature column, in a moderate sized, neat school hand, abbreviating his first name as "Wm."

He was the eldest of five children of the Rev. William and Mary (Dennie) Hooper, a Scots family from Kelso. Groomed to follow his father into the Ministry, William studied for seven years at Boston Latin School and entered Harvard as a sophomore in 1757. After graduation in 1760, he rejected the ministry as a profession and took up the study of Law under James Otis. He was admitted to the Bar in 1764, moved to Wilmington, NC, married the daughter of an early settler, and prospered in this new environment, traveling widely in the area.

By 1766, William Hooper was unanimously elected recorder of the Borough. In 1769 he was appointed Deputy Attorney General of the Salisbury District. His formal entry into politics began on 25 Jan 1773 when he sat in the Provincial Assembly as a delegate from Campbelltown, NC.[1] Hooper was selected in late 1773 to the important Committee of Correspondence, serving throughout the Revolutionary years, during which time he made signal contributions. When the First North Carolina Provincial Congress convened in New Bern on 25-28 Aug 1774, Hooper was named to represent North Carolina at the First Continental Congress. He was also elected on 2 Sep 1775 as a delegate to the important Second Continental Congress.[2] Although absent when the Declaration was actually debated and voted upon in early July, Hooper strongly approved and signed on 2 Aug 1776.

---

[1] *Dictionary of North Carolina Biography*, (UNC, Chapel Hill, NC), Vol. 3, pp. 199-202.
[2] *Letters of Delegates to Congress*, (Library of Congress, Washington, DC, 1979), Vol. 4, p. xix.

FIRST GENERATION

1. WILLIAM HOOPER was born in Boston, MA on 17 Jun 1742.[1] He married Anne CLARK, daughter of Thomas and Barbara (Murray) Clark in Boston, MA on 16 Aug 1767.[2] She was born in Wilmington, New Hanover County, NC about 1744[3], and died in New Hanover County, NC on 30 May 1795.[4] He died in Hillsborough, Orange County, NC on 14 Oct 1790.[5] Children:

+	2	i	William HOOPER, b. 1768
+	3	ii	Elizabeth HOOPER, b. 1770
	4	iii	Thomas HOOPER, b. 1772, d. c. 1806; unm
	5	iv	Anenas HOOPER, b. 1774, dy
	6	v	Son HOOPER, b. 1776, dy
	7	vi	Daughter HOOPER, b. 1778, dy

References:
[1] Della Gray Barthelmas, *The Signers of the Declaration of Independence, A Biographical and Genealogical Reference*, (Mcfarland & Company, Inc., Jefferson, NC, 1997), pp. 120-121; since all other sources report only William, Elizabeth, and Thomas as children of the signer, the other children, reported by Barthelmas had to have died young. Archibald Maclaine Hooper, *Life of William Hooper, Signer of the Declaration of Independence*, (1822), the usual ornate and flowery prose of the time, but at least an early view of this patriot. See also by the Rev. Charles A. Goodrich, *Lives of the Signers of the Declaration of Independence*, (R.G.H. Huntington, Hartford, CT, 1842), pp. 422-427, a Victorian era work without references or source citations. Another, more recent, biographical account is in Robert Kneip, *William Hooper, 1742-1790, Misunderstood Patriot*, (PhD dissertation, Tulane University, 1980). See also an article in the *Dictionary of North Carolina Biography*, (The University of North Carolina Press, Chapel Hill, NC, 1988), Vol. 3, pp.199-202. His birth is recorded in the *Records of Trinity Episcopal Church, Boston MA* and in the *Vital Records of Boston, MA, Births*. The Leach MSS material for William Hooper is recorded on microfilm through the FHL (Film # 0001756); and the hard copy is found in Volume 20, pp. 5950-5956. The Dictionary of American Biography (DAB) article on William Hooper is in Vol. IX, p. 204. The more recent *American National Biography*, (Oxford University Press, NY, 1999) has an article on William Hooper, Vol. 11, pp. 146-147. [2] The marriage is recorded in the *Records of King's Chapel, Boston, MA*. [3] Her exact date of birth is not known, only the place and parentage. [4] Will of Anne Hooper in the Orange County Courthouse, Hillsborough, NC. [5] Inscription on the gravestone of signer William Hooper in the Old Town Cemetery, Hillsborough, NC, gives both his dates of birth and death. Edwin Anderson Alderman, *Address on the life of William Hooper, The Prophet of American Independence*, (Guilford Battle Ground, 4 Jul 1894); a eulogy of the signer's life on the occasion of his re-interment.

SECOND GENERATION

2. WILLIAM HOOPER[2] (William Hooper[1]) son of William Hooper and Anne Clark was born in Wilmington, NC in 1768, and died in Brunswick County, NC on 15 Jul 1804.[1] He married Helen HOGG, daughter of James and -- McDowal (Alves) Hogg in Orange County, NC on 26 Jun 1791.[2] She was born in SCOTLAND about 1766, and died in North Carolina on 30 Oct 1846.[3] Children:

+ 8   i   William HOOPER, b. 31 Aug 1792
   9   ii Thomas Clark HOOPER, b. 1794, d. Nov 1828; dsp
   10   iii James Hogg HOOPER, b. Sep 1797, d. 26 Jun 1841; dsp

References:
[1] Leach MSS, p. 5951. [2] *Orange County Marriage Bonds*, NC, Vol. II, p. 195. Leach MSS, p. 5952; see also the Draper MSS in the DAR Library in Washington, DC, Addenda, p. 81. [3] After the death of her husband she married the Rev. Joseph Caldwell, but issue of that marriage would not be descendants of the body of the signer.

3. ELIZABETH HOOPER[2] (William Hooper[1]) daughter of William Hooper and Anne Clark was born in 1770, and died in Charlestown, MA on 30 Jun 1844.[1] She married Henry Hearne WATTERS, son of Joseph Watters in say 1790. He died in Wilmington, NC in Oct 1809.[2] Child:

   11   i   Henry Hearne WATTERS, Jr., b. 1791, dy 1 Nov 1809

References:
[1] Leach MSS, p. 5951. [2] Leach MSS, p. 5951; see also the Draper MSS in the DAR Library, pp. 81-82.

THIRD GENERATION

8. WILLIAM HOOPER[3] (William Hooper[2], William Hooper[1]) child of William Hooper and Helen Hogg was born in Hillsborough, Orange County, NC on 31 Aug 1792, and died in Chapel Hill, NC on 19 Aug 1876.[1] He married Frances Pollock JONES, daughter of Edward Jones in Dec 1814.[2] She was born in Chatham County, NC 1798, and died in Fayetteville, NC on 10 Mar 1863.[3] Children:

+ 12   i   William Wilberforce HOOPER, b. 2 Jan 1816
+ 13   ii   Edward Jones HOOPER, b. 24 Mar 1818
+ 14   iii Mary Elizabeth HOOPER, b. 26 Sep 1819
+ 15   iv   Joseph Caldwell HOOPER, b. 21 Jan 1821
   16   v   Elizabeth Watters HOOPER, b. 1824, d. c. 1869; unm
+ 17   vi   Thomas Clark HOOPER, b. 15 Nov 1827
   18   vii DuPonceau Jones HOOPER, b. 8 Jan 1831, d. 4 Apr 1863

References:
[1] Leach MSS, p. 5952. [2] Leach MSS, p. 5952 [3] Draper MSS in the DAR Library, pp. 81-82; DSDI Appl # 47.

FOURTH GENERATION

12. WILLIAM WILBERFORCE HOOPER[4] (William Hooper[3], William Hooper[2], William Hooper[1]) child of William Hooper and Frances Pollock Jones was born in Chatham County, NC on 2 Jan 1816, and died in Littleton, Warren County, NC on 15 Nov 1864.[1] He married Mary Jane KEARNEY, daughter of Edmond and Polly (Davis) Kearney in Warren County, NC on 23 Dec 1852.[2] Children:

19	i	William Edward HOOPER, b. 1854; unm
+ 20	ii	Louise Rencher HOOPER, b. 1856
+ 21	iii	James Havelock HOOPER, b. c. 1859
+ 22	iv	Charlotte Elizabeth HOOPER, b. c. 1862

References:
[1] Robert Charles Kneip, *William Hooper, 1742-1790, Misunderstood Patriot*, (Tulane University Doctoral Thesis, 1980). [2] A William Hooper descendant, Margie Amelia Wills, has researched and collected a very great deal of family history over the years, inherited a good deal more, and has most graciously made all of this available to the Author.
It is hereinafter cited as the Margie Amelia Wills Data, and is now a part of the Manuscript Collection of the New England Historic Genealogical Society in Boston, MA, available to future researchers.

13. EDWARD JONES HOOPER[4] (William Hooper[3], William Hooper[2], William Hooper[1]) child of William Hooper and Frances Pollock Jones was born in Chatham County, NC on 24 Mar 1818, and died in Littleton, Warren County, NC on 21 Oct 1850.[1] He married Amelia Virginia Jones MASSEY in Lancaster County, SC on 27 Nov 1845.[2] She was born about 1827, and died in Lowndes County, AL in Nov 1851.[3] Children:

23	i	Theresa HOOPER, b. c. 1846
+ 24	ii	William Edward HOOPER, b. 1847

References:
[1] DSDI Appl # 1816. [2] Data of Margie Amelia Willis. [3] Will of Amelia Hooper is found in *Alabama Genealogical Register*, Vo. 3, p. 7.

14. MARY ELIZABETH HOOPER[4] (William Hooper[3], William Hooper[2], William Hooper[1]) child of William Hooper and Frances Pollock Jones was born in Chapel Hill, NC on 26 Sep 1819, and died on 23 Jun 1894.[1] She married John DeBerniere HOOPER in Orange County, NC on 20 Dec

1837.[2] He was born in Wilmington, NC on 6 Sep 1811, and died in Chapel Hill, NC on 23 Jan 1886.[3] Children:

+ 25   i   Helen DeBerniere HOOPER, b. 29 Oct 1838
+ 26   ii   Frances DeBerniere HOOPER, b. 1 Feb 1840
   27   iii   Edward DeBerniere HOOPER, b. 23 Jul 1846, dy 10 Aug 1847
+ 28   iv   Henry DeBerniere HOOPER, b. 12 Jun 1848
   29   v   Mary Louise HOOPER, b. 20 Jul 1851, dy 10 Oct 1853
+ 30   vi   Julia Charlotte HOOPER, b. 24 Jul 1856

References:
[1] DSDI Appl # 2090. [2] The Marriage Bond is dated 19 Dec 1837, but the ceremony took place the next day, see *The Fayetteville Observer*; see also DSDI Appl # 1816. [3] *The John DeBerniere Hooper Papers, The Southern Historical Collection, # 835*, (UNC, Chapel Hill, NC).

15. JOSEPH CALDWELL HOOPER[4] (William Hooper[3], William Hooper[2], William Hooper[1]) child of William Hooper and Frances Pollock Jones was born in Chapel Hill, NC on 21 Jan 1821[1], and died in Jacksonville, FL on 12 Apr 1914. He married Mary Jones ECCLES in Fayetteville, NC on 23 Mar 1859.[1] Children:

   31   i   John Eccles HOOPER, b. c. 1860
   32   ii   Francis Charles HOOPER, b. 1862, dy 1865

References:
[1] Margie Amelia Wills Data.

17. THOMAS CLARK HOOPER[4] (William Hooper[3], William Hooper[2], William Hooper[1]) child of William Hooper and Frances Pollock Jones was born in Chapel Hill, NC on 15 Nov 1827, and died in Blackville, Barnwell County, SC on 27 Oct 1884.[1] He married Mary Elizabeth STEVENSON in New Bern, NC on 25 Nov 1849.[2] She was born in New Bern, NC on 10 Oct 1828, and died in Wilmington, NC on 20 Mar 1894.[2] Children:

+ 33   i   Susan Taylor HOOPER, b. 30 Apr 1852
   34   ii   Margaret B. HOOPER, b. 28 Jul 1855
+ 35   iii   Joseph Caldwell HOOPER, b. 24 May 1857
+ 36   iv   Sarah Jerkins HOOPER, b. 26 Aug 1859
   37   v   Annie Bryan HOOPER, b. 26 Aug 1859, dy 12 Oct 1860
   38   vi   George Stevenson HOOPER, b. 12 Feb 1861, dy Jun 1861
+ 39   vii   Amelia Jones HOOPER, b. 13 May 1862
   40   viii   James Stevenson HOOPER, b. 19 Aug 1865, d. 28 Apr 1928; unm
   41   ix   Clara Hughes HOOPER, b. 29 Aug 1867

References:
[1] DSDI Appl # 47. [2] Marriage Bond in Craven County, NC of 24 Nov 1849; see also DSDI Appl # 1855. [3] DSDI Appl# 1026.

FIFTH GENERATION

20. LOUISE RENCHER HOOPER[5] (William Wilberforce Hooper[4], William Hooper[3], William Hooper[2], William Hooper[1]) child of William Wilberforce Hooper and Mary Jane Kearney was born in 1856.[1] She married William Collin DAUGHTRY in say 1876. Children:

42	i	William Wilberforce DAUGHTRY, b. c. 1878
43	ii	Spier Whitaker DAUGHTRY, b. 1880
44	iii	Henry Lawrence DAUGHTRY, b. 1882, d. 1914; unm
45	iv	Ernest Moore DAUGHTRY, b. 1884, dy 1886
46	v	Florence Moore DAUGHTRY, b. 1886
47	vi	Joseph Skinner DAUGHTRY, b. 1888
48	vii	Vernon Kearney DAUGHTRY, b. 1891, d. 1914; unm
49	viii	Eunice DAUGHTRY, b. 1896, dy 1914

References:
[1] A Genealogical Chart prepared by Frances DeBerniere Hooper Whitaker.

21. JAMES HAVELOCK HOOPER[5] (William Wilberforce Hooper[4], William Hooper[3], William Hooper[2], William Hooper[1]) child of William Wilberforce Hooper and Mary Jane Kearney was born about 1859.[1] He married Frances DAUGHTRY in say 1884. Children:

50	i	James DuPonceau HOOPER, b. 1885
51	ii	Helen Alice HOOPER, b. 1887
52	iii	Virginia Jane HOOPER, b. 1890
53	iv	Martha Matilda HOOPER, b. 1892
54	v	William Henry HOOPER, b. 1897
55	vi	Bettie Sebel HOOPER, b. 1901

References:
[1] A Genealogical Chart prepared by Frances DeBerniere Hooper Whitaker.

22. CHARLOTTE ELIZABETH HOOPER[5] (William Wilberforce Hooper[4], William Hooper[3], William Hooper[2], William Hooper[1]) child of William Wilberforce Hooper and Mary Jane Kearney was born about 1862.[1] She married Benjamin Crowell ALSTON in say 1876. He was born in 1880.[1] Children:

56	i	Albert Robert ALSTON, b. 1881, d. 1903; unm

57   ii   Charles Cooke ALSTON, b. c. 1883
58   iii Malcolm L. E. ALSTON, b. c. 1884
59   iv   Robert Montford ALSTON, b. c. 1886 [twin]
60   v   John Crowell ALSTON, b. c. 1886 [twin]
61   vi   Bernadine ALSTON, b. c. 1889
62   vii Josephine ALSTON, b. c. 1890
63   viii DeBerniere Hooper ALSTON, b. c. 1892
64   ix   Marian L. B. ALSTON, b. c.1895

References:
[1] A Genealogical Chart prepared by Frances DeBerniere Hooper Whitaker.

24. WILLIAM EDWARD HOOPER[5] (Edward Jones Hooper[4], William Hooper[3], William Hooper[2], William Hooper[1]) child of Edward Jones Hooper and Amelia V. Massey was born in South Carolina in 1847[1], and died in Birmingham, AL on 9 Jan 1926. He married Martha Phillips MERI-WETHER, daughter of Dr. George Mathews and his 1st wife Sarah Ann (Fitzpatrick) Meriwether in Alabama about 1868.[2] She was born in Montgomery, AL on 23 Sep 1848[3], and died in Birmingham, AL on 1 Apr 1927. Children:

     65   i   William HOOPER, b. c. 1869, dy
+   66   ii Theresa Virginia HOOPER, b. 1871
+   67   iii May HOOPER, b. c. 1873
+   68   iv Kathleen HOOPER, b. 12 Feb 1875
     69   v   Ethel HOOPER, b. c. 1878, dy
+   70   vi Henry Johnston HOOPER, b. c. 1880

References:
[1] DSDI Appl # 1816, see also his Death Certificate, Bureau of Statistics and Vital Records, Birmingham, AL, File # 176-BH-1926. [2] N.H. Meriwether, *The Meriwethers and their Connections*, pp. 223-225; a compiled genealogy of the family. [3] The Family genealogy gives the date of birth as shown, her Death Certificate (1102-BH-1927) reports 24 Sep 1848; but was given by a Lige Loy, who may not have known.

25. HELEN DeBERNIERE HOOPER[5] (Mary Elizabeth Hooper[4], William Hooper[3], William Hooper[2], William Hooper[1]) child of Mary Elizabeth Hooper and John DeBerniere Hooper was born in Chapel Hill, NC on 29 Oct 1838[1], and died in Chapel Hill, NC on 24 Jun 1911. She married James WILLS in Wilson, NC on 12 Aug 1867.[2] He was born in 1835, and died in Chapel Hill, NC on 26 Oct 1884.[3] Children:

+   71   i   Henry Clarence WILLS, b. 8 May 1868
     72   ii George Blount WILLS, b. c. 1870

References:
[1] DSDI Appl # 2090. [2] Wilson, NC Marriage Register, Register of Deeds Office. [3] Parish Records Chapel of the Cross, Chapel Hill, NC.

26. FRANCES DeBERNIERE HOOPER[5] (Mary Elizabeth Hooper[4], William Hooper[3], William Hooper[2], William Hooper[1]) child of Mary Elizabeth Hooper and John DeBerniere Hooper was born in Chapel Hill, NC on 1 Feb 1840[1], and died in Birmingham, AL on 28 Nov 1911. She married Spier WHITAKER, son of Spier and Elizabeth (Lewis) Whitaker in Warren County, NC on 31 Jul 1866.[1] He was born in Halifax, NC on 15 Mar 1841[1], and died on 11 Jul 1901. Children:

73	i	DeBerniere WHITAKER, b. 5 Jul 1868, d. 25 Dec 1921
74	ii	Bessie Lewis WHITAKER, b. 10 Aug 1874, d. 19 Jan 1962; unm
75	iii	Percy DuPonceau WHITAKER, b. 12 Nov 1876, d. 27 Oct 1928
76	iv	David Spier WHITAKER, b. 18 Aug 1878, d. 29 Oct 1914
77	v	Vernon Edelen WHITAKER, b. 23 Feb 1881, d. 22 Oct 1929

References:
[1] Margie Amelia Wills Data.

28. HENRY DeBERNIERE HOOPER[5] (Mary Elizabeth Hooper[4], William Hooper[3], William Hooper[2], William Hooper[1]) child of Mary Elizabeth Hooper and John DeBerniere Hooper was born in Warren County, NC on 12 Jun 1848[1], and died in Raleigh, NC in 1909. He married Viola Jessica WRIGHT in Richmond, VA on 19 Dec 1876.[1] She was born in Norfolk, VA on 5 Mar 1856.[1] Children:

78	i	Henry DeBerniere HOOPER, b. 14 Apr 1881
+ 79	ii	Louise Maclaine HOOPER, b. c. 1884

References:
[1] DSDI Appl # 29.

30. JULIA CHARLOTTE HOOPER[5] (Mary Elizabeth Hooper[4], William Hooper[3], William Hooper[2], William Hooper[1]) child of Mary Elizabeth Hooper and John DeBerniere Hooper was born in Warren County, NC on 24 Jul 1856[1], and died in Chapel Hill, NC on 7 Nov 1944. She married Ralph Henry GRAVES, II, son of Ralph Henry and Emma (Taylor) Graves on 20 Jun 1877.[1] He was born on 1 Apr 1851, and died in 1889.[1] Children:

80	i	Ralph Henry GRAVES, III, b. 11 Jul 1878, d. 1 Dec 1939; dsp
+ 81	ii	Ernest GRAVES, b. 27 Mar 1880
82	iii	Louis GRAVES, b. 6 Aug 1883, d. Jan 1965; dsp
+ 83	iv	Mary DeBerniere GRAVES, b. 6 Jun 1886

References:
[1] Margie Amelia Wills Data.

33. SUSAN TAYLOR HOOPER[5] (Thomas Clark Hooper[4], William Hooper[3], William Hooper[2], William Hooper[1]) child of Thomas Clark Hooper and Mary Elizabeth Stevenson was born in New Bern, NC on 30 Apr 1852.[1] She married Charles Strong BRICE on 17 Dec 1874.[1] Children:

    84   i   William Robert BRICE, b. c. 1876
    85   ii Susan Annette BRICE, b. c. 1879

References:
[1] A Genealogical Chart prepared by Frances DeBerniere Hooper Whitaker.

35. JOSEPH CALDWELL HOOPER[5] (Thomas Clark Hooper[4], William Hooper[3], William Hooper[2], William Hooper[1]) child of Thomas Clark Hooper and Mary Elizabeth Stevenson was born in New Bern, NC on 24 May 1857.[1] He married Louise CUNNINGHAM about 1893.[1] Children:

    86   i   Mary Louise HOOPER, b. 1894
    87   ii James Caldwell HOOPER, b. 1896

References:
[1] A Genealogical Chart prepared by Frances DeBerniere Hooper Whitaker.

36. SARAH JERKINS HOOPER[5] (Thomas Clark Hooper[4], William Hooper[3], William Hooper[2], William Hooper[1]) child of Thomas Clark Hooper and Mary Elizabeth Stevenson was born in New Bern, NC on 26 Aug 1859[1], and died on 11 Jul 1924. She married William Weston WESTON, son of Isaac Tucker and Elizabeth (Moseley) Weston in Florence, SC on 27 Jan 1880.[2] He was born in Congaree, SC on 12 Dec 1853[1], and died on 31 Oct 1931. Children:

    88   i   Thomas Isaac WESTON, b. 15 Apr 1881, d. 22 Nov 1940; dsp
+ 89   ii William Stevenson WESTON, b. 27 Jul 1883
    90   iii Joseph Caldwell WESTON, b. 8 Jul 1885, dy 27 May 1886 [twin]
    91   iv Mary Elizabeth WESTON, b. 8 Jul 1885, dy 30 May 1886 [twin]
    92   v   John Tillinghast WESTON, b, 11 Sep 1887, dy 27 Feb 1905
+ 93   vi Christian Tucker WESTON, b. 12 Nov 1891
+ 94   vii Sarah Hooper WESTON, b. 28 Dec 1893

References:
[1] DSDI Appl # 47, 2218, 2238, 2239. [2] For the children of this marriage see Laura Jervey Hopkins, *Lower Richland Planters Hopkins, Adams, Weston and Related Families of South Carolina*, (The R. L. Bryan Company, Columbia, SC, 1976), p. 413.

39. AMELIA JONES HOOPER[5] (Thomas Clark Hooper[4], William Hooper[3], William Hooper[2], William Hooper[1]) child of Thomas Clark Hooper and Mary Elizabeth Stevenson was born in Fayetteville, NC on 13 May 1862[1], and died in Washington, DC on 31 Mar 1936. She married Winborn Lawton MELLICHAMPE, son of Edward Henry and Mary Theodosia (Vaughan) Mellichamp in Florence, SC on 20 May 1880.[2] He was born in James Island, SC on 8 Aug 1858[1], and died on 17 Oct 1920. Children:

+ 95 i Edward Winborn MELLICHAMPE, b. 25 Jul 1881
 96 ii Thomas Hooper MELLICHAMPE, b. 4 Jun 1883, dy 25 Jan 1884
+ 97 iii James Hooper MELLICHAMPE, b. 27 Sep 1885
 98 iv Joseph Stanley MELLICHAMPE, b. 28 Jan 1888, dy 31 May 1889
 99 v Augustus Chavasse MELLICHAMPE, b. 7 May 1890, d. 9 Nov 1957; dsp
 100 vi DeBerniere MELLICHAMPE, b. 7 Feb 1893, dy 23 Jul 1894
 101 vii Susanne Stevenson MELLICHAMPE, b. 17 Jun 1896, d. 31 Oct 1968; unm
 102 viii Emma Carolyn MELLICHAMPE, b. 29 Apr 1900, d. 29 May 1971; unm
 103 ix Hooper Prall MELLICHAMPE, b. 29 Aug 1902, dy 18 Jan 1905
+ 104 x Lawton Berkeley MELLICHAMPE, b. 16 Jun 1905

References:
[1] DSDI Appl # 101, 1026, 1855. [2] DSDI Appl # 101; note especially that Winborn Lawton Mellichamp [sic], changed the spelling of his name to add the "e", thus legally changing the family surname of his descendants to Mellichampe.

SIXTH GENERATION

66. THERESA VIRGINIA HOOPER[6] (William Edward Hooper[5], Edward Jones Hooper[4], William Hooper[3], William Hooper[2], William Hooper[1]) child of William Edward Hooper and Martha Phillips Meriwether was born in 1871[1], and died in 1959. She married Smith Morehead EVANS in say 1890. He was born in 1859, and died in 1896.[1] Children:

+ 105 i William Hooper EVANS, b. 2 Sep 1891
+ 106 ii Jonsie EVANS, b. 2 Sep 1893

References:
[1] N.H. Meriwether, *The Meriwethers and their Connections*, pp. 223-224.

67. MAY HOOPER[6] (William Edward Hooper[5], Edward Jones Hooper[4], William Hooper[3], William Hooper[2], William Hooper[1]) child of William

Edward Hooper and Martha Phillips Meriwether was born about 1873.[1] She married Thomas C. LAMAR in say 1892. Children:

   107   i Thomas C. LAMAR, Jr., b. c.1894

+ 108   ii Martha Meriwether LAMAR, b. c. 1896

References:
[1] N.H. Meriwether, *The Meriwethers and their Connections*, p. 224.

68. KATHLEEN HOOPER[6] (William Edward Hooper[5], Edward Jones Hooper[4], William Hooper[3], William Hooper[2], William Hooper[1]) child of William Edward Hooper and Martha Phillips Meriwether was born in Selma, AL on 12 Feb 1875[1], and died in Birmingham, AL on 15 Sep 1953. She married John Evander HARRIS in Birmingham, AL on 16 Nov 1898.[1] He was born in Sumterville, AL on 24 May 1870[1], and died in Livingston, AL on 24 Dec 1934.[1] Children:

   109   i John Evander HARRIS, Jr., b. 1897, d. 1918; unm

+ 110   ii Kathleen HARRIS, b. 18 Nov 1902

References:
[1] DSDI Appl # 1816.

70. HENRY JOHNSTON HOOPER[6] (William Edward Hooper[5], Edward Jones Hooper[4], William Hooper[3], William Hooper[2], William Hooper[1]) child of William Edward Hooper and Martha Phillips Meriwether was born about 1880.[1] He married Patricia CALLOWAY in say 1902. Children:

   111   i William M. HOOPER, b. c. 1904

   112   ii Frances HOOPER, b. c. 1907

References:
[1] N.H. Meriwether, *The Meriwethers and their Connections*, p. 225.

71. HENRY CLARENCE WILLS[6] (Helen DeBerniere Hooper[5], Mary Elizabeth Hooper[4], William Hooper[3], William Hooper[2], William Hooper[1]) child of Helen DeBerniere Hooper and James Wills was born in Wilson, NC on 8 May 1868[1], and died in Silver, SC on 18 Sep 1956. He married Rosa Christina JETTON, daughter of Charles P. and Victoria (Cole) Jetton in Durham, NC on 18 Dec 1889.[1] She was born in Durham, NC on 26 Mar 1869[1], and died in Summerville, SC on 15 Jun 1951. Children:

+ 113   i James WILLS, b. 19 Sep 1890

+ 114   ii Charles Battle WILLS, b. 28 Apr 1893

+ 115   iii Clarence Lucas WILLS, b. 11 Mar 1895

References:
[1] DSDI Appl # 1862, 2090.

79. LOUISE MACLAINE HOOPER[6] (Henry DeBerniere Hooper[5], Mary Elizabeth Hooper[4], William Hooper[3], William Hooper[2], William Hooper[1]) child of Henry DeBerniere Hooper and Viola Jessica Wright was born about 1884.[1] She married Arnold Edwin EWELL in Norfolk, VA on 8 Jan 1924. Child:

    116   i   Arnold Edwin EWELL, Jr., b. c. 1926

References:

[1] Mary Mellichampe data, conveyed through Irene Weston Croft.

81. ERNEST GRAVES[6] (Julia Charlotte Hooper[5], Mary Elizabeth Hooper[4], William Hooper[3], William Hooper[2], William Hooper[1]) child of Julia Charlotte Hooper and Ralph Henry Graves was born in Orange County, NC on 27 Mar 1880[1], and died in Washington, DC on 9 Jun 1953. He married Lucy Birnie HORGAN on 8 Jun 1923. Child:

    117   i   Ernest GRAVES, Jr., b. 6 Jul 1924

References:

[1] Mary Mellichampe data, conveyed through Irene Weston Croft. He was a graduate of USMA, see *Register of Graduates and Former Cadets of the United States Military Academy*, (Association of Graduates, West Point, NY, 1990), Class of 1905, Graduate # 4340, p. 329.

83. MARY DeBERNIERE GRAVES[6] (Julia Charlotte Hooper[5], Mary Elizabeth Hooper[4], William Hooper[3], William Hooper[2], William Hooper[1]) child of Julia Charlotte Hooper and Ralph Henry Graves was born in Orange County, NC on 6 Jun 1886[1], and died in Chapel Hill, NC on 28 Apr 1950. She married Arthur Dougherty REES in NYC on 18 Sep 1919. He was born in County Pembroke, WALES on 22 Aug 1878[1], and died in Brooklyn, NY on 28 Dec 1961. Child:

+ 118   i   Pembroke Graves REES, b. 21 Jul 1920

References:

[1] Margie Amelia Wills Data.

89. WILLIAM STEVENSON WESTON[6] (Sarah Jerkins Hooper[5], Thomas Clark Hooper[4], William Hooper[3], William Hooper[2], William Hooper[1]) child of Sarah Jerkins Hooper and William Weston Weston was born in "Grovewood", Congaree, Richland County, SC on 27 Jul 1883[1], and died in Columbia, SC on 3 Oct 1947. He married Mary Irene GABREY in Boston, MA on 7 Jan 1913. She was born in Middleboro, MA on 29 Jun 1894[2], and died in Columbia, SC on 28 Aug 1960. Children:

+ 119   i   William Stevenson WESTON, Jr., b. 10 Jan 1916

+ 120   ii   Irene Gabrey WESTON, b. 23 Jun 1918

    121   iii John Tillinghast WESTON, II, b. 1920, dy 1921

+ 122   iv Thomas Isaac WESTON, II, b. 9 Aug 1922
+ 123   v   James Caldwell WESTON, b. 18 May 1925
References:
[1] Laura Jervey Hopkins, *Lower Richland Planters Hopkins, Adams, Weston and Related Families of South Carolina*, (The R. L. Bryan Company, Columbia, SC, 1976), pp. 417-418.[2] DSDI Appl # 2218.

93. CHRISTIAN TUCKER WESTON[6] (Sarah Jerkins Hooper[5], Thomas Clark Hooper[4], William Hooper[3], William Hooper[2], William Hooper[1]) child of Sarah Jerkins Hooper and William Weston Weston was born in Congaree, SC on 12 Nov 1891[1], and died in Columbia, SC on 28 Jul 1977. He married Mary Postell HOPKINS in Congaree, SC on 26 Jun 1918. She was born in Hopkins, SC on 6 Sep 1890[1], and died in Columbia, SC on 20 Jan 1977. Children:
+ 124   i   Christian Tucker WESTON, Jr., b. 24 May 1919
+ 125   ii English Hopkins WESTON, b. 12 Dec 1920
   126   iii William Isaac Hopkins WESTON, b. 6 Aug 1922, dy 1 Jul 1924
References:
[1] DSDI Appl # 2238.

94. SARAH HOOPER WESTON[6] (Sarah Jerkins Hooper[5], Thomas Clark Hooper[4], William Hooper[3], William Hooper[2], William Hooper[1]) child of Sarah Jerkins Hooper and William Weston Weston was born in Gadsden, Richland County, SC on 28 Dec 1893[1], and died in Nashville, TN on 5 Sep 1988. She married Charles DePuy ROBISON in Columbia, SC on 8 Jun 1918. He was born in Geneva, Ontario County, NY on 4 Mar 1877[1], and died in Omaha, NE on 18 Apr 1959. Children:
+ 127   i   Sarah Weston ROBISON, b. 11 Mar 1919
+ 128   ii Charles DePuy ROBISON, Jr.b. 8 Feb 1921
+ 129   iii William Whitwell ROBISON, b. 15 May 1924
+ 130   iv Mary Elizabeth ROBISON, b. 1 Jun 1930
References:
[1] DSDI Appl # 2239.

95. EDWARD WINBORN MELLICHAMPE[6] (Amelia Jones Hooper[5], Thomas Clark Hooper[4], William Hooper[3], William Hooper[2], William Hooper[1]) child of Amelia Jones Hooper and Winborn Lawton Mellichampe was born in Florence, SC on 25 Jul 1881[1], and died in Alamogordo, NM on 16 May 1964. He married (1st) Bertha HAWORTH, daughter of Julius Jasper and Ella (Starbuck) Haworth in Knoxville, TN on 2 Mar 1908 She was born in Plainfield, IN on 27 Dec 1883[1], and died in Billings, MT on 23 Sep 1978. Children:

+ 131 　 i 　 Edward Winborn MELLICHAMPE, Jr., b. 29 May 1909
+ 132 　 ii 　 Samuel Haworth MELLICHAMPE, b. 16 Feb 1917

References:
[1] A Hooper descendant, James Hooper Mellichampe, Jr. has been most cooperative by furnishing the Author with a series of Family Group Sheets; hereinafter referenced as JHM Family Group Sheets.

97. JAMES HOOPER MELLICHAMPE[6] (Amelia Jones Hooper[5], Thomas Clark Hooper[4], William Hooper[3], William Hooper[2], William Hooper[1]) child of Amelia Jones Hooper and Winborn Lawton Mellichampe was born in Chester, SC on 27 Sep 1885[1], and died in Washington, DC on 3 Feb 1949. He married Frances Marion PICKETT, daughter of Francis Marion and Christina Eleanor (Charles) Pickett in High Point, NC on 29 Dec 1909. She was born in High Point, NC on 29 Oct 1890[1], and died in Rockville, MD on 18 Aug 1955. Children:

+ 133 　 i 　 Frances Marion MELLICHAMPE, b. 15 Jul 1912
　 134 　 ii 　 James Hooper MELLICHAMPE, Jr., b. 19 Mar 1915, sp
+ 135 　 iii 　 Eleanor Charles MELLICHAMPE, b. 30 Aug 1922

References:
[1] DSDI Appl # 1026, 1855.

104. LAWTON BERKELEY MELLICHAMPE[6] (Amelia Jones Hooper[5], Thomas Clark Hooper[4], William Hooper[3], William Hooper[2], William Hooper[1]) child of Amelia Jones Hooper and Winborn Lawton Mellichampe was born in High Point, NC on 16 Jun 1905, and died in Edgewater, MD on 17 Mar 1969. He married Margaret Regina WILSON, daughter of William Edward and Marietta (Vaughn) Wilson in Rockville, MD on 14 Sep 1934. She was born in Washington, DC on 22 Jun 1917. Children:

+ 136 　 i 　 Margaret Susanne MELLICHAMPE, b. 5 Nov 1935
　 137 　 ii 　 Lois Berkeley MELLICHAMPE, b. 27 Jun 1944; sp
　 138 　 iii 　 Lawton Berkeley MELLICHAMPE, Jr., b. 14 Sep 1946; sp

SEVENTH GENERATION

105. WILLIAM HOOPER EVANS[7] (Theresa Virginia Hooper[6], William Edward Hooper[5], Edward Jones Hooper[4], William Hooper[3], William Hooper[2], William Hooper[1]) child of Theresa Virginia Hooper and Smith

Morehead Evans was born on 2 Sep 1891.[1] He married Dorothy HART in 1926. Children:

+ 139   i   James Hart EVANS, b. 25 May 1927
+ 140   ii   Virginia Jonsie EVANS, b. 9 Jul 1931
+ 141   iii William Hooper EVANS, Jr., b. 19 Feb 1933
+ 142   iv   Robert Meriwether EVANS, b. 26 Feb 1934
   143   v   Blanche Darr EVANS, b. 29 Sep 1936, dy 21 Jun 1937
+ 144   vi   Clement Morehead EVANS, b. 9 May 1941

References:
[1] N.H. Meriwether, *The Meriwethers and their Connections*, pp. 223-224.

106. JONSIE EVANS[7] (Theresa Virginia Hooper[6], William Edward Hooper[5], Edward Jones Hooper[4], William Hooper[3], William Hooper[2], William Hooper[1]) child of Theresa Virginia Hooper and Smith Morehead Evans was born on 2 Sep 1893.[1] She married Arthur Davis ELSBERRY in 1913. Children:

   145   i   Arthur Davis ELSBERRY, Jr., b. 21 Jul 1916
   146   ii   William Evans ELSBERRY, b. 21 Nov 1919

References:
[1] N.H. Meriwether, *The Meriwethers and their Connections*, p. 224.

108. MARTHA MERIWETHER LAMAR[7] (May Hooper[6], William Edward Hooper[5], Edward Jones Hooper[4], William Hooper[3], William Hooper[2], William Hooper[1]) child of May Hooper and Thomas C. Lamar was born about 1896.[1] She married Alex T. CECIL in say 1920. Child:

   147   i   Alex T. CECIL, Jr., b. c. 1937

References:
[1] N.H. Meriwether, *The Meriwethers and their Connections*, p. 224.

110. KATHLEEN HARRIS[7] (Kathleen Hooper[6], William Edward Hooper[5], Edward Jones Hooper[4], William Hooper[3], William Hooper[2], William Hooper[1]) child of Kathleen Hooper and John Evander Harris was born in Birmingham, AL on 18 Nov 1902, and died in Birmingham, AL on 11 Aug 1969. She married George Magruder FOUCHE on 24 Apr 1925. He was born in Americus, GA on 25 Jun 1892[1], and died in Birmingham, AL on 24 Jul 1969. Child:

   148   i   Kathleen Ross FOUCHE, b. 2 Sep 1930

References:
[1] DSDI Appl # 1816.

113. JAMES WILLS[7] (Henry Clarence Wills[6], Helen DeBerniere Hooper[5], Mary Elizabeth Hooper[4], William Hooper[3], William Hooper[2], William

Hooper[1]) child of Henry Clarence Wills and Rosa Christina Jetton was born in Durham, NC on 19 Sep 1890[1], and died in Chapel Hill, NC on 22 Feb 1972. He married Ceclia Mae STROWD, daughter of Matthew Marshall and Adella (Andrews) Strowd on 31 Jul 1910. She was born in Orange County, NC on 17 May 1888[1], and died in Durham, NC on 9 Aug 1981. Children:

+ 149   i   Helen Faucett WILLS, b. 5 Dec 1911
+ 150   ii   Thelma Rhett WILLS, b. 27 Mar 1914
+ 151   iii James WILLS, b. 25 Aug 1917
+ 152   iv   Harold Bryant WILLS, b. 16 May 1920
+ 153   v   Henry Melvin WILLS, b. 19 Dec 1922
+ 154   vi   George DeBerniere WILLS, b. 28 Aug 1929
+ 155   vii Richard Hooper WILLS, b. 20 Jan 1933

References:
[1] DSDI Appl # 2090.

114. CHARLES BATTLE WILLS[7] (Henry Clarence Wills[6], Helen DeBerniere Hooper[5], Mary Elizabeth Hooper[4], William Hooper[3], William Hooper[2], William Hooper[1]) child of Henry Clarence Wills and Rosa Christina Jetton was born in Orange County, NC on 28 Apr 1893[1], and died in an American Hospital in FRANCE on 25 Dec 1918. He married Hulda Truit STALLINGS in Orange County, NC on 25 Dec 1915. She was born in Lenoir, NC on 16 Jun 1895[1], and died in Chapel Hill, NC on 6 Nov 1974. Child:

156   i   Charles Battle WILLS, Jr., b. 20 Mar 1917; unm

References:
[1] Margie Amelia Wills Data..

115. CLARENCE LUCAS WILLS[7] (Henry Clarence Wills[6], Helen DeBerniere Hooper[5], Mary Elizabeth Hooper[4], William Hooper[3], William Hooper[2], William Hooper[1]) child of Henry Clarence Wills and Rosa Christina Jetton was born in Durham, NC on 11 Mar 1895[1], and died in West Columbia, Lexington County, SC on 15 May 1981. He married Margie Louise RIDDLE in Burke County, NC on 15 Apr 1916. She was born in Bakersville, NC on 10 Oct 1900[1], and died in Darlington, SC on 9 Sep 1979. Children:

+ 157   i   Clarence Lucas WILLS, Jr., b. 30 Jun 1921
+ 158   ii   Harry DeBerniere WILLS, b. 15 Nov 1924
+ 159   iii Nora Louise WILLS, b. 27 Aug 1926
  160   iv   Margie Amelia WILLS, b. 12 Jan 1929; unm

References:
[1] DSDI Appl # 1862.

118. PEMBROKE GRAVES REES[7] (Mary DeBerniere Graves[6], Julia Charlotte Hooper[5], Mary Elizabeth Hooper[4], William Hooper[3], William Hooper[2], William Hooper[1]) child of Mary DeBerniere Graves and Arthur Dougherty Rees was born in Philadelphia, PA on 21 Jul 1920. He married Penley Christine PORTER, daughter of Lewis Stearns and Esther (Akeley) Porter in Normandy, MO on 9 Jun 1956. She was born in Houlton, Aroostook County, ME on 9 Jul 1934. Children:

    161   i   William Hooper REES, b. 21 Nov 1958; unm
    162   ii Thomas Pembroke REES, b. 9 Jan 1961; unm

119. WILLIAM STEVENSON WESTON, Jr.[7] (William Stevenson Weston[6], Sarah Jerkins Hooper[5], Thomas Clark Hooper[4], William Hooper[3], William Hooper[2], William Hooper[1]) child of William Stevenson Weston and Irene Gabrey was born in Columbia, SC on 10 Jan 1916, and died in Columbia, SC on 12 Dec1979. He married Capitola Catherine KING, daughter of William Eugene and Catherine (Carter) King in Aynor, SC on 23 Mar 1940. She was born on 3 Oct 1917, and died on 2 May 1981. Children:

+ 163   i   William Stevenson WESTON, III, b. 20 Jan 1941
+ 164   ii   Eugene King WESTON, b. 26 Apr 1943
+ 165   iii James Carter WESTON, b. 20 Jun 1948
+ 166   iv   Richard Holliday WESTON, b. 7 Jul 1951 [twin]
+ 167   v   Robert Gabrey WESTON, b. 7 Jul 1951 [twin]

120. IRENE GABREY WESTON[7] (William Stevenson Weston[6], Sarah Jerkins Hooper[5], Thomas Clark Hooper[4], William Hooper[3], William Hooper[2], William Hooper[1]) child of William Stevenson Weston and Irene Gabrey was born in Columbia, SC on 23 Jun 1918. She married Edward Stockton CROFT, Jr, in Congaree, SC on 22 Mar 1941. He was born in Atlanta, GA on 18 Mar 1916. Children:

+ 168   i   Edward Stockton CROFT, III, b. 12 Sep 1942
   169   ii   Irene Weston CROFT, b. 7 Dec 1943
+ 170   iii Lawrence McMahon CROFT, b. 16 Feb 1946
+ 171   iv   Stevenson Weston CROFT, b. 27 Jul 1952
   172   v   Sarah Crosswell CROFT, b. 26 Mar 1955, d. 11 Aug 1993;
               unm
+ 173   vi   Mary Gaillard CROFT, b. 13 Aug 1957

122. THOMAS ISAAC WESTON[7] (William Stevenson Weston[6], Sarah Jerkins Hooper[5], Thomas Clark Hooper[4], William Hooper[3], William Hooper[2], William Hooper[1]) child of William Stevenson Weston and Irene Gabrey was born in Columbia, SC on 9 Aug 1922. He married Peggy Louise HEDRICK, daughter of Grady Philip and Frances Edna (West) Hedrick in Columbia, SC on 17 Mar 1951. She was born in Atlanta, GA on 20 Sep 1930. Children:

+ 174   i   Peggy Louise WESTON, b. 24 Mar 1952
+ 175   ii   Thomas Isaac WESTON, Jr., b. 3 Oct 1956
   176   iii   Mark Alan WESTON, b. 24 Nov 1967

123. JAMES CALDWELL WESTON[7] (William Stevenson Weston[6], Sarah Jerkins Hooper[5], Thomas Clark Hooper[4], William Hooper[3], William Hooper[2], William Hooper[1]) child of William Stevenson Weston and Irene Gabrey was born in Columbia, SC on 18 May 1925. He married Carolyn Jean EDGAR in Columbia, SC on 25 Feb 1949. She was born in Columbia, SC on 2 Mar 1927, and died in Macon, GA in 1981. Children:

   177   i   Carolyn Jean WESTON, b. 26 Apr 1950
+ 178   ii   James Caldwell WESTON, Jr., b. 11 Nov 1951
+ 179   iii   Leslie Edgar WESTON, b. 12 Apr 1954
+ 180   iv   Elizabeth Anne WESTON, b. 16 Oct 1956

124. CHRISTIAN TUCKER WESTON, Jr.[7] (Christian Tucker Weston[6], Sarah Jerkins Hooper[5], Thomas Clark Hooper[4], William Hooper[3], William Hooper[2], William Hooper[1]) child of Christian Tucker Weston and Mary Postell Hopkins was born in Hopkins, SC on 24 May 1919. He married Pauline Hasell HANCKEL in Charleston, SC on 23 Jun 1943. She was born in Charleston, SC on 31 Jan 1922. Children:

   181   i   Pauline Hanckel WESTON, b. 8 Nov 1944, dy 3 Dec 1960
+ 182   ii   Mary Postell WESTON, b. 29 Oct 1947
+ 183   i   Christian Tucker WESTON, III, b. 28 Aug 1950
+ 184   ii   Frances Stuart WESTON, b. 21 May 1953
   185   iii   John Stuart WESTON, b. 2 Oct 1955

125. ENGLISH HOPKINS WESTON[7] (Christian Tucker Weston[6], Sarah Jerkins Hooper[5], Thomas Clark Hooper[4], William Hooper[3], William Hooper[2], William Hooper[1]) child of Christian Tucker Weston and Mary Postell Hopkins was born in Hopkins, SC on 12 Dec 1920. He married Sarah Catherine CRAWFORD in York, SC on 17 Jun 1953. She was born in West Palm Beach, FL on 22 Oct 1924. Children:

+ 186   i   Sarah Catherine WESTON, b. 12 Feb 1955
   187   ii   English Hopkins WESTON, Jr., b. 11 May 1958
+ 188   iii   Andrew Cornish WESTON, b. 14 Aug 1959
   189   iv   Laura Jervey WESTON, b. 29 Jun 1968

127. SARAH WESTON ROBISON[7] (Sarah Hooper Weston[6], Sarah Jerkins Hooper[5], Thomas Clark Hooper[4], William Hooper[3], William Hooper[2], William Hooper[1]) child of Sarah Hooper Weston and Charles DePuy Robison was born in Congaree, SC on 11 Mar 1919, and died in Atlanta, GA on 16 May 1979. She married Walter Gustaf ZIMMERMANN, Jr. on 12 Dec 1942. He was born on 4 Jan 1915. Children:

+ 190   i   Walter Herbert ZIMMERMANN, b. 17 Jun 1944
   191   ii   Mary Elizabeth ZIMMERMANN, b. 12 Jun 1945; sp
   192   iii   Sarah Joyce ZIMMERMANN, b. Aug 1946; dy

128. CHARLES DePUY ROBISON, Jr.[7] (Sarah Hooper Weston[6], Sarah Jerkins Hooper[5], Thomas Clark Hooper[4], William Hooper[3], William Hooper[2], William Hooper[1]) child of Sarah Hooper Weston and Charles DePuy Robison was born in South Orange, NJ on 8 Feb 1921. He married Elizabeth Jernigan BELL on 2 Sep 1944. She was born in Norfolk, VA on 21 Apr 1923. Children:

+ 193   i   Charles DePuy ROBISON, III, b. 5 Mar 1947
+ 194   ii   Alexander Bell ROBISON, b. 21 Jul 1950
+ 195   iii   Elizabeth Jernigan ROBISON, b. 19 Aug 1952

129. WILLIAM WHITWELL ROBISON[7] (Sarah Hooper Weston[6], Sarah Jerkins Hooper[5], Thomas Clark Hooper[4], William Hooper[3], William Hooper[2], William Hooper[1]) child of Sarah Hooper Weston and Charles DePuy Robison was born on 15 May 1924. He married (1st) Kathryn CRITCHFIELD on 6 Sep 1947. She was born on 29 Dec 1923. He married (2nd) Kathleen Kimberly MEYER on 16 Nov 1963. She was born in Davenport, IA on 22 Nov 1924.
Children by first marriage:
+ 196   i   Kathryn Diane ROBISON, b. 12 Jun 1949
+ 197   ii   William Whitwell ROBISON, III, b. 9 Sep 1953
+ 198   iii   James Critchfield ROBISON, b. 7 Jul 1955
Child by second marriage:
+ 199   iv   Marie Kimberly ROBISON, b. 19 Jun 1964

130. MARY ELIZABETH ROBISON[7] (Sarah Hooper Weston[6], Sarah Jerkins Hooper[5], Thomas Clark Hooper[4], William Hooper[3], William Hooper[2], William Hooper[1]) child of Sarah Hooper Weston and Charles DePuy Robison was born in Omaha, NE on 1 Jun 1930. She married Harold Doidge [sic] LOWRY in Omaha, NE on 2 May 1950. He was born in Pueblo, CO on 18 Dec 1927. Children:

+ 200   i   Harold Doidge LOWRY, Jr., b. 19 Jun 1952

+　201　　ii　Mary Susan LOWRY, b. 14 Dec 1954
　　202　　iii　Thomas Stone LOWRY, b. 2 May 1957; sp

131. EDWARD WINBORN MELLICHAMPE, Jr.[7] (Edward Winborn Mellichampe[6], Amelia Jones Hooper[5], Thomas Clark Hooper[4], William Hooper[3], William Hooper[2], William Hooper[1]) child of Edward Winborn Mellichampe and Bertha Haworth was born in Knoxville, TN on 29 May 1909, and died in Hopewell, VA on 9 Jun 1991. He married Julia Victoria CAMP, daughter of Joseph Pinckney and Juanita (Steel) Camp in Helena, AR on 3 Feb 1935. She was born in Morrilton, AR on 28 Oct 1906, and died in Billings, MT on 4 Nov 1982. Children:
　　203　　i　Edward Winborn MELLICHAMPE, III, b. 11 Aug 1937, dy
　　　　　　　12 Aug 1927
　　204　　ii　Joseph Haworth MELLICHAMPE, b. 17 Aug 1938, dy 18
　　　　　　　Aug 1938

132. SAMUEL HAWORTH MELLICHAMPE[7] (Edward Winborn Mellichampe[6], Amelia Jones Hooper[5], Thomas Clark Hooper[4], William Hooper[3], William Hooper[2], William Hooper[1]) child of Edward Winborn Mellichampe and Bertha Haworth was born in Pohick, VA on 16 Feb 1917, and died in Hopewell, VA on 7 Mar 1995. He married (2nd) Gladys ETHRIDGE, daughter of Charles Leon and Alma Elizabeth (Flowers) Ethridge in Petersburg, VA on 24 Oct 1938. She was born in Wilson, NC on 2 Aug 1917, and died in Prince George County, VA on 24 Nov 1989. Children:
+　205　　i　Aubrey Julian MELLICHAMPE, b. 9 Nov 1939
+　206　　ii　Edward MELLICHAMPE, b. 23 Dec 1946

133. FRANCES MARION MELLICHAMPE[7] (James Hooper Mellichampe[6], Amelia Jones Hooper[5], Thomas Clark Hooper[4], William Hooper[3], William Hooper[2], William Hooper[1]) child of James Hooper Mellichampe and Frances Marion Pickett was born in High Point, NC on 15 Jul 1912, and died in Fort Myers, FL on 8 Jun 1975. She married Fletcher Lamar SHEFFIELD, Jr., son of Fletcher Lamar and Eddye [sic] (Harris) Sheffield in Washington, DC on 22 Jun 1936. He was born in Macon, GA on 11 Feb 1914, and died in Fort Myers, FL on 10 May 1976. Child:
+　207　　i　Frances Marian ("Dolly") SHEFFIELD, b. 1 May 1937

135. ELEANOR CHARLES MELLICHAMPE[7] (James Hooper Mellichampe[6], Amelia Jones Hooper[5], Thomas Clark Hooper[4], William Hooper[3], William Hooper[2], William Hooper[1]) child of James Hooper Mellichampe and

Frances Marion Pickett was born in High Point, NC on 30 Aug 1922. She married (1st) Norman Griffith SMITH, son of Charles Henry and Jessica Marie (Griffith) Smith in Washington, DC on 11 Mar 1944. He was born in Washington, DC on 16 Jun 1917, and died in Bethesda, MD on 1 Jan 1970. Children:

    208   i   Norman Griffith SMITH, Jr., b. 20 May 1945
+ 209   ii Claudia Carol SMITH, b. 26 Jan 1947
+ 210   iii Randolph Hooper SMITH, b. 21 Feb 1952
    211   iv Amy Hope SMITH, b. 30 Jan 1963

136. MARGARET SUSANNE MELLICHAMPE[7] (Lawton Berkeley Mellichampe[6], Amelia Jones Hooper[5], Thomas Clark Hooper[4], William Hooper[3], William Hooper[2], William Hooper[1]) child of Lawton Berkeley Mellichampe and Margaret Regina Wilson was born in Washington, DC on 5 Nov 1935. She married (1st) Joseph E. BEATTY, son of Charles Francis and Pauline (Mieb) Beatty in Denver, CO on 24 Jul 1960. He was born in Denver, CO on 18 Aug 1934. Children:

    212   i   Joel Christian BEATTY, b. 21 Jun 1961
    213   ii Jonathan Lawton BEATTY, b. 26 Nov 1963
    214   iii Evan William BEATTY, b. 17 May 1969

EIGHTH GENERATION

139. JAMES HART EVANS[8] (William Hooper Evans[7], Theresa Virginia Hooper[6], William Edward Hooper[5], Edward Jones Hooper[4], William Hooper[3], William Hooper[2], William Hooper[1]) child of William Hooper Evans and Dorothy Hart was born on 25 May 1927. He married Betty HEBRANK in 1955. Children:

    215   i   William Morehead EVANS, b. 9 Apr 1956
    216   ii Kathryn Morehead EVANS, b. 3 Nov 1958
    217   iii Susan Hart EVANS, b. 5 Sep 1961
    218   iv Ann Meriwether EVANS, b. 11 Oct 1962

140. VIRGINIA JONSIE EVANS[8] (William Hooper Evans[7], Theresa Virginia Hooper[6], William Edward Hooper[5], Edward Jones Hooper[4], William Hooper[3], William Hooper[2], William Hooper[1]) child of William Hooper Evans and Dorothy Hart was born on 9 Jul 1931. She married Charles Preston NOELL, Jr. in 1954. Children:

    219   i   Charles Preston NOELL, III, b. 13 Oct 1955

220   ii   Dorothy Holloway NOELL, b. 30 Dec 1956
221   iii   Martha Meriwether NOELL, b. 23 Nov 1959
222   iv   James Lawrence Hart NOELL, b. 9 May 1962

141. WILLIAM HOOPER EVANS[8] (William Hooper Evans[7], Theresa Virginia Hooper[6], William Edward Hooper[5], Edward Jones Hooper[4], William Hooper[3], William Hooper[2], William Hooper[1]) child of William Hooper Evans and Dorothy Hart was born on 19 Feb 1933. He married Marian O'MEARA in 1955. Children:

223   i   Nancy Hart EVANS, b. 5 Apr 1957
224   ii   Timothy Marquette EVANS, b. 15 Dec 1958
225   iii   Madeleine Hayes EVANS, b. 30 Dec 1960
226   iv   Melissa EVANS, b. 12 May 1962

142. ROBERT MERIWETHER EVANS[8] (William Hooper Evans[7], Theresa Virginia Hooper[6], William Edward Hooper[5], Edward Jones Hooper[4], William Hooper[3], William Hooper[2], William Hooper[1]) child of William Hooper Evans and Dorothy Hart was born on 26 Feb 1934. He married Marilyn WEST-HUES in 1959. Children:

227   i   Helen Hart EVANS, b. 2 Jul 1960
228   ii   Henry Westhues EVANS, b. 10 Oct 1961

144. CLEMENT MOREHEAD EVANS[8] (William Hooper Evans[7], Theresa Virginia Hooper[6], William Edward Hooper[5], Edward Jones Hooper[4], William Hooper[3], William Hooper[2], William Hooper[1]) child of William Hooper Evans and Dorothy Hart was born on 9 May 1941. He married Nancy Von WEISE in 1960. Child:

229   i   William Hooper EVANS, II, b. 16 Jul 1961

149. HELEN FAUCETT WILLS[8] (James Wills[7], Henry Clarence Wills[6], Helen DeBerniere Hooper[5], Mary Elizabeth Hooper[4], William Hooper[3], William Hooper[2], William Hooper[1]) child of James Wills and Ceclia Mae Strowd was born in Chapel Hill, NC on 5 Dec 1911, and died on 23 Feb 1982. She married Robert JOHNSON in 1925. Children:

+ 230   i   Rachael JOHNSON, b. 1926
  231   ii   Shelton Abernathy JOHNSON, b. c. 1928

150. THELMA RHETT WILLS[8] (James Wills[7], Henry Clarence Wills[6], Helen DeBerniere Hooper[5], Mary Elizabeth Hooper[4], William Hooper[3], William Hooper[2], William Hooper[1]) child of James Wills and Ceclia Mae Strowd was born in Chapel Hill, NC on 27 Mar 1914. She married (1st)

Lonny Hubert BURGESS in Danville, VA on 30 Sep 1933. She married (2nd) Charles Stalford HICKS on 3 Jul 1954.

Children by first marriage:

+ 232   i   May Elizabeth BURGESS, b.25 Dec 1935
  233   ii   Margie Louise BURGESS, b. 25 Oct 1938
  234   iii   Lonny Hubert BURGESS, Jr., b. 22 Nov 1941
+ 235   iv   Doris Marie BURGESS, b. 11 Feb 1946
+ 236   v   Marvin L. BURGESS, b. 18 Jun 1948

Child by second marriage:

  237   vi   Stephen Robin HICKS, b. 16 Feb 1956

151. JAMES WILLS[8] (James Wills[7], Henry Clarence Wills[6], Helen DeBerniere Hooper[5], Mary Elizabeth Hooper[4], William Hooper[3], William Hooper[2], William Hooper[1]) child of James Wills and Ceclia Mae Strowd was born in Chapel Hill, NC on 25 Aug 1917, and died in Durham, NC on 11 Aug 1995. He married Cordelia WEAVER on 6 May 1942. Child:

  238   i   James Henry WILLS, b. 23 Feb 1946

152. HAROLD BRYANT WILLS[8] (James Wills[7], Henry Clarence Wills[6], Helen DeBerniere Hooper[5], Mary Elizabeth Hooper[4], William Hooper[3], William Hooper[2], William Hooper[1]) child of James Wills and Ceclia Mae Strowd was born in Chapel Hill, NC on 16 May 1920, and died in Durham, NC on 25 Aug 1999. He married Betty Mae LONG, daughter of Rubin and Mamie (Merrit) Long in Mebane, NC on 27 Apr 1942. She was born in VA on 29 Jun 1925. Children:

+ 239   i   Julia Ann WILLS, b. 16 Sep 1946
+ 240   ii   Ruby May WILLS, b. 22 Mar 1948
+ 241   iii   Matthew Marshall WILLS, b. 25 May 1950
  242   iv   Harold Bryant WILLS, Jr., b. 19 Jul 1952
  243   v   Dwight DeBerniere WILLS, b. 26 Dec 1953
+ 244   vi   Betty Sue WILLS, b. 25 Feb 1958
+ 245   vii   Wanda Kaye WILLS, b. 5 May 1960

153. HENRY MELVIN WILLS[8] (James Wills[7], Henry Clarence Wills[6], Helen DeBerniere Hooper[5], Mary Elizabeth Hooper[4], William Hooper[3], William Hooper[2], William Hooper[1]) child of James Wills and Ceclia Mae Strowd was born in Chapel Hill, NC on 19 Dec 1922. He married Pauline WILKINS, daughter of Edward and Lillian (Duke) Wilkins in Durham, NC on 1 Feb 1951. She was born in Durham, NC on 20 Jun 1929. Children:

  246   i   Henry Melvin WILLS, Jr., b. 19 May 1953; unm
  247   ii   Donald Thomas WILLS, b. 20 Jun 1957

154. GEORGE DeBERNIERE WILLS[8] (James Wills[7], Henry Clarence Wills[6], Helen DeBerniere Hooper[5], Mary Elizabeth Hooper[4], William Hooper[3], William Hooper[2], William Hooper[1]) child of James Wills and Ceclia Mae Strowd was born in Chapel Hill, NC on 28 Aug 1929. He married Helen ROBERTS on 5 Apr 1958. She was born on 23 Feb 1936. Child:

+ 248   i   Thomas WILLS, b. 8 Aug 1959

155. RICHARD HOOPER WILLS[8] (James Wills[7], Henry Clarence Wills[6], Helen DeBerniere Hooper[5], Mary Elizabeth Hooper[4], William Hooper[3], William Hooper[2], William Hooper[1]) child of James Wills and Ceclia Mae Strowd was born in Chapel Hill, NC on 20 Jan 1933. He married Shirleen PARROTT on 16 Dec 1955. She was born on 16 Jan 1936. Children:

+ 249   i   Deborah Fay WILLS, b. 17 Dec 1957
+ 250   ii   Beverly Karen WILLS, b. 12 Oct 1959
+ 251   iii Richard Hooper WILLS, Jr.,b. 30 Jun 1962
+ 252   iv   Kirby Spencer WILLS, b. 18 Feb 1969

157. CLARENCE LUCAS WILLS, Jr.[8] (Clarence Lucas Wills[7], Henry Clarence Wills[6], Helen DeBerniere Hooper[5], Mary Elizabeth Hooper[4], William Hooper[3], William Hooper[2], William Hooper[1]) child of Clarence Lucas Wills and Margie Louise Riddle was born in Chapel Hill, NC on 30 Jun 1921, and died in Wenatchee, Chelan County, WA on 8 Mar 1999. He married Mary Kathleen MAYO, daughter of John Thomas and Eva Undine (Coburn) Mayo in Seattle, WA on 16 Sep 1943. She was born in Worland, Washakie County, WY on 16 Jan 1919. Children:

+ 253   i   Cheryl Anne WILLS, b. 19 Sep 1944
+ 254   ii   Russell Steven WILLS, b. 5 Oct 1947

158. HARRY DeBERNIERE WILLS[8] (Clarence Lucas Wills[7], Henry Clarence Wills[6], Helen DeBerniere Hooper[5], Mary Elizabeth Hooper[4], William Hooper[3], William Hooper[2], William Hooper[1]) child of Clarence Lucas Wills and Margie Louise Riddle was born in Chapel Hill, NC on 15 Nov 1924. He married (1st) Virginia Lee RICKETSON, daughter of James Lee and Loretta (Willard) Ricketson in Charleston, SC on 18 Apr 1945. She was born in Macon, GA on 17 Sep 1927. Children:

+ 255   i   Carolyn Glenn WILLS, b. 11 Jun 1947
+ 256   ii   Laura Lee WILLS, b. 24 Sep 1950
  257   iii Miriam Heather WILLS, b. 12 Jan 1956
  258   iv   Harry DeBerniere WILLS, Jr., b. 9 May 1957, d. 26 Apr 1985; unm

159. NORA LOUISE WILLS[8] (Clarence Lucas Wills[7], Henry Clarence Wills[6], Helen DeBerniere Hooper[5], Mary Elizabeth Hooper[4], William Hooper[3], William Hooper[2], William Hooper[1]) child of Clarence Lucas Wills and Margie Louise Riddle was born in Chapel Hill, NC on 27 Aug 1926. She married Ted Marvin JOLLAY, son of the Rev. Charles and Loree (Gallamore) Jollay in Summerville, SC on 11 Jun 1951. He was born in Asheville, NC on 30 Jun 1917, and died in Charleston, SC on 6 Oct 1983. Children:

    259   i   Rebecca deLide JOLLAY, b. 25 Mar 1952
    260   ii David Earl JOLLAY, b. 2 Aug 1953
    261   iii Daniel Francis JOLLAY, b. 28 Jul 1957

163. WILLIAM STEVENSON WESTON, III[8] (William Stevenson Weston, Jr.[7], William Stevenson Weston[6], Sarah Jerkins Hooper[5], Thomas Clark Hooper[4], William Hooper[3], William Hooper[2], William Hooper[1]) child of William Stevenson Weston, Jr. and Capitola Catherine King was born in Aynor, Horry County, SC on 20 Jan 1941. He married (1st) Peggy Sue GARRETT, daughter of Gerald Alonzo and Mary Jane (Cole) Garrett in Conway, SC on 23 Jul 1963. She was born in Anderson, SC on 17 Feb 1944. Children:

+ 262   i   Tara Capitola WESTON, b. 20 Jan 1964
+ 263   ii Natalie Suzanne WESTON, b. 24 May 1965
    264   iii William Stevenson WESTON, IV, b. Sep 1968, dy Sep 1968
+ 265   iv William Stevenson WESTON, IV, b. 15 May 1972 [Again]
    266   v   Mary Catherine WESTON, b. 19 Sep 1973

164. EUGENE KING WESTON[8] (William Stevenson Weston, Jr.[7], William Stevenson Weston[6], Sarah Jerkins Hooper[5], Thomas Clark Hooper[4], William Hooper[3], William Hooper[2], William Hooper[1]) child of William Stevenson Weston, Jr. and Capitola Catherine King was born in Columbia, SC on 26 Apr 1943. He married (1st) Carmen Lucretia DUNCAN, daughter of Garret Davies and Christine (Carston) Duncan in Charleston, SC on 21 Jul 1967. She was born on 21 Jun 1944. He married (2nd) Elizabeth CRIBB in Apr 1979.

Children by first marriage:

+ 267   i   Eugene King WESTON, Jr., b. 18 Feb 1968
    268   ii Julia Catherine WESTON, b. 11 May 1969

Child by second marriage:

    269   iii Edward Andrew WESTON, b. 13 Apr 1981

165. JAMES CARTER WESTON[8] (William Stevenson Weston, Jr.[7], William Stevenson Weston[6], Sarah Jerkins Hooper[5], Thomas Clark Hooper[4],

William Hooper[3], William Hooper[2], William Hooper[1]) child of William Stevenson Weston, Jr. and Capitola Catherine King was born in Columbia, SC on 20 Jun 1948. He married Sandra LLOYD, daughter of James David and Sara (Cook) Lloyd in Columbia, SC on 5 Sep 1970. She was born in Columbia, SC on 7 Apr 1950. Children:

   270   i   James Carter WESTON, Jr., b. 9 May 1973
   271   ii   Lloyd David WESTON, b. 29 Apr 1976
   272   iii   King Sheely WESTON, b. 27 Jul 1978

166. RICHARD HOLLIDAY WESTON[8] (William Stevenson Weston, Jr.[7], William Stevenson Weston[6], Sarah Jerkins Hooper[5], Thomas Clark Hooper[4], William Hooper[3], William Hooper[2], William Hooper[1]) child of William Stevenson Weston, Jr. and Capitola Catherine King was born in Columbia, SC on 7 Jul 1951. He married Jennifer LOUD, daughter of John Merrill and Geneva (Vereen) Loud in Garden City, SC on 23 Apr 1977. She was born on 28 Aug 1953. Children:

   273   i   Capitola King WESTON, b. 10 Mar 1980
   274   ii   Jennifer Merrill WESTON, b. 12 Apr 1983
   275   iii   Richard Holliday WESTON, b. 6 Nov 1989

167. ROBERT GABREY WESTON[8] (William Stevenson Weston, Jr.[7], William Stevenson Weston[6], Sarah Jerkins Hooper[5], Thomas Clark Hooper[4], William Hooper[3], William Hooper[2], William Hooper[1]) child of William Stevenson Weston, Jr. and Capitola Catherine King was born in Columbia, SC on 7 Jul 1951. He married Elmira deGraffenried KEENAN, daughter of Richard deGraffenried and Lucia (Green) Keenan in Columbia, SC on 3 Jun 1972. She was born on 5 Mar 1952. Children:

   276   i   Robert Gabrey WESTON, Jr., b. 6 Feb 1977
   277   ii   Catherine Keenan WESTON, b. 12 Nov 1979

168. EDWARD STOCKTON CROFT, III[8] (Irene Gabrey Weston[7], William Stevenson Weston[6], Sarah Jerkins Hooper[5], Thomas Clark Hooper[4], William Hooper[3], William Hooper[2], William Hooper[1]) child of Irene Gabrey Weston and Edward Stockton Croft, Jr. was born in Columbia, SC on 12 Sep 1942. He married Susan Francez [sic] BRONSON in Shreveport, LA on 20 Jun 1964. She was born in Shreveport, LA on 14 Feb 1942. Children:

+ 278   i   Edward Stockton CROFT, IV, b. 3 Jan 1969
   279   ii   Francez Gabrey CROFT, b. 2 May 1970

170. LAWRENCE McMAHON CROFT[8] (Irene Gabrey Weston[7], William Stevenson Weston[6], Sarah Jerkins Hooper[5], Thomas Clark Hooper[4], William

Hooper[3], William Hooper[2], William Hooper[1]) child of Irene Gabrey Weston and Edward Stockton Croft, Jr. was born in Columbia, SC on 16 Feb 1946. He married Susan Lewis BRUSH in Lexington, VA on 31 Aug 1968. She was born in Lexington, VA on 11 Oct 1946. Children:

280   i   Susan Lewis CROFT, b. 11 Oct 1972
281   ii   Lawrence McMahon CROFT, b. 23 Jan 1976
282   iii   Marshall St. Julien CROFT, b. 22 Aug 1979
283   iv   Tucker Crosswell CROFT, b. 28 Jul 1982
284   v   Ann Carrington CROFT, b. 7 Oct 1987

171. STEVENSON WESTON CROFT[8] (Irene Gabrey Weston[7], William Stevenson Weston[6], Sarah Jerkins Hooper[5], Thomas Clark Hooper[4], William Hooper[3], William Hooper[2], William Hooper[1]) child of Irene Gabrey Weston and Edward Stockton Croft, Jr. was born in Atlanta, GA on 27 Jul 1952. He married Ouida Naomi COX in Lake Charles, LA on 27 Mar 1976. She was born in Houston, TX on 3 Oct 1951. Children:

285   i   Lee Sadler CROFT, b. 24 Aug 1982
286   ii   Stevenson Weston CROFT, Jr., b. 15 Apr 1984
287   iii   John Cox CROFT, b. 12 Jun 1987

173. MARY GAILLARD CROFT[8] (Irene Gabrey Weston[7], William Stevenson Weston[6], Sarah Jerkins Hooper[5], Thomas Clark Hooper[4], William Hooper[3], William Hooper[2], William Hooper[1]) child of Irene Gabrey Weston and Edward Stockton Croft, Jr. was born in Atlanta, GA on 13 Aug 1957. She married Gregory Rhey FERGUSON in Atlanta, GA on 3 May 1980. He was born in Independence, MO on 4 Aug 1949. Child:

288   i   Mary Elizabeth FERGUSON, b. 24 Oct 1985

174. PEGGY LOUISE WESTON[8] (Thomas Isaac Weston[7], William Stevenson Weston[6], Sarah Jerkins Hooper[5], Thomas Clark Hooper[4], William Hooper[3], William Hooper[2], William Hooper[1]) child of Thomas Isaac Weston and Peggy Louise Hedrick was born in Columbia, SC on 24 Mar 1952. She married Robert McElwee RAINEY in Columbia, SC on 1 Jan 1976. He was born in 1952. Children:

289   i   Weston McElwee RAINEY, b. 1980
290   ii   Robert Clark RAINEY, b. 1984
291   iii   Caroline Gabrey RAINEY, b. 1988

175. THOMAS ISAAC WESTON, Jr.[8] (Thomas Isaac Weston[7], William Stevenson Weston[6], Sarah Jerkins Hooper[5], Thomas Clark Hooper[4], William Hooper[3], William Hooper[2], William Hooper[1]) child of Thomas Isaac Weston and Peggy Louise Hedrick was born in Columbia, SC on 3 Oct 1956. He married Dianne Allee HANCOCK in Columbia, SC on 9 Jun 1984. She was born in 1957. Children:

292   i   Derek Thomas WESTON, b. 1986
293   ii William Tucker WESTON, b. 1988
294   iii John Reid WESTON, b. 1992

178. JAMES CALDWELL WESTON, Jr.[8] (James Caldwell Weston[7], William Stevenson Weston[6], Sarah Jerkins Hooper[5], Thomas Clark Hooper[4], William Hooper[3], William Hooper[2], William Hooper[1]) child of James Caldwell Weston and Carolyn Jean Edgar was born in Columbia, SC on 11 Nov 1951. He married Vicki OLIVER in Sanford, VA on 25 Apr 1987. She was born in Newport News, VA on 19 Oct 1955. Children:

295   i   April Nicole WESTON, b. 23 Feb 1988
296   ii Brooke Elizabeth WESTON, b. 19 May 1989

179. LESLIE EDGAR WESTON[8] (James Caldwell Weston[7], William Stevenson Weston[6], Sarah Jerkins Hooper[5], Thomas Clark Hooper[4], William Hooper[3], William Hooper[2], William Hooper[1]) child of James Caldwell Weston and Carolyn Jean Edgar was born in Columbia, SC on 12 Apr 1954. She married George Mark CUSHMAN in Macon, GA on 19 Mar 1977. He was born in Chattanooga, TN on 15 Mar 1954. Children:

297   i   Rebecca Corinne CUSHMAN, b. 1 May 1980
298   ii Christopher Weston CUSHMAN, b. 26 Sep 1981
299   iii Anna Elizabeth CUSHMAN, b. 8 Apr 1984

180. ELIZABETH ANNE WESTON[8] (James Caldwell Weston[7], William Stevenson Weston[6], Sarah Jerkins Hooper[5], Thomas Clark Hooper[4], William Hooper[3], William Hooper[2], William Hooper[1]) child of James Caldwell Weston and Carolyn Jean Edgar was born in Columbia, SC on 16 Oct 1956. She married Jeffrey Martin NOEL in Macon, GA on 14 Feb 1981. He was born in Houston, TX on 11 Jun 1957. Children:

300   i   Mark Jeffrey NOEL, b. 24 Oct 1983
301   ii Kate Elizabeth NOEL, b. 13 Mar 1986
302   iii William Weston NOEL, b. 27 Jan 1989

182. MARY POSTELL WESTON[8] (Christian Tucker Weston, Jr.[7], Christian Tucker Weston[6], Sarah Jerkins Hooper[5], Thomas Clark Hooper[4], William Hooper[3], William Hooper[2], William Hooper[1]) child of Christian Tucker Weston, Jr. and Pauline Hasell Hanckel was born in Columbia, SC on 29 Oct 1947. She married Edward Barnwell GRIMBALL in Columbia, SC on 11 Oct 1969. He was born in Charleston, SC on 13 May 1944. Child:

303   i   Edward Barnwell GRIMBALL, Jr., b. 15 Mar 1977

183. CHRISTIAN TUCKER WESTON, III[8] (Christian Tucker Weston, Jr.[7], Christian Tucker Weston[6], Sarah Jerkins Hooper[5], Thomas Clark Hooper[4], William Hooper[3], William Hooper[2], William Hooper[1]) child of Christian Tucker Weston, Jr. and Pauline Hasell Hanckel was born in Columbia, SC on 28 Aug 1950. He married Anne Chamblee THORNHILL in Charleston, SC on 3 Jun 1978. She was born in Charleston, SC on 31 Aug 1955. Children:

304   i   Sarah Jernigan WESTON, b. 11 Feb 1985
305   ii Drayton Chamblee WESTON, b. 2 Sep 1989

184. FRANCES STUART WESTON[8] (Christian Tucker Weston, Jr.[7], Christian Tucker Weston[6], Sarah Jerkins Hooper[5], Thomas Clark Hooper[4], William Hooper[3], William Hooper[2], William Hooper[1]) child of Christian Tucker Weston, Jr. and Pauline Hasell Hanckel was born in Columbia, SC on 21 May 1953. She married Walter Roy SMITH in Columbia, SC on 5 May 1979. He was born in GERMANY on 17 Nov 1957. Children:

306   i   Roy Walter SMITH, b. 24 Sep 1981
307   ii Robert Weston SMITH, b. 20 Nov 1984

186. SARAH CATHERINE WESTON[8] (English Hopkins Weston[7], Christian Tucker Weston[6], Sarah Jerkins Hooper[5], Thomas Clark Hooper[4], William Hooper[3], William Hooper[2], William Hooper[1]) child of English Hopkins Weston and Sarah Catherine Crawford was born in York, SC on 12 Feb 1955. She married John Taylor CONWAY on 28 Feb 1983. He was born in Washington, DC on 13 Dec 1956. Children:

308   i   Elisabeth Grace CONWAY, b. 28 Dec 1983
309   ii Edwin Jacob CONWAY, b. 25 Feb 1986 [twin]
310 iii James Samuel CONWAY, b. 25 Feb 1986 [twin]
311 iv Sarah Catherine CONWAY, b. 1 Jul 1994

188. ANDREW CORNISH WESTON[8] (English Hopkins Weston[7], Christian Tucker Weston[6], Sarah Jerkins Hooper[5], Thomas Clark Hooper[4], William Hooper[3], William Hooper[2], William Hooper[1]) child of English Hopkins Weston and Sarah Catherine Crawford was born in Chattanooga, TN on 14 Aug 1959. He married Rita Marie BACHMAN in Union, SC on 25 Dec 1982. She was born in Columbus, OH on 21 Jun 1957. Children:

312   i   Amanda Brianne WESTON, b. 19 Nov 1986
313   ii Brian Alexander WESTON, b. 1 Apr 1988

190. WALTER HERBERT ZIMMERMANN[8] (Sarah Weston Robison[7], Sarah Hooper Weston[6], Sarah Jerkins Hooper[5], Thomas Clark Hooper[4], William Hooper[3], William Hooper[2], William Hooper[1]) child of Sarah Weston Robison and Walter Gustaf Zimmermann, Jr. was born in Omaha, NE on 17 Jun 1944. He married (1st) Sharon Alice WETZEL on 10 Dec 1971. Child:

+ 314   i   Walter Troy ZIMMERMANN, b. 27 May 1973

193. CHARLES DePUY ROBISON, III[8] (Charles DePuy Robison, Jr.[7], Sarah Hooper Weston[6], Sarah Jerkins Hooper[5], Thomas Clark Hooper[4], William Hooper[3], William Hooper[2], William Hooper[1]) child of Charles DuPuy Robison, Jr. and Elizabeth Jernigan Bell was born in Charleston, SC on 5 Mar 1947. He married Katherine Grace DURRELL on 4 May 1974. She was born on 15 Jul 1959. Children:

315   i   Charles DePuy ROBISON, IV, b. 6 Mar 1979
316   ii   Katherine Bell ROBISON, b. 12 Mar 1981

194. ALEXANDER BELL ROBISON[8] (Charles DePuy Robison, Jr.[7], Sarah Hooper Weston[6], Sarah Jerkins Hooper[5], Thomas Clark Hooper[4], William Hooper[3], William Hooper[2], William Hooper[1]) child of Charles DuPuy Robison, Jr. and Elizabeth Jernigan Bell was born in Nashville, TN on 21 Jul 1950. He married Sharon Virginia DIVELEY on 6 Oct 1979. She was born in Nashville, TN on 30 Mar 1951. Children:

317   i   Alexander Lloyd ROBISON, b. 14 Nov 1984
318   ii   Elizabeth Diveley ROBISON, b. 9 May 1990

195. ELIZABETH JERNIGAN ROBISON[8] (Charles DePuy Robison, Jr.[7], Sarah Hooper Weston[6], Sarah Jerkins Hooper[5], Thomas Clark Hooper[4], William Hooper[3], William Hooper[2], William Hooper[1]) child of Charles DePuy Robison, Jr. and Elizabeth Jernigan Bell was born in Norfolk, VA on 19 Aug 1952. She married David Victor OTTERSON on 4 Aug 1979. He was born on 4 Oct 1954. Child:

319   i   John Hunter OTTERSON, b. 27 May 1989

196. KATHRYN DIANE ROBISON[8] (William Whitwell Robison[7], Sarah Hooper Weston[6], Sarah Jerkins Hooper[5], Thomas Clark Hooper[4], William Hooper[3], William Hooper[2], William Hooper[1]) child of William Whitwell Robison and his 1st wife Kathryn Critchfield was born on 12 Jun 1949. She married (1st) Gary Allen NELSON on 20 Dec 1969. He was born on 12 Jan 1949. Children:

320   i   Laura Alene NELSON, b. 10 Feb 1973
321   ii   Julie Anne NELSON, b. 10 Apr 1975

197. WILLIAM WHITWELL ROBISON, III[8] (William Whitwell Robison[7], Sarah Hooper Weston[6], Sarah Jerkins Hooper[5], Thomas Clark Hooper[4], William Hooper[3], William Hooper[2], William Hooper[1]) child of William Whitwell Robison and his 1st wife Kathryn Critchfield was born on 9 Sep 1953. He married Anne Denise CALLAHAN on 5 Aug 1978. Children:

- 322   i   Kathryn Anne ROBISON, b. 19 Jan 1982 [twin]
- 323   ii   Sarah Chandler ROBISON, b. 19 Jan 1982 [twin]
- 324   iii   William Whitwell ROBISON, IV, b. 21 Aug 1985
- 325   iv   Elizabeth Denise ROBISON, b. 29 May 1991

198. JAMES CRITCHFIELD ROBISON[8] (William Whitwell Robison[7], Sarah Hooper Weston[6], Sarah Jerkins Hooper[5], Thomas Clark Hooper[4], William Hooper[3], William Hooper[2], William Hooper[1]) child of William Whitwell Robison and his 1st wife Kathryn Critchfield was born on 7 Jul 1955. He married Carol Lynn LYLES on 8 Aug 1981. Children:

- 326   i   Haley Lynn ROBISON, b. 18 Aug 1985
- 327   ii   Holly Lee ROBISON, b. 9 Dec 1986
- 328   iii   Lacey Elizabeth ROBISON, b. 8 Oct 1990
- 329   iv   Parker Thomas ROBISON, b. 10 Feb 1993

199. MARIE KIMBERLY ROBISON[8] (William Whitwell Robison[7], Sarah Hooper Weston[6], Sarah Jerkins Hooper[5], Thomas Clark Hooper[4], William Hooper[3], William Hooper[2], William Hooper[1]) child of William Whitwell Robison and his 2nd wife Kathleen Kimberly Meyer was born on 19 Jun 1964. She married Stephan John MAGNELIA on 1 Oct 1983. He was born on 30 Oct 1961. Children:

- 330   i   Nichole Marie MAGNELIA, b. 21 Oct 1984
- 331   ii   Sarah Michelle MAGNELIA, b. 20 May 1989

200. HAROLD DOIDGE LOWRY, Jr.[8] (Mary Elizabeth Robison[7], Sarah Hooper Weston[6], Sarah Jerkins Hooper[5], Thomas Clark Hooper[4], William Hooper[3], William Hooper[2], William Hooper[1]) child of Mary Elizabeth Robison and Harold Doidge Lowry was born in Ames, IA on 19 Jun 1952. He married Leigh Ann WIESE in Bar Mills, York County, ME on 8 Jul 1978. She was born in Hartford, CT on 10 Dec 1954. Children:

- 332   i   Malcolm Clarke LOWRY, b. 8 Oct 1982
- 333   ii   Melissa Ross LOWRY, b. 13 Feb 1988

201. MARY SUSAN LOWRY[8] (Mary Elizabeth Robison[7], Sarah Hooper Weston[6], Sarah Jerkins Hooper[5], Thomas Clark Hooper[4], William Hooper[3],

William Hooper², William Hooper¹) child of Mary Elizabeth Robison and Harold Doidge Lowry was born in Rochester, NY on 14 Dec 1954. She married William Raymond MOREHOUSE in Rochester, NY on 27 Dec 1976. He was born in Akron, OH on 13 Mar 1943. Children:

   334   i   Sarah Ann MOREHOUSE, b. 22 Feb 1977
   335   ii Nathan Isaiah MOREHOUSE, b. 10 Dec 1978
   336   iii Johanna Elizabeth MOREHOUSE, b. 5 Sep 1981
   337   iv Joel David MOREHOUSE, b. 5 Nov 1983

205. AUBREY JULIAN MELLICHAMPE [8] (Samuel Haworth Mellichampe[7], Edward Winborn Mellichampe[6], Amelia Jones Hooper[5], Thomas Clark Hooper[4], William Hooper[3], William Hooper[2], William Hooper[1]) child of Samuel Haworth Mellichampe and Gladys Ethridge was born in Petersburg, VA on 9 Nov 1939. He married Rebecca LEWIS, daughter of Wesley Leroy and Mary (Temple) Lewis in Prince George County, VA on 24 Dec 1959. She was born in Dinwiddie County, VA on 29 Sep 1941. Children:

   338   i Rebecca Anne MELLICHAMPE, b. 2 Oct 1961
+ 339   ii Samuel Aubrey MELLICHAMPE, b. 31 May 1968

206. EDWARD MELLICHAMPE[8] (Samuel Haworth Mellichampe[7], Edward Winborn Mellichampe[6], Amelia Jones Hooper[5], Thomas Clark Hooper[4], William Hooper[3], William Hooper[2], William Hooper[1]) child of Samuel Haworth Mellichampe and Gladys Ethridge was born in Richmond, VA on 23 Dec 1946. He married (2nd) Annette RUSSELL, daughter of Walley and Ann (Westmoreland) Russell in Prince George County, VA on 5 Mar 1973. She was born in Petersburg, VA on 15 Mar 1953. Child:

   340   i Kelly Lynn MELLICHAMPE, b. 7 Jun 1975

207. FRANCES MARIAN ("Dolly") SHEFFIELD[8] (Frances Marion Mellichampe[7], James Hooper Mellichampe[6], Amelia Jones Hooper[5], Thomas Clark Hooper[4], William Hooper[3], William Hooper[2], William Hooper[1]) child of Frances Marion Mellichampe and Fletcher Lamsr Sheffield, Jr. was born on 1 May 1937. She married (1st) Frederick NEBRBAS, III on 24 Sep 1960. She married (2nd) Alexander MacINTYRE on 25 Oct 1972.
Child by first marriage:

   341   i Frances Marian NEBRBAS, b. c. 1963
Child by second marriage:

   342   ii Frances Marian MacINTYRE, b. 15 Feb 1978

209. CLAUDIA CAROL SMITH[8] (Eleanor Charles Mellichampe[7], James Hooper Mellichampe[6], Amelia Jones Hooper[5], Thomas Clark Hooper[4], William Hooper[3], William Hooper[2], William Hooper[1]) child of Eleanor Charles Mellichampe and Norman Griffith Smith was born on 26 Jan 1947. She married Michael Gordon DUFFY in say 1965. Children:

> 343   i   Aileen Archer DUFFY, b. 9 Sep 1966
> 344   ii   Barclay Patrick DUFFY, b. 3 Sep 1968
> 345   iii   Erin Brydges DUFFY, b. 7 Aug 1976

210. RANDOLPH HOOPER SMITH[8] (Eleanor Charles Mellichampe[7], James Hooper Mellichampe[6], Amelia Jones Hooper[5], Thomas Clark Hooper[4], William Hooper[3], William Hooper[2], William Hooper[1]) child of Eleanor Charles Mellichampe and Norman Griffith Smith was born on 21 Feb 1952. He married Barbara Lee WIDMAN in say 1978. Children:

> 346   i   Justin Elliot SMITH, b. 15 Feb 1981
> 347   ii   Timothy Asher SMITH, b. 3 Mar 1983
> 348   iii   Andrew Karsten SMITH, b. 4 Nov 1987

NINTH GENERATION

230. RACHAEL JOHNSON[9] (Helen Faucett Wills[8], James Wills[7], Henry Clarence Wills[6], Helen DeBerniere Hooper[5], Mary Elizabeth Hooper[4], William Hooper[3], William Hooper[2], William Hooper[1]) child of Helen Faucett Wills and Robert Johnson was born in 1926. She married (1st) Marvin RILEY in say 1944. Children:

> 349   i   Marvin Bryant RILEY, b. 1945
> 350   ii   Lucile RILEY, b. 1946

232. MAY ELIZABETH BURGESS[9] (Thelma Rhett Wills[8], James Wills[7], Henry Clarence Wills[6], Helen DeBerniere Hooper[5], Mary Elizabeth Hooper[4], William Hooper[3], William Hooper[2], William Hooper[1]) child of Thelma Rhett Wills and her 1st husband Lonny Hubert Burgess was born on 25 Dec 1935, and died on 30 May 1991. She married (1st) Alton HOWARD in say 1954. She married (2nd) Larry GREEN in say 1962.

Child by first marriage:

> 351   i   Patsy HOWARD, b. c. 1956

Children by second marriage:

> 352   ii   Brenda GREEN, b. c. 1964
> 353   iii   Linda GREEN, b. c. 1966
> 354   iv   Larry GREEN, Jr., b. c.1969

235. DORIS MARIE BURGESS[9] (Thelma Rhett Wills[8], James Wills[7], Henry Clarence Wills[6], Helen DeBerniere Hooper[5], Mary Elizabeth Hooper[4], William Hooper[3], William Hooper[2], William Hooper[1]) child of Thelma Rhett Wills and her 1st husband Lonny Hubert Burgess was born in Durham, NC on 11 Feb 1946. She married (1st) Lawrence HOWARD in say 1963. Children:

+ 355   i   Lisa Kay HOWARD, b. 9 Jul 1963
   356   ii   William HOWARD, b. 7 Aug 1964

236. MARVIN L. BURGESS[9] (Thelma Rhett Wills[8], James Wills[7], Henry Clarence Wills[6], Helen DeBerniere Hooper[5], Mary Elizabeth Hooper[4], William Hooper[3], William Hooper[2], William Hooper[1]) child of Thelma Rhett Wills and her 1st husband Lonny Hubert Burgess was born on 18 Jun 1948. He married Teresa GLADDEN on 23 Aug 1968. She was born on 23 Mar 1951. Child:

+ 357   i   Donnie BURGESS, b. 11 Aug 1971

239. JULIA ANN WILLS[9] (Harold Bryant Wills[8], James Wills[7], Henry Clarence Wills[6], Helen DeBerniere Hooper[5], Mary Elizabeth Hooper[4], William Hooper[3], William Hooper[2], William Hooper[1]) child of Harold Bryant Wills and Betty Mae Long was born in Durham, NC on 16 Sep 1946. She married Anthony Boone FISHER on 3 Jul 1966. Children:

+ 358`   i   LaTasha DeAnne [sic] FISHER, b. 20 Oct 1966
   359   ii   Kimberly Ann FISHER, b. c. 1968
   360   iii   Anthony Boone FISHER, Jr., b. c. 1970
   361   iv   Jeremy Alexander FISHER, b. c. 1973

240. RUBY MAY WILLS[9] (Harold Bryant Wills[8], James Wills[7], Henry Clarence Wills[6], Helen DeBerniere Hooper[5], Mary Elizabeth Hooper[4], William Hooper[3], William Hooper[2], William Hooper[1]) child of Harold Bryant Wills and Betty Mae Long was born in Durham, NC on 22 Mar 1948. She married Wade Ivey STONE on 31 Dec 1965. Child:

   362   i   Dale LaRee [sic] STONE, b. 1970, d. Nov 1991; unm

241. MATTHEW MARSHALL WILLS[9] (Harold Bryant Wills[8], James Wills[7], Henry Clarence Wills[6], Helen DeBerniere Hooper[5], Mary Elizabeth Hooper[4], William Hooper[3], William Hooper[2], William Hooper[1]) child of Harold Bryant Wills and Betty Mae Long was born in Durham, NC on 25 May 1950. He married Melinda Sue BROWN on 8 Oct 1966. Children:

   363   i   Deborah Leigh WILLS, b. c. 1968
   364   ii   Matthew Marshall WILLS, Jr., b. c. 1970
   365   iii   Mark Edwards WILLS, b. c. 1974

244. BETTY SUE WILLS[9] (Harold Bryant Wills[8], James Wills[7], Henry Clarence Wills[6], Helen DeBerniere Hooper[5], Mary Elizabeth Hooper[4], William Hooper[3], William Hooper[2], William Hooper[1]) child of Harold Bryant Wills and Betty Mae Long was born in Durham, NC on 25 Feb 1958. She married (1st) Michael Todd GOING in say 1976. She married (2nd) Kenneth Chester APPEL on 12 Sep 1982. He was born on 16 Oct 1959.
Children by first marriage:
    366   i   LaTasha Sheri GOING, b. 30 Apr 1977
+ 367   ii Michael Todd GOING, Jr., b. 2 Aug 1978
Child by second marriage:
    368   iii Kenni Alicia APPEL, b. 28 Jan 1984

245. WANDA KAYE WILLS[9] (Harold Bryant Wills[8], James Wills[7], Henry Clarence Wills[6], Helen DeBerniere Hooper[5], Mary Elizabeth Hooper[4], William Hooper[3], William Hooper[2], William Hooper[1]) child of Harold Bryant Wills and Betty Mae Long was born in Durham, NC on 5 May 1960. She married Thomas William NORTON on 24 Nov 1980. Children:
    369   i   Judith Nicole NORTON, b. 27 Jul 1981
    370   ii Jennifer Renee NORTON, b. 2 Aug 1982

248. THOMAS WILLS[9] (George DeBerniere Wills[8], James Wills[7], Henry Clarence Wills[6], Helen DeBerniere Hooper[5], Mary Elizabeth Hooper[4], William Hooper[3], William Hooper[2], William Hooper[1]) child of George DeBerniere Wills and Helen Roberts was born in NC on 8 Aug 1959. She married Tamera CONE in say 1983. Child:
    371   i   Tamera Nicole WILLS, b. 10 Jun 1985

249. DEBORAH FAY WILLS[9] (Richard Hooper Wills[8], James Wills[7], Henry Clarence Wills[6], Helen DeBerniere Hooper[5], Mary Elizabeth Hooper[4], William Hooper[3], William Hooper[2], William Hooper[1]) child of Richard Hooper Wills and Shirleen Parrott was born in Durham County, NC on 17 Dec 1957. She married David EBY on 12 Nov 1979. He was born on 25 Sep 1957. Children:
    372   i   Kristen EBY, b. 11 Sep 1984
    373   ii Lauren EBY, b. 5 Feb 1986

250. BEVERLY KAREN WILLS[9] (Richard Hooper Wills[8], James Wills[7], Henry Clarence Wills[6], Helen DeBerniere Hooper[5], Mary Elizabeth Hooper[4], William Hooper[3], William Hooper[2], William Hooper[1]) child of Richard Hooper Wills and Shirleen Parrott was born in Durham County, NC on 12

Oct 1959. She married Mitchell BAKER on 2 Jul 1983. He was born on 1 Mar 1958. Children:

374   i   Audra [sic] BAKER, b. 28 Sep 1985
375   ii   Sarah BAKER, b. 24 Jun 1987
376   iii Kaleb BAKER, b. 9 Feb 1989

251. RICHARD HOOPER WILLS, Jr.[9] (Richard Hooper Wills[8], James Wills[7], Henry Clarence Wills[6], Helen DeBerniere Hooper[5], Mary Elizabeth Hooper[4], William Hooper[3], William Hooper[2], William Hooper[1]) child of Richard Hooper Wills and Shirleen Parrott was born in Durham County, NC on 30 Jun 1962. He married Rebecca DAIGLE on 27 Jun 1980. Shje was born on 23 Aug 1957. Children:

377   i   Richard Hooper WILLS, III, b. 17 Jun 1982
378   ii   Ronald Harvey WILLS, b. 27 Nov 1983

252. KIRBY SPENCER WILLS[9] (Richard Hooper Wills[8], James Wills[7], Henry Clarence Wills[6], Helen DeBerniere Hooper[5], Mary Elizabeth Hooper[4], William Hooper[3], William Hooper[2], William Hooper[1]) child of Richard Hooper Wills and Shirleen Parrott was born in Durham County, NC on 18 Feb 1969. He married Tammy WAGONER in say 1993. Children:

379   i   Landon Daye WILLS, b. 12 Jan 1996
380   ii   Logan Bailey WILLS, b. 17 Aug 1998

253. CHERYL ANNE WILLS[9] (Clarence Lucas Wills, Jr.[8], Clarence Lucas Wills[7], Henry Clarence Wills[6], Helen DeBerniere Hooper[5], Mary Elizabeth Hooper[4], William Hooper[3], William Hooper[2], William Hooper[1]) child of Clarence Lucas Wills, Jr. and Mary Kathleen Mayo was born in Wenatchee, Chelan County, WA on 19 Sep 1944. She married (1st) Terry Dean ORCUTT on 11 May 1963. Children:

381   i   Patrick Raymond ORCUTT, b. 23 Nov 1963
+ 382 ii   Christopher Jon ORCUTT, b. 4 Apr 1965

254. RUSSELL STEVEN WILLS[9] (Clarence Lucas Wills, Jr.[8], Clarence Lucas Wills[7], Henry Clarence Wills[6], Helen DeBerniere Hooper[5], Mary Elizabeth Hooper[4], William Hooper[3], William Hooper[2], William Hooper[1]) child of Clarence Lucas Wills, Jr. and Mary Kathleen Mayo was born in Wenatchee, Chelan County, WA on 5 Oct 1947. He married Brenda Jean SPURLOCK in Monitor, WA on 9 Aug 1967. Children:

+ 383 i   Tawnya Faith WILLS, b. 4 Oct 1970
384   ii   Kiffin Lynn WILLS, b. 20 Sep 1974

255. CAROLYN GLENN WILLS[9] (Harry DeBerniere Wills[8], Clarence Lucas Wills[7], Henry Clarence Wills[6], Helen DeBerniere Hooper[5], Mary Elizabeth Hooper[4], William Hooper[3], William Hooper[2], William Hooper[1]) child of Harry DeBerniere Wills and Virginia Lee Ricketson was born in Asheville, NC on 11 Jun 1947. She married (1st) Charles E. TAYLOR on 29 Dec 1965. Children:

+ 385   i   Jennifer Anne TAYLOR, b. 4 Oct 1966
   386   ii   Julia Kay TAYLOR, b. 12 Jul 1968

256. LAURA LEE WILLS[9] (Harry DeBerniere Wills[8], Clarence Lucas Wills[7], Henry Clarence Wills[6], Helen DeBerniere Hooper[5], Mary Elizabeth Hooper[4], William Hooper[3], William Hooper[2], William Hooper[1]) child of Harry DeBerniere Wills and Virginia Lee Ricketson was born in Athens, GA on 24 Sep 1950. She married Michael Wayne EDWARDS in Oak Ridge, TN on 28 Jun 1968. Children:

   387   i   Russell Elliott EDWARDS, b. 19 Nov 1974
   388   ii   Matthew David EDWARDS, b. 13 Feb 1979

262. TARA CAPITOLA WESTON[9] (William Stevenson Weston, III[8], William Stevenson Weston, Jr.[7], William Stevenson Weston[6], Sarah Jerkins Hooper[5], Thomas Clark Hooper[4], William Hooper[3], William Hooper[2], William Hooper[1]) child of William Stevenson Weston, III and Peggy Sue Garrett was born in Columbia, SC on 20 Jan 1964. She married Mark R. HAWKINSON in Columbia, SC on 22 Apr 1989. Child:

   389   i   Sarah Elaine HAWKINSON, b. 25 Jun 1996

263. NATALIE SUZANNE WESTON[9] (William Stevenson Weston, III[8], William Stevenson Weston, Jr.[7], William Stevenson Weston[6], Sarah Jerkins Hooper[5], Thomas Clark Hooper[4], William Hooper[3], William Hooper[2], William Hooper[1]) child of William Stevenson Weston, III and Peggy Sue Garrett was born in Columbia, SC on 24 May 1965. She married Edward Cofton COKER in Columbia, SC on 5 Mar 1989. Children:

   390   i   Catherine Elise COKER, b. 22 Sep 1989
   391   ii   Weston Cofton COKER, b. 10 May 1995

265. WILLIAM STEVENSON WESTON, IV[9] (William Stevenson Weston, III[8], William Stevenson Weston, Jr.[7], William Stevenson Weston[6], Sarah Jerkins Hooper[5], Thomas Clark Hooper[4], William Hooper[3], William Hooper[2], William Hooper[1]) child of William Stevenson Weston, III and Peggy Sue Garrett was born in Columbia, SC on 15 May 1972. He married Nikki WILLIAMS in Nashville, TN in May 1994. Child:

   392   i   William Stevenson WESTON, V, b. 22 Nov 1994

267. EUGENE KING WESTON, Jr.[9] (Eugene King Weston[8], William Stevenson Weston, Jr.[7], William Stevenson Weston[6], Sarah Jerkins Hooper[5], Thomas Clark Hooper[4], William Hooper[3], William Hooper[2], William Hooper[1]) child of Eugene King Weston and Carmen Lucretia Duncan was born on 18 Feb 1968. He married Mary Susan BREWER in Washington, DC on 6 Jan 1996. She was born in Washington, DC on 18 Nov 1964. Child:

   393   i Amelia Brewer WESTON, b. 1 Dec 1999

278. EDWARD STOCKTON CROFT, IV[9] (Edward Stockton Croft, III[8], Irene Gabrey Weston[7], William Stevenson Weston[6], Sarah Jerkins Hooper[5], Thomas Clark Hooper[4], William Hooper[3], William Hooper[2], William Hooper[1]) child of Edward Stockton Croft, III and Susan Francez Bronson was born in Philadelphia, PA on 3 Jan 1969. He married Roberta Lee WICKER in Ponte Vedra, FL on 11 Oct 1997. She was born in Charlotte, NC in 1969. Children:

   394   i Sarah Adeline CROFT, b. 19 Mar 1998
   395   ii Edward Stockton CROFT, V, b. 29 Sep 1999

314. WALTER TROY ZIMMERMANN[9] (Walter Herbert Zimmermann[8], Sarah Weston Robison[7], Sarah Hooper Weston[6], Sarah Jerkins Hooper[5], Thomas Clark Hooper[4], William Hooper[3], William Hooper[2], William Hooper[1]) child of Walter Herbert Zimmermann and Sharon Alice Wetzel was born on 27 May 1973. He married Shani Elizabeth WEBB in say 1994. Children:

   396   i Danniella Jade ZIMMERMANN, b. 8 Jan 1995
   397   ii Hunter Troy ZIMMERMANN, b. Jun 1999

339. SAMUEL AUBREY MELLICHAMPE[9] (Aubrey Julian Mellichampe[8], Samuel Haworth Mellichampe[7], Edward Winborn Mellichampe[6], Amelia Jones Hooper[5], Thomas Clark Hooper[4], William Hooper[3], William Hooper[2], William Hooper[1]) child of Aubrey Julian Mellichampe and Rebecca Lewis was born in Petersburg, VA on 31 May 1968. He married Candice GORDON, daughter of Thomas Daniel and Mary Helen (Rich) Gordon on 18 Feb 1989. She was born in Heidelberg, GERMANY on 2 Feb 1968. Child:

   398   i Ashley Jordan MELLICHAMPE, b. 14 Jun 1989

TENTH GENERATION

355. LISA KAY BURGESS[10] (Doris Marie Burgesss[9], Thelma Rhett Wills[8], James Wills[7], Henry Clarence Wills[6], Helen DeBerniere Hooper[5], Mary

Elizabeth Hooper[4], William Hooper[3], William Hooper[2], William Hooper[1]) child of Doris Marie Burgess and Lawrence Howard was born in Chapel Hill, NC on 9 Jul 1963. She married Ronnie ANDREWS on 20 Jan 1986. He was born on 27 Dec 1961. Child:

   399   i   Thomas Wayne ANDREWS, b. 15 Feb 1993

357. DONNIE BURGESS[10] (Marvin L. Burgesss[9], Thelma Rhett Wills[8], James Wills[7], Henry Clarence Wills[6], Helen DeBerniere Hooper[5], Mary Elizabeth Hooper[4], William Hooper[3], William Hooper[2], William Hooper[1]) child of Marvin L. Burgess and Teresa Gladden was born on 11 Aug 1971. He married Cathy SHORT on 10 Mar 1990. She was born on 14 Jun 1974. Children:

   400   i   Haley BURGESS, b. 1 Aug 1990
   401   ii   Dustin BURGESS, b. 17 Jan 1995

358. LaTASHA DeANNE FISHER[10] (Julia Ann Wills[9], Harold Bryant Wills[8], James Wills[7], Henry Clarence Wills[6], Helen DeBerniere Hooper[5], Mary Elizabeth Hooper[4], William Hooper[3], William Hooper[2], William Hooper[1]) child of Julia Ann Wills and Anthony Boone Fisher was born on 20 Oct 1966. She married Paul MEES on 7 Jan 1984. He was born on 18 Nov 1960. Children:

   402   i   Robert MEES, b. 11 Jun 1984
   403   ii   Steven MEES, b. 22 Mar 1988
   404   iii   Amy MEES, b. 22 Jul 1993
   405   iv   David MEES, b. 14 Oct 1995

367. MICHAEL TODD GOING, Jr.[10] (Betty Sue Wills[9], Harold Bryant Wills[8], James Wills[7], Henry Clarence Wills[6], Helen DeBerniere Hooper[5], Mary Elizabeth Hooper[4], William Hooper[3], William Hooper[2], William Hooper[1]) child of Betty Sue Wills and her 1st husband Michael Todd Going was born on 2 Aug 1978. He married Jamie HOLDER on 7 Jun 1996. She was born on 8 Jul 1979. Children:

   406   i   Rebecca Lynn GOING, b. 19 Dec 1996
   407   ii   Michael Dylan GOING, b. 30 Jul 1998

382. CHRISTOPHER JON ORCUTT[10] (Cheryl Anne Wills[9], Clarence Lucas Wills, Jr.[8], Clarence Lucas Wills[7], Henry Clarence Wills[6], Helen DeBerniere Hooper[5], Mary Elizabeth Hooper[4], William Hooper[3], William Hooper[2], William Hooper[1]) child of Cheryl Anne Wills and Terry Dean Orcutt was born in Cashmere, Chelan County, WA on 4 Apr 1965. He married Tara SUNKEL in Chelan County, WA in say 1996. Children:

408   i   Christopher Jon ORCUTT, Jr., b. 4 Nov 1984
409   ii Joshua Dean ORCUTT, b. 21 Jul 1987
410   iii Bonnie Naomi ORCUTT, b. 26 Feb 1993
411   iv Rose Kathleen ORCUTT, b. 3 Feb 1995

383. TAWNYA FAITH WILLS[10] (Russell Steven Wills[9], Clarence Lucas Wills, Jr.[8], Clarence Lucas Wills[7], Henry Clarence Wills[6], Helen DeBerniere Hooper[5], Mary Elizabeth Hooper[4], William Hooper[3], William Hooper[2], William Hooper[1]) child of Russell Steven Wills and Brenda Jean Spurlock was born in Wenatchee, WA on 4 Oct 1970. She had a liaison with -- ROBINSON in say 1990. She married David SABEDRA on 19 Apr 1996. Child by liaison:
    412   i   Tyler Jay ROBINSON, b. c. 1991
Child by marriage:
    413   ii Austin James SABEDRA, b. c. 1997

385. JENNIFER ANNE TAYLOR[10] (Carolyn Glenn Wills[9], Harry DeBerniere Wills[8], Clarence Lucas Wills[7], Henry Clarence Wills[6], Helen DeBerniere Hooper[5], Mary Elizabeth Hooper[4], William Hooper[3], William Hooper[2], William Hooper[1]) child of Carolyn Glenn Wills and Charles E. Taylor was born in Oak Ridge, TN on 4 Oct 1966. She married (2nd) Michael Wesley FORTNER in Arlington, TX in Jun 1992. Child:
    414   i   Elizabeth DeBerniere FORTNER, b. 5 Feb 1993

Joseph Hewes

48: JOSEPH HEWES

"O Captain! My Captain! Our fearful trip is done."
                                          Walt Whitman

The signature of Joseph Hewes on the Declaration of Independence is among the uppermost grouping in the next in from the right-hand edge of the document, as the middle of the three names. He signed with his full name, no abbreviations, in a smallish, neat hand without flourishes.

Joseph Hewes was the son of Aaron Hewes and Providence Worth. He had an older sister Sarah, and a brother Josiah. The family had migrated from Connecticut to New Jersey about 1728. They were members of the Society of Friends (or Quakers), in which faith young Joseph was brought up and studied. He was apprenticed to a Philadelphia merchant, in whose office he learned the techniques of business accounting and shipping. When thirty years of age (1760), Hewes removed to the thriving port of Edenton, NC to establish his own shipping and mercantile business, taking his sister Sarah's son Nathaniel Allen, Jr. with him.[3]

In 1766, Hewes was elected to the North Carolina Provincial Assembly, and served in that colonial body until the end of Royal Government in 1775. He was a member of the Committee of Correspondence, a delegate to all five Provincial Congresses, and both the First and Second Continental Congress. At first a bit hesitant about the major step of independence, he fully supported the move after Bunker Hill, and voted for it [4]. In the Continental Congress, he rendered distinguished service. His work on numerous committees was endless. Every day required his attention to matters of shipping, naval matters, stores, commissary, and logistics. The work was so enormous and demanding that the overwork and irregular hours ruined his health - he literally died for his country.

---

[3] John and Katherine Bakeless, *Signers of the Declaration*, (Houghton Mifflin Company, Boston, MA, 1969), pp.267-269.
[4] *Dictionary of American Biography*, Vol. VIII, pp. 601-602.

FIRST GENERATION

1. JOSEPH HEWES was born in "Marbury Hill", Kingston (near Princeton), NJ on 23 Jan 1730.[1] He never married.[2] He died in Philadelphia, PA on 10 Nov 1779.[3]

References:
[1] There is no good biography of the Signer Joseph Hewes. Several sketches have been prepared over the decades, but most of them copy material from the earliest ones, such as John Sanderson, *Biographies of the Signers of the Declaration of Independence*, (Vol. VII, 1827); see Della Gray Bartherlmas, *The Signers of the Declaration of Independence, A Biographical and Genealogical Reference*, (Mcfarland & Company, Inc., Jefferson, NC, 1977), pp. 112-113. The Leach MSS for Joseph Hewes is microfilmed on FHL Film # 0001756, and the hard copy is found in Vol. #20, pp. 5940-5949. The DAB Article on Joseph Hewes is in Vol. VIII, pp. 601-602. [2] Joseph Hewes had been engaged to marry Isabella Johnson, but she died a few days before the wedding date, and he never after did marry; see the fuller exposition below. [3] Several writers of his day, report that Joseph Hewes worked for very long hours upon his various Committee assignments, often without food or drink, or adequate rest; his bachelor habits working against more regular and healthy approaches. In consequence of these poor work habits, his health failed completely, he collapsed from overwork, and died shortly thereafter. He was buried in Christ Church, Philadelphia, PA.

Joseph Hewes was a firm patriot, coming to fully support, vote for, and give his live to the independence and security of America. But he has no descendants!

Having moved himself to Edenton, NC, his gracious manner endearing him to the people, he quickly made connections with the best people. Among them was Samuel Johnson, President of the Provincial Assembly, and later a Governor of the State of North Carolina. Samuel Johnson had a lovely sister, Isabella, and it was not long before the very eligible Joseph Hewes and Isabella Johnson were engaged to be married, and a wedding date fixed.

Unfortunately, just a few days before the wedding, Isabella contracted a terrible fever and died. The distraught Joseph, overcome with grief, never, ever married, and died an unmarried bachelor at 49 years, 9 months, and 17 days of age. Thus, dear reader, there can be no descendants of the body of Signer Joseph Hewes.

John Pinn

49: JOHN PENN

"Exercise a power which is our human nature's highest dower."
William Wordsworth

The signature of John Penn on the Declaration of Independence is located with the other two North Carolina signers just to the left of John Hancock's large signature and in the second column in from the left edge of the document, He signed his full name in a small, clear hand.

John Penn was the only child of Moses Penn and Catherine Taylor, so he became the inheritor of his father's sizable estate, when he died at the time young Penn was 18 years old. However, the boy received only a few years of formal schooling, so he determined to continue his education by making use of the personal library of kinsmen Edmund Pendleton. Additionally he read for and studied law on his own and was admitted to the Virginia bar in 1761. He developed a successful law practice there for twelve or more years, moving to Granville County, North Carolina in 1774.

He quickly established himself in his new location and was elected to the Provincial Assembly in 1775. Within a matter of weeks he was also elected as a Delegate to the Continental Congress. Penn was an unassuming but efficient worker and quickly won the respect of not only his Provincial Assembly colleagues but also his Congressional colleagues. As he listened to the discussions and reports of the Representatives from the other Colonies, he soon recognized that any view of ever being able to work with the Royal Government was going to be difficult if not impossible. By July of 1776 all three of the North Carolina Delegates voted for Independence and signed the document in early August[5]. Recalled from Philadelphia in 1780 by the Governor of North Carolina, Penn was asked to sit on the Emergency Board of War for the State with responsibility for military affairs. The following year, in declining health, he passed up an offer for a Judgeship devoting his remaining energies to his law practice. Not one of the three North Carolina Signers ever lived to see his 50th birthday!

---

[5] John and Katherine Bakeless, *Signers of the Declaration*, (Houghton Mifflin Company, Boston, MA, 1969), p. 271.

FIRST GENERATION

1. JOHN PENN was born in Port Royal, Caroline County, VA on 6 May 1741[o.s.].[1] He married Susannah LYME, daughter of Henry Lyme in Granville County, NC on 28 Jul 1763.[2] She was born in Caroline County, VA about 1745, and died in Granville County, NC before 1 Mar 1784.[3] He died in Townsville, Granville County, NC on 14 Sep 1788.[4] Children:

    2   i   William PENN, b. c. 1764, dy
+ 3   ii Lucy PENN, b. 17 Oct 1766
    4   iii Son PENN, b. c. 1768, dy 1768

References:
[1] No standard biography of John Penn has ever been written. Something regarding his Taylor ancestors can be found in Della Gray Bartherlmas, *The Signers of the Declaration of Independence, A Biographical and Genealogical Reference*, (Mcfarland & Company, Inc., Jefferson, NC, 1977), pp. 214 -216. The Leach MSS for John Penn is microfilmed on FHL Film # 0001756, and the hard copy is found in Vol. #20, pp. 5957-6046. The DAB Article on John Penn is in Vol. XIV, p. 431. His birth is given in the Old Style, which is 11 days earlier than the New Style Calender that became effective in September 1752. [2] Leach MSS, p. 5957. [3] She was probably born as noted, since her father was still living there in 1747. She is not noted in John Penn's Will dated 1 Mar 1784, so she must have died before this date, nor does she appear in a Census of North Carolina of 1784-1787, confirming that she was almost certainly deceased by that time. It is quite possible that there were more children born of this marriage; however, no such listing has ever been discovered, nor did John Penn report any such other children in his notes or journals. If there were other children, they surely died in infancy, or early youth. The reader should note that only through his daughter Lucy does Signer of the Declaration of Independence John Penn have issue. [4] John Penn's date and place of death are reported by several authorities of the time.

SECOND GENERATION

3. LUCY PENN[2] (John Penn[1]) daughter of John Penn and Susannah Lyme was born in Mt. Airy, Caroline County, VA on 17 Oct 1766, and died in "Hazelwood", Caroline County, VA in Aug 1831.[1] She married John TAYLOR, son of James and Ann (Pollard) Taylor on 4 Dec 1783.[2] He was born in Orange County, VA on 19 Dec 1753, and died in "Hazelwood", Caroline County, VA on 20 Aug 1824.[2] Children:

+ 5   i   John TAYLOR, b. 7 Sep 1784
    6   ii Lucy TAYLOR, b. 2 Feb 1786, dy 16 Sep 1786

7   iii   Edmund Pendleton TAYLOR, b. 28 Sep 1787, d. 28 Sep 1820; dsp

8   iv   Elizabeth TAYLOR, b. 8 Mar 1789, dy 25 Aug 1794

9   v   William Penn TAYLOR, b. 25 Oct 1790, d. 18 Jun 1863; dsp

10   vi   Ann TAYLOR, b. 24 Jul 1792m dy 25 Sep 1794

+ 11   vii   Henry TAYLOR, b. 18 Feb 1794

12   viii James TAYLOR, b. 23 Nov 1797, dy 12 Nov 1805

+ 13   ix   George TAYLOR, b. 25 Feb 1799

References:
[1] Leach MSS, p. 5958 gives date and place of birth, Ralph Emmitt Fall, *Hidden Village*, reports month and year of death in data from St, Anne's Parish Register.[2] Leach MSS, p. 5958; see also Henry H. Simms, *Life of John Taylor*, (William Byrd Press, Richmond, VA, 1931).

THIRD GENERATION

5. JOHN TAYLOR [3] (Lucy Penn[2], John Penn[1]) child of Lucy Penn and John Taylor was born in Caroline County, VA on 7 Sep 1784, and died in "Liberty Hill", Caroline County, VA on 8 Aug 1853.[1] He married (1st) Lucy WOODFORD, daughter of John Thornton and Mary Turner (Taliaferio) Woodford on 25 Oct 1808.[1] She was born in "Windsor", Caroline County, VA on 11 Jul 1793, and died in "Liberty Hill", Caroline County, VA on 7 Sep 1832.[1] He married (2nd) Marion GORDON, daughter of Samuel and Susan Fitzhugh (Knox) Gordon on 13 Sep 1834.[1] She was born in Falmouth, VA on 21 Dec 1810, and died in "Liberty Hill", Caroline County, VA on 8 Nov 1843.[1]

Children by first marriage:

14   i   John TAYLOR, b. 24 Sep 1810, d. 12 Mar 1877; dsp

+ 15   ii   Lucy Penn TAYLOR, b. 29 May 1812

16   iii   Mary Woodford TAYLOR, b. 17 Mar 1819, dy Jun 1820

+ 17   iv   Edmund TAYLOR, b. 2 Nov 1822

Children by second marriage:

+ 18   v   Bazil Gordon TAYLOR, b. 3 Jul 1835

19   vi   Samuel Gordon TAYLOR, b. 29 Aug 1836, dy 8 Sep 1836

20   vii   William Knox TAYLOR, b. 31 Jul 1837, dy 4 Sep 1846

+ 21   viii Agnes TAYLOR, b. 5 Mar 1839

+ 22   ix   James TAYLOR, b. 5 Jun 1841

23   x   Bernard Moore TAYLOR, b. 30 Jan 1843, d. 21 Aug 1864; unm

References:
[1] Leach MSS, p. 5959.

11. HENRY TAYLOR[3] (Lucy Penn[2], John Penn[1]) child of Lucy Penn and John Taylor was born in Caroline County, VA on 18 Feb 1794, and died in Caroline County, VA on 10 Dec 1884.[1] He married Julia Dunlap LEIPER, daughter of Thomas and Elizabeth Coultas (Gray) Leiper on 9 Jun1825.[2] She was born in Philadelphia, PA on 11 Jan 1801, and died there on 21 Feb 1883.[1] Children:

24	i	William Penn TAYLOR, b. 1 Apr 1826, dy 10 Oct 1833
+ 25	ii	Henry TAYLOR, b. 19 Nov 1827
+ 26	iii	Lucy Penn TAYLOR, b. 3 Jan 1830
+ 27	iv	John TAYLOR, b. 7 Oct 1832
+ 28	v	William Penn TAYLOR, b. 16 Feb 1834
+ 29	vi	Thomas Leiper TAYLOR, b. 15 Sep 1836
30	vii	George Gray Leiper TAYLOR, b. 1838, dy 1838
31	viii	Edmund Pendleton TAYLOR, b. 10 Apr 1839, d. 2 May 1862; kia
32	ix	Elizabeth TAYLOR, b. 1840, dy 1840
+ 33	x	Julia Leiper TAYLOR, b. 5 Oct 1842

References:
[1] Leach MSS, p. 5967. [2] *Poulson's Advertiser* of 10 Jun 1825; see also Mary Stanley Field Liddell, *The Hon. George Gray, 4th of Philadelphia, His Ancestors & Descendants*, (Ann Arbor, MI, 1940), pp. 5, 17.

13. GEORGE TAYLOR[3] (Lucy Penn[2], John Penn[1]) child of Lucy Penn and John Taylor was born in Caroline County, VA on 25 Feb 1799, and died on 25 Sep 1872.[1] He married (1st) Catherine RANDOLPH, daughter of William and Anne (Andrews) Randolph on 20 Apr 1826.[1] She was born in "Wilton", Henrico County, VA on 25 Sep 1808, and died in Richmond, VA on 13 Jun 1865.[1] He married (2nd) Henrietta PENDLETON, daughter of Philip Henry and Ann Madison (Turner) Pendleton on 5 Mar 1868.[1] She was born in Port Royal, VA on 23 Dec 1840.[1]

Children by first marriage:

+ 34	i	Lucy Penn TAYLOR, b. 19 Jul 1827
+ 35	ii	Anne Randolph TAYLOR, b. 20 Aug 1829
+ 36	iii	Elizabeth Moore TAYLOR, b. 1 Sep 1831
37	iv	William Randolph TAYLOR, b. 1 Mar 1834, dy 21 Jan 1840
38	v	George TAYLOR, b. 28 Jul 1836, dy 3 Oct 1841
39	vi	John Penn TAYLOR, b. 14 Oct 1838
40	vii	Robert Randolph TAYLOR, b. 30 Nov 1840, dy 1 Dec 1840

41   viii Catherine Randolph TAYLOR, b. 10 Nov 1841, dy 13 Jun 1843
42   ix   George Henry TAYLOR, b. 15 Apr 1844; unm
Child by second marriage:
+ 43   x   Sallie Penn TAYLOR, b. 15 Dec 1870
References:
[1] Leach MSS, p. 5973, see also DSDI Appl # 1040.

FOURTH GENERATION

15. LUCY PENN TAYLOR[4] (John Taylor[3], Lucy Penn[2], John Penn[1]) child of John Taylor and his 1st wife Lucy Woodford was born in "Palestine", Caroline County, VA on 29 May 1812, and died in White Sulphur Springs, WV on 4 Aug 1870.[1] She married Bazil GORDON, son of Samuel and Susan Fitzhugh (Knox) Gordon on 5 Mar 1828.[1] He was born in Falmouth, VA on 4 Dec 1800, and died in Baltimore, MD on 3 Dec 1862.[1] Children:
44   i   Mary Wallace GORDON, b. 2 Feb 1829, dy 4 Apr 1830
45   ii   Battaile Fitzhugh GORDON, b. 7 Mar 1831, dy 28 Mar 1937
+ 46   iii   Lucy Woodford GORDON, b. 1 Dec 1836
47   iv   William Penn GORDON, b. 17 Jun 1838, dy 4 Aug 1840
+ 48   v   Agnes Armistead GORDON, b. 30 Apr 1843
49   vi   Margaret McKim GORDON, b. 10 Oct 1845; unm
50   vii   Graham GORDON, b. 4 Jan 1849; dsp
51   viii John Taylor GORDON, b. 9 Oct 1851, d. 4 Oct 1873; unm
52   ix   Bazil GORDON, b. 30 Apr 1854, d. 28 Apr 1884; unm
References:
[1] Leach MSS, p. 5960.

17. EDMUND TAYLOR[4] (John Taylor[3], Lucy Penn[2], John Penn[1]) child of John Taylor and his 1st wife Lucy Woodford was born in "Liberty Hill", Caroline County, VA on 2 Nov 1822, and died in Richmond, VA on 23 Sep 1880.[1] He married Susan Morris DABNEY, daughter of the Rev. John Blair and Elizabeth Lewis (Towles) Dabney on 29 May 1845.[1] She was born in "Vaucluse", Campbell County, VA on 4 Aug 1827.[1] Children:
+ 53   i   Blair TAYLOR, b. 15 Jan 1848
+ 54   ii   Lucy Woodford TAYLOR, b. 22 Jul 1849
+ 55   iii   Anne Montgomery TAYLOR, b. 1 Jul 1851
+ 56   iv   Elizabeth Lewis TAYLOR, b. 31 Jan 1853
57   v   John TAYLOR, b. 7 Dec 1854, dy 7 Jul 1857
58   vi   Edmund TAYLOR, b. 2 Oct 1856

59	vii	Caroline May TAYLOR, b. 2 May 1859
+ 60	viii	William Oliver TAYLOR, b. 3 Apr 1861
+ 61	ix	Agatha Bernard TAYLOR, b. 6 Aug 1866
62	x	Susan Morris TAYLOR, b. 24 Nov 1868; unm
63	xi	Maria Tallula TAYLOR, b. 10 Aug 1871, dy 19 Apr 1876

References:
[1] Leach MSS, p. 5962.

18. BAZIL GORDON TAYLOR[4] (John Taylor[3], Lucy Penn[2], John Penn[1]) child of John Taylor and his 2nd wife Marion Gordon was born in "Liberty Hill", Caroline County, VA on 3 Jul 1835, and died in Charlottesville, VA on 23 Nov 1862.[1] He married Fanny ASHBY, daughter of Marshall and Lucy (Cooke) Ashby on 27 Apr 1859.[1] She was born in Fauquier County, VA on 11 Jun 1838, and died in Savannah, GA in Mar 1881.[1] Child:

| 64 | i | Lucy Ashby TAYLOR, b. 9 Sep 1861 |

References:
[1] Leach MSS, p. 5965.

21. AGNES TAYLOR[4] (John Taylor[3], Lucy Penn[2], John Penn[1]) child of John Taylor and his 2nd wife Marion Gordon was born in "Liberty Hill", Caroline County, VA on 5 Mar 1839, and died in Fredericksburg, VA on 19 Aug 1895.[1] She married John Washington ASHBY, son of Marshall and Lucy (Cooke) Ashby on 28 Apr 1859.[1] He was born in Fauquier County, VA on 11 Mar 1822, and died in Bolivar County, MS on 7 Nov 1867.[1] Children:

65	i	Marion Gordon ASHBY, b. 20 Feb 1860, dy 18 Oct 1867
66	ii	Tallula ASHBY, b. 4 Jul 1864, dy 30 Oct 1864
67	iii	John Taylor ASHBY, b. 16 Oct 1865; unm

References:
[1] Leach MSS, p. 5966.

22. JAMES TAYLOR[4] (John Taylor[3], Lucy Penn[2], John Penn[1]) child of John Taylor and his 2nd wife Marion Gordon was born in "Liberty Hill", Caroline County, VA on 5 Jun 1841.[1] He married (1st) Belle Herndon STEVENSON, daughter of GEN Carter Littlepage and Martha (Griswold) Stevenson on 25 Apr 1867.[1] She was born in Detroit, MI on 26 Aug 1847, and died in Fredericksburg, VA on 26 Aug 1886.[1] He married (2nd) Susan Murray GRAY, daughter of Alexander Thomas and Anne Augusta (Stevens) Gray on 4 Jun 1889.[1] She was born in Janesville, Rock County, WI on 19 Jul 1857.[1]

Children by first marriage:

68   i   Carter Stevenson TAYLOR, b. 24 Jul 1871, dy 11 Aug 1872

69   ii Bernard Moore TAYLOR, b. 23 Sep 1880, dy 14 Jul 1882

Children by second marriage:

70   iii James Gray TAYLOR, b. 10 May 1890

+ 71   iv Marion Gordon TAYLOR, b. 4 Feb 1892

72   v   Murray Caldwell TAYLOR, b. 25 Jun 1895

73   vi Elizabeth Moore TAYLOR, b. 28 Sep 1898

References:

[1] DSDI Appl # 1414.

25. HENRY TAYLOR[4] (Henry Taylor[3], Lucy Penn[2], John Penn[1]) child of Henry Taylor and Julia Dunlap Leiper was born in "Hazelwood", Caroline County, VA on 19 Nov 1827[1], and died in Louisa County, VA on 7 Aug 1914. He married Mary Minor WATSON, daughter of Dr. James and Susan Dabney (Morris) Watson in Louisa County, VA on 14 Dec 1853.[1] She was born in "Bracketts", Louisa County, VA on 10 Dec 1832[1], and died in Richmond, VA on 10 Feb 1905. Children:

+ 74   i   Henry TAYLOR, b. 22 Sep 1854

+ 75   ii Susan Watson TAYLOR, b. 3 Nov 1856

+ 76   iii Julia Watson TAYLOR, b. 25 Dec 1858

77   iv Mary Watson TAYLOR, b. 28 Feb 1861, d. 1910; unm

+ 78   v   David Watson TAYLOR, b. 4 Mar 1864

79   vi Nancy Morris TAYLOR, b. 27 May 1866; unm

80   vii James Watson TAYLOR, b. 7 Jun 1868; unm

81   viii Lucy Penn TAYLOR, b. 1 Nov 1871; unm

82   ix Edmund Pendleton TAYLOR, b. 3 Mar 1874, d, 9 Sep 1894; unm

References:

[1] DSDI Appl # 341; see also Leach MSS, p. 5967.

26. LUCY PENN TAYLOR[4] (Henry Taylor[3], Lucy Penn[2], John Penn[1]) child of Henry Taylor and Julia Dunlap Leiper was born in "Hazelwood", Caroline County, VA on 3 Jan 1830[1], and died on 16 Dec 1913. She married Williams Carter WICKHAM, son of William Fanning and Anne (Carter) Wickham in Caroline County, VA on 11 Jan 1848.[2] He was born in Richmond, VA on 21 Sep 1820, and died there on 23 Jul 1888.[1] Children:

83   i   John WICKHAM, b. 12 Dec 1848, dy 13 Dec 1850

+ 84   ii Henry Taylor WICKHAM, b. 17 Dec 1849

+ 85   iii Anne Carter WICKHAM, b. 27 Oct 1851

86   iv Julia Leiper WICKHAM, b. 10 May 1859, dy 9 Jul 1873

+ 87   v   William Fanning WICKHAM, II, b. 24 Oct 1860
    88   vi   Son WICKHAM, b. 10 Jun 1864, dy 30 Jun 1864
References:
[1] Leach MSS, p. 5968. [2] *The National Intelligencer* of 19 Jan 1848.

27. JOHN TAYLOR[4] (Henry Taylor[3], Lucy Penn[2], John Penn[1]) child of
Henry Taylor and Julia Dunlap Leiper was born in "Bunker Hill", Westmoreland County, VA on 7 Oct 1832[1], and died in "Oak Grove", Westmoreland
County, VA on 5 Nov 1913. He married Isabella Nelson LOCKE, daughter
of the Rev. Thomas Estep and Lucy Armistead (Nelson) Locke on 20 Feb
1867.[1] She was born in "Mt. Holly", Lunenburg County, VA on 19 Nov
1843[1], and died on 24 Oct 1909. Children:
    89   i   Edmund Pendleton TAYLOR, b. 15 Dec 1867, d. 1935; unm
    90   ii   Thomas Locke TAYLOR, b. 25 Aug 1871, dy 23 Aug 1872
+ 91   iii   Lucy Nelson TAYLOR, b. 24 Jul 1873
+ 92   iv   Elizabeth Moore TAYLOR, b. 14 Feb 1875
+ 93   v   Anne ["Nannie"]Isaella TAYLOR, b. 7 Feb 1878
+ 94   vi   Margaret Locke TAYLOR, b. 27 Mar 1880
References:
[1] Leach MSS, p. 5969; see also Mary Stanley Field Liddell, *The Hon. George Gray, 4*[th]
of Philadelphia, His Ancestors & Descendants, (Ann Arbor, MI, 1940), p. 44.

28. WILLIAM PENN TAYLOR[4] (Henry Taylor[3], Lucy Penn[2], John Penn[1])
child of Henry Taylor and Julia Dunlap Leiper was born in "Bunker Hill",
Westmoreland County, VA on 16 Feb 1834 [1], and died on 30 Jul 1920. He
married Florence Ida CARTER, daughter of George Monroe and Mary
Tayloe (Rice) Carter on 23 Apr 1873.[1] She was born in "Oak Grove",
Westmoreland County, VA on 26 Jan 1849[1], and died in 1920. Children:
    95   i   George Carter TAYLOR, b. 26 Aug 1874, d. 1942; dsp
    96   ii   William Penn TAYLOR, b. 24 May 1876, d. 1901; unm
    97   iii   John Monroe TAYLOR, b. 28 Nov 1878, dy 23 Mar 2885
+ 98   iv   Henry Leiper TAYLOR, b. 23 Apr 1882
    99   v   Charlotte TAYLOR, b. 29 Feb 1884, d. 18 May 1982; unm
   100   vi   John Thomas TAYLOR, b. 5 Feb 1886, dy 21 Sep 1886
References:
[1] Leach MSS, p. 5969.

29. THOMAS LEIPER TAYLOR[4] (Henry Taylor[3], Lucy Penn[2], John
Penn[1]) child of Henry Taylor and Julia Dunlap Leiper was born in
Fredericksburg, VA on 15 Sep 1836[1], and died in 1901. He married Rosa
Van Doren LOCKE, daughter of the Rev. Thomas Estep and Lucy Armistead

(Nelson) Locke on 27 Oct 1868.[1] She was born in "Mt. Holly", Lunenburg County, VA on 17 Apr 1845[1], and died on 21 Aug 1924. Children:

101	i	Child TAYLOR, b. 1869, dy 1869
102	ii	Henry TAYLOR, b. 1 Jul 1870, dy 1 Jan 1877
103	iii	Robert Leiper TAYLOR, b. 25 Jan 1872, d. 1924; unm
104	iv	Julia Wickham TAYLOR, b. 23 Mar 1873, d. 1935; unm
+ 105	v	Thomas Locke TAYLOR, b. 5 Jun 1874
+ 106	vi	Henrietta TAYLOR, b. 17 Sep 1876
+ 107	vii	Bernard Pendleton TAYLOR, b. 28 Feb 1878
+ 108	viii	William Locke TAYLOR, b. 8 Apr 1880
109	ix	Ann Gray TAYLOR, b. 25 Jun 1881, d. 1930; dsp
110	x	Rosa Van Doren TAYLOR, b. 11 Mar 1886; dsp
+ 111	xi	John TAYLOR, b. 11 Sep 1888

References:
[1] Leach MSS, p. 5970.

33. JULIA LEIPER TAYLOR[4] (Henry Taylor[3], Lucy Penn[2], John Penn[1]) child of Henry Taylor and Julia Dunlap Leiper was born in "Montrose", Westmoreland County, VA on 5 Oct 1842[1], and died in 1918. She married Edmund Wilcox HUBARD, son of Robert Thruston and Susan Pocahontas (Bolling) Hubard on 25 Nov 1875.[1] He was born in "Rosny", Buckingham County, VA on 27 Feb 1841[1], and died in 1915. Children:

112	i	Julia Taylor HUBARD, b. 18 Aug 1877, d. 1904; unm
113	ii	Edmund Bolling HUBARD, b. 7 Jun 1880; dsp
114	iii	Robert Thruston HUBARD, b. 7 Jul 1881; dsp
115	iv	Henry Taylor HUBARD, b. 1 Mar 1883, dy 11 Aug 1883

References:
[1] Leach MSS, p. 5970.

34. LUCY PENN TAYLOR[4] (George Taylor[3], Lucy Penn[2], John Penn[1]) child of George Taylor and his 1st wife Catherine Randolph was born in "Hazelwood", Caroline County, VA on 19 Jul 1827.[1] She married Charles Carter LEE, son of Henry and Anne Hill (Carter) Lee on 13 May 1847.[2] He was born in "Stratford", Westmoreland County, VA on 8 Nov 1798, and died in "Windsor", Powhatan County, VA on 21 Mar 1871.[1] Children:

+ 116	i	George Taylor LEE, b. 8 Mar 1848
+ 117	ii	Henry LEE, b. 9 Jul 1849
+ 118	iii	Robert Randolph LEE, b. 22 May 1853
119	iv	Williams Carter LEE, b. 8 Sep 1855, d. 25 Jun 1882; unm
+ 120	v	Mildred LEE, b. 30 Nov 1857
+ 121	vi	Catherine Randolph LEE, b. 27 Aug 1865
122	vii	John Penn LEE, b. 11 Sep 1867

References:
[1] Leach MSS, p. 5973. [2] The National Intelligencer of 20 May 1847.

35. ANNE RANDOLPH TAYLOR[4] (George Taylor[3], Lucy Penn[2], John Penn[1]) child of George Taylor and his 1st wife Catherine Randolph was born in "Horn Quarter", King William County, VA on 20 Aug 1829.[1] She married Stephen Decatur WHITTLE, son of Fortesque and Mary Ann (Davies) Whittle on 18 Jun 1851.[1] He was born in Mecklenburg County, VA on 5 Dec 1821, and died in Powhatan County, VA on 5 Oct 1869.[1] Children:

    123   i   Katherine Randolph WHITTLE, b. 28 Sep 1852; unm
    124   ii Fortesque WHITTLE, b. 9 Jun 1854; unm
    125 iii Nannie Taylor WHITTLE, b. 26 Oct 1855, d. 7 Nov 1889; unm
    126 iv Mary Davies WHITTLE, b. 28 Jul 1858, d. 2 Jul 1878; unm

References:
[1] Leach MSS, p. 5975.

36. ELIZABETH MOORE TAYLOR[4] (George Taylor[3], Lucy Penn[2], John Penn[1]) child of George Taylor and his 1st wife Catherine Randolph was born in "Fighting Creek", Powhatan County, VA on 1 Sep 1831, and died in Powhatan County, VA on 30 May 1872.[1] She married John GILLIAM, son of Richard James and Catharine Elizabeth (Thornton) Gilliam on 20 Oct 1869.[1] He was born in Powhatan County, VA on 23 Jan 1843.[1] Child:

+ 127   i   Richard James GILLIAM, b. 3 Mar 1871

References:
[1] Leach MSS, p. 5975.

43. SALLIE PENN TAYLOR[4] (George Taylor[3], Lucy Penn[2], John Penn[1]) child of George Taylor and his 2nd wife Henrietta Pendleton was born in "Horn Quarter", King William County, VA on 15 Dec 1870[1], and died on 29 Jul 1961. She married Augustine Fitzhugh TURNER in Port Royal, VA on 9 Nov 1898.[1] He was born in King George County, VA on 6 Dec 1874.[1] Children:

    128   i   Anne Pendleton TURNER, b. 16 Jan 1900
+ 129   ii Taylor Fitzhugh TURNER, b. 17 Jun 1903

References:
[1] DSDI Appl # 1039, 1058.

FIFTH GENERATION

46. LUCY WOODFORD GORDON[5] (Lucy Penn Taylor[4], John Taylor[3], Lucy Penn[2], John Penn[1]) child of Lucy Penn Taylor and Bazil Gordon was born in "Kenmore", Spottsylvania County, VA on 1 Dec 1836.[1] She married Charles HERNDON, son of Dabney Minor and Elizabeth (Hull) Herndon on 25 Mar 1858.[1] He was born in Fredericksburg, VA on 14 Oct 1823, and died there on 17 Dec 1883.[1] Children:

	130	i	Lucy Taylor HERNDON, b. 6 Feb 1859; unm
	131	ii	Bazil Gordon HERNDON, b. 10 Jul 1861, d. 24 Feb 1883; unm
	132	iii	Ann Maury HERNDON, b. 11 Dec 1863
+	133	iv	Charles HERNDON, b. 11 Mar 1865
	134	v	William Lewis HERNDON, b. 3 Apr 1867, dy 4 Oct 1878

References:
[1] Leach MSS, p. 5961.

48. AGNES ARMISTEAD GORDON[5] (Lucy Penn Taylor[4], John Taylor[3], Lucy Penn[2], John Penn[1]) child of Lucy Penn Taylor and Bazil Gordon was born in "Kenmore", Spottsylvania County, VA on 30 Apr 1843, and died in Richmond, VA on 7 Jul 1884.[1] She married Francis Deane CUNNING-HAM, son of John Atkinson and Elizabeth (Dillon) Cunningham on 21 Sep 1864.[1] He was born in Goochland County, VA on 28 Jul 1836, and died in Richmond, VA on 9 Sep 1885.[1] Children:

135	i	Richard Hoope CUNNINGHAM, b. 1 Jul 1865; sp
136	ii	Francis Deane CUNNINGHAM, b. c. 1868, dy

References:
[1] Leach MSS, p. 5962.

53. BLAIR TAYLOR[5] (Edmund Taylor[4], John Taylor[3], Lucy Penn[2], John Penn[1]) child of Edmund Taylor and Susan Morris Dabney was born in Spottsylvania County, VA on 15 Jan 1848.[1] He married Mary Elizabeth ALLEN, daughter of Robert and Frances (Harvey) Allen on 12 Nov 1872.[1] She was born in Shenandoah County, VA on 25 Feb 1845.[1] Children:

137	i	Donald Allen TAYLOR, b. 18 Nov 1875
138	ii	Mary Blair TAYLOR, b. 2 Feb 1878

References:
[1] Leach MSS, p. 5963.

54. LUCY WOODFORD TAYLOR[5] (Edmund Taylor[4], John Taylor[3], Lucy Penn[2], John Penn[1]) child of Edmund Taylor and Susan Morris Dabney was born in "Vaucluse", Campbell County, VA on 22 Jul 1849, and died in "Aspenvale", Smyth County, VA on 22 Nov 1893.[1] She married Charles Henry Campbell PRESTON, son of John Montgomery and Maria Thornton Carter (Preston) Preston in Lynchburg, VA on 29 May 1885.[2] He was born in Abingdon, VA on 12 Sep 1840[2], and died in Goochland County, VA on 5 Jul 1932. Children:

+ 139   i   Susan Morris PRESTON, b. 4 Aug 1886
  140   ii Kitty Dabney PRESTON, b. 21 Mar 1888
  141 iii Anne Montgomery PRESTON, b. 12 Jan 1890
  142 iv Lucy Elizabeth PRESTON, b. 18 Oct 1893, dy 18 Jun 1894
References:
[1] Leach MSS, p. 5964. [2] DSDI Appl # 1034.

55. ANNE MONTGOMERY TAYLOR[5] (Edmund Taylor[4], John Taylor[3], Lucy Penn[2], John Penn[1]) child of Edmund Taylor and Susan Morris Dabney was born in "Greenwood", Orange County, VA on 1 Jul 1851.[1] She married James Callaway LANGHORNE, son of George Charles and Agnes McClanahan (White) Langhorne on 15 Apr 1875.[1] He was born in Roanoke County, VA on 7 Mar 1846.[1] Children:
  143   i   Lewis Ward LANGHORNE, b. 9 Jan 1878
  144 ii Anne Montgomery LANGHORNE, b. 11 Jun 1883
References:
[1] Leach MSS, p. 5964.

56. ELIZABETH LEWIS TAYLOR[5] (Edmund Taylor[4], John Taylor[3], Lucy Penn[2], John Penn[1]) child of Edmund Taylor and Susan Morris Dabney was born in "Greenwwod", Orange County, VA on 31 Jan 1853.[1] She married Charles Wadsworth CLENEAY, son of Francis and Caroline (Bland) Cleneay in Yuscaran, HONDURAS on 4 Nov 1889.[1] He was born in Maysville, KY on 11 Oct 1850.[1] Children:
+ 145   i   Norma Stewart CLENEAY, b. 2 Oct 1892
  146 ii Francis Bland CLENEAY, b. 4 Feb 1896
References:
[1] DSDI Appl # 891.

60. WILLIAM OLIVER TAYLOR[5] (Edmund Taylor[4], John Taylor[3], Lucy Penn[2], John Penn[1]) child of Edmund Taylor and Susan Morris Dabney was born in "Vaucluse". Orange County, VA on 3 Apr 1861.[1] He married Caroline Stevenson ROBERTS, daughter of George Hisler and Julia (Culbertson) Roberts on 19 Apr 1893.[1] She was born in Nebraska City, NE on 28 Jul 1871.[1] Child:
  147   i   Julia Culbertson TAYLOR, b. 17 Nov 1897

References:
[1] Leach MSS, p. 5965.

61. AGATHA BERNARD TAYLOR[5] (Edmund Taylor[4], John Taylor[3], Lucy Penn[2], John Penn[1]) child of Edmund Taylor and Susan Morris Dabney was born in "Vaucluse", Orange County, VA on 6 Aug 1866.[1] She married David WALKER, son of John Stewart and Lucy Wilhelmina (Otey) Walker in Aspenvale, Smyth County, VA on 14 Feb 1884.[1] He was born in Lynchburg, VA on 13 May 1854.[1] Children:

148	i	Norma Stewart WALKER, b. 25 May 1885, dy 15 Feb 1888
149	ii	John Otey WALKER, b. 6 Aug 1887
150	iii	David Stewart WALKER, b. 7 Oct 1889
151	iv	Agatha Lewis WALKER, b. 30 Aug 1892
152	v	Susan Dabney WALKER, b. 29 Jul 1895
+ 153	vi	Lucy WilhelminaWALKER, b. 3 Jan 1901

References:
[1] DSDI Appl # 380, see also Leach MSS, p. 5965.

71. MARION GORDON TAYLOR[5] (James Taylor[4], John Taylor[3], Lucy Penn[2], John Penn[1]) child of James Taylor and his 2nd wife Susan Murray Gray was born in Washington, DC on 4 Feb 1892.[1] She married Clayton Lyman DREW in Washington, DC on 20 Jan 1912. He was born in Ansonia, CT on 10 Dec 1890[1], and died in Vacaville, CA on 23 Aug 1967. Child:

+ 154	i	Dorris Lyman DREW, b. 13 Apr 1914

References:
[1] DSDI Appl # 1414.

74. HENRY TAYLOR[5] (Henry Taylor[4], Henry Taylor[3], Lucy Penn[2], John Penn[1]) child of Henry Taylor and Mary Minor Watson was born in "Westend", Louisa County, VA on 22 Sep 1854[1], and died in 1945. He married Virginia BAGBY, daughter of George William and Lucy Parke (Chamberlayne) Bagby on 6 Jun 1886.[1] She was born in Richmond, VA on 10 Jan 1864[1], and died in 1955. Children:

+ 155	i	Henry TAYLOR, b. 30 Apr 1887
156	ii	Lucy Parke Chamberlayne TAYLOR, b. 8 Aug 1888, d. 1938; unm
157	iii	Mary Minor Watson TAYLOR, b. 7 Apr 1890, d. 1976; unm
158	iv	Virginia TAYLOR, b. 1900, d. 1986; dsp

References:
[1] Leach MSS, p. 5971.

75. SUSAN WATSON TAYLOR[5] (Henry Taylor[4], Henry Taylor[3], Lucy Penn[2], John Penn[1]) child of Henry Taylor and Mary Minor Watson was born in "Montrose", Westmoreland County, VA on 3 Nov 1856, and died in "Mountain Green", Rappahannock County, VA on 22 Apr 1898.[1] She married John James MILLER, son of Benjamin Franklin and Sarah Eusebia (Browning) Miller on 12 Jun 1879.[1] He was born in Rappahannock County, VA on 26 Aug 1849.[1] Children:

159	i	Benjamin Franklin MILLER, b. 8 Jul 1880, d. 1937; dsp
160	ii	Henry Taylor MILLER, b. 23 Sep 1881; d. 1943; dsp
161	iii	John James MILLER, b. 20 Oct 1883, d. 1919; unm
162	iv	Mary Watson MILLER, b. 30 Oct 1884, dy 14 May 1885
163	v	Sarah Browning MILLER, b. 19 Aug 1886, d. 1921; unm

References:
[1] Leach MSS, p. 5971.

76. JULIA WATSON TAYLOR[5] (Henry Taylor[4], Henry Taylor[3], Lucy Penn[2], John Penn[1]) child of Henry Taylor and Mary Minor Watson was born in "Montrose", Westmoreland County, VA on 25 Dec 1858[1], and died in 1937. She married Thomas Shelton WATSON, II in 1885.[2] Child:

164	i	James WATSON, b. 1886, dy 1898

References:
[1] Leach MSS, p. 5971 as to place and date of birth. [2] Mary Stanley Field Liddell, *The Hon. George Gray, 4th of Philadelphia, His Ancestors & Descendants*, (Ann Arbor, MI, 1940), p. 89.

78. DAVID WATSON TAYLOR[5] (Henry Taylor[4], Henry Taylor[3], Lucy Penn[2], John Penn[1]) child of Henry Taylor and Mary Minor Watson was born in "Westend", Louisa County, VA on 4 Mar 1864[1], and died in 1940. He married Imogen Maury MORRIS, daughter of James Maury and Victoria Eulalia (Phillips) Morris in Waldrop, VA on 26 Oct 1892.[1] She was born in "Grassdale", Louisa County, VA on 10 Nov 1867[1], and died on 20 Aug 1940. Children:

+ 165	i	Dorothy Watson TAYLOR, b. 26 Nov 1895
+ 166	ii	Mary Coleman TAYLOR, b. 11 Nov 1900
+ 167	iii	David Watson TAYLOR, Jr., b. 14 Aug 1906
+ 168	iv	Imogen Morris TAYLOR, b. 1908

References:
[1] DSDI Appl # 551.

84. HENRY TAYLOR WICKHAM[5] (Lucy Penn Taylor[4], Henry Taylor[3], Lucy Penn[2], John Penn[1]) child of Lucy Penn Taylor and Williams Carter

Wickham was born in "Hickory Hill", Hanover County, VA on 17 Dec 1849[1], and died in 1943. He married Elise Warwick BARKSDALE, daughter of George Annesley and Elise Florence (Warwick) Barksdale on 17 Dec 1885.[1] She was born in Richmond, VA on 28 Aug 1861.[1] Children:
+ 169   i   Williams Carter WICKHAM, b. 17 Jul 1887
+ 170   ii   George Barksdale WICKHAM, b. 13 Sep 1888
References:
[1] Leach MSS, p. 5972.

85. ANNE CARTER WICKHAM[5] (Lucy Penn Taylor[4], Henry Taylor[3], Lucy Penn[2], John Penn[1]) child of Lucy Penn Taylor and Williams Carter Wickham was born in "Hickory Hill", Hanover County, VA on 27 Oct 1851[1], and died in 1939. She married Robert Henry RENSHAW, son of Benjamin and Francesca de Paula (de Orea) Renshaw on 9 Nov 1881.[1] He was born in Bristol, PA on 25 Apr 1833[1], and died in 1910. Children:
+ 171   i   Williams Carter Wickham RENSHAW, b. 19 Nov 1882
  172   ii   Francis Orea RENSHAW, b. 23 Aug 1884, d. 1920; dsp
+ 173   iii   Robert Henry RENSHAW, Jr., b. 15 Feb 1886
  174   iv   Benjamin Williams RENSHAW, b. 23 Sep 1887, dy 30 Jul 1888
  175   v   Julia Wickham RENSHAW, b. 8 Feb 1889; dsp
References:
[1] Leach MSS, p. 5972.

87. WILLIAM FANNING WICKHAM, II[5] (Lucy Penn Taylor[4], Henry Taylor[3], Lucy Penn[2], John Penn[1]) child of Lucy Penn Taylor and Williams Carter Wickham was born in "Hickory Hill", Hanover County, VA on 24 Oct 1860[1], and died in 1900. He married Anne Carter Leigh OLD, daughter of MAJ Charles and Anne Carter (Leigh) Old on 6 May 1896.[1] She was born in "Morewood" Powhatan County, VA on 25 Sep 1870[1], and died in 1903. Children:
  176   i   Lucien Penn WICKHAM, b. 21 Feb 1897, d. 1938; unm
+ 177   ii   Charles Leigh Old WICKHAM, b. 16 Mar 1898
+ 178   iii   Anne Carter WICKHAM, b. 13 Mar 1899
References:
[1] Leach MSS, p. 5972.

91. LUCY NELSON TAYLOR[5] (John Taylor[4], Henry Taylor[3], Lucy Penn[2], John Penn[1]) child of John Taylor and Isabella Nelson Locke was born in "Montrose", Westmoreland County, VA on 24 Jul 1873[1], and died on 7 May 1914. She married Chastine Gillespie WILLIAMS, son of William Arthur and Sallie Frances (Watts) Williams on 11 Jul 1912. He was born in Essex County, VA on 5 Nov 1871[2], and died in Westmoreland County, VA on 3 Oct 1942. Child:

+ 179   i   Lucy Nelson WILLIAMS, b. 12 Apr 1914

References:
[1] Leach MSS, p. 5969. [2] Family data graciously supplied by William G. Thompson; hereinafter cited as WGT data.

92. ELIZABETH MOORE TAYLOR[5] (John Taylor[4], Henry Taylor[3], Lucy Penn[2], John Penn[1]) child of John Taylor and Isabella Nelson Locke was born on 14 Feb 1875[1], and died in 1930. She married (1st) Robert Henry GOULDMAN, son of George and Ida (Stainback) Gouldman on 3 Jun 1905. He was born in 1879[2], and died in 1910. Child:

180   i   Robert Nelson GOULDMAN, b. 1908, d. 1966; unm

References:
[1] Leach MSS, p. 5969. [2] Mary Stanley Field Liddell, *The Hon. George Gray, 4th of Philadelphia, His Ancestors & Descendants*, (Ann Arbor, MI, 1940), p. 92.

93. ANNE ["NANNIE"] ISABELLA TAYLOR[5] (John Taylor[4], Henry Taylor[3], Lucy Penn[2], John Penn[1]) child of John Taylor and Isabella Nelson Locke was born on 7 Feb 1878[1], and died in 1963. She married Clarence Christopher SKEETER in Oak Grove, VA on 30 Jul 1902. Children:

+ 181   i   Margaret Pendleton SKEETER, b. 6 Jun 1903
182   ii   Taylor Page SKEETER, b. 19 Aug 1908, d. Jul 1974; unm

References:
[1] Leach MSS, p. 5969; see also WGT data.

94. MARGARET LOCKE TAYLOR[5] (John Taylor[4], Henry Taylor[3], Lucy Penn[2], John Penn[1]) child of John Taylor and Isabella Nelson Locke was born in "Montrose", Westmoreland County, VA on 27 Mar 1880[1], and died on 25 Aug 1940. She married Richard Vivian TURNER, son of Henry and Caroline (Smith) Turner in Oak Grove, VA on 9 Oct 1906. He was born in 1872[2], and died in 1943. Children:

+ 183   i   Harry Vivian TURNER, b. 26 Aug 1908
184   ii   Richard Nelson TURNER, b. 28 Aug 1911, d. 9 Sep 1976; unm

References:
[1] Leach MSS, p. 5969 [2] WGT data.

98. HENRY LEIPER TAYLOR[5] (William Penn Taylor[4], Henry Taylor[3], Lucy Penn[2], John Penn[1]) child of William Penn Taylor and Florence Ida

Carter was born on 23 Apr 1882[1], and died in 1956. He married Florence WHARTON in 1909. She was born in 1880.[2] Child:

185   i   Gwendolyn Hungerford TAYLOR, b. 1910, dy 1911

References:
[1] Leach MSS, p. 5969 [2] WGT data.

105. THOMAS LOCKE TAYLOR[5] (Thomas Leiper Taylor[4], Henry Taylor[3], Lucy Penn[2], John Penn[1]) child of Thomas Leiper Taylor and Rosa Van Doren Locke was born in Westmoreland County, VA on 5 Jun 1874[1], and died in 1916. He married Emily Winifred Whitby ALLEN, daughter of James and Emily (Whitby) Allen in 1904. She was born in 1886[2], and died in 1960. Children:

+ 186   i   Virginia Nelson TAYLOR, b. 1904
+ 187   ii   Constance California TAYLOR, b. 12 Dec 1906
  188   iii Thomas Locke TAYLOR, Jr., b. 1909; dsp
  189   iv   Leslie Milton TAYLOR, b. 1912

References:
[1] Leach MSS, p. 5970. [2] WGT data.

106. HENRIETTA TAYLOR[5] (Thomas Leiper Taylor[4], Henry Taylor[3], Lucy Penn[2], John Penn[1]) child of Thomas Leiper Taylor and Rosa Van Doren Locke was born on 17 Sep 1876[1], and died in 1960. She married Howard Wallace STUCH, son of LaFayette and Martha (Wallace) Stuch in 1903. He was born in 1876.[2] Child:

+ 190   i   Howard Taylor STUCH, b. 1907

References:
[1] Leach MSS, p. 5970. [2] WGT data.

107. BERNARD PENDLETON TAYLOR[5] (Thomas Leiper Taylor[4], Henry Taylor[3], Lucy Penn[2], John Penn[1]) child of Thomas Leiper Taylor and Rosa Van Doren Locke was born in Westmoreland County, VA on 28 Feb 1878[1], and died in 1940. He married Anna C. YOUNG in 1905. She was born in 1885[2], and died in 1921. Children:

191   i   Nettie TAYLOR, b. 1906
192   ii   Mildred TAYLOR, b. 1907

References:
[1] Leach MSS, p. 5970 reports place and date of birth. [2] WGT data reports only year of birth, no full date and no place.

108. WILLIAM LOCKE TAYLOR[5] (Thomas Leiper Taylor[4], Henry Taylor[3], Lucy Penn[2], John Penn[1]) child of Thomas Leiper Taylor and Rosa Van Doren Locke was born on 8 Apr 1880[1], and died in 1948. He married

Mary Deborah DIGGES, daughter of Eugene and Mary (Inglehart) Digges in 1927. She was born in 1892[2], and died in 1981. Child:
    193   i   Mary Inglehart TAYLOR, b. 1928
References:
[1] Leach MSS, p. 5970. [2] WGT data.

111. JOHN TAYLOR[5] (Thomas Leiper Taylor[4], Henry Taylor[3], Lucy Penn[2], John Penn[1]) child of Thomas Leiper Taylor and Rosa Van Doren Locke was born on 11 Sep 1888[1], and died in 1965. He married Margaret Deborah PARKER, daughter of Henry and Mary (Bragg) Parker in 1916. She was born in 1894[2], and died in 1983. Children:
    194   i   Joan TAYLOR, b. c. 1917
    195   ii   Mary Gordon TAYLOR, b. c. 1918, dy 1919
    196   iii   Marguerite Locke TAYLOR, b. 1921
    197   iv   Elizabeth Parker TAYLOR, b. 1922
References:
[1] Leach MSS, p. 5970. [2] WGT data.

116. GEORGE TAYLOR LEE[5] (Lucy Penn Taylor[4], George Taylor[3], Lucy Penn[2], John Penn[1]) child of Lucy Penn Taylor and Charles Carter Lee was born in Richmond, VA on 8 Mar 1848.[1] He married Ella Marion GOODRUM [widow of James Jefferson Fletcher], daughter of William and Caroline Elizabeth (Townsend) Goodrum on 15 May 1888.[1] She was born in Brownsville, AR on 30 Apr 1863.[1] Children:
    198   i   Charles Carter LEE, b. 9 Apr 1889
    199   ii   Lucy Randolph LEE, b. 19 Sep 1893
    200   iii   George Taylor LEE, b. 26 Dec 1895
References:
[1] Leach MSS, p. 5974.

117. HENRY LEE[5] (Lucy Penn Taylor[4], George Taylor[3], Lucy Penn[2], John Penn[1]) child of Lucy Penn Taylor and Charles Carter Lee was born in Richmond, VA on 9 Jul 1849.[1] He married Lillian Elizabeth WOOLLEN, daughter of James Anderson and Susan Caroline (Malcomb) Woollen on 19 Jul 1888.[1] She was born in Greensboro, NC on 23 Jun 1862.[1] Children:
    201   i   Charles Carter LEE, b. 18 May 1889, dy 25 May 1889
    202   ii   Robert Henry LEE, b. 3 Sep 1890
    203   iii   Virginia Lillian LEE, b. 26 Dec 1893
References:
[1] Leach MSS, p. 5974.

118. ROBERT RANDOLPH LEE[5] (Lucy Penn Taylor[4], George Taylor[3], Lucy Penn[2], John Penn[1]) child of Lucy Penn Taylor and Charles Carter Lee was born in Richmond, VA on 22 May 1853.[1] He married Alice WILKINSON, daughter of William Withers and Frances (Wilkinson) Wilkinson on 5 Feb 1886.[1] She was born in Madison County, FL on 2 Sep 1867.[1] Children:

   204   i   Williams Carter LEE, b. 14 Mar 1891
   205   ii   Robert Randolph LEE, b. 10 Sep 1892
   206 iii   Alice LEE, b. 10 Sep 1895

References:
[1] Leach MSS, p. 5974.

120. MILDRED LEE[5] (Lucy Penn Taylor[4], George Taylor[3], Lucy Penn[2], John Penn[1]) child of Lucy Penn Taylor and Charles Carter Lee was born in "Windsor", Powhatan County, VA on 30 Nov 1857.[1] She married John Taylor FRANCIS, son of Dr. John Taylor and Lucretia (Nash) Francis on 4 Feb 1888.[1] He was born in Norfolk, VA on 27 Nov 1859, and died there on 8 Jan 1893.[1] Children:

   207   i   Mildred Lee FRANCIS, b. 27 Dec 1888
   208   ii   John Taylor FRANCIS, b. 29 Dec 1889, dy 24 May 1890
   209 iii   Catherine Randolph FRANCIS, b. 3 Feb 1892, dy 26 Jun 1892

References:
[1] Leach MSS, p. 5974.

121. CATHERINE RANDOLPH LEE[5] (Lucy Penn Taylor[4], George Taylor[3], Lucy Penn[2], John Penn[1]) child of Lucy Penn Taylor and Charles Carter Lee was born in "Windsor", Powhatan County, VA on 27 Aug 1865.[1] She married John Reevely GUERRANT, son of Peter and Sarah (Saunders) Guerrant on 12 Jul 1892.[1] He was born in "Algoma", Franklin County, VA on 12 Jul 1865.[1] Children:

   210   i   Elizabeth Moore GUERRANT, b. 31 Dec 1893
   211   ii   Marie L'Orange GUERRANT, b. 1 Jun 1896

References:
[1] Leach MSS, p. 5975.

127. RICHARD JAMES GILLIAM[5] (Elizabeth Moore Taylor[4], George Taylor[3], Lucy Penn[2], John Penn[1]) child of Elizabeth Moore Taylor and John Gilliam was born on 3 Mar 1871, and died on 4 May 1897.[1] He married -- (--) in say 1893. Child:

   212   i   Randolph Moore GILLIAM, b. 27 Oct 1895

References:
[1] Leach MSS, p. 5975.

129. TAYLOR FITZHUGH TURNER[5] (Sallie Penn Taylor[4], George Taylor[3], Lucy Penn[2], John Penn[1]) child of Sallie Penn Taylor and Augustine Fitzhugh Turner was born in Port Royal, VA on 17 Jun 1903. He married Alice Lake ALEXANDER in Greenville, MS on 28 Dec 1932. She was born in Greenville, MS on 27 Aug 1908. Children:

+ 213   i   Taylor Fitzhugh TURNER, Jr., b. 21 Mar 1934
+ 214   ii   Alexander Pendleton TURNER, b. 6 Jan 1940

SIXTH GENERATION

133. CHARLES HERNDON[6] (Lucy Woodford Gordon[5], Lucy Penn Taylor[4], John Taylor[3], Lucy Penn[2], John Penn[1]) child of Lucy Woodford Gordon and Charles Herndon was born in Fredericksburg, VA on 11 Mar 1865.[1] He married (1st) Corinne DeForest YOUNG, daughter of Thomas Alexander and Susan (Hopkins) Young on 21 Jun 1890.[1] She was born in NYC on 31 Oct 1869, and died in Fredericksburg, VA on 11 Apr 1892.[1] Child:

215   i   Corinne Young HERNDON, b. 8 Mar 1892
References:
[1] Leach MSS, p. 5962.

139. SUSAN MORRIS PRESTON[6] (Lucy Woodford Taylor[5], Edmund Taylor[4], John Taylor[3], Lucy Penn[2], John Penn[1]) child of Lucy Woodford Taylor and Charles Henry Campbell Preston was born in "Aspenvale", Smyth County, VA on 4 Aug 1886.[1] She married Louis Knight LEAKE in Front Royal, VA on 29 Jun 1911. He was born on 29 Jun 1879.[1] Child:

216   i   Andrew Kean LEAKE, b. 31 Mar 1912
References:
[1] DSDI Appl # 1034.

145. NORMA STEWART CLENEAY[6] (Elizabeth Lewis Taylor[5], Edmund Taylor[4], John Taylor[3], Lucy Penn[2], John Penn[1]) child of Elizabeth Lewis Taylor and Charles Wadsworth Cleneay was born in Yuscaran, HONDURAS on 2 Oct 1892.[1] She married Robert White WILLIAMS in Washington, DC on 11 Nov 1920. He was born in Tallahassee, FL on 6 Dec 1878[1], and died in Washington, DC on 19 Sep 1940. Children:

217   i   Robert Willoughby WILLIAMS, b. 29 Sep 1921
218   ii   Elizabeth Cleneay WILLIAMS, b. 26 Oct 1924

References:
[1] DSDI Appl # 891, & 741.

153. LUCY WILHELMINA WALKER[6] (Agatha Bernard Taylor[5], Edmund Taylor[4], John Taylor[3], Lucy Penn[2], John Penn[1]) child of Agatha Bernard Taylor and David Walker was born in Lynchburg, VA on 3 Jan 1901, and died in Greenville, SC on 2 Nov 1987. She married James d'Alvigny McCULLOUGH in Lynchburg, VA on 3 Jan 1924. He was born in Greenville, SC on 20 Mar 1891[1] , and died the ` re on 11 Nov 1953. Children:

    219   i   Joseph Allen McCULLOUGH, b. 31 Dec 1924
+ 220   ii David Walker McCULLOUGH, b. 17 May 1927

References:
[1] DSDI Appl # 1372.

154. DORRIS LYMAN DREW[6] (Marion Gordon Taylor[5], James Taylor[4], John Taylor[3], Lucy Penn[2], John Penn[1]) child of Marion Gordon Taylor and Clayton Lyman Drew was born in Washington, DC on 13 Apr 1914. She married Walter Moulden EIKER in Washington, DC on 24 Jun 1937. He was born in Washington, DC on 22 May 1913. Child:

    221   i   Marion EIKER, b. 11 Feb 1940

155. HENRY TAYLOR[6] (Henry Taylor[5], Henry Taylor[4], Henry Taylor[3], Lucy Penn[2], John Penn[1]) child of Henry Taylor and Virginia Bagby was born on 30 Apr 1887[1], and died on 16 Dec 1982. He married Isabel DeLeon WILLIAMS, daughter of William and Alice (Taylor) Williams in 1925. She was born in 1897[2], and died in 1983. Children:

    222   i   Alice Marshall TAYLOR, b. 1926
    223   ii Henry TAYLOR, b. 1928
    224   iii George William Bagby TAYLOR, b. 1936

References:
[1] Leach MSS, p. 5972. [2] WGT data.

165. DOROTHY WATSON TAYLOR[6] (David Watson Taylor[5], Henry Taylor[4], Henry Taylor[3], Lucy Penn[2], John Penn[1]) child of David Watson Taylor and Imogen Maury Morris was born on 26 Nov 1895[1], and died in 1978. She married Robert Courtney HILLIARD, son of Alphonso and Eliza Armstrong (Courtney) Hilliard in 1916. He was born in 1893.[2] Children:

    225   i   Sylvia Taylor HILLIARD, b. 1917
    226   ii Robert Courtney HILLIARD, b. 1918
    227   iii Alphonso HILLIARD, Jr., b. 1923
    228   iv Dorothy Taylor HILLIARD, b. 1930

References:
[1] DSDI Appl # 551. [2] WGT data.

166. MARY COLEMAN TAYLOR[6] (David Watson Taylor[5], Henry Taylor[4], Henry Taylor[3], Lucy Penn[2], John Penn[1]) child of David Watson Taylor and Imogen Maury Morris was born on 11 Nov 1900, and died in 1939. She married George Paul TIDMARSH, son of Arthur William and Nell (Randle) Tidmarsh in 1927. He was born on 11 Jan 1896[1], and died in Jun 1959. Children:

   229   i Nell Randle TIDMARSH, b. 9 Jan 1928, d. Jan 1986; dsp
   230   ii Sallie Anne TIDMARSH, b. 1935

References:
[1] WGT data.

167. DAVID WATSON TAYLOR, Jr.[6] (David Watson Taylor[5], Henry Taylor[4], Henry Taylor[3], Lucy Penn[2], John Penn[1]) child of David Watson Taylor and Imogen Maury Morris was born on 14 Aug 1906[1], and died in Oct 1973. He married Mary DeFord BIGELOW, daughter of Horatio and Mary (Riese) Bigelow in 1928. She was born in 1908, and died in 1963. Children:

   231   i Mary DeFord TAYLOR, b. 1930 [twin]
   232   ii Nancy Bigelow TAYLOR, b. 1930 [twin]
+ 233 iii David Watson TAYLOR, III, b. 1931
   234 iv Imogen Morris TAYLOR, b. 1933

References:
[1] WGT data.

168. IMOGEN MORRIS TAYLOR[6] (David Watson Taylor[5], Henry Taylor[4], Henry Taylor[3], Lucy Penn[2], John Penn[1]) child of David Watson Taylor and Imogen Maury Morris was born in 1908, and died in 1970. She married (1st) John E. POWELL, son of William Henry and Alice (Walsh) Powell in 1928. She married (2nd) John DEVEREUX in 1943.
Children by first marriage:

   235   i Jean Taylor POWELL, b. 1929
   236   ii William Henry POWELL, b. 1930

Children by second marriage:

   237 iii Dorinda DEVEREUX, b. 1944
   238 iv Diana T. DEVEREUX, b. 1947

169. WILLIAMS CARTER WICKHAM[6] (Henry Taylor Wickham[5], Lucy Penn Taylor[4], Henry Taylor[3], Lucy Penn[2], John Penn[1]) child of Henry Taylor Wickham and Elise Warwick Barksdale was born in "Hickory Hill", Hanover

County, VA on 17 Jul 1887[1], and died in Jul 1985. He married Credilla MILLER, daughter of Lawrence Vernon and Carrie (Colton) Miller in 1912. She was born in 1890.[2] Children:

   239   i   William Carter WICKHAM, Jr., b. 1917; sp
\+ 240   ii Lawrence Vernon Miller WICKHAM, b. 17 Aug 1920
   241   iii Credilla Barksdale WICKHAM, b. 1922; sp

References:
[1] Date and place of birth is given in Leach MSS, p. 5972. [2] Her year of birth is reported in a PAF printout of Richard Ludwig.

170. GEORGE BARKSDALE WICKHAM[6] (Henry Taylor Wickham[5], Lucy Penn Taylor[4], Henry Taylor[3], Lucy Penn[2], John Penn[1]) child of Henry Taylor Wickham and Elise Warwick Barksdale was born in "Hickory Hill", Hanover County, VA on 13 Sep 1888[1], and died in 1928. He married Virginia Catherine CHESTERMAN in1916. She was born in 1895.[2] Children:

   242   i   Virginia Chesterman WICKHAM, b. 1918
\+ 243   ii Henry Taylor WICKHAM, b. 1919

References:
[1] Leach MSS, p. 5972. [2] Mary Stanley Field Liddell, *The Hon. George Gray, 4th of Philadelphia, His Ancestors & Descendants*, (Ann Arbor, MI, 1940), p. 160.

171. WILLIAMS CARTER WICKHAM RENSHAW[6] (Anne Carter Wickham[5], Lucy Penn Taylor[4], Henry Taylor[3], Lucy Penn[2], John Penn[1]) child of Anne Carter Wickham and Robert Henry Renshaw was born in Richmond, VA on 19 Nov 1882[1], and died in 1945. He married Martha CHAFIN in 1912. Children:

\+ 244   i   Carter Wickham RENSHAW, b. 1925 [twin]
\+ 245   ii Blair Vinson RENSHAW, b. 1925 [twin]

References:
[1] Leach MSS, p. 5972.

173. ROBERT HENRY RENSHAW, Jr.[6] (Anne Carter Wickham[5], Lucy Penn Taylor[4], Henry Taylor[3], Lucy Penn[2], John Penn[1]) child of Anne Carter Wickham and Robert Henry Renshaw was born in Richmond, VA on 15 Feb 1886[1], and died in 1973. He married Henrietta Buchanan ALBERT, daughter of Joseph Taylor and Mary Gittings Simmons (Buchanan) Albert in 1913. Children:

\+ 246   i   Mary Buchanan RENSHAW, b. 1914
\+ 247   ii Robert Henry RENSHAW, III, b. 14 Apr 1916
   248   iii Taylor Albert RENSHAW, b. 1918
\+ 249   iv Henrietta Gittings Albert RENSHAW, b. 1921

References:
[1] Leach MSS, p. 5972.

177. CHARLES LEIGH OLD WICKHAM[6] (William Fanning Wickham, II[5], Lucy Penn Taylor[4], Henry Taylor[3], Lucy Penn[2], John Penn[1]) child of William Fanning Wickham, II and Anne Carter Leigh Old was born on 16 Mar 1898.[1] He married Margaret Johnston STEWART in 1931. Child:
   250   i   Son WICKHAM, b. c. 1933, dy
References:
[1] Leach MSS, p. 5972.

178. ANNE CARTER WICKHAM[6] (William Fanning Wickham, II[5], Lucy Penn Taylor[4], Henry Taylor[3], Lucy Penn[2], John Penn[1]) child of William Fanning Wickham, II and Anne Carter Leigh Old was born on 13 Mar 1899[1], and died on 11 May 1994. She married Wallace Landon GRAVELY, son of Willis and Robert (Treadway) Gravely in 1925. Children:
   251   i   Julian Pruden GRAVELY, b. 1926
   252   ii   Roberta Treadway GRAVELY, b. 1928, dy
   253   iii   Anne Carter GRAVELY, b. 1931
   254   iv   Wallace Landon GRAVELY, Jr., b. c. 1934
References:
[1] Richard Ludwig PAF data.

179. LUCY NELSON WILLIAMS[6] (Lucy Nelson Taylor[5], John Taylor[4], Henry Taylor[3], Lucy Penn[2], John Penn[1]) child of Lucy Nelson Taylor and Chastine Gillespie Williams was born on 12 Apr 1914, and died on 7 Sep 1989. She married Thomas Muse THOMPSON, son of William Carroll and Sallie Deborah (Muse) Thompson on 18 Sep 1941. He was born on 31 Jul 1910, and died on 4 Dec 1952. Child:
   255   i   William Gillespie THOMPSON, b. 23 Aug 1944

181. MARGARET PENDLETON SKEETER[6] (Anne ["Nannie"]Isabella Taylor[5], John Taylor[4], Henry Taylor[3], Lucy Penn[2], John Penn[1]) child of Anne ["Nannie"]Isabella Taylor and Clarence Christopher Skeeter was born on 6 Jun 1903, and died in Reno, NV on 5 Jul 1999. She married (1st) Durey B. HOLMES, son of Milton and Martha (Dudman) Holmes in 1928. He was born in 1898.[1] Child:
   256   i   Mary Lee HOLMES, b. 1932
References:
[1] WGT data.

183. HARRY VIVIAN TURNER[6] (Margaret Locke Taylor[5], John Taylor[4], Henry Taylor[3], Lucy Penn[2], John Penn[1]) child of Margaret Locke Taylor and Richard Vivian Turner was born on 20 Aug 1908, and died in New Bern, NC on 22 May 1991. He married Virginia GREEN in say 1940. She was born on 5 Dec 1905, and died in Jan 1986. Child:

    257   i   David Richard TURNER, b. 1947

186. VIRGINIA NELSON TAYLOR[6] (Thomas Locke Taylor[5], Thomas Leiper Taylor[4], Henry Taylor[3], Lucy Penn[2], John Penn[1]) child of Thomas Locke Taylor and Winifred Whitby Allen was born in 1904, and died in 1979. She married Hugh Graham FINDLAY, son of Alexander Graham and Edith (Thompson) Findlay in 1925. Child:

    258   i   Hugh Graham FINDLAY, Jr., b. 1928

187. CONSTANCE CALIFORNIA TAYLOR[6] (Thomas Locke Taylor[5], Thomas Leiper Taylor[4], Henry Taylor[3], Lucy Penn[2], John Penn[1]) child of Thomas Locke Taylor and Winifred Whitby Allen was born on 12 Dec 1906, and died in Mar 1987. She married Alexander Von HERZEN, son of Pierre Alexander and Helen (Zoty) Von Herzen in 1929. Children:

+ 259   i   Alexander Taylor Von HERZEN, b. c. 1930
+ 260   ii   Virginia Ellen Von HERZEN, b. 1931
+ 261 iii   Jeannette Elizabeth Von HERZEN, b. 1932

190. HOWARD TAYLOR STUCH[6] (Henrietta Taylor[5], Thomas Leiper Taylor[4], Henry Taylor[3], Lucy Penn[2], John Penn[1]) child of Henrietta Taylor and Howard Wallace Stuch was born in 1907. He married (1st) Betty BIJUR in 1935. He married (3rd) Erma MONFORT in 1947.
Child by first marriage:

    262   i   Thomas Howard STUCH, b. 1936
Children by third marriage:

    263   i   Howard Walter STUCH, b. 1951
    264   ii   Robert Wayne STUCH, b. 1953

213. TAYLOR FITZHUGH TURNER, Jr.[6] (Taylor Fitzhugh Turner[5], Sallie Penn Taylor[4], George Taylor[3], Lucy Penn[2], John Penn[1]) child of Taylor Fitzhugh Turner and Alice Lake Alexander was born in Greenville, MS on 21 Mar 1934. He married Mary Elizabeth SLATER in Fredericksburg, VA on 7 Jun 1958. She was born in Petersburg, VA on 30 Oct 1935. Child:

+ 265   i   Elizabeth Robinette TURNER, b. 6 Jul 1964

214. ALEXANDER PENDLETON TURNER[6] (Taylor Fitzhugh Turner[5], Sallie Penn Taylor[4], George Taylor[3], Lucy Penn[2], John Penn[1]) child of Taylor Fitzhugh Turner and Alice Lake Alexander was born in Richmond, VA on 6 Jun 1940. He married Karen Diane LAHMANN in Alva, OK on 27 Jul 1969. She was born in Alva, OK on 8 Apr 1945. Children:

    266   i   John Alexander TURNER, b. 20 Sep 1974
    267   ii Michael Lee TURNER, b. 8 Jul 1979

SEVENTH GENERATION

220. DAVID WALKER McCULLOUGH[7] (Lucy Wilhelmina Walker[6], Agatha Bernard Taylor[5], Edmund Taylor[4], John Taylor[3], Lucy Penn[2], John Penn[1]) child of Lucy Wilhelmina Walker and James d'Alvigny McCullough was born in Greenville, SC on 17 May 1927. He married Ann Woltz CURRIE in Arden, Buncombe County, NC on 13 Aug 1960. She was born in Pinehurst, NC on 12 Oct 1933. Children:

    268   i   Lucy Lauchlin McCULLOUGH, b. 7 Sep 1961
    269   ii David Walker McCULLOUGH, Jr., b. 26 Nov 1963
    270   iii James Randolph McCULLOUGH, b. 28 Aug 1965

233. DAVID WATSON TAYLOR, III[7] (David Watson Taylor, Jr.[6], David Watson Taylor[5], Henry Taylor[4], Henry Taylor[3], Lucy Penn[2], John Penn[1]) child of David Watson Taylor, Jr. and Mary DeFord Bigelow was born in 1931, and died in 1962. He married Jean GEARY in 1954. Children:

    271   i   David Watson TAYLOR, IV, b. 1955
    272   ii Donna TAYLOR, b. 1957

240. LAWRENCE VERNON MILLER WICKHAM[7] (Williams Carter Wickham[6], Henry Taylor Wickham[5], Lucy Penn Taylor[4], Henry Taylor[3], Lucy Penn[2], John Penn[1]) child of Williams Carter Wickham and Credilla Miller was born in Washington, DC on 17 Aug 1920, and died on 30 Jan 1994. He married Marjorie Jean HEIDINGER in say 1944. She was born in 1921. Children:

    273   i   Marjorie Jean WICKHAM, b. 1946
    274   ii Andrew Carter WICKHAM, b. 1948
    275   iii John Graham WICKHAM, b. 1950

243. HENRY TAYLOR WICKHAM[7] (George Barksdale Wickham[6], Henry Taylor Wickham[5], Lucy Penn Taylor[4], Henry Taylor[3], Lucy Penn[2], John

Penn[1]) child of George Barksdale Wickham and Virginia Chesterman was born in Richmond, VA in 1919. He married Margaret Halsey GEARING in say 1945. Child:

276   i   Margaret Wallis WICKHAM, b. 1948

244. CARTER WICKHAM RENSHAW[7] (Williams Carter Wickham Renshaw[6], Anne Carter Wickham[5], Lucy Penn Taylor[4], Henry Taylor[3], Lucy Penn[2], John Penn[1]) child of Williams Carter Wickham Renshaw and Martha Chafin was born in 1925. She married W. Scott MOORE in 1950. Children:

277   i   Anne MOORE, b. 1951
278   ii   Martha Harvie MOORE, b. 1953

245. BLAIR VINSON RENSHAW[7] (Williams Carter Wickham Renshaw[6], Anne Carter Wickham[5], Lucy Penn Taylor[4], Henry Taylor[3], Lucy Penn[2], John Penn[1]) child of Williams Carter Wickham Renshaw and Martha Chafin was born in 1925. She married Frank H. WHEELER in 1948. Children:

279   i   Frank Renshaw WHEELER, b. 1949
280   ii   Mary Vinson WHEELER, b. 1953

246. MARY BUCHANAN RENSHAW[7] (Robert Henry Renshaw, Jr.[6], Anne Carter Wickham[5], Lucy Penn Taylor[4], Henry Taylor[3], Lucy Penn[2], John Penn[1]) child of Robert Henry Renshaw, Jr. and Henrietta Buchanan Albert was born in Preston, Caroline County, MD in 1914. She married Maurice Bixler LEONARD in say 1942. He was born in 1905. Children:

281   i   Robert Bixler LEONARD, b. 1945
282   ii   Buchanan Renshaw LEONARD, b. 1948

247. ROBERT HENRY RENSHAW, III[7] (Robert Henry Renshaw, Jr.[6], Anne Carter Wickham[5], Lucy Penn Taylor[4], Henry Taylor[3], Lucy Penn[2], John Penn[1]) child of Robert Henry Renshaw, Jr. and Henrietta Buchanan Albert was born in Baltimore, MD on 14 Apr 1916, and died in Naples, FL on 14 Oct 1998. He married Mildred Alice HOKE in say 1945. She was born in New Windsor, Carroll County, MD in 1921. Child:

283   i   Elsie Hoke RENSHAW, b. 1947
284   ii   Walter Hoke RENSHAW, b. c. 1950

249. HENRIETTA GITTINGS RENSHAW[7] (Robert Henry Renshaw, Jr.[6], Anne Carter Wickham[5], Lucy Penn Taylor[4], Henry Taylor[3], Lucy Penn[2], John Penn[1]) child of Robert Henry Renshaw, Jr. and Henrietta Buchanan Albert was born in Snow Hill, MD in 1921. She married Samuel Parran CARD in say 1945. He was born in Baltimore, MD in 1917. Children:

285   i   Carolynne Renshaw CARD, b. 1943
286   ii   Marianne Egerton CARD, b. 1945
287   iii   Daniel Parker CARD, II, b. 1947

259. ALEXANDER TAYLOR Von HERZEN[7] (Constance California Taylor[6], Thomas Locke Taylor[5], Thomas Leiper Taylor[4], Henry Taylor[3], Lucy Penn[2], John Penn[1]) child of Constance California Taylor and Alexander Von Herzen was born about 1929. He married Stepanie J. SARNO in say 1953. Child:
288   i   Elizabeth Von HERZEN, b. c. 1956

260. VIRGINIA ELLEN Von HERZEN[7] (Constance California Taylor[6], Thomas Locke Taylor[5], Thomas Leiper Taylor[4], Henry Taylor[3], Lucy Penn[2], John Penn[1]) child of Constance California Taylor and Alexander Von Herzen was born about 1932. She married Charles STUART in say 1952. Children:
289   i   Norman STUART, b. c. 1954
290   ii   Kathleen STUART, b. c. 1956
291   iii   William Nelson STUART, b. c. 1959

261. JEANNETTE ELIZABETH Von HERZEN[7] (Constance California Taylor[6], Thomas Locke Taylor[5], Thomas Leiper Taylor[4], Henry Taylor[3], Lucy Penn[2], John Penn[1]) child of Constance California Taylor and Alexander Von Herzen was born about 1935. She married H. Richard ERDMAN in say 1956. Children:
292   i   Scott ERDMAN, b. c. 1959
293   ii   Catherine ERDMAN, b. c. 1962
294   iii   Janice ERDMAN, b. c. 1966

265. ELIZABETH ROBINETTE TURNER[7] (Taylor Fitzhugh Turner, Jr.[6], Taylor Fitzhugh Turner[5], Sallie Penn Taylor[4], George Taylor[3], Lucy Penn[2], John Penn[1]) child of Taylor Fitzhugh Turner and Mary Elizabeth Slater was born in Charlottesville, VA on 6 Jul 1964. She married Jeffrey Scott WROBEL in Richmond, VA on 8 Oct 1994. He was born in Pasadena, CA on 11 Jul 1963. Children:
295   i   Jeffrey Scott WROBEL, Jr., b. 23 Jul 1996
296   ii   William Turner WROBEL, b. 31 Jan 1998

SOUTH CAROLINA

The territory within the present State of South Carolina was included in the Charter of Carolina [1663] that embraced North Carolina and much of what is now Georgia. A party of settlers under Joseph West came to the south shore of the Ashley River in April 1670, and ten years later moved to what was to become Charleston at the mouth of the Ashley and Cooper Rivers. Other settlements quickly developed along the coast, but there was considerable political unrest. With the weakening of proprietary control, the colonists urged a Crown appointment, which was proclaimed on 29 May 1721, thus erecting South Carolina as a Royal Colony, and separating it from North Carolina.

With the creation of the Royal Charter for Georgia on 20 Jun 1732, The King's Proclamation of 1763 giving the lands between the Althamha and St. Mary's River to Georgia, and the State's ceded strip of land about 12 miles wide to the United States in 1787, South Carolina assumes the size and shape we recognize today.[1] South Carolina elected five delegates to the 2nd Continental Congress on 16 Feb 1776: Thomas Heyward, Thomas Lynch, Sr., Arthur Middleton, Edward Rutledge, and John Rutledge. John Rutledge did not attend, Thomas Lynch, Sr. died before attending, and was replaced by the election of his son, Thomas Lynch, Jr. on 23 Mar 1776. Thus did South Carolina have four signers from that State!

During the Revolutionary War, there were several important battles on South Carolina soil, including Charleston, Ninety-six, and Cowpens, but the British were finally driven from the area. South Carolina ratified the Untied States Constitution on 23 May 1788, becoming the 8th State.[2] John C. Calhoun of South Carolina, while Secretary of State under President John Tyler, engineered a Joint Resolution of Congress that on 1 March 1845 annexed Texas to the United States.

---

[1] Franklin K. Van Zandt, *Boundaries of the United States and the Several States*, (Geological Survey Bulletin 1212, US Government Printing Office, Washington, DC, 1966), pp. 158-159.

[2] Richard B. Morris, *Encyclopedia of American History*, (Harper & Brothers, NY, 1953), p. 118.

Edward Rutledge

50: EDWARD RUTLEDGE

"He who has never hoped can never despair."
George Bernard Shaw

The signature of Edward Rutledge on the Declaration of Independence is in the second column in from the left edge, at the top of the second grouping of signatures, all from South Carolina. He wrote his name in a moderate modified school sized hand with a few curlicues and ended with a backwards slash and a period.

Edward Rutledge was the youngest child of seven , 5th son of John Rutledge and Sarah Hext. His father had emigrated from Ireland, probably County Kilkenny, but died when young Edward was just a year old. His early school lessons were under the tutelage of an Anglican Clergyman, and he also had a tutor in Charleston where he learned Greek and Latin. At nineteen he was sent to London to study law at the Middle Temple, returning to South Carolina in 1773 and was admitted to the Bar.

Well educated, well spoken, with strong Whig leanings, Rutledge was elected to the First Continental Congress in 1774.[1] Being included with a group of very important, mature men from all over the thirteen colonies broadened his understanding of the difficulties with the Mother Country. In February of 1776 he was again elected by the Provincial Congress of South Carolina to the Second Continental Congress where he was present, contributed to the arguments regarding independency, and voted for and later signed the Declaration of Independence.

Rutledge at first felt that the colonies should attempt to strengthen themselves with foreign alliances before committing to the perilous step of declaring independence. But realizing that a heavy majority of the colonies were in favor of such a move, young Rutledge, the youngest signer at barely over twenty six and a half years of age, persuaded the other South Carolina Delegates to approve, which they did on 2 July 1776.

---

[1] John and Katherine Bakeless, *Signers of the Declaration*, (Houghton Mifflin Company, Boston, MA, 1969), p. 281.

FIRST GENERATION

1. EDWARD RUTLEDGE was born in Charleston, SC on 23 Nov 1749.[1] He married (1st) Henrietta MIDDLETON, daughter of Henry and Mary (Williams) Middleton on 1 Mar 1774.[2] She was born in Charleston, SC on 15 Nov 1750[3], and died in Charleston, SC on 22 Apr 1792.[4] He died in Charleston, SC on 23 Jan 1800.[5] Children:

+ 2   i   Henry Middleton RUTLEDGE, b. 5 Apr 1775
   3   ii   Child RUTLEDGE, b. 22 Mar 1778. dy
   4   iii   Sarah RUTLEDGE, b. 1782, d. 15 Apr 1855; unm

References:
[1] The Rutledge and Middleton families are closely intertwined as can be seen from the fact that Edward Rutledge married a Middleton, and so did his son and only heir with issue, Henry Middleton. Little about the **ancestry** of Edward Rutledge is reported in the genealogical literature, and not much has been done by way of a good, quality life history. A quite recent biography of Edward Rutledge has been done by James Haw, *John and Edward Rutledge of South Carolina*, (University of Georgia Press, 1997); but it still contains some errors or incomplete research, particularly regarding the place of emigration. However, considering that no good biographical work had been attempted on this family for 100 years or more, Haw's work is a most welcome addition to the literature on the Signers. Most of the biographical information about Edward Rutledge is found in other compilations, or older works regarding the signers. These include: John Sanderson, *Biographies of the Signers of the Declaration of Independence*, (1823); The Rev. Charles A. Goodrich, *Lives of the Signers of the Declaration of Independence*, (Hartford, CT, 1842), pp. 436-440. See also Della Gray Bartherlmas, *The Signers of the Declaration of Independence, A Biographical and Genealogical Reference*, (Mcfarland & Company, Inc., Jefferson, NC, 1977), pp. 236 -238. The Leach MSS material for Edward Rutledge is microfilmed on FHL Film # 0001756, and the hard copy is found in Vol. #20, pp. 6376-6398. The DAB Article on Edward Rutledge is in Vol. XVI, pp. 257-258. [2] The second marriage of Edward Rutledge to Mary Shubrick [widow of Nicholas Eveleigh], daughter of Thomas Shubrick did not result in any issue, and is thus not reported in this Descendant Genealogical Register. His first marriage to Henrietta Middleton is reported in the Diary of Ann Manigault, and the *South Carolina Gazette and Country Journal* of 8 Mar 1774. See also *South Carolina Historical and Genealogical Magazine*, (Vol # 31), p. 23. There were probably other children born of this marriage, but they must have died young, since no mention of them has ever been located. [3] Her date of birth is reported in M. L. Webber, *Dr. John Rutledge and his Descendants*, (South Carolina Historical and Genealogical Magazine, Jan. 1930), p. 23. [4] M. L. Webber, *Dr. John Rutledge and his Descendants*, (South Carolina Historical and Genealogical Magazine, Jan. 1930), p. 23 as to her date of death. [5] His death is reported in *The Charleston City Gazette* of 25 Jan 1800. He is buried in St. Philip's Churchyard, Charleston, SC. The reader should note that

it is only through his son Henry Middleton Rutledge does Signer of the Declaration of Independence Edward Rutledge have issue!

SECOND GENERATION

2. HENRY MIDDLETON RUTLEDGE [2] (Edward Rutledge[1]) son of Edward Rutledge and Henrietta Middleton was born in Charleston, SC on 5 Apr 1775, and died in Nashville, TN on 20 Jan 1844.[1] He married Septima Sexta MIDDLETON [see also Sketch # 8, Chapter 53, this volume], daughter of Arthur and Mary (Izard) Middleton in Sullivan's Island, SC on 15 Oct 1799.[2] She was born in "Middleton Place", Charleston District, SC on 25 Oct 1783, and died in Nashville, TN on 12 Jun 1865.[3] Children:

+ 5   i   Mary Middleton RUTLEDGE, b. 18 Jun 1801
  6   ii Edward Augustus RUTLEDGE, b. c. Nov 1803, d. 16 Jul 1826; unm
+ 7   iii Henry Adolphus RUTLEDGE, b. 8 Aug 1805
+ 8   iv Henrietta Middleton RUTLEDGE, b. 1808
+ 9   v Emma Philadelphia Middleton RUTLEDGE, b. 1811/12
+ 10 vi Arthur Middleton RUTLEDGE, b. 1 Apr 1817
 11 vii Helen RUTLEDGE, b. Jun 1822, dy Jul 1826
 12 viii Cotesworth Pinckney RUTLEDGE, b. 1824, dy Jul 1826

References:
[1] M. L. Webber, *Dr. John Rutledge and his Descendants*, (South Carolina Historical and Genealogical Magazine, Jan. 1930), p. 96. [2] *Charleston City Gazette* of 18 Oct 1799. The reader should note that **all descendants** of South Carolina Signer Edward Rutledge are also descendants of South Carolina Signer Arthur Middleton through his daughter Septima Sexta Middleton. This is so because of her marriage to Edward Rutledge's only surviving child to have issue, his son Henry Middleton Rutledge. Dates of birth of the children of this marriage are rather well fixed, especially through careful research and the work of Mary Bray Wheeler and Genon Hickerson Neblett, *Chosen Exile, The Life and Times of Septima Sexta Middleton Rutledge*, (The Rutledge Compnay, Inc, Gadsden, AL, 1980), The three children who had no issue all died during July 1926 in Saratoga Springs, NY while the family was there on vacation. Correspondence reported in Wheeler notes the birth of Helen in Jun 1822, and further makes note that she was four years old when she died, It also notes that her younger brother Cotesworth Pinckney was two at the time. A letter from Arthur Peronneau Hayne to Andrew Jackson dated 20 July 1826 reports the death of Edward Augustus Rutledge on "Monday evening", [16 July 1826]. The young man, 22 years old at the time, suffered from severe depression, and perhaps resulting from the burden of the deaths of his two youngest siblings, committed suicide by blowing his brains out with a pistol. All three of these children are buried in the Putnam Cemetery in Saratoga Springs, NY. [3] M. L. Webber, *Dr. John Rutledge and his Descendants*, (South Carolina Historical and Genealogical Magazine, Jan. 1930), p. 96.

THIRD GENERATION

5. MARY MIDDLETON RUTLEDGE[3] (Henry Middleton Rutledge[2], Edward Rutledge[1]) child of Henry Middleton and Septima Sexta (Middleton) Rutledge was born in Charleston, SC on 18 Jan 1801, and died in Nashville, TN on 15 Mar 1872.[1] She married Francis Brinley FOGG, son of the Rev. Daniel and Deborah (Brinley) Fogg on 15 Oct 1823.[1] He was born in Brooklyn, Wingham County, CT on 21 Sep 1795, and died in Nashville, TN on 13 Apr 1880.[1] Children:

   13   i   Francis Brinley FOGG, Jr., b. 11 Jul 1825, d. 12 Feb 1848; unm

   14   ii Septima Sexta Middleton FOGG, b. 1826, d. 27 Oct 1851; unm

   15   iii Henry Middleton FOGG, b. 16 Sep 1830, d. 26 Jan 1862; kia

References:

[1] Leach MSS, p. 6379; see also M. L. Webber, *Dr. John Rutledge and his Descendants*, (South Carolina Historical and Genealogical Magazine, Jan. 1930), p. 97.

7. HENRY ADOLPHUS RUTLEDGE[3] (Henry Middleton Rutledge[2], Edward Rutledge[1]) child of Henry Middleton and Septima Sexta (Middleton) Rutledge was born in Charleston, SC on 8 Aug 1805, and died in "Rutledge Place", Talladega County, AL on 23 Sep 1883.[1] He married Caroline Belle NICHOLSON on 24 Nov 1831.[1] She was born in Davidson County, TN on 12 Apr 1812, and died in Selma, AL on 23 Dec 1878.[1] Children:

+ 16   i   Emma Philadelphia Middleton RUTLEDGE, b. 6 Aug 1833

+ 17   ii Septima Sexta Middleton RUTLEDGE, b. 3 Fe b 1836

References:

[1] Leach MSS, p. 6379.

8. HENRIETTA MIDDLETON RUTLEDGE[3] (Henry Middleton Rutledge[2], Edward Rutledge[1]) child of Henry Middleton and Septima Sexta (Middleton) Rutledge was born in Charleston, SC about 1808, and died in Flat Rock, NC on 27 Sep 1842.[1] She married Frederick RUTLEDGE, son of Frederick and Harriet Pinckney (Horry) Rutledge in Nashville, TN on 15 Oct 1825.[1] He was born in Charleston, SC on 28 Oct 1800, and died in Flat Rock, NC on 7 Jul 1884.[1] Children:

   18   i   Edward RUTLEDGE, b. Aug 1829, dy Aug 1829

19   ii   Elizabeth Pinckney RUTLEDGE, b. 8 Apr 1831, d. 23 Feb 1912; unm

20   iii   Frederick RUTLEDGE, b. 26 Sep 1832, dy 1832

+ 21   iv   Sarah Henrietta RUTLEDGE, b. 1 Oct 1834

22   v   Edward RUTLEDGE, b. 12 Apr 1836, dy 5 Aug 1856 [Again]

23   vi   Alice Izard RUTLEDGE, b. Jan 1838, dy Aug 1854

+ 24   vii   Henry Middleton RUTLEDGE, b. 5 Aug 1840

+ 25   viii   Emma Fredrika [sic] RUTLEDGE, b. 10 May 1842

References:

[1] Leach MSS, p. 6383.

9. EMMA PHILADELPHIA MIDDLETON RUTLEDGE[3] (Henry Middleton Rutledge[2], Edward Rutledge[1]) child of Henry Middleton and Septima Sexta (Middleton) Rutledge was born in "Cedar Grove", St. George's Parish, Charleston District, SC in 1811/12, and died in Flat Rock, NC on 23 Apr 1853.[1] She married Daniel BLAKE, son of Daniel and Anna Louisa (Middleton) Blake on 8 Jun 1831.[1] He was born in London, ENGLAND on 31 Jan 1803, and died in Henderson County, NC on 10 Aug 1873.[1] Children:

26   i   Daniel Henry BLAKE, b. 15 Jun 1832, dy 13 Aug 1832

+ 27   ii   Frederick Rutledge BLAKE, b. 24 Jan 1838

+ 28   iii   Daniel Francis BLAKE, b. 1 May 1841

29   iv   Frances Helen Caroline BLAKE, b. 10 Aug 1842

30   v   Henrietta Louisa BLAKE, b. 14 Oct 1843, d. 14 Sep 1872; dsp

+ 31   vi   Arthur Middleton BLAKE, b. May 1848

32   vii   Henry Middleton Rutledge BLAKE, b. 1851, dy Apr 1856

References:

[1] Leach MSS, p. 6385.

10. ARTHUR MIDDLETON RUTLEDGE[3] (Henry Middleton Rutledge[2], Edward Rutledge[1]) child of Henry Middleton and Septima Sexta (Middleton) Rutledge was born in "Cedar Grove", Charleston County, SC on 1 Apr 1817, and died in Sewanee, TN on 17 Jun 1876.[1] He married (1st) Eliza UNDERWOOD, daughter of Joseph Rogers and Eliza (Trotter) Underwood on 4 Nov 1851.[1] She was born in Bowling Green, KY on 23 Feb 1829, and died in Cuthbert, KY on 2 May 1865.[1] Children:

+ 33   i   Elizabeth Underwood RUTLEDGE, b. 29 Aug 1852

+ 34   ii   Emma Blake RUTLEDGE, b. 29 Mar 1854

+ 35   iii Arthur Middleton RUTLEDGE, b. 4 Nov 1855
   36   iv   Joseph Underwood Huger RUTLEDGE, b. 3 May 1859, dy
             31 Aug 1876
References:
[1] M. L. Webber, *Dr. John Rutledge and his Descendants*, (South Carolina Historical and Genealogical Magazine, Jan. 1930), pp. 102-103; see also Leach MSS, p. 6386.

FOURTH GENERATION

16. EMMA PHILADELPHIA MIDDLETON RUTLEDGE[4] (Henry Adolphus Rutledge[3], Henry Middleton Rutledge[2], Edward Rutledge[1]) child of Henry Adolphus and Caroline Belle (Nicholson) Rutledge was born in Nashville, TN on 6 Aug 1833, and died in Talladega County, AL on 28 Nov 1863.[1] She married Edwin Chiledes TURNER, son of Matthew and Mary Anne Eliza (Thomas) Turner on 7 Jul 1853.[1] He was born in Upshur County, GA on 31 Mar 1831, and died in Easta Boga, Talladega County, AL on 13 May 1890.[1] Children:
+ 37   i   Matthew TURNER, b. 24 May 1854
+ 38   ii   Emma Caroline TURNER, b. 9 Sep 1855
+ 39   iii Edwin Chiledes TURNER, Jr., b. 20 Mar 1857
+ 40   iv   Mary Anne Eliza TURNER, b. 5 Dec 1859
   41   v   Henry Adolphus TURNER, b. 19 Jul 1861, d. 6 Oct 1884;
             unm
References:
[1] Leach MSS, p. 6380.

17. SEPTIMA SEXTA MIDDLETON RUTLEDGE[4] (Henry Adolphus Rutledge[3], Henry Middleton Rutledge[2], Edward Rutledge[1]) child of Henry Adolphus and Caroline Belle (Nicholson) Rutledge was born in Talladega County, AL on 3 Feb 1836[1], and died in Jacksonville, Calhoun County, AL on 26 Mar 1920. She married John Horace FORNEY, son of Jacob and Sabina Swope (Hoke) Forney on 5 Feb 1863.[1] He was born in Lincoln County, NC on 12 Aug 1829[1], and died in Jacksonville, AL on 13 Dec 1902. Children:
   42   i   Emma Rutledge FORNEY, b. 30 May 1864
   43   ii   Henry Fogg FORNEY, b. 19 Apr 1867, dy 10 May 1867
+ 44   iii Jacob FORNEY, b. 8 Oct 1868
   45   iv   Mary Caroline FORNEY, b. 8 Feb 1871
+ 46   v   Sabina Swope FORNEY, b. 6 Aug 1873

+ 47   vi   Annie Rowan FORNEY, b. 1 Jun 1876
  48   vii Kathleen Theresa FORNEY, b. 8 Aug 1878, dy 20 Mar 1881
References:
[1] SAR Appl # 138041; M. L. Webber, *Dr. John Rutledge and his Descendants*, (South Carolina Historical and Genealogical Magazine, Jan. 1930), p. 102; Leach MSS, p. 6382.

21. SARAH HENRIETTA RUTLEDGE[4] (Henrietta Middleton Rutledge[3], Henry Middleton Rutledge[2], Edward Rutledge[1]) child of Henrietta Middleton Rutledge and Frederick Rutledge was born in Brooklands, NC on 1 Oct 1834[1], and died in 1908. She married Charles Cotesworth PINCKNEY, son of Charles Cotesworth and Carolina Phoebe (Elliott) Pinckney on 20 Sep 1866.[1] He was born in Charleston, SC on 31 Jul 1812.[1] Children:

+ 49   i   Edward Rutledge PINCKNEY, b. 27 Jun 1869
  50   ii   Thomas PINCKNEY, b. 28 Oct 1871
  51   iii Stephen Elliott PINCKNEY, b. 17 Feb 1874, dy 17 Jul 1875
References:
[1] Leach MSS, p. 6383.

24. HENRY MIDDLETON RUTLEDGE[4] (Henrietta Middleton Rutledge[3], Henry Middleton Rutledge[2], Edward Rutledge[1]) child of Henrietta Middleton Rutledge and Frederick Rutledge was born in Buncombe County, NC on 5 Aug 1840[1] , and died in McClellanville, SC on 10 Jun 1921. He married (1st) Anna Marie BLAKE, daughter of Walter and Anna Stead (Izard) Blake on 25 Nov 1863.[1] She was born in Henderson County, NC on 12 May 1842, and died on 21 Feb 1872.[1] He married (2nd) Margaret Hamilton SEABROOK, daughter of Archibald Hamilton and Caroline Phoebe (Pinckney) Seabrook in Charleston, SC on 18 Mar 1875.[2] She was born in Beaufort Island, SC on 24 Jan 1849[2], and died in Charleston, SC on 25 Feb 1925. Children by first marriage:

  52   i   Child RUTLEDGE, b. 1865, dy
+ 53   ii   Frederick RUTLEDGE, b. 10 Feb 1868
Children by second marriage:
  54   iii Caroline Phoebe RUTLEDGE, b. 27 Mar 1876
+ 55   iv   Harriott Horry RUTLEDGE, b. 8 Feb 1878
+ 56   v   Thomas Pinckney RUTLEDGE, b. 16 Feb 1879
  57   vi   Henry Middleton RUTLEDGE, b. 26 Aug 1882
+ 58   vii Archibald Hamilton RUTLEDGE, b. 23 Oct 1883
  59   viii Mary Pinckney RUTLEDGE, b. 10 Dec 1886
References:
[1] Leach MSS, p. 6384; SAR Appl # 56265. [2] DSDI Appl # 1535.

25. EMMA FREDRIKA RUTLEDGE[4] (Henrietta Middleton Rutledge[3], Henry Middleton Rutledge[2], Edward Rutledge[1]) child of Henrietta Middleton Rutledge and Frederick Rutledge was born in Charleston, SC on 10 May 1842[1], and died on 19 Jul 1919. She married William Brown REESE, Jr., son of William Brown and Sarah Maclin (Cooke) Reese on 14 Jun 1866.[1] He was born in Knoxville, TN on 17 Mar 1829[1], and died in 1891. Children:

+ 60   i   Mary Middleton Rutledge REESE, b. 20 Apr 1867
+ 61   ii Alice Sophia REESE, b. 4 Jun 1872

References:
[1] Leach MSS, p. 6385.

27. FREDERICK RUTLEDGE BLAKE[4] (Emma Philadelphia Middleton Rutledge[3], Henry Middleton Rutledge[2], Edward Rutledge[1]) child of Emma Philadelphia Middleton Rutledge and Daniel Blake was born in Charleston, SC on 24 Jan 1838.[1] He married Olivia MIDDLETON, daughter of Oliver Hering and Susan Matilda (Chisholm) Middleton on 6 Dec 1864.[1] She was born in Charleston SC on 26 Apr 1839.[1] Children:

+ 62   i   Edmund Molyneux BLAKE, b. 14 Jan 1866
  63   ii   Emma Middleton BLAKE, b. 31 Aug 1868, dy 16 Mar 1873
  64   iii Eliza Fisher BLAKE, b. 31 May 1870
+ 65   iv   Daniel BLAKE, b. 21 Oct 1872

References:
[1] Leach MSS, p. 6386.

28. DANIEL FRANCIS BLAKE[4] (Emma Philadelphia Middleton Rutledge[3], Henry Middleton Rutledge[2], Edward Rutledge[1]) child of Emma Philadelphia Middleton Rutledge and Daniel Blake was born in Henderson County, NC on 1 May 1841, and died in Henderson County, NC on 16 Oct 1872.[1] He married Sarah Hawkins POLK, daughter of the Rt. Rev. Leonidas and Frances Ann (Devereaux) Polk on 1 May 1866.[1] She was born in Maury County, TN on 24 Jun 1840.[1] Child:

  66   i   Frank Polk BLAKE, b. 1 Jun 1872

References:
[1] Leach MSS, p. 6386.

31. ARTHUR MIDDLETON BLAKE[4] (Emma Philadelphia Middleton Rutledge[3], Henry Middleton Rutledge[2], Edward Rutledge[1]) child of Emma Philadelphia Middleton Rutledge and Daniel Blake was born in May 1848.[1] He married Catherine MAXWELL in Nov 1872.[1] Children:

  67   i   Wade H. BLAKE, b. c. 1874
  68   ii   Francis H. BLAKE, b. c. 1877

69   iii   Charles BLAKE, b. c. 1879, dy 1891
70   iv   Emma BLAKE, b. c. 1882
71   v   Joseph BLAKE, b. c. 1884
72   vi   Z. Vance BLAKE, b. c. 1887
73   vii   Daniel BLAKE, b. c. 1890
+ 74   viii Florence Vernon BLAKE, b. 26 Aug 1893

References:
[1] South Carolina Historical and Genealogical Magazine, (Vol # 1, Issue # 3, July 1900), p. 166.

33. ELIZABETH UNDERWOOD RUTLEDGE[4] (Arthur Middleton Rutledge[3], Henry Middleton Rutledge[2], Edward Rutledge[1]) child of Arthur Middleton Rutledge and Eliza Underwood was born in "Chilhowie", Franklin County, TN on 29 Aug 1852[1], and died in Charleston, SC on 15 Feb 1918. She married Henry Edward YOUNG, son of the Rev. Thomas John and Rebecca (Gourdin) Young on 19 Nov 1873.[1] He was born in "Sherwood", Beaufort County, SC on 9 Aug 1831.[1] Children:

75   i   Eliza Underwood Rutledge YOUNG, b. 24 Nov 1874, dy 14 Apr 1878
+ 76   ii   Arthur Middleton Rutledge YOUNG, b. 3 Jul 1876
77   iii   Henry Gourdin YOUNG, b. 16 May 1878, dy 19 May 1878
78   iv   Henry Gourdin YOUNG, b. 7 Sep 1879, dy 25 Oct 1885 [Again]
+ 79   v   Joseph Underwood Rutledge YOUNG, b. 7 Jan 1881

References:
[1] Leach MSS, p. 6387; see also M. L. Webber, *Dr. John Rutledge and his Descendants*, (South Carolina Historical and Genealogical Magazine, Jan. 1930), p. 103.

34. EMMA BLAKE RUTLEDGE[4] (Arthur Middleton Rutledge[3], Henry Middleton Rutledge[2], Edward Rutledge[1]) child of Arthur Middleton Rutledge and Eliza Underwood was born in "Chilhowie", Franklin County, TN on 29 Mar 1854.[1] She married Henry Augustus Middleton SMITH, son of John Julius Pringle and Elizabeth (Middleton) Smith on 24 Jun 1879.[1] He was born in Charleston, SC on 30 Apr 1853[1], and died in 1924. Children:

80   i   Henry Augustus Middleton SMITH, b. 19 May 1882, dy 1 Dec 1901
+ 81   ii   John Julius Pringle SMITH, Jr., b. 14 Oct 1887

References:
[1] M. L. Webber, *Dr. John Rutledge and his Descendants*, (South Carolina Historical and Genealogical Magazine, Jan. 1930), p. 103.

35. ARTHUR MIDDLETON RUTLEDGE[4] (Arthur Middleton Rutledge[3], Henry Middleton Rutledge[2], Edward Rutledge[1]) child of Arthur Middleton Rutledge and Eliza Underwood was born in Bowling Green, KY on 4 Nov 1855.[1] He married Rosalie WINSTON, daughter of Joseph Pendleton and Lelia (Saunders) Winston in Richmond, VA on 12 Dec 1893.[1] She was born in Richmond, VA on 3 Dec 1866.[1] Children:

82	i	Arthur Middleton RUTLEDGE, b. 31 Dec 1896	
83	ii	Winston Underwood RUTLEDGE, b. 29 Mar 1898	
84	iii	Edward RUTLEDGE, b. 14 Jan 1901	

References:
[1] M. L. Webber, *Dr. John Rutledge and his Descendants*, (South Carolina Historical and Genealogical Magazine, Jan. 1930), p. 104.

FIFTH GENERATION

37. MATTHEW TURNER[5] (Emma Philadelphia Middleton Rutledge[4], Henry Adolphus Rutledge[3], Henry Middleton Rutledge[2], Edward Rutledge[1]) child of Emma Philadelphia Middleton Rutledge and Edwin Chiledes Turner was born in Marion County, TN on 24 May 1854.[1] He married Jane Scales CARPENTER, daughter of Charles Kendrick and Jane Emeline (Miller) Carpenter on 20 Nov 1877.[1] She was born in Talladega County, AL on 17 Jan 1854.[1] Children:

85	i	Emma Philadelphia Middleton TURNER, b. 12 Aug 1878	
86	ii	Henrietta TURNER, b. 7 May 1883	
87	iii	Jannie Belle TURNER, b. 17 Jan 1886	

References:
[1] Leach MSS, p. 6380.

38. EMMA CAROLINE TURNER[5] (Emma Philadelphia Middleton Rutledge[4], Henry Adolphus Rutledge[3], Henry Middleton Rutledge[2], Edward Rutledge[1]) child of Emma Philadelphia Middleton Rutledge and Edwin Chiledes Turner was born in Talladega County, AL on 9 Sep 1855.[1] She married John Thaddeus DONALDSON, son of Nimrod and Sallie Reid (McCullough) Donaldson on 4 Feb 1875.[1] He was born in Greenville County, SC on 20 Aug 1842.[1] Children:

88	i	Sallie Serresa DONALDSON, b. 18 Jun 1876
89	ii	Henry Rutledge DONALDSON, b. 13 Jul 1879
90	iii	Mana Lieze DONALDSON, b. 12 Aug 1881
91	iv	Hattie Louisa DONALDSON, b. 12 Aug 1884

92   v   John Arthur DONALDSON, b. 14 Feb 1887, dy 15 Jun 1887 [twin]
93   vi   James Quinton DONALDSON, b. 14 Feb 1887, dy 4 Jun 1887 [twin]
94   vii   Milton Levon DONALDSON, b. 18 Oct 1888
95   viii   Caspar Boyce DONALDSON, b. 23 Jul 1892, dy 24 Aug 1892

References:
[1] Leach MSS, pp. 6380-6381.

39. EDWIN CHILEDES TURNER, Jr.[5] (Emma Philadelphia Middleton Rutledge[4], Henry Adolphus Rutledge[3], Henry Middleton Rutledge[2], Edward Rutledge[1]) child of Emma Philadelphia Middleton Rutledge and Edwin Chiledes Turner was born in Talladega County, AL on 20 Mar 1857, and died in Talladega County, AL on 30 Dec 1881.[1] He married Emily BEAVERS on 21Feb 1877.[1] She was born in St. Clair County, AL on 18 Jul 1861.[1] Children:
96   i   Henry Adolphus TURNER, b. 5 Aug 1880
97   ii   Eddie Caroline TURNER, b. 5 Feb 1883

References:
[1] Leach MSS, p. 6381.

40. MARY ANNE ELIZA TURNER[5] (Emma Philadelphia Middleton Rutledge[4], Henry Adolphus Rutledge[3], Henry Middleton Rutledge[2], Edward Rutledge[1]) child of Emma Philadelphia Middleton Rutledge and Edwin Chiledes Turner was born in Talladega County, AL on 5 Dec 1859.[1] She married John Reed CUNNINGHAM, son of Joseph Christopher and Martha Roby (McClellan) Cunningham on 22 Nov 1877.[1] He was born in Talladega County, AL on 15 May 1856.[1] Children:
98   i   Frank McClellan CUNNINGHAM, b. 12 Sep 1878, dy 23 Jan 1883
99   ii   Septima Rutledge CUNNINGHAM, b. 31 Aug 1880
100   iii   Emma CUNNINGHAM, b. 20 Feb 1883
101   iv   Lide CUNNINGHAM, b. 21 Sep 1885
102   v   Joseph Christopher CUNNINGHAM, b. 6 Feb 1891

References:
[1] Leach MSS, p. 6382.

44. JACOB FORNEY[5] (Septima Sexta Middleton Rutledge[4], Henry Adolphus Rutledge[3], Henry Middleton Rutledge[2], Edward Rutledge[1]) child of Septima Sexta Middleton Rutledge and John Horace Forney was born in

Jacksonville, AL on 8 Oct 1868[1], and died in Springville, AL on 24 Dec 1902. He married Katherine Burt McLAUGHLIN in Springville, AL on 7 Jun 1899.[1] She was born in Springville, AL on 27 Mar 1877.[1] Children:

    103   i   Caroline FORNEY, b. 25 Mar 1900

+ 104   ii   John McLaughlin FORNEY, b. 19 Oct 1901

References:

[1] DSDI Appl # 1060; see also M. L. Webber, *Dr. John Rutledge and his Descendants*, (South Carolina Historical and Genealogical Magazine, Jan. 1930), p. 102.

46. SABINA SWOPE FORNEY[5] (Septima Sexta Middleton Rutledge[4], Henry Adolphus Rutledge[3], Henry Middleton Rutledge[2], Edward Rutledge[1]) child of Septima Sexta Middleton Rutledge and John Horace Forney was born in Jacksonville, AL on 6 Aug 1873.[1] She married Macon Abernathy STEVENSON on 16 Feb 1898.[1] He was born in Jacksonville, AL on 1 Nov 1867[1], and died in Anniston, AL on 14 Jan 1951. Children:

    105   i   John Forney STEVENSON, b. 6 Oct 1899

+ 106   ii   Horace Lee STEVENSON, b. 11 Jan 1902

+ 107   iii Mary Abernathy STEVENSON, b. 30 Dec 1903

    108   iv Eleanor Forney STEVENSON, b. 21 Aug 1905

    109   v   Child STEVENSON, b. c. 1907

    110   vi Child STEVENSON, b. c. 1910

References:

[1] DSDI Appl # 1061.

47. ANNIE ROWAN FORNEY[5] (Septima Sexta Middleton Rutledge[4], Henry Adolphus Rutledge[3], Henry Middleton Rutledge[2], Edward Rutledge[1]) child of Septima Sexta Middleton Rutledge and John Horace Forney was born in Jacksonville, AL on 1 Jun 1876[1], and died in Jacksonville, AL on 9 Nov 1974. She married Clarence William DAUGETTE on 22 Dec 1897.[1] He was born in Bell's Landing, AL on 14 Oct 1873[1], and died in Gadsden, AL on 9 Aug 1942. Children:

    111   i   Kathleen Forney DAUGETTE, b. 26 Oct 1898

+ 112   ii   Palmer DAUGETTE, b. 10 Jan 1900

+ 113   iii Clarence William DAUGETTE, Jr., b. 16 Sep 1903

+ 114   iv Forney Rutledge DAUGETTE, b. 28 Feb 1908

    115   v   Rankin Middleton DAUGETTE, b. 16 Sep 1910

References:

[1] DAR Appl # 522063, and SAR Appl # 138041; see also *South Carolina Historical and Genealogical Magazine*, (Vol. 31), pp. 7-14.

49. EDWARD RUTLEDGE PINCKNEY[5] (Sarah Henrietta Rutledge[4], Henrietta Middleton Rutledge[3], Henry Middleton Rutledge[2], Edward

Rutledge[1]) child of Sarah Henrietta Rutledge and Charles Cotesworth Pinckney was born in Charleston, SC on 27 Jun 1869[1], and died in 1944. He married Louise CLEVELAND in say 1918. Children:

 116 i Sarah Cleveland PINCKNEY, b. 24 Jan 1924; dsp
 117 ii Elizabeth Rutledge PINCKNEY, b. 24 Feb 1925; unm

References:
[1] Leach MSS, p. 6341 gives date and place of birth. Edmund B. Stewart very kindly made a Family Tree Program available with data on the spouse and children of this marriage.

53. FREDERICK RUTLEDGE[5] (Henry Middleton Rutledge[4], Henrietta Middleton Rutledge[3], Henry Middleton Rutledge[2], Edward Rutledge[1]) child of Henry Middleton Rutledge and his 1st wife Anna Marie Blake was born in Fletcher, Henderson County, NC on 10 Feb 1868.[1] He married Mable REEVES in 1892.[1] She was born in Oakland, CA in 1876.[1] Children:

+ 118 i Frederick Reeves RUTLEDGE, b. 17 Nov 1895
 119 ii John RUTLEDGE, b. 1899, dy 1900
 120 iii Reginald Edmund RUTLEDGE, b. 22 Nov 1902

References:
[1] SAR Appl # 56265.

55. HARRIOTT HORRY RUTLEDGE[5] (Henry Middleton Rutledge[4], Henrietta Middleton Rutledge[3], Henry Middleton Rutledge[2], Edward Rutledge[1]) child of Henry Middleton Rutledge and his 2nd wife Margaret Hamilton Seabrook was born in "Hampton Plantation", McClellanville, SC on 8 Feb 1878.[1] She married Paul Hamilton SEABROOK in say 1906. Children:

 121 i Margaret Hamilton SEABROOK, b. 1909
 122 ii Harriott SEABROOK, b. 1911

References:
[1] Leach MSS, p. 6341 gives date and place of birth. Edmund B. Stewart very kindly made a Family Tree Program available with data on the spouse and children of this marriage.

56. THOMAS PINCKNEY RUTLEDGE[5] (Henry Middleton Rutledge[4], Henrietta Middleton Rutledge[3], Henry Middleton Rutledge[2], Edward Rutledge[1]) child of Henry Middleton Rutledge and his 2nd wife Margaret Hamilton Seabrook was born on 16 Feb 1879[1], and died in 1954. He married Ethel Gary PARROTT in say 1908. She was born in 1879[1], and died in 1961. Child:

+ 123 i Henrietta Middleton RUTLEDGE, b. 1915

References:
[1] Richard Ludwig PAF data.

58. ARCHIBALD HAMILTON RUTLEDGE[5] (Henry Middleton Rutledge[4], Henrietta Middleton Rutledge[3], Henry Middleton Rutledge[2], Edward Rutledge[1]) child of Henry Middleton Rutledge and his 2nd wife Margaret Hamilton Seabrook was born in McClellanville, SC on 23 Oct 1883.[1] He married Florence Louise HART in Mercersburg, PA on 19 Dec 1907. She was born in Winchester, VA on 23 Jun 1870[1], and died in Charleston, SC on 9 Jan 1935. Children:

+ 124   i   Archibald Hamilton RUTLEDGE, Jr., b. 29 Sep 1908
+ 125   ii   Henry Middleton RUTLEDGE, b. 29 Jul 1910
+ 126   iii   Irving RUTLEDGE, b. c. 1913

References:
[1] DSDI Appl # 1293; 1535.

60. MARY MIDDLETON RUTLEDGE REESE[5] (Emma Fredrika Rutledge[4], Henrietta Middleton Rutledge[3], Henry Middleton Rutledge[2], Edward Rutledge[1]) child of Emma Fredrika Rutledge and William Brown Reese was born in Franklin, TN on 20 Apr 1867[1], and died in Montgomery, AL about 1950. She married Benjamin Bosworth SMITH, son of Samuel Bosworth and Caroline Castleman (Bacon) Smith in Nashville, TN on 1 Jun 1892.[1] He was born in Louisville, KY on 16 Jan 1863[1], and died in Montgomery, AL on 13 Jun 1926. Children:

   127   i   Benjamin Bosworth SMITH, Jr., b. 20 Mar 1893, d. 28 Dec 1918; unm
+ 128   ii   Elise Rutledge SMITH, b. 4 Dec 1894
+ 129   iii   Carol Castleman SMITH, b. 28 Dec 1896
+ 130   iv   Frederick Rutledge SMITH, b. 7 Jul 1899
   131   v   Alice Reese SMITH, b. 7 Sep 1900, d. 9 Jun 1925; unm
   132   vi   Mary Middleton SMITH, b. 6 Oct 1906, d. 1965; dsp

References:
[1] Leach MSS, p. 6385.

61. ALICE SOPHIA REESE[5] (Emma Fredrika Rutledge[4], Henrietta Middleton Rutledge[3], Henry Middleton Rutledge[2], Edward Rutledge[1]) child of Emma Fredrika Rutledge and William Brown Reese was born in Nashville, TN on 4 Jun 1872[1], and died in 1941. She married Edmund Bellinger FELDER in say 1896. Child:

+ 133   i   Katherine FELDER, b. 24 Dec 1900

References:
[1] Leach MSS, p. 6242.

62. EDMUND MOLYNEUX BLAKE[5] (Frederick Rutledge Blake[4], Emma Philadelphia Middleton Rutledge[3], Henry Middleton Rutledge[2], Edward Rutledge[1]) child of Frederick Rutledge Blake and Olivia Middleton was born on 14 Jan 1866[1], and died in Washington, DC on 20 Aug 1927. He married Eleanor FARLEY, daughter of COL -- Farley in Columbia, SC in 1895.[1] Children:

+   134   i   Ayliffe B. BLAKE, b. c. 1896
+   135   ii   Olivia Middleton BLAKE, b. c. 1898

References:
[1] Leach MSS, p. 6198; he was a graduate of USMA, see *Register of Graduates and Former Cadets of the United States Military Academy*, (Association of Graduates, West Point, NY, 1990), p. 310, Class of 1889, Graduate # 3288.

65. DANIEL BLAKE[5] (Frederick Rutledge Blake[4], Emma Philadelphia Middleton Rutledge[3], Henry Middleton Rutledge[2], Edward Rutledge[1]) child of Frederick Rutledge Blake and Olivia Middleton was born in "The Meadows", NC on 21 Oct 1872[1], and died in 1925. He married Mary Scott PERRY in 1900. She was born in 1877[2], and died in 1934. Child:

+   136   i   Daniel BLAKE, b. 1902

References:
[1] Leach MSS, p. 6198 reports date and place of birth. [2] Data from the Middleton Place Foundation Historian.

74. FLORENCE VERNON BLAKE[5] (Arthur Middleton Blake[4], Emma Philadelphia Middleton Rutledge[3], Henry Middleton Rutledge[2], Edward Rutledge[1]) Arthur Middleton Blake and Talulah Hazeltine Catherine Maxwell was born in Calhoun County, GA on 26 Aug 1893[1], and died in Ft. Worth, TX on 1 Nov 1979. She married William Bell HOFFMAN in Coleman, TX in say 1915. He was born in Bellville, TX on 19 Dec 1884[1], and died in Temple, TX on 14 Jan 1953. Child:

+   137   i   Willie Maxine HOFFMAN, b. 4 Jan 1923

References:
[1] DSDI Appl # 2171.

76. ARTHUR MIDDLETON RUTLEDGE YOUNG[5] (Elizabeth Underwood Rutledge[4], Arthur Middleton Rutledge[3], Henry Middleton Rutledge[2], Edward Rutledge[1]) child of Elizabeth Underwood Rutledge and Henry Edward Young was born on 3 Jul 1876.[1] He married Nannie Cabell CONNER on 19 Dec 1907. Children:

138   i   Arthur Middleton YOUNG, b. 8 Aug 1911
139   ii   James Conner YOUNG, b. 6 Mar 1914
140   iii   Joseph Rutledge YOUNG, b. 7 Jun 1916

References:
[1] M. L. Webber, *Dr. John Rutledge and his Descendants*, (South Carolina Historical and Genealogical Magazine, Jan. 1930), p. 103.

79. JOSEPH UNDERWOOD RUTLEDGE YOUNG[5] (Elizabeth Underwood Rutledge[4], Arthur Middleton Rutledge[3], Henry Middleton Rutledge[2], Edward Rutledge[1]) child of Elizabeth Underwood Rutledge and Henry Edward Young was born on 7 Jan 1881.[1] He married Julia Evelyn GRIMKE on 8 Jun 1905. Children:

   141   i   Julia Evelyn YOUNG, b. 28 Feb 1906, dy 17 Feb 1907
   142   ii   Joseph Rutledge YOUNG, b. Sep 1907, dy 26 Sep 1909
   143   iii Henry Gourdin YOUNG, b. 7 Dec 1909

References:
[1] M. L. Webber, *Dr. John Rutledge and his Descendants*, (South Carolina Historical and Genealogical Magazine, Jan. 1930), p. 103.

81. JOHN JULIUS PRINGLE SMITH, Jr.[5] (Emma Blake Rutledge[4], Arthur Middleton Rutledge[3], Henry Middleton Rutledge[2], Edward Rutledge[1]) child of Emma Blake Rutledge and John Julius Pringle Smith was born on 14 Oct 1887.[1] He married Heningham ELLETT, daughter of Tazewell Ellett on 25 Mar 1913. Child:

 + 144   i   Josephine Scott SMITH, b. 24 Dec 1913

References:
[1] M. L. Webber, *Dr. John Rutledge and his Descendants*, (South Carolina Historical and Genealogical Magazine, Jan. 1930), p. 103.

SIXTH GENERATION

104. JOHN McLAUGHLIN FORNEY[6] (Jacob Forney[5], Septima Sexta Middleton Rutledge[4], Henry Adolphus Rutledge[3], Henry Middleton Rutledge[2], Edward Rutledge[1]) child of Jacob Forney and Katherine Burt McLaughlin was born in Springville, AL on 19 Oct 1901, and died in NYC on 22 Dec 1964. He married Kathleen Clarke FOSTER in Chicago, IL on 4 Aug 1926. She was born in Tuscaloosa, AL on 4 Apr 1903, and died in Birmingham, AL on 12 Jun 1980. Child:

   145   i   John McLaughlin FORNEY, Jr., b. 4 Jun 1927

106. HORACE LEE STEVENSON[6] (Sabina Swope Forney[5], Septima Sexta Middleton Rutledge[4], Henry Adolphus Rutledge[3], Henry Middleton Rutledge[2], Edward Rutledge[1]) child of Sabina Swope Forney and Macon Abernathy Stevenson was born in Jacksonville, AL on 11 Jan 1902. He married Sara Katherine SEGREST in Luverne, AL on 17 Mar 1934. She was born in Brantley, AL on 12 Nov 1910. Child:

+ 146   i   Katherine Sabina STEVENSON, b. 27 Oct 1935

107. MARY ABERNATHY STEVENSON[6] (Sabina Swope Forney[5], Septima Sexta Middleton Rutledge[4], Henry Adolphus Rutledge[3], Henry Middleton Rutledge[2], Edward Rutledge[1]) child of Sabina Swope Forney and Macon Abernathy Stevenson was born in Jacksonville, AL on 30 Dec 1903. She married Arnold A. POLING on 26 Aug 1923. He was born in Athalia, OH on 13 Feb 1905. Child:

+ 147   i   Mary Caroline POLING, b. 15 Aug 1928

112. PALMER DAUGETTE[6] (Annie Rowan Forney[5], Septima Sexta Middleton Rutledge[4], Henry Adolphus Rutledge[3], Henry Middleton Rutledge[2], Edward Rutledge[1]) child of Annie Rowan Forney and Clarence William Daugette was born in Jacksonville, AL on 10 Jan 1900. She married William Jonathan CALVERT, Jr. on 22 Aug 1938. He was born in Pittsboro, NC on 3 Jul 1901. Child:

148   i   William Jonathan CALVERT, III, b. 10 Mar 1943

113. CLARENCE WILLLIAM DAUGETTE, Jr.[6] (Annie Rowan Forney[5], Septima Sexta Middleton Rutledge[4], Henry Adolphus Rutledge[3], Henry Middleton Rutledge[2], Edward Rutledge[1]) child of Annie Rowan Forney and Clarence William Daugette was born in Jacksonville, AL on 16 Sep 1903, and died in Gadsden, AL on 2 Oct 1988. He married Florence Earle THROCKMORTON in Birmingham, AL on 22 Jun 1946. She was born in Birmingham, AL on 12 Nov 1919. Children:

+ 149   i   Alburta [sic] Martin DAUGETTE, b. 25 Jun 1948
+ 150   ii   Florence Anne DAUGETTE, b. 14 Oct 1949
   151   iii   Clarence William DAUGETTE, III, b. 13 Mar 1951

114. FORNEY RUTLEDGE DAUGETTE[6] (Annie Rowan Forney[5], Septima Sexta Middleton Rutledge[4], Henry Adolphus Rutledge[3], Henry Middleton Rutledge[2], Edward Rutledge[1]) child of Annie Rowan Forney and Clarence William Daugette was born in Jacksonville, AL on 28 Feb 1908. He married Mary Elizabeth MOODY in Opelika, AL on 28 May 1929. She was born in Piedmont, AL on 23 Apr 1908. Child:

+ 152   i   Forney Rutledge DAUGETTE, Jr., b. 13 Nov 1932

118. FREDERICK REEVES RUTLEDGE[6] (Frederick Rutledge[5], Henry Middleton Rutledge[4], Henrietta Middleton Rutledge[3], Henry Middleton

Rutledge[2], Edward Rutledge[1]) child of Frederick Rutledge and Mable Reeves was born in Asheville, NC on 17 Nov 1895.[1] He married Beatrice Clyde EDWARDS in say 1929. Children:

    153   i   Frederick Reeves RUTLEDGE, Jr., b. 1 Nov 1932
    154   ii   Anne E. RUTLEDGE, b. 20 Nov 1935 [twin]
    155   iii Ruth P. RUTLEDGE, b. 20 Nov 1935 [twin]

References:
[1] SAR Appl # 56365.

123. HENRIETTA MIDDLETON RUTLEDGE[6] (Thomas Pinckney Rutledge[5], Henry Middleton Rutledge[4], Henrietta Middleton Rutledge[3], Henry Middleton Rutledge[2], Edward Rutledge[1]) child of Thomas Pinckney Rutledge and Ethel Gary Parrott was born in 1915, and died in 1976. She married Franklyn Clement MERRITT in say 1939. He was born in 1914, and died in 1975. Child:

+   156   i   Harrison Shelby MERRITT, b. 1942

124. ARCHIBALD HAMILTON RUTLEDGE[6] (Archibald Hamilton Rutledge[5], Henry Middleton Rutledge[4], Henrietta Middleton Rutledge[3], Henry Middleton Rutledge[2], Edward Rutledge[1]) child of Archibald Hamilton Rutledge and Florence Louise Hart was born in Mercersburg, PA on 29 Sep 1908, and died in McClellandville, SC on 3 Nov 1959. He married Margaret KINGSLEY in Chestertown, MD on 4 Jan 1932. She was born in Staten Island, NY on 11 Apr 1912. Child:

    157   i   Susan RUTLEDGE, b. 17 Aug 1934

125. HENRY MIDDLETON RUTLEDGE[6] (Archibald Hamilton Rutledge[5], Henry Middleton Rutledge[4], Henrietta Middleton Rutledge[3], Henry Middleton Rutledge[2], Edward Rutledge[1]) child of Archibald Hamilton Rutledge and Florence Louise Hart was born in Mercersburg, PA on 29 Jul 1910, and died in Laurens, SC on 3 Jan 1942. He married Flora McDONALD in Princeton, NJ on 8 Sep 1932. She was born in Philadelphia, PA on 7 Jul 1910. Children:

+   158   i   Donald Thropp RUTLEDGE, b. 27 Dec 1939
+   159   ii   Elise Pinckney RUTLEDGE, b. c. 1941

126. IRVING HART RUTLEDGE[6] (Archibald Hamilton Rutledge[5], Henry Middleton Rutledge[4], Henrietta Middleton Rutledge[3], Henry Middleton Rutledge[2], Edward Rutledge[1]) child of Archibald Hamilton Rutledge and Florence Louise Hart was born in Mercersburg, PA about 1913. He married Eleanor WHITE in say 1934. Children:

+ 160   i   Henry Middleton RUTLEDGE, b. c. 1936

   161   ii   Eleanor RUTLEDGE, b. c. 1940

128. ELISE RUTLEDGE SMITH[6] (Mary Middleton Rutledge Reese[5], Emma Fredricka Rutledge[4], Henrietta Middleton Rutledge[3], Henry Middleton Rutledge[2], Edward Rutledge[1]) child of Mary Middleton Rutledge Reese and Benjamin Bosworth Smith was born in Nashville, TN on 4 Dec 1894[1], and died in Anchorage, KY on 6 Apr 1977. She married Ewing Lloyd HARDY in say 1921. He died in Anchorage, KY on 6 Aug 1968. Children:

   162   i   Ewing Marshall HARDY, b. c. 1924

   163   ii   Benjamin Bosworth HARDY, b. c. 1927

+ 164   iii   Burwell Marshall HARDY, b. 4 Feb 1930

   165   iv   Elise HARDY, b. Feb 1936, dy 6 Mar 1936

References:

[1] Family Genealogical Report kindly furnished by the Rev. Benjamin B. Smith, a Rutledge descendant dated 22 Dec 1999.

129. CAROL CASTLEMAN SMITH[6] (Mary Middleton Rutledge Reese[5], Emma Fredricka Rutledge[4], Henrietta Middleton Rutledge[3], Henry Middleton Rutledge[2], Edward Rutledge[1]) child of Mary Middleton Rutledge Reese and Benjamin Bosworth Smith was born in Montgomery, AL on 28 Dec 1896[1], and died in Decatur, AL on 22 Sep 1966. He married Edith Manson STOLLENWERK in Greensboro, AL on 28 Apr 1928. She was born in Greensboro, AL on 18 Jul 1903, and died there on 11 Jun 1987. Children:

+ 166   i   Ann Cobbs SMITH, b. 6 Feb 1929

+ 167   ii   Carol Castleman SMITH, b. 7 Sep 1930

+ 168   iii   Alice Rutledge SMITH, b. 9 Mar 1932

+ 169   iv   Charles Stollenwerk SMITH, b. 9 Jan 1936

References:

[1] Family Genealogical Report kindly furnished by the Rev. Benjamin B. Smith, a Rutledge descendant dated 22 Dec 1999.

130. FREDERICK RUTLEDGE SMITH[6] (Mary Middleton Rutledge Reese[5], Emma Fredricka Rutledge[4], Henrietta Middleton Rutledge[3], Henry Middleton Rutledge[2], Edward Rutledge[1]) child of Mary Middleton Rutledge Reese and Benjamin Bosworth Smith was born in Montgomery, AL on 7 Jul 1899[1], and died in Tuscaloosa, AL on 7 May 1942. He married Mary Burton MATTHEWS, daughter of Lucien Tardy and Clara Winston (Burton) Matthews in Montgomery, AL on 10 Jun 1924. She was born in Huntsville, AL on 18 Jan 1902, and died in Louisville, KY on 18 Aug 1997. Children:

   170   i   Frederick Rutledge SMITH, Jr., b. 5 Apr 1925; unm

+ 171   ii   Mary Burton SMITH, b. 13 Aug 1926
+ 172   iii Benjamin Bosworth SMITH, b. 6 Dec 1929
References:
[1] Family Genealogical Report kindly furnished by the Rev. Benjamin B. Smith, a Rutledge descendant dated 22 Dec 1999.

133. KATHERINE FELDER[6] (Alice Sophia Reese[5], Emma Fredricka Rutledge[4], Henrietta Middleton Rutledge[3], Henry Middleton Rutledge[2], Edward Rutledge[1]) child of Alice Sophia Reese and Edmund Bellinger Felder was born in Montgomery, AL on 24 Dec 1900. She married (1st) Blackburn HUGHES in say 1922. She married (2nd) Francis Barretto STEWART in say 1931.
Child by first marriage:
     173   i   Blackburn HUGHES, Jr., b. 1923
Children by second marriage:
+ 174   ii   Edmund Bellinger STEWART, b. 30 Dec 1933 [twin]
+ 175   iii Francis Barretto STEWART, Jr., b. 30 Dec 1933 [twin]

134. AYLIFFE B. BLAKE[6] (Edmund Molyneux Blake[5], Frederick Rutledge Blake[4], Emma Philadelphia Middleton Rutledge[3], Henry Middleton Rutledge[2], Edward Rutledge[1]) child of Edmund Molyneux Blake and Eleanor Farley was born about 1896.[1] She married Nicholas Van Slyck MUMFORD in say 1916. Children:
+ 176   i   Eleanor MUMFORD, b. 1919
+ 177   ii   Nicholas Van Slyck MUMFORD, Jr., b. 1925
References:
[1] Data from Middleton Place Historian.

135. OLIVIA MIDDLETON BLAKE[6] (Edmund Molyneux Blake[5], Frederick Rutledge Blake[4], Emma Philadelphia Middleton Rutledge[3], Henry Middleton Rutledge[2], Edward Rutledge[1]) child of Edmund Molyneux Blake and Eleanor Farley was born about 1898[1], and died in 1977. She married Daniel Dee PULLEN in say 1920. He was born in 1885[1], and died in 1923. Child:
+ 178   i   Harriet Stuart PULLEN, b. 1922
References:
[1] Data from Middleton Place Historian.

136. DANIEL BLAKE[6] (Daniel Blake[5], Frederick Rutledge Blake[4], Emma Philadelphia Middleton Rutledge[3], Henry Middleton Rutledge[2], Edward Rutledge[1]) child of Daniel Blake and Mary Scott Perry was born in 1902[1], and died in 1986. He married Katharine Brooks SHANNON in 1926. She was born in 1900. Children:

+ 179　　i　Katharine Shannon BLAKE, b. 1927
+ 180　　ii　Daniel BLAKE, b. 1931

References:
[1] Data from Middleton Place Historian.

137. WILLIE MAXINE HOFFMAN[6] (Florence Vernon Blake[5], Arthur Middleton Blake[4], Emma Philadelphia Middleton Rutledge[3], Henry Middleton Rutledge[2], Edward Rutledge[1]) child of Florence Vernon Blake and William Bell Hoffman was born in Brownwood, TX on 4 Jan 1923. She married Clarence Milton CALDCLEUGH in Galveston, TX on 15 May 1944. He was born in San Marcos, TX on 15 Aug 1916. Child:

+ 181　　i　Robert Blake CLADCLEUGH, b. 16 Jun 1945

144. JOSEPHINE SCOTT SMITH[6] (John Julius Pringle Smith[5], Emma Blake Rutledge[4], Arthur Middleton Rutledge[3], Henry Middleton Rutledge[2], Edward Rutledge[1]) child of John Julius Pringle Smith and Heningham Ellett was born on 24 Dec 1913, and died on 27 Aug 1954. She married Charles DUELL, son of J. Holland and Mabel (Halliwell) Duell on 21 Oct 1933. He was born on 20 Jul 1905, and died on 10 Jul 1970. Children:

182　　i　Heningham Ann DUELL, b. 14 Aug 1934, d. 5 Dec 1987; dsp
183　　ii　Josephine Scott DUELL, b. 11 Mar 1936; unm
+ 184　　iii　Charles Halliwell Pringle DUELL, b. 10 Jun 1938

SEVENTH GENERATION

146. KATHERINE SABINA STEVENSON[7] (Horace Lee Stevenson[6], Sabina Swope Forney[5], Septima Sexta Middleton Rutledge[4], Henry Adolphus Rutledge[3], Henry Middleton Rutledge[2], Edward Rutledge[1]) child of Horace Lee Stevenson and Sara Katherine Segrest was born in Jacksonville, AL on 27 Oct 1935. She married William Powell PANNELL on 10 Jun 1956. He was born in Mobile, AL on 7 Aug 1934. Children:

185　　i　Katherine Suzanne PANNELL, b. 11 May 1957
186　　ii　William Powell PANNELL, Jr., b. 11 Jan 1960
187　　iii　John Lee PANNELL, b. 10 Nov 1961

147. MARY CAROLINE POLING[7] (Mary Abernathy Stevenson[6], Sabina Swope Forney[5], Septima Sexta Middleton Rutledge[4], Henry Adolphus

Rutledge[3], Henry Middleton Rutledge[2], Edward Rutledge[1]) child of Mary Abernathy Stevenson and Arnold A. Poling was born in Jacksonville, AL on 15 Aug 1928. She married Harry Alfred JOHNSON on 1 Dec 1945. He was born in Cambridge, MA on 2 Jul 1923. Child:

188   i   Forney Rutledge JOHNSON, b. 14 Mar 1948

149. ALBURTA MARTIN DAUGETTE[7] (Clarence William Daugette, Jr.[6], Annie Rowan Forney[5], Septima Sexta Middleton Rutledge[4], Henry Adolphus Rutledge[3], Henry Middleton Rutledge[2], Edward Rutledge[1]) child of Clarence William Daugette, Jr. and Florence Earle Throckmorton was born in Birmingham, AL on 25 Jun 1948. She married Marvin Lynn LOWE in Gadsden, AL on 2 Aug 1975. He was born in Bruceton, TN on 30 Dec 1947. Child:

189   i   Mary Kinney LOWE, b. 10 Jul 1981

150. FLORENCE ANNE DAUGETTE[7] (Clarence William Daugette, Jr.[6], Annie Rowan Forney[5], Septima Sexta Middleton Rutledge[4], Henry Adolphus Rutledge[3], Henry Middleton Rutledge[2], Edward Rutledge[1]) child of Clarence William Daugette, Jr. and Florence Earle Throckmorton was born in Birmingham, AL on 14 Oct 1949. She married Raymond R. RENFROW, Jr. in say 1972. Child:

190   i   Anne Clare RENFROW, b. 15 Apr 1974

152. FORNEY RUTLEDGE DAUGETTE, Jr.[7] (Forney Rutledge Daugette[6], Annie Rowan Forney[5], Septima Sexta Middleton Rutledge[4], Henry Adolphus Rutledge[3], Henry Middleton Rutledge[2], Edward Rutledge[1]) child of Forney Rutledge Daugette and Mary Elizabeth Moody was born in Anniston, AL on 13 Nov 1932. He married Mary Reed SIMPSON in Eagle Pass, TX on 6 Aug 1955. She was born in Eagle Pass, TX on 7 May 1934. Children:

191   i   Forney Rutledge DAUGETTE, III, b. 1 Sep 1956
192   ii   William Reed DAUGETTE, b. 27 Dec 1957
193   iii   Mary Elizabeth DAUGETTE, b. 18 Oct 1959
194   iv   Child DAUGETTE, b. c. 1962
195   v   Mona DAUGETTE, b. c. 1965

156. HARRISON SHELBY MERRITT [7] (Henrietta Middleton Rutledge[6], Thomas Pinckney Rutledge[5], Henry Middleton Rutledge[4], Henrietta Middleton Rutledge[3], Henry Middleton Rutledge[2], Edward Rutledge[1]) child of Henrietta Middleton Rutledge and Franklyn Clement Merritt was born in

1942. He married Anne Trapier DRAYTON in say 1968. She was born in 1945. Children:

   196   i   Harrison Shelby MERRITT, b. 1971
   197   ii Elizabeth Heyward MERRITT, b. 1974

158. DONALD THROPP RUTLEDGE[7] (Henry Middleton Rutledge[6], Archibald Hamilton Rutledge[5], Henry Middleton Rutledge[4], Henrietta Middleton Rutledge[3], Henry Middleton Rutledge[2], Edward Rutledge[1]) child of Henry Middleton Rutledge and Flora McDonald was born in Lumberton, NC on 27 Dec 1939. He married Leslie Townsend DOTTERER in Yonge's Island, SC on 6 Jun 1964. She was born in Charleston, SC on 1 Aug 1940. Children:

+ 198   i   Leslie Townsend RUTLEDGE, b. 3 Jul 1969
   199   ii Henry Middleton RUTLEDGE, b. 15 Oct 1970

159. ELISE PINCKNEY RUTLEDGE[7] (Henry Middleton Rutledge[6], Archibald Hamilton Rutledge[5], Henry Middleton Rutledge[4], Henrietta Middleton Rutledge[3], Henry Middleton Rutledge[2], Edward Rutledge[1]) child of Henry Middleton Rutledge and Flora McDonald was born about 1941. She married William Stewart BRADFORD in say 1963. Children:

+ 200   i   Robert Morris BRADFORD, b. c. 1967
   201   ii William Stewart BRADFORD, Jr., b. c. 1970
   202 iii Rutledge McDonald BRADFORD, b. c. 1975

160. HENRY MIDDLETON RUTLEDGE[7] (Irving Hart Rutledge[6], Archibald Hamilton Rutledge[5], Henry Middleton Rutledge[4], Henrietta Middleton Rutledge[3], Henry Middleton Rutledge[2], Edward Rutledge[1]) child of Irving Hart Rutledge and Eleanor White was born about 1936. He married -- (--) in say 1960. Children:

   203   i   Donald RUTLEDGE, b. c. 1963
   204   ii Macon RUTLEDGE, b. c. 1966

164. BURWELL MARSHALL HARDY[7] (Elise Rutledge Smith[6], Mary Middleton Rutledge Reese[5], Emma Fredricka Rutledge[4], Henrietta Middleton Rutledge[3], Henry Middleton Rutledge[2], Edward Rutledge[1]) child of Elise Rutledge Smith and Ewing Lloyd Hardy was born in Anchorage, KY on 4 Feb 1930, and died on 8 Feb 1989. He married Maria Jisela JANDI in 1954. Children:

   205   i   Viviana HARDY, b. 9 Feb 1969
   206   ii Laura HARDY, b. 24 May 1970
   207 iii Jose HARDY, b. 19 Sep 1972

166. ANN COBBS SMITH[7] (Carol Castleman Smith[6], Mary Middleton Rutledge Reese[5], Emma Fredricka Rutledge[4], Henrietta Middleton Rutledge[3], Henry Middleton Rutledge[2], Edward Rutledge[1]) child of Carol Castleman Smith and Edith Stollenwerk born in Montgomery, AL on 6 Feb 1929. She married Willis Duke WEATHERFORD, Jr. in Greensboro, AL on 28 Aug 1954. He was born in Asheville, NC on 24 Jun 1916, and died in Black Mountain, NC on 22 May 1996. Children:

+ 208   i   Edith Cobbs WEATHERFORD, b. 1 Jan 1957
+ 209   ii   Julia McCrory WEATHERFORD, b. 24 Jun 1958
+ 210   iii Willis Duke WEATHERFORD, III, b. 12 Apr 1960
  211   iv   Susan Parker WEATHERFORD, b. 9 Jan 1962 [twin]
+ 212   v   Alice Rutledge WEATHERFORD, b. 9 Jan 1962 [twin]

167. CAROL CASTLEMAN SMITH, Jr.[7] (Carol Castleman Smith[6], Mary Middleton Rutledge Reese[5], Emma Fredricka Rutledge[4], Henrietta Middleton Rutledge[3], Henry Middleton Rutledge[2], Edward Rutledge[1]) child of Carol Castleman Smith and Edith Stollenwerk born in Montgomery, AL on 7 Sep 1930, and died in Norfolk, VA on 15 Oct 1983. He married Sara Jane CLYDE in Pensacola, FL on 4 May 1957. She was born in Pensacola, FL on 21 Aug 1933. Children:

  213   i   Paul Rutledge SMITH, b. 14 Dec 1958
  214   ii   Carol Castleman SMITH, III, b. 7 Dec 1960
+ 215   iii Arthur Middleton SMITH, b. 2 Mar 1964
  216   iv   Laura Manson SMITH, b. 18 Nov 1969

168. ALICE RUTLEDGE SMITH[7] (Carol Castleman Smith[6], Mary Middleton Rutledge Reese[5], Emma Fredricka Rutledge[4], Henrietta Middleton Rutledge[3], Henry Middleton Rutledge[2], Edward Rutledge[1]) child of Carol Castleman Smith and Edith Stollenwerk born in Montgomery, AL on 9 Mar 1932. She married Richard Johnson RAMSEY in Tuscaloosa, AL on 3 Aug 1957. He was born in Atlanta, GA on 7 Feb 1932. Children:

+ 217   i   Richard Johnson RAMSEY, Jr. b. 18 Nov 1958
+ 218   ii   David Rutledge RAMSEY, b. 5 Apr 1960
+ 219   iii John Walden RAMSEY, b. 16 Feb 1964

169. CHARLES STOLLENWERK SMITH[7] (Carol Castleman Smith[6], Mary Middleton Rutledge Reese[5], Emma Fredricka Rutledge[4], Henrietta Middleton Rutledge[3], Henry Middleton Rutledge[2], Edward Rutledge[1]) child of Carol Castleman Smith and Edith Stollenwerk born in Montgomery, AL on 9 Jan 1936. He married Caroline Pauline BACKER in Zurich, SWITZER-LAND on 18 Apr 1961. She was born in NYC on 13 Jul 1938. Children:

+ 220   i   Jennifer Backer SMITH, b. 12 Mar 1962
  221   ii   Elise Avery SMITH, b. 8 Aug 1964; unm
  222   iii Charles Whelan Stollenwerk SMITH, b. 11 Dec 1970

171. MARY BURTON SMITH[7] (Frederick Rutledge Smith[6], Mary Middleton Rutledge Reese[5], Emma Fredricka Rutledge[4], Henrietta Middleton Rutledge[3], Henry Middleton Rutledge[2], Edward Rutledge[1]) child of Frederick Rutledge Smith and Mary Burton Matthews was born in Montgomery, AL on 13 Aug 1926. She married Henry Ewing HARRIS in Tuscaloosa, AL on 23 Sep 1949. He was born in Atlanta, GA on 9 Apr 1921. Children:
+ 223   i   Mary Burton HARRIS, b. 30 Jun 1950
+ 224   ii   Henry Ewing HARRIS, Jr., b. 13 Sep 1951
+ 225   iii Lucy Fairbanks HARRIS, b. 25 Jan 1953
+ 226   iv   Frederick Rutledge HARRIS, b. 23 May 1957
  227   v   John Bowen HARRIS, b. 22 Nov 1960; unm

172. BENJAMIN BOSWORTH SMITH[7] (Frederick Rutledge Smith[6], Mary Middleton Rutledge Reese[5], Emma Fredricka Rutledge[4], Henrietta Middleton Rutledge[3], Henry Middleton Rutledge[2], Edward Rutledge[1]) child of Frederick Rutledge Smith and Mary Burton Matthews was born in Montgomery, AL on 6 Dec 1929. He married Barbara Jane HAHN, daughter of Hebert Louis and Sarah Elizabeth (Ransom) Hahn in Birmingham, AL on 26 Oct 1954. She was born in Birmingham, AL on 28 Jun 1929. Children:
+ 228   i   Elizabeth Ransom SMITH, b. 20 Feb 1956
+ 229   ii   Mary Middleton SMITH, b. 29 Jan 1959
+ 230   iii Benjamin Bosworth SMITH, Jr., b. 16 Jun 1960
+ 231   iv   Barbara Beene SMITH, b. 18 Jul 1962

174. EDMUND BELLINGER STEWART [7] (Katherine Felder[6], Alice Sophia Reese[5], Emma Fredricka Rutledge[4], Henrietta Middleton Rutledge[3], Henry Middleton Rutledge[2], Edward Rutledge[1]) child of Katherine Felder and her 2nd husband Francis Barretto Stewart was born on 30 Dec 1933. He married Anita Maria Carolina WARING in say 1956. She was born in 1936. Children:
+ 232   i   Edmund Bellinger STEWART, Jr., b. 18 Jul 1958
  233   ii   Laura Katherine Coster STEWART, b. 13 Apr 1961

175. FRANCIS BARRETTO STEWART, Jr.[7] (Katherine Felder[6], Alice Sophia Reese[5], Emma Fredricka Rutledge[4], Henrietta Middleton Rutledge[3], Henry Middleton Rutledge[2], Edward Rutledge[1]) child of Katherine Felder and her 2nd husband Francis Barretto Stewart was born on 30 Dec 1933, and died in 1976. He married Susan SMITH in say 1958. Children:

    234   i   Francis Barretto STEWART, III, b. 1961
    235   ii   Geraldine Wilson STEWART, b. 1962
+ 236   iii   Sarah Rutledge STEWART, b. 1964

176. ELEANOR MUMFORD[7] (Ayliffe B. Blake[6], Edmund Molyneux Blake[5], Frederick Rutledge Blake[4], Emma Philadelphia Middleton Rutledge[3], Henry Middleton Rutledge[2], Edward Rutledge[1]) child of Ayliffe B. Blake and Nicholas Van Slylee Mumford was born in 1919. She married Harley Allen CASE in say 1942. She died in 1982. Children:

+ 237   i   Harley Allen CASE, Jr., 13 Nov 1944
+ 238   ii   Marshall CASE, b. 1947

177. NICHOLAS Van SLYCK MUMFORD, Jr.[7] (Ayliffe B. Blake[6], Edmund Molyneux Blake[5], Frederick Rutledge Blake[4], Emma Philadelphia Middleton Rutledge[3], Henry Middleton Rutledge[2], Edward Rutledge[1]) child of Ayliffe B. Blake and Nicholas Van Slyck Mumford was born in 1925. He married Rosemary DAVIS in say 1942. Children:

+ 239   i   Nicholas Van Slylee MUMFORD, III, b. 1948
    240   ii   Robert Blake MUMFORD, b. 1950
    241   iii   Ayliffe Blake MUMFORD, b. 1951
+ 242   iv   Elizabeth Davis MUMFORD, b. 1953

178. HARRIET STUART BLAKE[7] (Olivia Middleton Blake[6], Edmund Molyneux Blake[5], Frederick Rutledge Blake[4], Emma Philadelphia Middleton Rutledge[3], Henry Middleton Rutledge[2], Edward Rutledge[1]) child of Olivia Middleton Blake and Daniel Dee Pullen was born in 1922. She married J. Ormsby PHILLIPS in 1946. He was born in 1920. Children:

    243   i   Eleanor PHILLIPS, b. 1946
    244   ii   Virginia PHILLIPS, b. 1951
    245   iii   Charles PHILLIPS, b. 1952

179. KATHARINE SHANNON BLAKE[7] (Daniel Blake[6], Daniel Blake[5], Frederick Rutledge Blake[4], Emma Philadelphia Middleton Rutledge[3], Henry Middleton Rutledge[2], Edward Rutledge[1]) child of Daniel Blake and Katharine Brooks Shannon was born in 1927. She married Harvey Wilson JOHNSON in 1950. He was born in 1926. Children:

+ 246   i   Katharine Blake JOHNSON, b. 1953
+ 247   ii   Anna White JOHNSON, b. 1955
+ 248   iii   Jane Shannon JOHNSON, b. 1956

180. DANIEL BLAKE[7] (Daniel Blake[6], Daniel Blake[5], Frederick Rutledge Blake[4], Emma Philadelphia Middleton Rutledge[3], Henry Middleton Rutledge[2], Edward Rutledge[1]) child of Daniel Blake and Katharine Brooks Shannon was born in 1931. He married Virginia Ann FRASER in say 1955. She was born in 1934. Children:

    249   i   Daniel BLAKE, b. 1957
    250   ii   William Bratton BLAKE, b. 1958
    251   iii   Robert Fraser BLAKE, b. 1962
    252   iv   Frederick Rutledge BLAKE, b. 1965

181. ROBERT BLAKE CALDCLEUGH[7] (Willie Maxine Hoffman[6], Florence Vernon Blake[5], Arthur Middleton Blake[4], Emma Philadelphia Middleton Rutledge[3], Henry Middleton Rutledge[2], Edward Rutledge[1]) child of Willie Maxine Hoffman and Clarence Milton Caldcleugh was born in Colorado Springs, CO on 16 Jun 1945. He married Connie Ione LOWREY in Abilene, TX on 19 Jan 1968. She was born in Big Spring, TX on 25 Jan 1950. Child:

    253   i   Bobette CALDCLEUGH, b. 17 Sep 1971

184. CHARLES HALLIWELL PRINGLE DUELL[7] (Josephine Scott Smith[6], John Julius Pringle Smith[5], Emma Blake Rutledge[4], Arthur Middleton Rutledge[3], Henry Middleton Rutledge[2], Edward Rutledge[1]) child of Josephine Scott Smith and Charles Duell was born on 10 Jun 1938. He married Caroline Nichols WOOD on 31 Aug 1963. Children:

    254   i   Josephine Clark DUELL, b. 17 Jun 1966
    255   ii   June Heningham DUELL, b. 1968
    256   iii   Charles Holland DUELL, b. 1971
    257   iv   Caroline Middleton DUELL, b. 1974

EIGHTH GENERATION

198. LESLIE TOWNSEND RUTLEDGE[8] (Donald Thropp Rutledge[7], Henry Middleton Rutledge[6], Archibald Hamilton Rutledge[5], Henry Middleton Rutledge[4], Henrietta Middleton Rutledge[3], Henry Middleton Rutledge[2], Edward Rutledge[1]) child of Donald Thropp Rutledge and Leslie Townsend Dotterer was born in Charleston, SC on 3 Jul 1968. She married Thomas Morrison DICKINSON in "Hampton Plantation", SC on 6 Nov 1993. Child:

    258   i   Cole Rutledge DICKINSON, b. 10 Apr 1998

200. ROBERT MORRIS BRADFORD[8] (Elise Pinckney Rutledge[7], Henry Middleton Rutledge[6], Archibald Hamilton Rutledge[5], Henry Middleton Rutledge[4], Henrietta Middleton Rutledge[3], Henry Middleton Rutledge[2], Edward Rutledge[1]) child of Elise Pinckney Rutledge and William Stewart Bradford was born about 1967. He married Carolyn JOYE in say 1992. Children:

259   i   Elise BRADFORD, b. c. 1994
260   ii   Robert Bennett BRADFORD, b. c. 1996
261   iii Sarah Rutledge BRADFORD, b. c. 1999

208. EDITH COBBS WEATHERFORD[8] (Ann Cobbs Smith[7], Carol Castleman Smith[6], Mary Middleton Rutledge Reese[5], Emma Fredricka Rutledge[4], Henrietta Middleton Rutledge[3], Henry Middleton Rutledge[2], Edward Rutledge[1]) child of Ann Cobbs Smith and Willis Duke Weatherford, Jr. was born in Bryn Mawr, PA on 1 Jan 1957. She married Meredith Eugene HUNT in Berea, KY on 10 Jul 1982. He was born on 26 Nov 1952. Children:

262   i   Priscilla Dear HUNT, b. 16 Apr 1983
263   ii   Arthur Samuel HUNT, b. 1 Dec 1985
264   iii Anna Mary HUNT, b. 27 Jul 1987
265   iv   Jeffery Barnabas HUNT, b. 27 Feb 1989
266   v   Peter Malcolm HUNT, b. 18 Apr 1992
267   vi   Christopher Guard HUNT, b. 213 Jan 1995

209. JULIA McCRORY WEATHERFORD[8] (Ann Cobbs Smith[7], Carol Castleman Smith[6], Mary Middleton Rutledge Reese[5], Emma Fredricka Rutledge[4], Henrietta Middleton Rutledge[3], Henry Middleton Rutledge[2], Edward Rutledge[1]) child of Ann Cobbs Smith and Willis Duke Weatherford, Jr. was born in Bryn Mawr, PA on 24 Jun 1958. She married Mark MUELLER on 22 Mar 1980. Children:

268   i   Pearl Angeline MUELLER, b. 2 Nov 1980
269   ii   Vergil Christopher MUELLER, b. 27 Sep 1982

210. WILLIS DUKE WEATHERFORD, III[8] (Ann Cobbs Smith[7], Carol Castleman Smith[6], Mary Middleton Rutledge Reese[5], Emma Fredricka Rutledge[4], Henrietta Middleton Rutledge[3], Henry Middleton Rutledge[2], Edward Rutledge[1]) child of Ann Cobbs Smith and Willis Duke Weatherford, Jr. was born in Kuala Lumpur, MALAYSIA on 12 Apr 1960. He married Jane Elizabeth TURNBULL in Berea, KY on 22 Sep 1984. She was born on 18 Aug 1961. Children:

270   i   Frank Taylor WEATHERFORD, b. 2 Feb 1988

271   ii   Willis Duke WEATHERFORD, IV, b. 25 Apr 1990
272   iii Susanna Grace WEATHERFORD, b. 31 Jul 1994

212. ALICE RUTLEDGE WEATHERFORD[8] (Ann Cobbs Smith[7], Carol Castleman Smith[6], Mary Middleton Rutledge Reese[5], Emma Fredricka Rutledge[4], Henrietta Middleton Rutledge[3], Henry Middleton Rutledge[2], Edward Rutledge[1]) child of Ann Cobbs Smith and Willis Duke Weatherford, Jr. was born on 9 Jan 1962. She married Jeffrey DOWNS in Black Mountain, NC on 12 Aug 1984. He was born on 27 Apr 1952. Children:

273   i   Avery Anne DOWNS, b. 28 Oct 1986
274   ii   Rachel Justis DOWNS, b. 3 Feb 1988
275   iii Gretta Joy DOWNS, b. 3 Jan 1994
276   iv   Luke Daniel DOWNS, b. 9 Nov 1995

215. ARTHUR MIDDLETON SMITH[8] (Carol Castelman Smith, Jr.[7], Carol Castleman Smith[6], Mary Middleton Rutledge Reese[5], Emma Fredricka Rutledge[4], Henrietta Middleton Rutledge[3], Henry Middleton Rutledge[2], Edward Rutledge[1]) child of Carol Castelman Smith, Jr. and Sara Jane Clyde was born on 2 Mar 1964. He married -- (--). Children:

277   i   Krystle SMITH
278   ii   Lindsi SMITH
279   iii Arthur Middleton SMITH, II

217. RICHARD JOHNSON RAMSEY, Jr.[8] (Alice Rutledge Smith[7], Carol Castleman Smith[6], Mary Middleton Rutledge Reese[5], Emma Fredricka Rutledge[4], Henrietta Middleton Rutledge[3], Henry Middleton Rutledge[2], Edward Rutledge[1]) child of Alice Rutledge Smith and Richard Johnson Ramsey was born in Chattanooga, TN on 18 Nov 1958. He married Gretchen VAN DUSEN in Isleford, ME on 7 Sep 1991. She was born in Boston, MA on 24 Mar 1961. Children:

280   i   Eliza Cobbs Van Dusen RAMSEY, b. 20 Oct 1994
281   ii   Ian Lane RAMSEY, b. 2 Apr 1998

218. DAVID RUTLEDGE RAMSEY[8] (Alice Rutledge Smith[7], Carol Castleman Smith[6], Mary Middleton Rutledge Reese[5], Emma Fredricka Rutledge[4], Henrietta Middleton Rutledge[3], Henry Middleton Rutledge[2], Edward Rutledge[1]) child of Alice Rutledge Smith and Richard Johnson Ramsey was born in Chattanooga, TN on 5 Apr 1960. He married Nanette Starr PATTERSON in New Bloomfield, Perry County, PA on 11 May 1985. She was born in New Bloomfield, PA on 18 Feb 1958. Children:

282   i   Julia Alison RAMSEY, b. 18 Jun 1987
283   ii   Christopher Rutledge RAMSEY, b. 17 Mar 1990

219. JOHN WALDEN RAMSEY[8] (Alice Rutledge Smith[7], Carol Castleman Smith[6], Mary Middleton Rutledge Reese[5], Emma Fredricka Rutledge[4], Henrietta Middleton Rutledge[3], Henry Middleton Rutledge[2], Edward Rutledge[1]) child of Alice Rutledge Smith and Richard Johnson Ramsey was born in Chattanooga, TN on 16 Feb 1964. He married Birgit Elisabeth Marlies HASSE in Black Mountain, NC on 30 Mar 1991. She was born in Paderborn, GERMANY on 18 Oct 1966. Children:

    284   i   Jeremiah Engels RAMSEY, b. 21 Apr 1994
    285   ii   John Middleton RAMSEY, b. 21 Jan 1996

220. JENNIFER BACKER SMITH[8] (Charles Stollenwerk Smith[7], Carol Castleman Smith[6], Mary Middleton Rutledge Reese[5], Emma Fredricka Rutledge[4], Henrietta Middleton Rutledge[3], Henry Middleton Rutledge[2], Edward Rutledge[1]) child of Charles Stollenwerk Smith and Caroline Pauline Backer was born on 12 Mar 1962. She married Scott Charles GRIFFITH in Greensboro, AL on 15 Jul 1992. He was born on 30 Apr 1963. Children:

    286   i   Benjamin Charles Raymond GRIFFITH, b. 21 Jul 1994
    287   ii   Samuel Bosworth GRIFFITH, b. 13 Apr 1996

223. MARY BURTON HARRIS[8] (Mary Burton Smith[7], Frederick Rutledge Smith[6], Mary Middleton Rutledge Reese[5], Emma Fredricka Rutledge[4], Henrietta Middleton Rutledge[3], Henry Middleton Rutledge[2], Edward Rutledge[1]) child of Mary Burton Smith and Henry Ewing Harris was born in Louisville, KY on 30 Jun 1950. She married -- NASH in say 1978. Child:

    288   i   Lena Kai NASH, b. c. 1982

224. HENRY EWING HARRIS, Jr.[8] (Mary Burton Smith[7], Frederick Rutledge Smith[6], Mary Middleton Rutledge Reese[5], Emma Fredricka Rutledge[4], Henrietta Middleton Rutledge[3], Henry Middleton Rutledge[2], Edward Rutledge[1]) child of Mary Burton Smith and Henry Ewing Harris was born in Louisville, KY on 13 Sep 1951. He married Paula JOHNSON in say 1977. Child:

    289   i   Ruby Carol HARRIS, b. 10 Dec 1979

225. LUCY FAIRBANKS HARRIS[8] (Mary Burton Smith[7], Frederick Rutledge Smith[6], Mary Middleton Rutledge Reese[5], Emma Fredricka Rutledge[4], Henrietta Middleton Rutledge[3], Henry Middleton Rutledge[2], Edward Rutledge[1]) child of Mary Burton Smith and Henry Ewing Harris was born in Louisville, KY on 25 Jan 1953. She married Philip MERTZ in say 1976. Child:

    290   i   Luke Henry MERTZ, b. 9 Feb 1980

226. FREDERICK RUTLEDGE HARRIS[8] (Mary Burton Smith[7], Frederick Rutledge Smith[6], Mary Middleton Rutledge Reese[5], Emma Fredricka Rutledge[4], Henrietta Middleton Rutledge[3], Henry Middleton Rutledge[2], Edward Rutledge[1]) child of Mary Burton Smith and Henry Ewing Harris was born in Louisville, KY on 23 May 1957. He married Faye GRIFFIN in say 1984. Children:

 291   i   Evan Matthews HARRIS, b. 15 Feb 1987
 292   ii   Emily Meredith HARRIS, b. 10 Feb 1988
 293 iii   Abigail Victoria HARRIS, b. 10 Apr 1989

228. ELIZABETH RANSOM SMITH[8] (Benjamin Bosworth Smith[7], Frederick Rutledge Smith[6], Mary Middleton Rutledge Reese[5], Emma Fredricka Rutledge[4], Henrietta Middleton Rutledge[3], Henry Middleton Rutledge[2], Edward Rutledge[1]) child of Benjamin Bosworth Smith and Barbara Jane Hahn was born in Birmingham, AL on 20 Feb 1956. She married (2nd) Kurt Hans RITTERS, son of Vernon E. and Margie (Gosch) Ritters in say 1993. He was born in Randall, MN on 16 Nov 1954. Child:

 294   i   Elizabeth Rutledge RITTERS, b. 27 Dec 1995

229. MARY MIDDLETON SMITH[8] (Benjamin Bosworth Smith[7], Frederick Rutledge Smith[6], Mary Middleton Rutledge Reese[5], Emma Fredricka Rutledge[4], Henrietta Middleton Rutledge[3], Henry Middleton Rutledge[2], Edward Rutledge[1]) child of Benjamin Bosworth Smith and Barbara Jane Hahn was born in Mobile, AL on 29 Jan 1959. She married William Thompson JONES, Jr., son of William Thompson and Betty Lou (Rath) Jones in Charleston, SC on 21 Apr 1990. He was born in Ft. Lauderdale, FL on 11 Jul 1959. Children:

 295   i   William Middleton JONES, b. 23 Jan 1992
 296   ii   Benjamin Thompson JONES, b. 6 Mar 1995

230. BENJAMIN BOSWORTH SMITH, Jr.[8] (Benjamin Bosworth Smith[7], Frederick Rutledge Smith[6], Mary Middleton Rutledge Reese[5], Emma Fredricka Rutledge[4], Henrietta Middleton Rutledge[3], Henry Middleton Rutledge[2], Edward Rutledge[1]) child of Benjamin Bosworth Smith and Barbara Jane Hahn was born in Mobile, AL on 16 Jun 1960. He married Kimberly Susan MIXON in Charleston, SC in Oct 1983. She was born on 17 Mar 1960. Children:

 297   i   Kelly Elizabeth SMITH, b. 25 Feb 1989
 298   ii   Emily Jane SMITH, b. 20 Jan 1992
 299 iii   William Reese SMITH, b. 17 Nov 1995

231. BARBARA BEENE SMITH[8] (Benjamin Bosworth Smith[7], Frederick Rutledge Smith[6], Mary Middleton Rutledge Reese[5], Emma Fredricka Rutledge[4], Henrietta Middleton Rutledge[3], Henry Middleton Rutledge[2], Edward Rutledge[1]) child of Benjamin Bosworth Smith and Barbara Jane Hahn was born in Mobile, AL on 18 Jul 1962. She married David Byron RICE, son of the Rev. Richard Jordan and Nancy Lou (Booth) Rice in Charleston, SC on 19 Sep 1987. He was born in Riverhead, NY on 23 Apr 1959. Children:

　　300　　i　Richard Byron RICE, b. 8 Jun 1996
　　301　　ii　Samuel Bosworth RICE, b. 26 Feb 2000

232. EDMUND BELLINGER STEWART, Jr.[8] (Edmund Bellinger Stewart[7], Katherine Felder[6], Alice Sophia Reese[5], Emma Fredricka Rutledge[4], Henrietta Middleton Rutledge[3], Henry Middleton Rutledge[2], Edward Rutledge[1]) child of Edmund Bellinger Stewart and Anita Maria Carolina Waring was born in Winchester, TN on 18 Jul 1958. He married Mary Louanne BERK in say 1986. She was born in 1957. Child:

　　302　　i　Emma Katherine STEWART, b. 28 Mar 1992

236. SARAH RUTLEDGE STEWART[8] (Francis Barretto Stewart, Jr.[7], Katherine Felder[6], Alice Sophia Reese[5], Emma Fredricka Rutledge[4], Henrietta Middleton Rutledge[3], Henry Middleton Rutledge[2], Edward Rutledge[1]) child of Francis Barretto Stewart, Jr. and Susan Smith was born in 1964. She married John William Peter DYKSTRA in say 1993. He was born in 1964. Child:

　　303　　i　Matthew DYKSTRA, b. 1997

237. HARLEY ALLEN CASE[8] (Eleanor Mumford[7], Ayliffe B. Blake[6], Edmund Molyneux Blake[5], Frederick Rutledge Blake[4], Emma Philadelphia Middleton Rutledge[3], Henry Middleton Rutledge[2], Edward Rutledge[1]) child of Eleanor Mumford and Harley Allen Case was born on 13 Nov 1944, and died in Jan 1996. He married Cheryl (--) in 1967. Children:

　　304　　i　Heather Christine CASE, b. 1969
　　305　　ii　Jeffery CASE, b. 1973

238. MARSHALL CASE[8] (Eleanor Mumford[7], Ayliffe B. Blake[6], Edmund Molyneux Blake[5], Frederick Rutledge Blake[4], Emma Philadelphia Middleton Rutledge[3], Henry Middleton Rutledge[2], Edward Rutledge[1]) child of Eleanor Mumford and Harley Allen Case was born in 1947. He married Martha CUNNINGHAM in say 1971. Children:

　　306　　i　Brian CASE, b. 1975
　　307　　ii　Andrew CASE, b. 1980

239. NICHOLAS Van SLYCK MUMFORD, III[8] (Nicholas Van Slyck Mumford, Jr.[7], Ayliffe B. Blake[6], Edmund Molyneux Blake[5], Frederick Rutledge Blake[4], Emma Philadelphia Middleton Rutledge[3], Henry Middleton Rutledge[2], Edward Rutledge[1]) child of Nicholas Van Slylee Mumford, Jr. and Rosemary Davis was born in 1948. He married Catherine (--) in say 1973. Children:

　　308　　i　　Gregory MUMFORD, b. 1976
　　309　　ii　　Jennifer MUMFORD, b. 1979
　　310　　iii　Abigail MUMFORD, b. 1981

242. ELIZABETH DAVIS MUMFORD[8] (Nicholas Van Slyck Mumford, Jr.[7], Ayliffe B. Blake[6], Edmund Molyneux Blake[5], Frederick Rutledge Blake[4], Emma Philadelphia Middleton Rutledge[3], Henry Middleton Rutledge[2], Edward Rutledge[1]) child of Nicholas Van Slyck Mumford, Jr. and Rosemary Davis was born in 1953. She married Christopher BEEKMAN in say 1977. Children:

　　311　　i　　Emma BEEKMAN, b. 1981
　　312　　ii　　Eleanora BEEKMAN, b. 1984
　　313　　iii　Adam BEEKMAN, b. 1988
　　314　　iv　Melissa BEEKMAN, b. 1991

246. KATHARINE BLAKE JOHNSON[8] (Katharine Shannon Blake[7], Daniel Blake[6], Daniel Blake[5], Frederick Rutledge Blake[4], Emma Philadelphia Middleton Rutledge[3], Henry Middleton Rutledge[2], Edward Rutledge[1]) child of Katharine Shannon Blake and Harvey Wilson Johnson was born in 1953. She married Thomas A. BLANTON in say 1976. He was born in 1948. Children:

　　315　　i　　Katharine Johnson BLANTON, b. 1981
　　316　　ii　　Frances McKinley BLANTON, b. 1985

247. ANNA WHITE JOHNSON[8] (Katharine Shannon Blake[7], Daniel Blake[6], Daniel Blake[5], Frederick Rutledge Blake[4], Emma Philadelphia Middleton Rutledge[3], Henry Middleton Rutledge[2], Edward Rutledge[1]) child of Katharine Shannon Blake and Harvey Wilson Johnson was born in 1955. She married Steven Dunham SMITH in say 1977. He was born in 1950. Children:

　　317　　i　　Elizabeth Walters SMITH, b. 1980
　　318　　ii　　Anna Miles SMITH, b. 1984
　　319　　iii　Steven Dunham SMITH, Jr., b. 1985

248. JANE SHANNON JOHNSON[8] (Katharine Shannon Blake[7], Daniel Blake[6], Daniel Blake[5], Frederick Rutledge Blake[4], Emma Philadelphia

Middleton Rutledge[3], Henry Middleton Rutledge[2], Edward Rutledge[1]) child of Katharine Shannon Blake and Harvey Wilson Johnson was born in 1956. She married Raymond Daniel BRADY in say 1982. He was born in 1953. Child:

    320   i   Katharine Shannon BRADY, b. 1989

Tho⁵ Heyward Jun⁵

31: THOMAS HEYWARD, Jr.

"Well, honour is the subject of my story."

William Shakespeare

Thomas Heyward, Jr. signed his name to the Declaration of Independence along with all the other South Carolina Delegates on 2 August 1776. His is the second signature in that South Carolina grouping in which he abbreviated his first name as "Thos" and added the Junior as "Junr." in a somewhat disconnected, difficult to read and awkward hand.

He was the eldest son of Daniel Heyward and Mary Miles. His early education in South Carolina was the usual preparatory material in Greek and Latin that was provided by local academies and tutors of the wealthy plantation owner class. He was admitted to the Middle Temple, London for his more formal and finishing education on 10 January 1765 where he spent five years in study. Upon his return to South Carolina he was admitted to the Bar on 22 January 1771 and the following year he was elected to the Commons House of Assembly representing St. Helena's Parish.

Heyward was a Delegate to the Provincial Convention meeting at Charleston, South Carolina on 6 July 1774 when news of the blockading of the Port of Boston was received. He was a member of the Council of Safety and was later chosen when a Committee of the State Congress, a few months later took over the functions of Government from the Crown. He served on the Committee to prepare a Constitution for the state and was chosen to be one of the Delegates to the Second Continental Congress in Philadelphia[2].

He was present for and voted for independence on 2 July 1776. In 1779 he was wounded during the British attack on Port Royal Island and was captured a year later in defense of Charleston and imprisoned in St. Augustine, Florida until July 1781. He served as Circuit Court Judge from 1782 to 1789, and the balance of his years in maintaining his plantation.

---

[2] *Dictionary of American Biography*, (Vol. VIII), p. 609.

FIRST GENERATION

1. THOMAS HEYWARD, Jr. was born in "Old House", St. Helena's Parish, Beaufort District [now Jasper County], SC on 28 Jul 1746.[1] He married (1st) Elizabeth MATTHEWS, daughter of COL John and Sarah (Gibbes) Matthews in Charleston, SC on 20 Apr 1773.[2] She was born in St. John's Island, SC about 1753, and died in Philadelphia, PA on 16 Aug 1882.[3] He Married (2nd) Elizabeth SAVAGE, daughter of COL Thomas and Mary (Elliott) Savage in Charleston, SC on 4 May 1786.[4] She was born in 1769, and died in Beaufort County, SC in 1833.[5] He died in Beaufort County [now Jasper County], SC on 17 Apr 1809.[6]

Children by first marriage:

+	2	i	Daniel HEYWARD, b. 5 Feb 1774
	3	ii	Marie HEYWARD, b. 8 Aug 1775, dy 25 May 1776
	4	iii	Thomas HEYWARD, b. 8 Feb 1778, dy 17 Jul 1778
	5	iv	John HEYWARD, b. Jul 1779, dy Jul 1779
	6	v	Thomas HEYWARD, b. 13 Aug 1782, dy 23 Oct 1782 [Again]

Children by second marriage:

+	7	vi	Thomas HEYWARD, b. 14 Jul 1789
+	8	vii	James Hamilton HEYWARD, b. 17 Sep 1792
+	9	viii	Elizabeth Savage HEYWARD, b. 30 Oct 1794

References:
[1] There are several biographical sketches of Signer Thomas Heyward, Jr., but almost all of them are of the Victorian style: flowery, ornate, undocumented, and missing many facts about his life that would be truly interesting. John Sanderson, (1823); the Rev. Charles Goodrich, (1842); A. S. Salley, Jr., (1927) are all works of this nature. No good, quality, well supported biography of the Signer has been discovered. The best biographical sketch seems to be that found in Walter B. Edgar and N. Louise Bailey, *Biographical Directory of the South Carolina House of Representatives*, (1977), Vol. 2. A fair effort at a family genealogy was prepared by James Barnwell Heyward, II, *Heyward*, (Privately Printed, 1925). It, in turn, was a revision of an earlier compilation of the family, prepared by him in 1907; without references or a well understood and widely used numbering system. He acknowledged that he was trying to make use of facts only, without resort to imagination; but the results still contain many errors and omissions. *The South Carolina Historical Magazine*, (Charleston, SC , Oct 1958), Vol. LIX, # 4, p. 153, et seq., has tried to better document and reference information about this family, but the effort was only partially successful. See also Della Gray Bartherlmas, *The Signers of the Declaration of Independence, A Biographical and Genealogical Reference*, (Mcfarland & Company, Inc., Jefferson, NC, 1977), pp. 116-118. Leach gives his place of birth as "White Hall",

Beaufort County, SC, whereas J. B. Heyward and others give his place of birth as "Old House", Granville County, SC, or the Old House Plantation. The reader needs to know that before the First Federal Census of 1790, South Carolina had been organized as seven Districts (not Counties). The Old Heyward Plantation House was physically located in St. Helena's Parish, then in the Beaufort District, and now in Jasper County, SC. All authorities agree as to date of birth. Thomas Heyward was not named after his father, but styled himself as "Junr.", in order to distinguish him from his uncle Thomas Heyward. The Leach MSS data on Thomas Heyward, Jr. is microfilmed on FHL Film # 0001756; and the hard copy is found in Vol.# 20, pp. 6047-6185. The DAB article for Thomas Heyward, Jr. is in Vol. VIII, p. 609. See Leach MSS, p, 6049. [2] The date and place of this 1st marriage are reported in Leach MSS, p. 6049; Bartherlmas, p. 117; and DAB, p. 609. [3] The date of her birth is not known, Leach reports place only, her date and place of death is well recorded in Philadelphia, PA where she had gone to meet her husband upon his release from imprisonment at St. Augustine, FL. She is buried in St. Peter's Churchyard in Philadelphia, PA. [4] Leach MSS, p. 6049. [5] Bartherlmas, p. 117. [6] *The South Carolina Historical Magazine*, (Charleston, SC, 1940), Vol XLI, p. 75.

SECOND GENERATION

2. DANIEL HEYWARD[2] (Thomas Heyward, Jr.[1]) son of Thomas Heyward, Jr. and his 1st wife Elizabeth Matthews was born in "White Hall", Beaufort District, SC on 5 Feb 1774, and died in Savannah, GA on 25 Feb 1796.[1] He married Ann Sarah TREZEVANT, daughter of Theodore and Catherine (Crouch) Trezevant on 2 Nov 1795.[2] She was born in 1778, and died in Sullivan's Island, SC on 6 Jul 1828.[3] Child:

+ 10   i   Elizabeth Matthews HEYWARD, b. 24 Dec 1795

References:
[1] Leach MSS, p. 6050. [2] James Barnwell Heyward, II, *Heyward*, (Privately Printed, 1925), p. 78. [3] James Barnwell Heyward, II, *Heyward*, (Privately Printed, 1925), p. 79.

7. THOMAS HEYWARD[2] (Thomas Heyward, Jr.[1]) son of Thomas Heyward, Jr. and his 2nd wife Elizabeth Savage was born in Charleston, SC on 14 Jul 1789, and died in "White Hall", Beaufort County, SC on 15 Apr 1829.[1] He married Ann Elizabeth CUTHBERT [his second cousin], daughter of GEN John Alexander and Mary duPre (Heyward) Cuthbert on 7 Jan 1813.[2] She was born in "Bethel", Beaufort County, SC on 12 Mar 1792, and died in Charleston, SC on 16 Jan 1823.[3] Children:

11   i   John Cuthbert HEYWARD, b. 14 Nov 1813, dy 25 Nov 1825

+ 12   ii   Thomas Savage HEYWARD, b. 15 Oct 1815

13   iii   Nathaniel William HEYWARD, b. 4 Dec 1817, d. Nov 1850; unm

+ 14   iv Elizabeth Savage HEYWARD, b. 9 Nov 1819
+ 15   v George Cuthbert HEYWARD, b. 12 Jan 1822 [twin]
+ 16   vi Mary Caroline HEYWARD, b. 12 Jan 1822 [twin]
References:
[1] Leach MSS, p. 6059. [2] James Barnwell Heyward, II, *Heyward*, (Privately Printed, 1925), p. 79. [3] James Barnwell Heyward, II, *Heyward*, (Privately Printed, 1925), p. 74.

8. JAMES HAMILTON HEYWARD[2] (Thomas Heyward, Jr.[1]) son of Thomas Heyward, Jr. and his 2nd wife Elizabeth Savage was born in "White Hall", Beaufort County, SC on 17 Sep 1792, and died in "Chelsea:, Charleston County, SC on 2 Jul 1828.[1] He married Decima Cecilia SHUBRICK, daughter of COL Thomas and Mary Alicia (Branford) Shubrick on 12 Dec 1816.[2] She was born in "Belvidere", Charleston County, SC on 1 Feb 1796, and died in Washington, DC on 3 Mar 1867.[1] Children:
+ 17   i Mary Alicia HEYWARD, b. 16 Apr 1820
   18   ii Elizabeth HEYWARD, b. 24 Nov 1823, dy
   19   iii James Henry HEYWARD, b. 3 Mar 1826, dy
+ 20   iv James Francis HEYWARD, b. 30 Jul 1828
References:
[1] Leach MSS, p. 6069. [2] James Barnwell Heyward, II, *Heyward*, (Privately Printed, 1925), p. 80.

9. ELIZABETH SAVAGE HEYWARD[2] (Thomas Heyward, Jr.[1]) daughter of Thomas Heyward, Jr. and his 2nd wife Elizabeth Savage was born in "White Hall", Beaufort County, SC on 30 Oct 1794, and died in Grahamsville, SC on 3 Mar 1854.[1] She married Henry Middleton PARKER, son of John and Susan (Middleton) Parker on 5 Feb 1812.[2] He was born in Charleston, SC about 1785, and died there in Nov 1849.[1] Children:
   21   i Thomas Heyward PARKER, b. 15 Jul 1816, dy 18 Oct 1819
+ 22   ii Elizabeth Savage PARKER, b. 31 Jan 1821
+ 23   iii Emma Heyward PARKER, b. 15 Jul 1825
+ 24   iv Henry Middleton PARKER, Jr., b. 9 Jan 1831
   25   v Arthur Augustus PARKER, b. 17 Aug 1833, dy 14 Aug 1834
References:
[1] Leach MSS, p. 6074. [2] James Barnwell Heyward, II, *Heyward*, (Privately Printed, 1925), p. 83.

THIRD GENERATION

10. ELIZABETH MATTHEWS HEYWARD[3] (Daniel Heyward[2], Thomas Heyward, Jr.[1]) child of Daniel Heyward and Ann Sarah Trezevant was born

in Charleston, SC on 24 Dec 1795, and died in Albany, GA on 16 Dec 1862.[1] She married James HAMILTON, son of MAJ James and Elizabeth (Lynch) Hamilton on 15 Nov 1813.[1] He was born in Charleston, SC on 8 May 1786, and died at sea in the Gulf of Mexico on 16 Nov 1857.[1]
Children:

26	i	James HAMILTON, b. 9 Aug 1814, d. 10 Oct 1838; unm
+ 27	ii	Daniel Heyward HAMILTON, b. 12 May 1816
+ 28	iii	Thomas Lynch HAMILTON, b. 26 Dec 1817
+ 29	iv	Elizabeth Heyward HAMILTON, b. 28 Mar 1820
30	v	Oliver Perry HAMILTON, b. 25 Oct 1821, d. 28 Jun 1857; unm
31	vi	William Lowndes HAMILTON, b. 23 Jun 1823, d. 15 Dec 1855; dsp
+ 32	vii	Samuel Prioleau HAMILTON, b. 24 Jan 1826
+ 33	viii	John Randolph HAMILTON, b. 17 Nov 1828
34	ix	Henry Cruger HAMILTON, b. 20 Feb 1831; unm
35	x	Lewis Trevezant HAMILTON, b. 12 Mar 1833, 11 Jul 1855; unm
36	xi	Arthur St. Clair HAMILTON, b. 4 Jun 1836, d. 19 Mar 1879; unm

References:
[1] Leach MSS, p. 6050; see also James Barnwell Heyward, II, *Heyward*, (Privately Printed, 1925), pp. 109-110 for children not reported by Leach.

12. THOMAS SAVAGE HEYWARD[3] (Thomas Heyward[2], Thomas Heyward, Jr.[1]) child of Thomas Heyward and Ann Elizabeth Cuthbert was born in "The Bluff", Beaufort County, SC on 15 Oct 1815, and died in Charleston, SC on 26 May 1889.[1] He married (1st) Georgianna HASELL, daughter of Andrew and Hannah Cochran (Ashe) Hasell on 10 Mar 1836.[1] She was born in Charleston, SC on 3 May 1818, and died in Charleston, SC on 21 Jul 1858.[1] He married (2nd) Catherine Laing BOYKIN, daughter of John and Charlotte Adamson (Mortimer) Boykin on 15 Apr 1861.[2] She was born in Kershaw County, SC on 3 Jul 1822.[1]
Children by first marriage:

37	i	Anne Cuthbert HEYWARD, b. 24 Jan 1838, d. 1886; dsp
+ 38	ii	Thomas Savage HEYWARD, Jr., b. 2 Dec 1839
+ 39	iii	William Nathaniel HEYWARD, b. 26 Aug 1841
40	iv	Rosa Catherine HEYWARD, b. 15 Apr 1843, dy 26 Mar 1844
41	v	Henry Deas HEYWARD, b. 6 Mar 1845, dy 17 Apr 1846
+ 42	vi	Andrew Hasell HEYWARD, b. 25 Mar 1846

43   vii   Alfred Raoul HEYWARD, b. 17 Mar 1848, d. 23 Feb 1900; unm
44   viii Georgianna Hasell HEYWARD, b. 13 Jan 1850, dy 6 Jun 1866
45   ix   Elizabeth Catherine HEYWARD, b. 29 May 1852, d. 1892; dsp
46   x   Edward Percival HEYWARD, b. 31 Mar 1854, d. 13 Nov 1895; unm
+ 47   xi   Ella Louise HEYWARD, b. 5 Nov 1855
48   xii   Arthur Sydney HEYWARD, b. 2 Dec 1857, dy 13 Dec 1857
Children by second marriage:
+ 49   xiii John Boykin HEYWARD, b. 26 Aug 1862
50   xiv   Charlotte Boykin HEYWARD, b. 15 Feb 1864, dy 8 Jul 1864

References:
[1] Leach MSS, p. 6060. [2] James Barnwell Heyward, II, *Heyward*, (Privately Printed, 1925), p. 110.

14. ELIZABETH SAVAGE HEYWARD[3] (Thomas Heyward[2], Thomas Heyward, Jr.[1]) child of Thomas Heyward and Ann Elizabeth Cuthbert was born in "Pocotaligo", Beaufort County, SC on 9 Nov 1819, and died in Memphis, TN on 8 Oct 1884.[1] She married John WEBB, son of Daniel Cannon and Eliza (Ladson) Webb on 16 Apr 1839.[1] He was born in Charleston, SC on 26 Oct 1816, and died there on 8 Jul 1866.[1] Children:

51   i   Isabel Caroline WEBB, b. 7 Aug 1840, dy 13 Jul 1841
+ 52   ii   Annie Heyward WEBB, b. 7 Dec 1841
+ 53   iii   Martha Caroline WEBB, b. 13 Jun 1843
+ 54   iv   Elizabeth B. WEBB, b. 14 Dec 1844
55   v   John WEBB, b. 28 Jun 1846, dy 2 Oct 1849
56   vi   Mary Heyward WEBB, b. 14 Jun 1848, dy 5 Sep 1849
57   vii   William Nathaniel WEBB, b. 17 Apr 1850, dy Jun 1851
+ 58   viii Thomas Ladson WEBB, b. 25 Jun 1851
59   ix   George Heyward WEBB, b. 22 Mar 1853; unm
60   x   John WEBB, b. 14 Jan 1855, dy Mar 1861 [Again]
61   xi   Edward Screven WEBB, b. 8 Dec 1856, dy May 1857
62   xii   Charles Colcock WEBB, b. 2 Nov 1858; unm
63   xiii John WEBB, b. 7 Feb 1864, dy [Again]

References:
[1] Leach MSS, p. 6063.

15. GEORGE CUTHBERT HEYWARD[3] (Thomas Heyward[2], Thomas Heyward, Jr.[1]) child of Thomas Heyward and Ann Elizabeth Cuthbert was born in "The Bluff", Beaufort County, SC on 12 Jan 1822, and died in Bluffton, Beaufort County, SC on 1 Mar 1867.[1] He married Elizabeth Martha GUERARD, daughter of Dr. Jacob Deveaux and Alice (Screven) Guerard on 24 Feb 1842.[1] She was born in Beaufort County, SC on 1 Feb 1825, and died in Savannah, GA on 12 Nov 1875.[1] Children:

+ 64   i   Jacob Guerard HEYWARD, b. 5 Jan 1844
+ 65   ii   James Cuthbert HEYWARD, b. 2 May 1845
+ 66   iii   George Cuthbert HEYWARD, Jr., b. 24 Dec 1846
+ 67   iv   Robert Chisolm HEYWARD, b. 21 Jan 1848
   68   v   Thomas Savage HEYWARD, b. 1850, dy 1850
+ 69   vi   Thomas Daniel HEYWARD, b. 9 Jan 1852
   70   vii   Alice HEYWARD, b. 10 Oct 1854; unm
   71   viii   William Marion HEYWARD, b. 5 Dec 1856, d. 1907; dsp
+ 72   ix   Thomas Savage HEYWARD, b. 25 Jun 1858 [Again]
+ 73   x   Elizabeth Guerard HEYWARD, b. 7 Mar 1860
+ 74   xi   John Alexander HEYWARD, b. 16 May 1861
+ 75   xii   Mary Caroline HEYWARD, b. 6 Jun 1863
   76   xiii   Nathaniel William HEYWARD, b. 13 Jan 1866, d. 18 Mar 1890; unm

References:
[1] Leach MSS, pp. 6064-6065.

16. MARY CAROLINE HEYWARD[3] (Thomas Heyward[2], Thomas Heyward, Jr.[1]) child of Thomas Heyward and Ann Elizabeth Cuthbert was born in "The Bluff", Beaufort County, SC on 12 Jan 1822, and died in "Bonnie Doon", Beaufort County, SC on 24 Jun 1848.[1] She married Charles Jones COLCOCK, son of Thomas Huston and Mary Eliza (Hay) Colcock on 4 Nov 1839.[1] He was born in Barnwell County, SC on 30 Apr 1820, and died in "Elmwood", Hampton County, SC on 22 Oct 1891.[1] Children:

   77   i   John COLCOCK, b. 4 Aug 1843, d. 6 Mar 1877; unm
   78   ii   Caroline Ann COLCOCK, b. 4 Nov 1846, dy 18 Sep 1855

References:
[1] Leach MSS, p. 6068; note that both A.S. Salley, Jr. *Colcock Genealogy*, and *South Carolina Historical and Genalogical Magazine*, (Vol. 1, p. 420) give the name of Mary Eliza as Eliza Mary, however one was copying the other, and neither was well documented or referenced. The Author has used Leach in this case, because he was both closer in time to the event, and supported his work with Letters, and Newspaper accounts of the day.

17. MARY ALICIA HEYWARD[3] (James Hamilton Heyward[2], Thomas Heyward, Jr.[1]) child of James Hamilton Heyward and Decima Cecilia

Shubrick was born in Charleston, SC on 16 Jan 1820, and died in Wilmington, DE on 5 Apr 1848.[1] She married Edward Green BRADFORD, son of Moses and Phoebe (George) Bradford on 22 Dec 1842.[2] He was born in Cecil County, MD on 17 Jul 1819, and died in Wilmington, DE on 16 Jan 1884.[1] Children:

+ 79   i   James Heyward BRADFORD, b. 13 Oct 1844
   80   ii   Mary Cornelia BRADFORD, b. 28 May 1846, d. 1907; unm
+ 81   iii   Edward Green BRADFORD, b. 12 Mar 1848

References:
[1] Leach MSS, p. 6069. [2] James Barnwell Heyward, II, *Heyward*, (Privately Printed, 1925), p. 118.

20. JAMES FRANCIS HEYWARD[3] (James Hamilton Heyward[2], Thomas Heyward, Jr.[1]) child of James Hamilton Heyward and Decima Cecilia Shubrick was born in Charleston, SC on 30 Jul 1828, and died in St. Paul, MN on 23 May 1859.[1] He married Maria PRESTMAN, daughter of the Rev. Stephen Wilson and Ann (Brundige) Prestman on 4 Nov 1851.[1] She was born in New Castle, DE on 29 Jan 1828.[1] Children:

+ 82   i   Wilson Prestman HEYWARD, b. 6 Nov 1852
+ 83   ii   Decima Shubrick HEYWARD, b. 27 Apr 1854
   84   iii   James Francis HEYWARD, Jr., b. 19 Mar 1856, d. 1907; dsp
   85   iv   Shubrick HEYWARD, b. 9 Feb 1859, d. 13 Nov 1885; unm

References:
[1] Leach MSS, p. 6073.

22. ELIZABETH SAVAGE PARKER[3] (Elizabeth Savage Heyward[2], Thomas Heyward, Jr.[1]) child of Elizabeth Savage Heyward and Henry Middleton Parker was born in "Laurel Point", Beaufort County, SC on 31 Jan 1821, and died in Grahamsville, SC on 6 Apr 1885.[1] She married William Carr HOWARD [whose surname was changed by Act of the South Carolina Legislature], son of James and Sarah Hollinshead (Carr) Hogg on 30 Oct 1839.[1] He was born in Grahamsville, SC on 30 Sep 1817, and died on 10 Nov 1891.[1] Children:

+ 86   i   Emma Heyward HOWARD, b. 3 Sep 1840
   87   ii   William Henry HOWARD, b. 11 Nov 1842, dy 1856
+ 88   iii   Thomas Heyward HOWARD, b. 4 May 1844
+ 89   iv   Henry Parker HOWARD, b. 24 Apr 1846
   90   v   John HOWARD, b. 15 Mar 1854, dy May 1855
   91   vi   Sarah Elizabeth HOWARD, b. 11 Jun 1859, d. 1907; unm

References:
[1] Leach MSS, p. 6073.

23. EMMA HEYWARD PARKER[3] (Elizabeth Savage Heyward[2], Thomas Heyward, Jr.[1]) child of Elizabeth Savage Heyward and Henry Middleton Parker was born in "Laurel Point", Beaufort County, SC on 15 Jul 1825, and died in Walterboro, SC on 31 May 1867.[1] She married Clemm Chandos TRACY, son of Carlos and Jane Dollar (McLean) Tracy on 25 Oct 1852.[1] He was born in Beaufort, SC on 10 Feb 1828, and died there on 17 Jun 1859.[1] Children:

    92   i   Elizabeth Parker TRACY, b. 17 Sep 1854; unm
 + 93   ii   Carlos Chandos TRACY, b. 27 Jan 1856
    94   iii   Jean McLean TRACY, b. 29 Jun 1857

References:
[1] Leach MSS, p. 6076.

24. HENRY MIDDLETON PARKER, Jr.[3] (Elizabeth Savage Heyward[2], Thomas Heyward, Jr.[1]) child of Elizabeth Savage Heyward and Henry Middleton Parker was born in "Laurel Point", Beaufort County, SC on 9 Jan 1831, and died in Shangtung, CHINA in Oct 1861.[1] He married Mariana RHETT, daughter of James Smith and Charlotte (Haskell) Rhett on 3 Jan 1853.[1] She was born in Charleston, SC on 26 Feb 1829, and died in 1899.[1] Child:

 + 95   i   Henry Middleton PARKER, Jr., b. 27 Jul 1854

References:
[1] Leach MSS, p. 6077.

FOURTH GENERATION

27. DANIEL HEYWARD HAMILTON[4] (Elizabeth Matthews Heyward[3], Daniel Heyward[2], Thomas Heyward, Jr.[1]) child of Elizabeth Matthews Heyward and James Hamilton was born in Callawassie Island, SC on 12 May 1816, and died in Morristown, NJ on 29 Dec 1868.[1] He married Rebecca Motte MIDDLETON, daughter of John and Mary (Burroughs) Middleton in Charleston, SC on 26 Apr 1836.[1] She was born in Charleston, SC on 22 Nov 1818, and died in Hillsborough, NC on 27 Jan 1870.[1] Children:

 + 96   i   Mary Middleton HAMILTON, b. 14 Apr 1837
 + 97   ii   Daniel Heyward HAMILTON, Jr., b. 19 Mar 1838
 + 98   iii   Frances Motte HAMILTON, b. 25 Dec 1839
    99   iv   James HAMILTON, b. 20 Jul 1841, d. 15 Oct 1866; unm
 + 100   v   Elizabeth Heyward HAMILTON, b. 16 Nov 1844
 + 101   vi   John Middleton HAMILTON, b. 6 May 1847

102	vii	Arthur St. Clair HAMILTON, b. 8 Oct 1849, dy 10 Apr 1868
103	viii	George Elliott HAMILTON, b. 27 Mar 1853, dy 23 Sep 1867
+ 104	ix	Miles Brewton HAMILTON, b. 10 Apr 1856
+ 105	x	Rebecca Motte HAMILTON, b. 24 Jul 1857
106	xi	Caroline HAMILTON, b. 29 Feb 1860, dy 30 Jul 1861

References:
[1] DSDI Appl # 1564.

28. THOMAS LYNCH HAMILTON[4] (Elizabeth Matthews Heyward[3], Daniel Heyward[2], Thomas Heyward, Jr.[1]) child of Elizabeth Matthews Heyward and James Hamilton was born in Callawassie Island, SC on 26 Dec 1817[1], and died on 26 Nov 1894. He married Margaret Helen HETH, daughter of John and Margaret (Pickett) Heth on 1 Jun 1842.[1] She was born in "Black Heath", Chesterfield County, VA about 1822, and died in Savannah, GA in Mar 1855.[1] Children:

107	i	John Heth HAMILTON, b. c. 1845; unm
108	ii	Virginia HAMILTON, b. 1849, dy 1850
109	iii	Elizabeth ["Bessie"]HAMILTON, b. 1 May 1850, dy 15 Dec 1865

References:
[1] Leach MSS, p. 6051.

29. ELIZABETH HEYWARD HAMILTON[4] (Elizabeth Matthews Heyward[3], Daniel Heyward[2], Thomas Heyward, Jr.[1]) child of Elizabeth Matthews Heyward and James Hamilton was born in Charleston, SC on 28 Mar 1820, and died in Saugerties, NY on 15 Oct 1865.[1] She married Jacob Motte MIDDLETON, son of John and Mary (Burroughs) Middleton on 31 Mar 1841.[1] He was born in Charleston, SC on 23 Apr 1817, and died in Savannah, GA on 7 Jul 1871.[1] Child:

+ 110	i	John MIDDLETON, b. 27 Feb 1842

References:
[1] Leach MSS, p. 6057.

32. SAMUEL PRIOLEAU HAMILTON[4] (Elizabeth Matthews Heyward[3], Daniel Heyward[2], Thomas Heyward, Jr.[1]) child of Elizabeth Matthews Heyward and James Hamilton was born in Washington, DC on 24 Jan 1826, and died in Chester, SC in 1897.[1] He married Emma LEVY, daughter of Jacob C. and Fanny (Yates) Levy in Savannah, GA on 3 Dec 1851.[1] She was born in Charleston, SC on 13 Oct 1832, and died in Savannah, GA on 30 Mar 1873.[1] Children:

    111   i   Fanny HAMILTON, b. 12 Dec 1852, dy 30 Aug 1862
    112   ii   William Lowndes HAMILTON, b. 23 Aug 1855, d. 18 Nov 1880; unm
    113   iii   Henrietta HAMILTON, b. 10 Sep 1857, dy 9 Sep 1859
+ 114   iv   Annette Carolina HAMILTON, b. 14 Dec 1860
+ 115   v   James HAMILTON, b. 23 Sep 1865

References:
[1] DSDI Appl # 1315, see also Leach MSS, p. 6058.

33. JOHN RANDOLPH HAMILTON[4] (Elizabeth Matthews Heyward[3], Daniel Heyward[2], Thomas Heyward, Jr.[1]) child of Elizabeth Matthews Heyward and James Hamilton was born in Charleston, SC on 17 Nov 1828.[1] He married Mary Louisa WHALEY [widow of William Lowndes Hamilton], daughter of William Smith and Mary (Wilson) Whaley on 10 May 1859.[1] She was born in Charleston, SC on 3 May 1825, and died in London, ENGLAND on 11 Dec 1883.[1] Children:

    116   i   John Randolph HAMILTON, Jr., b. 21 Mar 1860; dsp
    117   ii   Mary Heyward HAMILTON, b. May 1866, dy 18 Aug 1866

References:
[1] Leach MSS, p. 6059.

38. THOMAS SAVAGE HEYWARD, Jr.[4] (Thomas Savage Heyward[3], Thomas Heyward[2], Thomas Heyward, Jr.[1]) child of Thomas Savage Heyward and his 1st wife Georgianna Hasell was born in "White Hall", St. Luke's Parish, Beaufort County, SC on 2 Dec 1839[1], and died in Charleston, SC on 11 Jul 1901. He married Louisa Virginia WATKINS, daughter of Edwin Franklin and Mildred Barbara (Johnson) Watkins on 17 Apr 1860.[1] She was born in "Round about Castle", Louisa County, VA on 31 Jul 1839[1], and died on Charleston, SC on 18 Sep 1926. Children:

    118   i   Thomas HEYWARD, b. 21 Aug 1861, dy 19 Sep 1871
+ 119   ii   Edwin Watkins HEYWARD, b. 6 Aug 1863
    120   iii   Louise Watkins HEYWARD, b. 14 Feb 1866, d. 1938; unm
    121   iv   Annie Cuthbert HEYWARD, b. 25 Jan 1868, dy 5 Oct 1871
+ 122   v   Wilmot Holmes HEYWARD, b. 5 Jan 1876

References:
[1] DSDI Appl # 1623 & Leach MSS, p. 6061.

39. WILLIAM NATHANIEL HEYWARD[4] (Thomas Savage Heyward[3], Thomas Heyward[2], Thomas Heyward, Jr.[1]) child of Thomas Savage Heyward and his 1st wife Georgianna Hasell was born in Grahamville, SC on 26 Aug 1841[1], and died on 13 May 1902. He married Louisa Chisolm GUERARD, daughter of George Henry and Alice (Cuthbert) Guerard on 7 May 1867.[1] She was born in Bluffton, SC on 23 May 1850[1], and died on 12 Feb 1912. Children:

123	i	William Nathaniel HEYWARD, Jr., b. 27 Apr 1868, dy 5 May 1868
124	ii	Georgianna Hasell HEYWARD, b. 26 Oct 1869; dsp
125	iii	Alice Cuthbert HEYWARD, b. 29 May 1871, d. 30 Jan 1914; dsp
+ 126	iv	Florence Percy HEYWARD, b. 9 Mar 1873
+ 127	v	William Nathaniel HEYWARD, Jr., b. 31 May 1874 [Again]
+ 128	vi	Henry Guerard HEYWARD, b. 12 May 1876
+ 129	vii	Louisa Guerard HEYWARD, b. 30 Sep 1877
130	viii	Gerald HEYWARD, b. 24 Jun 1887, dy 28 Dec 1887

References:
[1] Leach MSS, p. 6061 & DSDI Appl # 2555.

42. ANDREW HASELL HEYWARD[4] (Thomas Savage Heyward[3], Thomas Heyward[2], Thomas Heyward, Jr.[1]) child of Thomas Savage Heyward and his 1st wife Georgianna Hasell was born in Charleston, SC on 25 Mar 1846.[1] He married Frances Rosa SMITH, daughter of William Burroughs and Frances Susan (Jones) Smith on 1 Mar 1866.[1] She was born in Charleston, SC on 17 Feb 1843.[1] Children:

+ 131	i	William Burroughs Smith HEYWARD, b. 10 Jan 1867
132	ii	Georgianna Hasell HEYWARD, b. 23 Dec 1869
133	iii	Andrew Hasell HEYWARD, Jr., b. 22 Dec 1871, dy 13 Oct 1872
134	iv	Frances Smith HEYWARD, b. 22 Sep 1873
135	v	John Ashe HEYWARD, b. 22 Feb 1875
136	vi	Lillie Williman HEYWARD, b. 17 Feb 1877
137	vii	Catherine Lechmere HEYWARD, b. 8 Sep 1878
138	viii	Pauline Keith HEYWARD, b. 21 Sep 1880
+ 139	ix	Andrew Hasell HEYWARD, Jr., b. 11 Jan 1883 [Again]

References:
[1] Leach MSS, p. 6062.

47. ELLA LOUISE HEYWARD[4] (Thomas Savage Heyward[3], Thomas Heyward[2], Thomas Heyward, Jr.[1]) child of Thomas Savage Heyward and his 1st wife Georgianna Hasell was born in Charleston, SC on 5 Nov 1855[1], and died in Savannah, GA on 25 Jan 1925. She married John Heyward LYNAH, son of Edward and Eliza (Glover) Lynah in Charleston, SC on 7 Feb 1877.[1] He was born in Grahamville, SC on 10 May 1848[1], and died in Savannah, GA on 4 Feb 1935. Children:

+ 140   i   Savage Heyward LYNAH, b. 25 Jun 1879
+ 141   ii   James LYNAH, b. 6 Oct 1881
   142   iii   Lillie Heyward LYNAH, b. 5 Jul 1884, d. 21 Mar 1956; dsp
+ 143   iv   Eloise LYNAH, b. 15 Mar 1887
+ 144   v   John Heyward LYNAH, Jr., b. 1891
   145   vi   Maria Glover LYNAH, b. 1897, dy 1897 [twin]
   146   vii   Edward LYNAH, b. 1897, dy 1898 [twin]
+ 147   viii   Anne Cuthbert LYNAH, b. 8 Oct 1899

References:
[1] Leach MSS, p. 6062 & DSDI Appl # 2501; see also PAF printout for additional children of this marriage.

49. JOHN BOYKIN HEYWARD[4] (Thomas Savage Heyward[3], Thomas Heyward[2], Thomas Heyward, Jr.[1]) child of Thomas Savage Heyward and his 2nd wife Catherine Laing Boykin was born in Camden, SC on 26 Aug 1862[1], and died in Oakland, CA on 8 May 1928. He married Martha Hayes PYATT, daughter of John and Harriett (Newell) Pyatt on 15 Apr 1886.[1] She was born in Charleston, SC on 6 May 1862[1], and died in Oakland, CA on 19 Dec 1927. Children:

+ 148   i   John Boykin HEYWARD, Jr., b. 26 Feb 1887
   149   ii   Benjamin Alston HEYWARD, b. 23 May 1888

References:
[1]DSDI Appl # 2274.

52. ANNIE HEYWARD WEBB[4] (Elizabeth Savage Heyward[3], Thomas Heyward[2], Thomas Heyward, Jr.[1]) child of Elizabeth Savage Heyward and John Webb was born in Grahamville, SC on 7 Dec 1841[1], and died in 1925. She married (1st) James Witsell O'HEAR on 15 Mar 1860.[1] He died in Virginia on 28 May 1863 [kia].[1] She married (2nd) Thomas Heyward HOWARD [see sketch # 88], son of William Carr and Elizabeth Savage (Parker) Howard on 15 Jan 1867.[1] He was born in Grahamville, SC on 4 May 1844[1], and died in 1908.

Children by first marriage:
   150   i   James O'HEAR, b. 29 Jan 1861, dy 12 Sep 1861
   151   ii   James O'HEAR, b. 22 Jul 1863, dy 10 Mar 1865 [Again]

Children by second marriage:
   152   iii   William Carr HOWARD, b. 3 Mar 1868
   153   iv   John Webb HOWARD, b. 18 Dec 1869

+   154   v   Martha Horry HOWARD, b. 11 Jan 1872
    155   vi   Henry Parker HOWARD, b. 1 Apr 1874
    156   vii   Elizabeth HOWARD, b. 27 Feb 1876
    157   viii Thomas Heyward HOWARD, Jr., b. 26 Feb 1878
References:
[1] Leach MSS, p. 6063.

53. MARTHA CAROLINE WEBB[4] (Elizabeth Savage Heyward[3], Thomas Heyward[2], Thomas Heyward, Jr.[1]) child of Elizabeth Savage Heyward and John Webb was born in Grahamville, SC on 13 Jun 1843, and died in North Santee, SC on 28 Nov 1878.[1] She married Edward Shubrick HORRY, son of Elias and Mary (Shubrick) Horry on 23 May 1861.[1] He was born in Charleston, SC on 13 Jun 1827.[1] Children:
    158   i   Edward HORRY, b. 20 Mar 1862, dy 29 May 1863
    159   ii   Elias Edward HORRY, b. 10 Oct 1863
    160   iii   John Webb HORRY, b. 27 Dec 1865
    161   iv   Paul Trapler HORRY, b. 1 Mar 1867, dy 1 Nov 1867
    162   v   William Webb HORRY, b. 19 Dec 1868, dy 9 Jul 1871
    163   vi   Elizabeth Heyward HORRY, b. 8 Oct 1870
    164   vii   Mary Shubrick HORRY, b. 22 Jul 1872
    165   viii Heyward Howard HORRY, b. 17 Feb 1875, dy 25 Sep 1878
    166   ix   Martha Webb HORRY, b. 3 Mar 1877
References:
[1] Leach MSS, p. 6064.

54. ELIZABETH B. WEBB[4] (Elizabeth Savage Heyward[3], Thomas Heyward[2], Thomas Heyward, Jr.[1]) child of Elizabeth Savage Heyward and John Webb was born in "Bluff Plantation", Beaufort County, SC on 14 Dec 1844.[1] She married Abner Whatley LAMAR, son of Thomas Gresham and Mary (Whatley) Lamar on 8 Oct 1868.[1] He was born in Edgefield County, SC on 30 Mar 1847.[1] Children:
    167   i   Oralie LAMAR, b. 24 Aug 1870
    168   ii   Hamilton Hickman LAMAR, b. 11 Jun 1872, dy 12 Sep 1874
    169   iii   Abner Whatley LAMAR, Jr., b. 15 Mar 1875
    170   iv   Elizabeth Heyward LAMAR, b. 24 Jun 1877
    171   v   Mary Whatley LAMAR, b. 5 Aug 1880
    172   vi   Edward Horry LAMAR, b. 24 Jun 1883, dy 30 Aug 1886
    173   vii   William Bandrum LAMAR, b. 10 Oct 1885
References:
[1] Leach MSS, p. 6064.

58. THOMAS LADSON WEBB[4] (Elizabeth Savage Heyward[3], Thomas Heyward[2], Thomas Heyward, Jr.[1]) child of Elizabeth Savage Heyward and John Webb was born in Charleston, SC on 25 Jun 1851.[1] He married Rebecca M. LEACH in say 1867. She was born in 1849, and died in 1885.[2] Children:

174	i	Isabelle WEBB, b. 1868
175	ii	Elizabeth WEBB, b. 1870
176	iii	Pamella WEBB, b. 1871
177	iv	John WEBB, b. 1873
178	v	Frances Ann WEBB, b. 1878

References:
[1] Leach MSS, p. 6063. [2] Heyward Family Association HENRY data.

64. JACOB GUERARD HEYWARD[4] (George Cuthbert Heyward[3], Thomas Heyward[2], Thomas Heyward, Jr.[1]) child of George Cuthbert Heyward and Elizabeth Martha Guerard was born in Beaufort County, SC on 5 Jan 1844.[1] He married Pauline de CARADEUX, daughter of Achille and Elizabeth (Della Torre) de Caradeno on 6 Nov 1866.[1] She was born in Charleston, SC on 31 Oct 1844.[1] Children:

+ 179	i	Elise HEYWARD, b. 9 May 1868
180	ii	Rose HEYWARD, b. 2 Dec 1869, dy 9 Mar 1870 [twin]
181	iii	Pauline HEYWARD, b. 2 Dec 1869, dsp [twin]
182	iv	Margaret HEYWARD, b. 1 Sep 1871
183	v	Pauline HEYWARD, b. 22 Mar 1874 [Again]
184	vi	Jacob Guerard HEYWARD, Jr., b. 9 Apr 1876, dy 12 Jan 1881
+ 185	vii	Francis Caradeux HEYWARD, b. 22 Mar 1880
186	viii	Ethel HEYWARD, b. 28 Nov 1882, dy 9 May 1883
187	ix	Walter Screven HEYWARD, b. 9 Sep 1884

References:
[1] Leach MSS, p. 6066.

65. JAMES CUTHBERT HEYWARD[4] (George Cuthbert Heyward[3], Thomas Heyward[2], Thomas Heyward, Jr.[1]) child of George Cuthbert Heyward and Elizabeth Martha Guerard was born in Grahamville, SC on 2 May 1845[1], and died in Savannah, GA on 4 Feb 1904. He married Sarah Connelly TAYLOR, daughter of Ira Hamilton and Mary Street (Connelly) Taylor on 12 Nov 1873.[1] She was born in Macon, GA on 12 Nov 1855[1], and died in Savannah, GA on 21 May 1932. Children:

188	i	Mary Taylor HEYWARD, b. 21 Sep 1874
189	ii	James Cuthbert HEYWARD, Jr., b. 26 Sep 1875

+   190   iii   Roland Steiner HEYWARD, b. 9 Jul 1884
+   191   iv   Harvey Cuthbert HEYWARD, b. 18 Sep 1886
References:
[1] SAR Appl # 126053.

66. GEORGE CUTHBERT HEYWARD, Jr.[4](George Cuthbert Heyward[3], Thomas Heyward[2], Thomas Heyward, Jr.[1]) child of George Cuthbert Heyward and Elizabeth Martha Guerard was born in Charleston, SC on 24 Dec 1846[1], and died in Bluffton, SC on 21 Jan 1928. He married Margaret Evance DOAR, daughter of Stephen Duval and Charlotte Ann (Cordes) Doar in McClellanville, SC on 22 Jun 1875.[1] She was born in St. James Parish, Santee, SC on 28 Oct 1851[1], and died on Savannah, GA on 16 Mar 1938. Children:

        192   i   Elizabeth Guerard HEYWARD, b. 22 Jun 1876
+   193   ii   George Cuthbert HEYWARD, III, b. 7 Feb 1878
+   194   iii Stephen Doar HEYWARD, b. 30 Jun 1880
        195   iv   Edward Lee HEYWARD, b. 27 Jul 1881
        196   v   Cordes Withers HEYWARD, b. 14 Jan 1885, dy 1 Jul 1885
        197   vi   Arthur Smith HEYWARD, b. 28 Aug 1886
        198   vii Evance HEYWARD, b. 1888
References:
[1] DSDI Appl # 1888 & Leach MSS, p. 6067.

67. ROBERT CHISOLM HEYWARD[4] (George Cuthbert Heyward[3], Thomas Heyward[2], Thomas Heyward, Jr.[1]) child of George Cuthbert Heyward and Elizabeth Martha Guerard was born in Charleston, SC on 21 Jan 1848, and died in Bluffton, SC on 25 Dec 1886.[1] He married Mary Elizabeth STONEY, daughter of Joseph John and Mary Agnes (Kirk) Stoney in Bluffton, SC on 16 Apr 1871.[1] She was born in Hilton Head Island, SC on 18 Dec 1850[1], and died in Hendersonville, NC in Aug 1927. Children:

        199   i   Corinne HEYWARD, b. 3 Apr 1873
        200   ii   George Cuthbert HEYWARD, b. 12 Jan 1875
        201   iii Mary Agnes HEYWARD, b. 19 Aug 1876
+   202   iv   Robert Clarence HEYWARD, b. 12 Mar 1878
        203   v   Joseph Stoney HEYWARD, b. 14 Feb 1881
+   204   vi   Daniel Hasell HEYWARD, b. 30 Dec 1883
        205   vii Estelle Cottman HEYWARD, b. 9 Sep 1885
References:
[1] SAR Appl # 132490 & DSDI Appl # 2436.

69. THOMAS DANIEL HEYWARD[4](George Cuthbert Heyward[3], Thomas Heyward[2], Thomas Heyward, Jr.[1]) child of George Cuthbert Heyward and Elizabeth Martha Guerard was born in Charleston, SC on 9 Jan 1852[1], and died in Savannah, GA on 26 Oct 1916. He married Eliza Selina JOHNSTONE, daughter of William Clarkson and Alice Louisa (Fraser) Johnstone on 3 Jul 1884.[1] She was born in Georgetown, SC on 25 May 1861[1], and died in Savannah, GA on 27 Dec 1924. Children:

+ 206   i   Selina HEYWARD, b. 10 Mar 1887
+ 207   ii   Isabel HEYWARD, b. 20 Jun 1890
+ 208   iii   Elizabeth HEYWARD, b. 4 Sep 1894
   209   iv   Dorothy HEYWARD, b. c. 1897
   210   v   Helen Hasell HEYWARD, b. 1899

References:
[1] DSDI Appl # 2336 & Leach MSS, p. 6067; see also PAF data for additional children of this marriage.

72. THOMAS SAVAGE HEYWARD[4](George Cuthbert Heyward[3], Thomas Heyward[2], Thomas Heyward, Jr.[1]) child of George Cuthbert Heyward and Elizabeth Martha Guerard was born in Charleston, SC on 25 Jun 1858[1], and died in Savannah, GA on 1 Oct 1934. He married Mary Hamilton SEABROOK, daughter of Benjamin Whitemarsh and Adeline Clifford (Strobhart) Seabrook on 6 Dec 1882.[1] She was born in Grahamville, SC on 18 Apr 1860[1], and died in Savannah, GA on 28 May 1942. Children:

   211   i   Adeline Clifford HEYWARD, b. 8 Dec 1886
+ 212   ii   Mary Hamilton HEYWARD, b. 10 Sep 1888

References:
[1] DSDI Appl # 2177.

73. ELIZABETH GUERARD HEYWARD[4] (George Cuthbert Heyward[3], Thomas Heyward[2], Thomas Heyward, Jr.[1]) child of George Cuthbert Heyward and Elizabeth Martha Guerard was born in Charleston, SC on 7 Mar 1860[1], and died in Beaufort, SC on 25 Oct 1912. She married Edward Barnwell WALKER, son of Edward Tabb and Annie Bull (Barnwell) Walker on 13 Oct 1885.[1] He was born in Beaufort County, SC on 19 Apr 1859[1], and died in Charleston, SC on 16 Nov 1926. Children:

+ 213   i   Edward Barnwell WALKER, Jr., b. 3 Sep 1886
   214   ii   Anne Barnwell WALKER, b. c. 1888
   215   iii   Joseph Rogers HEYWARD, b. c. 1890
   216   iv   Daniel Heyward WALKER, b. c. 1891
   217   v   Carrie Heyward WALKER, b. c. 1893
+ 218   vi   George Heyward WALKER, b. c. 1895
   219   vii   Child Walker, b. c. 1898, dy

References:
[1] SAR Appl # 123204 & Leach MSS, p. 6068; see also PAF data for additional children of this marriage.

74. JOHN ALEXANDER HEYWARD[4] (George Cuthbert Heyward[3], Thomas Heyward[2], Thomas Heyward, Jr.[1]) child of George Cuthbert Heyward and Elizabeth Martha Guerard was born in Charleston, SC on 16 May 1861.[1] He married Helena MALLARD in say 1888. Children:

+ 220   i   William Guerard HEYWARD, b. c. 1890
+ 221   ii   Thomas Fleming HEYWARD, b. 18 Apr 1893
   222   iii   Mary HEYWARD, b. 18 Jan 1897, d. 3 Sep 1974; dsp

References:
[1] PAF data furnished the Author, dated 1 Jan 1980.

75. MARY CAROLINE HEYWARD[4](George Cuthbert Heyward[3], Thomas Heyward[2], Thomas Heyward, Jr.[1]) child of George Cuthbert Heyward and Elizabeth Martha Guerard was born in Aiken, SC on 6 Jun 1863, and died on 16 Feb 1894.[1] She married William LeSerurier GIGNILLIAT, son of William Robert and Hattie (Heyward) Gignilliat on 9 Jun 1891.[1] He was born in Aiken, SC on 21 Apr 1861[1], and died in Savannah, GA on 18 Nov 1930, Child:

+ 223   i   William Robert GIGNILLIAT, b. 29 Aug 1892

References:
[1] Leach MSS, p. 6065; see also PAF data furnished the Author, dated 1 Jan 1980.

79. JAMES HEYWARD BRADFORD[4] (Mary Alicia Heyward[3], James Hamilton Heyward[2], Thomas Heyward, Jr.[1]) child of Mary Alicia Heyward and Edward Green Bradford was born in Wilmington, DE on 13 Oct 1844.[1] He married Isabella Mitchell ELLIOT, daughter of James and Sarah Jordan (Mitchell) Elliot on 1 Mar 1871.[1] She was born in Jackson, MS on 24 May 1843.[1] Children:

   224   i   Isabella Middleton BRADFORD, b. 16 Nov 1872, dy 9 Oct
                 1873
   225   ii   James Heyward BRADFORD, Jr., b. 22 Mar 1874
   226   iii   Edward Elliot BRADFORD, b. 19 Jun 1875
   227   iv   William Shubrick BRADFORD, b. 5 Nov 1876
   228   v   Mary Eugenia BRADFORD, b. 13 May 1878
   229   vi   Elizabeth Elliot BRADFORD, b. 30 Nov 1881
   230   vii   Isabella BRADFORD, b. 27 May 1885

References:
[1] Leach MSS, p. 6070.

81. EDWARD GREEN BRADFORD[4] (Mary Alicia Heyward[3], James Hamilton Heyward[2], Thomas Heyward, Jr.[1]) child of Mary Alicia Heyward and Edward Green Bradford was born in Wilmington, DE on 12 Mar 1848[1], and died in Clifton Heights, PA on 30 Mar 1928. He married Eleuthera Paulina du PONT, daughter of Alexis Irenee and Joanna (Smith) du Pont on 18 Sep 1872.[1] She was born in Wilmington, DE on 3 Feb 1848[1], and died there on 6 Jun 1906. Children:

+ 231   i   Eleuthera du Pont BRADFORD, b. 12 Jul 1873
   232   ii Mary Alicia Heyward BRADFORD, b. 5 Aug 1876
   233   iii Edward Green BRADFORD, b. 11 Sep 1878
   234   iv Alexis Irenee du Pont BRADFORD, b. 14 Feb 1880, dy 13 Mar 1880
   235   v   Joanna du Pont BRADFORD, b. 17 Jul 1881

References:
[1] Leach MSS, p. 6070 & DSDI Appl # 642.

82. WILSON PRESTMAN HEYWARD[4] (James Francis Heyward[3], James Hamilton Heyward[2], Thomas Heyward, Jr.[1]) child of James Francis Heyward and Maria Prestman was born in Wilmington, DE on 6 Nov 1852.[1] He married Elizabeth Skinner WILSON, daughter of Henry Robert and Sallie Lloyd (Skinner) Wilson on 8 Jun 1882.[1] She was born in Baltimore, MD on 12 Jul 1852.[1] Children:

   236   i   Elizabeth Wilson HEYWARD, b. 30 Mar 1883
   237   ii Decima Shubrick HEYWARD, b. 16 Nov 1884
+ 238   iii Shubrick HEYWARD, b. 17 Jul 1886

References:
[1] Leach MSS, p. 6073.

83. DECIMA SHUBRICK HEYWARD[4] (James Francis Heyward[3], James Hamilton Heyward[2], Thomas Heyward, Jr.[1]) child of James Francis Heyward and Maria Presstman was born in Wilmington, DE on 27 Apr 1854.[1] She married Winfield Johns TAYLOR, son of Charles Rushman and Georgianna (Milliman) Taylor on 4 Oct 1876.[1] He was born in Baltimore, MD on 13 May 1850.[1] Children:

   239   i   Georgie May TAYLOR, b. 22 Jun 1877
   240   ii Maria Heyward TAYLOR, b. 24 Jan 1879, dy 24 Jul 1879
   241   iii James Heyward TAYLOR, b. 25 Jun 1880

References:
[1] Leach MSS, p. 6074.

86. EMMA HEYWARD HOWARD[4] (Elizabeth Savage Parker[3], Elizabeth Savage Heyward[2], Thomas Heyward, Jr.[1]) child of Elizabeth Savage Parker and William Carr Howard was born in Grahamville, SC on 3 Sep 1840[1], and died in Grahamviulle, SC on 8 Jan 1919. She married Henry DeSaussure BURNET on 23 Nov 1863.[1] He was born in Charleston, SC on 2 Jun 1842[1], and died in Grahamville, SC on 24 Nov 1915. Children:

+ 242   i   Nella BURNET, b. c. 1865
  243   ii   Emma BURNET, b. c. 1867
+ 244   iii Elizabeth Howard BURNET, b. 19 Aug 1870
+ 245   iv   Henry Heyward BURNET, b. 13 Feb 1873

References:
[1] DSDI Appl # 2523 & Leach MSS, p. 6075, see also PAF data.

88. THOMAS HEYWARD HOWARD[4] (Elizabeth Savage Parker[3], Elizabeth Savage Heyward[2], Thomas Heyward, Jr.[1]) child of Elizabeth Savage Parker and William Carr Howard was born in Grahamville, SC on 4 May 1844[1], and died in 1908. He married Annie Heyward WEBB [widow of James Witsell O'Hear], daughter of John and Elizabeth Savage (Heyward) Webb on 15 Jan 1867.[1] She was born in Grahamville, SC on 7 Dec 1841[1], and died in 1929. Children are as reported under the second marriage of Sketch # 52.

References:
[1] Leach MSS, p. 6076.

89. HENRY PARKER HOWARD[4] (Elizabeth Savage Parker[3], Elizabeth Savage Heyward[2], Thomas Heyward, Jr.[1]) child of Elizabeth Savage Parker and William Carr Howard was born in "Laurel Point", Beaufort County, SC on 24 Apr 1846[1], and died in 1907. He married Mary Huberly Glover JENKINS in say 1876. She was born in 1855[1], and died in 1929. Children:

  246   i   Adam Hubley HOWARD, b. 1877, d. 1923; unm
+ 247   ii   Henrietta Parker HOWARD, b. 1879
+ 248   iii   Robert Emmett Jenkins HOWARD, b. 10 Oct 1880
  249   iv   Maragaret ["Madge"] Glover HOWARD, b. c. 1882
  250   v   Ellen Fordney HOWARD, b. 1884, d. 1972; unm
  251   vi   Mary Craig HOWARD, b. c. 1889, d. 1970; unm
  252   vii   Emma Burnet HOWARD, b. 1891
+ 253   viii Henry Parker HOWARD, Jr., b. 1893
+ 254   ix   Lillian Jenkins HOWARD, b. c. 1895

References:
[1] Leach MSS, p. 6075, see also Heyward Family Association HENRY Chart for children of this marriage.

93. CARLOS CHANDOS TRACY[4] (Emma Heyward Parker[3], Elizabeth Savage Heyward[2], Thomas Heyward, Jr.[1]) child of Emma Heyward Parker and Clemm Chandos Tracy was born in Grahamville, SC on 27 Jan 1856.[1] He married Annie Caroline WILLIAMS, daughter of Oliver Perry and Annie Caroline (Campbell) Williams on 21 Apr 1880.[1] She was born in Walterboro, SC on 1 Dec 1858.[1] Children:

  255   i   Clemm Carlos TRACY, b. 8 Feb 1881, dy 11 Nov 1881
  256   ii   Emma Capers TRACY, b. Nov 1886
References:
[1] Leach MSS, p. 6076.

95. HENRY MIDDLETON PARKER, Jr.[4] (Henry Middleton Parker[3], Elizabeth Savage Heyward[2], Thomas Heyward, Jr.[1]) child of Henry Middleton Parker and Mariana Rhett was born in Charleston, SC on 27 Jul 1854.[1] He married Mary Montraville PATTON, daughter of Montraville and Maria Louisa (Hackett) Patton on 6 Mar 1883.[1] She was born in Asheville, NC on 3 Jan 1849.[1] Children:

  257   i   Henry Middleton PARKER, III, b. 20 May 1884
  258   ii   Katherine McDowell PARKER, b. 6 Aug 1886
  259   iii Mary Montraville PARKER, b. 6 Apr 1888
References:
[1] Leach MSS, p. 6077.

FIFTH GENERATION

96. MARY MIDDLETON HAMILTON[5] (Daniel Heyward Hamilton[4], Elizabeth Matthews Heyward[3], Daniel Heyward[2], Thomas Heyward, Jr.[1]) child of Daniel Heyward Hamilton and Rebecca Motte Middleton was born in Charleston, SC on 14 Apr 1837.[1] She married (1st) John Beaufaine IRVING, son of John Beaufaine and Emma Maria (Cruger) Irving on 21 Apr 1859.[1] He was born in Charleston, SC on 26 Nov 1825, and died in NYC on 20 Apr 1877.[1] Children:

  + 260   i   William Aemilius IRVING, b. 23 Feb 1860
  + 261   ii   Heyward Hamilton IRVING, b. 27 Sep 1861
  + 262   iii Emma Cruger IRVING, b. 17 Mar 1863
    263   iv   John Beaufaine IRVING, b. 29 Sep 1864, d. 1889; dsp
  + 264   v   Rebecca Middleton IRVING, b. 18 Jul 1866
  + 265   vi   Mary Elizabeth IRVING, b. 17 May 1871
    266   vii James Hamilton IRVING, b. 6 Aug 1872; unm
    267   viii Arthur Cruger IRVING, b. 3 Jul 1874

268   ix   Henry Cruger IRVING, b. 27 Apr 1876, dy 27 Apr 1876
269   x   Alfred Hawkins IRVING, b. 7 Jan 1878, dy 3 Nov 1879
References:
[1] Leach MSS, p. 6052.

97. DANIEL HEYWARD HAMILTON, Jr.[5] (Daniel Heyward Hamilton[4], Elizabeth Matthews Heyward[3], Daniel Heyward[2], Thomas Heyward, Jr.[1]) child of Daniel Heyward Hamilton and Rebecca Motte Middleton was born in Charleston, SC on 19 Mar 1838.[1] He married Frances Gray ROULHAC, daughter of Joseph Blount Gregorie and Catherine (Buffin) Roulhac on 8 Dec 1859.[1] She was born in Alamance, NC on 25 Aug 1839.[1] Children:

270   i   Katherine Roulhac HAMILTON, b. 21 Aug 1860, d. 6 Jul 1893; unm
271   ii   Elizabeth Roulhac HAMILTON, b. 3 Aug 1867
+ 272 iii Daniel Heyward HAMILTON, III, b. 14 Feb 1872
+ 273 iv   Joseph Gregorie Roulhac HAMILTON, b. 6 Aug 1878
References:
[1] Leach MSS, p. 6054.

98. FRANCES MOTTE HAMILTON[5] (Daniel Heyward Hamilton[4], Elizabeth Matthews Heyward[3], Daniel Heyward[2], Thomas Heyward, Jr.[1]) child of Daniel Heyward Hamilton and Rebecca Motte Middleton was born in Charleston, SC on 25 Dec 1839.[1] She married (1st) George Buist LAMB on 14 Sep 1857.[1] Child:

274   i   George Buist LAMB, Jr., b. 1 Mar 1859
References:
[1] Leach MSS, p. 6055.

100. ELIZABETH HEYWARD HAMILTON[5] (Daniel Heyward Hamilton[4], Elizabeth Matthews Heyward[3], Daniel Heyward[2], Thomas Heyward, Jr.[1]) child of Daniel Heyward Hamilton and Rebecca Motte Middleton was born in Charleston, SC on 16 Nov 1844, and died in Savannah, GA on 6 Apr 1873.[1] She married Albert Henry STODDARD, son of John and Mary Lavinia (Mongin) Stoddard on 22 May 1867.[1] He was born in Savannah, GA on 27 May 1838.[1] Children:

275   i   Mary Alice STODDARD, b. 4 Jul 1868, dy 2 Jan 1875
+ 276 ii   Albert Henry STODDARD, Jr., b. 15 Sep 1872
References:
[1] Leach MSS, p. 6056.

101. JOHN MIDDLETON HAMILTON[5] (Daniel Heyward Hamilton[4], Elizabeth Matthews Heyward[3], Daniel Heyward[2], Thomas Heyward, Jr.[1])

child of Daniel Heyward Hamilton and Rebecca Motte Middleton was born in Charleston, SC on 6 May 1847, and died in Ninety Six, SC on 16 Feb 1870.[1] He married Charlotte Marshall SMITH, daughter of Marshall Robert and Elizabeth Ann (Gillam) Smith on 4 Oct 1868.[1] She was born in Hamburg, SC on 18 Jan 1846.[1] Child:

277   i   Arthur St. CLAIR HAMILTON, b. 26 Nov 1869

References:
[1] Leach MSS, p. 6056.

104. MILES BREWTON HAMILTON[5] (Daniel Heyward Hamilton[4], Elizabeth Matthews Heyward[3], Daniel Heyward[2], Thomas Heyward, Jr.[1]) child of Daniel Heyward Hamilton and Rebecca Motte Middleton was born in "Lachland", Colleton County, SC on 10 Apr 1856[1], and died in Hyannis Port, MA on 13 Jun 1933. He married Mary Ravenal PRINGLE, daughter of Motte Alston and Gabriella (Ravenal) Pringle on 10 Apr 1883.[1] She was born in Charleston, SC on 6 Jun 1859[i], and died there on 11 Apr 1946. Children:

     278   i   James HAMILTON, b. 4 Sep 1884, dy 25 Jan 1885
     279   ii   Gabriella Ravenal HAMILTON, b. 11 May 1886
+ 280   iii   Daniel Heyward HAMILTON, b. 13 Feb 1893
     281   iv   Motte HAMILTON, b. c. 1894
+ 282   v   Mary Pringle HAMILTON, b. c. 1896
     283   vi   Francisca HAMILTON, b. c. 1899

References:
[1] Leach MSS, p. 6056 & DSDI Appl # 1564, see also PAF data for additional children of this marriage.

105. REBECCA MOTTE HAMILTON[5] (Daniel Heyward Hamilton[4], Elizabeth Matthews Heyward[3], Daniel Heyward[2], Thomas Heyward, Jr.[1]) child of Daniel Heyward Hamilton and Rebecca Motte Middleton was born in Greenville, SC on 24 Jul 1857.[1] She married Arthur Blackwell RYAN, son of William King and Martha Aurelia (Blackwell) Ryan on 3 Jun 1879.[1] He was born in Charleston, SC on 7 Jan 1854.[1] Children:

+ 284   i   Rebecca Hamilton RYAN, b. 18 Jun 1880
+ 285   ii   Martha RYAN, b. 30 Nov 1882
     286   iii   Ethel Middleton RYAN, b. 20 Mar 1885
+ 287   iv   Louise King RYAN, b. 31 Mar 1887
     288   v   Catherine Hamilton RYAN, b. 27 Jun 1889

References:
[1] Leach MSS, p. 6057.

110. JOHN MIDDLETON[5] (Elizabeth Heyward Hamilton[4], Elizabeth Matthews Heyward[3], Daniel Heyward[2], Thomas Heyward, Jr.[1]) child of Elizabeth Heyward Hamilton and Jacob Motte Middleton was born in Charleston, SC on 27 Feb 1842, and died in Savannah, GA on 27 Mar 1869.[1] He married Adele Allston KING, daughter of Henry Campbell and Susan (Petigru) King on 19 Dec 1865.[1] She was born in Charleston, SC on 20 Jun 1845, and died in Macon, GA on 8 Apr 1889.[1] Children:

> 289   i   Elizabeth Hamilton MIDDLETON, b. 8 Sep 1866, dy 28 Jun 1867
> 290   ii   Henry King MIDDLETON, b. 31 Aug 1867, dy 15 Jan 1872
> 291   iii   John MIDDLETON, b. 11 Apr 1869, dy 1 Dec 1874

References:
[1] Leach MSS, p. 6058.

114. ANNETTE CAROLINA HAMILTON[5] (Samuel Prioleau Hamilton[4], Elizabeth Matthews Heyward[3], Daniel Heyward[2], Thomas Heyward, Jr.[1]) child of Samuel Prioleau Hamilton and Emma Levy was born in Savannah, GA on 14 Dec 1860.[1] She married Theodore MUNRO, son of Robert and Margaret (Steele) Munro on 15 Jun 1882.[1] He was born in Marion, SC on 28 Feb 1848.[1] Children:

> 292   i   Theodore Hamilton MUNRO, b. 25 Mar 1883
> 293   ii   Annette Eleanor MUNRO, b. 16 Jul 1884, dy 10 Jan 1885

References:
[1] Leach MSS, p. 6058.

115. JAMES HAMILTON[5] (Samuel Prioleau Hamilton[4], Elizabeth Matthews Heyward[3], Daniel Heyward[2], Thomas Heyward, Jr.[1]) child of Samuel Prioleau Hamilton and Emma Levy was born in Chester, SC on 23 Sep 1865[1], and died in Chester, SC on 12 Oct 1918. He married Bessie Lee DUNBAR in Chester, SC on 24 Dec 1895.[1] She was born in Fairfield County, SC on 9 Mar 1876[1], and died in Chester, SC on 5 Jun 1951. Children:

> 294   i   Herman Prioleau HAMILTON, b. 24 Jun 1901
> 295   ii   James HAMILTON, Jr., b. c. 1904

References:
[1] DSDI Appl# 1315.

119. EDWIN WATKINS HEYWARD[5] (Thomas Savage Heyward, Jr.[4], Thomas Savage Heyward[3], Thomas Heyward[2], Thomas Heyward, Jr.[1]) child of Thomas Savage Heyward, Jr. and Louisa Virginia Watkins was born in Grahamville, SC on 6 Aug 1863, and died in Charleston, SC on 21 May 1888.[1] He married Jane Screven DuBOSE, daughter of Edwin and Jane

Edwards (Screven) DuBose on 15 Nov 1884.[1] She was born in "Harbin Plantation", St. John's, SC on 20 Dec 1864[1], and died on 11 Jun 1939. Children:

+ 296   i   Edwin DuBose HEYWARD, b. 31 Aug 1885
+ 297   ii   Jane DuBose HEYWARD, b. 3 Apr 1887

References:
[1] Leach MSS, p. 6062.

122. WILMOT HOLMES HEYWARD[5] (Thomas Savage Heyward, Jr.[4], Thomas Savage Heyward[3], Thomas Heyward[2], Thomas Heyward, Jr.[1]) child of Thomas Savage Heyward, Jr. and Louisa Virginia Watkins was born in Charleston, SC on 5 Jan 1876[1], and died in Miami, FL on 3 Jun 1936. He married Margaret Kennedy BOYKIN in Charleston, SC in say 1900. She was born in Camden, SC on 18 Nov 1878[1], and died in Decatur, GA on 2 Aug 1962. Children:

+ 298   i   Marguerite Boykin HEYWARD, b. 23 Jan 1901
   299   ii   Nellie Boykin HEYWARD, b. 28 Jul 1903, d. 1956; dsp
   300   iii   Louise Watkins HEYWARD, b. 28 Feb 1906, d. 1994; unm
+ 301   iv   Thomas Savage HEYWARD, b. 30 Mar 1910
   302   v   Martha Alexander HEYWARD, b. 9 Apr 1912 [twin]
   303   vi   Son HEYWARD, b. 9 Apr 1912, dy 9 Apr 1912 [twin]
+ 304   vii   Rives Boykin HEYWARD, b. 6 Nov 1915
   305   viii   Wilmot Holmes HEYWARD, Jr., b. 16 Oct 1919
+ 306   ix   Ned Watkins HEYWARD, b. 10 Nov 1920
+ 307   x   Hunter Boykin HEYWARD, b. 12 Sep 1922

References:
[1] DSDI Appl # 1662, see also PAF data for additional children of this marriage.

126. FLORENCE PERCY HEYWARD[5] (William Nathaniel Heyward[4], Thomas Savage Heyward[3], Thomas Heyward[2], Thomas Heyward, Jr.[1]) child of William Nathaniel Heyward and Louisa Chisolm Guerard was born in Savannah, GA on 9 Mar 1873[1], and died in Charleston, SC in Jan 1939. She married James Edward McTEER on 11 Dec 1894. He was born in Early Branch, SC on 23 Feb 1868[1], and died in Beaufort, SC on 2 Feb 1926. Children:

   308   i   Gerald Heyward McTEER, b. 22 Dec 1895, d. 14 Jan 1960; dsp
   309   ii   Lila Williams McTEER, b. 3 Aug 1897, dy 19 Sep 1897
+ 310   iii   Lila Williams McTEER, b. 6 Jan 1899
+ 311   iv   Louisa Guerard McTEER, b. 14 Feb 1901
+ 312   v   James Edwin McTEER, Jr., b. 2 May 1903

+ 313   vi   Margaret Williamson McTEER, b. 1906
+ 314   vii   Catherine Elliott McTEER, b. 22 Nov 1908
+ 315   viii   Georgianna Hasell McTEER, b. 4 Oct 1913
+ 316   ix   Walter William McTEER, b. 29 Mar 1914
+ 317   x   Florence Percy McTEER, b. 14 Jun 1917

References:
[1] DSDI Appl # 1813, see also PAF data for additional children of this marriage.

127. WILLIAM NATHANIEL HEYWARD, Jr.[5] (William Nathaniel Heyward[4], Thomas Savage Heyward[3], Thomas Heyward[2], Thomas Heyward, Jr.[1]) child of William Nathaniel Heyward and Louisa Chisolm Guerard was born Savannah, GA on 31 May 1874.[1] He married Minnie Louise PERRY-CLAIRE, daughter of William Ellis and Mary Alice (Eaton) Perryclaire on 29 Apr 1908. Children:

318   i   Virginia Eaton HEYWARD, b. 1911, d. 1999; unm
319   ii   William Nathaniel HEYWARD, III, b.10 Jun 1912
320   iii   George Henry HEYWARD, b. c. 1916

References:
[1] Leach MSS, p. 6061.

128. HENRY GUERARD HEYWARD[5] (William Nathaniel Heyward[4], Thomas Savage Heyward[3], Thomas Heyward[2], Thomas Heyward, Jr.[1]) child of William Nathaniel Heyward and Louisa Chisolm Guerard was born in Hardeeville, SC on 12 May 1876[1], and died in Savannah, GA on 13 Mar 1958. He married Floride Dupont PRITCHARD in Savannah, GA on 18 Oct 1907. She was born in Savannah, GA on 10 May 1886[1], and died there in Sep 1969. Children:

+ 321   i   Helen Perryclaire HEYWARD, b. 11 Jul 1908
322   ii   Margaret Pritchard HEYWARD, b. 2 Feb 1910, d, 1990; dsp
323   iii   Lulie Guerard HEYWARD, b. 2 Oct 1912
+ 324   iv   Henry Guerard HEYWARD, Jr., b. 28 Jul 1914
+ 325   v   Catherine Kirk HEYWARD, b. 26 Aug 1917
326   vi   Floride Dupont HEYWARD, b. 8 Mar 1919
327   vii   Thomas Cuthbert HEYWARD, b, 18 May 1921
+ 328   viii   Virginia Rutledge HEYWARD, b. 28 Mar 1923
+ 329   ix   Caroline Screven HEYWARD, b. 30 Apr 1926

References:
[1] DSDI Appl # 2555.

129. LOUISA GUERARD HEYWARD[5] (William Nathaniel Heyward[4], Thomas Savage Heyward[3], Thomas Heyward[2], Thomas Heyward, Jr.[1]) child of William Nathaniel Heyward and Louisa Chisolm Guerard was born in Hardeeville, SC on 30 Sep 1877[1], and died in 1927. She married George A. REEVES in Jun 1902. Child:

> 330   i   Alice Cuthbert Heyward REEVES, b. c. 1904

References:
[1] Leach MSS, p. 6061.

131. WILLIAM BURROUGHS SMITH HEYWARD[5] (Andrew Hasell Heyward[4], Thomas Savage Heyward[3], Thomas Heyward[2], Thomas Heyward, Jr.[1]) child of Andrew Hasell Heyward and Frances Rosa Smith was born in Charleston, SC on 1 Jan 1867, and died on 27 Feb 1896.[1] He married Mary Memminger PINCKNEY, daughter of Charles C. and Lucy (Memminger) Pinckney in say 1894. She was born in Charleston, SC on 26 Aug 1869[1], and died in Blowing Rock, NC on 7 Sep 1902. Child:

> +   331   i   William Smith HEYWARD, b. 23 Mar 1895

References:
[1] Leach MSS, p. 6061 as to date and place of birth; year of death from PAF data. [2] PAF data.

139. ANDREW HASELL HEYWARD, Jr.[5] (Andrew Hasell Heyward[4], Thomas Savage Heyward[3], Thomas Heyward[2], Thomas Heyward, Jr.[1]) child of Andrew Hasell Heyward and Frances Rosa Smith was born in Charleston, SC on 11 Jan 1883[1], and died in 1952. He married Marian SPEER in say 1903. She was born in 1874[2], and died in 1970. Children:

> +   332   i   Emory Speer HEYWARD, b. 3 May 1904
> +   333   ii   Andrew Hasell HEYWARD, III, b. 14 Jul 1905
> +   334   iii Eustace Willoughby Speer HEYWARD, b. 9 Jul 1908
> +   335   iv   Marion Speer HEYWARD, b. 17 Dec 1917

References:
[1] Leach MSS, p. 6061 as to date and place of birth. [2] Heyward Family Association HENRY data.

140. SAVAGE HEYWARD LYNAH[5] (Ella Louise Heyward[4], Thomas Savage Heyward[3], Thomas Heyward[2], Thomas Heyward, Jr.[1]) child of Ella Louise Heyward and John Heyward Lynah was born in Charleston, SC on 25 Jun 1879[1], and died on 27 Jul 1927. He married Anne Warren BUTLER in say 1906. She was born in 1879[2], and died on 17 Nov 1953. Child:

> 336   i   Mary Manning LYNAH, b. 3 Nov 1911

References:
[1] Leach MSS, p. 6062 as to date and place of birth. [2] Heyward Family Association HENRY data.

141. JAMES LYNAH[5] (Ella Louise Heyward[4], Thomas Savage Heyward[3], Thomas Heyward[2], Thomas Heyward, Jr.[1]) child of Ella Louise Heyward and John Heyward Lynah was born in Charleston, SC on 6 Oct 1881[1], and died in Savannah, GA on 24 Feb 1956. He married Elizabeth Eugenia BECK-WITH, daughter of Dr. George and Carrie (Kitchell) Beckwith on 23 Dec 1905. She was born in NYC on 8 Jan 1881[2], and died in Oct 1970. Children:

+ 337　　i　Elizabeth Beckwith LYNAH, b. 1906
+ 338　　ii　Maria Glover LYNAH, b. 1908
+ 339　　iii　Ella Louise Heyward LYNAH, b. 1910

References:
[1] Leach MSS, p. 6062 as to date and place of birth. [2] Heyward Family Association HENRY data.

143. ELOISE LYNAH[5] (Ella Louise Heyward[4], Thomas Savage Heyward[3], Thomas Heyward[2], Thomas Heyward, Jr.[1]) child of Ella Louise Heyward and John Heyward Lynah was born in Hardeeville, SC on 15 Mar 1887[1], and died in Savannah, GA on 18 Oct 1973. She married Paul Trapier PALMER in Savannah, GA on 29 Jun 1920. He was born in Woodruff, SC on 25 Oct 1886[1], and died in Wadmalaw Island, SC on 26 Dec 1948. Children:

+ 340　　i　Ella Heyward PALMER, b. 10 Jul 1921
+ 341　　ii　Paul Trapier PALMER, Jr., b. 24 Feb 1924
+ 342　　iii　Lilly Lynah PALMER, b. 20 Sep 1925
+ 343　　iv　James Lynah PALMER, b. 10 Feb 1927
+ 344　　v　Anne Cuthbert PALMER, b. 7 Aug 1930

References:
[1] DSDI Appl # 2501.

144. JOHN HEYWARD LYNAH, Jr.[5] (Ella Louise Heyward[4], Thomas Savage Heyward[3], Thomas Heyward[2], Thomas Heyward, Jr.[1]) child of Ella Louise Heyward and John Heyward Lynah was born on 19 Dec 1891[1], and died in Savannah, GA on 20 Sep 1935. He married Augusta Clayatt HOWARD on 14 Feb 1917. She was born on 25 Jan 1897[1], and died on 23 Aug 1967. Children:

+ 345　　i　John Heyward LYNAH, III, b. 1917
+ 346　　ii　Mary Howard LYNAH, b. 1923
+ 347　　iii　Savage Heyward LYNAH, b. 1924 [twin]
+ 348　　iv　Wallace Howard LYNAH, b. 1924 [twin]

References:
[1] Heyward Family Association HENRY data.

147. ANNE CUTHBERT LYNAH[5] (Ella Louise Heyward[4], Thomas Savage Heyward[3], Thomas Heyward[2], Thomas Heyward, Jr.[1]) child of Ella Louise Heyward and John Heyward Lynah was born on 8 Oct 1899.[1] She married Reider Arnold TROSDAL in say 1918. He was born on 14 Feb 1880.[1] Child:

+ 349   i   Reider TROSDAL, b. c. 1920
References:
[1] Heyward Family Association HENRY data.

148. JOHN BOYKIN HEYWARD, Jr.[5] (John Boykin Heyward[4], Thomas Savage Heyward[3], Thomas Heyward[2], Thomas Heyward, Jr.[1]) child of John Boykin Heyward and Martha Hayes Pyatt was born in Jacksonville, FL on 26 Feb 1887[1], and died in Oakland, CA on 22 Nov 1962. He married Jane Camp ATWOOD in Alameda, CA on 23 Apr 1914. She was born in Macon, GA on 14 Nov 1890[1], and died in Oakland, CA on 7 Dec 1958. Child:

+ 350   i   William Henry HEYWARD, b. 8 Oct 1916
References:
[1] DSDI Appl # 2274.

154. MARTHA HORRY HOWARD[5] (Annie Heyward Webb[4], Elizabeth Savage Heyward[3], Thomas Heyward[2], Thomas Heyward, Jr.[1]) child of Annie Heyward Webb and her 2nd husband Thomas Heyward Howard was born in Grahamville, SC on 11 Jan 1872.[1] She married John Elmore MARTIN in say 1893. He was born in 1858.[2] Children:

  351   i   Annie Webb MARTIN, b. c. 1895
+ 352   ii   Daisy Vincent MARTIN, b. c. 1897
  353   iii   Martha Soul MARTIN, b. c. 1899
+ 354   iv   John Vincent MARTIN, b. 1901
References:
[1] Leach MSS, p. 6063 as to date and place of birth. [2] Heyward Family Association HENRY data.

179. ELISE HEYWARD[5] (Jacob Guerard Heyward[4], George Cuthbert Heyward[3], Thomas Heyward[2], Thomas Heyward, Jr.[1]) child of Jacob Guerard Heyward and Pauline de Caradeux was born in Montmorenci, Aiken County, SC on 9 May 1868[1], and died in 1942. She married John Smallbrook HOWKINS in say 1890. He was born in 1858[2], and died in 1912. Children:

+ 355   i   John Smallbrook HOWKINS, Jr., b. 1892
+ 356   ii   Guerard Heyward HOWKINS, b. 1894
References:
[1] Leach MSS, p. 6066 as to date and place of birth. [2] Heyward Family Association HENRY data.

185. FRANCIS de CARADEUX HEYWARD[5] (Jacob Guerard Heyward[4], George Cuthbert Heyward[3], Thomas Heyward[2], Thomas Heyward, Jr.[1]) child of Jacob Guerard Heyward and Pauline de Caradeux was born in Savannah, GA on 22 Mar 1880.[1] He married Virginia KREICHBAUM in say 1903. Child:

+ 357   i   Francis de Caradeux HEYWARD, Jr., b. c. 1905

References:
[1] Leach MSS, p. 6066 as to date and place of birth. [2] Heyward Family Association HENRY data.

190. ROLAND STEINER HEYWARD[5] (James Cuthbert Heyward[4], George Cuthbert Heyward[3], Thomas Heyward[2], Thomas Heyward, Jr.[1]) child of James Cuthbert Heyward and Sarah Connelly Taylor was born in Holcombe, GA on 9 Jul 1884[1], and died in 1954. He married Theo Belle FARRAR in say 1910. She was born in 1893[2], and died in 1978. Children:

358   i   Roland Steiner HEYWARD, Jr., b. 1911, dy 1911
+ 359   ii   Evelyn HEYWARD, b. 1914
+ 360   iii   Benjamin Farrar HEYWARD, b. 8 Jul 1920

References:
[1] Leach MSS, p. 6066 as to date and place of birth. [2] Heyward Family Association HENRY data.

191. HARVEY CUTHBERT HEYWARD[5] (James Cuthbert Heyward[4], George Cuthbert Heyward[3], Thomas Heyward[2], Thomas Heyward, Jr.[1]) child of James Cuthbert Heyward and Sarah Connelly Taylor was born in Waynesboro, Burke County, GA on 18 Sep 1886[1], and died in Charleston, SC on 4 Aug 1941. He married Sarah Elizabeth HOWE in Savannah, GA on 29 Aug 1910. She was born in Chatham County, GA on 24 May 1891[1], and died in Charleston, SC on 8 Jan 1981. Child:

+ 361   i   Ethel Loraine HEYWARD, b. 23 Jun 1922

References:
[1] SAR Appl # 126053.

193. GEORGE CUTHBERT HEYWARD, III[5] (George Cuthbert Heyward, Jr.[4], George Cuthbert Heyward[3], Thomas Heyward[2], Thomas Heyward, Jr.[1]) child of George Cuthbert Heyward, Jr. and Margaret Evance Doar was born in Savannah, GA on 7 Feb 1878[1], and died in Savannah, GA on 13 Sep 1968. He married Alice Stuart HUNTER in Philadelphia, PA on 8 Nov 1911. She was born in Philadelphia, PA on 30 Jan 1887[1], and died in Savannah, GA on 18 Oct 1966. Children:

362   i   Stuart HEYWARD, b. 18 Nov 1912, dy 23 Nov 1912
363   ii   Margaret HEYWARD, b. 15 Dec 1913, dy 2 Jun 1918

364   iii   Alice Stuart HEYWARD, b. 7 Mar 1915, d. 2 Mar 1997;
             unm
365   iv   Anne Cuthbert HEYWARD, b. 7 Mar 1917, dy 15 Jun 1918
+ 366   v   Marjory HEYWARD, b. 16 Nov 1918
+ 367   vi   George Cuthbert HEYWARD, IV, b. 17 Oct 1920
+ 368   vii Allan McAlpin HEYWARD, b. 14 May 1922

References:
[1] DSDI Appl # 1888 & Heyward Family Association HENRY data for additional children of this marriage.

194. STEPHEN DOAR HEYWARD[5] (George Cuthbert Heyward, Jr.[4], George Cuthbert Heyward[3], Thomas Heyward[2], Thomas Heyward, Jr.[1]) child of George Cuthbert Heyward, Jr. and Margaret Evance Doar was born in Savannah, GA on 30 Jun 1880.[1] He married Blanche Eleanor ALLEN in say 1907. Children:

369   i   Helen Margaret HEYWARD, b. c. 1909
370   ii   Stephen Doar HEYWARD, Jr., b. c. 1912

References:
[1] Heyward Family Association HENRY data.

202. ROBERT CLARENCE HEYWARD[5] (Robert Chisolm Heyward[4], George Cuthbert Heyward[3], Thomas Heyward[2], Thomas Heyward, Jr.[1]) child of Robert Chisolm Heyward and Mary Elizabeth Stoney was born in Bluffton, SC on 12 Mar 1878[1], and died in Myrtle Beach, SC on 17 May 1960. He married Sallie Othello LONG in Pelzer, SC on 14 Mar 1899.[1] She was born in Greenville County, SC on 4 Sep 1882[1], and died in Pelzer, SC on 27 May 1924. Children:

371   i   Ralph Clarence HEYWARD, b. 11 Dec 1900, dy 1901
+ 372   ii   Mary Elizabeth HEYWARD, b. 14 Feb 1902
+ 373   iii   George Cuthbert HEYWARD, b. 25 Dec 1903
+ 374   iv   Thomas Savage HEYWARD, b. 4 Nov 1905
+ 375   v   Corinne HEYWARD, b. 8 Nov 1908
+ 376   vi   Josephine Stoney HEYWARD, b. 20 Dec 1911
377   vii   Robert Chisolm HEYWARD, b. 1914, dy 2 May 1914
+ 378   viii Robert Clarence HEYWARD, Jr., b. 12 Dec 1915

References:
[1] DSDI Appl # 1719 & SAR Appl # 132490.

204. DANIEL HASELL HEYWARD[5] (Robert Chisolm Heyward[4], George Cuthbert Heyward[3], Thomas Heyward[2], Thomas Heyward, Jr.[1]) child of Robert Chisolm Heyward and Mary Elizabeth Stoney was born in Bluffton, SC on 30 Dec 1883[1], and died in Bluffton, SC on 1 Apr 1963. He married

May MULLIGAN on 22 Apr 1906. She was born in Beaufort County, SC on 14 Jul 1890[2], and died in Hilton Head, SC on 22 Jul 1979. Children:

+ 379　　i　Gaillard Stoney HEYWARD, b. 8 Jan 1910
+ 380　　ii　James Edward HEYWARD, b. 2 Mar 1912
+ 381　　iii　Daniel Hasell HEYWARD, Jr., b. 13 Mar 1915
+ 382　　iv　Joseph Cuthbert HEYWARD, b. 24 Aug 1918
+ 383　　v　Ella Elizabeth HEYWARD, b. 8 Mar 1924

References:
[1] Leach MSS, p. 6067 as to place and date of birth, although several DSDI Applications report 31 Dec 1881. [2] DSDI Appl # 1634; see also Heyward Family Association HENRY System data for additional children of this marriage.

206. SELINA HEYWARD[5] (Thomas Daniel Heyward[4], George Cuthbert Heyward[3], Thomas Heyward[2], Thomas Heyward, Jr.[1]) child of Thomas Daniel Heyward and Eliza Selina Johnstone was born in Savannah, GA on 10 Mar 1887[1], and died on 25 Nov 1956. She married Rieman McNAMARA on 17 Oct 1922. He was born in NYC on 23 Sep 1890.[1] Child:

+ 384　　i　Rieman McNAMARA, Jr., b. 25 Jul 1928

References:
[1] DSDI Appl # 856.

207. ISABEL HEYWARD[5] (Thomas Daniel Heyward[4], George Cuthbert Heyward[3], Thomas Heyward[2], Thomas Heyward, Jr.[1]) child of Thomas Daniel Heyward and Eliza Selina Johnstone was born in Savannah, GA on 20 Jun 1890[1], and died in Savannah, GA on 5 May 1968. She married Emmet Cheatham WILSON on 14 Apr 1914. He was born in Dahlonaga, GA on 15 Feb 1887[1], and died in Richmond, VA on 7 Apr 1977. Children:

+ 385　　i　Isabel Heyward WILSON, b. 15 Mar 1915
+ 386　　ii　Dorothy Heyward WILSON, b. 26 Jun 1916
+ 387　　iii　Walter Stephen WILSON, b. 13 Jun 1918
　388　　iv　Caroline Price WILSON, b. 11 Sep 1920, d. 1994; dsp
+ 389　　v　Thomas Daniel Heyward WILSON, b. 19 May 1926
+ 390　　vi　Helen Heyward WILSON, b. 24 Oct 1928

References:
[1] DSDI Appl # 1919.

208. ELIZABETH HEYWARD[5] (Thomas Daniel Heyward[4], George Cuthbert Heyward[3], Thomas Heyward[2], Thomas Heyward, Jr.[1]) child of Thomas Daniel Heyward and Eliza Selina Johnstone was born in Savannah, GA on 4 Sep 1892[1], and died in Savannah, GA on 22 Oct 1972. She married George Hazelhurst LaBRUCE, Jr., son of George Hazelhurst and Katherine

(Fitzsimmons) LaBruce on 16 Dec 1920. He was born in Georgetown, SC on 1 Oct 1886[2], and died in Charleston, SC on 15 Jun 1953. Children:

+ 391   i   Elizabeth Heyward LaBRUCE, b. 30 Jul 1922
+ 392   ii   Katherine Fitzsimons LaBRUCE, b. 5 Oct 1923
+ 393   iii   Selina Johnstone LaBRUCE, b. 1 May 1927

References:
[1] DSDI Appl # 1079; although the year of birth is in error - it reports 1894, but should read 1892. [2] DSDI Appl # 1079. This sketch is a good example of much confusion generated by families that do not provide quality documentation of the events of their ancestors lives. The Genealogist for the Heyward Family Association has received information from the Gignilliat Genealogy, from individual family members (most of whom do not provide any sources or documentation), and from SAR and DAR applications these members supply. The reader should note that older such Society Applications usually do not contain the documentation required to prove matters regarding the place or date of the event recited. Therefore, these Societies have in more recent years, required new applicants, using the same ancestor, to research and discover the missing documentation. This same approach to proper research and documentation discovery will be a requirement in Family Histories of the future. If you cannot prove it, you cannot claim it!

212. MARY HAMILTON HEYWARD[5] (Thomas Savage Heyward[4], George Cuthbert Heyward[3], Thomas Heyward[2], Thomas Heyward, Jr.[1]) child of Thomas Savage Heyward and Mary Hamilton Seabrook was born in Grahamville, SC on 10 Sep 1888[1], and died in Savannah, GA on 21 Nov 1952. She married Edward Bell PATRICK in Savannah, GA on 10 May 1917. He was born in Grahamville, SC on 13 Jul 1893[1], and died in Savannah, GA on 20 Apr 1934. Children:

394   i   Edward Bell PATRICK, Jr., b. 15 Sep 1918
395   ii   Heyward PATRICK, b. c. 1920

References:
[1] DSDI Appl # 2177.

213. EDWARD BARNWELL WALKER, Jr.[5] (Elizabeth Guerard Heyward[4], George Cuthbert Heyward[3], Thomas Heyward[2], Thomas Heyward, Jr.[1]) child of Elizabeth Guerard Heyward and Edward Barnwell Walker was born in Beaufort, SC on 3 Sep 1886.[1] He married Sarah Donon PINCKNEY in Columbia, SC on 17 Jan 1912. Children:

+ 396   i   Pinckney Heyward WALKER, b. 11 May 1913
+ 397   ii   Joseph Rogers WALKER, b. c. 1915
+ 398   iii   Edward Barnwell WALKER, III, b. 26 Aug 1918

References:
[1] Leach MSS, p. 6068, see also SAR Appl # 79784.

218. GEORGE HEYWARD WALKER[5] (Elizabeth Guerard Heyward[4], George Cuthbert Heyward[3], Thomas Heyward[2], Thomas Heyward, Jr.[1]) child of Elizabeth Guerard Heyward and Edward Barnwell Walker was born about 1886.[1] He married Ellen WEST in say 1911. Child:

399   i   Elizabeth Heyward WALKER, b. c. 1913

References:
[1] Heyward Family Association HENRY data.

220. WILLIAM GUERARD HEYWARD[5] (John Alexander Heyward[4], George Cuthbert Heyward[3], Thomas Heyward[2], Thomas Heyward, Jr.[1]) child of John Alexander Heyward and Helen Mallard was born about 1890.[1] He married Gertrude EXLEY in say 1922. Children:

+ 400   i   Sarah Gertrude HEYWARD, b. 1925
+ 401   ii   Mary Katherine HEYWARD, b. 9 Sep 1927

References:
[1] Heyward Family Association HENRY data.

221. THOMAS FLEMING HEYWARD[5] (John Alexander Heyward[4], George Cuthbert Heyward[3], Thomas Heyward[2], Thomas Heyward, Jr.[1]) child of John Alexander Heyward and Helen Mallard was born in Darien, GA on 18 Apr 1893[1], and died on 16 Jan 1968. He married Ella Nora WALTON in say 1947. Children:

+ 402   i   Nora Lena HEYWARD, b. 19 Jan 1950
+ 403   ii   Thomas Fleming HEYWARD, Jr., b. 18 Jan 1953

References:
[1] Heyward Family Association HENRY data.

223. WILLIAM ROBERT GIGNILLIAT[5] (Mary Caroline Heyward[4], George Cuthbert Heyward[3], Thomas Heyward[2], Thomas Heyward, Jr.[1]) child of Mary Caroline Heyward and William LeSerurier Gignilliat was born in Pineora, Effingham County, GA on 29 Aug 1892[1], and died in Savannah, GA on 8 Mar 1965. He married Maria OLMSTEAD, daughter of Percival and Mina (Hetterich) Olmstead on 14 Oct 1914. She was born in Anniston, AL on 23 Mar 1890.[1] Children:

+ 404   i   Caroline Heyward GIGNILLIAT, b. 1 Aug 1915
+ 405   ii   William Robert GIGNILLIAT, Jr., 17 Jul 1918
+ 406   iii   Jean Frances GIGNILLIAT, b. 4 Dec 1927

References:
[1] Heyward Family Association HENRY data.

231. ELEUTHERA du PONT BRADFORD[5] (Edward Green Bradford[4], Mary Alicia Heyward[3], James Hamilton Heyward[2], Thomas Heyward, Jr.[1])

child of Edward Green Bradford and Eleuthera Paulina du Pont was born in Wilmington, DE on 12 Jul 1873[1], and died on 14 Feb 1953. She married Henry Belin du PONT in Wilmington, DE on 15 Sep 1897.[1] He was born in New Castle County, DE on 5 Nov 1873[1], and died in Phoenix, AZ on 8 Jul 1902. Child:

407   i   Henry Belin du PONT, b. 23 Jul 1898

References:
[1] DSDI Appl # 609.

238. SHUBRICK HEYWARD[5] (Wilson Prestman Heyward[4], James Francis Heyward[3], James Hamilton Heyward[2], Thomas Heyward, Jr.[1]) child of William Prestman Heyward and Elizabeth Skinner Wilson was born in Baltimore, MD on 17 Jul 1886.[1] He married Jean Sinclair VENABLE, daughter of Samuel Woodson and Jean Sinclair (Armistead) Venable in say 1915. She was born in Danville, VA on 19 Jun 1899.[2] Child:

+ 408   i   Jean Sinclair HEYWARD, b. 31 Jul 1917

References:
[1] Leach MSS, p. 6073 as to place and date of birth. [2] Heyward Family Association HENRY data.

242. NELLA BURNET[5] (Emma Heyward Howard[4], Elizabeth Savage Parker[3], Elizabeth Savage Heyward[2], Thomas Heyward, Jr.[1]) child of Emma Heyward Howard and Henry DeSaussure Burnet was born about 1865.[1] She married Alexander MacDougal STODDARD in say 1886. Children:

409   i   Anne Rutledge STODDARD, b. c. 1888
410   ii Florence STODDARD, b. c. 1890
411   iii Henri deSaussure STODDARD, b. c. 1894

References:
[1] Heyward Family Association HENRY data.

244. ELIZABETH HOWARD BURNET[5] (Emma Heyward Howard[4], Elizabeth Savage Parker[3], Elizabeth Savage Heyward[2], Thomas Heyward, Jr.[1]) child of Emma Heyward Howard and Henry DeSaussure Burnet was born in Grahamville, SC on 19 Aug 1870[1], and died in Camden, SC on 16 Jan 1920. She married Burwell Boykin CLARKE in Grahamville, SC on 19 Nov 1890.[1] He was born in Camden, SC on 21 Nov 1866[1], and died in Sumter, SC on 29 Mar 1928. Children:

+ 412   i   Burwell Boykin CLARKE, Jr., b. 23 Aug 1902
+ 413   ii Thomas Henry CLARKE, b. 1904
+ 414   iii Albertus Moore CLARKE, b. 1907

References:
[1] DSDI Appl # 2490, see also Heyward Family Association HENRY data for additional children of this marriage.

245. HENRY HEYWARD BURNET[5] (Emma Heyward Howard[4], Elizabeth Savage Parker[3], Elizabeth Savage Heyward[2], Thomas Heyward, Jr.[1]) child of Emma Heyward Howard and Henry DeSaussure Burnet was born in Grahamville, SC on 13 Feb 1873[1], and died in Waycross, GA on 7 Jun 1944. He married Valeria NORTH in Charleston, SCon 17 Jun 1900.[1] She was born in Charleston, SC on 5 Nov 1875[1], and died in Atlanta, GA on 12 Apr 1941. Children:

    415   i   Katherine Emory BURNET, b. 1901, d. 1992; dsp
+ 416   ii Henry Heyward BURNET, Jr., b. 23 Aug 1902
+ 417   iii Valeria North BURNET, b. 17 Mar 1905
+ 418   iv Emma Heyward BURNET, b. 25 May 1908

References:
[1] DSDI Appl # 2267.

247. HENRIETTA PARKER HOWARD[5] (Henry Parker Howard[4], Elizabeth Savage Parker[3], Elizabeth Savage Heyward[2], Thomas Heyward, Jr.[1]) child of Henry Parker Howard and Mary Huberly Glover Jenkins was born in Grahamville, SC in 1879[1], and died in 1963. She married Reuben Luckie ROCKWELL in say 1900. He was born in Thomasville, GA in 1858[1], and died in 1920. Children:

    419   i   Margaret Glover ROCKWELL, b. 1912, d. 1965; unm
+ 420   ii Reuben Luckie ROCKWELL, Jr., b. 1914

References:
[1] Heyward Family Association HENRY data.

248. ROBERT EMMETT JENKINS HOWARD[5] (Henry Parker Howard[4], Elizabeth Savage Parker[3], Elizabeth Savage Heyward[2], Thomas Heyward, Jr.[1]) child of Henry Parker Howard and Mary Huberly Glover Jenkins was born in Grahamville, SC on 10 Oct 1890[1], and died on 1 Jul 1916. He married Mary Josephine WATTERS on 7 Oct 1906. She was born in Burnswick, GA on 7 Mar 1883[1], and died in Savannah, GA on 10 Apr 1960. Children:

+ 421   i   Mary Louise Folliard HOWARD, b. 25 Aug 1907
    422   ii Robert Emmett HOWARD, b. 3 Oct 1909, d. 23 Feb 1979; unm
+ 423   iii Josephine Silverius HOWARD, b. 20 Jun 1912
+ 424   iv Katherine Anne HOWARD, b. 26 Jan 1915

References:
[1] Heyward Family Association HENRY data.

253. HENRY PARKER HOWARD, Jr.[5] (Henry Parker Howard[4], Elizabeth Savage Parker[3], Elizabeth Savage Heyward[2], Thomas Heyward, Jr.[1]) child of Henry Parker Howard and Mary Huberly Glover Jenkins was born in Grahamville, SC in 1893[1], and died in 1974. He married Norma LUBS in say 1919. Child:

    425   i   Elizabeth HOWARD, b. c. 1921
References:
[1] Heyward Family Association HENRY data.

254. LILLIAN JENKINS HOWARD[5] (Henry Parker Howard[4], Elizabeth Savage Parker[3], Elizabeth Savage Heyward[2], Thomas Heyward, Jr.[1]) child of Henry Parker Howard and Mary Huberly Glover Jenkins was born about 1895[1], and died in 1961. She married Martin STERLING in say 1900. Children:
+ 426   i   Hazel Howard STERLING, b. 1908
+ 427   ii   Virginia Dare STERLING, b. 1909
References:
[1] Heyward Family Association HENRY System data.

SIXTH GENERATION

260. WILLIAM AEMILIUS IRVING[6] (Mary Middleton Hamilton[5], Daniel Heyward Hamilton[4], Elizabeth Matthews Heyward[3], Daniel Heyward[2], Thomas Heyward, Jr.[1]) child of Mary Middleton Hamilton and John Beaufaine Irving was born in Charleston, SC on 23 Feb 1860.[1] He married Anna Josephine DAY, daughter of James and Annie (Dooley) Day on 11 Feb 1883.[1] She was born in Jersey City, NJ on 4 Jan 1866.[1] Children:
    428   i   William John IRVING, b. 19 Dec 1884, dy 9 Mar 1891
    429   ii   Mary Hamilton IRVING, b. 28 Oct 1886
    430   iii   Jane Wentworth IRVING, b. 18 Oct 1888
    431   iv   Anna IRVING, b. 6 Aug 1890, dy 11 Aug 1890
    432   v   John IRVING, b. 11 Nov 1891, dy 11 Nov 1891
    433   vi   Florence IRVING, b. 19 Oct 1893, dy 21 Oct 1893
References:
[1] Leach MSS, pp. 6052-6053.

261. HEYWARD HAMILTON IRVING[6] (Mary Middleton Hamilton[5], Daniel Heyward Hamilton[4], Elizabeth Matthews Heyward[3], Daniel Heyward[2], Thomas Heyward, Jr.[1]) child of Mary Middleton Hamilton and John Beaufaine Irving was born in Charleston, SC on 27 Sep 1861.[1] He married

Helen KEILEY, daughter of Jeremiah and Julia (Walsh) Keily on 14 Oct 1885.[1] She was born in Brooklyn, NY on 9 Nov 1865.[1] Child:

434   i   Lillian Middleton IRVING, b. 29 Oct 1886

References:
[1] Leach MSS, p. 6053.

262. EMMA CRÜGER IRVING⁶ (Mary Middleton Hamilton⁵, Daniel Heyward Hamilton⁴, Elizabeth Matthews Heyward³, Daniel Heyward², Thomas Heyward, Jr.¹) child of Mary Middleton Hamilton and John Beaufaine Irving was born in Columbia, SC on 17 Mar 1863.[1] She married George Dummer Brower ANCHER, daughter of Frederick Cornelius Brower and Georgine Lindsay (Dummer) Ancher on 3 Feb 1879.[1] He was born in Jersey City, NJ on 23 May 1856.[1] Children:

435   i   Frederick Lindsay ANCHER, b. 23 Sep 1880
436   ii   John Beaufaine ANCHER, b. 27 Sep 1881, dy 5 Jan 1882

References:
[1] Leach MSS, p. 6053.

264. REBECCA MIDDLETON IRVING⁶ (Mary Middleton Hamilton⁵, Daniel Heyward Hamilton⁴, Elizabeth Matthews Heyward³, Daniel Heyward², Thomas Heyward, Jr.¹) child of Mary Middleton Hamilton and John Beaufaine Irving was born in Greenville, NJ on 18 Jul 1866.[1] She married Arthur Joseph NOONAN, son of William and Margaret (Dobbins) Noonan on 22 Jun 1885.[1] He was born in NYC on 6 Jan 1861.[1] Children:

437   i   Rebecca Eleanor NOONAN, b. 1 Oct 1887
438   ii   Elizabeth Georgine NOONAN, b. 5 Oct 1890
439   iii   Arthur Joseph NOONAN, Jr., b. 19 Jul 1892

References:
[1] Leach MSS, p. 6053.

265. MARY ELIZABETH IRVING⁶ (Mary Middleton Hamilton⁵, Daniel Heyward Hamilton⁴, Elizabeth Matthews Heyward³, Daniel Heyward², Thomas Heyward, Jr.¹) child of Mary Middleton Hamilton and John Beaufaine Irving was born in Greenville, NJ on 17 May 1871.[1] She married Charles Cornelius NOONAN, son of William and Margaret (Dobbins) Noonan on 27 Dec 1891.[1] He was born in NYC on 9 Jan 1853.[1] Child:

440   i   Margaret Elizabeth NOONAN, b. 14 Apr 1893

References:
[1] Leach MSS, p. 6053.

272. DANIEL HEYWARD HAMILTON, III⁶ (Daniel Heyward Hamilton, Jr.⁵, Daniel Heyward Hamilton⁴, Elizabeth Matthews Heyward³, Daniel

Heyward[2], Thomas Heyward, Jr.[1]) child of Daniel Heyward Hamilton, Jr. and Frances Gray Roulhac was born in Hillsborough, NC on 14 Feb 1872.[1] He married Frances OUER in say 1897. Children:

    441   i   Daniel Heyward HAMILTON, IV, b. c. 1899
    442   ii   Frances HAMILTON, b. c. 1901
    443   iii   Adgate HAMILTON, b. c. 1904
    444   iv   James HAMILTON, b. c. 1907

References:
[1] Leach MSS, p. 6054 reports date and place of birth; James Heyward, Secretary of the Heyward Family Association furnished a PAF Data printout of names of members, but without much by way of dates, places, or documentation.

273. JOSEPH GREGORIE HAMILTON[6] (Daniel Heyward Hamilton, Jr.[5], Daniel Heyward Hamilton[4], Elizabeth Matthews Heyward[3], Daniel Heyward[2], Thomas Heyward, Jr.[1]) child of Daniel Heyward Hamilton, Jr. and Frances Gray Roulhac was born in Hillsborough, NC on 6 Aug 1878.[1] He married Mary THOMPSON in say 1903. Children:

    445   i   Roulhac HAMILTON, b. c. 1905
    446   ii   Daniel HAMILTON, b. c. 1908

References:
[1] Leach MSS, p. 6054.

276. ALBERT HENRY STODDARD, Jr.[6] (Elizabeth Heyward Hamilton[5], Daniel Heyward Hamilton[4], Elizabeth Matthews Heyward[3], Daniel Heyward[2], Thomas Heyward, Jr.[1]) child of Elizabeth Heyward Hamilton and Albert Henry Stoddard was born in Greenville, NJ on 15 Sep 1872.[1] He married Evelyn Byrd POLLARD in say 1901. Children:

    447   i   Daniel Heyward STODDARD, b. c. 1902
    448   ii   Spotswood STODDARD, b. c. 1903
    449   iii   Albert STODDARD, b. c. 1906

References:
[1] Leach MSS, p. 6056 reports date and place of birth; James Heyward, Secretary of the Heyward Family Association furnished a PAF Data printout of names of members, but without much by way of dates, places, or documentation.

280. DANIEL HEYWARD HAMILTON[6] (Miles Brewton Hamilton[5], Daniel Heyward Hamilton[4], Elizabeth Matthews Heyward[3], Daniel Heyward[2], Thomas Heyward, Jr.[1]) child of Miles Brewton Hamilton and Mary Ravenal Pringle was born in Charleston, SC on 13 Feb 1893[1], and died in Birmingham, AL on 2 May 1966. He married Margaret MUNSELL in Chestnut Hill, MA on 16 Jun 1917. She was born in Paris, FRANCE on 24 Mar 1897.[1] Children:

+   450   i   Daniel Heyward HAMILTON, Jr., b. 10 Apr 1918
+   451   ii Margot HAMILTON, b. 1 Aug 1920
References:
[1] DSDI Appl #1564

282. MARY PRINGLE HAMILTON[6] (Miles Brewton Hamilton[5], Daniel Heyward Hamilton[4], Elizabeth Matthews Heyward[3], Daniel Heyward[2], Thomas Heyward, Jr.[1]) child of Miles Brewton Hamilton and Mary Ravenal Pringle was born about 1896[1], and died in 1987. She married Edward MANIGAULT in say 1918. Children:
+   452   i   Mary MANIGAULT, b. c. 1921
+   453   ii Peter MANIGAULT, b. 13 Jan 1927
References:
[1] James Heyward, Secretary of the Heyward Family Association furnished a PAF Data printout in the HENRY numbering System, of names of members, but without much by way of dates, places, or documentation.

284. REBECCA HAMILTON RYAN[6] (Rebecca Motte Hamilton[5], Daniel Heyward Hamilton[4], Elizabeth Matthews Heyward[3], Daniel Heyward[2], Thomas Heyward, Jr.[1]) child of Rebecca Motte Hamilton and Arthur Blackwell Ryan was born in Charleston, SC on 18 Jun 1880.[1] She married Allan CLEPHONE in say 1900. Children:
    454   i   Mary CLEPHONE, b. c. 1901
    455   ii Arthur CELPHONE, b. c. 1904
References:
[1] Leach MSS, p. 6057 reports date and place of birth.

285. MARTHA RYAN[6] (Rebecca Motte Hamilton[5], Daniel Heyward Hamilton[4], Elizabeth Matthews Heyward[3], Daniel Heyward[2], Thomas Heyward, Jr.[1]) child of Rebecca Motte Hamilton and Arthur Blackwell Ryan was born in Charleston, SC on 30 Nov 1882.[1] She married Robert CATLETT in say 1901. Children:
    456   i   Robert CATLETT, Jr.,b. c. 1902
    457   ii   Martha CATLETT, b. c. 1904
    458   iii Rebecca CATLETT, b. c. 1907
    459   iv   Arthur CATLETT, b. c. 1910
References:
[1] Leach MSS, p. 6057 reports date and place of birth.

287. LOUISE KING RYAN[6] (Rebecca Motte Hamilton[5], Daniel Heyward Hamilton[4], Elizabeth Matthews Heyward[3], Daniel Heyward[2], Thomas Heyward, Jr.[1]) child of Rebecca Motte Hamilton and Arthur Blackwell Ryan was born in Charleston, SC on 31 Mar 1887.[1] She married William GILES in say 1906. Children:

    460   i William GILES, Jr., b. c. 1907
    461   ii Louise GILES, b. c. 1909

References:
[1] Leach MSS, p. 6057 reports date and place of birth.

296. EDWIN DuBOSE HEYWARD[6] (Edwin Watkins Heyward[5], Thomas Savage Heyward, Jr.[4], Thomas Savage Heyward[3], Thomas Heyward[2], Thomas Heyward, Jr.[1]) child of Edwin Watkins Heyward and Jane Screven DuBose was born in Charleston, SC on 31 Aug 1885[1], and died Tryon, Polk County, NC on 16 Jun 1940. He married Dorothy Hartzell KUHNS in say 1919. She was born in Wooster, OH in 1890[2], and died in 1961. Child:

    462   i Jennifer DuBosae HEYWARD, b. 1930

References:
[1] Leach MSS, p. 6062 reports date and place of birth. [2] Heyward Family Association PAF HENRY System data printout.

297. JANE DuBOSE HEYWARD[6] (Edwin Watkins Heyward[5], Thomas Savage Heyward, Jr.[4], Thomas Savage Heyward[3], Thomas Heyward[2], Thomas Heyward, Jr.[1]) child of Edwin Watkins Heyward and Jane Screven DuBose was born in Charleston, SC on 3 Apr 1887.[1] She married Edward Chauncy REGISTER in say 1910. He was born in Rose Hill, NC in 1884[2], and died in 1920. Child:

+   463   i Jane DuBose REGISTER, b. 1912

References:
[1] Leach MSS, p. 6062 reports date and place of birth. [2] Heyward Family Association HENRY System data printout.

298. MARGUERITE BOYKIN HEYWARD[6] (Wilmot Holmes Heyward[5], Thomas Savage Heyward, Jr.[4], Thomas Savage Heyward[3], Thomas Heyward[2], Thomas Heyward, Jr.[1]) child of Wilmot Holmes Heyward and Margaret Kennedy Boykin was born on 23 Jan 1901, and died on 19 Aug 1922. She married Ralph Wesley GORMAN in say 1919. He was born on 11 Nov 1895[1], and died in Dec 1963. Child:

    464   i Ralph Wesley GORMAN, Jr., b. 1920

References:
[1] Heyward Family Association data.

301. THOMAS SAVAGE HEYWARD[6] (Wilmot Holmes Heyward[5], Thomas Savage Heyward, Jr.[4], Thomas Savage Heyward[3], Thomas Heyward[2], Thomas Heyward, Jr.[1]) child of Wilmot Holmes Heyward and

Margaret Kennedy Boykin was born in East Point, GA on 30 Mar 1910, and died in 1989. He married Ethel Louise HODGE in Chattanooga, TN on 15 Aug 1936. She was born in Atlanta, GA on 17 Jan 1915. Children:

+ 465   i   Thomas Savage HEYWARD, Jr., b. 2 Aug 1939
+ 466   ii   Dorothy Louise HEYWARD, b. 3 Sep 1941
+ 467   iii Frances Virginia HEYWARD, b. 18 Jul 1945
+ 468   iv   Robert Brian HEYWARD, b. 17 Dec 1951

304. RIVES BOYKIN HEYWARD^6 (Wilmot Holmes Heyward^5, Thomas Savage Heyward, Jr.^{4}, Thomas Savage Heyward^3, Thomas Heyward^2, Thomas Heyward, Jr.^{1}) child of Wilmot Holmes Heyward and Margaret Kennedy Boykin was born in Atlanta, GA on 6 Nov 1915. She married Joseph Hinkle JOHNSTON on 27 Apr 1935. He was born in 1915, and died in 1991. Children:

   469   i   Ruth Marie JOHNSTON, b. 26 Dec 1935
+ 470   ii   Barbara Ann JOHNSTON, b. 12 Aug 1940
+ 471   iii Patricia Josephine JOHNSTON, b. 31 Mar 1942

306. NED WATKINS HEYWARD^6 (Wilmot Holmes Heyward^5, Thomas Savage Heyward, Jr.^{4}, Thomas Savage Heyward^3, Thomas Heyward^2, Thomas Heyward, Jr.^{1}) child of Wilmot Holmes Heyward and Margaret Kennedy Boykin was born in Atlanta, GA on 10 Nov 1920. He married Matelyn French LANDRUM, daughter of Herbert Otto and Willie Clyde (French) Landrum in Decatur, GA on 20 Sep 1946. She was born in Lexington, MS on 18 Aug 1920. Children:

+ 472   i   Ned Watkins HEYWARD, Jr., b. 1 Aug 1948
+ 473   ii   William Landrum HEYWARD, b. 15 Jun 1950

307. HUNTER BOYKIN HEYWARD^6 (Wilmot Holmes Heyward^5, Thomas Savage Heyward, Jr.^{4}, Thomas Savage Heyward^3, Thomas Heyward^2, Thomas Heyward, Jr.^{1}) child of Wilmot Holmes Heyward and Margaret Kennedy Boykin was born on 12 Sep 1922. He married Martha Jaunita WEISIGER in say 1920. She was born on 11 Jan 1925. Children:

+ 474   i   Eloise Vardery HEYWARD, b. 11 Sep 1951
+ 475   ii   Mark Weisiger HEYWARD, b. 8 Aug 1955
   476   iii Leslie Boykin HEYWARD, b. 27 Sep 1957

310. LILA WILLIAMS McTEER^6 (Florence Percy Heyward^5, William Nathaniel Heyward^4, Thomas Savage Heyward^3, Thomas Heyward^2, Thomas Heyward, Jr.^{1}) child of Florence Percy Heyward and James Edward McTeer was born in Beaufort, SC on 6 Jan 1899[1], and died in Beaufort, SC on 16

Jan 1971. She married George Holmes CROCKER in say 1925. He was born in Charleston, SC on 29 Jul 1888[1], and died in Beaufort, SC on 23 Feb 1940. Child:

+ 477   i   Julie Johnson CROCKER, b. 14 Mar 1929

References:
[1] Heyward Family Association HENRY System data.

311. LOUISA GUERARD McTEER[6] (Florence Percy Heyward[5], William Nathaniel Heyward[4], Thomas Savage Heyward[3], Thomas Heyward[2], Thomas Heyward, Jr.[1]) child of Florence Percy Heyward and James Edward McTeer was born on 14 Feb 1901. She married William Herbert OLTMANN in say 1916. Children:

+ 478   i   Anna Eckles OLTMANN, b. 1916
+ 479   ii   William Herbert OLTMANN, Jr., b. 1919
+ 480   iii   Lila Cuthbert OLTMANN, b. 1922
   481   iv   Zoe Guerard OLTMANN, b. 1926

312. JAMES EDWIN McTEER, Jr.[6] (Florence Percy Heyward[5], William Nathaniel Heyward[4], Thomas Savage Heyward[3], Thomas Heyward[2], Thomas Heyward, Jr.[1]) child of Florence Percy Heyward and James Edward McTeer was born in Hardeeville, SC on 2 May 1903, and died in Beaufort, SC on 24 Dec 1979. He married Jane Lucille LUPO, daughter of L. M. and Eula (Oliver) Lupo in Beaufort, SC on 3 Jun 1917. She was born in Dillon, SC on 28 Nov 1903. Children:

+ 482   i   Jane Lucille McTEER, b. 1 Apr 1928
+ 483   ii   Georgianna Hasell McTEER, b. 29 Dec 1930
+ 484   iii   Sally Guerard McTEER, b. 31 Aug 1934
+ 485   iv   James Edwin McTEER, III, b. 22 Sep 1938
+ 486   v   Thomas Heyward McTEER, b. 14 Aug 1944

313. MARGARET WILLIAMSON McTEER[6] (Florence Percy Heyward[5], William Nathaniel Heyward[4], Thomas Savage Heyward[3], Thomas Heyward[2], Thomas Heyward, Jr.[1]) child of Florence Percy Heyward and James Edward McTeer was born in Beaufort, SC in 1906, and died in 1977. She married James Leroy BUTLER in 1921. He was born In Rincon, GA in 1903, and died in 1943. Children:

+ 487   i   Frances Louise BUTLER, b. 27 Sep 1922
+ 488   ii   James Byron BUTLER, b. 4 Feb 1924
+ 489   iii   Margaret McTeer BUTLER, b. 1 Feb 1927
+ 490   iv   Robert Henry BUTLER, b. 10 Feb 1929
+ 491   v   Catherine BUTLER, b. 30 Jun 1930

+ 492 vi Florence Exley BUTLER, b. 4 Feb 1933 [twin]
  493 vii Evie Ryan BUTLER, b. 4 Feb 1933, dy 1933 [twin]
+ 494 viii Ann Lucille BUTLER, b. 3 May 1935
+ 495 ix James Leroy BUTLER, Jr., b. 14 Nov 1937
+ 496 x Carol McTeer BUTLER, b. 21 Oct 1940

314. CATHERINE ELLIOTT McTEER[6] (Florence Percy Heyward[5], William Nathaniel Heyward[4], Thomas Savage Heyward[3], Thomas Heyward[2], Thomas Heyward, Jr.[1]) child of Florence Percy Heyward and James Edward McTeer was born in Beaufort, SC on 22 Nov 1908. She married Mercade Adonis CRAMER in Beaufort, SC in say 1929. He was born in West Hartford, CT on 28 Feb 1901, and died on 24 Apr 1984. Children:
+ 497 i Mercade Adonis CRAMER, Jr., b. 24 Mar 1932
  498 ii James CRAMER, b. 8 Oct 1949

315. GEORGIANNA HASELL McTEER[6] (Florence Percy Heyward[5], William Nathaniel Heyward[4], Thomas Savage Heyward[3], Thomas Heyward[2], Thomas Heyward, Jr.[1]) child of Florence Percy Heyward and James Edward McTeer was born in Beaufort, SC on 6 Oct 1913. She married Charles Alfred LENGNICK in Beaufort, SC on 22 Dec 1932. He was born in Aiken, SC on 8 Jun 1913. Children:
+ 499 i Paula Wood LENGNICK, b. 7 Jan 1936
  500 ii Emilie Guerard LENGNICK, b. 4 Feb 1943, d. 28 Feb 1966; unm
  501 iii Susan LENGNICK, b. 31 Oct 1945, d. 12 Jul 1975; unm

316. WALTER WILLIAM McTEER[6] (Florence Percy Heyward[5], William Nathaniel Heyward[4], Thomas Savage Heyward[3], Thomas Heyward[2], Thomas Heyward, Jr.[1]) child of Florence Percy Heyward and James Edward McTeer was born in Beaufort, SC on 29 Mar 1914, and died in Waynesboro, GA on 29 Sep 1974. He married Mary Louise FOSTER, daughter of Joshua Banker and Louisa Kent (Follini) Foster in Jasper County, SC on 14 Jul 1934. She was born in Charleston, SC on 31 Jul 1916, and died in Waynesboro, GA on 29 Jan 1982. Children:
+ 502 i Walter Witridge McTEER, b.19 Sep 1937
+ 503 ii Louise Heyward McTEER, b. 12 Oct 1941
+ 504 iii Mary Adele McTEER, b. 7 Mar 1946
+ 505 iv William Guerard McTEER, b. 11 Jul 1950

317. FLORENCE PERCY McTEER[6] (Florence Percy Heyward[5], William Nathaniel Heyward[4], Thomas Savage Heyward[3], Thomas Heyward[2], Thomas

Heyward, Jr.[1]) child of Florence Percy Heyward and James Edward McTeer was born in Gray's Hill, SC on 14 Jun 1917. She married William Turner STEVENS in Barnwell, SC on 7 Nov 1935. He was born in Thomson, GA on 2 Sep 1913. Children:

+ 506   i   Florence Heyward STEVENS, b. 4 Oct 1936
  507   ii William Turner STEVENS, Jr., b. 14 Jun 1939
  508 iii Frances Herlong STEVENS, b. 10 Aug 1954

321. HELEN PERRYCLAIRE HEYWARD[6] (Henry Guerard Heyward[5], William Nathaniel Heyward[4], Thomas Savage Heyward[3], Thomas Heyward[2], Thomas Heyward, Jr.[1]) child of Henry Guerard Heyward and Floride Dupont Pritchard was born in Hardeeville, SC on 11 Jul 1908, and died in 1996. She married (1st) Jack Elquit ALTMAN in say 1935. He was born in Savannah, GA on 11 Oct 1905, and died there on 8 Apr 1952. Child:

+ 509   i   Jack Elquit ALTMAN, Jr., b. 11 Aug 1927

324. HENRY GUERARD HEYWARD, Jr.[6] (Henry Guerard Heyward[5], William Nathaniel Heyward[4], Thomas Savage Heyward[3], Thomas Heyward[2], Thomas Heyward, Jr.[1]) child of Henry Guerard Heyward and Floride Dupont Pritchard was born in Hardeeville, SC on 28 Jul 1914, and died on 7 Jul 1989. He married Kathryn Virginia BIRD in say 1935. She was born in Rincon, GA on 27 Nov 1921. Children:

+ 510   i   Henry Guerard HEYWARD, III, b. 16 Nov 1949
+ 511   ii Brenda Kay HEYWARD, b. 20 Nov 1950
+ 512   iii Virginia Lynn HEYWARD, b. 15 Aug 1952

325. CATHERINE KIRK HEYWARD[6] (Henry Guerard Heyward[5], William Nathaniel Heyward[4], Thomas Savage Heyward[3], Thomas Heyward[2], Thomas Heyward, Jr.[1]) child of Henry Guerard Heyward and Floride Dupont Pritchard was born on 26 Aug 1917. She married William Chandler SCONYERS, Jr. in say 1935. He was born on 10 Sep 1911, and died on 9 May 1960. Children:

+ 513   i   Kay Heyward SCONYERS, b. 23 Aug 1937
+ 514   ii William Chandler SCONYERS, III, b. 14 Feb 1941

328. VIRGINIA RUTLEDGE HEYWARD[6] (Henry Guerard Heyward[5], William Nathaniel Heyward[4], Thomas Savage Heyward[3], Thomas Heyward[2], Thomas Heyward, Jr.[1]) child of Henry Guerard Heyward and Floride Dupont Pritchard was born in Hardeeville, SC on 28 Mar 1923. She married James Leon McMURRAIN, Jr. in Ridgeland, SC on 13 Jun 1950. He was born in

Ridgeland, Stewart County, GA on 17 Jul 1916, and died in New Orleans, LA on 27 Aug 1967. Children:
+ 515   i   Deborah Heyward McMURRAIN, b. 21 Jan 1952
+ 516   ii Alice McMURRAIN, b. 25 Mar 1958 [twin]
+ 517   iii Norma McMURRAIN, b. 25 Mar 1958 [twin]

329. CAROLINE SCREVEN HEYWARD[6] (Henry Guerard Heyward[5], William Nathaniel Heyward[4], Thomas Savage Heyward[3], Thomas Heyward[2], Thomas Heyward, Jr.[1]) child of Henry Guerard Heyward and Floride Dupont Pritchard was born on 30 Apr 1926. She married Wallace GOETHE in say 1946. Child:
+ 518   i   Patricia Ann GOETHE, b. 15 Dec 1948

331. WILLIAM SMITH HEYWARD[6] (William Burroughs Smith Heyward[5], Andrew Hasell Heyward[4], Thomas Savage Heyward[3], Thomas Heyward[2], Thomas Heyward, Jr.[1]) child of William Burroughs Smith Heyward and Mary Memminger Pinckney was born in Summerville, SC on 23 Mar 1895[1], and died in Lakeland, FL on 2 Feb 1972. He married Annie Sinkler WALKER, daughter of B. Wilson and Anne Simons (Sinkler) Walker in Charleston, SC on 12 Apr 1916. She was born in Charleston, SC on 24 Aug 1895[1], and died in Scituate, MA on 22 Sep 1979. Children:
+ 519   i   Mary Anne HEYWARD, b. 25 Jul 1918
+ 520   ii Virginia Hughes HEYWARD, b. 12 Nov 1919
References:
[1] Heyward Family Association data.

332. EMORY SPEER HEYWARD[6] (Andrew Hasell Heyward, Jr.[5], Andrew Hasell Heyward[4], Thomas Savage Heyward[3], Thomas Heyward[2], Thomas Heyward, Jr.[1]) child of Andrew Hasell Heyward, Jr. and Marian Speer was born in Macon, GA in 1904, and died in 1990. He married Eugenia Louise POWELL in say 1933. She was born in Woodbury, GA in 1904, and died in 1980. Children:
+ 521   i   Marian Rochelle HEYWARD, b. 1935
+ 522   ii Eugenia Louise HEYWARD, b. 1938
+ 523   iii Emory Speer HEYWARD, Jr., b. 1941

333. ANDREW HASELL HEYWARD, III[6] (Andrew Hasell Heyward, Jr.[5], Andrew Hasell Heyward[4], Thomas Savage Heyward[3], Thomas Heyward[2], Thomas Heyward, Jr.[1]) child of Andrew Hasell Heyward, Jr. and Marian Speer was born on 14 Jul 1905, and died in 1990. He married Mildred GOODRUM in say 1932. She was born on 8 Feb 1909. Children:

+ 524   i   Andrew Hasell HEYWARD, IV, b. 20 Dec 1934
+ 525   ii   Mildred HEYWARD, b. 10 Apr 1941

334. EUSTACE WILLOUGHBY SPEER HEYWARD[6] (Andrew Hasell Heyward, Jr.[5], Andrew Hasell Heyward[4], Thomas Savage Heyward[3], Thomas Heyward[2], Thomas Heyward, Jr.[1]) child of Andrew Hasell Heyward, Jr. and Marian Speer was born on 9 Jul 1908, and died in 1992. He married Marcella MARTIN in say 1950. She died in 1982. Child:
+ 526   i   Marcella HEYWARD, b. 1957

335. MARION SPEER HEYWARD[6] (Andrew Hasell Heyward, Jr.[5], Andrew Hasell Heyward[4], Thomas Savage Heyward[3], Thomas Heyward[2], Thomas Heyward, Jr.[1]) child of Andrew Hasell Heyward, Jr. and Marian Speer was born in Macon, GA on 17 Dec 1917. He married Eleanor VANCE in say 1940. She was born in Macon, GA in 1918, and died in 1998. Children:
+ 527   i   Helen Vance HEYWARD, b. 1942
   528   ii   John Allen HEYWARD, b. 1949
   529   iii   Barbara Jean HEYWARD, b. 1951
   530   iv   Thomas Andrew HEYWARD, b. 1953

337. ELIZABETH BECKWITH LYNAH[6] (James Lynah[5], Ella Louise Heyward[4], Thomas Savage Heyward[3], Thomas Heyward[2], Thomas Heyward, Jr.[1]) child of James Lynah and Elizabeth Eugenia Beckwith was born in NYC on 27 Nov 1906, and died in Denver, CO on 4 Jul 1980. She married Bronson C. RUMSEY in say 1927. He was born in Buffalo, NY on 9 Jul 1879[1], and died in Cody, WY in Oct 1968. Children:
+ 531   i   Bronson C. RUMSEY, Jr., b. 8 Nov 1929
+ 532   ii   James Lynah RUMSEY, b. 31 Oct 1932

338. MARIA GLOVER LYNAH[6] (James Lynah[5], Ella Louise Heyward[4], Thomas Savage Heyward[3], Thomas Heyward[2], Thomas Heyward, Jr.[1]) child of James Lynah and Elizabeth Eugenia Beckwith was born on 8 Sep 1908, and died in 1983. She married George SHERRILL on 7 Jun 1930. He was born in 1902. Children:
+ 533   i   George SHERRILL, Jr., b. 11 Mar 1932
+ 534   ii   James Lynah SHERRILL, b. 14 Jun 1935

339. ELLA LOUISE HEYWARD LYNAH[6] (James Lynah[5], Ella Louise Heyward[4], Thomas Savage Heyward[3], Thomas Heyward[2], Thomas Heyward, Jr.[1]) child of James Lynah and Elizabeth Eugenia Beckwith was born on 4

May 1910, and died in 1999. She married Joseph Huger HARRISON in Savannah, GA on 26 Apr 1930. He was born in Atlanta, GA on 15 Aug 1906, and died on 15 Nov 1995. Children:

+ 535   i   Elizabeth Huger HARRISON, b. 29 Nov 1933
+ 536   ii   Robert Lynah HARRISON, b. 8 Dec 1939
+ 537   iii Joseph Huger HARRISON, Jr., b. 20 Oct 1943

340. ELLA HEYWARD PALMER[6] (Eloise Lynah[5], Ella Louise Heyward[4], Thomas Savage Heyward[3], Thomas Heyward[2], Thomas Heyward, Jr.[1]) child of Eloise Lynah and Paul Trapier Palmer was born in Charleston, SC on 10 Jul 1921. She married Samuel Emerson DOWDNEY on 17 Nov 1942. He was born in NYC on 19 Sep 1918. Children:

+ 538   i   Stephen Palmer DOWDNEY, b. 25 Dec 1943
+ 539   ii   John Heyward DOWDNEY, b. 11 Jun 1949

341. PAUL TRAPIER PALMER, Jr.[6] (Eloise Lynah[5], Ella Louise Heyward[4], Thomas Savage Heyward[3], Thomas Heyward[2], Thomas Heyward, Jr.[1]) child of Eloise Lynah and Paul Trapier Palmer was born on 24 Feb 1924, and died in 1981. He married Beaumont BARRINGER in say 1950. She was born in Columbia, SC on 12 Jul 1930. Child:

540   i   Paul Trapier PALMER, III, b. 1951

342. LILLY LYNAH PALMER[6] (Eloise Lynah[5], Ella Louise Heyward[4], Thomas Savage Heyward[3], Thomas Heyward[2], Thomas Heyward, Jr.[1]) child of Eloise Lynah and Paul Trapier Palmer was born in Charleston, SC on 20 Sep 1925. She married Earl BISCOE, Jr., son of Earl and Edith (Aldrich) Biscoe in Wadmalaw Island, SC on 28 May 1949. He was born in NYC on 12 Oct 1920. Children:

541   i   Earl BISCOE, III, b. 26 Apr 1952
542   ii   Eloise Palmer BISCOE, b. 5 May 1954

343. JAMES LYNAH PALMER[6] (Eloise Lynah[5], Ella Louise Heyward[4], Thomas Savage Heyward[3], Thomas Heyward[2], Thomas Heyward, Jr.[1]) child of Eloise Lynah and Paul Trapier Palmer was born in Charleston, SC on 10 Feb 1927. He married Patricia Semple BOURNE in Savannah, GA on 16 Mar 1951. She was born in Savannah, GA on 13 Jul 1931. Children:

543   i   James Lynah PALMER, Jr., b. 26 Jan 1952
+ 544   ii   Harry Timrod PALMER, b. 12 Aug 1955
+ 545   iii Patricia Bourne PALMER, b. 11 Jun 1958
+ 546   iv   Helen Strobahr PALMER, b. 29 Sep 1960

344. ANNE CUTHBERT PALMER[6] (Eloise Lynah[5], Ella Louise Heyward[4], Thomas Savage Heyward[3], Thomas Heyward[2], Thomas Heyward, Jr.[1]) child of Eloise Lynah and Paul Trapier Palmer was born in Charleston, SC on 7 Aug 1930. She married Jonathan Duncan BULKLEY in say 1956. He was born in NYC in on 5 Aug 1930. Children:

+ 547   i   Honor Heyward BULKLEY, b. 25 Feb 1958
  548   ii Peter BULKLEY, b. 8 Sep 1960
  549   iii Derrick Middleton BULKLEY, b. 1 Oct 1965

345. JOHN HEYWARD LYNAH[6] (John Heyward Lynah, Jr.[5], Ella Louise Heyward[4], Thomas Savage Heyward[3], Thomas Heyward[2], Thomas Heyward, Jr.[1]) child of John Heyward Lynah, Jr. and Augusta Clayatt Howard was born on 14 Nov 1917, and died on 5 Dec 1984. He married Anna Colquitt HUNTER on 18 Jun 1941. Children:

+ 550   i   Nancy Colquitt LYNAH, b. 9 Feb 1943
+ 551   ii Mary Savage LYNAH, b. 20 Feb 1945
  552   iii John Heyward LYNAH, IV, b. 30 Jan 1955

346. MARY HOWARD LYNAH[6] (John Heyward Lynah, Jr.[5], Ella Louise Heyward[4], Thomas Savage Heyward[3], Thomas Heyward[2], Thomas Heyward, Jr.[1]) child of John Heyward Lynah, Jr. and Augusta Clayatt Howard was born on 3 Jun 1923. She married David HIGGENBOTTOM on 9 Sep 1944. He was born in 1919. Children:

  553   i   David Wallace HIGGENBOTTOM, b. 27 Jun 1945
+ 554   ii Samuel Heyward HIGGENBOTTOM, b. 6 Sep 1946
  555   iii Nancy Savage HIGGENBOTTOM, b. 6 Feb 1948

347. SAVAGE HEYWARD LYNAH[6] (John Heyward Lynah, Jr.[5], Ella Louise Heyward[4], Thomas Savage Heyward[3], Thomas Heyward[2], Thomas Heyward, Jr.[1]) child of John Heyward Lynah, Jr. and Augusta Clayatt Howard was born in Savannah, GA on 2 Sep 1924, and died in 1995. He married Ruth Artley CAIN on 14 Sep 1948. She was born on 20 Jun 1927. Children:

+ 556   i   James LYNAH, b. 24 Jun 1950
+ 557   ii Thomas Ravenel LYNAH, b. 4 Nov 1952
+ 558   iii Katherine Savage LYNAH, b. 29 Apr 1955
+ 559   iv Savage Heyward LYNAH, Jr., b. 25 Oct 1961
  560   v   Ruth Artley LYNAH, b. 1965

348. WALLACE HOWARD LYNAH[6] (John Heyward Lynah, Jr.[5], Ella Louise Heyward[4], Thomas Savage Heyward[3], Thomas Heyward[2], Thomas

Heyward, Jr.[1]) child of John Heyward Lynah, Jr. and Augusta Clayatt Howard was born in Savannah, GA in 2 Sep 1924, and died in 1996. He married Helen ROWLAND 0n 16 Jul 1952. She was born in 1925. Children:

+ 561　　i　Helen Fairchild LYNAH, b. 15 Apr 1956
  562　　ii　Charles Wallace LYNAH, b. 12 Apr 1958
+ 563　　iii　Mary Rowland LYNAH, b. 1966

349. REIDER TROSDAL[6] (Anne Cuthbert Lynah[5], Ella Louise Heyward[4], Thomas Savage Heyward[3], Thomas Heyward[2], Thomas Heyward, Jr.[1]) child of Anne Cuthbert Lynah and Reider Arnold Trosdal was born about 1920, and died in 1963. He married Pamela SHARPLEY in say 1943. Children:

  564　　i　Karen TROSDAL, b. c. 1945
  565　　ii　Lynah TROSDAL, b. c. 1948

350. WILLIAM HENRY HEYWARD[6] (John Boykin Heyward, Jr.[5], John Boykin Heyward[4], Thomas Savage Heyward[3], Thomas Heyward[2], Thomas Heyward, Jr.[1]) child of John Boykin Heyward, Jr. and Jane Camp Atwood was born in Oakland, CA on 8 Oct 1916, and died in Greenbrae, CA on 8 Feb 1990. He married Betty Jean MARKLE in San Francisco, CA on 14 May 1957. She was born in Plymouth, Luzerne County, PA on 5 Aug 1921. Child:

+ 566　　i　Robert Edmund HEYWARD, b. 28 May 1945

352. DAISY VINCENT MARTIN[6] (Martha Horry Howard[5], Annie Heyward Webb[4], Elizabeth Savage Heyward[3], Thomas Heyward[2], Thomas Heyward, Jr.[1]) child of Martha Horry Howard and John Elmore Martin was born about 1897. She married R. Burke HAMMES in say 1919. Children:

+ 567　　i　R. Burke HAMMES, Jr., b. 1920
  568　　ii　John HAMMES, b. c. 1922
  569　　iii　Elmore HAMMES, b. c. 1926

354. JOHN VINCENT MARTIN[6] (Martha Horry Howard[5], Annie Heyward Webb[4], Elizabeth Savage Heyward[3], Thomas Heyward[2], Thomas Heyward, Jr.[1]) child of Martha Horry Howard and John Elmore Martin was born in Charleston, SC in 1901, and died in 1975. He married Elsie LEADBETTER in say 1924. She was born in Fleetwwood, ENGLAND in 1903, and died in 1988. Children:

+ 570　　i　Ann Cuthbert MARTIN, b. 1926
+ 571　　ii　Elsie Leadbetter MARTIN, b. 1928
+ 572　　iii　John Elmore MARTIN, b. 1929

355. JOHN SMALLBROOK HOWKINS, Jr.[6] (Elise Heyward[5], Jacob Guerard Heyward[4], George Cuthbert Heyward[3], Thomas Heyward[2], Thomas Heyward, Jr.[1]) child of Elsie Heyward and John Smallbrook Howkins was born in Savannah, GA in 1892[1], and died in 1968. He married Alice Keller HUGER in say 1923. She was born in Memphis, TN in 1902, and died in 1980. Children:

+ 573   i   John Smallbrook HOWKINS, III, b. 1925
+ 574   ii   John Huger HOWKINS, b. 1927
   575   iii   William Beekman HOWKINS, b. 1929

References:
[1] Heyward Family Association data.

356. GUERARD HEYWARD HOWKINS[6] (Elise Heyward[5], Jacob Guerard Heyward[4], George Cuthbert Heyward[3], Thomas Heyward[2], Thomas Heyward, Jr.[1]) child of Elsie Heyward and John Smallbrook Howkins was born in Savannah, GA in 1894[1], and died in 1975. He married Elizabeth Heyward CASSIDY in say 1918. She was born in Baltimore, MD in 1900, and died in 1975. Children:

+ 576   i   Guerard Heyward HOWKINS, Jr., b. 1919
+ 577   ii   John Henry Francis HOWKINS, b. 1921
   578   iii   Thomas Heyward HOWKINS, b. 1923
   579   iv   Anthony Chinn HOWKINS, b. 1924
   580   v   Elizabeth Heyward HOWKINS, b. 1930
   581   vi   Mary Ball HOWKINS, b. 1944

References:
[1] Heyward Family Association data.

357. FRANCIS de CARADEUX HEYWARD, Jr. [6] (Francis Heyward[5], Jacob Guerard Heyward[4], George Cuthbert Heyward[3], Thomas Heyward[2], Thomas Heyward, Jr.[1]) child of Francis Heyward and Virginia Kreichbaum was born about 1905. He married Lyne WILSON in say 1926. Child:

   582   i   Pauline Virginia HEYWARD, b. c. 1928

359. EVELYN HEYWARD[6] (Roland Steiner Heyward[5], James Cuthbert Heyward[4], George Cuthbert Heyward[3], Thomas Heyward[2], Thomas Heyward, Jr.[1]) child of Roland Steiner Heyward and Theo Belle Farrar was born in Birmingham, AL in 1914, and died on 30 May 1994. She married George Richard THOMAS in say 1946. He was born in 1913. Child:

+ 583   i   Karen Evelyn THOMAS, b. 1950

360. BENJAMIN FARRAR HEYWARD[6] (Roland Steiner Heyward[5], James Cuthbert Heyward[4], George Cuthbert Heyward[3], Thomas Heyward[2], Thomas Heyward, Jr.[1]) child of Roland Steiner Heyward and Theo Belle Farrar was born in Birmingham, AL on 8 Jul 1920. He married Eleanor Beverly HORNE on 15 Oct 1948. She was born in Spartanburg, SC on 3 May 1926. Children:

> 584   i   Susan Claudia HEYWARD, b. 15 Oct 1950
>
> 585   ii   Benjamin Farrar HEYWARD, Jr., b. 31 May 1953
>
> 586   iii   Jennifer Jane HEYWARD, b. 10 Jul 1957

361. ETHEL LORAINE HEYWARD[6] (Harvey Cuthbert Heyward[5], James Cuthbert Heyward[4], George Cuthbert Heyward[3], Thomas Heyward[2], Thomas Heyward, Jr.[1]) child of Harvey Cuthbert Heyward and Sarah Elizabeth Howe was born in Charleston, SC on 23 Jun 1922. She married Donald Wayne KENDRICK in Charleston, SC on 24 Nov 1943. He was born in Decatur, AL on 11 Jan 1920. Children:

> \+ 587   i   Dana KENDRICK, b. 1948
>
> 588   ii   Donald Wayne KENDRICK, Jr., b. 18 Jul 1953

366. MARJORY HEYWARD[6] (George Cuthbert Heyward, III[5], George Cuthbert Heyward, Jr.[4], George Cuthbert Heyward[3], Thomas Heyward[2], Thomas Heyward, Jr.[1]) child of George Cuthbert Heyward, III and Alice Stuart Hunter was born in Philadelphia, PA on 16 Nov 1918. She married Ralston Everett MINGLEDORFF in Savannah, GA on 2 May 1942. He was born in Savannah, GA on 9 Jul 1917. Children:

> 589   i   Elizabeth Percival MINGLEDORFF, b. 15 Dec 1945; sp
>
> \+ 590   ii   Anne Heyward MINGLEDORFF, b. 30 Oct 1948
>
> \+ 591   iii   Ralston Everett MINGLEDORFF, Jr., b. 10 Nov 1949
>
> 592   iv   George Heyward MINGLEDORFF, b. 21 Jan 1954, d. 13 Dec 1974; unm

367. GEORGE CUTHBERT HEYWARD, IV[6] (George Cuthbert Heyward, III[5], George Cuthbert Heyward, Jr.[4], George Cuthbert Heyward[3], Thomas Heyward[2], Thomas Heyward, Jr.[1]) child of George Cuthbert Heyward, III and Alice Stuart Hunter was born in Savannah, GA on 17 Oct 1920, and died in Washington, DC on 12 Jul 1947. He married Josephine Macon VINCENT in Charleston, SC on 27 Nov 1943. She was born in Cincinnati, OH on 14 Nov 1922. Children:

> \+ 593   i   Josephine de Rosset HEYWARD, b. 7 May 1945
>
> \+ 594   ii   George Cuthbert HEYWARD, V, b. 7 Dec 1947

368. ALLAN McALPIN HEYWARD[6] (George Cuthbert Heyward, III[5], George Cuthbert Heyward, Jr.[4], George Cuthbert Heyward[3], Thomas Heyward[2], Thomas Heyward, Jr.[1]) child of George Cuthbert Heyward, III and Alice Stuart Hunter was born in Savannah, GA on 14 May 1922. He married Marianna Chapin MARSHALL, daughter of Wayne and Eleanor Virginia Randolph (Chapin) Marshall in Philadelphia, PA on 2 Oct 1948. She was born in Wallingford, PA on 22 May 1928. Children:

+ 595   i   Allan McAlpin HEYWARD, Jr., b. 16 Apr 1950
   596   ii   Virginia Randolph Chapin HEYWARD, b. 20 Apr 1953
+ 597   iii   Roberta Guerard HEYWARD, b. 8 May 1956
   598   iv   Wayne Marshall HEYWARD, b. 3 Oct 1963

372. MARY ELIZABETH HEYWARD[6] (Robert Clarence Heyward[5], Robert Chisolm Heyward[4], George Cuthbert Heyward[3], Thomas Heyward[2], Thomas Heyward, Jr.[1]) child of Robert Clarence Heyward and Sallie Othello Long was born in Pelzer, SC on 14 Feb 1902, and died in 1988. She married John Housan FENNER, son of John Housan and Clara (Ferebee)Fenner in Spartanburg, SC on 1 Jan 1925. He was born in Halifax, NC on 24 Nov 1882[1], and died on 11 Nov 1949. Children:

+ 599   i   Clara Ferebee FENNER, b. 6 Nov 1925
+ 600   ii   John Housan FENNER, Jr., b. 1 Nov 1926
+ 601   iii   William Eaton FENNER, b. 17 Nov 1927

References:
[1] Heyward Family Association data.

373. GEORGE CUTHBERT HEYWARD, VI[6] (Robert Clarence Heyward[5], Robert Chisolm Heyward[4], George Cuthbert Heyward[3], Thomas Heyward[2], Thomas Heyward, Jr.[1]) child of Robert Clarence Heyward and Sallie Othello Long was born in Pelzer, SC on 25 Dec 1903, and died in Laurinburg, NC on 29 Oct 1954. He married Avis Irene BATSON in Girard, AL on 2 Jan 1932. She was born in Cedartown, GA on 17 Dec 1906, and died on 25 May 1997. Children:

+ 602   i   James Robert HEYWARD, b. 16 Nov 1932
+ 603   ii   George Cuthbert HEYWARD, VII, b. 29 Oct 1940

374. THOMAS SAVAGE HEYWARD[6] (Robert Clarence Heyward[5], Robert Chisolm Heyward[4], George Cuthbert Heyward[3], Thomas Heyward[2], Thomas Heyward, Jr.[1]) child of Robert Clarence Heyward and Sallie Othello Long was born in Pelzer, SC on 4 Nov 1905, and died in Sumter, SC on 1 May 1961. He married Mary McDANIEL, daughter of William Triplett and Gila

Mae (Crosby) McDaniel in Batesburg, SC on 5 Aug 1931. She was born on 17 Mar 1911, and died on 27 Aug 1992. Children:

+ 604   i   Mary Agnes HEYWARD, b. 16 Jan 1933
+ 605   ii   Thomas Savage HEYWARD, Jr., b. 11 Oct 1936
   606   iii   Charles Ralph HEYWARD, b. 28 Mar 1945
+ 607   iv   Deborah Crosby HEYWARD, b. 27 Apr 1951

375. CORINNE HEYWARD[6] (Robert Clarence Heyward[5], Robert Chisolm Heyward[4], George Cuthbert Heyward[3], Thomas Heyward[2], Thomas Heyward, Jr.[1]) child of Robert Clarence Heyward and Sallie Othello Long was born in Pelzer, SC on 8 Nov 1908, and died in 1971. She married Donald L. DENNISON in say 1927. Child:

   608   i   Donald L. DENNISON, Jr., b. c. 1929

376. JOSEPHINE STONEY HEYWARD[6] (Robert Clarence Heyward[5], Robert Chisolm Heyward[4], George Cuthbert Heyward[3], Thomas Heyward[2], Thomas Heyward, Jr.[1]) child of Robert Clarence Heyward and Sallie Othello Long was born in Pelzer, SC on 20 Dec 1911, and died in Batesburg, SC on 20 Mar 1986. She married David Edwin RAWL, son of David Baxter and Gussie Lee (Covin) Rawl in Lexington, SC on 25 Dec 1929. He was born in Batesburg, SC on 28 Nov 1908, and died there on 11 Aug 1992. Children:

+ 609   i   David Edwin RAWL, Jr., b. 16 May 1933
+ 610   ii   Joseph Heyward RAWL, b. 12 May 1938
+ 611   iii   Lee Covin RAWL, b. 12 Mar 1947

378. ROBERT CLARENCE HEYWARD, Jr.[6] (Robert Clarence Heyward[5], Robert Chisolm Heyward[4], George Cuthbert Heyward[3], Thomas Heyward[2], Thomas Heyward, Jr.[1]) child of Robert Clarence Heyward and Sallie Othello Long was born in Pelzer, SC on 15 Dec 1915, and died in 1984. He married Mary Ann CARTER in Charlotte, NC on 10 Jun 1944. She was born in Charlotte, NC on 13 May 1915. Children:

   612   i   Isabel Carter HEYWARD, b. 22 Aug 1945
   613   ii   Robert Clarence HEYWARD, III, b. 25 Oct 1951
+ 614   iii   Mary Ann HEYWARD, b. 2 Nov 1952

379. GAILLARD STONEY HEYWARD[6] (Daniel Hasell Heyward[5], Robert Chisolm Heyward[4], George Cuthbert Heyward[3], Thomas Heyward[2], Thomas Heyward, Jr.[1]) child of Daniel Hasell Heyward and May Mulligan was born in Bluffton, SC on 8 Jan 1910, and died in Bluffton, SC on 25 Oct 1987. He married Lila GRIFFIN, daughter of Wigfall and Anna (Evans) Griffin in

Bluffton, SC on 3 Jun 1934. She was born in Pinewood, SC on 30 Jun 1910.
Children:
+ 615   i   Ann Cuthbert HEYWARD, b. 31 Mar 1936
+ 616   ii Caroline Griffin HEYWARD, b. 13 Aug 1937
+ 617   iii Dorothy May HEYWARD, b. 14 Nov 1939
+ 618   iv Thomas Gaillard HEYWARD, b. 6 Mar 1942

380. JAMES EDWARD HEYWARD[6] (Daniel Hasell Heyward[5], Robert
Chisolm Heyward[4], George Cuthbert Heyward[3], Thomas Heyward[2], Thomas
Heyward, Jr.[1]) child of Daniel Hasell Heyward and May Mulligan was born
in Bluffton, SC on 2 Mar 1912, and died in Greenwood, SC on 20 Feb 1979.
He married Susanne Elise McKELLAR in say 1937. She was born in
Greenwood, SC on 4 Feb 1918. Children:
+ 619   i   Susanne McKellar HEYWARD, b. 28 Oct 1939
+ 620   ii Harriet McKellar HEYWARD, b. 15 Dec 1941
+ 621   iii James Edward HEYWARD, Jr., b. 17 Mar 1947
+ 622   iv Elaine McKellar HEYWARD, b. 17 Dec 1951

381. DANIEL HASELL HEYWARD, Jr.[6] (Daniel Hasell Heyward[5], Robert
Chisolm Heyward[4], George Cuthbert Heyward[3], Thomas Heyward[2], Thomas
Heyward, Jr.[1]) child of Daniel Hasell Heyward and May Mulligan was born
in Bluffton, SC on 13 Mar 1915, and died in 1997. He married Margaret
HAIR in Barnwell, SC on 21 Mar 1941. She was born in Barnwell County,
SC on 26 Jan 1922. Children:
+ 623   i   Frances Hasell HEYWARD, b. 10 Dec 1941
   624   ii Daniel Hasell HEYWARD, III, b. 8 Mar 1944, dy 25 Jan
             1959
+ 625   iii Dyan Margaret HEYWARD, b. 14 Jan 1946

382. JOSEPH CUTHBERT HEYWARD[6] (Daniel Hasell Heyward[5], Robert
Chisolm Heyward[4], George Cuthbert Heyward[3], Thomas Heyward[2], Thomas
Heyward, Jr.[1]) child of Daniel Hasell Heyward and May Mulligan was born
in Bluffton, SC on 24 Aug 1918, and died in Biloxi, MS on 28 Jan 1988. He
married Helen WILLIAMS in say 1941. Children:
   626   i   Joseph Cuthbert HEYWARD, Jr., b. c. 1944
   627   ii Maria Jo HEYWARD, b. c. 1947

383. ELLA ELIZABETH HEYWARD[6] (Daniel Hasell Heyward[5], Robert
Chisolm Heyward[4], George Cuthbert Heyward[3], Thomas Heyward[2], Thomas
Heyward, Jr.[1]) child of Daniel Hasell Heyward and May Mulligan was born
in Bluffton, SC on 8 Mar 1924. She married George Francis DeGAIN, Jr.,

son of George Francis and Grace (Carpenter) DeGain in Savannah, GA on 20 Jul 1946. He was born in Salamanca, NY on 27 Oct 1918. Children:

+ 628   i   Donald Edward DeGAIN, b. 22 Jun 1947
+ 629   ii   Grace Ann DeGAIN, b. 16 May 1950
  630   iii Richard Francis DeGAIN, b. 22 Feb 1955

384. RIEMAN McNAMARA, Jr.[6] (Selina Heyward[5], Thomas Daniel Heyward[4], George Cuthbert Heyward[3], Thomas Heyward[2], Thomas Heyward, Jr.[1]) child of Selina Heyward and Rieman McNamara was born in Richmond, VA on 25 Jul 1928. He married Merrily BROOKS, daughter of Allan Arthur and Lorraine (Wilmoth) Brooks in Franklin, NC on 2 Aug 1958. She was born in Alarka, Swain County, NC on 26 Apr 1926. Children:

  631   i   Brooks McNAMARA, b. 6 Aug 1960
  632   ii   Daniel Heyward McNAMARA, b. 28 Jul 1965

385. ISABEL HEYWARD WILSON[6] (Isabel Heyward[5], Thomas Daniel Heyward[4], George Cuthbert Heyward[3], Thomas Heyward[2], Thomas Heyward, Jr.[1]) child of Isabel Heyward and Emmet Cheatham Wilson was born in Savannah, GA on 15 Mar 1915. She married (1st) Marshall McCormick MILTON, Jr. in Birmingham, AL on 4 Aug 1938. He was born in Hagerstown, MD on 4 Oct 1912. Children:

+ 633   i   Isabel MILTON, b. 1 Jan 1941
  634   ii   Marshall McCormick MILTON, III, b. 6 Nov 1947
+ 635   iii William Byrd Lee MILTON, b. 11 Oct 1949

386. DOROTHY HEYWARD WILSON[6] (Isabel Heyward[5], Thomas Daniel Heyward[4], George Cuthbert Heyward[3], Thomas Heyward[2], Thomas Heyward, Jr.[1]) child of Isabel Heyward and Emmet Cheatham Wilson was born in Roanoke, VA on 26 Jun 1916. She married (1st) Pelham Hansard ANDERSON, Jr. in Birmingham, AL on 4 Aug 1938. He was born in Birmingham, AL on 14 Sep 1914. Children:

+ 636   i   Dorothy Fraser ANDERSON, b. 31 May 1940
+ 637   ii   Lucy Winston ANDERSON, b. 1 Apr 1945

387. WALTER STEPHEN WILSON[6] (Isabel Heyward[5], Thomas Daniel Heyward[4], George Cuthbert Heyward[3], Thomas Heyward[2], Thomas Heyward, Jr.[1]) child of Isabel Heyward and Emmet Cheatham Wilson was born in Savannah, GA on 13 Jun 1918. He married Alice Amy STEVENSON in Seattle, WA on 6 Mar 1944. She was born in Hamilton, Ontario, CANADA on 17 Nov 1919. Children:

+ 638   i   James Walter Stephen WILSON, b. 5 Oct 1945

639   ii   Richard Stevenson WILSON, b. 29 Jul 1951
640   iii   Mary Jeannette Copeland WILSON, b. 11 Aug 1952

389. THOMAS DANIEL HEYWARD WILSON[6] (Isabel Heyward[5], Thomas Daniel Heyward[4], George Cuthbert Heyward[3], Thomas Heyward[2], Thomas Heyward, Jr.[1]) child of Isabel Heyward and Emmet Cheatham Wilson was born on 19 May 1926. He married Peggy Ann GASTON on 9 Sep 1957. She was born in 1934. Child:
    641   i   Thomas Meredith WILSON, b. 9 Apr 1962

390. HELEN HEYWARD WILSON[6] (Isabel Heyward[5], Thomas Daniel Heyward[4], George Cuthbert Heyward[3], Thomas Heyward[2], Thomas Heyward, Jr.[1]) child of Isabel Heyward and Emmet Cheatham Wilson was born in Birmingham. AL on 24 Oct 1928. She married Robert Jennings STALL, Jr. in Atlanta, GA on 15 Apr 1946. He was born in Columbia, SC on 18 May 1918. Children:
    642   i   Robert Jennings STALL, III, b. 24 Apr 1947
+   643   ii   Eleanor Johnstone STALL, b. 12 Feb 1955
    644   iii   Walter Heard STALL, b. 13 Feb 1961; unm

391. ELIZABETH HEYWARD LaBRUCE[6] (Elizabeth Heyward[5], Thomas Daniel Heyward[4], George Cuthbert Heyward[3], Thomas Heyward[2], Thomas Heyward, Jr.[1]) child of Elizabeth Heyward and George Hazelhurst LaBruce was born in Savannah, GA in 30 Jul 1922. She married Albert Ellsworth PUGH on 4 Nov 1949. He was born on 17 Sep 1907. Children:
    645   i   Ellen Heyward PUGH, b. 22 Nov 1950; sp
+   646   ii   Robert Lewis PUGH, b. 1 Jan 1952
    647   iii   David William PUGH, b. 2 May 1954

392. KATHERINE FITZSIMONS LaBRUCE[6] (Elizabeth Heyward[5], Thomas Daniel Heyward[4], George Cuthbert Heyward[3], Thomas Heyward[2], Thomas Heyward, Jr.[1]) child of Elizabeth Heyward and George Hazelhurst LaBruce was born in Charleston, SC on 5 Oct 1923. She married Thomas Kenneth ROWE on 3 Sep 1945. He was born in Heathsville, VA on 22 Feb 1922. Children:
    648   i   Evelyn Fitzsimons ROWE, b. 17 Jul 1947
+   649   ii   Thomas Kenneth ROWE, Jr., b. 23 Sep 1950
+   650   iii   Elizabeth LaBruce ROWE, b. 22 Aug 1952
    651   iv   Priscilla Jett ROWE, b. 9 May 1960

393. SELINA JOHNSTONE LaBRUCE[6] (Elizabeth Heyward[5], Thomas Daniel Heyward[4], George Cuthbert Heyward[3], Thomas Heyward[2], Thomas Heyward, Jr.[1]) child of Elizabeth Heyward and George Hazelhurst LaBruce was born in Charlotte, NC on 1 May 1927. She married Hugh Richard JOHNSON, son of Hugh Richard and Gertrude (Bourne) Johnson in Charleston, SC on 5 Jun 1948. He was born in Georgetown, SC on 5 Jun 1921, and died in Savannah, GA on 24 Mar 1982. Children:

+ 652   i   Richard Elliot JOHNSON, b. 9 Mar 1949
  653   ii   George LaBruce JOHNSON, b. 21 Dec 1951, d. 1992; dsp
+ 654   iii Selina Heyward JOHNSON, b. 30 Jun 1962

396. PINCKNEY HEYWARD WALKER[6] (Edward Barnwell Walker, Jr.[5], Elizabeth Guerard Heyward[4], George Cuthbert Heyward[3], Thomas Heyward[2], Thomas Heyward, Jr.[1]) child of Edward Barnwell Walker, Jr. and Sarah Donon Pinckney was born in Charleston, SC on 11 May 1913. He married (1st) Ellen Marion JENNINGS, daughter of Dr. Curtis Herman and Ellen Marion (Hubbard) Jennings in Lexington, SC on 11 May 1933. She was born in Fitchburg, MA on 27 Jul 1911, and died on 4 Jan 1987. Children:

+ 655   i   Ellen Jael [sic] WALKER, b. 21 Aug 1935
+ 656   ii   Sarah Elizabeth WALKER, b. 27 Jul 1942
+ 657   iii Thomas Heyward WALKER, b. 24 Aug 1947

397. JOSEPH ROGERS WALKER[6] (Edward Barnwell Walker, Jr.[5], Elizabeth Guerard Heyward[4], George Cuthbert Heyward[3], Thomas Heyward[2], Thomas Heyward, Jr.[1]) child of Edward Barnwell Walker, Jr. and Sarah Donon Pinckney was born on 1 Apr 1915, and died on 25 Jul 1975. He married (1st) June LOMME in say 1939. Child:

  658   i   Joseph Rogers WALKER, Jr., b. c. 1941

398. EDWARD BARNWELL WALKER, III[6] (Edward Barnwell Walker, Jr.[5], Elizabeth Guerard Heyward[4], George Cuthbert Heyward[3], Thomas Heyward[2], Thomas Heyward, Jr.[1]) child of Edward Barnwell Walker, Jr. and Sarah Donon Pinckney was born in Charleston, SC on 26 Aug 1918, and died in 1996. He married (2nd) Shirley SASSO in Balboa, CANAL ZONE on 18 Jan 1943. She was born in Panama City, PANAMA on 13 Apr 1922. Children:

+ 659   i   Michelle Heyward WALKER, b. 3 Jan 1947
+ 660   ii   David Pinckney WALKER, b. 10 Aug 1948
  661   iii Dean Barnwell WALKER, b. c. 1951, dy
  662   iv   Rhett Barnwell WALKER, b. 24 Aug 1956

400. SARAH GERTRUDE HEYWARD[6] (William Guerard Heyward[5], John Alexander Heyward[4], George Cuthbert Heyward[3], Thomas Heyward[2], Thomas Heyward, Jr.[1]) child of William Guerard Heyward and Gertrude Exley was born in Savannah, GA on 26 Jan 1925, and died in Beaufort, SC on 24 Jun 1982. She married Frank John DROPLA on 12 Nov 1948.
Children:
+ 663   i   Frank EsDorn DROPLA, b. 17 Sep 1949
   664   ii   William Heyward DROPLA, b. 10 Jun 1951
   665   iii   Andrew Hasell DROPLA, b. 11 Jan 1967

401. MARY KATHERINE HEYWARD[6] (William Guerard Heyward[5], John Alexander Heyward[4], George Cuthbert Heyward[3], Thomas Heyward[2], Thomas Heyward, Jr.[1]) child of William Guerard Heyward and Gertrude Exley was born in Savannah, GA on 9 Sep 1927. She married EsDorn O'QUINN in Beaufort, SC on 2 Oct 1947. He was born on 24 Jun 1923.
Children:
+ 666   i   William EsDorn O'QUINN, b. 25 Sep 1947
+ 667   ii   Joseph Wales O'QUINN, b. 25 Sep 1964
+ 668   iii   John Thomas O'QUINN, b. 31 Dec 1965

402. NORA LENA HEYWARD[6] (Thomas Fleming Heyward[5], John Alexander Heyward[4], George Cuthbert Heyward[3], Thomas Heyward[2], Thomas Heyward, Jr.[1]) child of Thomas Fleming Heyward and Ella Nora Walton was born in Savannah, GA on 19 Jan 1950. She married (1st) Lonnie Brooks MUNCH in say 1969. Child:
   669   i   Emily Kathleen MUNCH, b. c. 1971

403. THOMAS FLEMING HEYWARD, Jr.[6] (Thomas Fleming Heyward[5], John Alexander Heyward[4], George Cuthbert Heyward[3], Thomas Heyward[2], Thomas Heyward, Jr.[1]) child of Thomas Fleming Heyward and Ella Nora Walton was born in Savannah, GA on 18 Jan 1953. He had a liason in say 1972. He married Cindy Lynn LEE on 23 Sep 1989. Child by liason:
   670   i   Charles Joseph HEYWARD, b. 14 Sep 1973
Children by spouse:
   671   ii   Janessa Lee HEYWARD, b. 21 Apr 1990
   672   iii   Jerica Lynn HEYWARD, b. 9 Apr 1992

404. CAROLINE HEYWARD GIGNILLIAT[6] (William Robert Gignilliat[5], Mary Caroline Heyward[4], George Cuthbert Heyward[3], Thomas Heyward[2], Thomas Heyward, Jr.[1]) child of William Robert Gignilliat and Maria Olmstead was born in Savannah, GA on 1 Aug 1915. She married W.

Chester SPARKS in Birmingham, AL on 4 Nov 1939. He was born in Russellville, AL in 1914. Children:

    673   i   Caroline Heyward SPARKS, b. 10 Jul 1943
+ 674   ii   Jean Marie SPARKS, b. 16 Sep 1945
    675   iii   Lois Virginia SPARKS, b. 24 Feb 1955

405. WILLIAM ROBERT GIGNILLIAT, Jr.[6] (William Robert Gignilliat[5], Mary Caroline Heyward[4], George Cuthbert Heyward[3], Thomas Heyward[2], Thomas Heyward, Jr.[1]) child of William Robert Gignilliat and Maria Olmstead was born in Savannah, GA on 16 Jul 1918. He married Ann Josephine HARRIS, daughter of Edward M. and Effie Harris on 16 May 1942. She was born in 1921. Children:

+ 676   i   William Robert GIGNILLIAT, III, b. 22 Mar 1943
+ 677   ii   Edward Harris GIGNILLIAT, b. 28 Aug 1944
+ 678   iii   Charles Olmstead GIGNILLIAT, b. 7 Mar 1946

406. JEAN FRANCES GIGNILLIAT[6] (William Robert Gignilliat[5], Mary Caroline Heyward[4], George Cuthbert Heyward[3], Thomas Heyward[2], Thomas Heyward, Jr.[1]) child of William Robert Gignilliat and Maria Olmstead was born in Tampa, FL on 4 Dec 1927. She married Thomas Preston COCKRELL on 3 Apr 1948. Children:

    679   i   Margaret Elizabeth COCKRELL, b. 22 May 1950
+ 680   ii   Patricia Anne COCKRELL, b. 16 Feb 1952
    681   iii   Thomas Preston COCKRELL, Jr., b. 8 Jan 1955
    682   iv   Jean Louise COCKRELL, b. 1 Sep 1960
    683   v   Ray Patrick COCKRELL, b. 17 Mar 1968

408. JEAN SINCLAIR HEYWARD[6] (Shubrick Heyward[5], Wilson Prestman Heyward[4], James Francis Heyward[3], James Hamilton Heyward[2], Thomas Heyward, Jr.[1]) child of Shubrick Heyward and Jean Sinclair Venable was born in Wilmington, DE on 31 Jul 1917. She married Charles Shoemaker TAYLOR, Jr., son of A. Merrit and Octavia M. (Reed) Taylor on 21 Oct 1939. He was born in Wayne, PA on 18 Sep 1912. Children:

    684   i   Charles Shoemaker TAYLOR, III, b. 1944
    685   ii   Anne Heyward TAYLOR, b. 1948

412. BURWELL BOYKIN CLARKE, Jr.[6] (Elizabeth Howard Burnet[5], Emma Howard Heyward[4], Elizabeth Savage Parker[3], Elizabeth Savage Heyward[2], Thomas Heyward, Jr.[1]) child of Elizabeth Howard Burnet and Burwell Boykin Clarke was born in Camden, SC on 23 Aug 1902, and died in Columbia, SC on 15 Jan 1960. He married Rosa Cantey HEYWARD in

Columbia, SC on 10 Sep 1929. She was born in Columbia, SC on 10 Sep 1905, and died there on 27 Nov 1987. Child:

+ 686   i   Elizabeth Howard CLARKE, b. 3 Aug 1930

413. THOMAS HENRY CLARKE[6] (Elizabeth Howard Burnet[5], Emma Howard Heyward[4], Elizabeth Savage Parker[3], Elizabeth Savage Heyward[2], Thomas Heyward, Jr.[1]) child of Elizabeth Howard Burnet and Burwell Boykin Clarke was born in 1904, and died in 1976. He married Sarah THURMOND in say 1942. She was born in 1910, and died in 1984. Children:

+ 687   i   Burwell Boykin CLARKE, II, b. 1941
+ 688   ii   William Lewis Bryant CLARKE, b. 1943
   689   iii   Thomas Henry CLARKE, III, b. 1946

414. ALBERTUS MOORE CLARKE[6] (Elizabeth Howard Burnet[5], Emma Howard Heyward[4], Elizabeth Savage Parker[3], Elizabeth Savage Heyward[2], Thomas Heyward, Jr.[1]) child of Elizabeth Howard Burnet and Burwell Boykin Clarke was born in Camden, SC on 15 Jan 1907, and died in Waycross, GA on 9 Jul 1986. He married Valeria North BURNET [see sketch # 417], daughter of Henry Heyward and Valeria (North) Burnet in Waycross, GA on 26 Oct 1929. She was born in Waycross, GA on 17 Mar 1905, and died there on 16 Dec 1991. Children:

+ 690   i   Henri deSaussure CLARKE, b. 13 Aug 1933
+ 691   ii   Heyward Burnet CLARKE, b. 21 Jun 1938

416. HENRY HEYWARD BURNET, Jr.[6] (Henry Heyward Burnet[5], Emma Howard Heyward[4], Elizabeth Savage Parker[3], Elizabeth Savage Heyward[2], Thomas Heyward, Jr.[1]) child of Henry Heyward Burnet and Valeria North was born in Waycross, GA on 23 Aug1902, and died in Waycross, GA on 14 Jul 1977. He married Catherine Margaret NORTH in Harrington Sound, BERMUDA on 25 Aug 1931. She was born in Harrington Sound, BER-MUDA on 7 May 1909. Children:

+ 692   i   Valeria North BURNET, b. 22 Mar 1934
+ 693   ii   Henry Heyward BURNET, III, b. 28 Mar 1939

417. VALERIA NORTH BURNET[6] (Henry Heyward Burnet[5], Emma Howard Heyward[4], Elizabeth Savage Parker[3], Elizabeth Savage Heyward[2], Thomas Heyward, Jr.[1]) child of Henry Heyward Burnet and Valeria North was born in Waycross, GA on 17 Mar 1905, and died in Waycross, GA on 16 Dec 1991. She married Albertus Moore CLARKE [see sketch # 414], son of Burwell Boykin and Elizabeth Howard (Burnet) Clarke in Waycroos, GA on 26 Oct 1929. He was born in Camden, SC on 15 Jan 1907, and died in Waycross, GA on 9 Jul 1986. Children are as reported under Sketch # 414.

418. EMMA HEYWARD BURNET[6] (Henry Heyward Burnet[5], Emma Howard Heyward[4], Elizabeth Savage Parker[3], Elizabeth Savage Heyward[2], Thomas Heyward, Jr.[1]) child of Henry Heyward Burnet and Valeria North was born in Waycross, GA on 25 May1908, and died in 1994. She married David Samuel WAINER in Thomas County, GA on 18 Jun 1933. He was born in Providence, RI on 27 Sep 1901, and died in Valdosta, GA on 30 Jan 1979. Children:

+ 694   i   Nancy Rutledge WAINER, b. 1934
+ 695   ii David Samuel WAINER, Jr., b. 20 Jan 1936
+ 696   iii Katherine Amory WAINER, b. 17 Jul 1944

420. REUBEN LUCKIE ROCKWELL, Jr.[6] (Henrietta Parker Howard[5], Henry Parker Howard[4], Elizabeth Savage Parker[3], Elizabeth Savage Heyward[2], Thomas Heyward, Jr.[1]) child of Henrietta Parker Howard and Reuben Luckie Rockwell was born in Augusta, GA on 5 Mar 1914, and died in Waynesboro, GA on 24 May 1963. He married Susan TUCKER in St. Louis, MO on 7 Feb 1943. She was born in Waynesboro, GA on 29 Jan 1920. Children:

     697   i   Memory Margaret ROCKWELL, b. c. 1953
+ 698   ii Reuben Luckie ROCKWELL, III, b. 22 Apr 1955
+ 699   iii Susan Tucker ROCKWELL, b. 26 Oct 1959

421. MARY LOUISE FOLLIARD HOWARD[6] (Robert Emmett Jenkins Howard[5], Henry Parker Howard[4], Elizabeth Savage Parker[3], Elizabeth Savage Heyward[2], Thomas Heyward, Jr.[1]) child of Robert Emmett Jenkins Howard and Mary Josephine Watters was born in Savannah, GA on 25 Aug 1907. She married Harry Hull SIMMONS on 2 Aug 1938. He was born in Savannah, GA on 21 Nov 1910, and died there on 24 Mar 1985. Children:

+ 700   i   Henry Howard SIMMONS, b. 20 Jul 1939
+ 701   ii Robert Emmett SIMMONS, b. 19 Sep 1942

423. JOSEPHINE SILVERIUS HOWARD[6] (Robert Emmett Jenkins Howard[5], Henry Parker Howard[4], Elizabeth Savage Parker[3], Elizabeth Savage Heyward[2], Thomas Heyward, Jr.[1]) child of Robert Emmett Jenkins Howard and Mary Josephine Watters was born in Savannah, GA on 20 Jun 1912, and died on 15 Dec 1976. She married John Francis ROBINSON in say 1949. He was born in Philadelphia, PA on 3 Dec 1914. Child:

+ 702   i   Josephine Ann ROBINSON, b. 11 Mar 1946

424. KATHERINE ANNE HOWARD[6] (Robert Emmett Jenkins Howard[5], Henry Parker Howard[4], Elizabeth Savage Parker[3], Elizabeth Savage Heyward[2], Thomas Heyward, Jr.[1]) child of Robert Emmett Jenkins Howard and Mary Josephine Watters was born in Savannah, GA on 26 Jan 1915. She married Arthur Michael BURKE in Utica, NY on 25 Apr 1946. Children:

    703   i   Arthur Michael BURKE, Jr., b. c. 1948
    704   ii   Kathleen Michaela BURKE, b. c. 1951
    705   iii Timothy Joseph BURKE, b. c. 1954

426. HAZEL HOWARD STERLING[6] (Lillian Jenkins Howard[5], Henry Parker Howard[4], Elizabeth Savage Parker[3], Elizabeth Savage Heyward[2], Thomas Heyward, Jr.[1]) child of Lillian Jenkins Howard and Martin Sterling was born in Washington, DC on 12 Jul 1908, and died in Ft. Lauderdale, FL in Feb 1989. She married Harold Sherlock HARWOOD in say 1928. He was born on 6 Feb 1906, and died in Jun 1955. Children:

    + 706   i   Harold Sherlock HARWOOD, Jr., b. 1929
    + 707   ii   Virginia Carolyn HARWOOD, b.1934

427. VIRGINIA DARE STERLING[6] (Lillian Jenkins Howard[5], Henry Parker Howard[4], Elizabeth Savage Parker[3], Elizabeth Savage Heyward[2], Thomas Heyward, Jr.[1]) child of Lillian Jenkins Howard and Martin Sterling was born in 1909, and died in 1987. She married Donald WOOLLEY in say 1934. He died in 1975. Child:

    708   i   Suzanne WOOLLEY, b. 1937

SEVENTH GENERATION

450. DANIEL HEYWARD HAMILTON, Jr. [7] (Daniel Heyward Hamilton[6], Miles Brewton Hamilton[5], Daniel Heyward Hamilton[4], Elizabeth Matthews Heyward[3], Daniel Heyward[2], Thomas Heyward, Jr.[1]) child of Daniel Heyward Hamilton and Margaret Munsell was born in NYC on 10 Apr 1918. He married Jane Stewart Evans NICHOLSON in Boston, MA on 12 Mar 1948. She was born in Arlington, MA on 21 May 1929. Children:

    + 709   i   Daniel Heyward HAMILTON, III, b. 1950
    + 710   ii   Margot Heyward HAMILTON, b. 1953
    + 711   iii Ann Hollister HAMILTON, b. 1955
      712   iv   Thomas Heyward Motte HAMILTON, b. 31 Mar 1969

451. MARGOT HAMILTON[7] (Daniel Heyward Hamilton[6], Miles Brewton Hamilton[5], Daniel Heyward Hamilton[4], Elizabeth Matthews Heyward[3], Daniel Heyward[2], Thomas Heyward, Jr.[1]) child of Daniel Heyward Hamilton and Margaret Munsell was born in 1920. She married James Walker COLEMAN, Jr. in say 1968. Children:

+ 713   i   James Walker COLEMAN, III, b. 1942
+ 714   ii   Heyward Hamilton COLEMAN, b. 1943
   715   iii   Alexander Chisolm COLEMAN, b. 1946
   716   iv   James Thomas COLEMAN, b. 1953

452. MARY MANIGAULT[7] (Mary Pringle Hamilton[6], Miles Brewton Hamilton[5], Daniel Heyward Hamilton[4], Elizabeth Matthews Heyward[3], Daniel Heyward[2], Thomas Heyward, Jr.[1]) child of Mary Pringle Hamilton and Edward Manigault was born about 1921. She married Frank GILBERTH in say 1953. Children:

   717   i   Rebecca Motte GILBERTH, b. 1956
   718   ii   Edward Manigault GILBERTH, b. 1959

453. PETER MANIGAULT[7] (Mary Pringle Hamilton[6], Miles Brewton Hamilton[5], Daniel Heyward Hamilton[4], Elizabeth Matthews Heyward[3], Daniel Heyward[2], Thomas Heyward, Jr.[1]) child of Mary Pringle Hamilton and Edward Manigault was born on 13 Jan 1927. He married (1st) Londine LeGENDRE in say 1959. Children:

   719   i   Gabriella MANIGAULT, b. 1960
   720   ii   Pierre MANIGAULT, b. 1962

463. JANE DuBOSE REGISTER[7] (Jane DuBose Heyward[6], Edwin Watkins Heyward[5], Thomas Savage Heyward, Jr.[4], Thomas Savage Heyward[3], Thomas Heyward[2], Thomas Heyward, Jr.[1]) child of Jane DuBose Heyward and Edward Chauncy Register was born in Atlanta, GA on 12 Apr 1912. She married John Ingram FISHBURNE in say 1959. He was born in Columbia, SC on 7 Dec 1913. Children:

+ 721   i   John Ingram FISHBURNE, Jr., b. 18 Aug 1937
+ 722   ii   Jane Heyward FISHBURNE, b. 12 Nov 1940

465. THOMAS SAVAGE HEYWARD, Jr.[7] (Thomas Savage Heyward[6], Wilmot Holmes Heyward[5], Thomas Savage Heyward, Jr.[4], Thomas Savage Heyward[3], Thomas Heyward[2], Thomas Heyward, Jr.[1]) child of Thomas Savage Heyward and Ethel Louise Hodge was born in Orlando, FL on 2 Aug 1939. He married (1st) Joanna COX in say 1959. He married (2nd) Susannah

Chapman HERBERT in Daytona, FL on 26 Nov 1964. She was born in Daytona, FL on 5 May 1937.

Child by first marriage:

723   i   Teri Lynne HEYWARD, b. 10 Apr 1961

Children by second marriage:

724   ii Alexandra Page HEYWARD, b. 4 Dec 1965

725   iii Thomas Savage HEYWARD, III, b. 15 Aug 1968 [twin]

726   iv Gratten Daniel HEYWARD, b. 15 Aug 1968 [twin]

466. DOROTHY LOUISE HEYWARD[7] (Thomas Savage Heyward[6], Wilmot Holmes Heyward[5], Thomas Savage Heyward, Jr., Thomas Savage Heyward[3], Thomas Heyward[2], Thomas Heyward, Jr.[1]) child of Thomas Savage Heyward and Ethel Louise Hodge was born in Orlando, FL on 3 Sep 1941, and died in 1982. She married James Edwin ROGERS in Auburn, AL on 30 Mar 1963. He was born in Tampa, FL on 2 Oct 1939. Children:

727   i   Allison Heyward ROGERS, b. 7 Mar 1964

728   ii Katherine Beryl ROGERS, b. 22 Feb 1967

467. FRANCES VIRGINIA HEYWARD[7] (Thomas Savage Heyward[6], Wilmot Holmes Heyward[5], Thomas Savage Heyward, Jr., Thomas Savage Heyward[3], Thomas Heyward[2], Thomas Heyward, Jr.[1]) child of Thomas Savage Heyward and Ethel Louise Hodge was born in Orlando, FL on 18 Jul 1945. She married Christopher J. PALMER in Orlando, FL on 7 Jun 1962. He was born on 28 Oct 1944. Children:

729   i   Cera Elizabeth PALMER, b. 12 Dec 1962

730   ii Deborah Anne PALMER, b. 1965

468. ROBERT BRIAN HEYWARD[7] (Thomas Savage Heyward[6], Wilmot Holmes Heyward[5], Thomas Savage Heyward, Jr., Thomas Savage Heyward[3], Thomas Heyward[2], Thomas Heyward, Jr.[1]) child of Thomas Savage Heyward and Ethel Louise Hodge was born in Orlando, FL on 17 Dec 1951. He married Alisa Gay PRICE in Burlington, Alamance County, NC on 15 Jun 1985. She was born on 1 Oct 1959. Child:

731   i   William Thomas HEYWARD, b. 28 Feb 1993

470. BARBARA MARIE JOHNSTON[7] (Rives Boykin Heyward[6], Wilmot Holmes Heyward[5], Thomas Savage Heyward, Jr., Thomas Savage Heyward[3], Thomas Heyward[2], Thomas Heyward, Jr.[1]) child of Rives Boykin Heyward and Joseph Hinkle Johnston was born on 12 Aug 1940. She married Robert PLAXICO in say 1962. Children:

732   i   Kelly Ann PLAXICO, b. 1965

733   ii Robert Jeff PLAXICO, b. 1968

471. PATRICIA JOSEPHINE JOHNSTON[7] (Rives Boykin Heyward[6], Wilmot Holmes Heyward[5], Thomas Savage Heyward, Jr., Thomas Savage Heyward[3], Thomas Heyward[2], Thomas Heyward, Jr.[1]) child of Rives Boykin Heyward and Joseph Hinkle Johnston was born on 31 Mar 1942. She married (1st) Thomas MOORE in say 1961. Child:

    734   i   Child MOORE, b. c. 1963

472. NED WATKINS HEYWARD, Jr.[7] (Ned Watkins Heyward[6], Wilmot Holmes Heyward[5], Thomas Savage Heyward, Jr., Thomas Savage Heyward[3], Thomas Heyward[2], Thomas Heyward, Jr.[1]) child of Ned Watkins Heyward and Matelyn French Landrum was born in Emory, GA on 1 Aug 1948. He married (1st) Jemille Reid WILLIAMS in Atlanta, GA on 11 Oct 1980. She was born on 22 May 1955. He married (2nd) Frieda Ann KIKER in say 1992. She was born in Hot Springs, AR in 1960.

Children by first marriage:

    735   i   Clayton Reid HEYWARD, b. 14 Sep 1983
    736   ii   Carlen Thomas HEYWARD, b. 5 Jul 1985

Child by second marriage:

    737   iii   Preston Watkins HEYWARD, b. 11 Aug 1994

473. WILLIAM LANDRUM HEYWARD[7] (Ned Watkins Heyward[6], Wilmot Holmes Heyward[5], Thomas Savage Heyward, Jr., Thomas Savage Heyward[3], Thomas Heyward[2], Thomas Heyward, Jr.[1]) child of Ned Watkins Heyward and Matelyn French Landrum was born in Emory, GA on 15 Jun 1950. He married (1st) Edith Strickland JOSLIN, daughter of George Stanley and Eleanor (Strickland) Joslin in Atlanta, GA on 26 May 1974. She was born in Emory, GA on 19 Mar 1952. Children:

    738   i   Joslin Elizabeth HEYWARD, b. 1 Dec 1982
    739   ii   Rebecca Matelyn HEYWARD, b. 3 Apr 1985

474. ELOISE VARDERY HEYWARD[7] (Hunter Boykin Heyward[6], Wilmot Holmes Heyward[5], Thomas Savage Heyward, Jr., Thomas Savage Heyward[3], Thomas Heyward[2], Thomas Heyward, Jr.[1]) child of Hunter Boykin Heyward and Martha Jaunita Weisiger was born on 11 Sep 1951. She married Charles Darold CORNELL in say 1972. Children:

    740   i   Mark David CORNELL, b. 22 Nov 1976
    741   ii   John Christopher CORNELL, b. 11 May 1979 [twin]
    742   iii   Bradley Heyward CORNELL, b. 11 May 1979 [twin]

475. MARK WEISIGER HEYWARD[7] (Hunter Boykin Heyward[6], Wilmot Holmes Heyward[5], Thomas Savage Heyward, Jr., Thomas Savage Heyward[3],

Thomas Heyward[2], Thomas Heyward, Jr.[1]) child of Hunter Boykin Heyward and Martha Jaunita Weisiger was born on 8 Aug 1955. He married Jane Beth ROGERS in say 1977. Children:

    743   i   John Weisiger HEYWARD, b. 1979
    744   ii Roger Joseph HEYWARD, b. 1981

477. JULIE JOHNSON CROCKER[7] (Lila Williams McTeer[6], Florence Percy Heyward[5], William Nathaniel Heyward, Thomas Savage Heyward[3], Thomas Heyward[2], Thomas Heyward, Jr.[1]) child of Lila Williams McTeer and George Holmes Crocker was born in Charleston, SC on 14 Mar 1929. She married Robert Lindeke SCHURMEIER on 14 Apr 1951. He was born in St. Paul, MN on 1 Oct 1926. Children:

    745   i   Sally Lindeke SCHURMEIER, b. 19 Mar 1952; sp
    746   ii Robert Lindeke SCHURMEIER, Jr., b. 25 Nov 1953
+ 747   iii Julie Susan SCHURMEIER, b. 21 Mar 1955
    748   iv Georgeanna SCHURMEIER, b. 17 Jun 1965

478. ANNA ECKLES OLTMANN[7] (Louisa Guerard McTeer[6], Florence Percy Heyward[5], William Nathaniel Heyward, Thomas Savage Heyward[3], Thomas Heyward[2], Thomas Heyward, Jr.[1]) child of Louisa Guerard McTeer and William Herbert Oltmann was born in Beaufort, SC on 25 Jan 1916. She married (1st) Elias Horry PALMER in say 1935. Child:

+ 749   i   Georgeanna Hasell PALMER, b. 24 Oct 1936

479. WILLIAM HERBERT OLTMANN, Jr.[7] (Louisa Guerard McTeer[6], Florence Percy Heyward[5], William Nathaniel Heyward, Thomas Savage Heyward[3], Thomas Heyward[2], Thomas Heyward, Jr.[1]) child of Louisa Guerard McTeer and William Herbert Oltmann was born on 30 Apr 1919, and died in 1980. He married Gertrude STEWART in say 1940. Children:

+ 750   i   William Herbert OLTMANN, III, b. 4 Apr 1941 [twin]
+ 751   ii Stewart Allen OLTMANN, b. 4 Apr 1941 [twin]
+ 752   iii Judy OLTMANN, b. 13 Nov 1945
+ 753   iv Linda OLTMANN, b. c. 1950

480. LILA CUTHBERT OLTMANN[7] (Louisa Guerard McTeer[6], Florence Percy Heyward[5], William Nathaniel Heyward, Thomas Savage Heyward[3], Thomas Heyward[2], Thomas Heyward, Jr.[1]) child of Louisa Guerard McTeer and William Herbert Oltmann was born in Beaufort, SC on 25 Jul 1922, and died in 1999. She married Francis Marion SEARSON, Jr. in Charleston, SC on 10 May 1940. He was born in Young's Island, SC on 20 Nov 1913, and died in Charleston, SC on 19 Jul 1964. Children:

+ 754   i   William Heyward SEARSON, b. 3 Mar 1941
+ 755   ii Francis Marion SEARSON, Jr., b. 1 Nov 1957

482. JANE LUCILLE McTEER[7] (James Edwin McTeer, Jr.[6], Florence Percy Heyward[5], William Nathaniel Heyward, Thomas Savage Heyward[3], Thomas Heyward[2], Thomas Heyward, Jr.[1]) child of James Edwin McTeer, Jr. and Jane Lucille Lupo was born in Beaufort, SC on 1 Apr 1928. She married John Sloman WOODS in Beaufort, SC on 12 Oct 1946. Children:
+ 756   i   Jane Lucille WOODS, b. 31 Jul 1948
+ 757   ii   Arline McTeer WOODS, b. 2 Sep 1949
+ 758   iii Lucille McTeer WOODS, b. 1 Feb 1958

483. GEORGIANNA HASELL McTEER[7] (James Edwin McTeer, Jr.[6], Florence Percy Heyward[5], William Nathaniel Heyward, Thomas Savage Heyward[3], Thomas Heyward[2], Thomas Heyward, Jr.[1]) child of James Edwin McTeer, Jr. and Jane Lucille Lupo was born in Beaufort, SC on 29 Dec 1930. She married Morris Dawes COOKE on 13 Jun 1953. Children:
+ 759   i   Morris Dawes COOKE, Jr., b. 20 Jul 1954
   760   ii   Elizabeth Meade COOKE, b. 21 Sep 1956

484. SALLY GUERARD McTEER[7] (James Edwin McTeer, Jr.[6], Florence Percy Heyward[5], William Nathaniel Heyward, Thomas Savage Heyward[3], Thomas Heyward[2], Thomas Heyward, Jr.[1]) child of James Edwin McTeer, Jr. and Jane Lucille Lupo was born in Beaufort, SC on 31 Aug 1934. She married Saxby Stowe CHAPLIN in Frogmore, SC on 4 Jul 1953. He was born in Birmingham, AL on 1 Aug 1926. Children:
   761   i   Saxby Stowe CHAPLIN, Jr., b. 27 Mar 1954
+ 762   ii   James McTeer CHAPLIN, b. 31 Mar 1957
+ 763   iii Gerald Jay CHAPLIN, b. 6 Aug 1958
   764   iv   Joseph Michael CHAPLIN, b. 18 Feb 1963, dy 20 Jul 1977

485. JAMES EDWIN McTEER, III[7] (James Edwin McTeer, Jr.[6], Florence Percy Heyward[5], William Nathaniel Heyward, Thomas Savage Heyward[3], Thomas Heyward[2], Thomas Heyward, Jr.[1]) child of James Edwin McTeer, Jr. and Jane Lucille Lupo was born in Charleston, SC on 22 Sep 1938. He married Glenda Gail ROBERTS in Anderson, SC on 4 Jun 1960. Children:
   765   i   Temple Ruth McTEER, b. 17 Apr 1961
   766   ii   Miranda Gail McTEER, b. 7 Jul 1962

486. THOMAS HEYWARD McTEER[7] (James Edwin McTeer, Jr.[6], Florence Percy Heyward[5], William Nathaniel Heyward, Thomas Savage

Heyward[3], Thomas Heyward[2], Thomas Heyward, Jr.[1]) child of James Edwin McTeer, Jr. and Jane Lucille Lupo was born in Parris Island, SC on 14 Aug 1944. He married (1st) Christine Elaine HELES in Beaufort, SC on 3 Jan 1968. He married (2nd) Eva Kathleen MARTIN in Frogmore, SC on 18 Jul 1980.

Children by first marriage:
767   i   Rebecca Oliver McTEER, b. 1 Jan 1973
768   ii Joshua Heyward McTEER, b. 10 Oct 1976

Children by second marriage:
769   iii Amanda Neil McTEER, b. 10 Jan 1982
770   iv James Edwin McTEER, II, b. 29 Dec 1983

487. FRANCES LOUISE BUTLER[7] (Margaret Williamson McTeer[6], Florence Percy Heyward[5], William Nathaniel Heyward, Thomas Savage Heyward[3], Thomas Heyward[2], Thomas Heyward, Jr.[1]) child of Margaret Williamson McTeer and James Leroy Butler was born in Beaufort, SC on 27 Sep 1922. She married (1st) Astle A. RYDER in 1940. She married (2nd) Papu TAPAO in 1963. He was born in Samoa, and died in 1998.

Child by first marriage:
771   i   Clark RYDER, b. 6 Jan 1943

Child by second marriage:
772   ii Robert Francis TAPAO, b. 3 Nov 1967

488. JAMES BYRON BUTLER[7] (Margaret Williamson McTeer[6], Florence Percy Heyward[5], William Nathaniel Heyward, Thomas Savage Heyward[3], Thomas Heyward[2], Thomas Heyward, Jr.[1]) child of Margaret Williamson McTeer and James Leroy Butler was born in Beaufort, SC on 4 Feb 1924. He married Ann STREET in say 1947. Children:
+ 773   i   Robert Byron BUTLER, b. 15 Oct 1948
   774   ii Gerald Leroy BUTLER, b. 3 Dec 1949
   775   iii John Edward BUTLER, b. 1 Dec 1950
   776   iv Richard Clark BUTLER, b. c. 1952
   777   v   Deborah Anne BUTLER, b. c. 1955

489. MARGARET McTEER BUTLER[7] (Margaret Williamson McTeer[6], Florence Percy Heyward[5], William Nathaniel Heyward, Thomas Savage Heyward[3], Thomas Heyward[2], Thomas Heyward, Jr.[1]) child of Margaret Williamson McTeer and James Leroy Butler was born in Beaufort, SC on 4 Feb 1927. She married Edgar E. THOMPSON in 1944. He died in 1998. Children:
+ 778   i   Suzanne Elizabeth THOMPSON, b. 28 Apr 1945

+ 779   ii   Patricia Ann THOMPSON, b. 5 May 1948
+ 780   iii Barbara Jean THOMPSON, b. 8 Feb 1954
   781   iv Margaret THOMPSON, b. 28 Dec 1962

490. ROBERT HENRY BUTLER[7] (Margaret Williamson McTeer[6], Florence Percy Heyward[5], William Nathaniel Heyward, Thomas Savage Heyward[3], Thomas Heyward[2], Thomas Heyward, Jr.[1]) child of Margaret Williamson McTeer and James Leroy Butler was born in Beaufort, SC on 10 Feb 1929. He married Iona C. McPHAIL on 6 Dec 1949. Child:
   782   i Debra Wallring BUTLER, b. 1951

491. CATHERINE BUTLER[7] (Margaret Williamson McTeer[6], Florence Percy Heyward[5], William Nathaniel Heyward, Thomas Savage Heyward[3], Thomas Heyward[2], Thomas Heyward, Jr.[1]) child of Margaret Williamson McTeer and James Leroy Butler was born in Beaufort, SC on 30 Jun 1930, and died in 1994. She married Howard Wesley ORWIG in say 1948. He was born in Baltimore, MD in 1923, and died in 1980. Children:
+ 783   i   Carol ORWIG, b. 1949
   784   ii Howard Wesley ORWIG, Jr., b. 2 Jun 1952
   785 iii Virginia ORWIG, b. 1954
   786   iv Larry ORWIG, b. 1959, d. 1983; unm
   787   v   Michael ORWIG, b. 1962
   788   vi Susan ORWIG, b. 1965

492. FLORENCE EXLEY BUTLER[7] (Margaret Williamson McTeer[6], Florence Percy Heyward[5], William Nathaniel Heyward, Thomas Savage Heyward[3], Thomas Heyward[2], Thomas Heyward, Jr.[1]) child of Margaret Williamson McTeer and James Leroy Butler was born in Beaufort, SC on 4 Feb 1933. She married (1st) Roy E. ALBERY in say 1948. She married (2nd) George McDURMON on 4 Jul 1959. He was born in Mount Vernon, IN on 22 Feb 1929.
Children by first marriage:
+ 789   i   Frances Geraldine ALBERY, b. 8 May 1949
+ 790   ii Roy Estle ALBERY, b. 16 Jul 1951
+ 791 iii Robert Henry ALBERY, b. 5 Jan 1955
Children by second marriage:
+ 792   iv Margaret Ann McDURMON, b. 14 Jul 1961
+ 793   v   Rosemary McDURMON, b. 18 Nov 1962
+ 794   vi Joseph Edward McDURMON, b. 13 Jun 1965

494. ANN LUCILLE BUTLER[7] (Margaret Williamson McTeer[6], Florence Percy Heyward[5], William Nathaniel Heyward, Thomas Savage Heyward[3], Thomas Heyward[2], Thomas Heyward, Jr.[1]) child of Margaret Williamson McTeer and James Leroy Butler was born in Beaufort, SC on 3 May 1935. She married Frank THOMPSON in say 1957. Children:

+ 795   i   Glenn Chester THOMPSON, b. 20 Apr 1958
   796   ii   Steven THOMPSON, b. c. 1960, d. 20 Feb 1992; unm

495. JAMES LEROY BUTLER, Jr.[7] (Margaret Williamson McTeer[6], Florence Percy Heyward[5], William Nathaniel Heyward, Thomas Savage Heyward[3], Thomas Heyward[2], Thomas Heyward, Jr.[1]) child of Margaret Williamson McTeer and James Leroy Butler was born in Beaufort, SC on 14 Nov 1937. He married Carol TOLLE in say 1960. She was born in OH in 1938. Children:

+ 797   i   James Leroy BUTLER, III, b. 23 Feb 1962
   798   ii   Vicki Lynn BUTLER, b. 14 Aug 1965

496. CAROL McTEER BUTLER[7] (Margaret Williamson McTeer[6], Florence Percy Heyward[5], William Nathaniel Heyward, Thomas Savage Heyward[3], Thomas Heyward[2], Thomas Heyward, Jr.[1]) child of Margaret Williamson McTeer and James Leroy Butler was born in Beaufort, SC on 21 Oct 1940. She married James Oliver SHIRLEY in say Feb 1956. Children:

+ 799   i   Faith Ann SHIRLEY, b. 12 Dec 1956
+ 800   ii   Terry Catherine SHIRLEY, b. 29 Sep 1959
+ 801   iii   Cheryl Marie SHIRLEY, b. 9 Jan 1961

497. MERCADE ADONIS CRAMER, Jr.[7] (Catherine Elliott McTeer[6], Florence Percy Heyward[5], William Nathaniel Heyward, Thomas Savage Heyward[3], Thomas Heyward[2], Thomas Heyward, Jr.[1]) child of Catherine Elliott McTeer and Mercade Adonis Cramer was born in Charleston, SC on 24 Mar 1932. He married Barbara Jean SPAULDING in Dayton, OH on 24 Jan 1959. She was born in West Hartford, CT on 7 Oct 1932, and died in Media, PA on 31 May 1984. Children:

   802   i   Gay Heyward CRAMER, b. 29 May 1959
   803   ii   Catherine Ruth CRAMER, b. 4 Dec 1960
   804   iii   Scott Tolman CRAMER, b. 10 May 1964

499. PAULA WOOD LENGNICK[7] (Georgianna Hasell McTeer[6], Florence Percy Heyward[5], William Nathaniel Heyward, Thomas Savage Heyward[3], Thomas Heyward[2], Thomas Heyward, Jr.[1]) child of Georgianna Hasell McTeer and Charles Alfred Lengnick was born in Charleston, SC on 7 Jan

1936. She married Colden Rhind BATTEY, Jr. in say 1956. He was born in Augusta, GA on 11 Jul 1935. Children:

+ 805   i   Colden Rhind BATTEY, III, b. 27 Aug 1957
+ 806   ii   Allison Paula BATTEY, b. 17 May 1959
  807   iii Alfred BATTEY, b. 12 Jul 1961
  808   iv   Susan Ella BATTEY, b. 17 Feb 1964

502. WALTER WITRIDGE McTEER[7] (Walter William McTeer[6], Florence Percy Heyward[5], William Nathaniel Heyward, Thomas Savage Heyward[3], Thomas Heyward[2], Thomas Heyward, Jr.[1]) child of Walter William McTeer and Mary Louise Foster was born in Charleston, SC on 19 Sep 1937. He married Mary JOHNSON, daughter of D. G. and Evelyn Johnson in say 1959. Children:

  809   i   Sheryl Marie McTEER, b. May 1961
  810   ii   Walter Witridge McTEER, Jr., b. Nov 1964

503. LOUISE HEYWARD McTEER[7] (Walter William McTeer[6], Florence Percy Heyward[5], William Nathaniel Heyward, Thomas Savage Heyward[3], Thomas Heyward[2], Thomas Heyward, Jr.[1]) child of Walter William McTeer and Mary Louise Foster was born in Florence, SC on 12 Oct 1941. She married John Lambeth FERGUSON, III, son of John Lambeth and Christine Viola (Franklin) Ferguson, Jr, in Waynesboro, GA on 19 Mar 1961. He was born in Nashville, TN on 23 Mar 1937. Children:

+ 811   i   Bonnie Louise FERGUSON, b. 15 Feb 1963
  812   ii   Meredith Gantt FERGUSON, b. 16 Sep 1969
  813   iii John Lambeth FERGUSON, IV, b. 12 Mar 1971

504. MARY ADELE McTEER[7] (Walter William McTeer[6], Florence Percy Heyward[5], William Nathaniel Heyward, Thomas Savage Heyward[3], Thomas Heyward[2], Thomas Heyward, Jr.[1]) child of Walter William McTeer and Mary Louise Foster was born in Hartsville, SC on 7 Mar 1946. She married Darvin DEASON, son of Neal Edward and Grace (Wilson) Deason in Aiken, SC on 3 Aug 1962. He was born in Millan, GA in 1941. Children:

+ 814   i   Mary Darlene DEASON, b. 16 Dec 1963
  815   ii   Cindy Marie DEASON, b. 13 Jul 1965, dy 13 Aug 1966
+ 816   iii Teresa Ann DEASON, b. 14 Dec 1967
  817   iv   Darvin DEASON, Jr., b. 29 Sep 1972

505. WILLIAM GUERARD McTEER[7] (Walter William McTeer[6], Florence Percy Heyward[5], William Nathaniel Heyward, Thomas Savage Heyward[3], Thomas Heyward[2], Thomas Heyward, Jr.[1]) child of Walter William McTeer

and Mary Louise Foster was born in Aiken, SC on 11 Jul 1950. He married
Marsha CHANCE, daughter of William Hardy and Inez Floyd (Waters)
Chance in say 1974. She was born on 15 Aug 1952. Children:

818   i   Jessica Ann McTEER, b. 4 Jun 1976
819   ii William Jeremy McTEER, b. 4 Oct 1978
820   iii Corey William McTEER, b. 19 Sep 1986

506. FLORENCE HEYWARD STEVENS[7] (Florence Percy McTeer[6],
Florence Percy Heyward[5], William Nathaniel Heyward, Thomas Savage
Heyward[3], Thomas Heyward[2], Thomas Heyward, Jr.[1]) child of Florence
Percy McTeer and William Turner Stevens was born in Beaufort, SC on 4
Oct 1936. She married Gene Wyman SANDERS in Barnwell, SC in say
1957. Child:

821   i   Florence Suzanne SANDERS, b. 1961

509. JACK ELQUIT ALTMAN, Jr.[7] (Helen Perry Claire Heyward[6], Henry
Guerard Heyward[5], William Nathaniel Heyward, Thomas Savage Heyward[3],
Thomas Heyward[2], Thomas Heyward, Jr.[1]) child of Helen Perryclaire
Heyward and Jack Elquit Altman was born in Savannah. GA on 11 Aug
1927. He married Ann Desbouillions MORGAN, daughter of Charles
Franklin and Louise (Desbouillions) Morganin Savannah, GA on 31 Mar
1951. She was born in Savannah, GA on 13 Oct 1931. Children:

+ 822   i   Jack Elquit ALTMAN, III, b. 2 Apr 1952
+ 823   ii Nancy Desbouillions ALTMAN, b. 4 Feb 1955
+ 824   iii Sally Ann ALTMAN, b. 2 Jan 1958
    825   iv Ann Morgan ALTMAN, b. 3 May 1963

510. HENRY GUERARD HEYWARD, III[7] (Henry Guerard Heyward,Jr.[6],
Henry Guerard Heyward[5], William Nathaniel Heyward, Thomas Savage
Heyward[3], Thomas Heyward[2], Thomas Heyward, Jr.[1]) child of Henry
Guerard Heyward, Jr. and Kathryn Virginia Bird was born in Savannah. GA
on 16 Nov 1949. He married Dell Charlene CROMER in say 1976. She was
born in Augusta, GA on 1 Jan 1953. Children:

826   i   Justin Guerard HEYWARD, b. 1980
827   ii Lauren Ashley HEYWARD, b. 1982

511. BRENDA KAY HEYWARD[7] (Henry Guerard Heyward,Jr.[6], Henry
Guerard Heyward[5], William Nathaniel Heyward, Thomas Savage Heyward[3],
Thomas Heyward[2], Thomas Heyward, Jr.[1]) child of Henry Guerard
Heyward, Jr. and Kathryn Virginia Bird was born in Savannah,GA on 20

Nov 1950. She married Robert D. GUNN in say 1975. He was born in Lake City, FL in 1930, and died in 1992. Children:

828   i   Matthew Robert GUNN, b. 21 Jan 1978
829   ii Heyward Elizabeth GUNN, b. 21 Feb 1980

512. VIRGINIA LYNN HEYWARD[7] (Henry Guerard Heyward, Jr.[6], Henry Guerard Heyward[5], William Nathaniel Heyward, Thomas Savage Heyward[3], Thomas Heyward[2], Thomas Heyward, Jr.[1]) child of Henry Guerard Heyward, Jr. and Kathryn Virginia Bird was born in Savannah. GA on 15 Aug 1952. She married Stacey THOMPSON in say 1981. He was born in Savannah, GA in 1957. Child:

830   i   Amanda THOMPSON, b. 19 Sep 1989

513. KAY HEYWARD SCONYERS[7] (Catherine Kirk Heyward[6], Henry Guerard Heyward[5], William Nathaniel Heyward, Thomas Savage Heyward[3], Thomas Heyward[2], Thomas Heyward, Jr.[1]) child of Catherine Kirk Heyward and William Chandler Sconyers, Jr. was born on 23 Aug 1937. She married Morris Eugene HUTCHINSON in say 1957. He was born on 2 Dec 1932, and died on 23 Sep 1967. Children:

+ 831   i   Ashley Kay HUTCHINSON, b. 8 Mar 1958
+ 832   ii Holly HUTCHINSON, b. 5 Feb 1961

514. WILLIAM CHANDLER SCONYERS, III[7] (Catherine Kirk Heyward[6], Henry Guerard Heyward[5], William Nathaniel Heyward, Thomas Savage Heyward[3], Thomas Heyward[2], Thomas Heyward, Jr.[1]) child of Catherine Kirk Heyward and William Chandler Sconyers, Jr. was born on 14 Feb 1941, and died on 28 Feb 1969. He married Lisa FINE in say 1960. Child:

+ 833   i   Lisa SCONYERS, b. 21 Oct 1962

515. DEBORAH HEYWARD McMURRAIN[7] (Virginia Rutledge Heyward[6], Henry Guerard Heyward[5], William Nathaniel Heyward, Thomas Savage Heyward[3], Thomas Heyward[2], Thomas Heyward, Jr.[1]) child of Virginia Rutledge Heyward and James Leon McMurrain, Jr. was born in Knoxville, TN on 21 Jan 1952. She married Clifford Carson CRUZE in Knoxville, TN on 19 Aug 1977. He was born on 11 Jan 1948. Children:

834   i   Jessica Louise CRUZE, b. 4 Apr 1980
835   ii Emily Heyward CRUZE, b. 6 Jun 1983

516. ALICE McMURRAIN[7] (Virginia Rutledge Heyward[6], Henry Guerard Heyward[5], William Nathaniel Heyward, Thomas Savage Heyward[3], Thomas Heyward[2], Thomas Heyward, Jr.[1]) child of Virginia Rutledge Heyward and

James Leon McMurrain, Jr. was born in Knoxville, TN on 25 Mar 1958. She married Gary Wayne BRANDON in say 1988. He was born on 16 Feb 1957. Child:

> 836   i   Matthew Wayne BRANDON, b. 30 Jun 1994

517. NORMA McMURRAIN[7] (Virginia Rutledge Heyward[6], Henry Guerard Heyward[5], William Nathaniel Heyward, Thomas Savage Heyward[3], Thomas Heyward[2], Thomas Heyward, Jr.[1]) child of Virginia Rutledge Heyward and James Leon McMurrain, Jr. was born in Knoxville, TN on 25 Mar 1958. She married Benjamin T. HARRINGTON in say 1985. He was born on 2 Dec 1959. Children:

> 837   i   Donovan James HARRINGTON, b. 28 Jun 1989
> 838   ii   Jackson Stewart HARRINGTON, b. 8 Apr 1994

518. PATRICIA ANN GOETHE[7] (Caroline Screven Heyward[6], Henry Guerard Heyward[5], William Nathaniel Heyward, Thomas Savage Heyward[3], Thomas Heyward[2], Thomas Heyward, Jr.[1]) child of Caroline Screven Heyward and Wallace Goethe was born on 15 Dec 1948. She married Frank HODGE, Jr. in say 1968. Children:

> 839   i   Perry HODGE, b. 20 Oct 1970
> 840   ii   Christopher Wallace HODGE, b. 23 Oct 1973

519. MARY ANNE HEYWARD[7] (William Smith Heyward[6], William Burroughs Smith Heyward[5], Andrew Hasell Heyward, Thomas Savage Heyward[3], Thomas Heyward[2], Thomas Heyward, Jr.[1]) child of William Smith Heyward and Annie Sinkler Walker was born in Charleston, SC on 25 Jul 1918. She married (2nd) Alfred Riggs FERGUSON, son of the Rev. John Bohn and Margaret Langley (Williams) Ferguson in Covington, KY on 23 May 1948. He was born in Hopewell, IN on 15 Aug 1915, and died on 5 May 1974. Children:

> + 841   i   Margaret Williams FERGUSON, b. 28 Dec 1948
> + 842   ii   Jean Heyward FERGUSON, b. 8 Feb 1951
> + 843   iii   Lucy Pinckney FERGUSON, b. 3 Oct 1954

520. VIRGINIA HUGHES HEYWARD[7] (William Smith Heyward[6], William Burroughs Smith Heyward[5], Andrew Hasell Heyward, Thomas Savage Heyward[3], Thomas Heyward[2], Thomas Heyward, Jr.[1]) child of William Smith Heyward and Annie Sinkler Walker was born in Charleston, SC on 12 Nov 1919, and died on 31 Dec 1967. She married David Yost COVERSTON, son of Harry Ethelbert and Mary Louise (Reed) Coverston on 11 Sep 1943. He was born in Shamrock, OK on 4 Feb 1920. Children:

844   i   John David COVERSTON, b. 28 Apr 1953, d. Jun 1979;
             unm
+ 845   ii Anne Heyward COVERSTON, b. 7 Mar 1955

521. MARIAN ROCHELLE HEYWARD[7] (Emory Speer Heyward[6], Andrew Hasell Heyward, Jr.[5], Andrew Hasell Heyward, Thomas Savage Heyward[3], Thomas Heyward[2], Thomas Heyward, Jr.[1]) child of Emory Speer Heyward and Eugenia Louise Powell was born in Macon, GA in 1935. She married William Joseph YEAGER, son of Otis Melton and Lula (Toone) Yeager in Washington, DC in 1954. He was born in Atlanta, GA in 1931, and died in 1982. Children:
+ 846   i   William Joseph YEAGER, Jr., b. 1956
+ 847   ii   Susan Ellen YEAGER, b. 1958
   848   iii Alan Winton YEAGER, b. 1963
+ 849   iv   Keith Heyward YEAGER, b. 1966

522. EUGENIA LOUISE HEYWARD[7] (Emory Speer Heyward[6], Andrew Hasell Heyward, Jr.[5], Andrew Hasell Heyward, Thomas Savage Heyward[3], Thomas Heyward[2], Thomas Heyward, Jr.[1]) child of Emory Speer Heyward and Eugenia Louise Powell was born in Macon, GA in 1938. She married Daniel Eleby DAVIS in say 1959. He was born in Miami, FL in 1930. Child:
   850   i   Laurie Louise DAVIS, b. 1961

523. EMORY SPEER HEYWARD, Jr.[7] (Emory Speer Heyward[6], Andrew Hasell Heyward, Jr.[5], Andrew Hasell Heyward, Thomas Savage Heyward[3], Thomas Heyward[2], Thomas Heyward, Jr.[1]) child of Emory Speer Heyward and Eugenia Louise Powell was born in Macon, GA in 1941. He married Sue TRAPNELL in say 1963. She was born in Lagrange, GA in 1943. Children:
   851   i   Julia Lynn HEYWARD, b. 1965, dy 1980
   852   ii   Emory Speer HEYWARD, III, b. 1969
   853   iii Janet Lea HEYWARD, b. 1972

524. ANDREW HASELL HEYWARD, IV[7] (Andrew Hasell Heyward, III[6], Andrew Hasell Heyward, Jr.[5], Andrew Hasell Heyward, Thomas Savage Heyward[3], Thomas Heyward[2], Thomas Heyward, Jr.[1]) child of Andrew Hasell Heyward, III and Mildred Goodrum was born in NYC on 20 Dec 1934. He married Carol INMAN, daughter of Richard M. and Laura R. Inman on 25 Jun 1960. She was born in Orlando, FL on 20 Feb 1936. Children:
   854   i   Andrew Hasell HEYWARD, V, b. 15 May 1961
+ 855   ii   Laura Ellen HEYWARD, b. 28 Jan 1963

525. MILDRED HEYWARD[7] (Andrew Hasell Heyward, III[6], Andrew Hasell Heyward, Jr.[5], Andrew Hasell Heyward, Thomas Savage Heyward[3], Thomas Heyward[2], Thomas Heyward, Jr.[1]) child of Andrew Hasell Heyward, III and Mildred Goodrum was born on 10 Apr 1941. She married George Clisby CLARKE, II in say 1967. Children:

   856   i   Katherine Lucinda CLARKE, b. 23 Feb 1969
   857   ii   Caroline Heyward CLARKE, b. 11 Nov 1970

526. MARCELLA HEYWARD[7] (Eustace Willoughby Speer Heyward[6], Andrew Hasell Heyward, Jr.[5], Andrew Hasell Heyward, Thomas Savage Heyward[3], Thomas Heyward[2], Thomas Heyward, Jr.[1]) child of Eustace Willoughby Speer Heyward and Marcella Martin was born in 1957. She married Alan L. KUYKENDALL in say 1981. He was born in 1954. Child:

   858   i   Marcella L. KUYKENDALL, b. 1986

527. HELEN VANCE HEYWARD[7] (Marion Speer Heyward[6], Andrew Hasell Heyward, Jr.[5], Andrew Hasell Heyward, Thomas Savage Heyward[3], Thomas Heyward[2], Thomas Heyward, Jr.[1]) child of Marion Speer Heyward and Eleanor Vance was born in Macon, GA in 1942. She married Jerry KILGO in say 1963. Children:

   859   i   Andrea A. KILGO, b. 1967
+ 860   ii   Angela Suzanne KILGO, b. 1975

531. BRONSON C. RUMSEY, Jr.[7] (Elizabeth Beckwith Lynah[6], James Lynah[5], Ella Louise Heyward, Thomas Savage Heyward[3], Thomas Heyward[2], Thomas Heyward, Jr.[1]) child of Elizabeth Beckwith Lynah and Bronson C. Rumsey was born on 8 Nov 1929. He married (1st) Martha Anne OSBORNE in say 1951. He married (2nd) Shirley WALTERS in say 1957. He married (3rd) Diana SWEET in say 1970.

Child by first marriage:
+ 861   i   Martha Elizabeth RUMSEY, b. 19 Aug 1952
Children by second marriage:
+ 862   ii   Bronson C. RUMSEY, III, b. 1 Jul 1959
   863 iii   Daniel Walters RUMSEY, b. 4 Apr 1961
Children by third marriage:
   864   iv   Georgina Beckwith RUMSEY, b. 28 Mar 1972
   865   v   Elizabeth Barron RUMSEY, b. 12 Dec 1974

532. JAMES LYNAH RUMSEY[7] (Elizabeth Beckwith Lynah[6], James Lynah[5], Ella Louise Heyward, Thomas Savage Heyward[3], Thomas Heyward[2], Thomas Heyward, Jr.[1]) child of Elizabeth Beckwith Lynah and

Bronson C. Rumsey was born in Billings, MT on 31 Oct 1932. He married Barbara MOORE in say 1956. He was born in Denver, CO on 9 Jan 1936. Children:

    866   i   Rebecca Brown RUMSEY, b. 12 Jan 1960
    867   ii   Robert Moore RUNSEY, b. 30 Jul 1966
    868   iii Suzanne Beckwith RUMSEY, b. 2 Jun 1970

533. GEORGE SHERRILL, Jr.[7] (Maria Glover Lynah[6], James Lynah[5], Ella Louise Heyward, Thomas Savage Heyward[3], Thomas Heyward[2], Thomas Heyward, Jr.[1]) child of Maria Glover Lynah and George Sherrill was born in Atlanta, GA on 11 Mar 1932. He married Claire Ridley GARDNER, daughter of Robert Emerson and Mary Cobb (Hunnicut) Gardner in Atlanta, GA on 12 Dec 1959. She was born in Atlanta, GA on 9 Dec 1937. Children:

+ 869   i   George SHERRILL, III, b. 15 Feb 1966
    870   ii   Robert Gardner SHERRILL, b. 18 Nov 1969

534. JAMES LYNAH SHERRILL[7] (Maria Glover Lynah[6], James Lynah[5], Ella Louise Heyward, Thomas Savage Heyward[3], Thomas Heyward[2], Thomas Heyward, Jr.[1]) child of Maria Glover Lynah and George Sherrill was born in Atlanta, GA on 14 Jun 1935. He married Mary Lou INGRAM, daughter of James Frederick and Jane (McConnell) Ingram in Beaver Falls, PA on 28 Dec 1957. She was born in Beaver Falls, PA on 19 Mar 1937. Children:

+ 871   i   Christine Lynah SHERRILL, b. 28 Jul 1959
    872   ii   Polly Ann SHERRILL, b. 26 Jun 1960
+ 873   iii James Lynah SHERRILL, Jr., b. 8 Apr 1962
+ 874   iv Jeffrey Ingram SHERRILL, b. 17 Oct 1963
    875   v   Mary Catherine SHERRILL, b. 1 Feb 1970

535. ELIZABETH HUGER HARRISON[7] (Ella Louise Heyward Lynah[6], James Lynah[5], Ella Louise Heyward, Thomas Savage Heyward[3], Thomas Heyward[2], Thomas Heyward, Jr.[1]) child of Ella Louise Heyward Lynah and Joseph Huger Harrison was born in Savannah, GA on 29 Nov 1933. She married Lawrence Miner AUSTIN, son of John Hogg and Helen Elizabeth (Miner) Austin in Savannah, GA on 22 Dec 1954. He was born in Ardmore, PA on 19 Jun 1930. Children:

+ 876   i   Elizabeth Huger AUSTIN, b. 13 Jan 1956
+ 877   ii   Lawrence Miner AUSTIN, Jr., b. 6 Dec 1957
    878   iii James Keighly AUSTIN, b. 6 Feb 1965

536. ROBERT LYNAH HARRISON[7] (Ella Louise Heyward Lynah[6], James Lynah[5], Ella Louise Heyward, Thomas Savage Heyward[3], Thomas Heyward[2], Thomas Heyward, Jr.[1]) child of Ella Louise Heyward Lynah and Joseph Huger Harrison was born in Savannah, GA on 8 Dec 1939. He married Susan Louise WOLFE, daughter of William and Jeanette (Bartels) Wolfe in Houston, TX on 20 Jun 1966. She was born in Pittsburgh, PA on 16 Apr 1942. Children:

  879   i   Eleanor Stuart HARRISON, b. 10 Jul 1970
  880   ii   Catherine Huger HARRISON, b. 31 Jul 1973
  881   iii   Margaret Lynah HARRISON, b. 10 Nov 1976

537. JOSEPH HUGER HARRISON[7] (Ella Louise Heyward Lynah[6], James Lynah[5], Ella Louise Heyward, Thomas Savage Heyward[3], Thomas Heyward[2], Thomas Heyward, Jr.[1]) child of Ella Louise Heyward Lynah and Joseph Huger Harrison was born in Savannah, GA on 20 Oct 1943. He married Gloria HORTON in Atlanta, GA on 11 Apr 1981. She was born in Atlanta, GA on 7 Nov 1947. Children:

  882   i   Isabelle Marie HARRISON, b. 22 Jul 1984
  883   ii   Benjamin Huger HARRISON, b. 19 Jul 1988

538. STEPHEN PALMER DOWDNEY[7] (Ella Heyward Palmer[6], Eloise Lynah[5], Ella Louise Heyward, Thomas Savage Heyward[3], Thomas Heyward[2], Thomas Heyward, Jr.[1]) child of Ella Heyward Palmer and Samuel Emerson Dowdney was born in Hyannis, MA on 25 Dec 1943. He married Mary Ellen JACKSON in Jan 1970. Children:

  884   i   Stephen Palmer DOWDNEY, Jr., b. 26 Oct 1970
  885   ii   Thomas Heyward DOWDNEY, b. 9 Oct 1973

539. JOHN HEYWARD DOWDNEY[7] (Ella Heyward Palmer[6], Eloise Lynah[5], Ella Louise Heyward, Thomas Savage Heyward[3], Thomas Heyward[2], Thomas Heyward, Jr.[1]) child of Ella Heyward Palmer and Samuel Emerson Dowdney was born in NYC on 11 Jun 1949. He married Marsha WEAVER in Apr 1978. Children:

  886   i   Samuel Emerson DOWDNEY, II, b. 26 Jun 1980
  887   ii   Matthew Heyward DOWDNEY, b. 31 Jan 1983

544. HARRY TIMROD PALMER[7] (James Lynah Palmer[6], Eloise Lynah[5], Ella Louise Heyward, Thomas Savage Heyward[3], Thomas Heyward[2], Thomas Heyward, Jr.[1]) child of James Lynah Palmer and Particia Semple Bourne was born in Charleston, SC on 12 Aug 1955. He married Diane

Marie NATALE in Philadelphia, PA in say 1980. She was born in Philadelphia, PA on 10 Nov 1953. Children:

888   i   Alison Heyward PALMER, b. 1983
889   ii   Kyle McKenzie PALMER, b. 1985 [twin]
890   iii Cody Lynah PALMER, b. 1985 [twin]

545. PATRICIA BOURNE PALMER[7] (James Lynah Palmer[6], Eloise Lynah[5], Ella Louise Heyward, Thomas Savage Heyward[3], Thomas Heyward[2], Thomas Heyward, Jr.[1]) child of James Lynah Palmer and Particia Semple Bourne was born in Charleston, SC on 11 Jun 1958. She married William WALPOLE in say 1979. Children:

891   i   John William Edings WALPOLE, b. 1981
892   ii   Ashley Addison Butler WALPOLE, b. 1983

546. HELEN STROBAHR PALMER[7] (James Lynah Palmer[6], Eloise Lynah[5], Ella Louise Heyward, Thomas Savage Heyward[3], Thomas Heyward[2], Thomas Heyward, Jr.[1]) child of James Lynah Palmer and Particia Semple Bourne was born in Charleston, SC on 29 Sep 1960. She married Randolph William COOPER in say 1980. He was born in Charleston, SC on 17 May 1957. Children:

893   i   Sarah Louise Churchill COOPER, b. c. 1982
894   ii   Randolph William COOPER, Jr., b. c. 1985

547. HONOR HEYWARD BULKLEY[7] (Anne Cuthbert Palmer[6], Eloise Lynah[5], Ella Louise Heyward, Thomas Savage Heyward[3], Thomas Heyward[2], Thomas Heyward, Jr.[1]) child of Anne Cuthbert Palmer and Jonathan Duncan Bulkley was born in San Francisco, CA on 25 Feb 1958. She married Juan Emanuel ARMAS in San Francisco, CA on 6 Nov 1986. He was born in Los Angeles, CA on 31 Jan 1955. Child:

895   i   Wynanda Heyward Bulkley ARMAS, b. c. 1987

550. NANCY COLQUITT LYNAH[7] (John Heyward Lynah[6], John Heyward Lynah, Jr.[5], Ella Louise Heyward, Thomas Savage Heyward[3], Thomas Heyward[2], Thomas Heyward, Jr.[1]) child of John Heyward Lynah and Anna Colquitt Hunter was born in Fort Sill, OK on 9 Feb 1943. She married Nowell STEBBING in say 1963. Children:

896   i   Claire Hunter STEBBING, b. 25 Jan 1964
897   ii   Zoe Elizabeth STEBBING, b. 8 Mar 1968
898   iii Jonathan Heyward STEBBING, b. c. 1973

551. MARY SAVAGE LYNAH[7] (John Heyward Lynah[6], John Heyward Lynah, Jr.[5], Ella Louise Heyward, Thomas Savage Heyward[3], Thomas Heyward[2], Thomas Heyward, Jr.[1]) child of John Heyward Lynah and Anna Colquitt Hunter [changed her name after a divorce to Mary Hunter Lynah] was born in Savannah, GA on 20 Feb 1945. She married Robert Russell POST, Jr. in say 1966. Children:

    899   i   Jeffrey POST, b. c. 1969
    900   ii Jennifer POST, b. c. 1972

554. SAMUEL HEYWARD HIGGENBOTTOM[7] (Mary Howard Lynah[6], John Heyward Lynah, Jr.[5], Ella Louise Heyward, Thomas Savage Heyward[3], Thomas Heyward[2], Thomas Heyward, Jr.[1]) child of Mary Howard Lynah and David Higgenbottom [after his parents divorce, his surname was changed to LYNAH] was born on 6 Sep 1946. He married Susan Eidson McKENZIE in say 1966. Child:

    901   i   Emily McKenzie LYNAH, b. 1984

556. JAMES LYNAH[7] (Savage Heyward Lynah[6], John Heyward Lynah, Jr.[5], Ella Louise Heyward, Thomas Savage Heyward[3], Thomas Heyward[2], Thomas Heyward, Jr.[1]) child of Savage Heyward Lynah and Ruth Artley Cain was born on 24 Jun 1950. He married Cindy ELLIS in say 1968. Children:

+ 902   i   Elizabeth LYNAH, b. 28 May 1968
    903   ii James LYNAH, Jr., b. 31 Oct 1970
    904 iii Wesley Morris LYNAH, b. 26 Nov 1978
    905   iv Jessica Cain LYNAH, b. 13 Feb 1984

557. THOMAS RAVENEL LYNAH[7] (Savage Heyward Lynah[6], John Heyward Lynah, Jr.[5], Ella Louise Heyward, Thomas Savage Heyward[3], Thomas Heyward[2], Thomas Heyward, Jr.[1]) child of Savage Heyward Lynah and Ruth Artley Cain was born on 4 Nov 1952. He married Mary Ann HENRY in say 1971. Children:

    906   i   Thomas Ravenel LYNAH, Jr., b. 22 Jun 1972
    907   ii John Collette LYNAH, b. 30 Oct 1977

558. KATHERINE SAVAGE LYNAH[7] (Savage Heyward Lynah[6], John Heyward Lynah, Jr.[5], Ella Louise Heyward, Thomas Savage Heyward[3], Thomas Heyward[2], Thomas Heyward, Jr.[1]) child of Savage Heyward Lynah and Ruth Artley Cain was born on 29 Apr 1955. She married William Baylus HOLLIDAY in say 1977. Children:

    908   i   Kathleen Lewis HOLLIDAY, b. 22 Sep 1980

909   ii   Emily Ruth HOLLIDAY, b. 13 Jul 1982
910   iii William Baylus HOLLIDAY, Jr., b. 19 Feb 1984

559. SAVAGE HEYWARD LYNAH, Jr.[7] (Savage Heyward Lynah[6], John Heyward Lynah, Jr.[5], Ella Louise Heyward, Thomas Savage Heyward[3], Thomas Heyward[2], Thomas Heyward, Jr.[1]) child of Savage Heyward Lynah and Ruth Artley Cain was born on 25 Oct 1961. He married Jill DeAnne FOUNTAIN in say 1986. Children:
911   i   Savage Heyward LYNAH, III, b. 14 Mar 1988
912   ii   Virginia Artley LYNAH, b. 25 Jun 1991

561. HELEN FAIRCHILD LYNAH[7] (Wallace Howard Lynah[6], John Heyward Lynah, Jr.[5], Ella Louise Heyward, Thomas Savage Heyward[3], Thomas Heyward[2], Thomas Heyward, Jr.[1]) child of Wallace Howard Lynah and Helen Rowland was born on 15 Apr 1956. She married Marshall STONE in say 1985. Children:
913   i   Wesley TenBroeck STONE, b. 1989
914   ii   Lynah Elizabeth STONE, b. 1991

563. MARY ROWLAND LYNAH[7] (Wallace Howard Lynah[6], John Heyward Lynah, Jr.[5], Ella Louise Heyward, Thomas Savage Heyward[3], Thomas Heyward[2], Thomas Heyward, Jr.[1]) child of Wallace Howard Lynah and Helen Rowland was born in 1966. She married Christian LEWIS in say 1989. Child:
915   i   Mary Rowland LEWIS, b. 1996

566. ROBERT EDMUND HEYWARD[7] (William Henry Heyward[6], John Boykin Heyward, Jr.[5], John Boykin Heyward[4], Thomas Savage Heyward[3], Thomas Heyward[2], Thomas Heyward, Jr.[1]) child of William Henry Heyward and Betty Jean Markle was born in East Orange, NJ on 28 May 1945. He married Cassandra Lee FRASER in Corte Madera, CA on 20 Apr 1968. She was born in Portland, OR on 16 Nov 1946. Children:
916   i   Robert Jon HEYWARD, b. 15 Dec 1969
917   ii   Jason Alexander HEYWARD, b. 10 Sep 1974

567. R. BURKE HAMMES, Jr.[7] (Daisy Vincent Martin[6], Martha Horry Howard[5], Annie Howard Webb[4], Elizabeth Savage Heyward[3], Thomas Heyward[2], Thomas Heyward, Jr.[1]) child of Daisy Vincent Martin and R. Burke Hammes was born in Charleston, SC in 1920. He married Jane Wynne TOUCHEY in Charleston, SC on 18 Apr 1942. She was born in Charleston, SC on 20 Oct 1925. Children:

+ 918   i   Roman Burchart HAMMES, b. 19 Feb 1943
   919   ii   Jane Marie HAMMES, b. 7 Apr 1944
   920   iii   Robert Touchey HAMMES, b. 3 Sep 1946
   921   iv   Louise Vincent HAMMES, b. 1 Nov 1950
   922   v   Michael L. HAMMES, b. 12 Nov 1952
   923   vi   John Martin HAMMES, b. 24 Mar 1960
   924   vii   Anne Walsh HAMMES, b. 13 Mar 1961

570. ANN CUTHBERT MARTIN[7] (John Vincent Martin[6], Martha Horry Howard[5], Annie Howard Webb[4], Elizabeth Savage Heyward[3], Thomas Heyward[2], Thomas Heyward, Jr.[1]) child of John Vincent Martin and Elsie Leadbetter was born in Washington, DC on 29 Oct 1926. She married John Wilbur PHENICIE, Jr. in say 1946. He was born in Sealy, TX on 27 Jan 1924. Children:

+ 925   i   John Vincent PHENICIE, b. 22 Jan 1948
+ 926   ii   William Martin PHENICIE, b. 28 Jan 1950
+ 927   iii   Thomas Heyward PHENICIE, b. 7 Apr 1953
+ 928   iv   Martha Ann PHENICIE, b. 14 Aug 1959
   929   v   James Middleton PHENICIE, b. 24 Apr 1962

571. ELSIE LEADBETTER MARTIN[7] (John Vincent Martin[6], Martha Horry Howard[5], Annie Howard Webb[4], Elizabeth Savage Heyward[3], Thomas Heyward[2], Thomas Heyward, Jr.[1]) child of John Vincent Martin and Elsie Leadbetter was born in Houston, TX in 1928, and died in 1994. She married Richard B. WALTON in say 1951. He was born in Glenridge, NJ in 1926, and died in 1963. Children:

   930   i   Robert Davenport WALTON, b. 1953
+ 931   ii   William Howard WALTON, b. 1957
   932   iii   Charles Martin WALTON, b. 1962, dy 1966

572. JOHN ELMORE MARTIN[7] (John Vincent Martin[6], Martha Horry Howard[5], Annie Howard Webb[4], Elizabeth Savage Heyward[3], Thomas Heyward[2], Thomas Heyward, Jr.[1]) child of John Vincent Martin and Elsie Leadbetter was born in Houston, TX in 1929. He married Margaret KIEBERGER in say 1952. She was born in Houston, TX in 1929. Children:

   933   i   John Vincent MARTIN, b. 1956
+ 934   ii   David Allan MARTIN, b. 1957

573. JOHN SMALLBROOK HOWKINS, III[7] (John Smallbrook Howkins, Jr.[6], Elise Heyward[5], Jacob Guerard Heyward[4], George Cuthbert Heyward[3], Thomas Heyward[2], Thomas Heyward, Jr.[1]) child of John Smallbrook

Howkins, Jr. and Alice Keller Huger was born in Savannah, GA in 1925. He married Virginia Ruth LYONS in say 1949. She was born in Hattiesburg, MS in 1926, and died in 1981. Children:

   935   i   Mary Alice HOWKINS, b. 1951
+ 936   ii Elizabeth Lyons HOWKINS, b. 1953

574. JOHN HUGER HOWKINS[7] (John Smallbrook Howkins, Jr.[6], Elise Heyward[5], Jacob Guerard Heyward[4], George Cuthbert Heyward[3], Thomas Heyward[2], Thomas Heyward, Jr.[1]) child of John Smallbrook Howkins, Jr. and Alice Keller Huger was born in Savannah, GA in 1927. He married Mary Louise KEY in say 1952. She was born in 1925. Child:

+ 937   i   John Huger HOWKINS, Jr., b. 1955

576. GUERARD HEYWARD HOWKINS, Jr.[7] (Guerard Heyward Howkins[6], Elise Heyward[5], Jacob Guerard Heyward[4], George Cuthbert Heyward[3], Thomas Heyward[2], Thomas Heyward, Jr.[1]) child of Guerard Heyward Howkins and Elizabeth Heyward Cassidy was born in 1919. He married Ann LORD in say 1952. Child:

   938   i   Mary Anne HOWKINS, b. 1954

577. JOHN HENRY FRANCIS HOWKINS[7] (Guerard Heyward Howkins[6], Elise Heyward[5], Jacob Guerard Heyward[4], George Cuthbert Heyward[3], Thomas Heyward[2], Thomas Heyward, Jr.[1]) child of Guerard Heyward Howkins and Elizabeth Heyward Cassidy was born in 1921. He married (1st) Phyllis DANA in say 1946. She was born in 1923, and died in 1971. He married (2nd) Agnes DEVINE in say 1972. She was born in 1943.
Children by first marriage:
+ 939   i   Elizabeth Heyward HOWKINS, b. 1948
+ 940   ii Ann Chinn HOWKINS, b. 1950
Children by second marriage:
   941   iii Reyna HOWKINS, b. 1972
   942   iv John Heyward HOWKINS, b. 1975

583. KAREN EVELYN THOMAS[7] (Evelyn Heyward[6], Roland Steiner Heyward[5], James Cuthbert Heyward[4], George Cuthbert Heyward[3], Thomas Heyward[2], Thomas Heyward, Jr.[1]) child of Evelyn Heyward and George Richard Thomas was born in Birmingham, AL in 1950. She married (1st) John Alexander TUCKER in say 1973. He was born in 1951. She married (2nd) Richard E. POWERS, Jr. in say 1986. He was born in 1951.
Child by first marriage:
   943   i   Kelly Rebecca TUCKER, b. 1977

Child by second marriage:
    944   ii   Michael Thomas POWERS, b. 1988

587. DANA KENDRICK[7] (Ethel Loraine Heyward[6], Harvey Cuthbert Heyward[5], James Cuthbert Heyward[4], George Cuthbert Heyward[3], Thomas Heyward[2], Thomas Heyward, Jr.[1]) child of Ethel Loraine Heyward and Donald Wayne Kendrick was born in Charleston, SC in 1948. She married James B. MOBLEY in say 1973. Children:
    945   i   Lauren MOBLEY, b. 1976
    946   ii   James Tyler MOBLEY, b. 1986

590. ANNE HEYWARD MINGLEDORFF[7] (Marjory Heyward[6], George Cuthbert Heyward, III[5], George Cuthbert Heyward, Jr.[4], George Cuthbert Heyward[3], Thomas Heyward[2], Thomas Heyward, Jr.[1]) child of Marjory Heyward and Ralston Everett Mingledorff was born in Savannah, GA on 30 Oct 1948. She married (1st) Lewis Craighill BLISS in Honolulu, HI on 30 Jun 1969. She married (2nd) Mark WILLIAMS in Savannah, GA in Apr 1983. Children by first marriage:
    947   i   Evelyn Cameron BLISS, b. 16 Dec 1969
    948   ii   Lewis Craighill BLISS, Jr., b. 28 Oct 1972
Child by second marriage:
    949   iii   Ralston McAlpin WILLIAMS, b. 19 Dec 1983

591. RALSTON EVERETT MINGLEDORFF, Jr.[7] (Marjory Heyward[6], George Cuthbert Heyward, III[5], George Cuthbert Heyward, Jr.[4], George Cuthbert Heyward[3], Thomas Heyward[2], Thomas Heyward, Jr.[1]) child of Marjory Heyward and Ralston Everett Mingledorff was born in Savannah, GA on 10 Nov 1949. He married (1st) Ellison BACKUS in Savannah, GA on 6 Aug 1971. He married (2nd) Carol Jan SIMON in Bluffton, SC on 6 Apr 1993.
Child by first marriage:
    950   i   George Heyward MINGLEDORFF, b. 29 Aug 1976
Child by second marriage:
    951   ii   Colton Everett MINGLEDORFF, b. 22 Aug 1993

593. JOSEPHINE de ROSSET HEYWARD[7] (George Cutbert Heyward, IV[6], George Cuthbert Heyward, III[5], George Cuthbert Heyward, Jr.[4], George Cuthbert Heyward[3], Thomas Heyward[2], Thomas Heyward, Jr.[1]) child of George Cuthbert Heyward, IV and Josephine Macon Vincent was born in Charleston, SC on 7 May 1945. She married Jonathan DYER in Devon, PA on 19 Aug 1967. Children:

952   i   Elizabeth Stuart DYER, b. 22 Jan 1969
953   ii Alexander Heyward DYER, b. Mar 1973

594. GEORGE CUTHBERT HEYWARD, V[7] (George Cutbert Heyward, IV[6], George Cuthbert Heyward, III[5], George Cuthbert Heyward, Jr. [4], George Cuthbert Heyward[3], Thomas Heyward[2], Thomas Heyward, Jr.[1]) child of George Cuthbert Heyward, IV and Josephine Macon Vincent was born in Savannah, GA on 7 Dec 1947. He married (1st) Hannah Hewson BRAD-FORD in Wellsboro, PA on 30 Apr 1968. She was born in Wellsboro, PA on 30 Mar 1947. Children:
+ 954   i   Alice Bradford HEYWARD, b. 30 Oct 1968
+ 955   ii Margaret HEYWARD, b. 10 Jun 1972

595. ALLAN McALPIN HEYWARD, Jr.[7] (Allan McAlpin Heyward[6], George Cuthbert Heyward, III[5], George Cuthbert Heyward, Jr. [4], George Cuthbert Heyward[3], Thomas Heyward[2], Thomas Heyward, Jr.[1]) child of Allan McAplin Heyward and Marianna Chapin Marshall was born in Philadelphia, PA on 16 Apr 1950. He married Laura Lowe PARRISH in San Francisco, CA on 10 Sep 1975. She was born in Rappahannock County, VA on 30 Apr 1950. Children:
956   i   Georgia Lowe HEYWARD, b. 11 Feb 1978
957   ii   Isabelle McAlpin HEYWARD, b. 1 Sep 1980
958   iii Thomas Bentley HEYWARD, b. 16 Apr 1983 [twin]
959   iv   Daniel Chandler HEYWARD, b. 16 Apr 1983 [twin]

597. ROBERTA GUERARD HEYWARD[7] (Allan McAlpin Heyward[6], George Cuthbert Heyward, III[5], George Cuthbert Heyward, Jr. [4], George Cuthbert Heyward[3], Thomas Heyward[2], Thomas Heyward, Jr.[1]) child of Allan McAplin Heyward and Marianna Chapin Marshall was born in Newport News, VA on 8 May 1956. She married Stephen Barry PERKINS in Richmond, VA on 4 Feb 1984. He was born in Kidderminster, Worcester-shire, ENGLAND on 8 Sep 1954. Children:
960   i   Sarah Heyward PERKINS, b. 23 Aug 1988
961   ii   Hannah Marie McAlpin PERKINS, b. 3 Mar 1990
962   iii Katherine Randolph PERKINS, b. 13 May 1991

599. CLARA FEREBEE FENNER[7] (Mary Elizabeth Heyward[6], Robert Clarence Heyward[5], Robert Chisolm Heyward[4], George Cuthbert Heyward[3], Thomas Heyward[2], Thomas Heyward, Jr.[1]) child of Mary Elizabeth Heyward and John Housan Fenner was born in Nash County, NC on 6 Nov 1925. She married Herbert Leslie MANNING in Rocky Mount, NC on 8 Mar 1953. He was born in Martin County, NC in 1923. Children:

+ 963   i   Herbert Leslie MANNING, Jr., b. 1955
+ 964   ii   Mary Whitley MANNING, b. 1959

600. JOHN HOUSAN FENNER, Jr.[7] (Mary Elizabeth Heyward[6], Robert Clarence Heyward[5], Robert Chisolm Heyward[4], George Cuthbert Heyward[3], Thomas Heyward[2], Thomas Heyward, Jr.[1]) child of Mary Elizabeth Heyward and John Housan Fenner was born in Nash County, NC on 1 Nov 1926. He married Joan Mildred BACKAT in Rocky Mount, NC on 28 Jun 1959. She was born in GERMANY on 4 Apr 1935. Child:

+ 965   i   John Housan FENNER, III, b. 20 Dec 1960

601. WILLIAM EATON FENNER[7] (Mary Elizabeth Heyward[6], Robert Clarence Heyward[5], Robert Chisolm Heyward[4], George Cuthbert Heyward[3], Thomas Heyward[2], Thomas Heyward, Jr.[1]) child of Mary Elizabeth Heyward and John Housan Fenner was born in Halifax County, NC on 17 Nov 1927. He married Doris Jeanne TUCKER in Greenville, SC on 15 Mar 1953. She was born in Silver Springs, MD in 1933. Children:

+ 966   i   William Eaton FENNER, Jr., b. 26 Jan 1954
+ 967   ii   Elizabeth Heyward FENNER, b. 26 Apr 1955
+ 968   iii   Edwin Ferebee FENNER, b. 8 Oct 1956
+ 969   iv   Thomas Shaw FENNER, b. 1 Jan 1959
   970   v   Jeanne Ashley FENNER, b. 15 Sep 1965

602. JAMES ROBERT HEYWARD[7] (George Cuthbert Heyward, VI[6], Robert Clarence Heyward[5], Robert Chisolm Heyward[4], George Cuthbert Heyward[3], Thomas Heyward[2], Thomas Heyward, Jr.[1]) child of George Cuthbert Heyward, VI and Avis Irene Batson was born in Columbus, GA on 16 Nov 1932. He married Linnie Mae STALLINGS, daughter of James Noah and Eva (Driver) Stallings in Middlesex, NC on 17 Jul 1955. She was born in Middlesex, Nash County, NC on 16 Sep 1930. Children:

+ 971   i   James Robert HEYWARD, Jr., b. 7 Jul 1956
+ 972   ii   Eva Jeannette HEYWARD, b. 2 Jan 1958

603. GEORGE CUTHBERT HEYWARD, VII[7] (George Cuthbert Heyward, VI[6], Robert Clarence Heyward[5], Robert Chisolm Heyward[4], George Cuthbert Heyward[3], Thomas Heyward[2], Thomas Heyward, Jr.[1]) child of George Cuthbert Heyward, VI and Avis Irene Batson was born in Wadesboro, NC on 29 Oct 1940. He married Trudy Aliene DAVIS, daughter of Ralph Wilton and Billie (Hayes) Davis in Asheville, NC on 16 Aug 1970. She was born in Canton, NC on 18 Mar 1944. Children:

 973 i George Cuthbert HEYWARD, VIII, b, 21 Jul 1974
 974 ii Brian Thomas HEYWARD, b. 10 Nov 1976

604. MARY AGNES HEYWARD[7] (Thomas Savage Heyward[6], Robert Clarence Heyward[5], Robert Chisolm Heyward[4], George Cuthbert Heyward[3], Thomas Heyward[2], Thomas Heyward, Jr.[1]) child of Thomas Savage Heyward and Mary McDaniel was born in Rockingham, NC on 16 Jan 1933. She married Joseph Carter JOHNS, son of Ray Lee and Margaret Christine Johns in Aiken, SC on 13 Jun 1953. He was born in Loudon, TN on 24 Jul 1925. Children:

 975 i Susan Heyward JOHNS, b. 26 Jun 1954
+ 976 ii David Michael JOHNS, b. 30 Mar 1957
+ 977 iii Joseph Carter JOHNS, Jr., b. 25 Feb 1959
+ 978 iv Margaret Ann JOHNS, b. 21 Feb 1961
+ 979 v Mary Elizabeth JOHNS, b. 6 Dec 1965

605. THOMAS SAVAGE HEYWARD, Jr.[7] (Thomas Savage Heyward[6], Robert Clarence Heyward[5], Robert Chisolm Heyward[4], George Cuthbert Heyward[3], Thomas Heyward[2], Thomas Heyward, Jr.[1]) child of Thomas Savage Heyward and Mary McDaniel was born in Rockingham, NC on 11 Oct 1936. He married (1st) Betty JOHNSON in Sumter, SC on 13 Jan 1962. Children:

 980 i Terri Lynne HEYWARD, b. 15 Nov 1962
+ 981 ii Thomas Savage HEYWARD, III, b. 3 Dec 1963

607. DEBORAH CROSBY HEYWARD[7] (Thomas Savage Heyward[6], Robert Clarence Heyward[5], Robert Chisolm Heyward[4], George Cuthbert Heyward[3], Thomas Heyward[2], Thomas Heyward, Jr.[1]) child of Thomas Savage Heyward and Mary McDaniel was born in Aiken, SC on 27 Apr 1951. She married Gerald Gant SMITH in Sumter , SC on 13 Nov 1971. Children:

 982 i Larry Heyward SMITH, b. 1974
 983 ii Cynthia Anne SMITH, b. 1982

609. DAVID EDWIN RAWL, Jr.[7] (Josephine Stoney Heyward[6], Robert Clarence Heyward[5], Robert Chisolm Heyward[4], George Cuthbert Heyward[3], Thomas Heyward[2], Thomas Heyward, Jr.[1]) child of Josephine Stoney Heyward and David Edwin Rawl was born in Batesburg, SC on 16 May 1933, and died in 1999. He married Joan Annette MASSEY, daughter of

John W. and Jeanette (Cruxton) Massey in Kershaw, SC on 27 Jul 1956. She was born in Taxahaw, SC on 22 Dec 1933. Child:

    984   i   David Edwin RAWL, III, b. 28 Nov 1957

610. JOSEPH HEYWARD RAWL[7] (Josephine Stoney Heyward[6], Robert Clarence Heyward[5], Robert Chisolm Heyward[4], George Cuthbert Heyward[3], Thomas Heyward[2], Thomas Heyward, Jr.[1]) child of Josephine Stoney Heyward and David Edwin Rawl was born in Batesburg, SC on 22 May 1938. He married (1st) Ruth Anne KEARNS in say 1962. She was born in 1941. Children:

    985   i   Robin Leigh RAWL, b. 2 Sep 1964
+ 986   ii   Kimberly Michelle RAWL, b. 1967
+ 987 iii Michael Heyward RAWL, b. 1969

611. LEE COVIN RAWL[7] (Josephine Stoney Heyward[6], Robert Clarence Heyward[5], Robert Chisolm Heyward[4], George Cuthbert Heyward[3], Thomas Heyward[2], Thomas Heyward, Jr.[1]) child of Josephine Stoney Heyward and David Edwin Rawl was born in Batesburg, SC on 12 Mar 1947. He married (1st) Kathy K. KAISER in say 1971. He married (2nd) Mary Margaret McMILLAN on 10 Aug 1980. She was born Honea Path, Anderson County, SC on 30 May 1948.

Children by first marriage:

    988   i   Holly Kaiser RAWL, b. 24 Dec 1974
    989   ii   Jason L. RAWL, b. 3 May 1979

Child by second marriage:

    990 iii Amanda M. RAWL, b. 2 Jun 1985

614. MARY ANN HEYWARD[7] (Robert Clarence Heyward, Jr.[6], Robert Clarence Heyward[5], Robert Chisolm Heyward[4], George Cuthbert Heyward[3], Thomas Heyward[2], Thomas Heyward, Jr.[1]) child of Robert Clarence Heyward, Jr. and Mary Ann Carter was born in Hendersonville, NC on 2 Nov 1952. She married (1st) Bruce Alton DRINKWATER in say 1980. Children:

    991   i   Robert Heyward DRINKWATER, b. 1984
    992   ii   Isabel Alton DRINKWATER, b. 1988

615. ANN CUTHBERT HEYWARD[7] (Gaillard Stoney Heyward[6], Daniel Hasell Heyward[5], Robert Chisolm Heyward[4], George Cuthbert Heyward[3], Thomas Heyward[2], Thomas Heyward, Jr.[1]) child of Gaillard Stoney Heyward and Lila Griffin was born in Beaufort Count, SC on 31 Mar 1936. She married Thomas E. TRYBALSKI in say 1978. Children:

993 i Karen Lorraine TRYBALSKI, b. 12 Jul 1961, sp
+ 994 ii Rhonda Susan TRYBALSKI, b. 10 Jun 1965
+ 995 iii Amy Laura TRYBALSKI, b. 30 Mar 1969

616. CAROLINE GRIFFIN HEYWARD[7] (Gaillard Stoney Heyward[6], Daniel Hasell Heyward[5], Robert Chisolm Heyward[4], George Cuthbert Heyward[3], Thomas Heyward[2], Thomas Heyward, Jr.[1]) child of Gaillard Stoney Heyward and Lila Griffin was born in Ridgeland, SC on 13 Aug 1937. She married (1st) Thomas Bentley MOFFETT, Jr. in say 1956. Child:
996 i Teresa Lynn MOFFETT, b. 23 Nov 1957

617. DOROTHY MAY HEYWARD[7] (Gaillard Stoney Heyward[6], Daniel Hasell Heyward[5], Robert Chisolm Heyward[4], George Cuthbert Heyward[3], Thomas Heyward[2], Thomas Heyward, Jr.[1]) child of Gaillard Stoney Heyward and Lila Griffin was born in Hardeeville, SC on 14 Nov 1939, and died in 1995. She married (1st) Robert Ray HAAG in say 1958. Children:
+ 997 i Lee Ray HAAG, b. 5 Jul 1959
998 ii Henry Robert HAAG, b. 28 May 1963

618. THOMAS GAILLARD HEYWARD[7] (Gaillard Stoney Heyward[6], Daniel Hasell Heyward[5], Robert Chisolm Heyward[4], George Cuthbert Heyward[3], Thomas Heyward[2], Thomas Heyward, Jr.[1]) child of Gaillard Stoney Heyward and Lila Griffin was born in Bluffton, SC on 6 Mar 1942. He married (1st) Clare Frances WALKER in Columbia, SC on 11 Aug 1967. She was born in Shenandoah, PA on 31 Dec 1944, and died in 1991. Children:
+ 999 i Thomas Gaillard HEYWARD, Jr., b. 31 Mar 1968
+ 1000 ii Melanie Clare HEYWARD, b. 21 Jul 1970
1001 iii Laura Ashley HEYWARD, b. 1984

619. SUSANNE McKELLAR HEYWARD[7] (James Edward Heyward[6], Daniel Hasell Heyward[5], Robert Chisolm Heyward[4], George Cuthbert Heyward[3], Thomas Heyward[2], Thomas Heyward, Jr.[1]) child of James Edward Heyward and Susanne Elise McKellar was born in Greenwood, SC on 28 Oct 1939. She married James Turner KEY, Jr., son of James Turner and Isabel Foster (DePass) Key on 15 Nov 1969. He was born in Columbia, SC on 8 May 1931. Children:
1002 i Jason Heyward KEY, III, b. 22 Oct 1973
1003 ii Martin Victor KEY, b. 22 Sep 1975

620. HARRIET McKELLAR HEYWARD[7] (James Edward Heyward[6], Daniel Hasell Heyward[5], Robert Chisolm Heyward[4], George Cuthbert Heyward[3], Thomas Heyward[2], Thomas Heyward, Jr.[1]) child of James Edward Heyward and Susanne Elise McKellar was born in Greenwood, SC on 15 Dec 1941. She married John Clarence ADAMS, son of Frank Turner and Katherine (Ivester) Adams in Greenwood, SC on 6 Nov 1965. He was born in Atlanta, GA on 7 Aor 1941. Children:

    1004   i Katherine Elise ADAMS, b. 29 Aug 1967
    1005 ii Heyward Turner ADAMS, b. 27 Jul 1971

621. JAMES EDWARD HEYWARD, Jr.[7] (James Edward Heyward[6], Daniel Hasell Heyward[5], Robert Chisolm Heyward[4], George Cuthbert Heyward[3], Thomas Heyward[2], Thomas Heyward, Jr.[1]) child of James Edward Heyward and Susanne Elise McKellar was born in Greenwood, SC on 17 Mar 1947. He married Margaret McKee FLEISCHMAN, daughter of Keith M. and Elizabeth K. (Spratt) Fleischman in Ninety Six, SC on 3 Jul 1976. She was born in Georgetown, SC in 1951. Children:

    1006   i James Edward HEYWARD, III, b. 9 Apr 1981
    1007 ii Ellen Elizabeth HEYWARD, b. 27 Nov 1982
    1008 iii Keith McKellar HEYWARD, b. 30 Oct 1984

622. ELAINE McKELLAR HEYWARD[7] (James Edward Heyward[6], Daniel Hasell Heyward[5], Robert Chisolm Heyward[4], George Cuthbert Heyward[3], Thomas Heyward[2], Thomas Heyward, Jr.[1]) child of James Edward Heyward and Susanne Elise McKellar was born in Greenwood, SC on 17 Dec 1951. She married William Augustus BARNETTE, III in Greenwood, SC on 3 Feb 1973. He was born in Greenwood, SC on 8 Dec 1949. Children:

    1009   i Katherine Heyward BARNETTE, b. 5 Apr 1982
    1010 ii William Augustus BARNETTE, IV, b. 9 Jan 1986

623. FRANCES HASELL HEYWARD[7] (Daniel Hasell Heyward, Jr.[6], Daniel Hasell Heyward[5], Robert Chisolm Heyward[4], George Cuthbert Heyward[3], Thomas Heyward[2], Thomas Heyward, Jr.[1]) child of Daniel Hasell Heyward, Jr. and Margaret Hair was born in Charleston, SC on 10 Dec 1941. She married Elmer Hainesworth SMITH, Jr. in Bluffton, SC on 30 Jul 1961. He was born in Savannah, GA on 3 Jan 1938. Children:

+ 1011   i Georgia Leigh SMITH, b. 16 Dec 1963
    1012 ii Margaret Daniel SMITH, b. 16 Sep 1966

625. DYAN MARGARET HEYWARD[7] (Daniel Hasell Heyward, Jr.[6], Daniel Hasell Heyward[5], Robert Chisolm Heyward[4], George Cuthbert

Heyward[3], Thomas Heyward[2], Thomas Heyward, Jr.[1]) child of Daniel Hasell Heyward, Jr. and Margaret Hair was born in Ridgeland, SC on 14 Jan 1946. She married Palmer HODGES in say 1966. Child:

+ 1013   i   Daniel Lee HODGES, b. 10 Jun 1968

628. DONALD EDWARD DeGAIN[7] (Ella Elizabeth Heyward[6], Daniel Hasell Heyward[5], Robert Chisolm Heyward[4], George Cuthbert Heyward[3], Thomas Heyward[2], Thomas Heyward, Jr.[1]) child of Ella Elizabeth Heyward and George Francis DeGain, Jr. was born in Salamanca, Cattaraugus County, NY on 22 Jun 1947. He married Deborah Ann WEIGLE in Tampa, FL on 11 Mar 1978. Children:

   1014   i   Danielle Christine DeGAIN, b. 9 Oct 1979
   1015   ii   Donna Michelle DeGAIN, b. 1982
   1016   iii   Derek Justin DeGAIN, b. 1984

629. GRACE ANN DeGAIN[7] (Ella Elizabeth Heyward[6], Daniel Hasell Heyward[5], Robert Chisolm Heyward[4], George Cuthbert Heyward[3], Thomas Heyward[2], Thomas Heyward, Jr.[1]) child of Ella Elizabeth Heyward and George Francis DeGain, Jr. was born in Salamanca, Cattaraugus County, NY on 16 May 1950. She married Ronald W. FRANK in say 1971. Children:

   1017   i   Kurt Wade FRANK, b. 1973
   1018   ii   Amie Lynn FRANK, b. 1976

633. ISABEL MILTON[7] (Isabel Heyward Wilson[6], Isabel Heyward[5], Thomas Daniel Heyward[4], George Cuthbert Heyward[3], Thomas Heyward[2], Thomas Heyward, Jr.[1]) child of Isabel Heyward Wilson and Marshall McCormick Milton, Jr. was born on 1 Jan 1941. She married Eric Ellis MARCUSSON in say 1967. He was born in 1948. Child:

   1019   i   Lia Milton MARCUSSON, b. 1968

635. WILLIAM BYRD LEE MILTON[7] (Isabel Heyward Wilson[6], Isabel Heyward[5], Thomas Daniel Heyward[4], George Cuthbert Heyward[3], Thomas Heyward[2], Thomas Heyward, Jr.[1]) child of Isabel Heyward Wilson and Marshall McCormick Milton, Jr. was born on 11 Oct 1949. He married Carolyn TIDLER in say 1969. Child:

   1020   i   William Byrd Lee MILTON, Jr., b. 1970

636. DOROTHY FRASER ANDERSON[7] (Dorothy Heyward Wilson[6], Isabel Heyward[5], Thomas Daniel Heyward[4], George Cuthbert Heyward[3], Thomas Heyward[2], Thomas Heyward, Jr.[1]) child of Dorothy Heyward Wilson and Pelham Hansard Anderson, Jr. was born in Birmingham, AL on

31 May 1940. She married George Michael GIANARAS in say 1971. He was born in Tampa, FL in 1941, and died in 1985. Children:

    1021   i   Diana Fraser GIANARAS, b. 1978

    1022   ii Christopher Michael GIANARAS, b. 1984

637. LUCY WINSTON ANDERSON[7] (Dorothy Heyward Wilson[6], Isabel Heyward[5], Thomas Daniel Heyward[4], George Cuthbert Heyward[3], Thomas Heyward[2], Thomas Heyward, Jr.[1]) child of Dorothy Heyward Wilson and Pelham Hansard Anderson, Jr. was born in Newport News, VA on 1 Apr 1945. She married Robert Arthur ROY, son of Joseph Albert and Cecile (Marois) Roy in Winter Park, FL on 12 Mar 1966. He was born in Hampton, VA on 6 Dec 1943. Children:

    1023   i   Robert Anderson ROY, b. 14 Dec 1966

    1024   ii   Heather Winston ROY, b. 22 Mar 1969

    1025   iii Molly Fraser ROY, b. 16 Nov 1974

638. JAMES WALTER STEPHEN WILSON[7] (Walter Stephen Wilson[6], Isabel Heyward[5], Thomas Daniel Heyward[4], George Cuthbert Heyward[3], Thomas Heyward[2], Thomas Heyward, Jr.[1]) child of Walter Stephen Wilson and Alice Amy Stevenson was born in Berkeley, CA on 5 Sep 1945. He married Diana M. BRIDGES, daughter of Joseph W. and Maria Bridges on 11 Nov 1966. She was born in Norfolk, VA in 1946. Child:

    1026   i   Lesley Ann WILSON, b. 24 Sep 1978

643. ELEANOR JOHNSTONE STALL[7] (Helen Heyward Wilson[6], Isabel Heyward[5], Thomas Daniel Heyward[4], George Cuthbert Heyward[3], Thomas Heyward[2], Thomas Heyward, Jr.[1]) child of Helen Heyward Wilson and Robert Jennings Stall, Jr. was born on 12 Feb 1955. She married Glenn Roberts NORTHERN on 14 Apr 1973. He was born on 24 Dec 1952. Child:

    1027   i   Katherine Heyward NORTHERN, b. 15 Feb 1975

646. ROBERT LEWIS PUGH[7] (Elizabeth Heyward LaBruce[6], Elizabeth Heyward[5], Thomas Daniel Heyward[4], George Cuthbert Heyward[3], Thomas Heyward[2], Thomas Heyward, Jr.[1]) child of Elizabeth Heyward LaBruce and Albert Ellsworth Pugh was born in Baltimore, MD on 1 Jan 1952. He married Katherine KEARNEY in Mt. Pleasant, SC on 22 Oct 1980. She was born in Feb 1952. Child:

    1028   i   Emily De Leon PUGH, b. 17 Jul 1984

649. THOMAS KENNETH ROWE, Jr.[7] (Katherine Fitzsimons LaBruce[6], Elizabeth Heyward[5], Thomas Daniel Heyward[4], George Cuthbert Heyward[3],

Thomas Heyward[2], Thomas Heyward, Jr.[1]) child of Katherine Fitzsimons LaBruce and Thomas Kenneth Rowe was born in Richmond, VA on 28 Sep 1950. He married (1st) Jane BLOODWORTH on 3 Sep 1977. Child:

   1029   i Megan BLOODWORTH, b. 4 Jul 1983

650. ELIZABETH LaBRUCE ROWE[7] (Katherine Fitzsimons LaBruce[6], Elizabeth Heyward[5], Thomas Daniel Heyward[4], George Cuthbert Heyward[3], Thomas Heyward[2], Thomas Heyward, Jr.[1]) child of Katherine Fitzsimons LaBruce and Thomas Kenneth Rowe was born in Richmond, VA on 22 Aug 1952. She married Michael Daniel LAMBERTSON in Richmond, VA on 4 Jun 1983. Child:

   1030   i Katherine Flowers LAMBERTSON, b. 1991

652. RICHARD ELLIOT JOHNSON[7] (Selina Johnstone LaBruce[6], Elizabeth Heyward[5], Thomas Daniel Heyward[4], George Cuthbert Heyward[3], Thomas Heyward[2], Thomas Heyward, Jr.[1]) child of Selina Johnstone LaBruce and Hugh Richard Johnson was born in Ann Arbor, MI on 9 Dec 1949. He married Eleanor Elmira BLACKMON, daughter of Stephen and Eleanor (--) Blackmon in Washington, GA on 24 May 1975. Child:

   1031   i Richard Blackmon JOHNSON, b. 3 Sep 1977

654. SELINA HEYWARD JOHNSON[7] (Selina Johnstone LaBruce[6], Elizabeth Heyward[5], Thomas Daniel Heyward[4], George Cuthbert Heyward[3], Thomas Heyward[2], Thomas Heyward, Jr.[1]) child of Selina Johnstone LaBruce and Hugh Richard Johnson was born in Savannah, GA on 30 Jun 1962. She married Luther Don LOUGHRIDGE, III, son of Luther Don and Louise (Grilton) Loughridge, Jr. in Savannah, GA on 26 Jul 1986. He was born in Atlanta, GA in 1961. Children:

   1032   i Selina Elizabeth LOUGHRIDGE, b. 1988
   1033 ii Luther Don LOUGHRIDGE, IV, b. 1989

655. ELLEN JAEL WALKER[7] (Pinckney Heyward Walker[6], Edward Barnwell Walker, Jr.[5], Elizabeth Guerard Heyward[4], George Cuthbert Heyward[3], Thomas Heyward[2], Thomas Heyward, Jr.[1]) child of Pinckney Heyward Walker and Ellen Marion Jennings was born in Boston, MA on 21 Aug 1935. She married A. Frankland BRANDT in say 1958. Children:

   1034   i David Lawrence Adams BRANDT, b. 1962
   1035 ii Zoe Elizabeth Rea BRANDT, b. 1964
   1036 iii John Edward Barnwell BRANDT, b. 1966

656. SARAH ELIZABETH WALKER[7] (Pinckney Heyward Walker[6], Edward Barnwell Walker, Jr.[5], Elizabeth Guerard Heyward[4], George Cuthbert Heyward[3], Thomas Heyward[2], Thomas Heyward, Jr.[1]) child of Pinckney Heyward Walker and Ellen Marion Jennings was born in Roanoke, VA on 27 Jul 1942. She married David A. FRANZ in say 1965. Children:

    1037   i   Alan Edward FRANZ, b. 1968
    1038   ii Katherine Jennings FRANZ, b. 1972

657. THOMAS HEYWARD WALKER[7] (Pinckney Heyward Walker[6], Edward Barnwell Walker, Jr.[5], Elizabeth Guerard Heyward[4], George Cuthbert Heyward[3], Thomas Heyward[2], Thomas Heyward, Jr.[1]) child of Pinckney Heyward Walker and Ellen Marion Jennings was born in Richmond, VA on 24 Aug 1947. He married Mary Margarite DAILY in San Antonio, TX on 23 Jun 1973. She was born in San Antonio, TX on 5 Feb 1951. Child:

    1039   i   Edward Thomas WALKER, b. 26 Dec 1977

659. MICHELLE HEYWARD WALKER[7] (Edward Barnwell Walker, III[6], Edward Barnwell Walker, Jr.[5], Elizabeth Guerard Heyward[4], George Cuthbert Heyward[3], Thomas Heyward[2], Thomas Heyward, Jr.[1]) child of Edward Barnwell Walker, III and Shirley Sasso was born in Philadelphia, PA on 3 Jan 1947. She married Paul LUND in say 1968. Children:

    1040   i   Heather Heyward LUND, b. 1970
    1041   ii Holly Jensen LUND, b. 1972
    1042 iii Marc Vernon LUND, b. 1974

660. DAVID PINCKNEY WALKER[7] (Edward Barnwell Walker, III[6], Edward Barnwell Walker, Jr.[5], Elizabeth Guerard Heyward[4], George Cuthbert Heyward[3], Thomas Heyward[2], Thomas Heyward, Jr.[1]) child of Edward Barnwell Walker, III and Shirley Sasso was born in Sao Paulo, BRAZIL on 10 Aug 1948. He married Rosemary LAMONT in say 1976. Child:

    1043   i   David Alexander WALKER, b. 1983

663. FRANK EsDORN DROPLA[7] (Sarah Gertrude Heyward[6], William Guerard Heyward[5], John Alexander Heyward[4], George Cuthbert Heyward[3], Thomas Heyward[2], Thomas Heyward, Jr.[1]) child of Sarah Gertrude Heyward and Frank John Dropla was born in New Bern, NC on 17 Sep 1949. He married Gwen NELSON in say 1981. Children:

    1044   i   Melissa DROPLA, b. c. 1985
    1045   ii Melaine DROPLA, b. c. 1988

1046   iii   Lauren DROPLA, b. 30 Sep 1990
1047   iv   Michael DROPLA, b. 12 Dec 1991

666. WILLIAM EsDORN O'QUINN[7] (Mary KatherineHeyward[6], William Guerard Heyward[5], John Alexander Heyward[4], George Cuthbert Heyward[3], Thomas Heyward[2], Thomas Heyward, Jr.[1]) child of Mary Katherine Heyward and EsDorn O'Quinn was born in Beaufort, SC on 25 Sep 1947. He married Cynthia HUGGINS in Branchville, SC on 12 Jun 1970. Children:

    1048   i   William EsDorn O'QUINN, Jr., b. 9 Dec 1972
    1049   ii   Brian Lowell O'QUINN, b. 7 Oct 1976
    1050   iii   Brandi Lafaye O'QUINN, b. 5 Nov 1981

667. JOSEPH WALES O'QUINN[7] (Mary KatherineHeyward[6], William Guerard Heyward[5], John Alexander Heyward[4], George Cuthbert Heyward[3], Thomas Heyward[2], Thomas Heyward, Jr.[1]) child of Mary Katherine Heyward and EsDorn O'Quinn was born in Charleston, SC on 25 Sep 1964. He married Sherri Lynn PADGETT, daughter of Jerry Frank and Jean Laverne (Walsh) Padgett in Hampton, SC on 14 Jun 1986. Children:

    1051   i   Emily Margaret O'QUINN, b. 29 May 1994
    1052   ii   Joseph Wales O'QUINN, Jr., b. 11 Oct 1996, dy 3 Jan 1997 [twin]
    1053   iii   Abigail Lynn O'QUINN, b. 11 Oct 1996 [twin]
    1054   iv   Lindsay Grace O'QUINN, b. 31 Dec 1997

668. JOHN THOMAS O'QUINN[7] (Mary KatherineHeyward[6], William Guerard Heyward[5], John Alexander Heyward[4], George Cuthbert Heyward[3], Thomas Heyward[2], Thomas Heyward, Jr.[1]) child of Mary Katherine Heyward and EsDorn O'Quinn was born in Charleston, SC on 31 Dec 1965. He married Melissa NELSON in Hampton County, SC on 4 Mar 1989. Child:

    1055   i   Jordan Alexandria O'QUINN, b. 29 Jan 1995

674 JEAN MARIE SPARKS[7] (Caroline Heyward Gignilliat[6], William Robert Gignilliat[5], Mary Caroline Heyward[4], George Cuthbert Heyward[3], Thomas Heyward[2], Thomas Heyward, Jr.[1]) child of Caroline Heyward Gignilliat and W. Chester Sparks was born in Florence, AL on 16 Sep 1945. She married Joseph William STANFIELD, Jr. on 4 Jun 1966. Children:

+   1056   i   Jean Rebecca STANFIELD, b. 4 Nov 1967
    1057   ii   Joseph William STANFIELD, III, b. 28 Apr 1970
    1058   iii   Christopher Heyward STANFIELD, b. 1 Nov 1975

676. WILLIAM ROBERT GIGNILLIAT, III[7] (William Robert Gignilliat, Jr.[6], William Robert Gignilliat[5], Mary Caroline Heyward[4], George Cuthbert Heyward[3], Thomas Heyward[2], Thomas Heyward, Jr.[1]) child of William Robert Gignilliat, Jr. and Ann Josephine Harris was born in Sebring, FL on 22 Mar 1943. He married (1st) Rosemary BERSCH in say 1969. He married (2nd) Laura LIEBERMAN in say 1983.
Child by first marriage:
   1059   i   Meighan Rebecca GIGNILLIAT, b. 1973
Children by second marriage:
   1060   ii   William Robert GIGNILLIAT, IV, b. 1985
   1061   iii   Elizabeth Ann GIGNILLIAT, b. 1988

677. EDWARD HARRIS GIGNILLIAT[7] (William Robert Gignilliat, Jr.[6], William Robert Gignilliat[5], Mary Caroline Heyward[4], George Cuthbert Heyward[3], Thomas Heyward[2], Thomas Heyward, Jr.[1]) child of William Robert Gignilliat, Jr. and Ann Josephine Harris was born in Augusta, GA on 28 Aug 1944. He married Marguerite Montford McKENZIE, daughter of Edwin Myers McKenzie on 23 Jun 1975. Children:
   1062   i   Harris McKenzie GIGNILLIAT, b. 1977
   1063   ii   William Stuart GIGNILLIAT, b. 1980

678. CHARLES OLMSTEAD GIGNILLIAT[7] (William Robert Gignilliat, Jr.[6], William Robert Gignilliat[5], Mary Caroline Heyward[4], George Cuthbert Heyward[3], Thomas Heyward[2], Thomas Heyward, Jr.[1]) child of William Robert Gignilliat, Jr. and Ann Josephine Harris was born in Gainesville, GA on 7 Mar 1946. He married Nora Linda WHITE, daughter of Darrell Sidney White on 31 Aug 1974. Children:
   1064   i   Charles Heyward GIGNILLIAT, b. 26 Dec 1975
   1065   ii   Darrell White GIGNILLIAT, b. 1979

680. PATRICIA ANNE COCKRELL[7] (Jean Frances Gignilliat[6], William Robert Gignilliat[5], Mary Caroline Heyward[4], George Cuthbert Heyward[3], Thomas Heyward[2], Thomas Heyward, Jr.[1]) child of Jean Frances Gignilliat and Thomas Preston Cockrell was born in Jacksonville, FL on 16 Feb 1953. She married William Earl WILLIS in say 1976. Children:
   1066   i   Kimberly Anne WILLIS, b. 1979
   1067   ii   Christopher Robert WILLIS, b. 1981
   1068   iii   Sallie Elizabeth WILLIS, b. 1988

686. ELIZABETH HOWARD CLARKE[7] (Burwell Boykin Clarke, Jr.[6], Elizabeth Howard Burnet[5], Emma Howard Heyward[4], Elizabeth Savage

Parker[3], Elizabeth Heyward[2], Thomas Heyward, Jr.[1]) child of Burwell Boykin Clarke, Jr. and Rosa Cantey Heyward was born in Columbia, SC on 3 Aug 1930. She married George Cameron TODD, son of Benjamin Harris and Mary Cameron (Cole) Todd in Columbia, SC on 18 Oct 1950. He was born in Columbia, SC on 8 Jan 1926. Children:

    1069   i   Elizabeth Clarke TODD, b. 24 Feb 1953
+ 1070   ii George Cameron TODD, Jr., b. 4 Oct 1954
+ 1071 iii Albert Rhett Heyward TODD, b. 25 May 1956
+ 1072 iv Rosa Cantey Heyward TODD, b. 8 Mar 1960

687. BURWELL BOYKIN CLARKE, II[7] (Thomas Henry Clarke[6], Elizabeth Howard Burnet[5], Emma Howard Heyward[4], Elizabeth Savage Parker[3], Elizabeth Heyward[2], Thomas Heyward, Jr.[1]) child of Thomas Henry Clarke and Sarah Thurmond was born in 1941. He married Molly Miller CALHOUN in say 1950. She was born in 1981. Child:

    1073   i   Burwell Boykin CLARKE, III, b. 1984

688. WILLIAM LEWIS BRYANT CLARKE[7] (Thomas Henry Clarke[6], Elizabeth Howard Burnet[5], Emma Howard Heyward[4], Elizabeth Savage Parker[3], Elizabeth Heyward[2], Thomas Heyward, Jr.[1]) child of Thomas Henry Clarke and Sarah Thurmond was born in 1943. He married Sheryl Malvina HUTCHINSON in say 1950. She was born in 1969. Child:

    1074   i   Heather Robyn CLARKE, b. 1970

690. HENRI deSAUSSURE CLARKE[7] (Albertus Moore Clarke[6], Elizabeth Howard Burnet[5], Emma Howard Heyward[4], Elizabeth Savage Parker[3], Elizabeth Heyward[2], Thomas Heyward, Jr.[1]) child of Albertus Moore Clarke and Valeria North Burnet was born in Waycroos, GA on 13 Aug 1933. He married Elizabeth Janet JAMES, daughter of Frederick and Sophia (Duchak) James on 23 Nov 1959. She was born in Winnipeg, CANADA on 30 Jan 1937. Child:

+ 1075   i   Burnet Todd CLARKE, b. 12 Feb 1964

691. HEYWARD BURNET CLARKE[7] (Albertus Moore Clarke[6], Elizabeth Howard Burnet[5], Emma Howard Heyward[4], Elizabeth Savage Parker[3], Elizabeth Heyward[2], Thomas Heyward, Jr.[1]) child of Albertus Moore Clarke and Valeria North Burnet was born in Waycroos, GA on 21 Jun 1938. He married Margaret Annette WILLIAMS in Waycross, GA on 20 Apr 1963. She was born in Waycross, GA on 6 Mar 1942. Children:

+ 1076   i   David Burnet CLARKE, b. 1964
    1077   ii Andrew Rhett CLARKE, b. 28 Mar 1968
    1078 iii Margaret Laurens CLARKE, b. 1973

692. VALERIA NORTH BURNET[7] (Henry Heyward Burnet. Jr.[6], Henry Heyward Burnet[5], Emma Howard Heyward[4], Elizabeth Savage Parker[3], Elizabeth Heyward[2], Thomas Heyward, Jr.[1]) child of Henry Heyward Burnet, Jr. and Catherine Margaret North was born in Waycross, GA on 22 Mar 1934. She married Charles Joseph ORR in Waycross, GA on 31 Mar 1956. He was born in Athens, GA on 5 Feb 1927, and died in Augusta, GA on 10 Oct 1992. Children:

    1079   i   Charles Joseph ORR, Jr., b. 28 Jan 1957, d. 6 Nov 1984; unm

    1080   ii   Elizabeth Burnet ORR, b. 21 Aug 1960

693. HENRY HEYWARD BURNET, III[7] (Henry Heyward Burnet. Jr.[6], Henry Heyward Burnet[5], Emma Howard Heyward[4], Elizabeth Savage Parker[3], Elizabeth Heyward[2], Thomas Heyward, Jr.[1]) child of Henry Heyward Burnet, Jr. and Catherine Margaret North was born in Waycross, GA on 28 Mar 1939. He married Alice Marie MUSGROVE in Homerville, GA on 5 Sep 1964. She was born in Metter, GA on 2 Jul 1944. Children:

    1081   i   Julie Rutledge BURNET, b. 6 Nov 1965

+ 1082   ii   Henry Heyward BURNET, IV, b. 27 Mar 1968

694. NANCY RUTLEDGE WAINER[7] (Emma Heyward Burnet[6], Henry Heyward Burnet[5], Emma Howard Heyward[4], Elizabeth Savage Parker[3], Elizabeth Heyward[2], Thomas Heyward, Jr.[1]) child of Emma Heyward Burnet and David Samuel Wainer was born in Valdosta, GA in 1934. She married Jesse L. PARROTT in say 1954. He was born in Salley, SC in 1918. Children:

+ 1083   i   Jonathan Rutledge PARROTT, b. 1956

+ 1084   ii   Stephen Price PARROTT, b. 1959

695. DAVID SAMUEL WAINER, Jr.[7] (Emma Heyward Burnet[6], Henry Heyward Burnet[5], Emma Howard Heyward[4], Elizabeth Savage Parker[3], Elizabeth Heyward[2], Thomas Heyward, Jr.[1]) child of Emma Heyward Burnet and David Samuel Wainer was born in Valdosta, GA on 20 Jan 1936. He married Patricia McCORMICK in Jacksonville Beach, FL on 3 Feb 1968. She was born in Jacksonville, FL on 16 Mar 1944. Children:

    1085   i   David Samuel WAINER. III, b. 15 Mar 1970

    1086   ii   John Benjamin WAINER, b. 5 Jun 1972

    1087   iii   Michael Judah WAINER, b. 1975

    1088   iv   Joseph Asher WAINER, b. 1978

    1089   v   Selah Jean WAINER, b. 1980

696. KATHERINE AMORY WAINER[7] (Emma Heyward Burnet[6], Henry Heyward Burnet[5], Emma Howard Heyward[4], Elizabeth Savage Parker[3], Elizabeth Heyward[2], Thomas Heyward, Jr.[1]) child of Emma Heyward Burnet and David Samuel Wainer was born in Valdosta, GA on 17 Jul 1944. She married James Herbert OWENS in Valdosta, GA on 20 Jul 1968. He was born in Valdosta, GA on 1 Jan 1941. Children:

    1090   i   Marilois Hitch OWENS, b. 12 Jan 1970
+ 1091 ii Elizabeth Heyward OWENS, b. 9 Apr 1973
    1092 iii Katherine Amory OWENS, b. 20 May 1974

698. REUBEN LUCKIE ROCKWELL, III[7] (Reuben Luckie Rockwell, Jr.[6], Henrietta Parker Howard[5], Henry Parker Howard[4], Elizabeth Savage Parker[3], Elizabeth Heyward[2], Thomas Heyward, Jr.[1]) child of Reuben Luckie Rockwell, Jr. and Susan Tucker was born in Augusta, GA on 22 Apr 1955. He married Martha Gail SCOTT in say 1978. She was born in Waynesboro, GA in 1954. Children:

    1093   i   Reuben Luckie ROCKWELL, IV, b. c. 1980
    1094 ii Hugh Scott ROCKWELL, b. c. 1983
    1095 iii Stephen Whitehead ROCKWELL, b. c. 1987

699. SUSAN TUCKER ROCKWELL[7] (Reuben Luckie Rockwell, Jr.[6], Henrietta Parker Howard[5], Henry Parker Howard[4], Elizabeth Savage Parker[3], Elizabeth Heyward[2], Thomas Heyward, Jr.[1]) child of Reuben Luckie Rockwell, Jr. and Susan Tucker was born in Augusta, GA on 26 Oct 1959. She married Matthew Blaine BOLTON in say 1984. He was born in Johnson City, TN in 1958. Children:

    1096   i   Catherine Tucker BOLTON, b. c. 1989
    1097 ii Matthew Blaine BOLTON, Jr., b. c. 1993

700. HENRY HOWARD SIMMONS[7] (Mary Louise Folliard Howard[6], Robert Emmett Jenkins Howard[5], Henry Parker Howard[4], Elizabeth Savage Parker[3], Elizabeth Heyward[2], Thomas Heyward, Jr.[1]) child of Mary Louise Folliard Howard and Harry Hull Simmons was born in Savannah, GA on 20 Jul 1939. He married Bette Jo BENNETT in say 1964. She was born in Walterboro, SC in 1938. Children:

    1098   i   Patrick Howard SIMMONS, b. c. 1968
    1099 ii Barry Bennett SIMMONS, b. c. 1970

701. ROBERT EMMETT SIMMONS[7] (Mary Louise Folliard Howard[6], Robert Emmett Jenkins Howard[5], Henry Parker Howard[4], Elizabeth Savage Parker[3], Elizabeth Heyward[2], Thomas Heyward, Jr.[1]) child of Mary Louise

Folliard Howard and Harry Hull Simmons was born on 19 Sep 1942. He married (1st) Rosemary CRAFT in say 1962. She was born in Iva, SC in 1944. He married (2nd) Mary Arden NEIDLINGER in say 1967. She was born in Savannah, GA in 1946.

Child by first marriage:

    1100   i   Julie Ann SIMMONS, b. 1963

Child by second marriage:

    1101   ii   Therese Marie SIMMONS, b. 1969

702. JOSEPHINE ANN ROBINSON[7] (Josephine Silverius Howard[6], Robert Emmett Jenkins Howard[5], Henry Parker Howard[4], Elizabeth Savage Parker[3], Elizabeth Heyward[2], Thomas Heyward, Jr.[1]) child of Josephine Silverius Howard and John Francis Robinson was born on 11 Mar 1946. She married Michael A. SLATER in say 1969. Child:

    1102   i   Michael John SLATER, b. c. 1973

706. HAROLD SHERLOCK HARWOOD, Jr.[7] (Hazel Howard Sterling[6], Lillian Jenkins Howard[5], Henry Parker Howard[4], Elizabeth Savage Parker[3], Elizabeth Heyward[2], Thomas Heyward, Jr.[1]) child of Hazel Howard Sterling and Harold Sherlock Harwood was born in Washington, DC in 1929. He married Joan Carol VOSS in say 1955. She was born in Winston-Salem, NC in 1927. Child:

    1103   i   Sterling Voss HARWOOD, b. 1958

707. VIRGINIA CAROLYN HARWOOD[7] (Hazel Howard Sterling[6], Lillian Jenkins Howard[5], Henry Parker Howard[4], Elizabeth Savage Parker[3], Elizabeth Heyward[2], Thomas Heyward, Jr.[1]) child of Hazel Howard Sterling and Harold Sherlock Harwood was born in Washington, DC in 1929. She married Richard Ferris BUSCH in say 1953. He was born in Buffalo, NY in 1930. Children:

+   1104   i   Linda Jean BUSCH, b. 1955
       1105   ii   Deborah Anne BUSCH, b. 1957
       1106   iii   Richard Howard BUSCH, b. 1961

EIGHTH GENERATION

709. DANIEL HEYWARD HAMILTON, III[8] (Daniel Heyward Hamilton, Jr.[7], Daniel Heyward Hamilton[6], Miles Brewton Hamilton[5], Daniel Heyward Hamilton[4], Elizabeth Matthews Heyward[3], Daniel Heyward[2], Thomas

Heyward, Jr.[1]) child of Daniel Heyward Hamilton, Jr. and Jane Stewart Evans Nicholson was born in 1950. He married Joanne NASTASI in say 1970. Children:

    1107   i   Joel HAMILTON, b. 1971

    1108   ii   Elizabeth HAMILTON, b. 1973

710. MARGOT HEYWARD HAMILTON[8] (Daniel Heyward Hamilton, Jr.[7], Daniel Heyward Hamilton[6], Miles Brewton Hamilton[5], Daniel Heyward Hamilton[4], Elizabeth Matthews Heyward[3], Daniel Heyward[2], Thomas Heyward, Jr.[1]) child of Daniel Heyward Hamilton, Jr. and Jane Stewart Evans Nicholson was born in 1953. She married Kenneth SPAAR in say 1976. Child:

    1109   i   Jason SPAAR, b. 1978

711. ANN HOLLISTER HAMILTON[8] (Daniel Heyward Hamilton, Jr.[7], Daniel Heyward Hamilton[6], Miles Brewton Hamilton[5], Daniel Heyward Hamilton[4], Elizabeth Matthews Heyward[3], Daniel Heyward[2], Thomas Heyward, Jr.[1]) child of Daniel Heyward Hamilton, Jr. and Jane Stewart Evans Nicholson was born in 1955. She married Sumner Kittelle MOORE, Jr. in say 1977. He was born on 1952. Children:

    1110   i   Samantha Grosvenor MOORE, b. 1990 [twin]

    1111   ii   Cornelia Robinson MOORE, b. 1990 [twin]

713. JAMES WALKER COLEMAN, III[8] (Margot Hamilton[7], Daniel Heyward Hamilton[6], Miles Brewton Hamilton[5], Daniel Heyward Hamilton[4], Elizabeth Matthews Heyward[3], Daniel Heyward[2], Thomas Heyward, Jr.[1]) child of Margot Hamilton and James Walker Coleman was born in 1942. He married Betty LARKIN in say 1962. Children:

    1112   i   James Walker COLEMAN, IV, b. 20 Dec 1963

    1113   ii   Chisolm Larkin COLEMAM, b. 16 May 1966

714. HEYWARD HAMILTON COLEMAN[8] (Margot Hamilton[7], Daniel Heyward Hamilton[6], Miles Brewton Hamilton[5], Daniel Heyward Hamilton[4], Elizabeth Matthews Heyward[3], Daniel Heyward[2], Thomas Heyward, Jr.[1]) child of Margot Hamilton and James Walker Coleman was born in 1943. He married Charlotte BLACKWELL in say 1970. Children:

    1114   i   Heyward Hamilton COLEMAN, Jr., b. 28 Jan 1973

    1115   ii   Alexander COLEMAN, b. 7 Apr 1976

    1116 iii   Margaret Hamilton COLEMAN, b. 9 Mar 1979

721. JOHN INGRAM FISHBURNE, Jr.[8] (Jane DuBose Register[7], Jane DuBose Heyward[6], Edwin Watkins Heyward[5], Thomas Savage Heyward, Jr.[4], Thomas Savage Heyward[3], Thomas Heyward[2], Thomas Heyward, Jr.[1]) child of Jane DuBose Register and John Ingram Fishburne was born in Charleston, SC on 18 Aug 1937. He married Jean Rachel CRAWFORD in say 1960. She was born in Savannah, GA in 1939. Children:

    1117   i   John Ingram FISHBURNE, III, b. 12 Mar 1962
    1118   ii   Barron Crawford FISHBURNE, b. 12 Apr 1965
    1119   iii   Virginia Heyward FISHBURNE, b. 13 mar 1973

722. JANE HEYWARD FISHBURNE[8] (Jane DuBose Register[7], Jane DuBose Heyward[6], Edwin Watkins Heyward[5], Thomas Savage Heyward, Jr.[4], Thomas Savage Heyward[3], Thomas Heyward[2], Thomas Heyward, Jr.[1]) child of Jane DuBose Register and John Ingram Fishburne was born in Charleston, SC on 12 Nov 1940. She married George Allen COLLIER in say 1961. He was born in Washington, DC in 1942. Children:

    1120   i   David John COLLIER, b. 18 Jun 1963
    1121   ii   Lucy Jane COILLIER, b. 20 May 1965

747. JULIE SUSAN SCHURMEIER[8] (Julie Johnson Crocker[7], Lila Williams McTeer[6], Florence Percy Heyward[5], William Nathaniel Heyward[4], Thomas Savage Heyward[3], Thomas Heyward[2], Thomas Heyward, Jr.[1]) child of Julie Johnson Crocker and Robert Lindeke Schurmeier was born in Philadelphia, PA on 21 Mar 1955. She married Stephen Patrick NORRIS in say 1981. He was born in Rocky Mount, NC in 1951. Children:

    1122   i   Sarah Christine NORRIS, b. 1985
    1123   ii   Lila Rebecca NORRIS, b. 1987

749. GEORGEANNA HASELL PALMER[8] (Anna Eckles Oltmann[7], Lila Williams McTeer[6], Florence Percy Heyward[5], William Nathaniel Heyward[4], Thomas Savage Heyward[3], Thomas Heyward[2], Thomas Heyward, Jr.[1]) child of Anna Eckles Oltmann and Elias Horry Palmer was born on 24 Oct 1936. She married Joseph Herbert PEELE, Jr. on 3 Nov 1956. Children:

    1124   i   Janna Patrice PEELE, b. 1958
    1125   ii   Joseph Herbert PEELE, III, b. 1960

750. WILLIAM HERBERT OLTMANN, III[8] (William Herbert Oltmann, Jr.[7], Louisa Guerard McTeer[6], Florence Percy Heyward[5], William Nathaniel Heyward[4], Thomas Savage Heyward[3], Thomas Heyward[2], Thomas Heyward, Jr.[1]) child of William Herbert Oltmann, Jr. and Gertrude Stewart was born on 4 Apr 1941. He married Glenda MOORE in say 1962. Child:

+   1126   i   William Herbert OLTMANN, IV, b. 18 Dec 1964

751. STEWART ALLEN OLTMANN[8] (William Herbert Oltmann, Jr.[7], Louisa Guerard McTeer[6], Florence Percy Heyward[5], William Nathaniel Heyward[4], Thomas Savage Heyward[3], Thomas Heyward[2], Thomas Heyward, Jr.[1]) child of William Herbert Oltmann, Jr. and Gertrude Stewart was born in Charleston, SC on 4 Apr 1941. He married (1st) Betty RODDENBERRY, daughter of Marvin and Grace Roddenberry in Charleston, SC on 3 Nov 1962. She was born in Charleston, SC on 14 Mar 1941. Children:

    1127   i   Stewart Allen OLTMANN, Jr., b. 16 Sep 1964
+ 1128   ii Leslie English OLTMANN, b. 29 Jun 1968

752. JUDY OLTMANN[8] (William Herbert Oltmann, Jr.[7], Louisa Guerard McTeer[6], Florence Percy Heyward[5], William Nathaniel Heyward[4], Thomas Savage Heyward[3], Thomas Heyward[2], Thomas Heyward, Jr.[1]) child of William Herbert Oltmann, Jr. and Gertrude Stewart was born on 13 Nov 1943. She married John Deneil WILKINS in say 1960. Children:

+ 1129   i   Loren Deneil WILKINS, b. 16 Nov 1960
+ 1130   ii Kelly Lynn WILKINS, b. 30 Nov 1962

753. LINDA OLTMANN[8] (William Herbert Oltmann, Jr.[7], Louisa Guerard McTeer[6], Florence Percy Heyward[5], William Nathaniel Heyward[4], Thomas Savage Heyward[3], Thomas Heyward[2], Thomas Heyward, Jr.[1]) child of William Herbert Oltmann, Jr. and Gertrude Stewart was born about 1950. She married (2nd) Frederick GAUCH in say 1973. Child:

    1131   i   Tiffany Oltmann GAUCH, b. 17 Jul 1974

754. WILLIAM HEYWARD SEARSON[8] (Lila Cuthbert Oltmann[7], Louisa Guerard McTeer[6], Florence Percy Heyward[5], William Nathaniel Heyward[4], Thomas Savage Heyward[3], Thomas Heyward[2], Thomas Heyward, Jr.[1]) child of Lila Cuthbert Oltmann and Francis Marion Searson was born in Charleston, SC on 3 Mar 1941. He married Jacqueline COPELAND in say 1966. Children:

    1132   i   Christy L. SEARSON, b. c. 1970
    1133   ii Sally SEARSON, b. c. 1974

755. FRANCIS MARION SEARSON, Jr.[8] (Lila Cuthbert Oltmann[7], Louisa Guerard McTeer[6], Florence Percy Heyward[5], William Nathaniel Heyward[4], Thomas Savage Heyward[3], Thomas Heyward[2], Thomas Heyward, Jr.[1]) child of Lila Cuthbert Oltmann and Francis Marion Searson was born in Charleston, SC on 1 Nov 1957. He married Cynthia Adele ALBRIGHT in Charleston, SC on 10 Nov 1984 She was born in Charleston, SC on 14 Nov 1960. Child:

    1134   i   Layne Adele SEARSON, b. 23 Jun 1987

756. JANE LUCILLE WOODS[8] (Jane Lucille McTeer[7], James Edwin McTeer, Jr.[6], Florence Percy Heyward[5], William Nathaniel Heyward[4], Thomas Savage Heyward[3], Thomas Heyward[2], Thomas Heyward, Jr.[1]) child of Jane Lucille McTeer and John Sloman Woods was born in Beaufort, SC on 31 Jul 1948. She married (1st) Roger Dale HELMS in Beaufort, SC on 20 Jul 1967. She married (2nd) Clifford Thomas HERRING on 31 Aug 1974.
Children by first marriage:
+ 1135   i   Jane Lucille HELMS, b. 27 Feb 1968
+ 1136   ii   Laura Eve HELMS, b. 24 Dec 1969
Child by second marriage:
   1137   iii   John Thomas HERRING, b. 20 Nov 1978

757. ARLINE McTEER WOODS[8] (Jane Lucille McTeer[7], James Edwin McTeer, Jr.[6], Florence Percy Heyward[5], William Nathaniel Heyward[4], Thomas Savage Heyward[3], Thomas Heyward[2], Thomas Heyward, Jr.[1]) child of Jane Lucille McTeer and John Sloman Woods was born in Beaufort, SC on 2 Sep 1949. She married Kent Winner NICKERSON in say 1969 Child:
   1138   i   Allison Lynn NICKERSON, b. 5 Jul 1970

758. LUCILLE McTEER WOODS[8] (Jane Lucille McTeer[7], James Edwin McTeer, Jr.[6], Florence Percy Heyward[5], William Nathaniel Heyward[4], Thomas Savage Heyward[3], Thomas Heyward[2], Thomas Heyward, Jr.[1]) child of Jane Lucille McTeer and John Sloman Woods was born in Beaufort, SC on 1 Feb 1958. She married Robert Gibbes McDOWELL, Jr. in say 1982 Children:
   1139   i   Robert Gibbes McDOWELL, III, b. 21 Jan 1985
   1140   ii   Ashley Rebecca McDOWELL, b. 1 Aug 1988

759. MORRIS DAWES COOKE, Jr.[8] (Georgianne Hasell McTeer[7], James Edwin McTeer, Jr.[6], Florence Percy Heyward[5], William Nathaniel Heyward[4], Thomas Savage Heyward[3], Thomas Heyward[2], Thomas Heyward, Jr.[1]) child of Georgianna Hasell McTeer and Morris Dawes Cooke was born in Beaufort, SC on 20 Jul 1954. He married Helen HAFFEY on 16 May 1981 Children:
   1141   i   Morris Dawes COOKE, III, b. 22 Feb 1985
   1142   ii   George Henry COOKE, b. 11 Jan 1987
   1143   iii   Ellen Cecilia COOKE, b. 1994

762. JAMES McTEER CHAPLIN[8] (Sally Guerard McTeer[7], James Edwin McTeer, Jr.[6], Florence Percy Heyward[5], William Nathaniel Heyward[4], Thomas Savage Heyward[3], Thomas Heyward[2], Thomas Heyward, Jr.[1]) child of Sally Guerard McTeer and Saxby Stowe Chaplin was born in Beaufort, SC on 31 Mar 1957. He married Jamie Lillian REMBERT in Beaufort, SC on 7 Apr 1984. She was born on 12 Jul 1961 Children:

    1144   i   Sally McTeer CHAPLIN, b. 14 May 1986

    1145   ii   James McTeer CHAOLIN, Jr., b. 1990

763. GERALD JAY CHAPLIN[8] (Sally Guerard McTeer[7], James Edwin McTeer, Jr.[6], Florence Percy Heyward[5], William Nathaniel Heyward[4], Thomas Savage Heyward[3], Thomas Heyward[2], Thomas Heyward, Jr.[1]) child of Sally Guerard McTeer and Saxby Stowe Chaplin was born in Beaufort, SC on 6 Aug 1958. He married Cathy Charlene SAULS in Beaufort, SC on 12 Jun 1978. She was born on 24 Dec 1960. Child:

    1146   i   Gerald Jay CHAPLIN, Jr., b. 9 Jun 1979

773. ROBERT BYRON BUTLER[8] (James Byron Butler[7], Margaret Williamson McTeer[6], Florence Percy Heyward[5], William Nathaniel Heyward[4], Thomas Savage Heyward[3], Thomas Heyward[2], Thomas Heyward, Jr.[1]) child of James Bryon Butler and Ann Street was born in Hartford, CT on 15 Oct 1948. He married Cindy June DEWEY in say 1969 Children:

    1147   i   Michael Robert BUTLER, b. 1970

    1148   ii   Jeffrey Byron BUTLER, b. 1977

778. SUZANNE ELIZABETH THOMPSON[8] (Margaret McTeer Butler[7], Margaret Williamson McTeer[6], Florence Percy Heyward[5], William Nathaniel Heyward[4], Thomas Savage Heyward[3], Thomas Heyward[2], Thomas Heyward, Jr.[1]) child of Margaret McTeer Butler and Edgar E. Thompson was born in Parris Island, SC on 28 Apr 1945. She married Robert W. NEWSOME in say 1963 Child:

    1149   i   Thomas Eugene NEWSOME, b. 1964

779. PATRICIA ANN THOMPSON[8] (Margaret McTeer Butler[7], Margaret Williamson McTeer[6], Florence Percy Heyward[5], William Nathaniel Heyward[4], Thomas Savage Heyward[3], Thomas Heyward[2], Thomas Heyward, Jr.[1]) child of Margaret McTeer Butler and Edgar E. Thompson was born in Coronada, CA on 5 May 1948. She married William BARKSDALE in say 1972 Child:

    1150   i   William Jason BARKSDALE, b. 1979

780. BARBARA JEAN THOMPSON[8] (Margaret McTeer Butler[7], Margaret Williamson McTeer[6], Florence Percy Heyward[5], William Nathaniel Heyward[4], Thomas Savage Heyward[3], Thomas Heyward[2], Thomas Heyward,

Jr.[1]) child of Margaret McTeer Butler and Edgar E. Thompson was born in Thomson, GA on 8 Feb 1954. She married Patrick EPPS in say 1982 Child:
    1151   i   Kelly Christine EPPS, b. 1988

783. CAROL ORWIG[8] (Catherine Butler[7], Margaret Williamson McTeer[6], Florence Percy Heyward[5], William Nathaniel Heyward[4], Thomas Savage Heyward[3], Thomas Heyward[2], Thomas Heyward, Jr.[1]) child of Catherine Butler and Howard Wesley Orwig was born in 1949. She married (1st) Michael THOMPSON in say 1971 Children:
    1152   i   Jennifer THOMPSON, b. 1973
    1153   ii Kristen THOMPSON, b. 1974

789. FRANCES GERALDINE ALBERY[8] (Florence Exley Butler[7], Margaret Williamson McTeer[6], Florence Percy Heyward[5], William Nathaniel Heyward[4], Thomas Savage Heyward[3], Thomas Heyward[2], Thomas Heyward, Jr.[1]) child of Florence Exley Butler and her 1st husband Roy E. Albery was born in Beaufort, SC on 8 May 1949. She married Michael RAINEY in say 1967 Children:
+ 1154   i   Kina Marie RAINEY, b. 1967
+ 1155   ii Georgianne RAINEY, b. 1969
    1156   iii Timothy Michael RAINEY, b. c. 1972

790. ROY ESTLE ALBERY, Jr.[8] (Florence Exley Butler[7], Margaret Williamson McTeer[6], Florence Percy Heyward[5], William Nathaniel Heyward[4], Thomas Savage Heyward[3], Thomas Heyward[2], Thomas Heyward, Jr.[1]) child of Florence Exley Butler and her 1st husband Roy Estle Albery was born in El Paso, TX on 16 Jul 1951. He married Andrea HERRICK in say 1973 Child:
    1157   i   Adam Royce ALBERY, b. c. 1975

791. ROBERT HENRY ALBERY[8] (Florence Exley Butler[7], Margaret Williamson McTeer[6], Florence Percy Heyward[5], William Nathaniel Heyward[4], Thomas Savage Heyward[3], Thomas Heyward[2], Thomas Heyward, Jr.[1]) child of Florence Exley Butler and her 1st husband Roy E. Albery was born in Beaufort, SC on 5 Jan 1955. He married Lee FUTRELL in say 1976 Child:
    1158   i   Robert James ALBERY, b. c. 1979

792. MARGARET ANN McDURMON[8] (Florence Exley Butler[7], Margaret Williamson McTeer[6], Florence Percy Heyward[5], William Nathaniel Heyward[4], Thomas Savage Heyward[3], Thomas Heyward[2], Thomas Heyward,

Jr.[1]) child of Florence Exley Butler and her 2nd husband George McDurmon was born in Beaufort, SC on 14 Jul 1961. She married Sean Bernard MOONEY in say 1980 Children:

    1159   i   Nicholas Judah MOONEY, b. c. 1982
    1160   ii Benjamin Reed MOONEY, b. c. 1984

793. ROSEMARY McDURMON[8] (Florence Exley Butler[7], Margaret Williamson McTeer[6], Florence Percy Heyward[5], William Nathaniel Heyward[4], Thomas Savage Heyward[3], Thomas Heyward[2], Thomas Heyward, Jr.[1]) child of Florence Exley Butler and her 2nd husband George McDurmon was born in Jacksonville, NC on 18 Nov 1962. She married James SMITH in say 1982 Children:

    1161   i   Stephanie SMITH, b. c. 1985
    1162   ii Allison SMITH, b. c. 1987

794. JOSEPH EDWARD McDURMON[8] (Florence Exley Butler[7], Margaret Williamson McTeer[6], Florence Percy Heyward[5], William Nathaniel Heyward[4], Thomas Savage Heyward[3], Thomas Heyward[2], Thomas Heyward, Jr.[1]) child of Florence Exley Butler and her 2nd husband George McDurmon was born in Camp Pendelton, CA on 13 Jun 1965. He married Tracey KOONCE in say 1988 Children:

    1163   i   Kasey Joseph McDURMON, b. c. 1990
    1164   ii Dalton James McDURMON, b. c. 1993

795. GLENN CHESTER THOMPSON[8] (Ann Lucille Butler[7], Margaret Williamson McTeer[6], Florence Percy Heyward[5], William Nathaniel Heyward[4], Thomas Savage Heyward[3], Thomas Heyward[2], Thomas Heyward, Jr.[1]) child of Ann Lucille Butler and Frank Thompson was born on 20 Apr 1958. He married Joan SULLIVAN in say 1988 Children:

    1165   i   Emily Catherine THOMPSON, b. 1993
    1166   ii Chole Danielle THOMPSON, b. 1995
    1167 iii Mackenzie Elizabeth THOMPSON, b. 1999

797. JAMES LEROY BUTLER, III[8] (James Leroy Butler, Jr.[7], Margaret Williamson McTeer[6], Florence Percy Heyward[5], William Nathaniel Heyward[4], Thomas Savage Heyward[3], Thomas Heyward[2], Thomas Heyward, Jr.[1]) child of James Leroy Butler, Jr. and Carol Tolle was born on 23 Feb 1962. He married Vicki Lee BUTLER in say 1988 Children:

    1168   i   Laura Elizabeth BUTLER, b. 1989
    1169   ii Christopher James BUTLER, b. 1992

799. EDITH ANN SHIRLEY[8] (Carol McTeer Butler[7], Margaret Williamson McTeer[6], Florence Percy Heyward[5], William Nathaniel Heyward[4], Thomas Savage Heyward[3], Thomas Heyward[2], Thomas Heyward, Jr.[1]) child of Carol McTeer Butler and James Oliver Shirley was born in Beaufort, SC on 12 Dec 1956. She married Michael HATFIELD in say 1982. Child:

    1170   i   Matthew Ryan HATFIELD, b. 1988

800. TERRY CATHERINE SHIRLEY[8] (Carol McTeer Butler[7], Margaret Williamson McTeer[6], Florence Percy Heyward[5], William Nathaniel Heyward[4], Thomas Savage Heyward[3], Thomas Heyward[2], Thomas Heyward, Jr.[1]) child of Carol McTeer Butler and James Oliver Shirley was born in Beaufort, SC on 29 Sep 1959. She married Richard MURPHY in say 1987. Children:

    1171   i   Megan Catherine MURPHY, b. 1992
    1172   ii   Brandon Taylor MURPHY, b. 1994

801. CHERYL MARIE SHIRLEY[8] (Carol McTeer Butler[7], Margaret Williamson McTeer[6], Florence Percy Heyward[5], William Nathaniel Heyward[4], Thomas Savage Heyward[3], Thomas Heyward[2], Thomas Heyward, Jr.[1]) child of Carol McTeer Butler and James Oliver Shirley was born in Beaufort, SC on 9 Jan 1961. She married Steven Benjamin CATOE in say 1984. Children:

    1173   i   Christen Marie CATOE, b. 1988
    1174   ii   Benjamin James CATOE, b. 1992

805. COLDEN RHIND BATTEY, III[8] (Paula Wood Lengnick[7], Georgianna Hasell McTeer[6], Florence Percy Heyward[5], William Nathaniel Heyward[4], Thomas Savage Heyward[3], Thomas Heyward[2], Thomas Heyward, Jr.[1]) child of Paula Wood Lengnick and Colden Rhind Battey, Jr. was born in Beaufort, SC on 27 Aug 1957. He married Kathryn WHITE in say 1983. She was born on 19 Sep 1957. Children:

    1175   i   Caroline Jordan BATTEY, b. 31 Aug 1989
    1176   ii   Rebecca Wood BATTEY, b. 25 May 1993

806. ALLISON PAULA BATTEY[8] (Paula Wood Lengnick[7], Georgianna Hasell McTeer[6], Florence Percy Heyward[5], William Nathaniel Heyward[4], Thomas Savage Heyward[3], Thomas Heyward[2], Thomas Heyward, Jr.[1]) child of Paula Wood Lengnick and Colden Rhind Battey, Jr. was born in Trinidad on 17 May 1959. She married Dayle MARSHALL in say 1985. Children:

    1177   i   Joshua MARSHALL, b. 4 Se p 1989
    1178   ii   Emily MARSHALL, b. 28 Mar 1991
    1179   iii   Jason MARSHALL, b. Feb 1993

811. BONNIE LOUISE FERGUSON[8] (Louise Heyward McTeer[7], Walter William McTeer[6], Florence Percy Heyward[5], William Nathaniel Heyward[4], Thomas Savage Heyward[3], Thomas Heyward[2], Thomas Heyward, Jr.[1]) child of Louise Heyward McTeer and John Lambeth Ferguson, III was born in Athens, GA on 15 Feb 1963. She married Gary DOUGLAS in say 1981˙ Child:

    1180   i   Leonora Bailey DOUGLAS, b. 1981

814. MARY DARLENE DEASON[8] (Mary Adele McTeer[7], Walter William McTeer[6], Florence Percy Heyward[5], William Nathaniel Heyward[4], Thomas Savage Heyward[3], Thomas Heyward[2], Thomas Heyward, Jr.[1]) child of Mary Adele McTeer and Darvin Deason was born in Waynesboro, GA on 16 Oct 1963. She married William ELLIS in say 1981˙ Child:

    1181   i   Mary Christina ELLIS, b. 1982

816. TERESA ANN DEASON[8] (Mary Adele McTeer[7], Walter William McTeer[6], Florence Percy Heyward[5], William Nathaniel Heyward[4], Thomas Savage Heyward[3], Thomas Heyward[2], Thomas Heyward, Jr.[1]) child of Mary Adele McTeer and Darvin Deason was born in Waynesboro, GA on 14 Dec 1967. She married Gregory A. COOKE in Jun 1987˙ Child:

    1182   i   Cody Anthony COOKE, b. 17 Nov 1988

822. JACK ELQUIT ALTMAN, III[8] (Jack Elquit Altman, Jr.[7], Helen Perry Claire Heyward[6], Henry Guerard Heyward[5], William Nathaniel Heyward[4], Thomas Savage Heyward[3], Thomas Heyward[2], Thomas Heyward, Jr.[1]) child of Jack Elquit Altman, Jr. and Ann Desbouillions Morgan was born in Savannah, GA on 2 Apr 1952. He married Margaret Lee BRYSON in Decatur, AL on 12 Jun 1976. She was born in Montgomery, AL in 1954˙ Children:

    1183   i   John Heyward ALTMAN, b. 1981
    1184   ii   Charles Bryson ALTMAN, b. 1984

823. NANCY DESBOUILLIONS ALTMAN[8] (Jack Elquit Altman, Jr.[7], Helen Perry Claire Heyward[6], Henry Guerard Heyward[5], William Nathaniel Heyward[4], Thomas Savage Heyward[3], Thomas Heyward[2], Thomas Heyward, Jr.[1]) child of Jack Elquit Altman, Jr. and Ann Desbouillions Morgan was born in Savannah, GA on 4 Feb 1955. She married Scottie Randall RUFFINGTON, son of Allen and Bena Mae (Murphy) Ruffington in Savannah, GA on 3 Jan 1976. He was born in Gainesville, GA on 29 Aug 1950. Children:

    1185   i   Katherine Louise RUFFINGTON, b. 1 Feb 1980
    1186   ii   Scott Allen RUFFINGTON, b. 2 Jul 1982

824. SALLY ANN ALTMAN[8] (Jack Elquit Altman, Jr.[7], Helen Perry Claire Heyward[6], Henry Guerard Heyward[5], William Nathaniel Heyward[4], Thomas Savage Heyward[3], Thomas Heyward[2], Thomas Heyward, Jr.[1]) child of Jack Elquit Altman, Jr. and Ann Desbouillions Morgan was born in Savannah, GA on 2 Jan 1958. She married Harry David BRIGDON, Jr., son of Harry David and Barbara (Cribbs) Brigdon in Savannah, GA on 30 Jul 1983. He was born in Savannah, GA on 14 Jun 1959. Children:

    1187   i   Hunter Moore BRIGDON, b. 9 May 1985
    1188   ii Emily Lucille BRIGDON, b. 14 Jan 1987
    1189 iii Sarah Elizabeth BRIGDON, b. 9 Oct 1990

831. ASHLEY KAY HUTCHINSON[8] (Kay Heyward Sconyers[7], Catherine Kirk Heyward[6], Henry Guerard Heyward[5], William Nathaniel Heyward[4], Thomas Savage Heyward[3], Thomas Heyward[2], Thomas Heyward, Jr.[1]) child of Kay Heyward Sconyers and Morris Eugene Hutchinson was born on 8 Mar 1958. She married Charles Michael SEVERANCE say1981. He was born in 1956. Children:

    1190   i   William Chandler SEVERANCE, b. 1987
    1191   ii Michael Heyward SEVERANCE, b. 1990

832. HOLLY HUTCHINSON[8] (Kay Heyward Sconyers[7], Catherine Kirk Heyward[6], Henry Guerard Heyward[5], William Nathaniel Heyward[4], Thomas Savage Heyward[3], Thomas Heyward[2], Thomas Heyward, Jr.[1]) child of Kay Heyward Sconyers and Morris Eugene Hutchinson was born on 5 Feb 1961. She married Robert Thomas McMANUS say1982. He was born in 1959. Children:

    1192   i   Mallory Ashley McMANUS, b. 1985
    1193   ii Thomas Clayton McMANUS, b. 1988
    1194 iii Catherine Wade McMANUS, b. 1995

833. LISA SCONYERS[8] (William Chandler Sconyers, III[7], Catherine Kirk Heyward[6], Henry Guerard Heyward[5], William Nathaniel Heyward[4], Thomas Savage Heyward[3], Thomas Heyward[2], Thomas Heyward, Jr.[1]) child of William Chandler Sconyers, III and Lisa Fine was born on 21 Oct 1962. She married Michael COPLAN say1987. Children:

    1195   i   Lewis Jacob COPLAN, b. 1992
    1196   ii Dorothy Kate COPLAN, b. 1996

841. MARGARET WILLIAMS FERGUSON[8] (Mary Anne Heyward[7], William Smith Heyward[6], William Burroughs Smith Heyward[5], Andrew Hasell Heyward[4], Thomas Savage Heyward[3], Thomas Heyward[2], Thomas

Heyward, Jr.[1]) child of Mary Anne Heyward and Alfred Riggs Ferguson was born in Columbus, OH on 28 Dec 1948. She married David Edward SIMPSON say1984. He was born in Swaffham, Norfolk, ENGLAND on 30 Sep 1951. Children:

    1197   i   Susanna Elizabeth SIMPSON, b. 2 Sep 1987

    1198   ii Christina Rose SIMPSON, b. 1997 [twin]

    1199   iii Marianne Sarah SIMPSON, b. 1997 [twin]

842. JEAN HEYWARD FERGUSON[8] (Mary Anne Heyward[7], William Smith Heyward[6], William Burroughs Smith Heyward[5], Andrew Hasell Heyward[4], Thomas Savage Heyward[3], Thomas Heyward[2], Thomas Heyward, Jr.[1]) child of Mary Anne Heyward and Alfred Riggs Ferguson was born in Columbus, OH on 8 Feb 1951. She married Stephen Leo CARR, son of Leo John and Marguerite (Cahill) Carr in Scituate, MA on 7 Jun 1975. He was born in Cambridge, MA on 9 Nov 1950. Children:

    1200   i   Margaret Ferguson CARR, b. 5 Mar 1984

    1201   ii Julie Cahill CARR, b. 25 Oct 1992

843. LUCY PINCKNEY FERGUSON[8] (Mary Anne Heyward[7], William Smith Heyward[6], William Burroughs Smith Heyward[5], Andrew Hasell Heyward[4], Thomas Savage Heyward[3], Thomas Heyward[2], Thomas Heyward, Jr.[1]) child of Mary Anne Heyward and Alfred Riggs Ferguson was born in Delaware, OH on 3 Oct 1954. She married (1st) Thomas Richard ALLEN on 17 Jul 1976. He was born in Morrisville, NJ in 1953. She married (2nd) Philip Carl TENENBAUM, son of Abbot and Irma (Marcus) Tenenbaum in Middletown, VT on 13 Aug 1988. He was born in Exeter, NH on 25 Apr 1955.

Child by first marriage:

    1202   i   Nathaniel Ferguson ALLEN, b. 28 Mar 1981

Child by second marriage:

    1203   ii Ruth Ellen TENENBAUM, b. 23 Mar 1990

845. ANNE HEYWARD COVERSTON[8] (Virginia Hughes Heyward[7], William Smith Heyward[6], William Burroughs Smith Heyward[5], Andrew Hasell Heyward[4], Thomas Savage Heyward[3], Thomas Heyward[2], Thomas Heyward, Jr.[1]) child of Virginia Hughes Heyward and David Yost Coverston was born on 7 Mar 1955. She married William Rueben BROWN say1976. He was born in 1950. Children:

    1204   i   Stephanie Virginia BROWN, b. c. 1978

    1205   ii Sheri Frances BROWN, b. c. 1980

    1206   iii William Robert BROWN, b. c. 1984

846. WILLIAM JOSEPH YEAGER, Jr.[8] (Marian Rochelle Heyward[7], Emory Speer Heyward[6], Andrew Hasell Heyward, Jr.[5], Andrew Hasell Heyward[4], Thomas Savage Heyward[3], Thomas Heyward[2], Thomas Heyward, Jr.[1]) child of Marian Rochelle Heyward and William Joseph Yeager was born in Norfolk, VA in 1956. He married Reba REYNOLDS in Candor, NC in 1979. She was born in Candor, NC in 1960. Children:

   1207   i   William Joseph YEAGER, III, b. 1984
   1208   ii Andrew Heyward YEAGER, b. 1986
   1209 iii Emily Michelle YEAGER, b. 1991

847. SUSAN ELLEN YEAGER[8] (Marian Rochelle Heyward[7], Emory Speer Heyward[6], Andrew Hasell Heyward, Jr.[5], Andrew Hasell Heyward[4], Thomas Savage Heyward[3], Thomas Heyward[2], Thomas Heyward, Jr.[1]) child of Marian Rochelle Heyward and William Joseph Yeager was born in St. Simons Island, GA in 1958. She married William Franklin BERRY in Warner Robins, Houston County, GA in say 1982. He was born in 1958. Children:

   1210   i   William Franklin BERRY, Jr., b. 1985
   1211   ii Brett Yeager BERRY, b. 1988
   1212 iii Kelsey Claire BERRY, b. 1990

849. KEITH HEYWARD YEAGER[8] (Marian Rochelle Heyward[7], Emory Speer Heyward[6], Andrew Hasell Heyward, Jr.[5], Andrew Hasell Heyward[4], Thomas Savage Heyward[3], Thomas Heyward[2], Thomas Heyward, Jr.[1]) child of Marian Rochelle Heyward and William Joseph Yeager was born in Warner Robins, GA in 1966. He married Karen HERRING say1991. She was born in West Palm Beach, FL in 1968. Children:

   1213   i   Brian Emory YEAGER, b. 1996
   1214   ii Mark Alan YEAGER, b. 1998

855. LAURA ELLEN HEYWARD[8] (Andrew Hasell Heyward, IV[7], Andrew Hasell Heyward, III[6], Andrew Hasell Heyward, Jr.[5], Andrew Hasell Heyward[4], Thomas Savage Heyward[3], Thomas Heyward[2], Thomas Heyward, Jr.[1]) child of Andrew Hasell Heyward, IV and Carol Inman was born in Atlanta, GA on 28 Jan 1963. She married James Todd McLOCHLIN , son of James Francis and Carol (Yeich) McLochlin in Atlanta, GA on 4 May 1991. He was born in Logansport, IN on 31 Jul 1964. Children:

   1215   i   Caroline Heyward McLOCHLIN, b. 2 Feb 1994
   1216   ii Elizabeth Inman McLOCHLIN, b. 1997

860. ANGELA SUZANNE KILGO[8] (Helen Vance Heyward[7], Marion Speer Heyward[6], Andrew Hasell Heyward, Jr.[5], Andrew Hasell Heyward[4], Thomas Savage Heyward[3], Thomas Heyward[2], Thomas Heyward, Jr.[1]) child of Helen Vance Heyward and Jerry Kilgo was born in Atlanta, GA in 1975. She married Brian ADLER say1993. He was born in 1967. Children:

 1217   i   Brian ADLER, Jr., b. 1993
 1218   ii   Michael ADLER, b. 1995

861. MARTHA ELIZABETH RUMSEY[8] (Bronson C. Rumsey, Jr.[7], Elizabeth Beckwith Lynah[6], James Lynah[5], Ella Louise Heyward[4], Thomas Savage Heyward[3], Thomas Heyward[2], Thomas Heyward, Jr.[1]) child of Bronson C. Rumsey, Jr. and his 1st wife Martha Anne Osborne was born on 19 Aug 1952. She married James WHITLEY in say 1977. Children:

 1219   i   James Bronson WHITLEY, b. 1979
 1220   ii   Christopher John WHITLEY, b. 1980

862. BRONSON C. RUMSEY, III[8] (Bronson C. Rumsey, Jr.[7], Elizabeth Beckwith Lynah[6], James Lynah[5], Ella Louise Heyward[4], Thomas Savage Heyward[3], Thomas Heyward[2], Thomas Heyward, Jr.[1]) child of Bronson C. Rumsey, Jr. and his 2nd wife Shirley Walters was born on 1 Jul 1959. He married Heidi PETERSON in say 1988. Child:

 1221   i   Sarah Louise RUMSEY, b. 21 Nov 1995

869. GEORGE SHERRILL, III[8] (George Sherrill, Jr.[7], Maria Glover Lynah[6], James Lynah[5], Ella Louise Heyward[4], Thomas Savage Heyward[3], Thomas Heyward[2], Thomas Heyward, Jr.[1]) child of George Sherrill, Jr. and Claire Ridley Gardner was born in Atlanta, GA on 15 Feb 1966. He married Sara BOONE in say 1992. Child:

 1222   i   George SHERRILL, IV, b. 1997

871. CHRISTINE LYNAH SHERRILL[8] (James Lynah Sherrill[7], Maria Glover Lynah[6], James Lynah[5], Ella Louise Heyward[4], Thomas Savage Heyward[3], Thomas Heyward[2], Thomas Heyward, Jr.[1]) child of James Lynah Sherrill and Mary Lou Ingram was born on 27 Jul 1959. She married John Sharp VASS in Apr 1983. Child:

 1223   i   John Sharp VASS, Jr., b. 3 Jul 1994

873. JAMES LYNAH SHERRILL, Jr.[8] (James Lynah Sherrill[7], Maria Glover Lynah[6], James Lynah[5], Ella Louise Heyward[4], Thomas Savage Heyward[3], Thomas Heyward[2], Thomas Heyward, Jr.[1]) child of James Lynah

Sherrill and Mary Lou Ingram was born on 8 Apr 1962. He married Anne Marie SHARBAUGH 31 Dec 1994. Child:

    1224   i   James Lynah SHERRILL, III, b. 29 Mar 1996

874. JEFFREY INGRAM SHERRILL[8] (James Lynah Sherrill[7], Maria Glover Lynah[6], James Lynah[5], Ella Louise Heyward[4], Thomas Savage Heyward[3], Thomas Heyward[2], Thomas Heyward, Jr.[1]) child of James Lynah Sherrill and Mary Lou Ingram was born on 17 Oct 1963. He married Celeste EMBRY in Atlanta, GA on 25 Apr 1987. Child:

    1225   i   Emily Jane SHERRILL, b. 8 Mar 1996

876. ELIZABETH HUGER AUSTIN[8] (Elizabeth Huger Harrison[7], Ella Louise Heyward Lynah[6], James Lynah[5], Ella Louise Heyward[4], Thomas Savage Heyward[3], Thomas Heyward[2], Thomas Heyward, Jr.[1]) child of Elizabeth Huger Harrison and Lawrence Miner Austin was born in Savannah, GA on 13 Jan 1956. She married Peter Michael DAILEY in Savannah, GA on 30 Apr 1983. He was born in Mexico City, MEXICO in 1952. Children:

    1226   i   Austin Michael DAILEY, b. 1988
    1227   ii   Caroline Beckwith DAILEY, b. 1994

877. LAWRENCE MINER AUSTIN, Jr.[8] (Elizabeth Huger Harrison[7], Ella Louise Heyward Lynah[6], James Lynah[5], Ella Louise Heyward[4], Thomas Savage Heyward[3], Thomas Heyward[2], Thomas Heyward, Jr.[1]) child of Elizabeth Huger Harrison and Lawrence Miner Austin was born in Savannah, GA on 6 Dec 1957. He married Donna Marie NIEMAN in Alexandria, VA in May 1985. She was born in Mar 1962. Children:

    1228   i   Elizabeth Gail AUSTIN, b. 1990
    1229   ii   Margaret Elliott AUSTIN, b. 1992

902. ELIZABETH LYNAH[8] (James Lynah[7], Savage Heyward Lynah[6], John Heyward Lynah, Jr.[5], Ella Louise Heyward[4], Thomas Savage Heyward[3], Thomas Heyward[2], Thomas Heyward, Jr.[1]) child of James Lynah and Cindy Ellis was born on 28 May 1968. She married Mark Alton REAVIS in say 1991. Child:

    1230   i   Mark Alton REAVIS, Jr., b. 1994

918. ROMAN BURCHART HAMMES[8] (R. Burke Hammes, Jr.[7], Daisy Vincent Martin[6], Martha Horry Howard[5], Annie Howard Webb[4], Elizabeth Savage Heyward[3], Thomas Heyward[2], Thomas Heyward, Jr.[1]) child of R. Burke Hammes, Jr. and Jane Wynne Touchey was born in Savannah, GA on 19 Feb 1943. He married (1st) Yvonne MICHEL in say 1967. She was born in 1947. He married (2nd) Ruth Anne GLOVER in say 1976. She was born in 1950.

Child by first marriage:

    1231   i   Michel HAMMES, b. 22 Jun 1969

Children by second marriage:

    1232   ii   Francis Rutledge HAMMES, b. 4 Mar 1978

    1233   iii Andrew Burchart HAMMES, b. 18 Ap 1980

    1234   iv Roman Vincent HAMMES, b. 30 Dec 1981

    1235   v   Claire Elizabeth HAMMES, b. 20 Sep 1983

    1236   vi Dayne Martin HAMMES, b. 22 Jul 1985

    1237   vii Abram Glover HAMMES, b. 28 Nov 1987

    1238   viii Drayton Marshall HAMMES, b. 24 Sep 1989

925. JOHN VINCENT PHENICIE[8] (Ann Cuthbert Martin[7], John Vincent Martin[6], Martha Horry Howard[5], Annie Howard Webb[4], Elizabeth Savage Heyward[3], Thomas Heyward[2], Thomas Heyward, Jr.[1]) child of Ann Cuthbert Martin and John Wilbur Phenicie was born in Oklahoma City, OK on 22 Jan 1948. He married Tamera Leigh JUERGENS in say 1970. She was born in Miami, OK in 1949. Children:

    1239   i   John Christopher PHENICIE, b. 30 Apr 1972 [twin]

+ 1240   ii Tiffany Kathleen PHENICIE, b. 30 Apr 1972 [twin]

    1241   iii Joshua Vincent PHENICIE, b. 26 Jul 1975

    1242   iv Kelly Michelle PHENICIE, b. 1983

926. WILLIAM MARTIN PHENICIE[8] (Ann Cuthbert Martin[7], John Vincent Martin[6], Martha Horry Howard[5], Annie Howard Webb[4], Elizabeth Savage Heyward[3], Thomas Heyward[2], Thomas Heyward, Jr.[1]) child of Ann Cuthbert Martin and John Wilbur Phenicie was born in Houston, TX on 28 Jan 1950, and died on 25 May 1974. He married Sara Ann RAGSDALE in say 1968. She was born in Tulsa, OK in 1950. Child:

+ 1243   i   Michael Vincent PHENICIE, b. 16 Dec 1969

927. THOMAS HEYWARD PHENICIE[8] (Ann Cuthbert Martin[7], John Vincent Martin[6], Martha Horry Howard[5], Annie Howard Webb[4], Elizabeth Savage Heyward[3], Thomas Heyward[2], Thomas Heyward, Jr.[1]) child of Ann Cuthbert Martin and John Wilbur Phenicie was born in Houston, TX on 7 Apr 1953. He married Pamela Ann GARRISON in say 1981. She was born in Tulsa, OK in 1952. Children:

    1244   i   Jennifer Marie PHENICIE, b. 1984

    1245   ii Thomas Heyward PHENICIE, Jr., b. 1986

928. MARTHA ANN PHENICIE[8] (Ann Cuthbert Martin[7], John Vincent Martin[6], Martha Horry Howard[5], Annie Howard Webb[4], Elizabeth Savage Heyward[3], Thomas Heyward[2], Thomas Heyward, Jr.[1]) child of Ann Cuthbert Martin and John Wilbur Phenicie was born in Casper, WY on 14 Aug 1949. She married (1st) Randall CALLAHAN in say 1975. He was born in Corpus Christi, TX in 1953. She married (2nd) Michael Laurence NEWSOME in say 1986. He was born in Atlanta, GA in 1955.
Child by first marriage:
    1246   i   Christina Lynn CALLAHAN, b. 16 Feb 1977
Child by second marriage:
    1247   ii   Jonathan Michael NEWSOME, b. 1988

931. WILLIAM HOWARD WALTON[8] (Elise Leadbetter Martin[7], John Vincent Martin[6], Martha Horry Howard[5], Annie Howard Webb[4], Elizabeth Savage Heyward[3], Thomas Heyward[2], Thomas Heyward, Jr.[1]) child of Elise Leadbetter Martin and Richard B. Walton was born in Houston, TX in 1957. He married Mary Jean WILSON in say 1979. She was born in Houston, TX in 1956. Children:
    1248   i   Ryan Matthew WALTON, b. 1981
    1249   ii   William Reid WALTON, b. 1985

934. DAVID ALLAN MARTIN[8] (John Elmore Martin[7], John Vincent Martin[6], Martha Horry Howard[5], Annie Howard Webb[4], Elizabeth Savage Heyward[3], Thomas Heyward[2], Thomas Heyward, Jr.[1]) child of John Elmore Martin and Margaret Kieberger was born in Houston, TX in 1957. He married Catherine CARLTON in say 1979. She was born in Midland, TX in 1955. Child:
    1250   i   Michael Carlton MARTIN, b. 1992

936. ELIZABETH LYONS HOWKINS[8] (John Smallbrook Howkins, III[7], John Smallbrook Howkins, Jr.[6], Elise Heyward[5], Jacob Guerard Heyward[4], George Cuthbert Heyward[3], Thomas Heyward[2], Thomas Heyward, Jr.[1]) child of John Smallbrook Howkins, III and Virginia Ruth Lyons was born in Pascagoula, MS in 1953. She married Jeffrey Hall PARKINGTON in say 1980. He was born in 1951 Children:
    1251   i   Christopher Lyons PARKINGTON, b. 1984
    1252   ii   Matthew Benjamin PARKINGTON, b. 1987

937. JOHN HUGER   HOWKINS, Jr.[8] (John Huger Howkins[7], John Smallbrook Howkins, Jr.[6], Elise Heyward[5], Jacob Guerard Heyward[4], George Cuthbert Heyward[3], Thomas Heyward[2], Thomas Heyward, Jr.[1]) child of John Huger Howkins and Mary Louise Key was born in Savannah, GA in 1955. He married Catherine ALLEY in say 1978. She was born in 1956. Children:

    1253   i   John Huger HOWKINS, III, b. 1981
    1254   ii Catherine Alexander HOWKINS, b. 1983

939. ELIZABETH HEYWARD HOWKINS[8] (John Henry Francis Howkins[7], Guerard Heyward Howkins[6], Elise Heyward[5], Jacob Guerard Heyward[4], George Cuthbert Heyward[3], Thomas Heyward[2], Thomas Heyward, Jr.[1]) child of John Henry Francis Howkins and his 1st wife Phyllis Dana was born in 1948. She married Wes REED in say 1968. He was born in 1947 Children:

    1255   i   Joseph REED, b. 1970
    1256   ii Amy REED, b. 1973

940. ANN CHINN HOWKINS[8] (John Henry Francis Howkins[7], Guerard Heyward Howkins[6], Elise Heyward[5], Jacob Guerard Heyward[4], George Cuthbert Heyward[3], Thomas Heyward[2], Thomas Heyward, Jr.[1]) child of John Henry Francis Howkins and his 1st wife Phyllis Dana was born in 1950. She married Ronald HALDEMAN in say 1976. He was born in 1949 Children:

    1257   i   Benjamin HALDEMAN, b. 1980
    1258   ii Christen HALDEMAN, b. 1983

954. ALICE BRADFORD HEYWARD[8] (George Cuthbert Heyward, V[7], George Cuthbert Heyward, IV[6], George Cuthbert Heyward, III[5], George Cuthbert Heyward, Jr.[4], George Cuthbert Heyward[3], Thomas Heyward[2], Thomas Heyward, Jr.[1]) child of George Cuthbert Heyward, V and Hannah Hewson Bradford was born in Bethlehem, PA on 30 Oct 1968. She married Fletcher Carl DERRICK, III in say 1993. He was born in 1968. Child:

    1259   i   Heyward Fletcher DERRICK, b. 1997

955. MARGARET HEYWARD[8] (George Cuthbert Heyward, V[7], George Cuthbert Heyward, IV[6], George Cuthbert Heyward, III[5], George Cuthbert Heyward, Jr.[4], George Cuthbert Heyward[3], Thomas Heyward[2], Thomas Heyward, Jr.[1]) child of George Cuthbert Heyward, V and Hannah Hewson Bradford was born in Phoenixville, PA on 10 Jun 1972. She married (2nd) Mark CAPORINI in say 1996. He was born in 1970. Child:

    1260   i   Isabella Hewson CAPORINI, b. 1998

963. HERBERT LESLIE MANNING, Jr.[8] (Clara Ferebee Fenner[7], Mary Elizabeth Heyward[6], Robert Clarence Heyward[5], Robert Chisolm Heyward[4],

George Cuthbert Heyward[3], Thomas Heyward[2], Thomas Heyward, Jr.[1]) child of Clara Ferebee Fenner and Herbert Leslie Manning was born in Rocky Mount, NC in 1955. He married (2nd) Paige WOLTZEN in say 1991. She was born in 1965. Child:

 1261 i Margot Elizabeth MANNING, b. 16 Aug 1995

964. MARY WHITLEY MANNING[8] (Clara Ferebee Fenner[7], Mary Elizabeth Heyward[6], Robert Clarence Heyward[5], Robert Chisolm Heyward[4], George Cuthbert Heyward[3], Thomas Heyward[2], Thomas Heyward, Jr.[1]) child of Clara Ferebee Fenner and Herbert Leslie Manning was born in Rocky Mount, NC in 1959. She married C. David GARNETT in say 1984. He was born in 1957. Children:

 1262 i Nathan David GARNETT, b. 3 Sep 1989
 1263 ii Samuel Thomas GARNETT, b. 14 Jan 1994

965. JOHN HOUSAN FENNER, III[8] (John Housan Fenner, Jr.[7], Mary Elizabeth Heyward[6], Robert Clarence Heyward[5], Robert Chisolm Heyward[4], George Cuthbert Heyward[3], Thomas Heyward[2], Thomas Heyward, Jr.[1]) child of John Housan Fenner, Jr. and Joan Mildred Backat was born in Rocky Mount, NC on 20 Dec 1960. He married Catherine St. PIERRE in say 1987. Children:

 1264 i Jessica Catherine FENNER, b. 1991
 1265 ii Rachel Claire FENNER, b. 1996

966. WILLIAM EATON FENNER, Jr.[8] (William Eaton Fenner[7], Mary Elizabeth Heyward[6], Robert Clarence Heyward[5], Robert Chisolm Heyward[4], George Cuthbert Heyward[3], Thomas Heyward[2], Thomas Heyward, Jr.[1]) child of William Eaton Fenner and Doris Jeanne Tucker was born in Dallas, TX on 26 Jan 1954. He married Janice DARLINGTON in say 1986. Children:

 1266 i William Eaton FENNER, III, b. 2 Oct 1990
 1267 ii Jordan Marie FENNER, b. May 1993

967. ELIZABETH HEYWARD FENNER[8] (William Eaton Fenner[7], Mary Elizabeth Heyward[6], Robert Clarence Heyward[5], Robert Chisolm Heyward[4], George Cuthbert Heyward[3], Thomas Heyward[2], Thomas Heyward, Jr.[1]) child of William Eaton Fenner and Doris Jeanne Tucker was born in Dallas, TX on 26 Apr 1955. She married James STUDDARD in say 1983. Child:

 1268 i Ashley STUDDARD, b. 25 Sep 1987

968. EDWIN FEREBEE FENNER[8] (William Eaton Fenner[7], Mary Elizabeth Heyward[6], Robert Clarence Heyward[5], Robert Chisolm Heyward[4],

George Cuthbert Heyward[3], Thomas Heyward[2], Thomas Heyward, Jr.[1]) child of William Eaton Fenner and Doris Jeanne Tucker was born in Dallas, TX on 8 Oct 1956. He married Linda PHARRINGTON in say 1982. Child:

    1269   i   Edwin Ferebee FENNER, Jr., b. c. 1985

969. THOMAS SHAW FENNER[8] (William Eaton Fenner[7], Mary Elizabeth Heyward[6], Robert Clarence Heyward[5], Robert Chisolm Heyward[4], George Cuthbert Heyward[3], Thomas Heyward[2], Thomas Heyward, Jr.[1]) child of William Eaton Fenner and Doris Jeanne Tucker was born in Raleigh, NC on 1 Jan 1959. He married Denny Lynn LEACH in say 1986. Children:

    1270   i   Kristina Marie FENNER, b. 14 Apr 1989
    1271   ii   Rachel Elizabeth FENNER, b. Apr 1992
    1272   iii   Brandon Thomas FENNER, b. 16 Sep 1995
    1273   iv   Chad Heyward FENNER, b. 1996

971. JAMES ROBERT HEYWARD, Jr.[8] (James Robert Heyward[7], George Cuthbert Heyward, VI[6], Robert Clarence Heyward[5], Robert Chisolm Heyward[4], George Cuthbert Heyward[3], Thomas Heyward[2], Thomas Heyward, Jr.[1]) child of James Robert Heyward and Linnie Mae Stallings was born in Fort Knox, KY on 7 Jul 1956. He married Cynthia Faye MICHAL, daughter of Joseph Lewis and Edna Faye (Shaw) Michal, Jr. in Asheville, NC on 24 May 1980. She was born in Asheville, NC on 18 Sep 1959. Children:

    1274   i   Andrew James HEYWARD, b. 15 Sep 1986
    1275   ii   Christine Michal HEYWARD, b. c. 1989

972. EVA JEANNETTE HEYWARD[8] (James Robert Heyward[7], George Cuthbert Heyward, VI[6], Robert Clarence Heyward[5], Robert Chisolm Heyward[4], George Cuthbert Heyward[3], Thomas Heyward[2], Thomas Heyward, Jr.[1]) child of James Robert Heyward and Linnie Mae Stallings was born in Fort Knox, KY on 2 Jan 1958. She married Bonum Sams WILSON, III in say 1985. Children:

    1276   i   Jenkins Heyward WILSON, b. 5 Sep 1989
    1277   ii   Sams Noah WILSON, b. 1 Jul 1993
    1278   iii   Anna Bailey WILSON, b. 22 Aug 1996

976. DAVID MICHAEL JOHNS[8] (Mary Agnes Heyward[7], Thomas Savage Heyward[6], Robert Clarence Heyward[5], Robert Chisolm Heyward[4], George Cuthbert Heyward[3], Thomas Heyward[2], Thomas Heyward, Jr.[1]) child of Mary Agnes Heyward and Joseph Carter Johns was born in Aiken, SC on 30

Mar 1957. He married Margaret Elizabeth GUYER in Newark, DE on 27
May 1980. She was born in Wilmington, DE in 1959. Children:
 1279   i   Matthew David JOHNS, b. 29 Nov 1983
 1280   ii Michael Robert JOHNS, b. 25 Mar 1986
 1281   iii Daniel Joseph JOHNS, b. Jun 1994

977. JOSEPH CARTER JOHNS, Jr.[8] (Mary Agnes Heyward[7], Thomas
Savage Heyward[6], Robert Clarence Heyward[5], Robert Chisolm Heyward[4],
George Cuthbert Heyward[3], Thomas Heyward[2], Thomas Heyward, Jr.[1]) child
of Mary Agnes Heyward and Joseph Carter Johns was born in Parkersburg,
WV on 25 Feb 1959. He married Frances Ann JACKSON, daughter of
Charles Klair and Mary (Evans) Jackson in Wilmington, DE on 13 Sep 1980.
She was born in Wilmington, DE on 22 Jun 1959. Children:
 1282   i   Jennifer Frances JOHNS, b. 31 May 1982
 1283   ii Randall Savage JOHNS, b. 10 Apr 1987
 1284   iii Mary Rebecca JOHNS, b. 26 Jan 1989

978. MARGARET ANN JOHNS[8] (Mary Agnes Heyward[7], Thomas Savage
Heyward[6], Robert Clarence Heyward[5], Robert Chisolm Heyward[4], George
Cuthbert Heyward[3], Thomas Heyward[2], Thomas Heyward, Jr.[1]) child of
Mary Agnes Heyward and Joseph Carter Johns was born in Orange, TX on
21 Feb 1961. She married Steven James SCHUESSLER on 31 Jan 1998. He
was born in Sheboygan, WI in 1962. Child:
 1285   i   Erin Nicole SCHUESSLER, b. May 1998

979. MARY ELIZABETH JOHNS[8] (Mary Agnes Heyward[7], Thomas
Savage Heyward[6], Robert Clarence Heyward[5], Robert Chisolm Heyward[4],
George Cuthbert Heyward[3], Thomas Heyward[2], Thomas Heyward, Jr.[1]) child
of Mary Agnes Heyward and Joseph Carter Johns was born in Orange, TX
on 6 Dec 1965. She married Kenneth Paul HOVIS in Waynesboro, PA on 11
Sep 1993. Child:
 1286   i   Megan Elizabeth HOVIS, b. Feb 1995

981. THOMAS SAVAGE HEYWARD, III[8] (Thomas Savage Heyward,
Jr.[7], Thomas Savage Heyward[6], Robert Clarence Heyward[5], Robert Chisolm
Heyward[4], George Cuthbert Heyward[3], Thomas Heyward[2], Thomas
Heyward, Jr.[1]) child of Thomas Savage Heyward, Jr. and Betty Johnson was
born in Greensboro, NC on 3 Dec 1963. He married Brenda SMITH in say
1986. She was born in Thomaston, Upson County, GA in 1964. Children:
 1287   i   Thomas Savage HEYWARD, IV, b. 1988
 1288   ii Travis Paul HEYWARD, b. 1993

986. KIMBERLY MICHELLE RAWL[8] (Joseph Heyward Rawl[7], Josephine Stoney Heyward[6], Robert Clarence Heyward[5], Robert Chisolm Heyward[4], George Cuthbert Heyward[3], Thomas Heyward[2], Thomas Heyward, Jr.[1]) child of Joseph Heyward Rawl and Ruth Anne Kearns was born in 1967. She married Donald MILLS in say 1992. She was born in 1962. Child:

    1289   i   Brent Eugene MILLS, b. 1996

987. MICHAEL HEYWARD RAWL[8] (Joseph Heyward Rawl[7], Josephine Stoney Heyward[6], Robert Clarence Heyward[5], Robert Chisolm Heyward[4], George Cuthbert Heyward[3], Thomas Heyward[2], Thomas Heyward, Jr.[1]) child of Joseph Heyward Rawl and Ruth Anne Kearns was born in 1969. He married Wendy Gale NEELEY in say 1994. She was born in 1970. Child:

    1290   i   Taylor Madison RAWL, b. 1996

994. RHONDA SUSAN TRYBALSKI[8] (Ann Cuthbert Heyward[7], Gaillard Stoney Heyward[6], Daniel Hasell Heyward[5], Robert Chisolm Heyward[4], George Cuthbert Heyward[3], Thomas Heyward[2], Thomas Heyward, Jr.[1]) child of Ann Cuthbert Heyward and Thomas E. Trybalski was born on 10 Jun 1965. She married Robert LEPLEY in say 1985. Child:

    1291   i   Justin Grant LEPLEY, b. 5 Oct 1987

995. AMY LAURA TRYBALSKI[8] (Ann Cuthbert Heyward[7], Gaillard Stoney Heyward[6], Daniel Hasell Heyward[5], Robert Chisolm Heyward[4], George Cuthbert Heyward[3], Thomas Heyward[2], Thomas Heyward, Jr.[1]) child of Ann Cuthbert Heyward and Thomas E. Trybalski was born on 30 Mar 1969. She married James BROACH in say 1989. Children:

    1292   i   Savanah BROACH, b. 16 May 1991
    1293 ii   Stoney BROACH, b. 13 Oct 1993

997. LEE RAY HAAG[8] (Dorothy May Heyward[7], Gaillard Stoney Heyward[6], Daniel Hasell Heyward[5], Robert Chisolm Heyward[4], George Cuthbert Heyward[3], Thomas Heyward[2], Thomas Heyward, Jr.[1]) child of Dorothy May Heyward and Robert Ray Haag was born on 5 Jul 1959. He married Sarah Christine McLEOD in say 1979. Children:

    1294   i   Christian HAAG, b. 1980
    1295 ii   Sarah Lee HAAG, b. 1982

999. THOMAS GAILLARD HEYWARD, Jr.[8] (Thomas Gaillard Heyward[7], Gaillard Stoney Heyward[6], Daniel Hasell Heyward[5], Robert Chisolm 7Heyward[4], George Cuthbert Heyward[3], Thomas Heyward[2], Thomas

Heyward, Jr.[1]) child of Thomas Gaillard Heyward and Clare Frances Walker was born on 31 Mar 1968. He married Diana SPAHR in say 1993. Child:

    1296   i   Thomas Gaillard HEYWARD, III, b. 21 Oct 1995

1000. MELANIE CLARE HEYWARD[8] (Thomas Gaillard Heyward[7], Gaillard Stoney Heyward[6], Daniel Hasell Heyward[5], Robert Chisolm Heyward[4], George Cuthbert Heyward[3], Thomas Heyward[2], Thomas Heyward, Jr.[1]) child of Thomas Gaillard Heyward and Clare Frances Walker was born on 21 Jul 1970. She married Brad DOBYNS in say 1991. Children:

    1297   i   Mari Clare DOBYNS, b. Feb 1993
    1298   ii   Kelsey Elizabethy DOBYNS, b. 16 Oct 1995

1011. GEORGIA LEIGH SMITH[8] (Frances Hasell Heyward[7], Daniel Hasell Heyward, Jr.[6], Daniel Hasell Heyward[5], Robert Chisolm Heyward[4], George Cuthbert Heyward[3], Thomas Heyward[2], Thomas Heyward, Jr.[1]) child of Frances Hasell Heyward and Elmer Hainesworth Smith was born on 16 Dec 1963. She married (1st) James STREIT in say 1983. Child:

    1299   i   James Andrew STREIT, b. 6 Apr 1984

1013. DANIEL LEE HODGES[8] (Dyan Margaret Heyward[7], Daniel Hasell Heyward, Jr.[6], Daniel Hasell Heyward[5], Robert Chisolm Heyward[4], George Cuthbert Heyward[3], Thomas Heyward[2], Thomas Heyward, Jr.[1]) child of Dyan Margaret Heyward and Palmer Hodges was born in Savannah, GA on 10 Jun 1968. He married Karen FLUERY in say 1993. Child:

    1300   i   Chelsea Marie HODGES, b. 1998

1056. JEAN REBECCA STANFIELD[8] (Jean Marie Sparks[7], Caroline Heyward Gignilliat[6], William Robert Gignilliat[5], Mary Caroline Heyward[4], George Cuthbert Heyward[3], Thomas Heyward[2], Thomas Heyward, Jr.[1]) child of Jean Marie Sparks and Joseph William Stanfield was born in Huntsville, AL on 4 Nov 1967. She married Richard David CRAGO in say 1992. Child:

    1301   i   David William CRAGO, b. 1997

1070. GEORGE CAMERON TODD, Jr.[8] (Elizabeth Howard Clarke[7], Burwell Boykin Clarke, Jr.[6], Elizabeth Howard Burnet[5], Emma Howard Heyward[4], Elizabeth Savage Parker[3], Elizabeth Heyward[2], Thomas Heyward, Jr.[1]) child of Elizabeth Howard Clarke and George Cameron Todd was born in Columbia, SC on 4 Oct 1954. He married (2nd) Sara Welsh HALL, daughter of Eugene Evey and Margaret Esther (Durant) Hall, Jr. on 20 Feb 19821. She was born in Florence, SC on 21 Oct 1955. Children:

    1302   i   George Cameron TODD, III, b. 28 Mar 1984

1303   ii   Eugene Hall TODD, b. 17 Aug 1987
1304   iii Burwell Boykin Clarke TODD, b. 29 Jan 1990

1071. ALBERT RHETT HEYWARD TODD[8] (Elizabeth Howard Clarke[7], Burwell Boykin Clarke, Jr.[6], Elizabeth Howard Burnet[5], Emma Howard Heyward[4], Elizabeth Savage Parker[3], Elizabeth Heyward[2], Thomas Heyward, Jr.[1]) child of Elizabeth Howard Clarke and George Cameron Todd was born in Columbia, SC on 25 May 1956. He married (2nd) Serena WHITFIELD in say 1995. She was born in 1969. Child:
1305   i   Albert Rhett Heyward TODD, Jr., b. 1998

1072. ROSA CANTEY HEYWARD TODD[8] (Elizabeth Howard Clarke[7], Burwell Boykin Clarke, Jr.[6], Elizabeth Howard Burnet[5], Emma Howard Heyward[4], Elizabeth Savage Parker[3], Elizabeth Heyward[2], Thomas Heyward, Jr.[1]) child of Elizabeth Howard Clarke and George Cameron Todd was born in Columbia, SC on 8 Mar 1960. She married Eugene Dewey FOXWORTH, III, son of Eugene Dewey and Elizabeth (Hubbard) Foxworth, Jr. on 10 Dec 1983. He was born in Beaufort, SC on 18 Dec 1954. Children:
1306   i   Eugene Dewey FOXWORTH, IV, b. 1 Oct 1987
1307   ii   Heyward Boykin FOXWORTH, b. 25 May 1990

1075. BURNET TODD CLARKE[8] (Henri deSaussure Clarke[7], Albertus Moore Clarke[6], Elizabeth Howard Burnet[5], Emma Howard Heyward[4], Elizabeth Savage Parker[3], Elizabeth Heyward[2], Thomas Heyward, Jr.[1]) child of Henri deSaussure Clarke and Elizabeth Janet James was born in Beaumont, TX on 12 Feb 1964. He married Criss Ann ARMSTRONG in say 1989. She was born in 1962. Children:
1308   i   Zachary Heyward CLARKE, b. 1992
1309   ii   Caroline Elizabeth CLARKE, b. 1994

1076. DAVID BURNET CLARKE[8] (Heyward Burnet Clarke[7], Albertus Moore Clarke[6], Elizabeth Howard Burnet[5], Emma Howard Heyward[4], Elizabeth Savage Parker[3], Elizabeth Heyward[2], Thomas Heyward, Jr.[1]) child of Heyward Burnet Clarke and Margaret Annette Williams was born in 1964. He married Sharon WALTERS in say 1988. She was born in 1967. Children:
1310   i   Hunter Burnet CLARKE, b. 1992
1311   ii   Madison Susan CLARKE, b. 1996
1312   iii Preston Daniel CLARKE, b. 1999

1082. HENRY HEYWARD BURNET, IV[8] (Henry Heyward Burnet, III[7], Henry Heyward Burnet, Jr.[6], Henry Heyward Burnet[5], Emma Howard Heyward[4], Elizabeth Savage Parker[3], Elizabeth Heyward[2], Thomas Heyward, Jr.[1]) child of Henry Heyward Burnet, III and Alice Marie Musgrove was born in Waycross, GA on 27 Mar 1968. He married Virginia BRYAN in say 1993. Child:

    1313   i   Henry Heyward BURNET, V, b. 1998

1083. JONATHAN RUTLEDGE PARROTT[8] (Nancy Rutledge Wainer[7], Emma Heyward Burnet[6], Henry Heyward Burnet[5], Emma Howard Heyward[4], Elizabeth Savage Parker[3], Elizabeth Heyward[2], Thomas Heyward, Jr.[1]) child of Nancy Rutledge Wainer and Jesse L. Parrott was born in Hahira, Lowndes County, GA on 10 Nov 1956. He married Sarah Kathryn BARBARE in say 1992. She was born in Chapel Hill, NC on 24 Feb 1966. Children:

    1314   i   Jonathan Rutledge PARROTT, Jr., b. 21 Mar 1996
    1315   ii   Emma Kathryn PARROTT, b. 1998
    1316   iii   Sarah Bray PARROTT, b. 1999

1084. STEPHEN PRICE PARROTT[8] (Nancy Rutledge Wainer[7], Emma Heyward Burnet[6], Henry Heyward Burnet[5], Emma Howard Heyward[4], Elizabeth Savage Parker[3], Elizabeth Heyward[2], Thomas Heyward, Jr.[1]) child of Nancy Rutledge Wainer and Jesse L. Parrott was born in Hahira, Lowndes County, GA on 31 May 1959. He married Karen Ann RAMSBOTTOM in say 1985. She was born in Atlanta, GA on 15 Oct 1960. Children:

    1317   i   Jessica Lyle PARROTT, b. 6 Apr 1988
    1318   ii   Samuel Price PARROTT, b. 1993
    1319   iii   Bonnie Elizabeth PARROTT, b. 1998

1091. ELIZABETH HEYWARD OWENS[8] (Katherine Amory Wainer[7], Emma Heyward Burnet[6], Henry Heyward Burnet[5], Emma Howard Heyward[4], Elizabeth Savage Parker[3], Elizabeth Heyward[2], Thomas Heyward, Jr.[1]) child of Katherine Amory Wainer and James Herbert Owens was born in Valdosta, GA on 9 Apr 1973. She married Charles Joseph STEEDLEY in say 1992. He was born in Valdosta, GA in 1967. Children:

    1320   i   Laura Laci STEEDLEY, b. 1995
    1321   ii   Heyward Rebecca STEEDLEY, b. 1997

1104. LINDA JEAN BUSCH[8] (Virginia Carolyn Harwood[7], Hazel Howard Sterling[6], Lillian Jenkins Howard[5], Henry Parker Howard[4], Elizabeth Savage Parker[3], Elizabeth Heyward[2], Thomas Heyward, Jr.[1]) child of Virginia

Carolyn Harwood and Richard Ferris Busch was born in 1955. She married Michael DILEMBO in say 1987. Child:
 1322 i Zachariah DILEMBO, b. 1994

NINTH GENERATION

1126. WILLIAM HERBERT OLTMANN, IV[9] (William Herbert Oltmann, III[8], William Herbert Oltmann, Jr.[7], Louisa Guerard McTeer[6], Florence Percy Heyward[5], William Nathaniel Heyward[4], Thomas Savage Heyward[3], Thomas Heyward[2], Thomas Heyward, Jr.[1]) child of William Herbert Oltmann, III and Glenda Moore was born in 1964. He married Joyce (–) in in say 1988. Children:
 1323 i Caylin Marie OLTMANN, b. 18 Dec 1990
 1324 ii William Herbert OLTMANN, V, b. 15 Feb 1995

1128. LESLIE ENGLISH OLTMANN[9] (Stewart Allen Oltmann[8], William Herbert Oltmann, Jr.[7], Louisa Guerard McTeer[6], Florence Percy Heyward[5], William Nathaniel Heyward[4], Thomas Savage Heyward[3], Thomas Heyward[2], Thomas Heyward, Jr.[1]) child of Stewart Allen Oltmann and Betty Roddenberry was born in 1968. She married Lawrence ELSEY in say 1988. Child:
 1325 i Chase ELSEY, b. 15 Jun 1989

1129. LOREN DENEIL WILKINS[9] (Judy Oltmann[8], William Herbert Oltmann, Jr.[7], Louisa Guerard McTeer[6], Florence Percy Heyward[5], William Nathaniel Heyward[4], Thomas Savage Heyward[3], Thomas Heyward[2], Thomas Heyward, Jr.[1]) child of Judy Oltmann and John Deneil Wilkins was born in 1960. She married John BETHEA in say 1989. Child:
 1326 i Zachary Tristam BETHEA, b. 20 Aug 1996

1130. KELLY LYNN WILKINS[9] (Judy Oltmann[8], William Herbert Oltmann, Jr.[7], Louisa Guerard McTeer[6], Florence Percy Heyward[5], William Nathaniel Heyward[4], Thomas Savage Heyward[3], Thomas Heyward[2], Thomas Heyward, Jr.[1]) child of Judy Oltmann and John Deneil Wilkins was born in 1962. She married Scott E. BEAM in say 1985. Children:
 1327 i Joshua Scott BEAM, b. 1988
 1328 ii Jesse BEAM, b. 1991

1135. JANE LUCILLE HELMS[9] (Jane Lucille Woods[8], Jane Lucille McTeer[7], James Edwin McTeer, Jr.[6], Florence Percy Heyward[5], William

Nathaniel Heyward[4], Thomas Savage Heyward[3], Thomas Heyward[2], Thomas Heyward, Jr.[1]) child of Jane Lucille Woods and her 1st husband Roger Dale Helms was born in 1968. She married Thomas FOGLE in say 1988. Child:

    1329   i   Roger Dale FOGLE, b. 1992

1136. LAURA EVE HELMS[9] (Jane Lucille Woods[8], Jane Lucille McTeer[7], James Edwin McTeer, Jr.[6], Florence Percy Heyward[5], William Nathaniel Heyward[4], Thomas Savage Heyward[3], Thomas Heyward[2], Thomas Heyward, Jr.[1]) child of Jane Lucille Woods and her 1st husband Roger Dale Helms was born in Beaufort, SC in 1969. She married Charles CRUCIATA in say 1992. Child:

    1330   i   Jonathan Charles CRUCIATA, b. 1996

1154. KINA MARIE RAINEY[9] (Frances Geraldine Albery[8], Florence Exley Butler[7], Margaret Williamson McTeer[6], Florence Percy Heyward[5], William Nathaniel Heyward[4], Thomas Savage Heyward[3], Thomas Heyward[2], Thomas Heyward, Jr.[1]) child of Frances Geraldine Albery and Michael Rainey was born in New Britian, CT in 1967. She married Donald CAMPBELL in say 1983. Children:

    1331   i   Joshua CAMPBELL, b. 1984
    1332   ii   Debra CAMPBELL, b. 1985
    1333   iii   Rebecca CAMPBELL, b. 1987
    1334   iv   Donald CAMPBELL, Jr., b. 1989
    1335   v   Laura CAMPBELL, b. 1991

1155. GEORGIANNE RAINEY[9] (Frances Geraldine Albery[8], Florence Exley Butler[7], Margaret Williamson McTeer[6], Florence Percy Heyward[5], William Nathaniel Heyward[4], Thomas Savage Heyward[3], Thomas Heyward[2], Thomas Heyward, Jr.[1]) child of Frances Geraldine Albery and Michael Rainey was born in New Britian, CT in 1969. She married Shannon HARJES in say 1988. Children:

    1336   i   Emily Nicole HARJES, b. 1990 [twin]
    1337   ii   Taylor Jordon HARJES, b. 1990 [twin]
    1338   iii   Zachary Paul HARJES, b. 1995
    1339   iv   Shane Michael HARJES, b. 1998

1240. TIFFANY KATHLEEN PHENICIE[9] (John Vincent Phenicie[8], Ann Cuthbert Martin[7], John Vincent Martin[6], Martha Horry Howard[5], Annie Howard Webb[4], Elizabeth Savage Heyward[3], Thomas Heyward[2], Thomas Heyward, Jr.[1]) child of John Vincent Phenicie and Tamera Leigh Juergens was born in New Orleans, LA on 30 Apr 1972. She married Jeffery Alan CONRAD in say 1994. He was born in 1971. Child:

    1340   i   Cale Jeffery CONRAD, b. 1998

1243. MICHAEL VINCENT PHENICIE[9] (William Martin Phenicie[8], Ann Cuthbert Martin[7], John Vincent Martin[6], Martha Horry Howard[5], Annie Howard Webb[4], Elizabeth Savage Heyward[3], Thomas Heyward[2], Thomas Heyward, Jr.[1]) child of William Martin Phenicie and Pamela Ann Garrison was born in Norman, OK on 16 Dec 1969. He married Melissa Marie RICHARDS in say 1995. She was born in Murfreesboro, TN in 1969. Child:

    1341   i   Kaitlyn Nicole PHENICIE, b. 1998

Thomas Lynch Junr

52: THOMAS LYNCH, Jr.

"We are such stuff as dreams are made on."

William Shakespeare

Thomas Lynch, Jr. signed the Declaration of Independence in the same grouping with the other South Carolina Delegates in the bottom portion of the second column from the left of the Document. His is the next to the last signature in that column. He signed in a rather small, non-flourished hand, in which he abbreviated Junior as "Junr".

He was the only son of Thomas Lynch and Elizabeth H. Alston. His early education was through locally retained tutors and his more formal earlier education was through the Indigo Society School at nearby George-town, Georgia. He was sent to Eton College as a lad of fifteen, and from there to Gonville and Caius College, Cambridge University; after which he studied law at the Middle Temple in London. He returned to South Carolina in 1772.

Young Lynch, however, did not practice law upon his return, but entered public life being a member of the Provincial Congresses of South Carolina and a Captain of the First South Carolina Regiment. While his father served in the Continental Congress, the son attended to state politics and Constitutional Committees. Unfortunately, on a recruiting trip into North Carolina, young Lynch contracted malaria ("swamp fever") from which he never fully recovered and which affected him for the remainder of his short life[3].

Early in 1776, while at Philadelphia, the elder Lynch suffered a stroke, that incapacitated him for further public service. The concerned South Carolina Assembly elected the son, both to take care of the father and to act on his behalf as needed. Although ill himself, the younger Lynch traveled to Philadelphia and was there to vote for and later sign the Declaration. Returning home later in the year, the father died in Annapolis, Maryland.

---

[3] John and Katherine Bakeless, *Signers of the Declaration*, (Houghton Mifflin Company, Boston, MA, 1969), p. 283.

FIRST GENERATION

1. THOMAS LYNCH, Jr. was born in "Hopsewee Plantation", at Winyaw on the North Santee River, Prince George's Parish, Georgetown District, SC on 5 Aug 1749.[1] He married Elizabeth SHUBRICK, daughter of Thomas and Mary (Baker) Shubrick on 14 May 1772[2]. She died at sea in Dec 1779.[3] He died at sea in Dec 1779.[3] No issue.

References:
[1] No standard Biography of Thomas Lynch, Jr. is known. A. S. Salley, Jr., *Delegates to the Continental Congress from South Carolina, 1774-1789, with sketches of the Four who signed the Declaration of Independence*, (South Carolina Historical Commission, 1927) contains only a short sketch of Thomas Lynch, Jr. The DAB Article on Thomas Lynch, Jr. is in Vol. XI, pp. 523-524. The LDS microfilm of the Leach MSS for Thomas Lynch, Jr. is on Film # 0001756; and the hard copy is in Vol. # 20, pp. 6186-6188. Leach MSS, p. 6187 gives date and place of birth. See also Della Gray Bartherlmas, *The Signers of the Declaration of Independence, A Biographical and Genealogical Reference*, (Mcfarland & Company, Inc., Jefferson, NC, 1977), pp. 168-169. [2] *Marriage Notices in the South Carolina Gazette and Country Journal, 1765-1775.*The father gave the son a property known as "Peach Tree", located on the North Santee River in St. James Parish, about 4 miles south of "Hopsewee Plantation" (now in Charleston County, SC) as a gift for young Lynch's wedding. [3] Near the end of the year 1779, in failing health, Lynch and his wife boarded ship for passage to the West Indies, from which place, they expected to take passage to southern France. There, it was hoped, the climate would be conducive to improving his health. They were never heard from again, and both must have died at sea.

The reader should note from this genealogical sketch that signer from South Carolina Thomas Lynch, Jr. can have no descendants. This is because he had no children. He died with his wife at sea without issue. While he was an **only** son, he did have siblings - a sister Elizabeth Lynch, for example, who married Daniel H. Hamilton and had children. Other sisters include: Sabina Lynch, and Esther Lynch. There were no brothers, he was an only son! Occasionally, someone reports that they are a descendant of "Thomas Lynch, the Signer". That obviously cannot be. Perhaps it is descent from the father, Thomas Lynch, through a daughter, but Thomas Lynch, the father was never a Signer of the Declaration of Independence. There can be no descendants from Signer of the Declaration of Independence Thomas Lynch, Jr.!

Arthur Middleton

ARTHUR MIDDLETON

"To Make mankind in conscious virtue old."

Arthur Middleton was the last of the four South Carolina signers, whose signature is at the bottom of the second column from the left edge of the document. He wrote his full name in a moderately large, very neat hand.

He was the eldest of 11 children of Henry Middleton and Mary Williams. The family are descendants of Edward Middleton who came to Carolina in 1678 and had large land holdings obtained through a grant. When young Arthur was twelve he was sent to England to attend the Hackney School and Trinity Hall, Cambridge. He then was admitted to the Middle Temple where he studied law and returned to South Carolina on 24 December 1763. He had been away for nine years!

His return brought him to the growing political conflict with the home country with the passage of the Proclamation Act of 1763 and the later Stamp Act of 1765. Arthur found that even the conservative leaning members of his social circle were embracing the patriot cause. In 1764 he became a Justice of the Peace and a member of the Committee to Correspond with the colonial agent in London. He traveled again to England and thence to Europe for more than three years from May 1768-Sep 1771. He was elected to the House of Assembly and later to the First Provincial Congress representing Charleston. In June of 1775 Arthur Middleton was chosen for the Council of Safety and in the following year to the Committee to prepare a Constitution for South Carolina.[1]

Arthur Middleton succeeded his father as a South Carolina Delegate to the Second Continental Congress and voted for and signed the Declaration. Taken prisoner along with fellow Signers Heyward and Rutledge at the capture of Charleston, he was sent to St. Augustine, FL until July 1781.

---

[1] John and Katherine Bakeless, *Signers of the Declaration*, (Houghton Mifflin Company, Boston, MA, 1969), p. 278; see also *Dictionary of American Biography*, Vol. XII, p. 599.

FIRST GENERATION

1. ARTHUR MIDDLETON was born in "Middleton Place", St. Andrew's Parish, Charleston District, SC on 26 Jun 1742.[1] He married Mary IZARD, daughter of Walter and Elizabeth (Gibbes) Izard on 19 Aug 1764.[2] She was born in "Cedar Grove", St. George's Parish, Charleston District, SC on 31 Jul 1747[3], and died in Charleston, SC on 12 Jul 1814.[4] He died at his home on the Ashley River, near Charleston, SC on 1 Jan 1787.[5] Children:

+	2	i	Henry MIDDLETON, b. 28 Sep 1770
	3	ii	Maria Henrietta MIDDLETON, b. 30 Aug 1772, d. 14 Jan 1791; dsp
	4	iii	Eliza Carolina MIDDLETON, b. 6 Oct 1774, dy 7 Feb 1792
+	5	iv	Emma Philadelphia MIDDLETON, b. 22 Oct 1776
+	6	v	Anna Louisa MIDDLETON, b. 26 Mar 1778
+	7	vi	Isabella Johannes MIDDLETON, b. 26 Nov 1780
+	8	vii	Septima Sexta MIDDLETON, b. 15 Oct 1783
+	9	viii	John Izard MIDDLETON, b. 13 Aug 1785
	10	ix	Son MIDDLETON, b. 12 Jun 1787, dy 22 Jun 1787

References:
[1] Some biographical material about the Signer Arthur Middleton is found in Langdon Cheves, *Middleton of South Carolina, a Middleton Family Genealogy*, (Middleton Place Foundation, Charleston, SC), an essay reprinted from *The South Carolina Historical and Genealogical Magazine*, (Vol. 1, # 3, July 1900) as revised in 1979 by Harriot Cheves Leland. Some of the genealogical data reported in the *South Carolina Historical and Genealogical Magazine* (Vol. 1, # 3, July 1900), pp. 228 - 262 contains errors, and does not include the female lines. The Leach MSS material on Arthur Middleton is microfilmed on FHL Film # 0001756; and the hard copy will be found in Volume # 20, pp. 6189 -6375. The DAB Article on Arthur Middleton is in Vol. XVI, pp. 257-258. See also Della Gray Bartherlmas, *The Signers of the Declaration of Independence, A Biographical and Genealogical Reference*, (Mcfarland & Company, Inc., Jefferson, NC, 1977), pp. 178-180. The reader needs to know that before the First Federal Census of 1790, South Carolina had been organized as seven Districts (not Counties). The Middleton Family property known as "Middleton Place" was physically located in St. Andrew's Parish, then in the Charleston District, and now in Charleston County, SC. Date and place of birth given in *South Carolina Historical and Genealogical Magazine* (Vol. 1, # 3, July 1900), pp. 242. [2] Date of marriage reported in Leach MSS, p. 6192. [3] Her place and date of birth are reported in Leach MSS, p. 6192. [4] Her death is given in *The Charleston Courier* of 12 Jul 1814. [5] He died at his home on the Ashley River and is buried in the Middleton Tomb on the grounds of "Middleton Place", as reported in Della Gray Bartherlmas, *The Signers of the Declaration of Independence, A Biographical and Genealogical Reference*, (Mcfarland &

Company, Inc., Jefferson, NC, 1977), p. 178, and in *South Carolina Gazette* of 3 Jan 1787.

SECOND GENERATION

2. HENRY MIDDLETON [2] (Arthur Middleton[1]) son of Arthur Middleton and Mary Izard was born in London, ENGLAND on 28 Sep 1770, and died in Charleston, SC on 14 Jun 1846.[1] He married Mary Helen HERING, daughter of CAPT Julines and Mary (Inglis) Hering in Bath, ENGLAND on 13 Nov 1794.[1] She was born in Jamaica, BWI on 25 Jul 1772, and died in Philadelphia, PA on 24 May 1850.[1] Children:

+ 11   i   Arthur MIDDLETON, b. 28 Oct 1795
  12   ii   Henry MIDDLETON, b. 16 Mar 1797, d. 15 Mar 1876; dsp
+ 13   iii Oliver Hering MIDDLETON, b. 12 Aug 1798
+ 14   iv   John Izard MIDDLETON, b. 4 Feb 1800
+ 15   v   Maria Henrietta MIDDLETON, b. 14 Nov 1802
  16   vi   Eleanor Isabella MIDDLETON, b. 18 Jul 1804, d. 25 Jan 1827; unm
  17   vii Emma MIDDLETON, b. 16 Jun 1806, dy 3 Jul 1807
+ 18   viii Williams MIDDLETON, b. 26 Jul 1809
+ 19   ix   Edward MIDDLETON, b. 11 Dec 1810
  20   x   Catherine MIDDLETON, b. 10 Sep 1812, d. May 1894; unm
+ 21   xi   Elizabeth Izard MIDDLETON, b. 9 Jun 1815

References:
[1] Leach MSS, p. 6192.

5. EMMA PHILADELPHIA MIDDLETON[2] (Arthur Middleton[1]) daughter of Arthur Middleton and Mary Izard was born in Philadelphia, PA on 22 Oct 1776, and died in Charleston, SC on 1 May 1813.[1] She married Henry IZARD, son of Ralph and Alice (DeLancey) Izard on 1 Jun 1795.[1] He was born at sea on 15 May 1771, and died in Charleston, SC on 30 Dec 1826.[1] Children:

  22   i   Henry IZARD, b. 12 May 1796, dy Oct 1796
  23   ii   Henry IZARD, b. 6 Aug 1797, dy 1807 [Again]
  24   iii Mary IZARD, b. 7 Nov 1798, d. 27 Sep 1822; dsp
  25   iv   Walter IZARD, b. 6 May 1800, dy 1800
  26   v   Alice IZARD, b. 2 Mar 1802, d. Oct 1863; dsp
+ 27   vi   Walter IZARD, b. 7 Aug 1804 [Again]
  28   vii Eliza Caroline IZARD, b. 15 Jan 1808, dy Oct 1823
+ 29   viii Margaret Emma IZARD, b. 3 Aug 1811
  30   ix   Martha IZARD, b. 18 Apr 1813, dy 1813

References:
[1] Leach MSS, p. 6192.

6. ANNA LOUISA MIDDLETON[2] (Arthur Middleton[1]) daughter of Arthur Middleton and Mary Izard was born in "Middleton Place", St. Andrew's Parish, Charleston District, SC on 26 Mar 1778, and died in London, ENGLAND in 1818.[1] She married Daniel BLAKE, son of William and Ann (Izard) Blake on 1 Jan 1800.[1] He was born in ENGLAND in 1775, and died in Savannah, GA in Oct 1834.[1] Children:

+ 31   i   Daniel BLAKE, b. 31 Jan 1803
+ 32   ii   Maria Louisa BLAKE, b. 1810
  33   iii Arthur Middleton BLAKE, b. 1812, d. 13 Mar 1881; unm
  34   iv   Frances Middleton BLAKE, b. 1818, d. 14 Jun 1836; dsp

References:
[1] Leach MSS, p. 6218.

7. ISABELLA JOHANNES MIDDLETON[2] (Arthur Middleton[1]) daughter of Arthur Middleton and Mary Izard was born in "Middleton Place", Charleston District, SC on 26 Nov 1780, and died in Athens, GA on 25 Aug 1865.[1] She married Daniel Elliott HUGER, son of Daniel and Sabina (Elliott) Huger on 26 Nov 1800.[1] He was born in Charleston, SC on 29 Jun 1779, and died in Sullivan's Island, SC on 21 Aug 1854.[1] Children:

+ 35   i   Mary Middleton HUGER, b. 9 Jul 1802
  36   ii   William Elliott HUGER, b. 1 Jan 1804, d. 28 Jun 1833; unm
+ 37   iii Daniel Elliott HUGER, b. 10 Mar 1806
+ 38   iv   John Izard HUGER, b. 12 Nov 1808
+ 39   v   Sabina Elliott HUGER, b. 30 Nov 1810
  40   vi   Emma Middleton HUGER, b. 30 May 1813, d. 15 Nov 1892; dsp
+ 41   vii Joseph Alston HUGER, b. 15 May 1815
+ 42   viii Sarah Elliott HUGER, b. 19 Oct 1818
+ 43   ix   Arthur Middleton HUGER, b. 17 Sep 1821
+ 44   x   Eliza Caroline Middleton HUGER, b. 6 Sep 1824

References:
[1] Leach MSS, p. 6222.

8. SEPTIMA SEXTA MIDDLETON[2] (Arthur Middleton[1]) daughter of Arthur Middleton and Mary Izard was born in Charleston, SC on 15 Oct 1783, and died in Nashville, TN on 12 Jun 1865.[1] She married Henry Middleton RUTLEDGE [see Sketch # 2, Chapter 50, this volume], son of Edward and Henrietta (Middleton) Rutledge in Sullivan's Island, SC on 15

Oct 1799.[1] He was born in Charleston, SC on 5 Apr 1775, and died in Nashville, TN on 20 Jan 1844.[1] Children:

+ 45   i   Mary Middleton RUTLEDGE, b. 18 Jun 1801
   46   ii   Edward Augustus RUTLEDGE, b., c. Nov 1803, d. 16 Jul 1826; unm
+ 47   iii   Henry Adolphus RUTLEDGE, b. 8 Aug 1805
+ 48   iv   Henrietta Middleton RUTLEDGE, b. 1808
+ 49   v   Emma Philadelphia Middleton RUTLEDGE, b. 1810
   50   vi   Helen RUTLEDGE, b. c. 1812, dy 1826
   51   vii   Cotesworth Pinckney RUTLEDGE, b. c. 1815, dy 1826
+ 52   viii   Arthur Middleton RUTLEDGE, b. 1 Apr 1817

References:
[1] Leach MSS, p. 6235. The reader should note that **all descendants** of South Carolina Signer Arthur Middleton, through his daughter Septima Sexta Middleton, are also descendants of South Carolina Signer Edward Rutledge. This is so because of her marriage to Henry Middleton Rutledge, the son of and only surviving child of Edward Rutledge to have issue.

9. JOHN IZARD MIDDLETON[2] (Arthur Middleton[1]) son of Arthur Middleton and Mary Izard was born in "Middleton Place", St. Andrew's Parish, Charleston District, SC on 13 Aug 1785, and died in Paris, FRANCE on 5 Oct 1849.[1] He married Eliza Augusta dePalazieux FALCONNET, daughter of Jean Theodore and Anne Falconnet on 11 Jun 1810.[2] Child:

   53   i   Anna MIDDLETON, b. c. Mar 1815, dy 9 Jun 1815

References:
[1] Leach MSS, p. 6192. Note that Leach reports an un-named son of this marriage, and an incorrect early SAR Application reports another son [Wesley Middleton] of this marriage, but the Middleton Place Foundation reports that there was one, and one only child of this marriage! [2] Marriage License.

THIRD GENERATION

11. ARTHUR MIDDLETON[3] (Henry Middleton[2], Arthur Middleton[1]) child of Henry Middleton and Mary Helen Hering was born in Clifton, Gloucestershire, ENGLAND on 27 Oct 1795, and died in Naples, ITALY on 9 Jun 1853.[1] He married (2nd) Paolina BENTIVOGLIO, daughter of GEN Count Domenico and Angela (Sandri) Bentivoglio on 4 May 1841.[1] She was born in Rome, ITALY on 20 Mar 1821, and died there on 14 Nov 1883.[1] Children:

+ 54   i   Henry Bentivoglio MIDDLETON, b. 10 Mar 1843
   55   ii   Anna Costanza Angela MIDDLETON, b. 2 Jan 1845, d. 1920; dsp

References:
[1] Leach MSS, p. 6194.

13. OLIVER HERING MIDDLETON[3] (Henry Middleton[2], Arthur Middleton[1]) child of Henry Middleton and Mary Helen Hering was born in Clifton, Gloucestershire, ENGLAND on 12 Aug 1798, and died in Charleston, SC on 17 Jan 1892.[1] He married Susan Matilda Harriet CHISOLM, daughter of Robert Trail and Mary Elizabeth (Edings) Chisolm on 5 Apr 1827.[1] She was born in Edisto Island, SC on 4 Sep 1806, and died in Columbia, SC on 18 Oct 1865.[1] Children:

+ 56   i   Mary Julia MIDDLETON, b. 1 Feb 1829
   57   ii   Susan Matilda MIDDLETON, b. 2 Jan 1830, d. 11 Jan 1880; unm
+ 58   iii   Eleanor Maria MIDDLETON, b. 17 Apr 1831
+ 59   iv   Olivia MIDDLETON, b. 25 Apr 1839
   60   v   Emma MIDDLETON, b. 4 Mar 1841, d. 2 May 1913; unm
   61   vi   Oliver Hering MIDDLETON, Jr., b. 17 Jul 1845, d. 31 May 1864; kia

References:
[1] Leach MSS, p. 6195, see also DSDI Appl # 238 & 2351.

14. JOHN IZARD MIDDLETON[3] (Henry Middleton[2], Arthur Middleton[1]) child of Henry Middleton and Mary Helen Hering was born in Charleston, SC on 4 Feb 1800, and died in Summerville, SC on 12 Jan 1877.[1] He married Sarah McPherson ALSTON, daughter of John Ashe and Sarah (McPherson) Alston on 28 Mar 1828.[1] She died in Charleston, SC on 28 May 1878.[1] Children:

   62   i   Henry MIDDLETON, b. 9 Dec 1828, dy 21 Jan 1847
   63   ii   Sarah McPherson MIDDLETON, b. 30 Jun 1830. D. 9 Jul 1855; unm
   64   iii   Mary Helen MIDDLETON, b. 4 Apr 1832, dy 18 Jun 1837
+ 65   iv   John Izard MIDDLETON, Jr., b. 16 Feb 1834
+ 66   v   Thomas Alston MIDDLETON, b. 16 Jun 1836
   67   vi   Arthur MIDDLETON, b. 1838, dy Sep 1839
   68   vii   Mary Helen MIDDLETON, b. 23 Oct 1839, d. 10 Nov 1925; unm [Again]
   69   viii   Maria Henrietta MIDDLETON, b. 18 Apr 1841, d. 1928; unm

References:
[1] Leach MSS, p. 6200, see also DSDI Appl # 1317.

15. MARIA HENRIETTA MIDDLETON[3] (Henry Middleton[2], Arthur Middleton[1]) child of Henry Middleton and Mary Helen Hering was born in "Cedar Grove", St. George's Parish, Charleston District, SC on 14 Nov 1802, and died at sea on 14 Jun 1838.[1] She married Edward Jenkins PRINGLE, son of John Julius and Susannah (Reid) Pringle in 1834.[1] He was born in Charleston, SC 16 Dec 1796, and died at sea on 14 Jun 1838.[2] Children:

    70   i   Bethia PRINGLE, b. c. 1835, d. 14 Jun 1838
    71   ii Edward PRINGLE, b. c. 1837, d. 14 Jun 1838

References:
[1] Leach MSS, p. 6200. [2] Both parents and their children were lost in the wreck of the steamer "Pulaski", when it's boiler exploded at sea on its way from Charleston, SC to NYC and it went down on 14 Jun 1838.

18. WILLIAMS MIDDLETON[3] (Henry Middleton[2], Arthur Middleton[1]) child of Henry Middleton and Mary Helen Hering was born in Sullivan's Island, SC on 26 Jul 1809, and died in Greenville, SC on 23 Aug 1883.[1] He married Susan Pringle SMITH, daughter of Robert and Elizabeth (Pringle) Smith on 11 Jan 1849.[1] She was born in Charleston, SC on 1 Dec 1822, and died on 10 Jan 1900.[2] Children:

    72   i   Elizabeth Smith MIDDLETON, b. 7 Nov 1849, d. 15 Jun 1915; dsp
+ 73   ii Henry MIDDLETON, b. 10 Mar 1851

References:
[1] Leach MSS, p. 6201. [2] Middleton Place Foundation Data.

19. EDWARD MIDDLETON[3] (Henry Middleton[2], Arthur Middleton[1]) child of Henry Middleton and Mary Helen Hering was born in Charleston, SC on 11 Dec 1810, and died in Washington, DC on 27 Apr 1883.[1] He married (1st) Edwardina de NORMAN on 13 Jan 1845.[1] He married (2nd) Ellida Juell DAVISON, daughter of Edward and Emeline (Leland) Davison in NYC on 10 Oct 1865.[2] She was born in Charlestown, MA on 6 Sep 1842.[2] Child by first marriage:

    74   i   Edward MIDDLETON, b. 6 Jun 1846, dy

Children by second marriage:
+ 75   ii Emeline Virginia MIDDLETON, b. 31 Jan 1869
+ 76   iii Arthur Edward Henry MIDDLETON, b. 25 Jul 1872

References:
[1] Leach MSS, p. 6202. [2] DSDI Appl # 118.

21. ELIZABETH IZARD MIDDLETON[3] (Henry Middleton[2], Arthur Middleton[1]) child of Henry Middleton and Mary Helen Hering was born in

Charleston, SC on 9 Jun 1815, and died in Philadelphia, PA on 19 Feb 1890.[1] She married Joshua Francis FISHER, son of Joshua and Elizabeth Francis (Powel) Fisher in "Middleton Place", Charleston, SC on 12 Mar 1839.[1] He was born in Philadelphia, PA on 17 Feb 1807, and died there on 21 Jan 1873.[1] Children:

+ 77   i   Elizabeth Francis FISHER, b. 29 Jun 1840
  78   ii   Sophia Georgina FISHER, b. 26 Nov 1841, d. 1 Mar 1926;
             dsp
+ 79   iii Mary Helen FISHER, b. 1 Jul 1844
+ 80   iv   Maria Middleton FISHER, b. 20 Dec 1847
+ 81   v   George Harrison FISHER, b. 25 Jun 1849
+ 82   vi   Henry Middleton FISHER, b. 29 May 1851

References:
[1] DSDI Appl # 2263, see also Leach MSS, pp. 6204-6205.

27. WALTER IZARD[3] (Emma Philadelphia Middleton[2], Arthur Middleton[1]) child of Emma Philadelphia Middleton and Henry Izard was born in "The Elms", Charleston, SC on 7 Aug 1804, and died in "Rose Hill", Chester County, SC on 22 Jun 1835.[1] He married Mary Cadwallader [two ll's] GREEN, daughter of Allen Jones and Lucy Pride (Jones) Green on 10 Oct 1827.[2] She was born in Halifax, NC on 8 Aug 1808, and died in Goodes, Bedford County, VA in Dec 1889.[2] Children:

+ 83   i   Walter IZARD, b. 28 Sep 1828
  84   ii   Henry IZARD, b. 29 May 1830, dy 16 Nov 1830
+ 85   iii Henry IZARD, b. 25 Sep 1831 [Again]
+ 86   iv   Lucy IZARD, b. 26 Feb 1833
+ 87   v   Allen Cadwallader IZARD, b. 13 Jul 1834

References:
[1] DSDI Appl # 855. [2] Leach MSS, p. 6211.

29. MARGARET EMMA IZARD[3] (Emma Philadelphia Middleton[2], Arthur Middleton[1]) child of Emma Philadelphia Middleton and Henry Izard was born in "The Elms", Charleston, SC on 3 Aug 1811, and died in Charleston, SC on 18 Jul 1836.[1] She married Nathaniel Russell MIDDLETON [her second cousin], son of Arthur and Alicia Hopton (Russell) Middleton on 18 Jan 1832.[1] He was born in Charleston, SC on 1 Apr 1810, and died there on 6 Sep 1890.[1] Children:

+ 88   i   Arthur MIDDLETON, b. 28 Dec 1832
  89   ii   Henry Izard MIDDLETON, b. 12 Oct 1834; unm
  90   iii Walter Izard MIDDLETON, b. 25 Jan 1836, d. 20 Sep 1871;
             unm

References:
[1] DSDI Appl # 1495.

31. DANIEL BLAKE[3] (Anna Louisa Middleton[2], Arthur Middleton[1]) child of Anna Louisa Middleton and Daniel Blake was born in London, ENGLAND on 31 Jan 1803, and died in Henderson County, NC on 10 Aug 1873.[1] He married (1st) Emma Philadelphia Middleton RUTLEDGE, daughter of Henry Middleton and Septima Sexta (Middleton) Rutledge on 8 Jun 1831.[1] She was born in "Cedar Grove", St. George's Parish, Charleston District, SC in 1810, and died in Flat Rock, NC on 23 Apr 1853.[1] He married (2nd) Helen Elizabeth CRAIG, daughter of Samuel and Helen (Bayley) Craig on 22 Jul 1856.[1] She was born in NYC on 23 Oct 1825.[1] Children by first marriage:

  91   i   Daniel Henry BLAKE, b. 15 Jun 1832, dy 13 Aug 1832
+ 92   ii   Frederick Rutledge BLAKE, b. 24 Jan 1838
+ 93   iii   Daniel Francis BLAKE, b. 1 May 1841
  94   iv   Frances Helen Caroline BLAKE, b. 13 Aug 1842, d. 1920; unm
  95   v   Henrietta Louisa BLAKE, b. 14 Oct 1843, d. 14 Sep 1872; dsp
+ 96   vi   Arthur Middleton BLAKE, b. May 1848
  97   viii   Henry Middleton Rutledge BLAKE, b. 1851, dy Apr 1856
Children by second marriage:
  98   vi   Robert Bunch BLAKE, b. 23 Jan 1861
+ 99   vii   Emma Craig BLAKE, b. 30 Jan 1865
+ 100 viii   Helen Bayley BLAKE, b. 10 Nov 1867

References:
[1] Leach MSS, p. 6219.

32. MARIA LOUISA BLAKE[3] (Anna Louisa Middleton[2], Arthur Middleton[1]) child of Anna Louisa Middleton and Daniel Blake was born in London, ENGLAND in 1810, and died in Savannah, GA on 10 Feb 1854.[1] She married Arthur HEYWARD, son of Nathaniel and Henrietta (Manigault) Heyward in say 1834.[1] He was born in Charleston, SC on 31 Oct 1805, and died there on 2 Dec 1852.[1] Children:

  101   i   Walter Blake HEYWARD, b. 17 Feb 1837, d. 5 Nov 1870; dsp
  102   ii   Arthur HEYWARD, b. 4 Feb 1839, dy 6 Feb 1843
+ 103   iii   Daniel Blake HEYWARD, b. 28 Feb 1840

References:
[1] Leach MSS, p. 6221.

35. MARY MIDDLETON HUGER[3] (Isabella Johannes Middleton[2], Arthur Middleton[1]) child of Isabella Johannes Middleton and Daniel Elliott Huger was born in Charleston, SC on 9 Jul 1802, and died in Charleston, SC on 29 Aug 1831.[1] She married Joseph MANIGAULT, son of Josaeph and Charlotte (Drayton) Manigault in say 1826.[1] He was born in Charleston, SC in 1801, and died in Sullivan's Island, SC on 27 Jul 1829.[1] Child:

104   i   Joseph MANIGAULT, b. 11 Jul 1827; unm

References:
[1] Leach MSS, p. 6223.

37. DANIEL ELLIOTT HUGER[3] (Isabella Johannes Middleton[2], Arthur Middleton[1]) child of Isabella Johannes Middleton and Daniel Elliott Huger was born in Charleston, SC on 10 Mar 1806, and died in "White Oak", North Santee, SC on 25 Dec 1874.[1] He married Carolina PROCTOR, daughter of Stephen Royer and Mary (Screven) Proctor in New Orleans, LA on 21 Mar 1832.[1] She was born in Savannah, GA on 27 Mar 1814, and died in Charleston, SC on 5 Mar 1875.[1] Children:

+ 105   i   Mary Proctor HUGER, b. 6 Feb 1833
   106   ii   Daniel Elliott HUGER, b. 16 Nov 1839, d. 20 Sep 1863; kia
   107   iii   Stephen Proctor HUGER, b. 22 Feb 1842, dy 25 Jan 1862
+ 108   iv   William Elliott HUGER, b. 8 Jan 1844
   109   v   Joseph Proctor HUGER, b. 16 Oct 1846, d. 13 Apr 1864; kia
+ 110   vi   Richard Proctor HUGER, b. 15 Mar 1850
+ 111   vii   Caroline Proctor HUGER, b. 15 Sep 1852
   112   viii   Isabella Izard HUGER, b. 26 Jul 1855; unm

References:
[1] Leach MSS, p. 6224 & DSDI Appl # 1190.

38. JOHN IZARD HUGER[3] (Isabella Johannes Middleton[2], Arthur Middleton[1]) child of Isabella Johannes Middleton and Daniel Elliott Huger was born in Charleston, SC on 12 Nov 1808, and died in NYC on 24 Feb 1894.[1] He married Elizabeth Allen DEAS, daughter of James Sutherland and Margaret (Chestnut) Deas on 12 Apr 1832.[1] She was born in Camden, SC on 5 Jul 1811, and died in NYC on 7 Dec 1890.[1] Children:

   113   i   Margaret Deas HUGER, b. 28 Feb 1833; unm
+ 114   ii   Daniel Elliott HUGER, b. 30 Nov 1834
+ 115   iii   Isabella Johannes Middleton HUGER, b. 24 Apr 1837
   116   iv   James Sutherland Deas HUGER, b. 22 Feb 1839, d. 30 Dec
                 1881; unm
+ 117   v   William Elliott HUGER, b. 17 Apr 1841
+ 118   vi   Charles Lowndes HUGER, b. 27 Apr 1844

119   vii   Allen Deas HUGER, b. 31 Mar 1847, dy 7 Aug 1854
120   viii   Arthur Middleton HUGER, b. 18 Mar 1850, dy 23 Dec 1858
121   ix   Emma Middleton HUGER, b. 31 Jul 1852; unm
122   x   Allen Deas HUGER, b. 7 May 1855, dy 10 Dec 1858
      [Again]
References:
[1] Leach MSS, p. 6228.

39. SABINA ELLIOTT HUGER[3] (Isabella Johannes Middleton[2], Arthur Middleton[1]) child of Isabella Johannes Middleton and Daniel Elliott Huger was born in Charleston, SC on 30 Nov 1810, and died in Charleston, SC on 15 Jun 1874.[1] She married Charles Tidyman LOWNDES in Charleston, SC on 31 Dec 1829.[1] He was born in Charleston, SC on 6 Jun 1808, and died in "Oaklands", Charleston, SC on 13 Nov 1882.[1] Children:

+   123   i   Rawlins LOWNDES, b. 23 Jul 1838
+   124   ii   Emma Middleton Huger LOWNDES, b. Sep 1847
    125   iii   Mary Huger LOWNDES, b. c. 1850
References:
[1] DSDI Appl # 378 & 770.

41. JOSEPH ALSTON HUGER[3] (Isabella Johannes Middleton[2], Arthur Middleton[1]) child of Isabella Johannes Middleton and Daniel Elliott Huger was born in Charleston, SC on 15 May 1815, and died in Savannah, GA on 29 Mar 1895.[1] He married Mary Esther HUGER [Cousin], daughter of Francis Kinloch and Harriet Lucas (Pinckney) Huger in Charleston, SC on 21 May 1840.[1] She was born in Charleston, SC on 13 Sep 1820, and died in Sewanee, TN on 17 Jun 1898.[1] Children:

    126   i   Arthur Middleton HUGER, b. 20 Mar 1842
+   127   ii   Joseph Alston HUGER, Jr., b. 15 Jun 1843
    128   iii   Francis Kinloch HUGER, b. 5 Dec 1844; dsp
+   129   iv   Lynch Prioleau HUGER, b. 16 Jan 1846
+   130   v   Harriet Lucas Pinckney HUGER, b. 6 Aug 1848
    131   vi   Thomas Pinckney HUGER, b. 22 Jan 1850; dsp
    132   vii   Katharine Mackay HUGER, b. 13 Nov 1853; unm
    133   viii   Mary Esther HUGER, b. 6 Jan 1858; unm
+   134   ix   John Wells HUGER, b. 4 Jul 1859
    135   x   Harriet Horry HUGER, b. 3 Mar 1861; dsp
References:
[1] Leach MSS, p. 6231 & DSDI Appl # 2487.

42. SARAH ELLIOTT HUGER[3] (Isabella Johannes Middleton[2], Arthur Middleton[1]) child of Isabella Johannes Middleton and Daniel Elliott Huger was born in Charleston, SC on 19 Oct 1818[1], and died in Charleston, SC in 1904. She married James Withers WILKINSON, son of Willis and Eleonora (Withers) Wilkinson on 14 Feb 1839.[2] He was born in Georgetown, SC on 7 May 1816, and died in Orlando, FL on 23 May 1884.[1] Children:

136	i	Willis WILKINSON, b. 25 Jul 1842
+ 137	ii	William Withers WILKINSON, b. 7 Feb 1844
+ 138	iii	Isabella Middleton WILKINSON, b. 27 Mar 1848
+ 139	iv	Maria Louisa WILKINSON, b. 25 Feb 1850
+ 140	v	Daniel Elliott Huger WILKINSON, b. 18 Oct 1852
141	vi	James Withers WILKINSON, b. 12 Dec 1854, dy 22 Jan 1855

References:
[1] SAR Appl # 88948, see also Leach MSS, p. 6233.

43. ARTHUR MIDDLETON HUGER[3] (Isabella Johannes Middleton[2], Arthur Middleton[1]) child of Isabella Johannes Middleton and Daniel Elliott Huger was born in Sullivan's Island, SC on 17 Sep 1821, and died in Charleston, SC on 15 May 1870.[1] He married Margaret Campbell KING, daughter of Mitchell and Susannah (Campbell) King on 6 May 1846.[1] She was born in Charleston, SC on 31 May 1824.[1] Children:

142	i	Daniel Elliott HUGER, b. 26 Jun 1847, d. 3 Oct 1876; unm
143	ii	Mitchell King HUGER, b. 5 Sep 1848, dy 17 Sep 1858
144	iii	Charles Lowndes HUGER, b. 24 Dec 1849, dy 10 Sep 1858
145	iv	Arthur Middleton HUGER, b. 17 Jul 1851; unm
146	v	Kirkwood King HUGER, b. 8 Jan 1854; unm
147	vi	Margaret Campbell HUGER, b. 14 Jan 1856, dy 23 Nov 1857
148	vii	Margaret Campbell HUGER, b. 24 Jan 1858; unm [Again]
149	viii	Mitchell King HUGER, b. 6 Sep 1860, dy 23 Aug 1868 [Again]
150	ix	Alfred Huger HUGER, b. 28 Feb 1863, dy 14 May 1864

References:
[1] Leach MSS, p. 6232.

44. ELIZA CAROLINE MIDDLETON HUGER[3] (Isabella Johannes Middleton[2], Arthur Middleton[1]) child of Isabella Johannes Middleton and Daniel Elliott Huger was born in Sullivan's Island, SC on 6 Sep 1824[1], and died in 1919. She married William Mason SMITH, son of Robert and

Elizabeth (Pringle) Smith on 10 Feb 1842.[1] He was born in Charleston, SC on 6 Sep 1818, and died there on 11 May 1851.[1] Children:

    151   i   William Mason SMITH, b. 18 Jul 1843, d. 16 Aug 1864
    152   ii   Robert Tilghman SMITH, b. 9 Apr 1845, d. 1932; unm
+ 153   iii   Daniel Elliott Huger SMITH, b. 2 Apr 1846
    154   iv   Isabella Johannes Middleton SMITH, b. 1 Dec 1847, d. 1920; unm
+ 155   v   Anna Elizabeth Mason SMITH, b. 25 Sep 1849
    156   vi   Joseph Allen SMITH, b. 30 Aug 1851, dy 30 Aug 1863

References:
[1] Leach MSS, p. 6234.

45. MARY MIDDLETON RUTLEDGE[3] (Septima Sexta Middleton[2], Arthur Middleton[1]) child of Septima Sexta Middleton and Henry Middleton Rutledge was born in Charleston, SC on 19 Jun 1801, and died in Nashville, TN on 15 Mar 1872.[1] She married Francis Brinley FOGG, son of the Rev. Daniel and Deborah (Brinley) Fogg on 15 Oct 1823.[1] He was born in Brooklyn, CT on 21 Sep 1795, and died in Nashville, TN on 13 Apr 1880.[1] Children:

    157   i   Francis Brinley FOGG, Jr., b. 11 Jul 1825, d. 12 Feb 1848; unm
    158   ii   Septima Sexta Middleton FOGG, b. 1826, d. 26 Oct 1851; unm
    159   iii   Henry Middleton Rutledge FOGG, b. 16 Sep 1830, d. 26 Jan 1962; kia

References:
[1] Leach MSS, p. 6236.

47. HENRY ADOLPHUS RUTLEDGE[3] (Septima Sexta Middleton[2], Arthur Middleton[1]) child of Septima Sexta Middleton and Henry Middleton Rutledge was born in Charleston, SC on 8 Aug 1805, and died in "Rutledge Place", Talladega County, AL on 23 Sep 1883.[1] He married Caroline Belle NICHOLSON in Nashville, TN on 24 Nov 1831.[1] She was born in Davidson County, TN on 12 Apr 1812, and died in Selma, AL on 23 Dec 1878.[1] Children:

+ 160   i   Emma Philadelphia Middleton RUTLEDGE, b. 6 Aug 1833
+ 161   ii   Septima Sexta Middleton RUTLEDGE, b. 3 Feb 1836

References:
[1] DSDI Appl # 1042.

48. HENRIETTA MIDDLETON RUTLEDGE[3] (Septima Sexta Middleton[2], Arthur Middleton[1]) child of Septima Sexta Middleton and Henry Middleton Rutledge was born in Charleston, SC in 1808, and died in Flat Rock, NC on

27 Sep 1842.[1] She married Frederick RUTLEDGE, son of Frederick and Harriet Pinckney (Horry) Rutledge in Nashville, TN on 15 Oct 1825.[1] He was born in Charleston, SC on 26 Oct 1800, and died in Flat Rock, NC on 7 Jul 1884.[1] Children:

- 162   i   Edward RUTLEDGE, b. Aug 1829, dy Aug 1829
- 163   ii   Elizabeth Pinckney RUTLEDGE, b. 8 Apr 1831, dy 1832
- 164   iii Frederick RUTLEDGE, b. 26 Sep 1832, dy 1832
- + 165 iv   Sarah Henrietta RUTLEDGE, b. 1 Oct 1834
- 166   v   Edward RUTLEDGE, b. 12 Apr 1836, dy 5 Aug 1856 [Again]
- 167   vi   Alice Izard RUTLEDGE, b. Jan 1838, dy Aug 1854
- + 168 vii Henry Middleton RUTLEDGE, b. 5 Aug 1840
- + 169 viii Emma Fredrika RUTLEDGE, b. 10 May 1842

References:
[1] DSDI Appl # 1293, see also Leach MSS, p. 6240.

49. EMMA PHILADELPHIA MIDDLETON RUTLEDGE[3] (Septima Sexta Middleton[2], Arthur Middleton[1]) child of Septima Sexta Middleton and Henry Middleton Rutledge was born in "Cedar Grove", St. George's Parish, Charleston District, SC in 1810, and died in Charleston, SC on 23 Apr 1853.[1] She married Daniel BLAKE [see sketch # 31], son of Daniel and Anna Louisa (Middleton) Blake on 8 Jun 1831.[1] He was born in London, ENGLAND on 31 Jan 1803, and died in Henderson County, NC on 10 Aug 1873.[1] Children are as reported under Sketch # 31, this Chapter.
References:
[1] Leach MSS, p. 6243.

52. ARTHUR MIDDLETON RUTLEDGE[3] (Septima Sexta Middleton[2], Arthur Middleton[1]) child of Septima Sexta Middleton and Henry Middleton Rutledge was born in "Cedar Grove", St, George's Parish, Charleston District, SC on 1 Apr 1817, and died in Sewanee, TN on 17 Jun 1876.[1] He married (1st) Eliza UNDERWOOD, daughter of Joseph Rogers and Eliza (Trotter) Underwood on 4 Nov 1851.[1] She was born in Bowling Green, KY on 23 Feb 1829, and died in Cuthbert, KY on 2 May 1865.[1] Children:

- + 170 i   Elizabeth Underwood RUTLEDGE, b. 29 Aug 1852
- + 171 ii   Emma Blake RUTLEDGE, b. 29 Mar 1854
- + 172 iii Arthur Middleton RUTLEDGE, b. 4 Nov 1855
- 173   iv   Joseph Underwood Huger RUTLEDGE, b. 3 May 1859, dy 31 Aug 1876

References:
[1] Leach MSS, p. 6244.

FOURTH GENERATION

54. HENRY BENTIVOGLIO MIDDLETON[4] (Arthur Middleton[3], Henry Middleton[2], Arthur Middleton[1]) child of Arthur Middleton and Paolina Bentivoglio was born in Charleston, SC on 10 Mar 1843.[1] He married Beatrice CINI, daughter of COUNT Filippo and Guilla (Prosperi-Buzi) Cini on 7 Jun 1869.[1] She was born in Rome, ITALY on 17 Nov 1850.[1] Children:

+ 174   i   Costanza MIDDLETON, b. 7 May 1870
   175   ii   Maria Elisa MIDDLETON, b. 8 Jul 1871, d. 1950
+ 176   iii   Virginia MIDDLETON, b. 10 Oct 1872
+ 177   iv   Arthur Giulio MIDDLETON, b. 1 Nov 1873

References:
[1] Leach MSS, p. 6194.

56. MARY JULIA MIDDLETON [4] (Oliver Hering Middleton[3], Henry Middleton[2], Arthur Middleton[1]) child of Oliver Hering Middleton and Susan Matilda Harriet Chisolm was born in Charleston, SC on 1 Feb 1829[1], and died on 19 Dec 1904. She married Benjamin Huger READ, son of John Harleston and Emily Ann (Huger) Read on 16 Feb 1854.[1] He was born in Maryville, SC on 17 Mar 1823, and died in Henderson County, NC on 11 Oct 1887.[1] Children:

+ 178   i   Oliver Middleton READ, b. 6 Nov 1855
+ 179   ii   Benjamin Huger READ, b. 16 Dec 1856
+ 180   iii   Emily Anne READ, b. 14 Jan 1858
   181   iv   Susan Chisolm READ, b. 9 Nov 1864

References:
[1] Leach MSS, p. 6195.

58. ELEANOR MARIA MIDDLETON[4] (Oliver Hering Middleton[3], Henry Middleton[2], Arthur Middleton[1]) child of Oliver Hering Middleton and Susan Matilda Harriet Chisolm was born in Charleston, SC on 17 Apr 1831[1], and died in Charleston, SC on 25 Dec 1905. She married Benjamin Huger RUTLEDGE, son of Benjamin Huger and Alice Ann (Weston) Rutledge in Charleston, SC on 25 Jan 1858.[1] He was born in Statesburg, SC on 4 Jun 1829, and died in Charleston, SC on 30 Apr 1893.[1] Children:

+ 182   i   Benjamin Huger RUTLEDGE, b. 4 Sep 1861
+ 183   ii   Oliver Middleton RUTLEDGE, b. 1 Sep 1862
   184   iii   Alice Weston RUTLEDGE, b. 18 Dec 1865; dsp
   185   iv   Eleanor RUTLEDGE, b. 10 Mar 1867, dy 28 Mar 1867

186   v   Hugh RUTLEDGE, b. 30 Jan 1869, dy 10 Nov 1870
+ 187   vi   Edward RUTLEDGE, b. 28 Jun 1870
188   vii Mary Helen RUTLEDGE, b. 25 Jan 1872, d. 25 May 1872
References:
[1] Leach MSS, p. 6196.

59. OLIVIA MIDDLETON[4] (Oliver Hering Middleton[3], Henry Middleton[2], Arthur Middleton[1]) child of Oliver Hering Middleton and Susan Matilda Harriet Chisolm was born in Charleston, SC on 25 Apr 1839[1], and died in 1920. She married Frederick Rutledge BLAKE [see sketch # 92], son of Daniel and Emma Philadelphia Middleton (Rutledge) Blake on 6 Dec 1864.[1] He was born in Charleston, SC on 24 Jan 1838[1], and died in 1907. Children:
+ 189   i   Edmund Molyneux BLAKE, b. 14 Jan 1866
190   ii   Emma Middleton Rutledge BLAKE, b. 31 Aug 1868, dy 16 Mar 1873
191   iii Eliza Fisher BLAKE, b. 31 May 1870
+ 192   iv   Daniel BLAKE, b. 21 Oct 1872
References:
[1] Leach MSS, p. 6198 & 6220.

65. JOHN IZARD MIDDLETON, Jr.[4] (John Izard Middleton[3], Henry Middleton[2], Arthur Middleton[1]) child of John Izard Middleton and Sarah McPherson Alston was born in Charleston, SC on 16 Feb 1834[1], and died in Baltimore, MD in Aug 1907. He married Harriet Sterrett GITTINGS, daughter of Lambert and Harriet (Tenant) Gittings in Baltimore, MD on 26 Apr 1866.[1] She was born in Baltimore, MD on 15 Dec 1838[1], and died in NYC in Apr 1911. Children:
+ 193   i   John Izard MIDDLETON, III, b. 14 Feb 1867
194   ii   Mary Alston MIDDLETON, b. 2 Nov 1872, d. 28 Mar 1893; unm
195   iii Lambert Gittings MIDDLETON, b. 4 Aug 1875, dy 21 Aug 1875
References:
[1] DSDI Appl # 1317, see also Leach MSS, p. 6199.

66. THOMAS ALSTON MIDDLETON[4] (John Izard Middleton[3], Henry Middleton[2], Arthur Middleton[1]) child of John Izard Middleton and Sarah McPherson Alston was born in Charleston, SC on 16 Jun 1836, and died in "Clermont", SC on 6 Feb 1896.[1] He married Mary Grey BEIRNE, daughter of Andrew and Ellen (Grey) Beirne on 26 Jul 1864.[1] She was born about 1840, and died in "Clermont", SC on 6 Feb 1895.[1] Children:

196	i	Andrew Beirne MIDDLETON, b. 30 Apr 1866, d. 9 Jul 1895; unm
197	ii	John Izard MIDDLETON, b. 7 Jan 1868, d. 1930; dsp
198	iii	Thomas Alston MIDDLETON, b. 22 May 1870; dsp
199	iv	Sarah McPherson MIDDLETON, b. 14 Jun 1873, d. 1959; unm

References:
[1] Leach MSS, p. 6199.

73. HENRY MIDDLETON[4] (Williams Middleton[3], Henry Middleton[2], Arthur Middleton[1]) child of Williams Middleton and Susan Pringle Smith was born on 10 Mar 1851[1], and died on 26 Feb 1932. He cohabited with (1st) Mary Elizabeth HEATLY, daughter of COL -- Heatly in say 1883.[1] She was born in 1858[1], and died on 11 May 1920. He cohabited with (2nd) Beatrice Esther Florence LIFT in say 1895. She died on 12 Oct 1900.

Children by first partner:

200	i	Mary Helen Angelina MIDDLETON, b. 30 Jan 1885, d. 27 Jan 1970; dsp
+ 201	ii	Maud Muriel MIDDLETON, b. 24 Jan 1886
+ 202	iii	Henry MIDDLETON, b. 18 Apr 1887
203	iv	Arthur John Williams MIDDLETON, b. 14 Apr 1888, d. c. 1970; unm
+ 204	v	Algernon Manfred MIDDLETON, b. 17 May 1889
205	vi	Reginald Rupert Dare MIDDLETON, b. 19 Dec 1890, d. 16 Dec 1970; unm
206	vii	George Broke MIDDLETON, b. 28 Jan 1892
+ 207	viii	Edward Thomas Francis MIDDLETON, b. 10 May 1893
+ 208	ix	Lilian Nora MIDDLETON, b. 19 Aug 1895
209	x	Emily Eliza Florence MIDDLETON, b. 18 Jun 1897, dy 1914
+ 210	xi	Dorothy Emma MIDDLETON, b. 25 Nov 1898
211	xii	Ruby MIDDLETON, b. c. 1899

Children by second partner:

+ 212	xiii	Ronald Williams MIDDLETON, b. 2 Sep 1897
+ 213	xiv	Basil Bernard Norman MIDDLETON, b. 14 Oct 1898
+ 214	xv	Catherine Eleanor Mabel MIDDLETON, b. 15 May 1900

References:
[1] Data from Middleton Place Foundation.

75. EMELINE VIRGINIA MIDDLETON[4] (Edward Middleton[3], Henry Middleton[2], Arthur Middleton[1]) child of Edward Middleton and his 2nd wife

Ellida Juell Davison was born on 31 Jan 1869[1], and died on 29 Aug 1948. She married Edgar M. DAVISON on 27 Jul 1910. Child:

+ 215   i   Emmeline Ellida DAVISON, b. 12 Jun 1911
References:
[1] Data from Middleton Place Foundation.

76. ARTHUR EDWARD HENRY MIDDLETON[4] (Edward Middleton[3], Henry Middleton[2], Arthur Middleton[1]) child of Edward Middleton and his 2nd wife Ellida Juell Davison was born on 25 Jul 1872[1], and died on 21 Apr 1919. He married Nancy Anne ASHBY on 22 Aug 1910. She was born in 1879.[1] Children:

   216   i   Ellida Juell MIDDLETON, b. 12 Oct 1913, d. 8 Nov 1991; dsp
+ 217   ii   Nancy Reeves MIDDLETON, b. 1 Jun 1915
References:
[1] Data from Middleton Place Foundation.

77. ELIZABETH FRANCIS FISHER[4] (Elizabeth Izard Middleton[3], Henry Middleton[2], Arthur Middleton[1]) child of Elizabeth Izard Middleton and Joshua Francis Fisher was born in Philadelphia, PA on 29 Jun 1840[1], and died in 1919. She married Robert Patterson KANE, son of John Kintzing and Jean DuVal (Leiper) Kane on 31 Oct 1861.[1] He was born in Philadelphia, PA on 9 Jun 1827.[1] Children:

+ 218   i   Eliza Middleton KANE, b. 8 Apr 1863
   219   ii   Joshua Francis KANE, b. 1 Aug 1864, dy 29 Nov 1864
   220   iii   Francis Fisher KANE, b. 17 Jun 1866, d. 1955; unm
References:
[1] Leach MSS, p. 6207.

79. MARY HELEN FISHER[4] (Elizabeth Izard Middleton[3], Henry Middleton[2], Arthur Middleton[1]) child of Elizabeth Izard Middleton and Joshua Francis Fisher was born in Philadelphia, PA on 1 Jul 1844[1], and died in Philadelphia, PA on 29 Dec 1937. She married John CADWALADER [one L], son of JUDGE John and Henrietta Maria (Banker) Cadwalader on 17 Apr 1866.[1] He was born in Philadelphia, PA on 27 Jun 1843[1], and died there on 11 Mar 1925. Children:

   221   i   Sophia CADWALADER, b. 6 Feb 1867, d. 1955; unm
   222   ii   Mary Helen CADWALADER, b. 19 Mar 1871, d. 1944; unm
+ 223   iii   John CADWALADER, b. 24 Feb 1874
+ 224   iv   Thomas Francis CADWALADER, b. 22 Sep 1880

References:
[1] DSDI Appl # 2263.

80. MARIA MIDDLETON FISHER[4] (Elizabeth Izard Middleton[3], Henry Middleton[2], Arthur Middleton[1]) child of Elizabeth Izard Middleton and Joshua Francis Fisher was born in Philadelphia, PA on 20 Dec 1847[1], and died in Drifton, PA on 16 Jan 1933. She married Brinton COXE, son of Charles Sidney and Ann Maria (Brinton) Coxe on 12 Oct 1872.[1] He was born in Philadelphia, PA on 3 Aug 1833, and died in Drifton, PA on 15 Sep 1892.[1] Children:

225	i	Charlotte D. COXE, b. 21 Nov 1873; dsp
+ 226	ii	Eliza Middleton COXE, b. 7 Nov 1875
+ 227	iii	Mary Rebecca COXE, b. 29 Jan 1877
+ 228	iv	Edmund James COXE, b. 3 May 1881

References:
[1] DSDI Appl # 1184 & Leach MSS, p. 6208.

81. GEORGE HARRISON FISHER[4] (Elizabeth Izard Middleton[3], Henry Middleton[2], Arthur Middleton[1]) child of Elizabeth Izard Middleton and Joshua Francis Fisher was born in "Alverthorpe", Montgomery County, PA on 25 Jun 1849.[1] He married Betsey RIDDLE, daughter of Robert Moore and Mary Johnston (Dickinson) Riddle on 20 Apr 1876.[1] She was born in Pittsburgh, PA on 19 Jul 1852.[1] Children:

+ 229	i	Anna Scott FISHER, b. 12 Mar 1877
230	ii	Francis FISHER, b. 29 Oct 1881, dy

References:
[1] Leach MSS, p. 6209.

82. HENRY MIDDLETON FISHER[4] (Elizabeth Izard Middleton[3], Henry Middleton[2], Arthur Middleton[1]) child of Elizabeth Izard Middleton and Joshua Francis Fisher was born on 29 May 1851.[1] He married Mary E. WHARTON in say 1880. Child:

+ 231	i	Mary FISHER, b. c. 1884

References:
[1] Data from Middleton Place Foundation.

83. WALTER IZARD[4] (Walter Izard[3], Emma Philadelphia Middleton[2], Arthur Middleton[1]) child of Walter Izard and Mary Cadwallader Green was born in "Rose Hill", Chester County, SC on 28 Sep 1828[1], and died in Fredericksburg, VA in Jan 1912. He married Sallie GOODE, daughter of John and Ann (Leftwitch) Goode on 22 Oct 1853.[1] She was born in Bedford County, VA on 9 Nov 1832, and died there in Sep 1899.[1] Children:

+ 232   i   Walter IZARD, b. 12 Oct 1854
+ 233   ii   John IZARD, b. 17 Aug 1856
   234   iii   Lucy IZARD, b. 31 Jul 1858, dy 30 Apr 1874
+ 235   iv   Ralph IZARD, b. 19 Mar 1860
References:
[1] DSDI Appl # 1234 & 855.

85. HENRY IZARD[4] (Walter Izard[3], Emma Philadelphia Middleton[2], Arthur Middleton[1]) child of Walter Izard and Mary Cadwallader Green was born in Chester County, SC on 25 Sep 1831.[1] He married Laura LIPSCOMB, daughter of Dr. Dabney and Jane Elizabeth (Hardwick) Lipscomb on 9 May 1860.[1] She was born in Columbus, MS on 1 Apr 1841.[1] Children:

   236   i   Mary Elizabeth IZARD, b. 3 Mar 1861, dy 7 Jul 1862
   237   ii   Annie Laura IZARD, b. 27 Mar 1864, dy 22 Feb 1865
+ 238   iii   George Lipscomb IZARD, b. 7 Nov 1865
   239   iv   Henry IZARD, b. 1 Sep 1867
   240   v   William Lowndes IZARD, b. 6 Sep 1870, dy 23 Mar 1871
   241   vi   Tallulah IZARD, b. 3 Dec 1872, dy 5 Dec 1874
   242   vi   Irene Middleton IZARD, b. 4 Jan 1880
References:
[1] Leach MSS, p. 6212.

86. LUCY IZARD[4] (Walter Izard[3], Emma Philadelphia Middleton[2], Arthur Middleton[1]) child of Walter Izard and Mary Cadwallader Green was born in Chester County, SC on 26 Feb 1833, and died in Columbia, SC on 20 Jun 1859.[1] She married Edward Barnwell HEYWARD, son of Charles and Emma (Barnwell) Heyward on 7 Nov 1850.[1] He was born in Charleston, SC on 4 May 1827, and died there on 19 Feb 1871.[1] Children:

+ 243   i   Walter Izard HEYWARD, b. 31 Oct 1851
   244   ii   Arthur HEYWARD, b. c. 1852, dy 1854
   245   iii   Lucy Izard HEYWARD, b. c. 1854, dy 1863
   246   iv   Emma Barnwell HEYWARD, b. c. 1856, dy 1862
References:
[1] Leach MSS, p. 6212.

87. ALLEN CADWALLADER IZARD[4] (Walter Izard[3], Emma Philadelphia Middleton[2], Arthur Middleton[1]) child of Walter Izard and Mary Cadwallader Green was born in Chester County, SC on 13 Jul 1834[1], and died in Walterboro, SC on 28 Feb 1901. He married Julia Davis BEDON, daughter of Richard Stobo and Julia (Davis) Bedon on 19 Nov 1857.[1] She was born in Columbia, SC on 10 Dec 1840.[1] Children:

+ 247   i   Julia Davis IZARD, b. 31 Dec 1858
   248   ii   Mary Green IZARD, b. 5 Jan 1861
   249   iii   Allen Cadwallader IZARD, Jr., b. 19 Feb 1864
   250   iv   Alice Heyward IZARD, b. 1 Oct 1866
   251   v   Josephine Bedon IZARD, b. 9 Dec 1867
   252   vi   Martha Perry IZARD, b. 1 May 1870
   253   vii   Ralph De Lancey IZARD, b. 15 Mar 1872
+ 254   viii   Mary Rutherford IZARD, b. 27 Jan 1874

References:
[1] Leach MSS, p. 6213.

88. ARTHUR MIDDLETON[4] (Margaret Emma Izard[3], Emma Philadelphia Middleton[2], Arthur Middleton[1]) child of Margaret Emma Izard and Nathaniel Russell Middleton was born in Charleston, SC on 28 Dec 1832[1], and died in Charleston, SC on 24 Jan 1910. He married Julia Emma RHETT, daughter of James Smith and Charlotte (Haskell) Rhett on on 27 Jan 1853.[1] She was born in Charleston, SC on 27 Jan 1835[1], and died in Greenwood, SC on 16 Dec 1908. Children:

   255   i   Arthur MIDDLETON, b. 18 May 1854
+ 256   ii   James Smith MIDDLETON, b. 26 May 1856
+ 257   iii   Margaret Emma MIDDLETON, b. 3 Feb 1858
+ 258   iv   Julia Emma MIDDLETON, b. 30 Jan 1860
+ 259   v   William Dehon MIDDLETON, b. 6 Nov 1862
+ 260   vi   Lucy Izard MIDDLETON, b. 14 Sep 1866
   261   vii   Alice Izard MIDDLETON, b. 3 Oct 1868
+ 262   viii   Helen MIDDLETON, b. 2 Jul 1872
+ 263   ix   Walter Izard MIDDLETON, b. 12 Sep 1874

References:
[1]DSDI Appl # 1772.

92. FREDERICK RUTLEDGE BLAKE[4] (Daniel Blake[3], Anna Louisa Middleton[2], Arthur Middleton[1]) child of Daniel Blake and his 1st wife Emma Philadelphia Middleton Rutledge was born in Charleston, SC on 24 Jan 1838.[1] He married Olivia MIDDLETON [see sketch # 59], daughter of Oliver Hering and Susan Matilda (Chisholm) Middleton on 6 Dec 1864.[1] She was born in Charleston, SC on 26 Apr 1839.[1] Children are as reported under Sketch # 59.

References:
[1]Leach MSS, p. 6220.

93. DANIEL FRANCIS BLAKE[4] (Daniel Blake[3], Anna Louisa Middleton[2], Arthur Middleton[1]) child of Daniel Blake and his 1st wife Emma Philadelphia Middleton Rutledge was born in Henderson County, NC on 1 May 1841, and died in Henderson County, NC on 16 Oct 1872.[1] He married Sarah Hawkins POLK, daughter of the Rt. Rev. Leonidas and Frances Ann (Devereux) Polk on 1 May 1866.[1] She was born in Maury County, TN on 24 Jun 1840.[1]
Child:
    264　　　i　Frank Polk BLAKE, b. 1 Jun 1872
References:
[1]Leach MSS, p. 6220.

96. ARTHUR MIDDLETON BLAKE[4] (Daniel Blake[3], Anna Louisa Middleton[2], Arthur Middleton[1]) child of Daniel Blake and his 1st wife Emma Philadelphia Middleton Rutledge was born in Columbia, SC on 9 May 1848[1], and died in Santa Anna, TX on 12 Oct 1921. He married Tallulah Hazeltine Catherine MAXWELL on 7 Nov 1872.[1] She was born in Henderson County, NC on 23 Jun 1854[1], and died in Santa Anna, TX on 28 May 1909. Children:
    265　　　i　Wade H. BLAKE, b. c. 1874
    266　　ii　Francis H. BLAKE, b. c. 1877
    267　iii　Charles BLAKE, b. c. 1879, dy 1891
    268　iv　Emma BLAKE, b. c. 1882
    269　　v　Joseph BLAKE, b. c. 1884
    270　vi　Z. Vance BLAKE, b. c. 1887
    271　vii　Daniel BLAKE, b. c. 1890
+　272　viii　Florence Vernon BLAKE, b. 26 Aug 1893
References:
[1]DSDI Appl # 2171; see also South Carolina Historical and Genealogical Magazine, (Vol. # 1, issue # 3, July 1900), p. 166.

99. EMMA CRAIG BLAKE[4] (Daniel Blake[3], Anna Louisa Middleton[2], Arthur Middleton[1]) child of Daniel Blake and his 2nd wife Helen Elizabeth Craig was born in "The Meadows", Henderson County, NC on 30 Jan 1865[1], and died in 1935. She married Benjamin Huger RUTLEDGE [see sketch # 182], son of Benjamin Huger and Eleanor Maria (Middleton) Rutledge on 5 Oct 1892.[1] He was born in Charleston, SC on 4 Sep 1861[1], and died in 1925. Children:
    273　　　i　Eleanor Middleton RUTLEDGE, b. 24 Mar 1894; dsp
    274　　ii　Emma RUTLEDGE, b. 1897, d. 1989; unm
+　275　iii　Alice RUTLEDGE, b. 1899
+　276　iv　Benjamin Huger RUTLEDGE, b. 1902

+ 277   v   Amelia Van Cortlandt RUTLEDGE, b. 1904
+ 278   vi Susan Middleton RUTLEDGE, b. 1906
+ 279   vii Anne Blake RUTLEDGE, b. 1910
References:
[1]Leach MSS, p. 6220; data on most of the children of this marriage came from the
Middleton Place Foundation.

100. HELEN BAYLEY BLAKE[4] (Daniel Blake[3], Anna Louisa Middleton[2],
Arthur Middleton[1]) child of Daniel Blake and his 2nd wife Helen Elizabeth
Craig was born in "The Meadows", Henderson County, NC on 10 Nov
1867[1], and died in 1955. She married Oliver Middleton RUTLEDGE [see
sketch # 183], son of Benjamin Huger and Eleanor Maria (Middleton)
Rutledge on 5 Oct 1892.[1] He was born in Columbia, SC on 1 Sep 1862[1],
and died in 1928. Children:
       280   i   Helen Bayley RUTLEDGE, b. 10 Aug 1893; dsp
+ 281   ii Frances Bayley Blake RUTLEDGE, b. 1895
+ 282   iii Oliver Middleton RUTLEDGE , Jr., b. 1900
+ 283   iv Elise RUTLEDGE, b. 1903
+ 284   v   Dorothea Barclay RUTLEDGE, b. 1905
References:
[1]Leach MSS, p. 6220.

103. DANIEL BLAKE HEYWARD[4] (Maria Louisa Blake[3], Anna Louisa
Middleton[2], Arthur Middleton[1]) child of Maria Louisa Blake and Arthur
Heyward was born in Charleston, SC on 28 Feb 1840, and died in Charles-
ton, SC on 31 May 1870.[1] He married Louisa Patience BLAKE, daughter
of Walter and Anna Stead (Izard) Blake on 18 May 1861.[1] She was born in
Naples, ITALY on 29 Jan 1839.[1] Children:
       285   i   Ann Louise HEYWARD, b. 27 Dec 1865
       286   ii Henrietta Maria HEYWARD, b. 8 Sep 1867, dy 31 Dec 1881
       287   iii Josephine Izard HEYWARD, b. 10 Aug 1869
References:
[1]Leach MSS, p. 6221.

105. MARY PROCTOR HUGER[4] (Daniel Elliott Huger[3], Isabella Johannes
Middleton[2], Arthur Middleton[1]) child of Daniel Elliott Huger and Carolina
Proctor was born in New Orleans, LA on 6 Feb 1833, and died in Charleston, SC on 14 Jul 1893.[1] She married Arthur Middleton MANIGAULT, son
of Joseph and Charlotte (Drayton) Manigault on 18 Apr 1850.[1] He was born
in Charleston, SC on 26 Oct 1824, and died in South Island, Georgetown, SC
on 16 Aug 1886.[1] Children:
+ 288   i   Arthur Middleton MANIGAULT, b. 30 Jul 1851

289   ii Carolina MANIGAULT, b. 7 Feb 1853, dy 25 Jul 1860
290   iii Daniel Elliott MANIGAULT, b. 14 Aug 1866
291   iv Stephen MANIGAULT, b. 24 Sep 1868
292   v   Mary Huger MANIGAULT, b. 21 Mar 1870
References:
[1]Leach MSS, p. 6225.

108. WILLIAM ELLIOTT HUGER[4] (Daniel Elliott Huger[3], Isabella Johannes Middleton[2], Arthur Middleton[1]) child of Daniel Elliott Huger and Carolina Proctor was born in Charleston, SC on 8 Jan 1844.[1] He married Elizabeth Pringle SMITH, daughter of John Julius Pringle and Elizabeth (Middleton) Smith on 15 Apr 1869.[1] She was born in Charleston, SC on 18 Feb 1847.[1] Children:

    293   i   Elizabeth Smith HUGER, b. 8 Feb 1870, dy 16 Aug 1870
+   294   ii Daniel Elliott HUGER, b. 8 Nov 1871
    295   iii William Elliott HUGER, b. 28 Nov 1874
    296   iv Carolina Proctor HUGER, b. 26 Apr 1876, dy 4 May 1882
References:
[1]Leach MSS, p. 6226.

110. RICHARD PROCTOR HUGER[4] (Daniel Elliott Huger[3], Isabella Johannes Middleton[2], Arthur Middleton[1]) child of Daniel Elliott Huger and Carolina Proctor was born in Charleston, SC on 15 Mar 1850[1], and died in Anniston, AL on 2 Jun 1922. He married (1st) Mary Cornelia ALSTON, daughter of Lemuel Lovett and Sarah French (Jackson) Alston on 11 Jan 1876.[1] She was born in "Grove Hill", Clarke County, AL on 15 Aug 1855, and died in Orrville, Dallas County, AL on 1 Feb 1881.[1] He married (2nd) Eliza Alwera NOBLE, daughter of John Ward and Alwera Sarah (Abbott) Noble in Anniston, AL on 29 Sep 1884.[1] She was born in Rome, GA on 5 Sep 1859, and died in Anniston, AL on 16 Jan 1896.[1]
Children by first marriage:
    297   i   Mary Williams Alston HUGER, b. 18 Aug 1877
    298   ii   Richard Proctor HUGER, Jr., b. 16 Apr 1879
Children by second marriage:
+   299   iii Alwera HUGER, b. 4 Jul 1885
    300   iv   Stella Noble HUGER, b. 31 Jan 1887
    301   v   Isabella Middleton HUGER, b. 4 Aug 1888
    302   vi   John Noble HUGER, b. 24 Feb 1890
+   303   vii Joseph Proctor HUGER, b. 25 Oct 1891
+   304   viii Stephen Proctor HUGER, b. 30 May 1894
    305   ix   Eliza Alwera HUGER, b. 30 Dec 1895

References:
[1]DSDI Appl # 1190.

111. CAROLINE PROCTOR HUGER[4] (Daniel Elliott Huger[3], Isabella Johannes Middleton[2], Arthur Middleton[1]) child of Daniel Elliott Huger and Carolina Proctor was born in Charleston, SC on 15 Sep 1852.[1] She married William Withers WILKINSON, son of James Withers and Sarah Elliott (Huger) Wilkinson on 30 Apr 1877.[1] He was born in Charleston, SC on 7 Feb 1844.[1] Children:

306   i   James Withers WILKINSON, b. 28 Jul 1880
307   ii   William Withers WILKINSON, b. 8 Mar 1882
308   iii   Willis WILKINSON, b. 24 Nov 1883
309   iv   Arthur Manigault WILKINSON, b. 11 Oct 1892

References:
[1]Leach MSS, p. 6227.

114. DANIEL ELLIOTT HUGER[4] (John Izard Huger[3], Isabella Johannes Middleton[2], Arthur Middleton[1]) child of John Izard Huger and Elizabeth Allen Deas was born in Camden, SC on 30 Nov 1834.[1] He married Harriet WITHERS, daughter of Jones Mitchell and Rebecca Eloisa (Forney) Withers in Nov 1860.[1] Children:

+ 310   i   Eloise HUGER, b. 11 Apr 1864
  311   ii   Allen HUGER, b. 29 Jul 1866
  312   iii   Deas Nott HUGER, b. 5 Mar 1868

References:
[1]Leach MSS, p. 6229.

115. ISABELLA JOHANNES MIDDLETON HUGER[4] (John Izard Huger[3], Isabella Johannes Middleton[2], Arthur Middleton[1]) child of John Izard Huger and Elizabeth Allen Deas was born in Mobile, AL on 24 Apr 1837.[1] She married Alexander Fraser WARLEY, son of Jacob and Sophia Miles (Fraser) Warley on 1 Dec 1862.[1] Children:

+ 313   i   Allen Deas Huger WARLEY, b. 4 Aug 1864
  314   ii   Sophia Maud WARLEY, b. 13 Dec 1866
  315   iii   Arthur Middleton Huger WARLEY, b. 24 Sep 1869, dy 12 May 1871
  316   iv   Theodore Dehon Wagner WARLEY, b. 7 May 1872
  317   v   Felix WARLEY, b. 29 Feb 1876

References:
[1]Leach MSS, p. 6229.

117. WILLIAM ELLIOTT HUGER[4] (John Izard Huger[3], Isabella Johannes Middleton[2], Arthur Middleton[1]) child of John Izard Huger and Elizabeth Allen Deas was born in Mobile, AL on 17 Apr 1841.[1] He married Elizabeth Devereux POLK, daughter of the Rt. Rev. Leonidas and Frances Ann (Devereux) Polk on 27 Apr 1864.[1] She was born in Maury County, TN on 29 Jun 1843.[1] Children:

    318   i   Leonide Polk HUGER, b. 3 Jul 1865, dy 11 Aug 1866
    319   ii   Frances Devereux HUGER, b. 24 Mar 1867
    320   iii   John Middleton HUGER, b. 1 May 1868
    321   iv   Lucia Polk HUGER, b. 29 Oct 1870; dsp
    322   v   Emily Hamilton HUGER, b. 11 Jan 1876
    323   vi   Arthur Middleton HUGER, b. 26 Aug 1878
    324   vii   William Elliott HUGER, b. 22 Oct 1882

References:
[1]Leach MSS, p. 6230.

118. CHARLES LOWNDES HUGER[4] (John Izard Huger[3], Isabella Johannes Middleton[2], Arthur Middleton[1]) child of John Izard Huger and Elizabeth Allen Deas was born in Mobile, AL on 27 Apr 1844.[1] He married Ruth DARGAN, daughter of Edmund Strother and Roxana (Brack) Dargan on 15 Apr 1868.[1] She was born in Mobile, AL on 16 Jul 1847.[1] Children:

    325   i   Meta Deas HUGER, b. 1 Dec 1869
    326   ii   Edmund Dargan HUGER, b. 22 Jul 1871
    327   iii   Charles Lowndes HUGER, Jr., b. 1 Jul 1877
    328   iv   Ruth Dargan HUGER, b. 21 Oct 1881

References:
[1]Leach MSS, p. 6230.

123. RAWLINS LOWNDES[4] (Sabina Elliott Huger[3], Isabella Johannes Middleton[2], Arthur Middleton[1]) child of Sabina Elliott Huger and Charles Tidyman Lowndes was born in Charleston, SC on 23 Jul 1838[1], and died in Charleston, SC on 31 Dec 1919. He married Sarah Buchanan PRESTON in Columbia, SC on 10 Mar 1868.[1] Child:

  +   329   i   Caroline Hampton LOWNDES, b. 12 Nov 1872

References:
[1]DSDI Appl # 378.

124. EMMA MIDDLETON HUGER LOWNDES[4] (Sabina Elliott Huger[3], Isabella Johannes Middleton[2], Arthur Middleton[1]) child of Sabina Elliott Huger and Charles Tidyman Lowndes was born in Charleston, SC in Sep 1847[1], and died in Asheville, NC on 30 Oct 1902. She married James

Munroe SCOTT in Charleston, SC on 16 May 1879.[1] He died in Macon, GA in 1884.[1] Child:

+ 330   i   May Sabina Lowndes SCOTT, b. 1 May 1880

References:
[1]DSDI Appl # 770.

127. JOSEPH ALSTON HUGER, Jr.[4] (Joseph Alston Huger[3], Isabella Johannes Middleton[2], Arthur Middleton[1]) child of Joseph Alston Huger and Mary Esther Huger was born in Pendleton, SC on 15 Jun 1843[1], and died in Bluffton, SC on 10 Dec 1915. He married Mary Stiles ELLIOTT, daughter of Ralph Emms and Margaret Cowper (Mackay) Elliott in Savannah, GA on 17 Feb 1874.[2] She was born in Savannah, GA on 29 Nov 1838[1], and died in Bluffton, SC on 7 Feb 1919. Children:

+ 331   i   Eliza Mackay HUGER, b. 30 Aug 1875
    332   ii   Caroline Pinckney HUGER, b. 31 Aug 1877, d. 1954; unm
+ 333   iii   Emma Middleton Izard HUGER, b. 19 Oct 1879
    334   iv   Percival Elliott HUGER, b. 26 Mar 1881; dsp
+ 335   v   Clermont Kinloch HUGER, b. 19 Apr 1883

References:
[1]Leach MSS, p. 6231. [2] DSDI Appl # 2471.

129. LYNCH PRIOLEAU HUGER[4] (Joseph Alston Huger[3], Isabella Johannes Middleton[2], Arthur Middleton[1]) child of Joseph Alston Huger and Mary Esther Huger was born in "Clydesdale", Beaufort County, SC on 16 Jan 1846[1], and died in NYC on 1 Jun 1909. He married Emily Keese BAILEY, daughter of Floyd and Amelia Kirk (Newton) Bailey in NYC on 6 Apr 1892.[2] She was born in "Valley View", Rockland County, NY on 10 Aug 1865[1], and died in NYC on 14 Feb 1923. Children:

    336   i   Floyd Bailey HUGER, b. 24 Feb 1894
+ 337   ii   Daniel Elliott HUGER, b. 31 Jul 1897

References:
[1]Leach MSS, p. 6232, see also SAR Appl # 57486. [2] DSDI Appl # 524.

130. HARRIET LUCAS PINCKNEY HUGER[4] (Joseph Alston Huger[3], Isabella Johannes Middleton[2], Arthur Middleton[1]) child of Joseph Alston Huger and Mary Esther Huger was born in Savannah, GA on 6 Aug 1848[1], and died in Highlands, NC on 8 Oct 1931. She married John Barnwell ELLIOTT, son of the Rt. Rev. Stephen and Charlotte Bull (Barnwell) Elliott in Greenborough, GA on 26 Jan 1870.[2] He was born in Beaufort, SC on 26 Sep 1841[1], and died in Highlands, NC in Jun 1921. Children:

+ 338   i   John Barnwell ELLIOTT, Jr., b. 30 Oct 1870

339   ii   Esther Huger ELLIOTT, b. 4 Jun 1872
340   iii   Joseph Huger ELLIOTT, b. 15 Dec 1873
341   iv   Charlotte Barnwell ELLIOTT, b. 15 Aug 1875
342   v   Robert Huger ELLIOTT, b. 15 Oct 1877
343   vi   Stephen ELLIOTT, b. 8 Aug 1880, dy 8 Aug 1881
+   344   vii   Lucy Pinckney ELLIOTT, b. 24 Jan 1885
    345   viii   Percival ELLIOTT, b. 24 May 1891
References:
[1]Leach MSS, p. 6232. [2] DSDI Appl # 707.

134. JOHN WELLS HUGER[4] (Joseph Alston Huger[3], Isabella Johannes Middleton[2], Arthur Middleton[1]) child of Joseph Alston Huger and Mary Esther Huger was born on 4 Jul 1859[1], and died in 1915. He married Catherine A. BEEKMAN in 1901. Children:

346   i   Alice Kellar HUGER, b. c. 1902
347   ii   Frances Kinloch HUGER, b. c. 1904
348   iii   William Beekman HUGER, b. c. 1907
References:
[1]Data from the Middleton Place Foundation.

137. WILLIAM WITHERS WILKINSON[4] (Sarah Elliott Huger[3], Isabella Johannes Middleton[2], Arthur Middleton[1]) child of Sarah Elliott Huger and James Withers Wilkinson was born in Charleston, SC on 7 Feb 1844.[1] He married Caroline Proctor HUGER [see sketch # 111], daughter of Daniel Elliott and Caroline (Proctor) Huger on 30 Apr 1877.[1] She was born in Charleston, SC on 15 Sep 1852.[1] Children are as reported under Sketch # 111, this Chapter.
References:
[1]Leach MSS, p. 6233.

138. ISABELLA MIDDLETON WILKINSON[4] (Sarah Elliott Huger[3], Isabella Johannes Middleton[2], Arthur Middleton[1]) child of Sarah Elliott Huger and James Withers Wilkinson was born in Charleston, SC on 27 Mar 1848[1], and died in 1918. She married Eugene Postell JERVEY, son of James Postell and Emma Gough (Smith) Jervey on 16 Dec 1869.[1] He was born in Charleston, SC on 8 May 1843[1], and died in 1921. Children:

349   i   Susan D. JERVEY, b. 31 Oct 1870, dy 4 Mar 1873
350   ii   Eugene Postell JERVEY, Jr., b. 19 Oct 1872
+   351   iii   James Wilkinson JERVEY, b. 19 Oct 1874
    352   iv   Isabella Wilkinson JERVEY, b. 6 Nov 1876, dy 14 Nov 1881

353   v   Huger Wilkinson JERVEY, b. 26 Sep 1878
354   vi Emma Smith JERVEY, b. 21 Jan 1880
355   vii Sarah Huger JERVEY, b. 24 Feb 1882
356   viii Anna Laight JERVEY, b. 2 Oct 1883
357   ix Edward Darrell JERVEY, b. 31 Oct 1885
358   x   Henrietta Postell JERVEY, b. 2 Apr 1887
References:
[1]Leach MSS, p. 6233, see also SAR Appl # 88948.

139. MARIA LOUISA WILKINSON[4] (Sarah Elliott Huger[3], Isabella Johannes Middleton[2], Arthur Middleton[1]) child of Sarah Elliott Huger and James Withers Wilkinson was born on 25 Feb 1850[1], and died in 1926. She married Arthur BARNWELL in 1871.[1] He was born in 1845[1], and died in 1918. Children:

359   i   Arthur BARNWELL, Jr., b. 1872, dy 1878
360   ii Louis BARNWELL, b. 1873, d. 1895; unm
361   iii Margaret Manigault BARNWELL, b. 1875, d. 1895; unm
+ 362   iv Maria Louisa Wilkinson BARNWELL, b. 1876
363   v   Arthur BARNWELL, Jr., b. 1878, d. 1955; dsp [Again]
+ 364   vi Marie Louise BARNWELL, b. 1879
References:
[1]Data from the Middleton Place Foundation.

140. DANIEL ELLIOTT HUGER WILKINSON[4] (Sarah Elliott Huger[3], Isabella Johannes Middleton[2], Arthur Middleton[1]) child of Sarah Elliott Huger and James Withers Wilkinson was born in Charleston, SC on 18 Oct 1852.[1] He married Mary Mildred DUNCAN, daughter of John Randolph and Mary Jane (Duncan) Duncan on 1 May 1880.[1] She was born in Platt County, MO on 5 May 1854, and died there on 13 Aug 1890.[1] Children:

365   i   Sarah Mildred WILKINSON, b. 5 May 1881, dy 5 May1888
366   ii Willis WILKINSON, b. 17 Jun 1883, dy 17 May 1889
367   iii Louella WILKINSON, b. 17 Oct 1885
368   iv John Cacique WILKINSON, b. 19 Sep 1889, dy 13 Sep 1890
References:
[1]Leach MSS, p. 6234.

153. DANIEL ELLIOTT HUGER SMITH[4] (Eliza Caroline Middleton Huger[3], Isabella Johannes Middleton[2], Arthur Middleton[1]) child of Eliza Caroline Middleton Huger and William Mason Smith was born in Charleston, SC on 2 Apr 1846.[1] He married Caroline Ravenel RAVENEL, daughter of

James and Augusta (Winthrop) Ravenel on 16 Nov 1869.[1] She was born in Charleston, SC on 7 Nov 1844, and died there on 17 Jun 1889.[1] Children:

369   i   Eliza Huger SMITH, b. 16 Mar 1871, d. 1940; unm
370   ii   Caroline Ravenel SMITH, b. 7 Dec 1872
+ 371 iii William Mason SMITH, b. 15 Nov 1874
372   iv   Alice Ravenel Huger SMITH, b. 14 Jul 1876, d. 1958; unm
373   v   James Ravenel SMITH, b. 11 Feb 1878, d. 1924; dsp
References:
[1]Leach MSS, p. 6235.

155. ANNA ELIZABETH MASON SMITH[4] (Eliza Caroline Middleton Huger[3], Isabella Johannes Middleton[2], Arthur Middleton[1]) child of Eliza Caroline Middleton Huger and William Mason Smith was born in Charleston, SC on 25 Sep 1849[1], and died on 15 Sep 1924. She married Edward Laight WELLS, son of Thomas Lawrence and Julia (Laight) Wells on 3 Aug 1869.[1] He was born in NYC on 27 Nov 1839.[1] Children:

374   i   Julian Lawrence WELLS, b. 20 Jul 1870
+ 375 ii   Eliza Huger WELLS, b. 18 Aug 1872
376   iii Sabina Elliott WELLS, b. 5 Jul 1876
377   iv   John WELLS, b. 17 Aug 1878, dy 10 Apr 1882
378   v   Edward Lawrence WELLS, b. 7 Aug 1886
References:
[1]Leach MSS, p. 6235.

160. EMMA PHILADELPHIA MIDDLETON RUTLEDGE[4] (Henry Adolphus Rutledge[3], Septima Sexta Middleton[2], Arthur Middleton[1]) child of Henry Adolphus Rutledge and Caroline Bell Nicholson was born in Nashville, TN on 6 Aug 1833, and died in Talladega County, AL on 28 Nov 1863.[1] She married Edwin Chiledes TURNER, son of Matthew and Mary Anne Eliza (Thomas) Turner on 7 Jul 1853.[1] He was born in Upshur County, GA on 31 Mar 1831, and died in Easta Boga, Talladega County, AL on 13 May 1890.[1] Children:

+ 379 i   Matthew TURNER, b. 24 May 1854
+ 380 ii   Emma Caroline TURNER, b. 9 Sep 1855
+ 381 iii Edwin Chiledes TURNER, Jr., b. 20 Mar 1857
+ 382 iv   Mary Ann Eliza TURNER, b. 5 Dec 1859
383   v   Henry Adolphus TURNER, b. 19 Jul 1861, d. 6 Oct 1884; unm
References:
[1] Leach MSS, p. 6237.

161. SEPTIMA SEXTA MIDDLETON RUTLEDGE[4] (Henry Adolphus Rutledge[3], Septima Sexta Middleton[2], Arthur Middleton[1]) child of Henry Adolphus Rutledge and Caroline Bell Nicholson was born in Talladega County, AL on 3 Feb 1836[1], and died in Jacksonville, Calhoun County, AL on 26 Mar 1920. She married John Horace FORNEY, son of Jacob and Sabina Swope (Hoke) Forney on 5 Feb 1863.[1] He was born in Lincoln County, NC on 12 Aug 1829[1], and died in Jacksonville, AL on 13 Dec 1902. Children:

384	i	Emma Rutledge FORNEY, b. 30 May 1864
385	ii	Henry Fogg FORNEY, b. 19 Apr 1867, dy 10 May 1867
+ 386	iii	Jacob FORNEY, b. 8 Oct 1868
387	iv	Mary Caroline FORNEY, b. 8 Feb 1871
+ 388	v	Sabina Swope FORNEY, b. 6 Aug 1873
+ 389	vi	Annie Rowan FORNEY, b. 1 Jun 1876
390	vii	Kathleen Theresa FORNEY, b. 8 Aug 1878, dy 20 Mar 1881

References:
[1] DSDI Appl # 1042.

165. SARAH HENRIETTA RUTLEDGE[4] (Henrietta Middleton Rutledge[3], Septima Sexta Middleton[2],Arthur Middleton[1]) child of Henrietta Middleton Rutledge and Frederick Rutledge was born in Brooklands, NC on 1 Oct 1834.[1] She married Charles Cotesworth PINCKNEY, son of Charles Cotesworth and Carolina Phoebe (Elliott) Pinckney on 20 Sep 1866.[1] He was born in Charleston, SC on 31 Jul 1812.[1] Children:

+ 391	i	Edward Rutledge PINCKNEY, b. 27 Jun 1869
392	ii	Thomas PINCKNEY, b. 28 Oct 1871, d. 1899; unm
393	iii	Stephen Elliott PINCKNEY, b. 17 Feb 1874, dy 17 Jul 1875

References:
[1] Leach MSS, p. 6341.

168. HENRY MIDDLETON RUTLEDGE[4] (Henrietta Middleton Rutledge[3], Septima Sexta Middleton[2], Arthur Middleton[1]) child of Henrietta Middleton Rutledge and Frederick Rutledge was born in Buncombe County, NC on 5 Aug 1840[1] , and died in McClellanville, SC on 10 Jun 1921. He married (1st) Anna Marie BLAKE, daughter of Walter and Anna Stead (Izard) Blake on 25 Nov 1863.[1] She was born in Henderson County, NC on 12 May 1842, and died on 21 Feb 1872.[1] He married (2nd) Margaret Hamilton SEABROOK, daughter of Archibald Hamilton and Caroline Phoebe (Pinckney) Seabrook in Charleston, SC on 18 Mar 1875.[2] She was born in Beaufort, SC on 24 Jan 1849[2], and died in Charleston, SC on 25 Feb 1925.

Children by first marriage:
    394   i   Child RUTLEDGE, b. 1865, dy
+ 395   ii Frederick RUTLEDGE, b. 10 Feb 1868
Children by second marriage:
    396   iii Caroline Phoebe RUTLEDGE, b. 27 Mar 1876
+ 397   iv Harriott Horry RUTLEDGE, b. 8 Feb 1878
+ 398   v   Thomas Pinckney RUTLEDGE, b. 16 Feb 1879
    399   vi Henry Middleton RUTLEDGE, b. 26 Aug 1882, dy 1893
+ 400   vii Archibald Hamilton RUTLEDGE, b. 23 Oct 1883
    401   viii Mary Pinckney RUTLEDGE, b. 10 Dec 1886
References:
[1] Leach MSS, p. 6241; SAR Appl # 56265. [2] DSDI Appl # 1535 & 1293.

169. EMMA FREDRIKA RUTLEDGE[4] (Henrietta Middleton Rutledge[3], Septima Sexta Middleton[2], Arthur Middleton[1]) child of Henrietta Middleton Rutledge and Frederick Rutledge was born in Charleston, SC on 10 May 1842[1], and died on 19 Jul 1919. She married William Brown REESE, son of William Brown and Sarah Maclin (Cooke) Reese on 14 Jun 1866.[1] He was born in Knoxville, TN on 17 Mar 1829.[1] Children:
+ 402   i   Mary Middleton Rutledge REESE, b. 20 Apr 1867
+ 403   ii Alice Sophia REESE, b. 4 Jun 1872
References:
[1] Leach MSS, p. 6242.

170. ELIZABETH UNDERWOOD RUTLEDGE[4] (Arthur Middleton Rutledge[3], Septima Sexta Middleton[2], Arthur Middleton[1]) child of Arthur Middleton Rutledge and Eliza Underwood was born in "Chilhowee", Franklin County, TN on 29 Aug 1852[1], and died in Charleston, SC on 15 Feb 1918. She married Henry Edward YOUNG, son of the Rev. Thomas John and Rebecca (Gourdin) Young on 19 Nov 1873.[1] He was born in "Sherwood", Beaufort County, SC on 9 Aug 1831.[1] Children:
    404   i   Eliza Underwood Rutledge YOUNG, b. 24 Nov 1874, dy 14
                Apr 1878
+ 405   ii Arthur Middleton Rutledge YOUNG, b. 3 Jul 1876
    406   iii Henry Gourdin YOUNG, b. 16 May 1878, dy 19 May 1878
    407   iv Henry Gourdin YOUNG, b. 7 Sep 1879, dy 25 Oct 1885
                [Again]
+ 408   v   Joseph Underwood Rutledge YOUNG, b. 7 Jan 1881
References:
[1] Leach MSS, p. 6244; see also M. L. Webber, *Dr. John Rutledge and his Descendants*, (South Carolina Historical and Genealogical Magazine, Jan. 1930), p. 103.

171. EMMA BLAKE RUTLEDGE[4] (Arthur Middleton Rutledge[3], Septima Sexta Middleton[2], Arthur Middleton[1]) child of Arthur Middleton Rutledge and Eliza Underwood was born in "Chilhowee", Franklin County, TN on 29 Mar 1854.[1] She married Henry Augustus Middleton SMITH, son of John Julius Pringle and Elizabeth (Middleton) Smith on 24 Jun 1879.[1] He was born in Charleston, SC on 30 Apr 1853[1], and died in 1924. Children:

409   i   Henry Augustus Middleton SMITH, Jr., b. 19 May 1882, dy 1 Dec 1901

+ 410   ii   John Julius Pringle SMITH, b. 14 Oct 1887

References:
[1] M. L. Webber, *Dr. John Rutledge and his Descendants*, (South Carolina Historical and Genealogical Magazine, Jan. 1930), p. 103.

172. ARTHUR MIDDLETON RUTLEDGE[4] (Arthur Middleton Rutledge[3], Septima Sexta Middleton[2], Arthur Middleton[1]) child of Arthur Middleton Rutledge and Eliza Underwood was born in Bowling Green, KY on 4 Nov 1855.[1] He married Rosalie WINSTON, daughter of Joseph Pendleton and Lelia (Saunders) Winston in Richmond, VA on 12 Dec 1893.[1] She was born in Richmond, VA on 3 Dec 1866.[1] Children:

411   i   Arthur Middleton RUTLEDGE, b. 31 Dec 1896

412   ii   Winston Underwood RUTLEDGE, b. 29 Mar 1898

413   iii   Edward RUTLEDGE, b. 14 Jan 1901

References:
[1] M. L. Webber, *Dr. John Rutledge and his Descendants*, (South Carolina Historical and Genealogical Magazine, Jan. 1930), p. 104.

FIFTH GENERATION

174. COSTANZA MIDDLETON[5] (Henry Bentivoglio Middleton[4], Arthur Middleton[3], Henry Middleton[2], Arthur Middleton[1]) child of Henry Bentivoglio Middleton and Beatrice Cini was born in Rome, ITALY on 7 May 1870[1], and died on 8 Apr 1912. She married John Bowring SPENCE in 1895.[1] He was born in Rome, ITALY on 26 Feb 1861[1], and died in TRIPOLI on 26 Sep 1917. Children:

414   i   Edgar SPENCE, b. 2 Jun 1896; dsp

415   ii   George Bentivoglio Middleton SPENCE, b. 17 Sep 1898, d. 30 Oct 1994; dsp

References:
[1] Data from Middleton Place Foundation.

176. VIRGINIA MIDDLETON[5] (Henry Bentivoglio Middleton[4], Arthur Middleton[3], Henry Middleton[2], Arthur Middleton[1]) child of Henry Bentivoglio Middleton and Beatrice Cini was born in Rome, ITALY on 10 Oct 1872[1], and died in 1963. She married Piero Masetti de Dainella de BAGNAMO in 1893.[1] He was born on 11 Oct 1872[1], and died on 23 Sep 1963. Children:

```
     416      i    Julio Masetti de BAGNAMO, b. 1894, d. 1926; dsp
 +   417      ii   Carlo Masetti de BAGNAMO, b. 1897
 +   418      iii  Maria Grazia Masetti de BAGNAMO, b. 1901
```
References:
[1] Data from Middleton Place Foundation.

177. ARTHUR GIULIO MIDDLETON[5] (Henry Bentivoglio Middleton[4], Arthur Middleton[3], Henry Middleton[2], Arthur Middleton[1]) child of Henry Bentivoglio Middleton and Beatrice Cini was born in Rome, ITALY on 1 Nov 1873[1], and died on 5 Feb 1925. He married Carolina RESPIGLIOSA in say 1915. Child:

```
 +   419      i    Henry Bentivoglio MIDDLETON, b. 14 Dec 1923
```
References:
[1] Data from Middleton Place Foundation.

178. OLIVER MIDDLETON READ[5] (Mary Julia Middleton[4], Oliver Hering Middleton[3], Henry Middleton[2], Arthur Middleton[1]) child of Mary Julia Middleton and Benjamin Huger Read was born in Charleston, SC on 6 Nov 1855.[1] He married (1st) Mary Louise GREGORIE in 1886.[1] She was born in Abbeville County, SC on 19 Aug 1864, and died in Charleston, SC on 23 Apr 1892.[1] He married (2nd) Edith Matthew GLOVER in say 1896. Children by first marriage:

```
     420      i    Mary Louise READ, b. 5 Nov 1887
 +   421      ii   Oliver Middleton READ, Jr., b. 12 Jan 1889
 +   422      iii  Eliza Baker READ, b. 3 Jun 1890
     423      iv   Julia Middleton READ, b. 17 Apr 1892, d. 1983; unm
```
Children by second marriage:
```
     424      v    Benjamin Huger READ, b. 1899
     425      vi   Sanders Glover READ, b. 1903
```
References:
[1] Leach MSS, p. 6197.

179. BENJAMIN HUGER READ[5] (Mary Julia Middleton[4], Oliver Hering Middleton[3], Henry Middleton[2], Arthur Middleton[1]) child of Mary Julia Middleton and Benjamin Huger Read was born in Charleston, SC on 16 Dec 1856.[1] He married Anne Cleland SMITH, daughter of John Julius Pringle and Elizabeth (Middleton) Smith on 9 Dec 1884.[1] She was born in Charleston, SC on 10 Jun 1860.[1] Children:

+ 426   i   Elizabeth Middleton READ, b. 31 Aug 1885
   427   ii   Benjamin Huger READ, Jr., b. 11 Jun 1888, dy 11 Jan 1892
   428   iii   Francis Kinloch READ, b. 19 Mar 1891, dy 5 Jan 1892
   429   iv   Mary Middleton READ, b. 22 Dec 1893
   430   v   Anne Cleland READ, b. 1894

References:
[1] Leach MSS, p. 6197.

180. EMILY ANNE READ[5] (Mary Julia Middleton[4], Oliver Hering Middleton[3], Henry Middleton[2], Arthur Middleton[1]) child of Mary Julia Middleton and Benjamin Huger Read was born in Charleston, SC on 14 Jan 1858[1], and died in Philadelphia, PA on 23 Jun 1942. She married Joseph Mickle [sic] FOX, son of Samuel Mickle and Mary Rodman (Fisher) Fox in Charleston, SC on 10 May 1883.[1] He was born in Philadelphia, PA on 4 Feb 1853[1], and died there on 3 Sep 1918. Children:

   431   i   Mary Lindley FOX, b. 25 Dec 1884; dsp
   432   ii   Emily Read FOX, b. 7 Jun 1887; dsp
+ 433   iii   Eliza Middleton FOX, b. 23 Feb 1890
   434   iv   William Logan FOX, b. 15 Nov 1892

References:
[1] DSDI Appl # 2351.

182. BENJAMIN HUGER RUTLEDGE[5] (Eleanor Maria Middleton[4], Oliver Hering Middleton[3], Henry Middleton[2], Arthur Middleton[1]) child of Eleanor Maria Middleton and Benjamin Huger Rutledge was born in Charleston, SC on 4 Sep 1861.[1] He married Emma Craig BLAKE [see sketch # 99], daughter of Daniel and his 2nd wife Helen Elizabeth (Craig) Blake on 5 Oct 1892.[1] She was born in "The Meadows", Henderson County, NC on 30 Jun 1865.[1] Children are as reported under Sketch # 99.

183. OLIVER MIDDLETON RUTLEDGE[5] (Eleanor Maria Middleton[4], Oliver Hering Middleton[3], Henry Middleton[2], Arthur Middleton[1]) child of Eleanor Maria Middleton and Benjamin Huger Rutledge was born in Columbia, SC on 1 Sep 1862.[1] He married Helen Bayley BLAKE [see sketch # 100], daughter of Daniel and his 2nd wife Helen Elizabeth (Craig) Blake on 5 Oct 1892.[1] She was born in "The Meadows", Henderson County, NC on 10 Nov 1867.[1] Children are as reported under Sketch # 100.

187. EDWARD RUTLEDGE[5] (Eleanor Maria Middleton[4], Oliver Hering Middleton[3], Henry Middleton[2], Arthur Middleton[1]) child of Eleanor Maria Middleton and Benjamin Huger Rutledge was born on 28 Jan 1870[1], and died in 1942. He married Eliza Huger WELLS [see sketch # 375], daughter of Edward Laight and Anna Elizabeth Mason (Smith) Wells in 1906. She was born on 18 Aug 1872.[1] Children:

    435   i   Anna Wells RUTLEDGE, b. c. 1907
    436   ii Ella Middleton RUTLEDGE, b. 1909
    437 iii Eliza Huger RUTLEDGE, b. 1911

References:
[1] DATA from Middleton Place Foundation.

189. EDMUND MOLYNEUX BLAKE[5] (Olivia Middleton[4], Oliver Hering Middleton[3], Henry Middleton[2], Arthur Middleton[1]) child of Olivia Middleton and Frederick Rutledge Blake was born on 14 Jan 1866[1], and died in Washington, DC on 20 Aug 1927. He married Eleanor FARLEY, daughter of Col -- Farley in Columbia, SC in 1895.[1] Children:

+ 438   i   Ayliffe B. BLAKE, b. c. 1896
+ 439   ii Olivia Middleton BLAKE, b. c. 1898

References:
[1] Leach MSS, p. 6198; he was a graduate of USMA, see *Register of Graduates and Former Cadets of the United States Military Academy*, (Association of Graduates, West Point, NY, 1990), p. 310, Class of 1889, Graduate # 3288.

192. DANIEL BLAKE[5] (Olivia Middleton[4], Oliver Hering Middleton[3], Henry Middleton[2], Arthur Middleton[1]) child of Olivia Middleton and Frederick Rutledge Blake was born in "The Meadows", NC on 21 Oct 1872[1], and died in 1925. He married Mary Scott PERRY in 1900. She was born in 1877[2], and died in 1934. Child:

+ 440   i   Daniel BLAKE, b. 1902

References:
[1] Leach MSS, p. 6198 reports date and place of birth. [2] Data from Middleton Place Foundation.

193. JOHN IZARD MIDDLETON, III[5] (John Izard Middleton, Jr.[4], John Izard Middleton[3], Henry Middleton[2], Arthur Middleton[1]) child of John Izard Middleton, Jr. and Harriet SterrettGittings was born in Baltimore, MD on 14 Feb 1867[1], and died in NYC on 20 Mar 1953. He married Elena de APEZTEGUIA in NYC on 15 Jul 1905. She was born in San Sebastian, SPAIN on 5 Sep 1882[1], and died in Far Rockaway, LI, NY on 16 Jul 1954. Child:

    441   i   John Izard MIDDLETON, IV, b. 10 Dec 1907, d. Sep 1981;
               unm

References:
[1] DSDI Appl # 1317.

201. MAUD MURIEL MIDDLETON[5] (Henry Middleton[4], Williams Middleton[3], Henry Middleton[2], Arthur Middleton[1]) child of Henry Middleton and his 1st partner Mary Elizabeth Heatly was born on 24 Jan 1886.[1] She married -- BARTLETT in say 1905. Children:

    442   i   William BARTLETT, b. c. 1907
    443   ii   Elizabeth BARTLETT, b. c. 1909

References:
[1] Data from Middleton Place Foundation.

202. HENRY MIDDLETON[5] (Henry Middleton[4], Williams Middleton[3], Henry Middleton[2], Arthur Middleton[1]) child of Henry Middleton and his 1st partner Mary Elizabeth Heatly was born on 18 Apr 1887[1], and died on 14 Aug 1977. He married Eva CAMERON in say 1918. She was born on 28 May 1889[1], and died on 5 Feb 1985. Children:

    444   i   Henry Heatly MIDDLETON, b. 24 Jun 1921
+ 445   ii   Shirley MIDDLETON, b. 13 Oct 1928
    446   iii   Royalind MIDDLETON, b. 23 Jun 1933

References:
[1] Data from Middleton Place Foundation.

204. ALGERNON MANFRED MIDDLETON[5] (Henry Middleton[4], Williams Middleton[3], Henry Middleton[2], Arthur Middleton[1]) child of Henry Middleton and his 1st partner Mary Elizabeth Heatly was born on 17 May 1889[1], and died in 1959. He married Elise SIMS in say 1920. Children:

    447   i   Williams Ian MIDDLETON, b. c. 1923
+ 448   ii   Mary MIDDLETON, b. 21 Oct 1925

References:
[1] Data from Middleton Place Foundation.

207. EDWARD THOMAS FRANCIS MIDDLETON[5] (Henry Middleton[4], Williams Middleton[3], Henry Middleton[2], Arthur Middleton[1]) child of Henry Middleton and his 1st partner Mary Elizabeth Heatly was born on 10 May 1893[1], and died on 23 Sep 1975. He married Amelia HOMANN in say 1919. Children:

    449   i   David E. MIDDLETON, b. c. 1921
    450   ii   Child MIDDLETON, b. c. 1923
    451   iii   Child MIDDLETON, b. c. 1926
    452   iv   Child MIDDLETON, b. c. 1930
    453   v   Child MIDDLETON, b. c. 1933

References:
[1] Data from Middleton Place Foundation.

208. LILIAN NORA MIDDLETON[5] (Henry Middleton[4], Williams Middleton[3], Henry Middleton[2], Arthur Middleton[1]) child of Henry Middleton and his 1st partner Mary Elizabeth Heatly was born on 19 Aug 1895.[1] She married Nigel Vivien JOHNSTON in say 1916. Children:

    454   i   Sally JOHNSTON, b. c. 1919
    455   ii Anthony JOHNSTON, b. c. 1922

References:
[1] Data from Middleton Place Foundation.

210. DOROTHY EMMA MIDDLETON[5] (Henry Middleton[4], Williams Middleton[3], Henry Middleton[2], Arthur Middleton[1]) child of Henry Middleton and his 1st partner Mary Elizabeth Heatly was born on 25 Nov 1898[1], and died in 1960. She married Gordon Bryce Seymour COUSENS on 12 Aug 1925. He was born on 14 Feb 1885[1], and died in Nov 1956. Children:

+ 456   i   Marion Barbara Dorothy COUSENS, b. 27 Aug 1926
+ 457   ii Pamela Helen Margaret COUSENS, b. 28 Dec 1927
+ 458   iii George Edward Heatly COUSENS, b. 22 Apr 1929
+ 459   iv Colin Arthur Middleton COUSENS, b. 22 Mar 1930

References:
[1] Data from Middleton Place Foundation.

212. RONALD WILLIAMS MIDDLETON[5] (Henry Middleton[4], Williams Middleton[3], Henry Middleton[2], Arthur Middleton[1]) child of Henry Middleton and his 2nd partner Beatrice Esther Florence Lift was born on 2 Sep 1897[1], and died on 15 Feb 1980. He married Elsie Mary HAWKINS in say 1905. She was born on 20 Nov 1910. Children:

+ 460   i   Ronald David MIDDLETON, b. 30 Apr 1932
+ 461   ii Jean Patricia MIDDLETON, b. 17 Mar 1934

References:
[1] Data from Middleton Place Foundation.

213. BASIL BERNARD NORMAN MIDDLETON[5] (Henry Middleton[4], Williams Middleton[3], Henry Middleton[2], Arthur Middleton[1]) child of Henry Middleton and his 2nd partner Beatrice Esther Florence Lift was born on 14 Oct 1898[1], and died on 21 Feb 1952. He married Evelyn WOOD in say 1930. She was born on 28 May 1889[1], and died on 5 Feb 1985. Children:

+ 462   i   Paul Frederick MIDDLETON, b. 6 Jun 1932
+ 463   ii Anthony Hugh MIDDLETON, b. 30 Jun 1933 [twin]
+ 464   iii Brian Neil MIDDLETON, b. 30 Jun 1933 [twin]
+ 465   iv Ian Keith MIDDLETON, b. 3 Dec 1934

References:
[1] Data from Middleton Place Foundation.

214. CATHERINE ELEANOR MABEL MIDDLETON⁵ (Henry Middleton⁴, Williams Middleton³, Henry Middleton², Arthur Middleton¹) child of Henry Middleton and his 2nd partner Beatrice Esther Florence Lift was born on 15 May 1900. She married Samuel MEPHAM in say 1922. Child:
+ 466   i   Raymond Christoher MEPHAM, b. c. 1925

215. EMMELINE ELLIDA DAVISON⁵ (Emeline Virginia Middleton⁴, Edward Middleton³, Henry Middleton², Arthur Middleton¹) child of Emeline Virginia Middleton and Edgar M. Davison was born on 12 Jun 1911. She married John M. REA on 22 Jun 1935. He was born on 22 Jun 1909. Children:
+ 467   i   Child REA, b. c. 1937
+ 468   ii Paul REA, b. c. 1940
+ 469   iii Edward Middleton REA, b. c. 1945

217. NANCY REEVES MIDDLETON⁵ (Arthur Edward Henry Middleton⁴, Edward Middleton³, Henry Middleton², Arthur Middleton¹) child of Arthur Edward Henry Middleton and Nancy Anne Ashby was born on 1 Jun 1915, and died on 19 May 1988. She married William Saxton MYERS on 1 Jul 1939. He was born on 16 Feb 1914. Children:
+ 470   i   David Saxton MYERS, b. 27 Mar 1941
+ 471   ii Susan Ellen MYERS, b. 20 Mar 1942
  472   iii Christopher Middleton MYERS, b. 22 Dec 1947

218. ELIZA MIDDLETON KANE⁵ (Elizabeth Francis Fisher⁴, Elizabeth Izard Middleton³, Henry Middleton², Arthur Middleton¹) child of Elizabeth Francis Fisher and Robert Patterson Kane was born in Philadelphia, PA on 8 Apr 1863[1], and died in 1953. She married Walter COPE, son of Thomas Pym and Elizabeth Waln (Stokes) Cope on 2 May 1893.[1] He was born in Philadelphia, PA on 1 Oct 1860[1], and died in 1902. Children:
+ 473   i   Thomas Pym COPE, b. 1896
+ 474   ii Elizabeth Francis COPE, b. 1898
+ 475   iii Anne Francis COPE, b. 1900
+ 476   iv Oliver COPE, b. 1902

References:
[1] Leach MSS, p. 6207, supported by data from Middleton Place Foundation.

223. JOHN CADWALADER[5] (Mary Helen Fisher[4], Elizabeth Izard Middleton[3], Henry Middleton[2], Arthur Middleton[1]) child of Mary Helen Fisher and John Cadwalader was born on 24 Sep 1874[1], and died on 10 Jun 1934. He married Margaret NICOLL on 28 Aug 1908. She was born on 24 Jul 1875[1], and died on 19 Oct 1962. Child:

+   477   i   John CADWALADER, b. 8 Jan 1910
References:
[1] Data from Middleton Place Foundation.

224. THOMAS FRANCIS CADWALADER[5] (Mary Helen Fisher[4], Elizabeth Izard Middleton[3], Henry Middleton[2], Arthur Middleton[1]) child of Mary Helen Fisher and John Cadwalader was born in Philadelphia, PA on 22 Sep 1880[1], and died in Joppa, Harford County, MD on 24 Feb 1970. He married Elizabeth Middleton READ [see sketch # 426], daughter of Benjamin Huger and Anne Cleland (Smith) Read in Baltimore, MD on 23 Nov 1911. She was born in Baltimore, MD on 31 Aug 1885[1], and died in Joppa, Harford County, MD on 27 Jun 1952. Children:

+   478   i   Thomas Francis CADWALADER, Jr., b. 18 Nov 1912
    479   ii   Mary Helen CADWALADER, b. 20 Dec 1915
+   480   iii Ann Cleland CADWALADER, b. 24 Dec 1918
    481   iv   Benjamin Read CADWALADER, b. 13 Mar 1922
References:
[1] DSDI Appl # 2263.

226. ELIZA MIDDLETON COXE[5] (Maria Middleton Fisher[4], Elizabeth Izard Middleton[3], Henry Middleton[2], Arthur Middleton[1]) child of Maria Middleton Fisher and Brinton Coxe was born on 7 Nov 1875[1], and died in 1950. She married Charles Morris YOUNG on 18 Nov 1903. He was born in 1869[1], and died about 1964. Children:

    482   i   Arthur M. YOUNG, b. 1905
    483   ii   Christopher YOUNG, b. c. 1907
    484   iii Philip YOUNG, b. c. 1910
    485   iv   Brinton O. C. YOUNG, b. c. 1914
References:
[1] Data from Middleton Place Foundation.

227. MARY REBECCA COXE[5] (Maria Middleton Fisher[4], Elizabeth Izard Middleton[3], Henry Middleton[2], Arthur Middleton[1]) child of Maria Middleton Fisher and Brinton Coxe was born in Philadelphia, PA on 29 Jan 1877[1], and died in Philadelphia, PA on 28 Dec 1925. She married Arthur Howell

GERHARD on 9 Dec 1903. He was born in Philadelphia, PA on 15 Apr 1877[1], and died there in Aug 1949. Child:

486   i   Arthur Howell GERHARD, Jr., b. 7 Nov 1909

References:
[1] DSDI Appl # 1184.

228. EDMUND JAMES COXE[5] (Maria Middleton Fisher[4], Elizabeth Izard Middleton[3], Henry Middleton[2], Arthur Middleton[1]) child of Maria Middleton Fisher and Brinton Coxe was born on 3 May 1881.[1] He married -- (--) in say 1905. Children:

487   i   Daniel COXE, b. c. 1907
488   ii   Brinton COXE, Jr., b. c. 1910, dy
489   iii Maria COXE, b. c. 1914

References:
[1] Data from Middleton Place Foundation.

229. ANNA SCOTT FISHER[5] (George Harrison Fisher[4], Elizabeth Izard Middleton[3], Henry Middleton[2], Arthur Middleton[1]) child of George Harrison Fisher and Betsey Riddle was born in Philadelphia, PA on 12 Mar 1877.[1] She married William Howard HART on 18 Jan 1899.[1] Children:

490   i   Harry Carlton HART, b. c. 1900
+ 491   ii   Eleanor HART, b. 1902
492   iii Francis Fisher HART, b. c. 1905
493   iv   Mary Montgomery HART, b. c. 1908
494   v   George Harrison HART, b. c. 1910

References:
[1] Leach MSS, p. 6209.

231. MARY FISHER[5] (Henry Middleton Fisher[4], Elizabeth Izard Middleton[3], Henry Middleton[2], Arthur Middleton[1]) child of Henry Middleton Fisher and Mary E. Wharton was born about 1884. She married James Blathwaite DRINKER on 20 Oct 1917. He was born on 23 Oct 1882.[1] Children:

+ 495   i   Henry Middleton DRINKER, b. 19 Nov 1919
496   ii   Sandwith DRINKER, b. 7 Oct 1922
+ 497   iii Mary Elwyn DRINKER, b. 2 May 1927
+ 498   iv   James DRINKER, b. 11 Dec 1928

References:
[1] Data from Middleton Place Foundation.

232. WALTER IZARD[5] (Walter Izard[4], Walter Izard[3], Emma Philadelphia Middleton[2], Arthur Middleton[1]) child of Walter Izard and Sallie Goode was born in Bedford County, VA on 12 Oct 1854.[1] He married Annie Wharton

SALE, daughter of John Wharton and Anne Rebecca (Campbell) Sale on 5 Jan 1881.[1] She was born in Liberty, VA on 19 Jan 1862.[1] Children:
   499   i   Lucy IZARD, b. 21 Nov 1881
   500   ii   Walter IZARD, b. 7 Nov 1882
   501 iii   John IZARD, b. 9 Oct 1884
References:
[1] Leach MSS, p. 6214.

233. JOHN IZARD[5] (Walter Izard[4], Walter Izard[3], Emma Philadelphia Middleton[2], Arthur Middleton[1]) child of Walter Izard and Sallie Goode was born in Bedford County, VA on 17 Aug 1856.[1] He married Roberta Pearis JOHNSTON, daughter of James David and Mary Ann (Fowler) Johnston on 23 Jun 1886.[1] She was born in Pearisburg, Giles County, VA on 15 Nov 1858.[1] Children:
   502   i   John IZARD, b. 7 Apr 1887
   503   ii   Alice De Lancy IZARD, b. 11 Jul 1888
   504 iii   James Johnston IZARD, b. 14 Jun 1890, dy 19 Jul 1890
   505 iv   Mary Fowler IZARD, b. 11 May 1892
References:
[1] Leach MSS, p. 6214.

235. RALPH IZARD[5] (Walter Izard[4], Walter Izard[3], Emma Philadelphia Middleton[2], Arthur Middleton[1]) child of Walter Izard and Sallie Goode was born in Goodes, VA on 19 Mar 1860[1], and died in Richmond, VA on 17 Feb 1942. He married Nannie Theresa LYONS in Tazewell, VA on 25 Mar 1891.[1] She was born in Tazewell, VA on 10 Dec 1870.[1] Children:
+ 506   i   Sarah Lyons IZARD, b. 14 May 1892
+ 507   ii   Rita IZARD, b. 14 Aug 1894
+ 508 iii   Laura Elizabeth IZARD, b. 3 Feb 1903
References:
[1] DSDI Appl # 1234.

238. GEORGE LIPSCOMB IZARD[5] (Henry Izard[4], Walter Izard[3], Emma Philadelphia Middleton[2], Arthur Middleton[1]) child of Henry Izard and Laura Lipscomb was born in Garlandville, MS on 7 Nov 1860.[1] He married Emma A. DANTZLER, daughter of L. W. and -- (Griffin) Dantzler on 21 Jan 1891.[1] She was born in Moss Point, MS on 8 Jul 1868.[1] Child:
   509   i   George Dantzler IZARD, b. 6 Jul 1892
References:
[1] Leach MSS, p. 6214.

243. WALTER IZARD HEYWARD[5] (Lucy Izard[4], Walter Izard[3], Emma Philadelphia Middleton[2], Arthur Middleton[1]) child of Lucy Izard and Edward Barnwell Heyward was born in Charleston, SC on 31 Oct 1851.[1] He married (1st) Susan Gruning BRUMBY, daughter of Arnoldus Vander Horst and Anne (Wallis) Brumby on 8 Apr 1874.[1] She was born in Marietta, GA about 1856, and died in Atlanta, GA on 18 Jun 1876.[1] Child:

510   i   Mary Izard HEYWARD, b. 11 May 1876, dy 14 Jun 1876

References:
[1] Leach MSS, p. 6215.

247. JULIA DAVIS IZARD[5] (Allen Cadwallader Izard[4], Walter Izard[3], Emma Philadelphia Middleton[2], Arthur Middleton[1]) child of Allen Cadwallader Izard and Julia Davis Bedon was born in Walterboro, SC on 31 Dec 1858.[1] She married William Taylor WILLIAMS, son of Henry Reuben and Amelia Sarah (Richards) Williams on 23 Dec 1880.[1] He was born in Hardeeville, SC on 23 Apr 1855.[1] Children:

511   i   Allen Izard WILLIAMS, b. 16 Oct 1881
512   ii   Henrietta Ruby WILLIAMS, b. 16 Jul 1884
513   iii Edith WILLIAMS, b. 22 Nov 1885

References:
[1] Leach MSS, p. 6215.

254. MARY RUTHERFORD IZARD[5] (Allen Cadwallader Izard[4], Walter Izard[3], Emma Philadelphia Middleton[2], Arthur Middleton[1]) child of Allen Cadwallader Izard and Julia Davis Bedon was born in Walterboro, SC on 27 Jan 1874.[1] She married Julius August KLEIN, son of Franz and Elizabetha (Hatling) Klein on 21 Jul 1892.[1] He was born in Frankenthal, Platinate, GERMANY on 19 Aug 1866.[1] Child:

514   Rutherford Izard KLEIN, b. 14 Oct 1893

References:
[1] Leach MSS, p. 6215.

256. JAMES SMITH MIDDLETON[5] (Arthur Middleton[4], Margaret Emma Izard[3], Emma Philadelphia Middleton[2], Arthur Middleton[1]) child of Arthur Middleton and Julia Emma Rhett was born in Charleston, SC on 26 May 1856.[1] He married Pauline LEE, daughter of Hutson and Eliza Lucilla (Haskell) Lee on 2 May 1882.[1] She was born in Charleston, SC on 7 Jun 1856.[1] Children:

515   i   Pauline Lee MIDDLETON, b. 13 Jan 1883
516   ii   Lucilla MIDDLETON, b. 29 Dec 1885
517   iii Julia MIDDLETON, b. 6 Jul 1887

518   iv   Charlotte Haskell MIDDLETON, b. 14 Nov 1888
519   v   Margaret MIDDLETON, b. 16 Aug 1891
520   vi   Caroline MIDDLETON, b. 4 Apr 1893
References:
[1] Leach MSS, p. 6217.

257. MARGARET EMMA MIDDLETON[5] (Arthur Middleton[4], Margaret Emma Izard[3], Emma Philadelphia Middleton[2], Arthur Middleton[1]) child of Arthur Middleton and Julia Emma Rhett was born in Charleston, SC on 3 Feb 1858, and died on 28 Sep 1890.[1] She married William Cotesworth Pinckney FERGUSON, son of John and Rebecca Witter (McCants) Ferguson on 21 Apr 1881.[1] He was born in Monticello, Jefferson County, FL on 15 Sep 1852[1], and died on 4 Oct 1927. Children:
521   i   Arthur Middleton FERGUSON, b. 21 Dec 1882
+ 522   ii   Margaret Izard FERGUSON, b. 27 Jan 1885
References:
[1] Leach MSS, p. 6217.

258. JULIA EMMA MIDDLETON[5] (Arthur Middleton[4], Margaret Emma Izard[3], Emma Philadelphia Middleton[2], Arthur Middleton[1]) child of Arthur Middleton and Julia Emma Rhett was born in Charleston, SC on 30 Jan 1860.[1] She married Thomas Hall Jervey WILLIAMS, son of David Ramsay and Mary Anne (Whitesides) Williams on 29 Jun 1880.[1] He was born in Mt. Pleasant, SC on 21 May 1856.[1] Children:
523   i   Marion WILLIAMS, b. 9 Jul 1881
524   ii   Arthur Middleton WILLIAMS, b. 5 Feb 1883
525   iii Thomas Hall WILLIAMS, b. 5 Sep 1835
526   iv   Julian Rhett WILLIAMS, b. 28 Sep 1887
527   v   Lucy Middleton WILLIAMS, b. 28 Oct 1889
528   vi   Margaret Middleton WILLIAMS, b. 13 Dec 1891
References:
[1] Leach MSS, p. 6218.

259. WILLIAM DEHON MIDDLETON[5] (Arthur Middleton[4], Margaret Emma Izard[3], Emma Philadelphia Middleton[2], Arthur Middleton[1]) child of Arthur Middleton and Julia Emma Rhett was born in Pickens District, SC [redesignated Pickens County in 1868] on 6 Nov 1862[1], and died in Charleston, SC on 30 Nov 1942. He married Julia Porcher BLAKE, daughter of COL Julius A. and Julia (Lewis) Blake in Charleston, SC on 20 Oct 1890.[1] She was born in Charleston, SC on 7 Nov 1867[1], and died there on 18 Jan 1953. Children:

+ 529   i   Arthur MIDDLETON, b. 23 Aug 1897
   530   ii   Charles Haskell MIDDLETON, b. 19 Oct 1899, dy 15 Feb 1900
+ 531   iii   Julius Blake MIDDLETON, b. 9 Nov 1900
+ 532   iv   William MIDDLETON, b. 8 Oct 1902
+ 533   v   Julia Porcher MIDDLETON, b. 27 Dec 1905
+ 534   vi   Robert Cuthbert MIDDLETON, b. 14 Sep 1907
+ 535   vii   Lewis Blake MIDDLETON, b. 9 Dec 1909

References:
[1] DSDI Appl # 1772.

260. LUCY IZARD MIDDLETON[5] (Arthur Middleton[4], Margaret Emma Izard[3], Emma Philadelphia Middleton[2], Arthur Middleton[1]) child of Arthur Middleton and Julia Emma Rhett was born on 14 Sep 1866[1], and died on 16 Dec 1954. She married William Wilson MUNNERLYN on 24 May 1898.[1] He was born on 8 Mar 1869[1], and died on 20 Mar 1921. Children:
   536   i   Lucy Middleton MUNNERLYN, b. 16 Feb 1899, d. 2 Sep 1926; unm
+ 537   ii   Benjamin MUNNERLYN, b. 16 Sep 1901

References:
[1] Data from Middleton Place Foundation.

262. HELEN MIDDLETON[5] (Arthur Middleton[4], Margaret Emma Izard[3], Emma Philadelphia Middleton[2], Arthur Middleton[1]) child of Arthur Middleton and Julia Emma Rhett was born on 2 Jul 1872.[1] She married Theodore DEHON, Jr. on 8 Feb 1893.[1] He was born on 11 Feb 1871.[1] Children:
   538   i   Julia Middleton DEHON, b. 27 Nov 1893; unm
   539   ii   Helen DEHON, b. 30 Apr 1897, dy 9 Sep 1898
+ 540   iii   Anna Bertha DEHON, b. 17 Feb 1899
   541   iv   Alice Ford DEHON, b. c. 1900
+ 542   v   Eva Russell DEHON, b. c. 1902
+ 543   vi   Charlotte DEHON, b. c. 1905
+ 544   vii   Arthur Middleton DEHON, b. c. 1907
+ 545   viii   Mary DEHON, b. c. 1910

References:
[1] Data from Middleton Place Foundation.

263. WALTER IZARD MIDDLETON[5] (Arthur Middleton[4], Margaret Emma Izard[3], Emma Philadelphia Middleton[2], Arthur Middleton[1]) child of

Arthur Middleton and Julia Emma Rhett was born on 12 Sep 1874[1], and died on 14 Jan 1921. He married Mary Brown BRIDGE on 1 Jun 1898.[1] She was born on 30 Aug 1876[1], and died on 1 Oct 1951. Children:

        546   i   Walter Izard MIDDLETON, b. 25 Jul 1899
+   547   ii   Miriam Bridge MIDDLETON, b. 12 Apr 1902
        548   iii Margaret Izard MIDDLETON, b. 5 Sep 1904
        549   iv   Mary Brown MIDDLETON, b. 5 Sep 1906

References:
[1] Data from Middleton Place Foundation.

272. FLORENCE VERNON BLAKE[5] (Arthur Middleton Blake[4], Daniel Blake[3], Anna Louisa Middleton[2], Arthur Middleton[1]) child of Arthur Middleton Blake and Talulah Hazeltine Catherine Maxwell was born in Calhoun County, GA on 26 Aug 1893[1], and died in Ft. Worth, TX on 1 Nov 1979. She married William Bell HOFFMAN in Coleman, TX in say 1915. He was born in Bellville, TX on 19 Dec 1884[1], and died in Temple, TX on 14 Jan 1953. Child:

+   550   i   Willie Maxine HOFFMAN, b. 4 Jan 1923

References:
[1] DSDI Appl # 2171.

275. ALICE RUTLEDGE[5] (Emma Craig Blake[4], Daniel Blake[3], Anna Louisa Middleton[2], Arthur Middleton[1]) child of Emma Craig Blake and Benjamin Huger Rutledge was born in 1899.[1] She married Edward TILLMAN in say 1920. Child:

+   551   i   Alice TILLMAN, b. c. 1922

References:
[1] Data from Middleton Place Foundation.

276. BENJAMIN HUGER RUTLEDGE[5] (Emma Craig Blake[4], Daniel Blake[3], Anna Louisa Middleton[2], Arthur Middleton[1]) child of Emma Craig Blake and Benjamin Huger Rutledge was born in 1902. He married Eleanor OLIVER in say 1927. Child:

+   552   i   Eleanor Oliver RUTLEDGE, b. 1930

277. AMELIA Van CORTLANDT RUTLEDGE[5] (Emma Craig Blake[4], Daniel Blake[3], Anna Louisa Middleton[2], Arthur Middleton[1]) child of Emma Craig Blake and Benjamin Huger Rutledge was born in 1904. She married Asa DAVIS in say 1925. Children:

+   553   i   Asa DAVIS, Jr., b. c. 1928
        554   ii   Eleanor DAVIS, b. c. 1932

278. SUSAN MIDDLETON RUTLEDGE[5] (Emma Craig Blake[4], Daniel Blake[3], Anna Louisa Middleton[2], Arthur Middleton[1]) child of Emma Craig Blake and Benjamin Huger Rutledge was born in 1906. She married Benjamin Allston MOORE in 1929. He was born in 1900. Child:

+ 555   i   Benjamin Allston MOORE, Jr., b. 1930

279. ANNE BLAKE RUTLEDGE[5] (Emma Craig Blake[4], Daniel Blake[3], Anna Louisa Middleton[2], Arthur Middleton[1]) child of Emma Craig Blake and Benjamin Huger Rutledge was born in 1910. She married Albert MOORE in say 1932. Children:

+ 556   i   Emma MOORE, b. c. 1935
   557   ii   Adele MOORE, b. c. 1938

281. FRANCES BAYLEY BLAKE RUTLEDGE[5] (Helen Bayley Blake[4], Daniel Blake[3], Anna Louisa Middleton[2], Arthur Middleton[1]) child of Helen Bayley Blake and Oliver Middleton Rutledge was born in 1895[1], and died in 1954. She married Theophilus Parker CHESHIRE in say 1922. Children:

+ 558   i   Frances CHESHIRE, b. 1924
+ 559   ii   John Rutledge CHESHIRE, b. 1925
+ 560   iii   Katherine Blount CHESHIRE, b. 1928

References:
[1] Data from Middleton Place Foundation.

282. OLIVER MIDDLETON RUTLEDGE[5] (Helen Bayley Blake[4], Daniel Blake[3], Anna Louisa Middleton[2], Arthur Middleton[1]) child of Helen Bayley Blake and Oliver Middleton Rutledge was born in 1900. He married Clementina KOHN in say 1924. Child:

+ 561   i   Clementina RUTLEDGE, b. c. 1927

283. ELISE RUTLEDGE[5] (Helen Bayley Blake[4], Daniel Blake[3], Anna Louisa Middleton[2], Arthur Middleton[1]) child of Helen Bayley Blake and Oliver Middleton Rutledge was born in 1903. She married Channing SWAN in 1927. He was born in 1898.[1] Children:

+ 562   i   Helen Blake Rutledge SWAN, b. 1928
+ 563   ii   Josephine Cutter SWAN, b. 1930
+ 564   iii   Elizabeth Middleton Rutledge SWAN, b. c. 1933

284. DOROTHEA BARCLAY RUTLEDGE[5] (Helen Bayley Blake[4], Daniel Blake[3], Anna Louisa Middleton[2], Arthur Middleton[1]) child of Helen Bayley Blake and Oliver Middleton Rutledge was born in 1905. She married Overton PRICE in say 1925. Children:

+ 565   i   Overton PRICE, Jr., b. c. 1928
+ 566   ii   Alice PRICE, b. c. 1931

288. ARTHUR MIDDLETON MANIGAULT[5] (Mary Proctor Huger[4], Daniel Elliott Huger[3], Isabella Johannes Middleton[2], Arthur Middleton[1]) child of Mary Proctor Huger and Arthur Middleton Manigault was born in Charleston, SC on 30 Jul 1851.[1] He married Harriott Kinloch SMITH, daughter of John Julius Pringle and Elizabeth (Middleton) Smith on 30 Mar 1891.[1] She was born in Charleston, SC on 15 Oct 1855.[1] Children:

+ 567   i   Caroline MANIGAULT, b. 5 Apr 1892
   568   ii   Arthur Middleton MANIGAULT, b. 17 Oct 1893
+ 569   iii   Edward MANIGAULT, b. 1896
   570   iv   Robert Smith MANIGAULT, b. c. 1900, d. 1945; dsp

References:
[1] Leach MSS, p. 6227.

294. DANIEL ELLIOTT HUGER[5] (William Elliott Huger[4], Daniel Elliott Huger[3], Isabella Johannes Middleton[2], Arthur Middleton[1]) child of William Elliott Huger and Elizabeth Pringle Smith was born in Charleston, SC on 8 Nov 1871.[1] He married Louisa S. CHISOLM in 1900. Child:

+ 571   i   Daniel Elliott HUGER, Jr., b. c. 1903

References:
[1] Leach MSS, p. 6226.

299. ALWERA HUGER[5] (Richard Proctor Huger[4], Daniel Elliott Huger[3], Isabella Johannes Middleton[2], Arthur Middleton[1]) child of Richard Proctor Huger and his 2nd wife Eliza Alwera Noble was born in Anniston, AL on 4 Jul 1885[1], and died in Anniston, AL on 14 Nov 1913. She married Edward Ennis ROBERTS on 28 Dec 1912. He was born in Anniston, AL on 27 Sep 1884.[1] Child:

   572   i   Edward Huger ROBERTS, b. 4 Nov 1913

References:
[1] DSDI Appl # 1190.

303. JOSEPH PROCTOR HUGER[5] (Richard Proctor Huger[4], Daniel Elliott Huger[3], Isabella Johannes Middleton[2], Arthur Middleton[1]) child of Richard Proctor Huger and his 2nd wife Eliza Alwera Noble was born in Anniston, AL on 25 Oct 1891[1], and died in Wilmington, DE on 22 Feb 1930. He married Florine DOUGLAS in Anniston, AL on 15 Jul 1914. She was born in Anniston, AL on 1 Oct 1891.[1] Children:

   573   i   Florine Douglas HUGER, b. 28 Sep 1916
   574   ii   Ruth Noble HUGER, b. 16 Aug 1920

References:
[1] DSDI Appl # 1199.

304. STEPHEN PROCTOR HUGER[5] (Richard Proctor Huger[4], Daniel Elliott Huger[3], Isabella Johannes Middleton[2], Arthur Middleton[1]) child of Richard Proctor Huger and his 2nd wife Eliza Alwera Noble was born in Anniston, AL on 30 May 1894[1], and died in Anniston, AL on 27 Aug 1950. He married Mary Willard HALL in Dothan, AL on 28 Nov 1925. She was born in Geneva, AL on 13 Mar 1898[1], and died in Anniston, AL on 19 Jun 1958. Child:

    575   i   Eliza Alwera HUGER, b. 14 Oct 1927
References:
[1] DSDI Appl # 1229.

310. ELOSIE HUGER[5] (Daniel Elliott Huger[4], John Izard Huger[3], Isabella Johannes Middleton[2], Arthur Middleton[1]) child of Daniel Elliott Huger and Harriet Withers was born on 11 Apr 1864.[1] She married Cleland Kinloch SMITH in 1895.[1] Child:

    576   i   Harriet SMITH, b. c. 1897
References:
[1] Data from Middleton Place Foundation.

313. ALLEN DEAS HUGER WARLEY[5] (Isabella Johannes Middleton Huger[4], John Izard Huger[3], Isabella Johannes Middleton[2], Arthur Middleton[1]) child of Isabella Johannes Middleton Huger and Alexander Fraser Warley was born in Pendleton, SC on 4 Aug 1864.[1] He married Helen Elmore RUNDLE, daughter of Samuel Elmore and Helen (Toulmin) Rundle on 30 Jan 1890.[1] She was born in New Orleans, LA on 25 Dec 1868.[1] Children:

    577   i   Helen Toulmin WARLEY, b. 27 Nov 1890
    578   ii   Deas Huger WARLEY, b. 31 Jan 1893
References:
[1] Leach MSS, p. 6230.

329. CAROLINE HAMPTON LOWNDES[5] (Rawlins Lowndes[4], Sabina Elliott Huger[3], Isabella Johannes Middleton[2], Arthur Middleton[1]) child of Rawlins Lowndes and Sarah Buchanan Preston was born in Charleston, SC on 12 Nov 1872[1], and died in 1963. She married Lane MULLALLY in Charleston, SC on 6 Nov 1894.[1] He was born in Pendleton, SC on 12 Mar 1867[1], and died in Charleston, SC on 23 Mar 1920. Children:

    579   i   Charles Lowndes MULLALLY, b. 1897
 + 580   ii   Caroline Hampton MULLALLY, b. 9 Jul 1903
References:
[1] DSDI Appl # 378.

330. MAY SABINA LOWNDES SCOTT[5] (Emma Middleton Huger Lowndes[4], Sabina Elliott Huger[3], Isabella Johannes Middleton[2], Arthur Middleton[1]) child of Emma Middleton Huger Lowndes and James Munroe Scott was born in Charleston, SC on 1 May 1880.[1] She married Joseph Brackin TATE in Asheville, NC on 24 Apr 1909. He was born in Mountain Island, NC on 13 Jun 1882[1], and died in Asheville, NC on 3 Jun 1924. Child:

    581   i   Charles Lowndes TATE, b. 30 Sep 1914

References:
[1] DSDI Appl # 770.

331. ELIZA MACKAY HUGER[5] (Joseph Alston Huger, Jr.[4], Joseph Alston Huger[3], Isabella Johannes Middleton[2], Arthur Middleton[1]) child of Joseph Alston Huger, Jr. and Mary Stiles Elliott was born in Savannah, GA on 30 Aug 1875[1], and died in 1952. She married Robert Clifford HARRISON in say 1901. Children:

    582   i   Joseph H. HARRISON, b. c. 1903
    583   ii   Child HARRISON, b. c. 1906

References:
[1] Data from Middleton Place Foundation.

333. EMMA MIDDLETON IZARD HUGER[5] (Joseph Alston Huger, Jr.[4], Joseph Alston Huger[3], Isabella Johannes Middleton[2], Arthur Middleton[1]) child of Joseph Alston Huger, Jr. and Mary Stiles Elliott was born in Savannah, GA on 19 Oct 1879[1], and died in Savannah, GA on 26 Oct 1956. She married David Crenshaw BARROW in Savannah, GA on 10 Dec 1907. He was born in Oglethorpe County, GA on 6 Jun 1874[1], and died in Savannah, GA on 25 Sep 1949. Children:

+   584   i   Middleton Pope BARROW, b. 31 Dec 1909
    585   ii   Mary BARROW, b. c. 1912
    586   iii   David Crenshaw BARROW, Jr., b. c. 1915
    587   iv   Arthur E. BARROW, b. c. 1919

References:
[1] DSDI Appl # 2487.

335. CLERMONT KINLOCH HUGER[5] (Joseph Alston Huger, Jr.[4], Joseph Alston Huger[3], Isabella Johannes Middleton[2], Arthur Middleton[1]) child of Joseph Alston Huger, Jr. and Mary Stiles Elliott was born in Savannah, GA on 19 Apr 1883[1], and died in Savannah, GA on 21 Jan 1962. She married Lawrence LEE in Savannah, GA on 10 Nov 1910. He was born in Charles-

ton, SC on 3 Mar 1880[1], and died in Savannah, GA on 11 Jan 1953.
Children:
   588   i Clermont LEE, b. 1914; unm
+ 589   ii Lawrence LEE, Jr., b. 16 Aug 1915
   590   iii James Moultrie LEE, b. c. 1917
References:
[1] DSDI Appl # 2480.

337. DANIEL ELLIOTT HUGER[5] (Lynch Prioleau Huger[4], Joseph Alston
Huger[3], Isabella Johannes Middleton[2], Arthur Middleton[1]) child of Lynch
Prioleau Huger and Emily Keese Bailey was born in NYC on 31 Jul 1897.[1]
He married Elizabeth KRESS in NYC on 25 Nov 1927. She was born in
Atlanta, GA on 27 Nov 1903. Children:
   591   i Daniel Elliott HUGER, Jr., b. 23 Sep 1928
   592   ii Beatrice Kress HUGER, b. 2 Mar 1930
References:
[1] SAR Appl # 57486 & DSDI Appl # 524.

338. JOHN BARNWELL ELLIOTT, Jr.[5] (Harriet Lucas Pinckney Huger[4],
Joseph Alston Huger[3], Isabella Johannes Middleton[2], Arthur Middleton[1])
child of Harriet Lucas Pinckney Huger and John Barnwell Elliott was born
on 30 Oct 1870.[1] He married Noel Elizabeth FORSYTHE in say 1894.
Children:
   593   i Douglas F. ELLIOTT, b. c. 1896
   594   ii Sarah Rice ELLIOTT, b. c. 1898
References:
[1] Data from Middleton Place Foundation.

344. LUCY PINCKNEY ELLIOTT[5] (Harriet Lucas Pinckney Huger[4],
Joseph Alston Huger[3], Isabella Johannes Middleton[2], Arthur Middleton[1])
child of Harriet Lucas Pinckney Huger and John Barnwell Elliott was born
on 24 Jan 1885.[1] She married Warren W. CUNNINGHAM in say 1913.
Children:
   595   i William W. CUNNINGHAM, b. c. 1915
   596   ii Esther E. CUNNINGHAM, b. c. 1917
   597   iii Charles CUNNINGHAM, b. c. 1920
References:
[1] Data from Middleton Place Foundation.

351. JAMES WILKINSON JERVEY[5] (Isabella Middleton Wilkinson[4],
Sarah Elliott Huger[3], Isabella Johannes Middleton[2], Arthur Middleton[1]) child
of Isabella Middleton Wilkinson and Eugene Postell Jervey was born in

Charleston, SC on 19 Oct 1874[1], and died in Charleston, SC on 15 Nov 1945. He married Helen Doremus SMITH in Charleston, SC on 26 Oct 1899.[1] She was born in Charleston, SC on 29 Feb 1876[1], and died in Greenville, SC on 24 Feb 1936. Children:

+   598   i   James Wilkinson JERVEY, Jr., b. 19 Feb 1901
    599   ii   Helen JERVEY, b. 1902
References:
[1] SAR Appl # 88948.

362. MARIA LOUISA WILKINSON BARNWELL[5] (Maria Louisa Wilkinson[4], Sarah Elliott Huger[3], Isabella Johannes Middleton[2], Arthur Middleton[1]) child of Maria Louisa Wilkinson and Arthur Barnwell was born in 1876[1], and died in 1961. She married Macmillan Campbell KING in 1901. He was born in 1873[1], and died in 1951. Child:

+   600   i   Marguerite Barnwell KING, b. 1903
References:
[1] Data from Middleton Place Foundation.

364. MARIE LOUISE BARNWELL[5] (Maria Louisa Wilkinson[4], Sarah Elliott Huger[3], Isabella Johannes Middleton[2], Arthur Middleton[1]) child of Maria Louisa Wilkinson and Arthur Barnwell was born in 1879[1], and died in 1965. She married Arthur Bright MARSTON in 1908. He was born in 1885[1], and died in 1961. Child:

+   601   i   Arthur Bright MARSTON, Jr., b. 16 Feb 1909
References:
[1] Data from Middleton Place Foundation.

371. WILLIAM MASON SMITH[5] (Daniel Elliott Huger Smith[4], Eliza Caroline Middleton Huger[3], Isabella Johannes Middleton[2], Arthur Middleton[1]) child of Daniel Elliott Huger Smith and Caroline Ravenel Ravenel was born on 15 Nov 1874.[1] He married Mary A. SWAN in 1906. Children:

    602   i   Caroline SMITH, b. 1907, d. 1983; unm
    603   ii   Eleanor SMITH, b. 1909, d. 1999; dsp
+   604   iii William Mason SMITH, III, b. 1910
References:
[1] Data from Middleton Place Foundation.

375. ELIZA HUGER WELLS[5] (Anna Elizabeth Mason Smith[4], Eliza Caroline Middleton Huger[3], Isabella Johannes Middleton[2], Arthur Middleton[1]) child of Anna Elizabeth Mason Smith and Edward Laight Wells was born on 18 Aug 1872.[1] She married Edward RUTLEDGE in 1906. He was born in 1870[1], and died in 1942. Children:

605   i   Anna Wells RUTLEDGE, b. c. 1907
606   ii   Ella Middleton RUTLEDGE, b. 1909
607   iii   Eliza Huger RUTLEDGE, b. 1911
References:
[1] Data from Middleton Place Foundation.

379. MATTHEW TURNER[5] (Emma Philadelphia Middleton Rutledge[4], Henry Adolphus Rutledge[3], Septima Sexta Middleton[2], Arthur Middleton[1]) child of Emma Philadelphia Middleton Rutledge and Edwin Chiledes Turner was born in Marion County, TN on 24 May 1854.[1] He married Jane Scales CARPENTER, daughter of Charles Kendrick and Jane Emeline (Miller) Carpenter on 20 Nov 1877.[1] She was born in Talladega County, AL on 17 Jan 1854.[1] Children:
608   i   Emma Philadelphia Middleton TURNER, b. 12 Aug 1878
609   ii   Henrietta TURNER, b. 7 May 1883
610   iii   Jannie Belle TURNER, b. 17 Jan 1886
References:
[1] Leach MSS, p. 6237.

380. EMMA CAROLINE TURNER[5] (Emma Philadelphia Middleton Rutledge[4], Henry Adolphus Rutledge[3], Septima Sexta Middleton[2], Arthur Middleton[1]) child of Emma Philadelphia Middleton Rutledge and Edwin Chiledes Turner was born in Talladega County, AL on 9 Sep 1855.[1] She married John Thaddeus DONALDSON, son of Nimrod and Sallie Reid (McCullough) Donalson on 4 Feb 1875.[1] He was born in Greenville, SC on 20 Aug 1842.[1] Children:
611   i   Sallie Serresa DONALDSON, b. 18 Jun 1876
612   ii   Henry Rutledge DONALDSON, b. 13 Jul 1878
613   iii   Mana Lieze [sic] DONALDSON, b. 12 Aug 1881
614   iv   Hattie Louisa DONALDSON, b. 12 Aug 1884
615   v   John Arthur DONALDSON, b. 14 Feb 1887, dy 15 Jun 1887 [twin]
616   vi   James Quinton DONALDSON, b. 14 Feb 1887, dy 4 Jun 1887 [twin]
617   vii   Milton Levon DONALDSON, b. 18 Oct 1888
618   viii   Caspar Boyce DONALDSON, b. 23 Jul 1892, dy 24 Aug 1892
References:
[1] Leach MSS, p. 6238.

381. EDWIN CHILEDES TURNER, Jr.[5] (Emma Philadelphia Middleton Rutledge[4], Henry Adolphus Rutledge[3], Septima Sexta Middleton[2], Arthur

Middleton[1]) child of Emma Philadelphia Middleton Rutledge and Edwin Chiledes Turner was born in Talladega County, AL on 20 Mar 1857, and died in Talladega County, AL on 30 Dec 1884.[1] He married Emily BEAVERS on 21 Feb 1877.[1] She was born in St. Clair County, AL on 16 Jul 1861.[1] Children:

    619   i   Henry Adolphus TURNER, b. 5 Aug 1880
    620   ii Eddie Caroline TURNER, b. 5 Feb 1883

References:
[1] Leach MSS, p. 6239.

382. MARY ANN ELIZA TURNER[5] (Emma Philadelphia Middleton Rutledge[4], Henry Adolphus Rutledge[3], Septima Sexta Middleton[2], Arthur Middleton[1]) child of Emma Philadelphia Middleton Rutledge and Edwin Chiledes Turner was born in Talladega County, AL on 5 Dec 1859.[1] She married John Reed CUNNINGHAM, son of Joseph Christopher and Martha Roby (McClellan) Cunningham on 22 Nov 1877.[1] He was born in Talladega County, AL on 15 May 1856.[1] Children:

    621   i   Frank McClellan CUNNINGHAM, b. 12 Sep 1878, dy 23 Jan 1883
    622   ii Septima Rutledge CUNNINGHAM, b. 31 Aug 1880
    623 iii Emma CUNNINGHAM, b. 20 Feb 1883
    624 iv Lide [sic] CUNNINGHAM, b. 21 Sep 1885
    625   v Joseph Christopher CUNNINGHAM, b. 6 Feb 1891

References:
[1] Leach MSS, p. 6239.

386. JACOB FORNEY[5] (Septima Sexta Middleton Rutledge[4], Henry Adolphus Rutledge[3], Septima Sexta Middleton[2], Arthur Middleton[1]) child of Septima Sexta Middleton Rutledge and John Horace Forney was born in Jacksonville, AL on 8 Oct 1868[1], and died in Springville, AL on 24 Dec 1902. He married Roberta McLAUGHLIN in Springville, AL on 7 Jun 1899.[1] She was born in Springville, AL on 27 Mar 1877.[1] Children:

    626   i   Caroline FORNEY, b. 25 Mar 1900
+ 627   ii John McLaughlin FORNEY, b. 19 Oct 1901

References:
[1] DSDI Appl # 1060.

388. SABINA SWOPE FORNEY[5] (Septima Sexta Middleton Rutledge[4], Henry Adolphus Rutledge[3], Septima Sexta Middleton[2], Arthur Middleton[1]) child of Septima Sexta Middleton Rutledge and John Horace Forney was born in Jacksonville, AL on 6 Aug 1873.[1] She married Macon Abernathy STEVENSON in Jacksonville, AL on 16 Feb 1898.[1] He was born in

Jacksonville, AL on 1 Nov 1867[1], and died in Anniston, AL on 14 Jan 1951. Children:

628   i   John Forney STEVENSON, b. 6 Oct 1899
+ 629   ii   Horace Lee STEVENSON, b. 11 Jan 1902
+ 630   iii   Mary Abernathy STEVENSON, b. 30 Dec 1903
631   iv   Eleanor STEVENSON, b. 21 Aug 1905
632   v   Child STEVENSON, b. c. 1907
633   vi   Child STEVENSON, b. c. 1910

References:
[1] DSDI Appl # 1061.

389. ANNIE ROWAN FORNEY[5] (Septima Sexta Middleton Rutledge[4], Henry Adolphus Rutledge[3], Septima Sexta Middleton[2], Arthur Middleton[1]) child of Septima Sexta Middleton Rutledge and John Horace Forney was born in Jacksonville, AL on 1 Jun 1876[1], and died in Jacksonville, AL on 9 Nov 1974. She married Clarence William DAUGETTE in Jacksonville, AL on 22 Dec 1897.[1] He was born in Bell's Landing, AL on 14 Oct 1873[1], and died in Gadsden, AL on 9 Aug 1942. Children:

634   i   Kathleen Forney DAUGETTE, b. 26 Oct 1898
+ 635   ii   Palmer DAUGETTE, b. 10 Jan 1900
+ 636   iii   Clarence William DAUGETTE, Jr., b. 16 Sep 1903
+ 637   iv   Forney Rutledge DAUGETTE, b. 28 Feb 1908
638   v   Rankin Middleton DAUGETTE, b. 16 Sep 1910

References:
[1] DSDI Appl # 1042.

391. EDWARD RUTLEDGE PINCKNEY[5] (Sarah Henrietta Rutledge[4], Henrietta Middletron Rutledge[3], Septima Sexta Middleton[2], Arthur Middleton[1]) child of Sarah Henrietta Rutledge and Charles Cotesworth Pinckney was born in Charleston, SC on 27 Jun 1869[1], and died in 1954. He married Louise CLEVELAND in 1920. Children:

639   i   Sarah PINCKNEY, b. 1924
640   ii   Elise Rutledge PINCKNEY, b. 1925; unm

References:
[1] Leach MSS, p. 6341.

395. FREDERICK RUTLEDGE[5] (Henry Middleton Rutledge[4], Henrietta Middleton Rutledge[3], Septima Sexta Middleton[2], Arthur Middleton[1]) child of Henry Middleton Rutledge and his 1st wife Anna Marie Blake was born in Fletcher, Henderson County, NC on 10 Feb 1868.[1] He married Mable REEVES in 1892.[1] She was born in Oakland, CA in 1876.[1] Children:

+   641   i   Frederick Reeves RUTLEDGE, b. 17 Nov 1895
    642   ii   John RUTLEDGE, b. 1899, dy 1900
    643   iii Reginald Edmund RUTLEDGE, b. 22 Nov 1902
References:
[1] SAR Appl # 56265.

397. HARRIOTT HORRY RUTLEDGE[5] (Henry Middleton Rutledge[4], Henrietta Middleton Rutledge[3], Septima Sexta Middleton[2], Arthur Middleton[1]) child of Henry Middleton Rutledge and his 2nd wife Margaret Hamilton Seabrook was born in "Hampton", Charleston, SC on 8 Feb 1878.[1] She married Paul Hamilton SEABROOK in say 1906. Children:
    644   i   Margaret Hamilton SEABROOK, b. 1909
    645   ii   Harriott SEABROOK, b. 1911
References:
[1] Leach MSS, p. 6341 gives date and place of birth. Edmund B. Stewart very kindly made a Family Tree Program available with data on the spouse and children of this marriage.

398. THOMAS PINCKNEY RUTLEDGE[5] (Henry Middleton Rutledge[4], Henrietta Middleton Rutledge[3], Septima Sexta Middleton[2], Arthur Middleton[1]) child of Henry Middleton Rutledge and his 2nd wife Margaret Hamilton Seabrook was born on 16 Feb 1879[1], and died in 1954. He married Ethel Gary PARROTT in say 1908. She was born in 1879[1], and died in 1961. Child:
+   646   i   Henrietta Middleton RUTLEDGE, b. 1915
References:
[1] Richard Ludwig PAF data.

400. ARCHIBALD HAMILTON RUTLEDGE[5] (Henry Middleton Rutledge[4], Henrietta Middleton Rutledge[3], Septima Sexta Middleton[2], Arthur Middleton[1]) child of Henry Middleton Rutledge and his 2nd wife Margaret Hamilton Seabrook was born in McClellanville, SC on 23 Oct 1883.[1] He married Florence Louise HART in Mercersburg, PA on 19 Dec 1907. She was born in Winchester, VA on 23 Jun 1870[1], and died in Charleston, SC on 9 Jan 1935. Children:
+   647   i   Archibald Hamilton RUTLEDGE, Jr., b. 29 Sep 1908
+   648   ii   Henry Middleton RUTLEDGE, b. 29 Jul 1910
+   649   iii Irving RUTLEDGE, b. c. 1913
References:
[1] DSDI Appl # 1293; 1535.

402. MARY MIDDLETON RUTLEDGE REESE[5] (Emma Fredrika Rutledge[4], Henrietta Middleton Rutledge[3], Septima Sexta Middleton[2], Arthur Middleton[1]) child of Emma Fredrika Rutledge and William Brown Reese was born in Franklin, TN on 20 Apr 1867[1], and died in Montgomery, AL about 1950. She married Benjamin Bosworth SMITH, son of Samuel Bosworth and Caroline Castleman (Bacon) Smith in Nashville, TN on 1 Jun 1892.[1] He was born in Louisville, KY on 16 Jan 1864[1], and died in Montgomery, AL on 13 Jun 1926. Children:

650	i	Benjamin Bosworth SMITH, Jr., b. 20 Mar 1893, d. 28 Dec 1918; unm
+ 651	ii	Elise Rutledge SMITH, b. 4 Dec 1894
+ 652	iii	Carol Castleman SMITH, b. 28 Dec 1897
+ 653	iv	Frederick Rutledge SMITH, b. 7 Jul 1899
654	v	Alice Reese SMITH, b. 7 Sep 1900, d. 9 Jun 1925; unm
655	vi	Mary Middleton SMITH, b. 6 Oct 1906, d. 1965; dsp

References:
[1] Leach MSS, p. 6385, see also Leach MSS, p. 6242.

403. ALICE SOPHIA REESE[5] (Emma Fredrika Rutledge[4], Henrietta Middleton Rutledge[3], Septima Sexta Middleton[2], Arthur Middleton[1]) child of Emma Fredrika Rutledge and William Brown Reese was born in Nashville, TN on 4 Jun 1872[1], and died in 1941. She married Edmund Bellinger FELDER in say 1896. Child:

+ 656	i	Katherine FELDER, b. 24 Dec 1900

References:
[1] Leach MSS, p. 6242.

405. ARTHUR MIDDLETON RUTLEDGE YOUNG[5] (Elizabeth Underwood Rutledge[4], Arthur Middleton Rutledge[3], Septima Sexta Middleton[2], Arthur Middleton[1]) child of Elizabeth Underwood Rutledge and Henry Edward Young was born on 3 Jul 1876.[1] He married Nannie Cabell CONNER on 19 Dec 1907. Children:

657	i	Arthur Middleton YOUNG, b. 8 Aug 1911
658	ii	James Conner YOUNG, b. 6 Mar 1914
659	iii	Joseph Rutledge YOUNG, b. 7 Jun 1916

References:
[1] M. L. Webber, *Dr. John Rutledge and his Descendants*, (South Carolina Historical and Genealogical Magazine, Jan. 1930), p. 103.

408. JOSEPH UNDERWOOD RUTLEDGE YOUNG[5] (Elizabeth Underwood Rutledge[4], Arthur Middleton Rutledge[3], Septima Sexta

Middleton[2], Arthur Middleton[1]) child of Elizabeth Underwood Rutledge and Henry Edward Young was born on 7 Jan 1881.[1] He married Julia Evelyn GRIMKE on 8 Jun 1905. Children:

   660   i   Julia Evelyn YOUNG, b. 28 Feb 1906, dy 17 Feb 1907
   661   ii   Joseph Rutledge YOUNG, b. Sep 1907, dy 26 Sep 1909
   662   iii   Henry Gourdin YOUNG, b. 7 Dec 1909

References:
[1] M. L. Webber, *Dr. John Rutledge and his Descendants*, (South Carolina Historical and Genealogical Magazine, Jan. 1930), p. 103.

410. JOHN JULIUS PRINGLE SMITH[5] (Emma Blake Rutledge[4], Arthur Middleton Rutledge[3], Septima Sexta Middleton[2], Arthur Middleton[1]) child of Emma Blake Rutledge and Henry Augustus Middleton Smith was born on 14 Oct 1887[1], and died on 21 Dec 1969. He married Heningham ELLETT, daughter of Tazewell and Josephine Lyons (Scott) Ellett on 25 Mar 1913. She was born on 25 May 1890[2], and died on 20 Jun 1957. Child:

+ 663   i   Josephine Scott SMITH, b. 24 Dec 1913

References:
[1] M. L. Webber, *Dr. John Rutledge and his Descendants*, (South Carolina Historical and Genealogical Magazine, Jan. 1930), p. 103. [2] Data from Middleton Place Foundation.

SIXTH GENERATION

417. CARLO MASETTI de BAGNAMO[6] (Virginia Middleton[5], Henry Bentivoglio Middleton[4], Arthur Middleton[3], Henry Middleton[2], Arthur Middleton[1]) child of Virginia Middleton and Piero Masetti de Dainella de Bagnamo was born in 1897[1], and died in 1965. He married Daisy FIORINI in say 1923. Children:

+ 664   i   Dainella de BAGNAMO, b. 2 Jul 1925
+ 665   ii   Piera de BAGNAMO, b. 22 Mar 1928

References:
[1] Data from Middleton Place Foundation.

418. MARIA GRAZIA MASETTI de BAGNAMO[6] (Virginia Middleton[5], Henry Bentivoglio Middleton[4], Arthur Middleton[3], Henry Middleton[2], Arthur Middleton[1]) child of Virginia Middleton and Piero Masetti de Dainella de Bagnamo was born in 1901. She married Francesco CASTELBARCO in say 1923. Child:

   666   i   Briano CASTELBARCO, b. 24 Jun 1924

References:
[1] Data from Middleton Place Foundation.

419. HENRY BENTIVOGLIO MIDDLETON[6] (Arthur Giulio Middleton[5], Henry Bentivoglio Middleton[4], Arthur Middleton[3], Henry Middleton[2], Arthur Middleton[1]) child of Arthur Giulio Middleton and Carolina Respigliosa was born on 14 Dec 1923. He married Payne Whitney PAYSON in 1957. Children:

  667   i   Julia MIDDLETON, b. 17 Aug 1958
  668   ii   Laurinda Payson MIDDLETON, b. 14 May 1960
  669   iii   Alison Hay MIDDLETON, b. 21 Jan 1968

421. OLIVER MIDDLETON READ, Jr.[6] (Oliver Middleton Read[5], Mary Julia Middleton[4], Oliver Hering Middleton[3], Henry Middleton[2], Arthur Middleton[1]) child of Oliver Middleton Read and his 1st wife Mary Louise Gregorie was born on 12 Jan 1889[1], and died in 1972. He married Constance SEARS in 1918. Children:

  670   i   Mary Louise READ, b. c. 1920
  671   ii   Oliver Middleton READ, III, b. c. 1923

References:
[1] Data from Middleton Place Foundation.

422. ELIZA BAKER READ[6] (Oliver Middleton Read[5], Mary Julia Middleton[4], Oliver Hering Middleton[3], Henry Middleton[2], Arthur Middleton[1]) child of Oliver Middleton Read and his 1st wife Mary Louise Gregorie was born on 3 Jun 1890.[1] She married Walter MANGUM in 1912. Child:

 + 672   i   Anne MANGUM, b. c. 1915

426. ELIZABETH MIDDLETON READ[6] (Benjamin Huger Read[5], Mary Julia Middleton[4], Oliver Hering Middleton[3], Henry Middleton[2], Arthur Middleton[1]) child of Benjamin Huger Read and Anne Cleland Smith was born in Baltimore, MD on 31 Aug 1885[1], and died in Joppa, Harford County, MD on 27 Jun 1952. She married Thomas Francis CADWALADER [see sketch # 224], son of John and Mary Helen (Fisher) Cadwalader in Baltimore, MD on 23 Nov 1911. He was born in Philadelphia, PA on 22 Sep 1880[1], and died in Joppa, MD on 24 Feb 1970. Children are as reported under Sketch # 224.

References:
[1] DSDI Appl # 2263.

433. ELIZA MIDDLETON FOX[6] (Emily Anne Read[5], Mary Julia Middleton[4], Oliver Hering Middleton[3], Henry Middleton[2], Arthur Middleton[1]) child of Emily Anne Read and Joseph Mickle Fox was born in Philadelphia, PA on 23 Feb 1890[1], and died in Philadelphia, PA on 24 Apr 1961. She married Benjamin Chew TILGHMAM, III in Philadelphia, PA on 23 Jun

1916. He was born in London, ENGLAND on 16 Jan 1890[1], and died in Hamilton, BERMUDA on 6 Oct 1953. Child:

+ 673   i   Richard Albert TILGHMAN, b. 8 Mar 1920
References:
[1] DSDI Appl # 2351.

438. AYLIFFE B. BLAKE[6] (Edmund Molyneux Blake[5], Olivia Middleton[4], Oliver Hering Middleton[3], Henry Middleton[2], Arthur Middleton[1]) child of Edmund Molyneux Blake and Eleanor Farley was born about 1896.[1] She married Nicholas Van Slyck MUMFORD in say 1916. Children:

+ 674   i   Eleanor MUMFORD, b. 1919
+ 675   ii Nicholas Van Slyck MUMFORD, Jr., b. 1925
References:
[1] Data from Middleton Place Foundation.

439. OLIVIA MIDDLETON BLAKE[6] (Edmund Molyneux Blake[5], Olivia Middleton[4], Oliver Hering Middleton[3], Henry Middleton[2], Arthur Middleton[1]) child of Edmund Molyneux Blake and Eleanor Farley was born about 1898[1], and died in 1977. She married Daniel Dee PULLEN in say 1920. He was born in 1885[1], and died in 1923. Child:

+ 676   i   Harriet Stuart PULLEN, b. 1922
References:
[1] Data from Middleton Place Foundation.

440. DANIEL BLAKE[6] (Daniel Blake[5], Olivia Middleton[4], Oliver Hering Middleton[3], Henry Middleton[2], Arthur Middleton[1]) child of Daniel Blake and Mary Scott Perry was born in 1902[1], and died in 1986. He married Katharine Brooks SHANNON in 1926. She was born in 1900. Children:

+ 677   i   Katharine Shannon BLAKE, b. 1927
+ 678   ii Daniel BLAKE, b. 1931
References:
[1] Data from Middleton Place Foundation.

445. SHIRLEY MIDDLETON[6] (Henry Middleton[5], Henry Middleton[4], Williams Middleton[3], Henry Middleton[2], Arthur Middleton[1]) child of Henry Middleton and Eva Cameron was born on 13 Oct 1928, and died in 1989. She married William John HENDRY on 26 Jan 1952. He was born on 8 Jul 1923. Children:

+ 679   i   Shirleigh HENDRY, b. 3 Oct 1954
   680   ii Alison HENDRY, b. 31 Aug 1961; sp

448. MARY MIDDLETON[6] (Algernon Manfred Middleton[5], Henry Middleton[4], Williams Middleton[3], Henry Middleton[2], Arthur Middleton[1]) child of Algernon Manfred Middleton and Elise Sims was born on 21 Oct 1925, and died on 5 Nov 1998. She married Kenneth E. MARTIN in say 1950. Children:

  681   i   Kenneth MARTIN, Jr., b. c. 1952
  682   ii Gillian MARTIN, b. c. 1955

456. MARION BARBARA DOROTHY COUSENS[6] (Dorothy Emma Middleton[5], Henry Middleton[4], Williams Middleton[3], Henry Middleton[2], Arthur Middleton[1]) child of Dorothy Emma Middleton and Gordon Bryce Seymour Cousens was born on 27 Aug 1926. She married Keith Joseph DUNCAN on 11 Sep 1948. He was born on 27 Jan 1927. Children:

+ 683   i   Janet Elizabeth DUNCAN, b. 18 Jun 1950
  684   ii   Gregory Keith DUNCAN, b. 21 Nov 1951
+ 685   iii Ellen Barbara DUNCAN, b. 1 Nov 1953
+ 686   iv   Maureen Patricia DUNCAN, b. 25 Aug 1955
+ 687   v   Kelly Jeanne DUNCAN, b. 7 Jan 1958

457. PAMELA HELEN MARGARET COUSENS[6] (Dorothy Emma Middleton[5], Henry Middleton[4], Williams Middleton[3], Henry Middleton[2], Arthur Middleton[1]) child of Dorothy Emma Middleton and Gordon Bryce Seymour Cousens was born on 28 Dec 1927. She married Edward Sinclair RUTTER on 6 May 1950. He was born on 6 Apr 1926. Children:

+ 688   i   Diane Elaine RUTTER, b. 5 Apr 1951
+ 689   ii   Brian Edward RUTTER, b. 15 Mar 1953
+ 690   iii Joanne Barbara RUTTER, b. 4 Jun 1954
+ 691   iv   Bryce George RUTTER, b. 4 Jan 1957
+ 692   v   Pamela Ann RUTTER, b. 8 May 1960
  693   vi   Sandra Lee RUTTER, b. 29 Jun 1963 [twin]
  694   vii Susan Lynn RUTTER, b. 29 Jun 1963 [twin]

458. GEORGE EDWARD HEATLY COUSENS[6] (Dorothy Emma Middleton[5], Henry Middleton[4], Williams Middleton[3], Henry Middleton[2], Arthur Middleton[1]) child of Dorothy Emma Middleton and Gordon Bryce Seymour Cousens was born on 22 Apr 1929. He married Joan Elizabeth MACON on 28 Jun 1958. She was born on 18 Apr 1935. Children:

+ 695   i   Geoffrey Gordon Henry COUSENS, b. 4 Aug 1961
  696   ii   David Colin Allan COUSENS, b. 25 Jul 1963
  697   iii John George Edward COUSENS, b. 8 Nov 1967
  698   iv   Jennifer Joan Elizabeth COUSENS, b. 13 Jun 1972

459. COLIN ARTHUR MIDDLETON COUSENS[6] (Dorothy Emma Middleton[5], Henry Middleton[4], Williams Middleton[3], Henry Middleton[2], Arthur Middleton[1]) child of Dorothy Emma Middleton and Gordon Bryce Seymour Cousens was born on 22 Mar 1930. He married Emelia Bernadette NAULT on 24 Oct 1953. She was born on 4 Jun 1935. Children:

+ 699   i   George Robert COUSENS, b. 1 Jan 1955
+ 700   ii Dianne Bernadette COUSENS, b. 8 Apr 1956
+ 701   iii Donald Gordon COUSENS, b. 8 Dec 1957
+ 702   iv Douglas Victor COUSENS, b. 25 Jan 1962

460. RONALD DAVID MIDDLETON[6] (Ronald Williams Middleton[5], Henry Middleton[4], Williams Middleton[3], Henry Middleton[2], Arthur Middleton[1]) child of Ronald Williams Middleton and Elise Mary Hawkins was born on 30 Apr 1932. He married (1st) Ann Elizabeth HUGHES in say 1956. She was born on 4 Aug 1929, and died on 27 Jun 1976. Children:

+ 703   i   Jean Elizabeth Philippa MIDDLETON, b. 2 May 1959
+ 704   ii Alison Patricia Sian MIDDLETON, b. 19 Feb 1961
  705   iii Judith Ann MIDDLETON, b. 2 May 1963

461. JEAN PATRICIA MIDDLETON[6] (Ronald Williams Middleton[5], Henry Middleton[4], Williams Middleton[3], Henry Middleton[2], Arthur Middleton[1]) child of Ronald Williams Middleton and Elise Mary Hawkins was born on 17 Mar 1934. She married Leo Patrick SULLIVAN in say 1955. Child:

  706   i   Anthony John SULLIVAN, b. 10 Jan 1957

462. PAUL FREDERICK MIDDLETON[6] (Basil Bernard Norman Middleton[5], Henry Middleton[4], Williams Middleton[3], Henry Middleton[2], Arthur Middleton[1]) child of Basil Bernard Norman Middleton and Evelyn Wood was born on 6 Jun 1932. He married Audrey Margaret BORRELL on 15 Feb 1958. Children:

  707   i   Adrian Paul Borrell MIDDLETON, b. 22 Apr 1962
  708   ii Sarah Lee MIDDLETON, b. 23 Mar 1964

463. ANTHONY HUGH MIDDLETON[6] (Basil Bernard Norman Middleton[5], Henry Middleton[4], Williams Middleton[3], Henry Middleton[2], Arthur Middleton[1]) child of Basil Bernard Norman Middleton and Evelyn Wood was born on 30 Jun 1933. He married Elizabeth Mary NUTMAN in say 1959. Children:

+ 709   i   Deborah Rose MIDDLETON, b. 6 Aug 1961
+ 710   ii Petrea Mary MIDDLETON, b. 26 May 1963
  711   iii Bernard Robin Neil MIDDLETON, b. 18 Sep 1965

464. BRIAN NEIL MIDDLETON[6] (Basil Bernard Norman Middleton[5], Henry Middleton[4], Williams Middleton[3], Henry Middleton[2], Arthur Middleton[1]) child of Basil Bernard Norman Middleton and Evelyn Wood was born on 30 Jun 1933. He married (1st) Doreen BATES in say 1957. He married (2nd) Claire VEETCH in say 1964.
Child by first marriage:
712   i   Nicholas MIDDLETON, b. c. 1959
Child by second marriage:
713   ii Brian Clive MIDDLETON, b. 19 Feb 1966

465. IAN KEITH MIDDLETON[6] (Basil Bernard Norman Middleton[5], Henry Middleton[4], Williams Middleton[3], Henry Middleton[2], Arthur Middleton[1]) child of Basil Bernard Norman Middleton and Evelyn Wood was born on 3 Dec 1934. He married Suzanne Romaine FOX in say 1957. Children:
+ 714   i   Amanda Zoe MIDDLETON, b. 15 Oct 1959
    715   ii Karen Lucy MIDDLETON, b. 10 Apr 1962
    716   iii Fiona Gay MIDDLETON, b. 3 Jan 1964
    717   iv Keith Bernard Hugh MIDDLETON, b. 19 Apr 1965
    718   v Graeme Ian David MIDDLETON, b. 4 Sep 1966

466. RAYMOND CHRISTOPHER MEPHAM[6] (Catherine Eleanor Mabel Middleton[5], Henry Middleton[4], Williams Middleton[3], Henry Middleton[2], Arthur Middleton[1]) child of Catherine Eleanor Mabel Middleton and Samuel Mepham was born about 1925. He married Iris (--) in say 1948. Children:
719   i   Theresa MEPHAM, b. c. 1950
720   ii Sarah MEPHAM, b. c. 1953

467. CHILD REA[6] (Emmeline Ellida Davison[5], Emeline Virginia Middleton[4], Edward Middleton[3], Henry Middleton[2], Arthur Middleton[1]) child of Emmeline Ellida Davison and John M. Rea was born about 1937. He married-- (--) in say 1959. Children:
721   i   Susan REA, b. c. 1962
722   ii John REA, b. c. 1964
723   iii Andrew REA, b. c. 1968

468. PAUL REA[6] (Emmeline Ellida Davison[5], Emeline Virginia Middleton[4], Edward Middleton[3], Henry Middleton[2], Arthur Middleton[1]) child of Emmeline Ellida Davison and John M. Rea was born about 1940. He married -- (--) in say 1964. Children:
724   i   Arthur REA, b. c. 1965
725   ii Daughter REA, b. c. 1968

469. EDWARD MIDDLETON REA[6] (Emmeline Ellida Davison[5], Emeline Virginia Middleton[4], Edward Middleton[3], Henry Middleton[2], Arthur Middleton[1]) child of Emmeline Ellida Davison and John M. Rea was born about 1945. He married Karen (--) in say 1969. Children:

726   i   Christopher Middleton REA, b. 17 Dec 1973
727   ii   Melissa REA, b. 10 May 1978

470. DAVID SAXTON MYERS[6] (Nancy Reeves Middleton[5], Arthur Edward Henry Middleton[4], Edward Middleton[3], Henry Middleton[2], Arthur Middleton[1]) child of Nancy Reeves Middleton and William Saxton Myers was born on 27 Mar 1941. He married Charlene GOFREY on 19 Oct 1968. She was born on 25 Sep 1945. Children:

728   i   Catherine Allison MYERS, b. 22 Aug 1972
729   ii   Meagan Leigh MYERS, b. 11 Sep 1982

471. SUSAN ELLEN MYERS[6] (Nancy Reeves Middleton[5], Arthur Edward Henry Middleton[4], Edward Middleton[3], Henry Middleton[2], Arthur Middleton[1]) child of Nancy Reeves Middleton and William Saxton Myers was born on 20 Mar 1942. She married H. Dewar BURBAGE on 6 Jun 1964. He was born on 13 Apr 1941. Children:

730   i   Scott Middleton BURBAGE, b. 16 Dec 1967
731   ii   Lee Patrick BURBAGE, b. 20 Nov 1970

473. THOMAS PYM COPE[6] (Eliza Middleton Kane[5], Elizabeth Francis Fisher[4], Elizabeth Izard Middleton[3], Henry Middleton[2], Arthur Middleton[1]) child of Eliza Middleton Kane and Walter Cope was born in 1896[1], and died in 1977. He married Elizabeth W. BARRINGER in say 1931. Child:

+   732   i   Felicity COPE, b. 1934

References:
[1] Data from Middleton Place Foundation.

474. ELIZABETH FRANCIS PYM COPE[6] (Eliza Middleton Kane[5], Elizabeth Francis Fisher[4], Elizabeth Izard Middleton[3], Henry Middleton[2], Arthur Middleton[1]) child of Eliza Middleton Kane and Walter Cope was born in 1898[1], and died in 1977. She married Joseph C. AUB in 1925. He died in 1973. Children:

+   733   i   Elizabeth Francis AUB, b. 1926
+   734   ii   Frances AUB, b. 1930
+   735   iii   Nancy Cope AUB, b. 1934

References:
[1] Data from Middleton Place Foundation.

475. ANNE FRANCIS COPE[6] (Eliza Middleton Kane[5], Elizabeth Francis Fisher[4], Elizabeth Izard Middleton[3], Henry Middleton[2], Arthur Middleton[1]) child of Eliza Middleton Kane and Walter Cope was born in 1900. She married Thomas Pierrepont HAZARD in say 1920. Children:

+ 736   i   Sophia HAZARD, b. c. 1923
   737   ii   Thomas HAZARD, b. c. 1925
+ 738   iii   Mary Pierrepont HAZARD, b. c. 1928
+ 739   iv   Anne HAZARD, b. c. 1930
+ 740   v   Oliver Cope HAZARD, b. c. 1933

476. OLIVER COPE[6] (Eliza Middleton Kane[5], Elizabeth Francis Fisher[4], Elizabeth Izard Middleton[3], Henry Middleton[2], Arthur Middleton[1]) child of Eliza Middleton Kane and Walter Cope was born in 1902. He married Alice de NORMANDIE in 1932. Children:

+ 741   i   Robert de Normandie COPE, b. 1935
+ 742   ii   Eliza Middleton COPE, b. 1936

477. JOHN CADWALADER[6] (John Cadwalader[5], Mary Helen Fisher[4], Elizabeth Izard Middleton[3], Henry Middleton[2], Arthur Middleton[1]) child of John Cadwalader and Margaret Nicoll was born on 8 Jan 1910, and died in 1999. He married (1st) Beatrice d'Este PENROSE on 22 Apr 1935. She was born on 11 Jul 1913, and died on 5 Jan 1944. He married (2nd) Lea Thom ASPINWALL on 4 May 1946. She was born on 17 Jun 1922.
Children by first marriage:

+ 743   i   John CADWALADER, b. 28 Jun 1937
+ 744   ii   George CADWALADER, b. 10 May 1939
   745   iii   David CADWALADER, b. c. 1942
Children by second marriage:
   746   iv   Sandra Lea CADWALADER, b. 11 Jul 1947
+ 747   v   Gardner Aspinwall CADWALADER, b. 29 Jul 1948

478. THOMAS FRANCIS CADWALADER, Jr.[6] (Thomas Francis Cadwalader[5], Mary Helen Fisher[4], Elizabeth Izard Middleton[3], Henry Middleton[2], Arthur Middleton[1]) child of Thomas Francis Cadwalader and Elizabeth Middleton Read was born in Baltimore, MD on 18 Nov 1912. He married Phyllis Jane CLEGG in St. Helier, Island of Jersey, GB on 31 Jan 1946. She was born in Treorchy, WALES on 11 Jul 1924. Children:

+ 748   i   Elizabeth Jane CADWALADER, b. 16 Nov 1946
+ 749   ii   Sophia Francis CADWALADER, b. 4 Jan 1951

480. ANN CLELAND CADWALADER[6] (Thomas Francis Cadwalader[5], Mary Helen Fisher[4], Elizabeth Izard Middleton[3], Henry Middleton[2], Arthur Middleton[1]) child of Thomas Francis Cadwalader and Elizabeth Middleton Read was born on 24 Dec 1918. She married Richard Blair EARLE on 5 Aug 1944. He was born on 11 Jun 1915. Children:

+   750   i   Stephen Jackson EARLE, b. 2 Dec 1949
    751   ii   Richard Blair EARLE, Jr., b. 12 Jul 1951
+   752   iii   Thomas Cadwalader EARLE, b. 20 Oct 1953
+   753   iv   Cleland Kinloch EARLE, b. 20 Jan 1956

491. ELEANOR HART[6] (Anna Scott Fisher[5], George Harrison Fisher[4], Elizabeth Izard Middleton[3], Henry Middleton[2], Arthur Middleton[1]) child of Anna Scott Fisher and William Howard Hart was born in 1902. She married George Appleton ROBBINS in 1924. He was born in 1898[1], and died in 1968. Children:

+   754   i   Virginia ROBBINS, b. 1931
    755   ii   George Howard ROBBINS, b. 1936
    756   iii   Eleanor Arden ROBBINS, b. 1940

References:
[1] Data from Middleton Place Foundation.

495. HENRY MIDDLETON DRINKER[6] (Mary Fisher[5], Henry Middleton Fisher[4], Elizabeth Izard Middleton[3], Henry Middleton[2], Arthur Middleton[1]) child of Mary Fisher and James Blathwaite Drinker was born on 19 Nov 1919, and died on 26 May 1999. He married Marilyn ROWE in 1947. Children:

    757   i   John DRINKER, b. c. 1947
    758   ii   Edward DRINKER, b. c. 1950
    759   iii   Sandwith DRINKER, b. c. 1955

497. MARY ELWYN DRINKER[6] (Mary Fisher[5], Henry Middleton Fisher[4], Elizabeth Izard Middleton[3], Henry Middleton[2], Arthur Middleton[1]) child of Mary Fisher and James Blathwaite Drinker was born on 2 May 1927. She married Peter S. ELEK in say 1949. Children:

    760   i   Daphne Drinker ELEK, b. c. 1950
    761   ii   Frances Wharton ELEK, b. c. 1952
    762   iii   Henry Drinker ELEK, b. c. 1955
    763   iv   Susanna Middleton ELEK, b. c. 1959

498. JAMES DRINKER[6] (Mary Fisher[5], Henry Middleton Fisher[4], Elizabeth Izard Middleton[3], Henry Middleton[2], Arthur Middleton[1]) child of Mary

Fisher and James Blathwaite Drinker was born on 11 Dec 1928. He married Margaret (--) in say 1951. Child:

764   i   Philip DRINKER, b. c. 1953

506. SARAH LYONS IZARD[6] (Ralph Izard[5], Walter Izard[4], Walter Izard[3], Emma Philadelphia Middleton[2], Arthur Middleton[1]) child of Ralph Izard and Nannie Theresa Lyons was born in Tazewell, VA on 14 May 1892[1], and died in 1988. She married Marsden Churchill SMITH in Fredericksburg, VA on 14 Sep 1916. He was born in Lexington, VA on 15 Dec 1888.[1]Children:

765   i   Anne Marsden SMITH, b. 10 May 1919
766   ii   Sarah Izard SMITH, b. 24 Oct 1922
767   iii   Elizabeth Friend SMITH, b. 8 Sep 1927

References:
[1] DSDI Appl # 855 & 1216.

507. RITA IZARD[6] (Ralph Izard[5], Walter Izard[4], Walter Izard[3], Emma Philadelphia Middleton[2], Arthur Middleton[1]) child of Ralph Izard and Nannie Theresa Lyons was born in Tazewell, VA on 14 Aug 1894[1], and died in Aug 1981. She married William Blair HUNTER in Gastonia, NC on 22 Dec 1926. He was born in Dallas, NC on 22 Feb 1886.[1] Child:

+ 768   i   Rita Izard HUNTER, b. 28 Jan 1928

References:
[1] DSDI Appl # 1253.

508. LAURA ELIZABETH IZARD[6] (Ralph Izard[5], Walter Izard[4], Walter Izard[3], Emma Philadelphia Middleton[2], Arthur Middleton[1]) child of Ralph Izard and Nannie Theresa Lyons was born in Jamaica, LI, NY on 3 Feb 1903. She married (1st) Albert Winfree HAWKINS in 1925. She married (2nd) John Edmund HARRIS in Upper Marlboro, Prince George's County, MD on 23 Jul 1938. He was born in Richmond, VA on 4 May 1904.

Child by first marriage:

+ 769   i   Nancy Ware HAWKINS, b. 13 Mar 1929

Child by second marriage:

+ 770   ii   Alice DeLancey HARRIS, b. 14 Mar 1939

522. MARGARET IZARD FERGUSON[6] (Margaret Emma Middleton[5], Arhtur Middleton[4], Margaret Emma Izard[3], Emma Philadelphia Middleton[2], Arthur Middleton[1]) child of Margaret Emma Middleton and William Cotesworth Pinckney Ferguson was born on 27 Jan 1885[1], and died on 11 Dec 1983. She married Richard Henry PRATT on 2 Apr 1913. He was born on 4 Dec 1885[1], and died on 10 Dec 1961. Children:

771   i   Margaret Middleton PRATT, b. 11 Feb 1916
772   ii   Virginia Elwyn PRATT, b. 20 Apr 1924

References:
[1] Data from Middleton Place Foundation.

529. ARTHUR MIDDLETON[6] (William Dehon Middleton[5], Arthur Middleton[4], Emma Izard[3], Emma Philadelphia Middleton[2], Arthur Middleton[1]) child of William Dehon Middleton and Julia Porcher Blake was born in Charleston, SC on 23 Aug 1897[1], and died in West Chester, PA on 31 Aug 1969. He married Patience Campbell HURD in Charleston, SC on 20 Nov 1923. She was born in Pawling, NY on 14 Jul 1905, and died in West Chester , PA on 9 Oct 1983. Children:

+ 773   i   Patience Hurd MIDDLETON, b. 19 Sep 1924
+ 774   ii   Sally Horton MIDDLETON, b. 2 Mar 1927
+ 775   iii Annely Blake MIDDLETON, b. 9 Dec 1928
+ 776   iv   Gay Van Assendelft MIDDLETON, b. 28 May 1933
   777   v   Hope Campbell MIDDLETON, b. 1 Oct 1940; sp

References:
[1] Obituary, *West Chester Daily Local News* of 2 Sep 1969; see also DSDI Appl # 1495.

531. JULIUS BLAKE MIDDLETON[6] (William Dehon Middleton[5], Arthur Middleton[4], Emma Izard[3], Emma Philadelphia Middleton[2], Arthur Middleton[1]) child of William Dehon Middleton and Julia Porcher Blake was born on 9 Nov 1900, and died on 12 Apr 1986. He married Margaret Lane GOODWYN on 13 Feb 1926. She was born on 17 Oct 1904, and died on 14 Apr 1998. Children:

+ 778   i   Julius Blake MIDDLETON, Jr., b. 15 Aug 1932
+ 779   ii   Charlie Lane MIDDLETON, b. 9 Apr 1938

532. WILLIAM MIDDLETON[6] (William Dehon Middleton[5], Arthur Middleton[4], Emma Izard[3], Emma Philadelphia Middleton[2], Arthur Middleton[1]) child of William Dehon Middleton and Julia Porcher Blake was born on 8 Oct 1902, and died on 26 Nov 1997. He married Frances Gaillard HANAHAN on 1 Sep 1926. She was born on 5 Jan 1905. Children:

+ 780   i   William MIDDLETON, Jr., b. 21 Dec 1931
+ 781   ii   Francis Gaillard MIDDLETON, b. 25 Mar 1940

533. JULIA PORCHER MIDDLETON[6] (William Dehon Middleton[5], Arthur Middleton[4], Emma Izard[3], Emma Philadelphia Middleton[2], Arthur Middleton[1]) child of William Dehon Middleton and Julia Porcher Blake was born in Charleston, SC on 27 Dec 1905. She married Charles Brewster

PRENTISS, Jr. in Charleston, SC on 19 Apr 1927. He was born in Charleston, SC on 7 Apr 1902, and died there on 11 Jan 1972. Children:
+ 782   i   Charles Brewster PRENTISS, III, b. 14 Dec 1929
+ 783   ii   Julia Blake PRENTISS, b. 23 Feb 1932

534. ROBERT CUTHBERT MIDDLETON[6] (William Dehon Middleton[5], Arthur Middleton[4], Emma Izard[3], Emma Philadelphia Middleton[2], Arthur Middleton[1]) child of William Dehon Middleton and Julia Porcher Blake was born on 14 Sep 1907, and died on 26 Dec 1998. He married Isabell Delores BROWN on 1 Dec 1939. Child:
   784   i   Betsy Blake MIDDLETON, b. 19 Oct 1943; sp

535. LEWIS BLAKE MIDDLETON[6] (William Dehon Middleton[5], Arthur Middleton[4], Emma Izard[3], Emma Philadelphia Middleton[2], Arthur Middleton[1]) child of William Dehon Middleton and Julia Porcher Blake was born on 9 Dec 1909, and died on 19 Dec 1987. He married Elizabeth Ingram LACHICOTTE on 19 Oct 1946. She was born on 15 May 1921, and died on 6 Dec 1965. Children:
+ 785   i   Lewis Blake MIDDLETON, Jr., b. 13 Nov 1947
+ 786   ii   Julia Porcher MIDDLETON, b. 15 Jan 1951

537. BENJAMIN MUNNERLYN[6] (Lucy Izard Middleton[5], Arthur Middleton[4], Emma Izard[3], Emma Philadelphia Middleton[2], Arthur Middleton[1]) child of Lucy Izard Middleton and William Wilson Munnerlyn was born on 16 Sep 1901, and died in 1954. He married Margaret Elizabeth SPRING in say 1924. She was born in 1901. Children:
   787   i   Margaret Middleton MUNNERLYN, b. 7 Oct 1926
+ 788   ii   Jane Morris MUNNERLYN, b. 15 Jan 1929

540. ANNA BERTHA DEHON[6] (Helen Middleton[5], Arthur Middleton[4], Margaret Emma Izard[3], Emma Philadelphia Middleton[2], Arthur Middleton[1]) child of Helen Middleton and Theodore Dehon was born on 17 Feb 1899[1], and died in Oct 1929. She married Wilbur C. DuBOIS in say 1920. Children:
+ 789   i   Wilbur C. DuBOIS, Jr., b. 2 Oct 1923
+ 790   ii   Helen Middleton DuBOIS, b. 1 Aug 1926
   791   iii   Ellsworth DuBOIS, b. 2 Oct 1929

References:
[1] Data from Middleton Place Foundation.

542. EVA RUSSELL DEHON[6] (Helen Middleton[5], Arthur Middleton[4], Margaret Emma Izard[3], Emma Philadelphia Middleton[2], Arthur Middleton[1]) child of Helen Middleton and Theodore Dehon was born about 1902. She married Charles B. ARBOGAST in say 1921. Children:

   792   i   Middleton Dehon ARBOGAST, b. c. 1923, d. 1955; unm
+ 793   ii Charles B. ARBOGAST, Jr., b. c. 1925

543. CHARLOTTE DEHON[6] (Helen Middleton[5], Arthur Middleton[4], Margaret Emma Izard[3], Emma Philadelphia Middleton[2], Arthur Middleton[1]) child of Helen Middleton and Theodore Dehon was born about 1905. She married Charles SWAYNE in say 1925. Children:

   794   i   Charles SWAYNE, b. c. 1927
   795   ii Charlotte SWAYNE, b. c. 1930

544. ARTHUR MIDDLETON DEHON[6] (Helen Middleton[5], Arthur Middleton[4], Margaret Emma Izard[3], Emma Philadelphia Middleton[2], Arthur Middleton[1]) child of Helen Middleton and Theodore Dehon was born about 1907. He married Betty Kay MORGAN in say 1930. Children:

   796   i   Arthur Middleton DEHON, Jr., b. c. 1933
   797   ii Sandra DEHON, b. c. 1936

545. MARY DEHON[6] (Helen Middleton[5], Arthur Middleton[4], Margaret Emma Izard[3], Emma Philadelphia Middleton[2], Arthur Middleton[1]) child of Helen Middleton and Theodore Dehon was born about 1910, and died on 28 Feb 1996. She married Wilbur Hamilton MAULDIN in say 1931. Children:

+ 798   i   Mary MAULDIN, b. c. 1934
+ 799   ii Harriet MAULDIN, b. c. 1937
   800   iii Helen Dehon MAULDIN, b. c. 1939
+ 801   iv Ann MAULDIN, b. c. 1942

547. MIRIAM BRIDGE MIDDLETON[6] (Walter Izard Middleton[5], Arthur Middleton[4], Margaret Emma Izard[3], Emma Philadelphia Middleton[2], Arthur Middleton[1]) child of Walter Izard Middleton and Mary Brown Bridge was born on 12 Apr 1902, and died on 19 Apr 1965. She married Harry Hightower HALLMAN on 16 Dec 1925. He was born on 23 Aug 1895[1], and died on 6 Jun 1966. Children:

+ 802   i   Miriam Middleton HALLMAN, b. 23 Sep 1926
   803   ii Harriett HALLMAN, b. 23 Nov 1932

References:
[1] Data from Middleton Place Foundation.

550. WILLIE MAXINE HOFFMAN[6] (Florence Vernon Blake[5], Arthur Middleton Blake[4], Daniel Blake[3], Anna Louisa Middleton[2], Arthur Middleton[1]) child of Florence Vernon Blake and William Bell Hoffman was born in Brownwood, TX on 4 Jan 1923. She married Clarence Milton CALD-CLEUGH in Galveston, TX on 15 May 1944. He was born in San Marcos, TX on 15 Aug 1916. Child:

+ 804   i   Robert Blake CLADCLEUGH, b. 16 Jun 1945

551. ALICE TILLMAN[6] (Alice Rutledge[5], Emma Craig Blake[4], Daniel Blake[3], Anna Louisa Middleton[2], Arthur Middleton[1]) child of Alice Rutledge and Edward Tillman was born about 1922. She married George BAIRD in say 1943· Children:

805   i   Alice BAIRD, b. c. 1945
806   ii Laura BAIRD, b. c. 1948

552. ELEANOR OLIVER RUTLEDGE[6] (Benjamin Huger Rutledge[5], Emma Craig Blake[4], Daniel Blake[3], Anna Louisa Middleton[2], Arthur Middleton[1]) child of Benjamin Huger Rutledge and Eleanor Oliver was born in 1930. She married Arnold Rich HOLT in 1953· Children:

+ 807   i   Olivia Caldwell HOLT, b. 1954
808   ii Susan Middleton HOLT, b. 1956
809 iii Eliza Rutledge HOLT, b. 1960

553. ASA DAVIS, Jr.[6] (Amelia Van Cortlandt Rutledge[5], Emma Craig Blake[4], Daniel Blake[3], Anna Louisa Middleton[2], Arthur Middleton[1]) child of Amelia Van Cortlandt Rutledge and Asa Davis was born about 1928. He married Deborah CARSON in say 1952· Children:

810   i   Amanda DAVIS, b. c. 1955
811   ii Katherine DAVIS, b. c. 1959

555. BENJAMIN ALLSTON MOORE, Jr.[6] (Susan Middleton Rutledge[5], Emma Craig Blake[4], Daniel Blake[3], Anna Louisa Middleton[2], Arthur Middleton[1]) child of Susan Middleton Rutledge and Benjamin Allston Moore was born in 1930. He married Frida BARROW in say 1954. Children:

812   i   Frida MOORE, b. c. 1955
813   ii Emma MOORE, b. c. 1957
814   ii Eleanor MOORE, b, c. 1960

556. EMMA MOORE[6] (Anne Blake Rutledge[5], Emma Craig Blake[4], Daniel Blake[3], Anna Louisa Middleton[2], Arthur Middleton[1]) child of Anne Blake Rutledge and Albert Moore was born about 1935. She married James KELLOCK in say 1957. Children:

815   i   James Albert KELLOCK, b. c. 1960
816   ii Adele KELLOCK, b. c. 1964

558. FRANCES CHESHIRE[6] (Frances Bayley Blake Rutledge[5], Helen Bayley Blake[4], Daniel Blake[3], Anna Louisa Middleton[2], Arthur Middleton[1]) child of Frances Bayley Blake Rutledge and Theophilus Parker Cheshire was born in 1924. She married Francis RHETT in say 1948. Children:

+ 817   i   Francis P. RHETT, b. 1951
+ 818   ii   Joseph Cheshire RHETT, b. 1953
   819   iii   Helen Rutledge RHETT, b. 1956
   820   iv   Thomas Barnwell RHETT, b. c. 1960

559. JOHN RUTLEDGE CHESHIRE[6] (Frances Bayley Blake Rutledge[5], Helen Bayley Blake[4], Daniel Blake[3], Anna Louisa Middleton[2], Arthur Middleton[1]) child of Frances Bayley Blake Rutledge and Theophilus Parker Cheshire was born in 1925. He married Julie DAVIDSON in say 1954. Children:

   821   i   John Rutledge CHESHIRE, Jr., b. 1958
   822   ii   Mary Patterson CHESHIRE, b. 1961

560. KATHERINE BLOUNT CHESHIRE[6] (Frances Bayley Blake Rutledge[5], Helen Bayley Blake[4], Daniel Blake[3], Anna Louisa Middleton[2], Arthur Middleton[1]) child of Frances Bayley Blake Rutledge and Theophilus Parker Cheshire was born in 1928. She married Amory PARKER in say 1952. Children:

+ 823   i   Frances PARKER, b. 1955
+ 824   ii   Oliver Ames PARKER, b. 1956

561. CLEMENTINA RUTLEDGE[6] (Oliver Middleton Rutledge[5], Helen Bayley Blake[4], Daniel Blake[3], Anna Louisa Middleton[2], Arthur Middleton[1]) child of Oliver Middleton Rutledge and Clementina Kohn was born about 1927. She married Howard EDWARDS in say 1952. Children:

   825   i   Tina EDWARDS, b. 1954
   826   ii   Howard EDWARDS, Jr., b. c. 1957
+ 827   iii   Oliver Rutledge EDWARDS, b. c. 1961

562. HELEN BLAKE RUTLEDGE SWAN[6] (Elise Rutledge[5], Helen Bayley Blake[4], Daniel Blake[3], Anna Louisa Middleton[2], Arthur Middleton[1]) child of Elise Rutledge and Channing Swan was born in 1928. She married John Lee MERRILL, Jr. in say 1948. Children:

+ 828   i   John Lee MERRILL, III, b. 1950
+ 829   ii   Elizabeth Rutledge MERRILL, b. 1952

563. JOSEPHINE CUTTER SWAN[6] (Elise Rutledge[5], Helen Bayley Blake[4], Daniel Blake[3], Anna Louisa Middleton[2], Arthur Middleton[1]) child of Elise Rutledge and Channing Swan was born in 1930. She married George BLAGDEN in say 1951. Children:

+ 830   i   Timothy Swan BLAGDEN, b. c. 1952
  831   ii Julia Whitney BLAGDEN, b. c. 1954

564. ELIZABETH MIDDLETON RUTLEDGE SWAN[6] (Elise Rutledge[5], Helen Bayley Blake[4], Daniel Blake[3], Anna Louisa Middleton[2], Arthur Middleton[1]) child of Elise Rutledge and Channing Swan was born about 1933. She married John Patterson WEITZEL in say 1955. Children:

  832   i   Mary Middleton WEITZEL, b. c. 1957
  833   ii Paul Patterson WEITZEL, b. c. 1960

565. OVERTON PRICE, Jr.[6] (Dorothea Barclay Rutledge[5], Helen Bayley Blake[4], Daniel Blake[3], Anna Louisa Middleton[2], Arthur Middleton[1]) child of Dorothea Barclay Rutledge and Overton Price was born about 1928. He married Nancy (--) in say 1952. Children:

  834   i   Julia PRICE, b. c. 1955
  835   ii Thomas Oliver PRICE, b. c. 1960

566. ALICE PRICE[6] (Dorothea Barclay Rutledge[5], Helen Bayley Blake[4], Daniel Blake[3], Anna Louisa Middleton[2], Arthur Middleton[1]) child of Dorothea Barclay Rutledge and Overton Price was born about 1931. She married Jerry MADDEN in say 1951. Children:

  836   i   Katharine Andrea MADDEN, b. c. 1953
  837   ii Daniel MADDEN, b. c. 1955
  838   iii John M. MADDEN, b. c. 1958

567. CAROLINE MANIGAULT[6] (Arthur Middleton Manigault[5], Mary Proctor Huger[4], Daniel Elliott Huger[3], Isabella Johannes Middleton[2], Arthur Middleton[1]) child of Arthur Middleton Manigault and Harriott Kinloch Smith was born on 5 Apr 1892[1], and died on 19 Feb 1985. She married John Walter WILCOX in say 1919. Children:

+ 839   i   Arthur Manigault WILCOX, b. 2 May 1922
+ 840   ii Mary Huger Manigault WILCOX, b. 5 Jul 1930

References:
[1] Data from Middleton Place Foundation.

569. EDWARD MANIGAULT[6] (Arthur Middleton Manigault[5], Mary Proctor Huger[4], Daniel Elliott Huger[3], Isabella Johannes Middleton[2], Arthur

Middleton[1]) child of Arthur Middleton Manigault and Harriott Kinloch Smith was born in 1896[1], and died in 1983. He married Mary Pringle HAMILTON in say 1920. Children:

    841   i   Peter MANIGAULT, b. c. 1923
    842   ii Mary MANIGAULT, b. c. 1927

References:
[1] Data from Middleton Place Foundation.

571. DANIEL ELLIOTT HUGER, Jr.[6] (Daniel Elliott Huger[5], William Elliott Huger[4], Daniel Elliott Huger[3], Isabella Johannes Middleton[2], Arthur Middleton[1]) child of Daniel Elliott Huger and Louisa S. Chisolm was born about 1903. He married Frances PELZER in say 1927. Children:

+ 843   i   Frances Pelzer HUGER, b. c. 1930
    844   ii Louisa C. HUGER, b. c. 1932
    845 iii Mary Randolph HUGER, b. c. 1935
+ 846 iv Elizabeth Pelzer HUGER, b. c. 1940

580. CAROLINE HAMPTON MULLALLY[6] (Caroline Hampton Lowndes[5], Rawlins Lowndes[4], Sabina Elliott Huger[3], Isabella Johannes Middleton[2], Arthur Middleton[1]) child of Caroline Hampton Lowndes and Lane Mullally was born in Charleston, SC on 9 Jul 1903. She married (2nd) Lawrence Knight LADUE in say 1928. Children:

+ 847   i   Caroline Hampton LADUE, b. 22 Aug 1930
    848   ii Lawrence Knight LADUE, Jr., b. 1935

584. MIDDLETON POPE BARROW[6] (Emma Middleton Izard Huger[5], Joseph Alston Huger, Jr.[4], Joseph Alston Huger[3], Isabella Johannes Middleton[2], Arthur Middleton[1]) child of Emma Middleton Izard Huger and David Crenshaw Barrow was born in Savannah, GA on 31 Dec 1909, and died in Black Mountain, NC on 24 Dec 1991. He married Katherine Winchester FORSYTHE in Ellicott City, MD on 4 Jun 1938. She was born in Baltimore, MD on 27 Oct 1913. Child:

+ 849   i   Middleton Pope BARROW, Jr., b. 26 Dec 1942

589. LAWRENCE LEE, Jr.[6] (Clermont Kinloch Huger[5], Joseph Alston Huger, Jr.[4], Joseph Alston Huger[3], Isabella Johannes Middleton[2], Arthur Middleton[1]) child of Clermont Kinloch Huger and Lawrence Lee was born in Savannah, GA on 16 Aug 1915. He married Elizabeth Middleton ANDREWS in Flat Rock, NC on 27 Aug 1949. She was born in Flat Rock, NC on 24 May 1926. Children:

+ 850   i   Alice Lowndes LEE, b. 12 May 1951

851   ii   Lawrence E. LEE, b. 1952
852   iii   Robert Mackay LEE, b. 1957

598. JAMES WILKINSON JERVEY, Jr.[6] (James Wilkinson Jervey[5], Isabella Middleton Wilkinson[4], Sarah Elliott Huger[3], Isabella Johannes Middleton[2], Arthur Middleton[1]) child of James Wilkinson Jervey and Helen Doremus Smith was born in Greenville, SC on 19 Feb 1901. He married Laura Aletta WOOD on 20 Apr 1929. She was born on 23 Oct 1903. Children:

+ 853   i   Aletta Wood JERVEY, b. 13 Apr 1930
   854   ii   James Wilkinson JERVEY, III, b. 17 May 1931
+ 855   iii Edward Darrell JERVEY, b. 23 Aug 1936
   856   iv   Mary Gardiner JERVEY, b. 28 Feb 1946

600. MARGUERITE BARNWELL KING[6] (Maria Louisa Wilkinson Barnwell[5], Maria Louisa Wilkinson[4], Sarah Elliott Huger[3], Isabella Johannes Middleton[2], Arthur Middleton[1]) child of Maria Louisa Wilkinson Barnwell and Macmillan Campbell King was born in 1903. She married William W. ELLIOTT in 1922. Children:

+ 857   i   Louise Barnwell ELLIOTT, b. 1928
+ 858   ii   William W. ELLIOTT, III, b. 1932

601. ARTHUR BRIGHT MARSTON, Jr.[6] (Marie Louise Barnwell[5], Maria Louisa Wilkinson[4], Sarah Elliott Huger[3], Isabella Johannes Middleton[2], Arthur Middleton[1]) child of Marie Louise Barnwell and Arthur Bright Marston was born on 16 Feb 1909. He married Hazel Ernestine FACKLER on 2 Oct 1938. She was born in 1919. Children:

   859   i   Arthur Dennis Fackler MARSTON, b. 1940
   860   ii   Sherry Lynn Fackler MARSTON, b. 1944
   861   iii Deborah Kay Fackler MARSTON, b. 1946

604. WILLIAM MASON SMITH, III[6] (William Mason Smith[5], Daniel Elliott Huger Smith[4], Eliza Caroline Middleton Huger[3], Isabella Johannes Middleton[2], Arthur Middleton[1]) child of William Mason Smith and Mary A. Swan was born in 1910. He married Jane PROUTY in say 1937. Children:

   862   i   William Mason SMITH, IV, b. 1939
   863   ii   Olivia SMITH, b. c. 1942

627. JOHN McLAUGHLIN FORNEY[6] (Jacob Forney[5], Septima Sexta Middleton Rutledge[4], Henry Adolphus Rutledge[3], Septima Sexta Middleton[2], Arthur Middleton[1]) child of Jacob Forney and Katherine Burt McLaughlin was born in Springville, AL on 19 Oct 1901, and died in NYC on 22 Dec 1964. He married Kathleen Clarke FOSTER in Chicago, IL on 4 Aug 1926. She was born in Tuscaloosa, AL on 4 Apr 1903, and died in Birmingham, AL on 12 Jun 1980. Child:

    864   i   John McLaughlin FORNEY, Jr., b. 4 Jun 1927

629. HORACE LEE STEVENSON[6] (Sabina Swope Forney[5], Septima Sexta Middleton Rutledge[4], Henry Adolphus Rutledge[3], Septima Sexta Middleton[2], Arthur Middleton[1]) child of Sabina Swope Forney and Macon Abernathy Stevenson was born in Jacksonville, AL on 11 Jan 1902. He married Sara Katherine SEGREST in Luverne, AL on 17 Mar 1934. She was born in Brantley, AL on 12 Nov 1910. Child:

+ 865   i   Katherine Sabina STEVENSON, b. 27 Oct 1935

630. MARY ABERNATHY STEVENSON[6] (Sabina Swope Forney[5], Septima Sexta Middleton Rutledge[4], Henry Adolphus Rutledge[3], Septima Sexta Middleton[2], Arthur Middleton[1]) child of Sabina Swope Forney and Macon Abernathy Stevenson was born in Jacksonville, AL on 30 Dec 1903. She married Arnold A. POLING on 26 Aug 1923. He was born in Athalia, OH on 13 Feb 1905. Child:

+ 866   i   Mary Caroline POLING, b. 15 Aug 1928

635. PALMER DAUGETTE[6] (Annie Rowan Forney[5], Septima Sexta Middleton Rutledge[4], Henry Adolphus Rutledge[3], Septima Sexta Middleton[2], Arthur Middleton[1]) child of Annie Rowan Forney and Clarence William Daugette was born in Jacksonville, AL on 10 Jan 1900. She married William Jonathan CALVERT, Jr. on 22 Aug 1938. He was born in Pittsboro, NC on 3 Jul 1901. Child:

    867   i   William Jonathan CALVERT, III, b. 10 Mar 1943

636. CLARENCE WILLLIAM DAUGETTE, Jr.[6] (Annie Rowan Forney[5], Septima Sexta Middleton Rutledge[4], Henry Adolphus Rutledge[3], Septima Sexta Middleton[2], Arthur Middleton[1]) child of Annie Rowan Forney and Clarence William Daugette was born in Jacksonville, AL on 16 Sep 1903, and died in Gadsden, AL on 2 Oct 1988. He married Florence Earle THROCKMORTON in Birmingham, AL on 22 Jun 1946. She was born in Birmingham, AL on 12 Nov 1919. Children:

+ 868   i   Alburta [sic] Martin DAUGETTE, b. 25 Jun 1948
+ 869   ii   Florence Anne DAUGETTE, b. 14 Oct 1949
    870 iii   Clarence William DAUGETTE, III, b. 13 Mar 1951

637. FORNEY RUTLEDGE DAUGETTE[6] (Annie Rowan Forney[5], Septima Sexta Middleton Rutledge[4], Henry Adolphus Rutledge[3], Septima Sexta Middleton[2], Arthur Middleton[1]) child of Annie Rowan Forney and Clarence William Daugette was born in Jacksonville, AL on 28 Feb 1908. He married Mary Elizabeth MOODY in Opelika, AL on 28 May 1929. She was born in Piedmont, AL on 23 Apr 1908. Child:

+ 871   i   Forney Rutledge DAUGETTE, Jr., b. 13 Nov 1932

641. FREDERICK REEVES RUTLEDGE[6] (Frederick Rutledge[5], Henry Middleton Rutledge[4], Henrietta Middleton Rutledge[3], Septima Sexta Middleton[2], Arthur Middleton[1]) child of Frederick Rutledge and Mable Reeves was born in Asheville, NC on 17 Nov 1895.[1] He married Beatrice Clyde EDWARDS in say 1929. Children:

872   i   Frederick Reeves RUTLEDGE, Jr., b. 1 Nov 1932
873   ii   Anne E. RUTLEDGE, b. 20 Nov 1935 [twin]
874   iii   Ruth P. RUTLEDGE, b. 20 Nov 1935 [twin]

References:
[1] SAR Appl # 56365.

646. HENRIETTA MIDDLETON RUTLEDGE[6] (Thomas Pinckney Rutledge[5], Henry Middleton Rutledge[4], Henrietta Middleton Rutledge[3], Septima Sexta Middleton[2], Arthur Middleton[1]) child of Thomas Pinckney Rutledge and Ethel Gary Parrott was born in 1915, and died in 1976. She married Franklyn Clement MERRITT in say 1939. He was born in 1914, and died in 1975. Child:

+ 875   i   Harrison Shelby MERRITT, b. 1942

647. ARCHIBALD HAMILTON RUTLEDGE[6] (Archibald Hamilton Rutledge[5], Henry Middleton Rutledge[4], Henrietta Middleton Rutledge[3], Septima Sexta Middleton[2], Arthur Middleton[1]) child of Archibald Hamilton Rutledge and Florence Louise Hart was born in Mercersburg, PA on 29 Sep 1908, and died in McClellanville, SC on 3 Nov 1959. He married Margaret KINGSLEY in Chestertown, MD on 4 Jan 1932. She was born in Staten Island, NY on 11 Apr 1912. Child:

876   i   Susan RUTLEDGE, b. 17 Aug 1934

648. HENRY MIDDLETON RUTLEDGE[6] (Archibald Hamilton Rutledge[5], Henry Middleton Rutledge[4], Henrietta Middleton Rutledge[3], Septima Sexta Middleton[2], Arthur Middleton[1]) child of Archibald Hamilton Rutledge and Florence Louise Hart was born in Mercersburg, PA on 29 Jul 1910, and died in Laurens, SC on 3 Jan 1942. He married Flora McDONALD in Princeton,

NJ on 8 Sep 1932. She was born in Philadelphia, PA on 7 Jul 1910. Children:
+ 877   i   Donald Thropp RUTLEDGE, b. 27 Dec 1939
+ 878   ii   Elise Pinckney RUTLEDGE, b. c. 1941

649. IRVING HART RUTLEDGE[6] (Archibald Hamilton Rutledge[5], Henry Middleton Rutledge[4], Henrietta Middleton Rutledge[3], Septima Sexta Middleton[2], Arthur Middleton[1]) child of Archibald Hamilton Rutledge and Florence Louise Hart was born in Mercersburg, PA about 1913. He married Eleanor WHITE in say 1934. Children:
+ 879   i   Henry Middleton RUTLEDGE, b. c. 1936
   880   ii   Eleanor RUTLEDGE, b. c. 1940

651. ELISE RUTLEDGE SMITH[6] (Mary Middleton Rutledge Reese[5], Emma Fredricka Rutledge[4], Henrietta Middleton Rutledge[3], Septima Sexta Middleton[2], Arthur Middleton[1]) child of Mary Middleton Rutledge Reese and Benjamin Bosworth Smith was born in Nashville, TN on 4 Dec 1894[1], and died in Anchorage, KY on 6 Apr 1977. She married Ewing Lloyd HARDY in say 1921. He died in Anchorage, KY on 6 Aug 1968. Children:
   881   i   Ewing Marshall HARDY, b. c. 1924
   882   ii   Benjamin Bosworth HARDY, b. c. 1927
+ 883   iii   Burwell Marshall HARDY, b. 4 Feb 1930
   884   iv   Elise HARDY, b. Feb 1936, dy 6 Mar 1936

References:
[1] Family Genealogical Report kindly furnished by the Rev. Benjamin B. Smith, a Rutledge descendant dated 22 Dec 1999.

652. CAROL CASTLEMAN SMITH[6] (Mary Middleton Rutledge Reese[5], Emma Fredricka Rutledge[4], Henrietta Middleton Rutledge[3], Septima Sexta Middleton[2], Arthur Middleton[1]) child of Mary Middleton Rutledge Reese and Benjamin Bosworth Smith was born in Montgomery, AL on 28 Dec 1897[1], and died in Decatur, AL on 22 Sep 1966. He married Edith STOLLEN-WERK in Greensboro, AL on 28 Apr 1928. She was born in Greensboro, AL on 18 Jul 1903, and died there on 11 Jun 1987. Children:
+ 885   i   Ann Cobbs SMITH, b. 6 Feb 1929
+ 886   ii   Carol Castleman SMITH, 7 Sep 1930
+ 887   iii   Alice Rutledge SMITH, b. 9 Mar 1932
+ 888   iv   Charles Stollenwerk SMITH, b. 9 Jan 1936

References:
[1] Family Genealogical Report kindly furnished by the Rev. Benjamin B. Smith, a Rutledge descendant dated 22 Dec 1999.

653. FREDERICK RUTLEDGE SMITH[6] (Mary Middleton Rutledge Reese[5], Emma Fredricka Rutledge[4], Henrietta Middleton Rutledge[3], Septima Sexta Middleton[2], Arthur Middleton[1]) child of Mary Middleton Rutledge Reese and Benjamin Bosworth Smith was born in Montgomery, AL on 7 Jul 1899[1], and died in Tuscaloosa, AL on 7 May 1942. He married Mary Burton MATTHEWS, daughter of Lucien Tardy and Clara Winston (Burton) Matthews in Montgomery, AL on 10 Jun 1924. She was born in Huntsville, AL on 18 Jan 1902, and died in Louisville, KY on 18 Aug 1997. Children:

    889   i   Frederick Rutledge SMITH, Jr., b. 5 Apr 1925; unm
+ 890   ii   Mary Burton SMITH, b. 13 Aug 1926
+ 891   iii   Benjamin Bosworth SMITH, b. 6 Dec 1929

References:
[1] Family Genealogical Report kindly furnished by the Rev. Benjamin B. Smith, a Rutledge descendant dated 22 Dec 1999.

656. KATHERINE FELDER[6] (Alice Sophia Reese[5], Emma Fredricka Rutledge[4], Henrietta Middleton Rutledge[3], Septima Sexta Middleton[2], Arthur Middleton[1]) child of Alice Sophia Reese and Edmund Bellinger Felder was born in Montgomery, AL on 24 Dec 1900. She married (1st) Blackburn HUGHES in say 1922. She married (2nd) Francis Barretto STEWART in say 1931.

Child by first marriage:

    892   i   Blackburn HUGHES, Jr., b. 1923

Children by second marriage:

+ 893   ii   Edmund Bellinger STEWART, b. 30 Dec 1933 [twin]
+ 894   iii   Francis Barretto STEWART, Jr., b. 30 Dec 1933 [twin]

663. JOSEPHINE SCOTT SMITH[6] (John Julius Pringle Smith[5], Emma Blake Rutledge[4], Arthur Middleton Rutledge[3], Septima Sexta Middleton[2], Arthur Middleton[1]) child of John Julius Pringle Smith and Heningham Ellett was born on 24 Dec 1913, and died on 27 Aug 1954. She married Charles DUELL, son of J. Holland and Mabel (Halliwell) Duell on 21 Oct 1933. He was born on 20 Jul 1905, and died on 10 Jul 1970. Children:

    895   i   Heningham Ann DUELL, b. 14 Aug 1934, d. 5 Dec 1987; dsp
    896   ii   Josephine Scott DUELL, b. 11 Mar 1936; unm
+ 897   iii   Charles Halliwell Pringle DUELL, b. 10 Jun 1938

SEVENTH GENERATION

664. DAINELLA de BAGNAMO[7] (Carlo Masetti de Bagnamo[6], Virginia Middleton[5], Henry Bentivoglio Middleton[4], Arthur Middleton[3], Henry Middleton[2], Arthur Middleton[1]) child of Carlo Masetti de Bagnamo and Daisy Fiorini was born on 2 Jul 1925. She married Ferdinando GAETANI in say 1947. Children:

898	i	Bonifacio GAETANI. b. 9 Feb 1950
899	ii	Isabella GAETANI, b. 1952
900	iii	Gailla GAETANI, b. 1957

665. PIERA de BAGNAMO[7] (Carlo Masetti de Bagnamo[6], Virginia Middleton[5], Henry Bentivoglio Middleton[4], Arthur Middleton[3], Henry Middleton[2], Arthur Middleton[1]) child of Carlo Masetti de Bagnamo and Daisy Fiorini was born on 22 Mar 1928. She married Giorgio San Just di TEU-LADA in say 1950. Children:

901	i	Giovanni di TEULADA, b. 13 Mar 1953
902	ii	Carlo di TEULADA, b. 10 Feb 1955
903	iii	Pietro di TEULADA, b. 1958

672. ANNE MANGUM[7] (Eliza Baker Read[6], Oliver Middleton Read[5], Mary Julia Middleton[4], Oliver Hering Middleton[3], Henry Middleton[2], Arthur Middleton[1]) child of Eliza Baker Read and Walter Mangum was born about 1915. She married William McKissick CHAPMAN in say 1938. Children:

+ 904	i	Benjamin Chapin CHAPMAN, b. c. 1940
+ 905	ii	John Harleston CHAPMAN, b. c. 1943
+ 906	iii	Alexander Gregorie CHAPMAN, b. c. 1948

673. RICHARD ALBERT TILGHMAN[7] (Eliza Middleton Fox[6], Emily Anne Read[5], Mary Julia Middleton[4], Oliver Hering Middleton[3], Henry Middleton[2], Arthur Middleton[1]) child of Eliza Middleton Fox and Benjamin Chew Tilghman, III was born in Manchester, ENGLAND on 8 Mar 1920. He married Diana DISSTON in Philadelphia, PA on 26 Feb 1944. She was born in Philadelphia, PA on 5 Jul 1923. Child:

+ 907	i	Richard Albert TILGHMAN, Jr., b. 6 Jan 1945

674. ELEANOR MUMFORD[7] (Ayliffe B. Blake[6], Edmund Molyneux Blake[5], Olivia Middleton[4], Oliver Hering Middleton[3], Henry Middleton[2], Arthur Middleton[1]) child of Ayliffe B. Blake and Nicholas Van Slyck

Mumford was born in 1919. She married Harley Allen CASE in say 1942. He died in 1982. Children:

+ 908   i   Harley Allen CASE, Jr., 13 Nov 1944
+ 909   ii   Marshall CASE, b. 1947

675. NICHOLAS Van SLYCK MUMFORD, Jr.[7] (Ayliffe B. Blake[6], Edmund Molyneux Blake[5], Olivia Middleton[4], Oliver Hering Middleton[3], Henry Middleton[2], Arthur Middleton[1]) child of Ayliffe B. Blake and Nicholas Van Slyck Mumford was born in 1925. He married Rosemary DAVIS in say 1942. Children:

+ 910   i   Nicholas Van Slyck MUMFORD, III, b. 1948
   911   ii   Robert Blake MUMFORD, b. 1950
   912   iii   Ayliffe Blake MUMFORD, b. 1951
+ 913   iv   Elizabeth Davis MUMFORD, b. 1953

676. HARRIET STUART BLAKE[7] (Olivia Middleton Blake[6], Edmund Molyneux Blake[5], Olivia Middleton[4], Oliver Hering Middleton[3], Henry Middleton[2], Arthur Middleton[1]) child of Olivia Middleton Blake and Daniel Dee Pullen was born in 1922. She married J. Ormsby PHILLIPS in 1946. He was born in 1920. Children:

+ 914   i   Eleanor PHILLIPS, b. 1948
   915   ii   Virginia PHILLIPS, b. 1951
   916   iii   Charles PHILLIPS, b. 1952

677. KATHARINE SHANNON BLAKE[7] (Daniel Blake[6], Daniel Blake[5], Olivia Middleton[4], Oliver Hering Middleton[3], Henry Middleton[2], Arthur Middleton[1]) child of Daniel Blake and Katharine Brooks Shannon was born in 1927. She married Harvey Wilson JOHNSON in 1950. He was born in 1926. Children:

+ 917   i   Katharine Blake JOHNSON, b. 1953
+ 918   ii   Anna White JOHNSON, b. 1955
+ 919   iii   Jane Shannon JOHNSON, b. 1956

678. DANIEL BLAKE[7] (Daniel Blake[6], Daniel Blake[5], Olivia Middleton[4], Oliver Hering Middleton[3], Henry Middleton[2], Arthur Middleton[1]) child of Daniel Blake and Katharine Brooks Shannon was born in 1931. He married Virginia Ann FRASER in say 1955. She was born in 1934. Children:

   920   i   Daniel BLAKE, b. 1957
   921   ii   William Bratton BLAKE, b. 1958
   922   iii   Robert Fraser BLAKE, b. 1962
   923   iv   Frederick Rutledge BLAKE, b. 1965

679. SHIRLEIGH HENDRY[7] (Shirley Middleton[6], Henry Middleton[5], Henry Middleton[4], Williams Middleton[3], Henry Middleton[2], Arthur Middleton[1]) child of Shirley Middleton and William John Hendry was born on 3 Oct 1954. She married Kenneth MATHERS on 2 Feb 1974. He was born on 29 Apr 1953. Children:

 924 i Andrew MATHERS, b. 15 May 1976
 925 ii Christopher MATHERS, b. 22 Oct 1979
 926 iii Glen MATHERS, b. 13 Mar 1985

683. JANET ELIZABETH DUNCAN[7] (Marion Barbara Dorothy Cousens[6], Dorothy Emma Middleton[5], Henry Middleton[4], Williams Middleton[3], Henry Middleton[2], Arthur Middleton[1]) child of Marion Barbara Dorothy Cousens and Keith Joseph Duncan was born on 18 Jun 1950. She married David Patrick WYLLIE on 2 Nov 1970. He was born on 3 Jun 1948. Children:

 927 i Nathan Michael Duncan WYLLIE, b. 21 Feb 1979
 928 ii Cameron James Marshall WYLLIE, b. 31 Aug 1981

685. ELLEN BARBARA DUNCAN[7] (Marion Barbara Dorothy Cousens[6], Dorothy Emma Middleton[5], Henry Middleton[4], Williams Middleton[3], Henry Middleton[2], Arthur Middleton[1]) child of Marion Barbara Dorothy Cousens and Keith Joseph Duncan was born on 1 Nov 1953. She married Donald George ROSS on 7 May 1977. He was born on 9 Jan 1950. Children:

 929 i Colin Andrew ROSS, b. 7 Aug 1979
 930 ii Bryce Derek ROSS, b. 11 Dec 1985

686. MAUREEN PATRICIA DUNCAN[7] (Marion Barbara Dorothy Cousens[6], Dorothy Emma Middleton[5], Henry Middleton[4], Williams Middleton[3], Henry Middleton[2], Arthur Middleton[1]) child of Marion Barbara Dorothy Cousens and Keith Joseph Duncan was born on 25 Aug 1955. She married Real Gerhard LEBLOND on 4 Aug 1979. He was born on 7 Apr 1954. Children:

 931 i Simon Mathieu LEBLOND, b. 29 Jan 1982
 932 ii Patrick Real LEBLOND, b. 10 Jul 1986
 933 iii Mathieu Lucien LEBLOND, b. 18 Oct 1990

687. KELLY JEANNE DUNCAN[7] (Marion Barbara Dorothy Cousens[6], Dorothy Emma Middleton[5], Henry Middleton[4], Williams Middleton[3], Henry Middleton[2], Arthur Middleton[1]) child of Marion Barbara Dorothy Cousens and Keith Joseph Duncan was born on 7 Jan 1958. She married Philip Thomas BARTLETT on 23 Dec 1988. He was born on 6 Jul 1962. Children:

 934 i Kalyn Rose BARTLETT, b. 27 Apr 1990
 935 ii Trevor Keegan BARTLETT, b. 3 Jun 1992

688. DIANE ELAINE RUTTER[7] (Pamela Helen Margaret Cousens[6], Dorothy Emma Middleton[5], Henry Middleton[4], Williams Middleton[3], Henry Middleton[2], Arthur Middleton[1]) child of Pamela Helen Margaret Cousens and Edward Sinclair Rutter was born on 5 Apr 1951. She married Bernard Jeudy HUGO on 14 Aug 1976. He was born on 23 Oct 1937. Children:

    936   i   Chad Gavin HUGO, b. 21 May 1978
    937   ii   Kent Derek HUGO, b. 11 May 1981

689. BRIAN EDWARD RUTTER[7] (Pamela Helen Margaret Cousens[6], Dorothy Emma Middleton[5], Henry Middleton[4], Williams Middleton[3], Henry Middleton[2], Arthur Middleton[1]) child of Pamela Helen Margaret Cousens and Edward Sinclair Rutter was born on 15 Mar 1953. He married Catherine Anne ODEN on 25 Aug 1973. She was born on 29 Jun 1953. Children:

    938   i   Martin Edward RUTTER, b. 20 Dec 1979
    939   ii   Brianne Nicole RUTTER, b. 26 Mar 1981

690. JOANNE BARBARA RUTTER[7] (Pamela Helen Margaret Cousens[6], Dorothy Emma Middleton[5], Henry Middleton[4], Williams Middleton[3], Henry Middleton[2], Arthur Middleton[1]) child of Pamela Helen Margaret Cousens and Edward Sinclair Rutter was born on 4 Jun 1954. She married Kirk Russell ARCHER on 21 Aug 1982. He was born on 20 Apr 1955. Children:

    940   i   Jeffrey Russell ARCHER, b. 4 Jun 1984
    941   ii   Katelyn Elizabeth ARCHER, b. 6 Sep 1988
    942   iii   Colin Edward ARCHER, b. 31 Jan 1990
    943   iv   Stephanie Ann ARCHER, b. 8 Jul 1992

691. BRYCE GEORGE RUTTER[7] (Pamela Helen Margaret Cousens[6], Dorothy Emma Middleton[5], Henry Middleton[4], Williams Middleton[3], Henry Middleton[2], Arthur Middleton[1]) child of Pamela Helen Margaret Cousens and Edward Sinclair Rutter was born on 4 Jan 1957. He married Joyce SAMSON on 11 Jan 1986. She was born on 18 Dec 1957. Children:

    944   i   Megan Marie RUTTER, b. 5 May 1988
    945   ii   Erin Elizabeth RUTTER, b. 9 May 1991

692. PAMELA ANN RUTTER[7] (Pamela Helen Margaret Cousens[6], Dorothy Emma Middleton[5], Henry Middleton[4], Williams Middleton[3], Henry Middleton[2], Arthur Middleton[1]) child of Pamela Helen Margaret Cousens and Edward Sinclair Rutter was born on 8 May 1960. She married Peter Neil MUCHMORE on 10 Oct 1987. He was born on 1 Jan 1962. Children:

    946   i   Alyssa Ann MUCHMORE, b. 20 Feb 1990
    947   ii   Adam Peter MUCHMORE, b. 20 Mar 1992

695. GEOFFREY GORDON HENRY COUSENS[7] (George Edward Heatly Cousens[6], Dorothy Emma Middleton[5], Henry Middleton[4], Williams Middleton[3], Henry Middleton[2], Arthur Middleton[1]) child of George Edward Heatly Cousens and Joan Elizabeth Macon was born on 4 Aug 1961. He married Keri OAKLEY on 9 Sep 1990. She was born on 20 Jun 1963. Child:

> 948   i   Braden Geoffrey Thomas COUSENS, b. 15 Apr 1991

699. GEORGE ROBERT COUSENS[7] (Colin Arthur Middleton Cousens[6], Dorothy Emma Middleton[5], Henry Middleton[4], Williams Middleton[3], Henry Middleton[2], Arthur Middleton[1]) child of Colin Arthur Middleton Cousens and Emelia Bernadette Nault was born on 1 Jan 1955. He married Katharyn Louise RYAN on 14 Oct 1978. She was born on 22 Jun 1957. Children:

> 949   i   Julie Ann COUSENS, b. 31 Jul 1981
> 950   ii   John Robert COUSENS, b. 20 Apr 1984

700. DIANNE BERNADETTE COUSENS[7] (Colin Arthur Middleton Cousens[6], Dorothy Emma Middleton[5], Henry Middleton[4], Williams Middleton[3], Henry Middleton[2], Arthur Middleton[1]) child of Colin Arthur Middleton Cousens and Emelia Bernadette Nault was born on 8 Apr 1956. She married Morris Peter ELBERS on 1 Jun 1979. He was born on 13 Aug 1954. Children:

> 951   i   Brent Colin ELBERS, b. 31 Jul 1980
> 952   ii   Jason Matthew ELBERS, b. 30 Oct 1984
> 953   iii Ryan James ELBERS, b. 19 Sep 1987

701. DONALD GORDON COUSENS[7] (Colin Arthur Middleton Cousens[6], Dorothy Emma Middleton[5], Henry Middleton[4], Williams Middleton[3], Henry Middleton[2], Arthur Middleton[1]) child of Colin Arthur Middleton Cousens and Emelia Bernadette Nault was born on 8 Dec 1957. He married Sandra Aileen COPELAND on 18 Sep 1981. She was born on 14 Sep 1958. Children:

> 954   i   Stephanie Aileen COUSENS, b. 14 Apr 1985
> 955   ii   Deron Gordon COUSENS, b. 21 Mar 1987

702. DOUGLAS VICTOR COUSENS[7] (Colin Arthur Middleton Cousens[6], Dorothy Emma Middleton[5], Henry Middleton[4], Williams Middleton[3], Henry Middleton[2], Arthur Middleton[1]) child of Colin Arthur Middleton Cousens and Emelia Bernadette Nault was born on 25 Jan 1962. He married Debra Lynn GUNBY in say 1984. She was born on 5 Sep 1955. Children:

> 956   i   Scott Russell COUSENS, b. 8 Jun 1986
> 957   ii   Sean Douglas COUSENS, b. 20 Aug 1988

703. JEAN ELIZABETH PHILIPPA MIDDLETON[7] (Ronald David Middleton[6], Ronald Williams Middleton[5], Henry Middleton[4], Williams Middleton[3], Henry Middleton[2], Arthur Middleton[1]) child of Ronald David Middleton and Ann Elizabeth Hughes was born on 2 May 1959. She married Stephen CROFT in 1985. He was born on 16 Dec 1958. Children:

    958   i   Alexander Henry Gordon CROFT, b. 12 Nov 1990
    959   ii   Rupert Charles Tristan CROFT, b. 22 Mar 1993

704. ALISON PATRICIA SIAN MIDDLETON[7] (Ronald David Middleton[6], Ronald Williams Middleton[5], Henry Middleton[4], Williams Middleton[3], Henry Middleton[2], Arthur Middleton[1]) child of Ronald David Middleton and Ann Elizabeth Hughes was born on 19 Feb 1961. She married Christopher COOKS in say 1990. He was born on 1 May 1952. Children:

    960   i   Camilla Ann COOKS, b. 27 Apr 1989
    961   ii   Cosmo James Middleton COOKS, b. 13 Feb 1991

709. DEBORAH ROSE MIDDLETON[7] (Anthony Hugh Middleton[6], Basil Bernard Norman Middleton[5], Henry Middleton[4], Williams Middleton[3], Henry Middleton[2], Arthur Middleton[1]) child of Anthony Hugh Middleton and Elizabeth Mary Nutman was born on 6 Aug 1961. She married (1st) Jonathan Paul JAMES in say 1979. Child:

    962   i   Benjamin Alexander John JAMES, b. 25 Feb 1980

710. PETREA MARY MIDDLETON[7] (Anthony Hugh Middleton[6], Basil Bernard Norman Middleton[5], Henry Middleton[4], Williams Middleton[3], Henry Middleton[2], Arthur Middleton[1]) child of Anthony Hugh Middleton and Elizabeth Mary Nutman was born on 26 May 1963. She married Michael Henry NORTH in say 1982. Children:

    963   i   Matthew Henry NORTH, b. 7 Aug 1984
    964   ii   Elizabeth Mary NORTH, b. 4 Jul 1986

714. AMANDA ZOE MIDDLETON[7] (Ian Keith Middleton[6], Basil Bernard Norman Middleton[5], Henry Middleton[4], Williams Middleton[3], Henry Middleton[2], Arthur Middleton[1]) child of Ian Keith Middleton and Suzanne Romaine Fox was born on 15 Oct 1959. She married (1st) Bruce STEWART on 4 Jan 1979. She married by Common Law (2nd) Vincent STEWART in say 1986. Children by first marriage:

    965   i   Karl Bruce STEWART, b. 12 Jul 1979
    966   ii   Zoe Sarah STEWART, b. 18 Jul 1981

Child by Common Law marriage:

    967   iii   Kirsty Isabel STEWART, b. 6 May 1988

732. FELICITY COPE[7] (Thomas Pym Cope[6], Eliza Middleton Kane[5], Elizabeth Francis Fisher[4], E lizabeth Izard Middleton[3], Henry Middleton[2], Arthur Middleton[1]) child of Thomas Pym Cope and Elizabeth W. Barringer was born in 1934. She married Shepherd K. ROBERTS in say 1954. Children:

    968   i   Elizabeth ROBERTS, b. 1956 [twin]
    969   ii   Ann ROBERTS, b. 1956 [twin]
    970   iii Oliver ROBERTS, b. c. 1958
    971   iv   Alison ROBERTS, b. 1963

733. ELIZABETH FRANCIS AUB[7] (Elizabeth Francis Pym Cope[6], Eliza Middleton Kane[5], Elizabeth Francis Fisher[4], Elizabeth Izard Middleton[3], Henry Middleton[2], Arthur Middleton[1]) child of Elizabeth Francis Pym Cope and Joseph C. Aub was born in 1926. She married Robert C. REID in 1954. Children:

    972   i   Child REID, b. c. 1957
    973   ii   Child REID, b. c. 1960
    974   iii Child Reid, b. c. 1964

734. FRANCES AUB[7] (Elizabeth Francis Pym Cope[6], Eliza Middleton Kane[5], Elizabeth Francis Fisher[4], Elizabeth Izard Middleton[3], Henry Middleton[2], Arthur Middleton[1]) child of Elizabeth Francis Pym Cope and Joseph C. Aub was born in 1930. She married Daniel K. BLOOMFIELD in 1955. Children:

    975   i   Louis BLOOMFIELD, b. 1956
    976   ii   Ruth BLOOMFIELD, b. 1958
    977   iii Anne BLOOMFIELD, b. 1962

735. NANCY COPE AUB[7] (Elizabeth Francis Pym Cope[6], Eliza Middleton Kane[5], Elizabeth Francis Fisher[4], Elizabeth Izard Middleton[3], Henry Middleton[2], Arthur Middleton[1]) child of Elizabeth Francis Pym Cope and Joseph C. Aub was born in 1934. She married Herbert P. GLEASON in 1954. Children:

    978   i   David Hollis GLEASON, b. 1960
    979   ii   Alice Hamilton GLEASON, b. 1963

736. SOPHIA HAZARD[7] (Anne Francis Cope[6], Eliza Middleton Kane[5], Elizabeth Francis Fisher[4], E lizabeth Izard Middleton[3], Henry Middleton[2], Arthur Middleton[1]) child of Anne Francis Cope and Thomas Pierrepont Hazard was born about 1923. She married Philip BARRINGER in 1948. Children:

980   i   Thomas BARRINGER, b. c. 1950
981   ii   Frances BARRINGER, b. c. 1953
982   iii Paul BARRINGER, b. c. 1958

738. MARY PIERREPONT HAZARD[7] (Anne Francis Cope[6], Eliza Middleton Kane[5], Elizabeth Francis Fisher[4], E lizabeth Izard Middleton[3], Henry Middleton[2], Arthur Middleton[1]) child of Anne Francis Cope and Thomas Pierrepont Hazard was born about 1928. She married (1st) Edwin HOYT in say 1948. She married (2nd) James K. CONRAD in say 1960. Children by first marriage:

983   i   William HOYT, b. c. 1950
+ 984   ii   Maria Louisa HOYT, b. c. 1952
985   iii Emily HOYT, b. c. 1955
Child by second marriage:
986   iv   Benjamin CONRAD, b. c. 1962

739. ANNE HAZARD[7] (Anne Francis Cope[6], Eliza Middleton Kane[5], Elizabeth Francis Fisher[4], Elizabeth Izard Middleton[3], Henry Middleton[2], Arthur Middleton[1]) child of Anne Francis Cope and Thomas Pierrepont Hazard was born about 1930. She married Elliott RICHARDSON in say 1950. Children:

987   i   Henry RICHARDSON, b. c. 1952
988   ii   Nancy RICHARDSON, b. c. 1954
989   iii Michael RICHARDSON, b. c. 1957

740. OLIVER COPE HAZARD[7] (Anne Francis Cope[6], Eliza Middleton Kane[5], Elizabeth Francis Fisher[4], Elizabeth Izard Middleton[3], Henry Middleton[2], Arthur Middleton[1]) child of Anne Francis Cope and Thomas Pierrepont Hazard was born about 1933. He married Sally PELL in say 1955. Children:

990   i   Elizabeth HAZARD, b. c. 1958
991   ii   Caroline HAZARD, b. c. 1960
992   iii Son HAZARD, b. c. 1964

741. ROBERT de NORMANDIE COPE[7] (Oliver Cope[6], Eliza Middleton Kane[5], Elizabeth Francis Fisher[4], Elizabeth Izard Middleton[3], Henry Middleton[2], Arthur Middleton[1]) child of Oliver Cope and Alice de Normandie was born in 1935. He married Margaret GRUENWALD in 1955. Children:

993   i   Oliver COPE, b. 1958
+ 994   ii   Eliza Middleton COPE, b. c. 1960
995   iii Thomas Pym COPE, b. c. 1964

742. ELIZA MIDDLETON COPE[7] (Oliver Cope[6], Eliza Middleton Kane[5], Elizabeth Francis Fisher[4], Elizabeth Izard Middleton[3], Henry Middleton[2], Arthur Middleton[1]) child of Oliver Cope and Alice de Normandie was born in 1936. She married Timothy HARRISON in 1960. Children:

   996   i   Abigail HARRISON, b. 1962
   997   ii   Emily HARRISON, b. 1964

743. JOHN CADWALADER[7] (John Cadwalader[6], John Cadwalader[5], Mary Helen Fisher[4], Elizabeth Izard Middleton[3], Henry Middleton[2], Arthur Middleton[1]) child of John Cadwalader and his 1st wife Beatrice d'Este Penrose was born on 28 Jun 1937. He married Deborah Dean RICHARDS in Sep 1986. She was born on 10 Jun 1953. Child:

   998   i   Susannah CADWALADER, b. 11 Dec 1988

744. GEORGE CADWALADER[7] (John Cadwalader[6], John Cadwalader[5], Mary Helen Fisher[4], Elizabeth Izard Middleton[3], Henry Middleton[2], Arthur Middleton[1]) child of John Cadwalader and his 1st wife Beatrice d'Este Penrose was born on 10 May 1939. He married Yara TELLES on 28 Mar 1969. She was born on 18 Jul 1939.Children:

   999   i   George CADWALADER, Jr., b. 4 Sep 1969
  1000   ii   Thomas CADWALADER, b. 22 Jan 1972

745. GARDNER ASPINWALL CADWALADER[7] (John Cadwalader[6], John Cadwalader[5], Mary Helen Fisher[4], Elizabeth Izard Middleton[3], Henry Middleton[2], Arthur Middleton[1]) child of John Cadwalader and his 2nd wife Lea Thom Aspinwall was born on 29 Jul 1948. He married Kathryn Louise KAERSHER on 4 Sep 1976. Children:

  1001   i   Genevieve Aspinwall CADWALADER, b. 28 Sep 1982
  1002   ii   Gardner Owen CADWALADER, b. 22 Feb 1985

748. ELIZABETH JANE CADWALADER[7] (Thomas Francis Cadwalader, Jr.[6], Thomas Francis Cadwalader[5], Mary Helen Fisher[4], Elizabeth Izard Middleton[3], Henry Middleton[2], Arthur Middleton[1]) child of Thomas Francis Cadwalader, Jr. and Phyllis Jane Clegg was born on 16 Nov 1946. She married Eugene Stanley BARON on 21 Jun 1981. He was born on 20 Feb 1952. Child:

  1003   i   Owen David Cadwalader BARON, b. 23 Nov 1987

749. SOPHIA FRANCIS CADWALADER[7] (Thomas Francis Cadwalader, Jr.[6], Thomas Francis Cadwalader[5], Mary Helen Fisher[4], Elizabeth Izard Middleton[3], Henry Middleton[2], Arthur Middleton[1]) child of Thomas Francis

Cadwalader, Jr. and Phyllis Jane Clegg was born in Baltimore, MD on 4 Jan 1951. She married James Stoddard HAYES, Jr. on 5 Jun 1971. He was born in Ridley Park, PA on 8 Mar 1948. Children:

    1004   i   James Stoddard HAYES, III, b. 26 Jun 1972

    1005   ii   Joshua Francis HAYES, b. 5 May 1976

750. STEPHEN JACKSON EARLE[7] (Ann Cleland Cadwalader[6], Thomas Francis Cadwalader[5], Mary Helen Fisher[4], Elizabeth Izard Middleton[3], Henry Middleton[2], Arthur Middleton[1]) child of Ann Cleland Cadwalader and Richard Blair Earle was born on 2 Dec 1949. He married Akemi OGAWA on 21 Mar 1974. She was born on 18 May 1949. Children:

    1006   i   Lieko EARLE, b. 20 Jan 1975

    1007   ii   Sayako EARLE, b. 15 Sep 1980

752. THOMAS CADWALADER EARLE[7] (Ann Cleland Cadwalader[6], Thomas Francis Cadwalader[5], Mary Helen Fisher[4], Elizabeth Izard Middleton[3], Henry Middleton[2], Arthur Middleton[1]) child of Ann Cleland Cadwalader and Richard Blair Earle was born on 20 Oct 1953. He married Elizabeth C. WELDON on 21 Jul 1979. She was born on 22 Mar 1948, and died on 17 Nov 1994. Children:

    1008   i   Sarah Elizabeth EARLE, b. 22 Aug 1981

    1009   ii   Katherine Cadwalader EARLE, b. 23 Mar 1984

753. CLELAND KINLOCH EARLE[7] (Ann Cleland Cadwalader[6], Thomas Francis Cadwalader[5], Mary Helen Fisher[4], Elizabeth Izard Middleton[3], Henry Middleton[2], Arthur Middleton[1]) child of Ann Cleland Cadwalader and Richard Blair Earle was born on 20 Jan 1956. He married Miriam Elizabeth NELSON on 23 Jan 1988. She was born on 3 May 1960. Children:

    1010   i   Kinloch Mason EARLE, b. 6 Aug 1988

    1011   ii   Eliza Middleton EARLE, b. 30 Mar 1990

    1012   iii   Alexander Jackson EARLE, b. 29 Apr 1992

754. VIRGINIA ROBBINS[7] (Eleanor Hart[6], Anna Scott Fisher[5], George Harrison Fisher[4], Elizabeth Izard Middleton[3], Henry Middleton[2], Arthur Middleton[1]) child of Eleanor Hart and George Appleton Robbins was born in 1931. She married Edward John GAUSS in 1955. He was born in 1932. Children:

    1013   i   Christy Ann GAUSS, b. 1959

    1014   ii   George Harry GAUSS, b. 1962

768. RITA IZARD HUNTER[7] (Rita Izard[6], Ralph Izard[5], Walter Izard[4], Walter Izard[3], Emma Philadelphia Middleton[2], Arthur Middleton[1]) child of Rita Izard and William Blair Hunter was born in Gastonia, NC on 28 Jan 1928. She married Lyle Vincent WADE in Lillington, NC on 24 Nov 1950. He was born in Greensboro, NC on 12 Feb 1925. Children:
+ 1015   i   Nancy Theresa WADE, b. 4 Sep 1954
+ 1016   ii Anne Berry WADE, b. 29 Oct 1955

769. NANCY WARE HAWKINS[7] (Laura Elizabeth Izard[6], Ralph Izard[5], Walter Izard[4], Walter Izard[3], Emma Philadelphia Middleton[2], Arthur Middleton[1]) child of Laura Elizabeth Izard and her 1st husband Albert Winfree Hawkins was born in Richmond, VA on 13 Mar 1929. She married Playford BOYLE in Richmond, VA on 2 Jul 1949. He was born in Uniontown, PA on 11 Mar 1924. Child:
     1017   i   Laura Louise BOYLE, b. 15 Aug 1963

770. ALICE DeLANCEY HARRIS[7] (Laura Elizabeth Izard[6], Ralph Izard[5], Walter Izard[4], Walter Izard[3], Emma Philadelphia Middleton[2], Arthur Middleton[1]) child of Laura Elizabeth Izard and her 2nd husband John Edmund Harris was born on 14 Mar 1939. She married Jonathan HILL in 1960. Children:
     1018   i   Peter C. HILL, b. 1962
     1019   ii Cabell HILL, b. 1963

773. PATIENCE HURD MIDDLETON[7] (Arthur Middleton[6], William Dehon Middleton[5], Arthur Middleton[4], Emma Izard[3], Emma Philadelphia Middleton[2], Arthur Middleton[1]) child of Arthur Middleton and Patience Campbell Hurd was born in Charleston, SC on 19 Sep 1924. She married Ernest Arthur HAYDEN, Jr in Augusta, GA on 23 May 1947. He was born in North Augusta, SC on 27 Dec 1919. Children:
     1020   i   Ernest Arthur HAYDEN, III, b. 20 Nov 1947
     1021   ii Robert Campbell HAYDEN, b. 9 Aug 1952

774. SALLY HORTON MIDDLETON[7] (Arthur Middleton[6], William Dehon Middleton[5], Arthur Middleton[4], Emma Izard[3], Emma Philadelphia Middleton[2], Arthur Middleton[1]) child of Arthur Middleton and Patience Campbell Hurd was born in Charleston, SC on 2 Mar 1927. She married Robert McLain HAWKRIDGE in Augusta, GA on 28 May 1955. He was born in Boston, MA on 26 Jul 1926. Children:
+ 1022   i   Robert McLain HAWKRIDGE, Jr., b. 12 May 1958
+ 1023   ii Sally Horton HAWKRIDGE, b. 20 Aug 1961

775. ANNELY BLAKE MIDDLETON[7] (Arthur Middleton[6], William Dehon Middleton[5], Arthur Middleton[4], Emma Izard[3], Emma Philadelphia Middleton[2], Arthur Middleton[1]) child of Arthur Middleton and Patience Campbell Hurd was born in Charleston, SC on 9 Dec 1928. She married (1st) Samuel Mack RAMSEY, Jr. in Augusta, GA on 16 Apr 1947. He was born in Augusta, GA on 9 Dec 1924. She married (2nd) Richard Burton HAYES, Jr. on 7 Oct 1955. He was born on 31 Oct 1923, and died on 23 May 1976. Childen by first marriage:
+ 1024   i   Samuel Mack RAMSEY, III, b. 30 Mar 1948
+ 1025   ii   Arthur Middleton RAMSEY, b. 1 Dec 1950
+ 1026   iii   Annely Blake RAMSEY, b. 20 Feb 1952
Children by second marriage:
+ 1027   iv   Hope Gardner HAYES, b. 8 Nov 1956
   1028   v   Patience Hurd HAYES, b. 9 Jan 1958
+ 1029   vi   Richard Burton HAYES, III, b. 20 May 1959

776. GAY Van ASSENDELFT MIDDLETON[7] (Arthur Middleton[6], William Dehon Middleton[5], Arthur Middleton[4], Emma Izard[3], Emma Philadelphia Middleton[2], Arthur Middleton[1]) child of Arthur Middleton and Patience Campbell Hurd was born in Charleston, SC on 28 May 1933. She married Frank Nichols MASON in Augusta, GA on 28 Feb 1953. He was born in Waynesboro, VA on 28 Jan 1931. Children:
+ 1030   i   Gay Middleton MASON, b. 26 Jul 1954
+ 1031   ii   Lemuel Wyatt MASON, b. 31 May 1959
+ 1032   iii   Frank Nichols MASON, Jr., b. 19 Mar 1961
   1033   iv   Arthur Middleton MASON, b. 8 Apr 1968

778. JULIUS BLAKE MIDDLETON, Jr.[7] (Julius Blake Middleton[6], William Dehon Middleton[5], Arthur Middleton[4], Emma Izard[3], Emma Philadelphia Middleton[2], Arthur Middleton[1]) child of Julius Blake Middleton and Margaret Lane Goodwyn was born on 15 Aug 1932. He married Nancy King DANIELS on 15 Sep 1954. Children:
   1034   i   Julius Blake MIDDLETON, III, b. 12 Feb 1959
   1035   ii   Mark Tyler MIDDLETON, b. 15 Sep 1960
   1036   iii   Gardner King MIDDLETON, b. 10 May 1962
   1037   iv   Lane Goodwyn MIDDLETON, b. 16 Sep 1964

779. CHARLIE LANE MIDDLETON[7] (Julius Blake Middleton[6], William Dehon Middleton[5], Arthur Middleton[4], Emma Izard[3], Emma Philadelphia Middleton[2], Arthur Middleton[1]) child of Julius Blake Middleton and Margaret

Lane Goodwyn was born on 9 Apr 1938. She married Francis John Morland KINSMAN on 7 Aug 1959. He was born on 28 Aug 1934. Children:

 1038   i   Julius Blake Middleton KINSMAN, b. 10 Dec 1960, d. 17 Nov 1983; unm
 1039   ii   Emmeline Hibbery KINSMAN, b. 29 Mar 1962
 1040   iii   John Francis Morland KINSMAN, b. 28 Sep 1964

780. WILLIAM MIDDLETON, Jr.[7] (William Middleton[6], William Dehon Middleton[5], Arthur Middleton[4], Emma Izard[3], Emma Philadelphia Middleton[2], Arthur Middleton[1]) child of William Middleton and Frances Gaillard Hanahan was born on 21 Dec 1931, and died on 20 Jan 1996. He married Mary Ann ERWIN on 5 Jun 1957. Children:

 1041   i   William MIDDLETON, III, b. 15 Oct 1958
 1042   ii   Mary Ann MIDDLETON, b. 6 Mar 1962
 1043   iii   Harriet Addie MIDDLETON, b. 8 Dec 1963

781. FRANCIS GAILLARD MIDDLETON[7] (William Middleton[6], William Dehon Middleton[5], Arthur Middleton[4], Emma Izard[3], Emma Philadelphia Middleton[2], Arthur Middleton[1]) child of William Middleton and Frances Gaillard Hanahan was born on 25 Mar 1940. He married Allison Jaycocks JONES on 27 Apr 1968. Children:

 1044   i   Ethel Allison MIDDLETON, b. 4 Mar 1969
 1045   ii   Francis Gaillard MIDDLETON, Jr., b. 2 Apr 1972
 1046   iii   Arthur Dehon MIDDLETON, b. 8 Aug 1979

782. CHARLES BREWSTER PRENTISS, III[7] (Julia Porcher Middleton[6], William Dehon Middleton[5], Arthur Middleton[4], Emma Izard[3], Emma Philadelphia Middleton[2], Arthur Middleton[1]) child of Julia Porcher Middleton and Charles Brewster Prentiss was born on 14 Dec 1929. He married Margaret Naomi ORTMANN on 8 Oct 1951. He was born on 24 Feb 1931. Child:

 + 1047   i   Eugenia Kirkland PRENTISS, b. 14 Jul 1955

783. JULIA BLAKE PRENTISS[7] (Julia Porcher Middleton[6], William Dehon Middleton[5], Arthur Middleton[4], Emma Izard[3], Emma Philadelphia Middleton[2], Arthur Middleton[1]) child of Julia Porcher Middleton and Charles Brewster Prentiss was born in Charleston, SC on 23 Feb 1932. She married Paul Amberg HAGEN, Jr. in Charleston, SC on 11 Jul 1953. He was born in Madison, WI on 19 Aug 1930. Children:

 + 1048   i   Julie Ann HAGEN, b. 16 Mar 1955
 + 1049   ii   Lars Romoren HAGEN, b. 10 Mar 1957 [twin]
 1050   iii   Lynn Prentiss HAGEN, b. 10 Mar 1957 [twin]

785. LEWIS BLAKE MIDDLETON, Jr.[7] (Lewis Blake Middleton[6], William Dehon Middleton[5], Arthur Middleton[4], Emma Izard[3], Emma Philadelphia Middleton[2], Arthur Middleton[1]) child of Lewis Blake Middleton and Elizabeth Ingram Lachicotte was born on 12 Nov 1947. He married Mary Catherine POWELL on 18 May 1974. She was born on 20 Apr 1953. Children:

 1051 i Arthur Blake MIDDLETON, b. 8 Sep 1977
 1052 ii Mary Porcher MIDDLETON, b. 15 Apr 1981

786. JULIA PORCHER MIDDLETON[7] (Lewis Blake Middleton[6], William Dehon Middleton[5], Arthur Middleton[4], Emma Izard[3], Emma Philadelphia Middleton[2], Arthur Middleton[1]) child of Lewis Blake Middleton and Elizabeth Ingram Lachicotte was born on 15 Jan 1951. She married John Edward ROYALL, Jr. on 5 Nov 1977. He was born on 15 Dec 1947. Children:

 1053 i John Edward ROYALL, III, b. 24 Jul 1980
 1054 ii Robert Lewis ROYALL, b. 20 Sep 1982

788. JANE MORRIS MUNNERLYN[7] (Benjamin Munnerlyn[6], Lucy Izard Middleton[5], Arthur Middleton[4], Emma Izard[3], Emma Philadelphia Middleton[2], Arthur Middleton[1]) child of Benjamin Munnerlyn and Elizabeth Spring was born on 15 Jan 1929. She married Frank CARTER, Jr. in 1949. He died in 1991. Children:

+ 1055 i Frank CARTER, III, b. 16 Sep 1950
+ 1056 ii Benjamin Munnerlyn CARTER, b. 26 Dec 1953
 1057 iii Wilson Munnerlyn CARTER, b. 15 Apr 1957
 1058 iv Jane Stewart CARTER, b. 10 Oct 1961

789. WILBUR C. DuBOIS, Jr.[7] (Anna Bertha Dehon[6], Helen Middleton[5], Arthur Middleton[4], Margaret Emma Izard[3], Emma Philadelphia Middleton[2], Arthur Middleton[1]) child of Anna Bertha Dehon and Wilbur C. Dubois was born on 2 Oct 1923. He married Anne HAMMER in say 1948. Children:

 1059 i Wilbur C. DuBOIS, b. c. 1950
 1060 ii William Hammer DuBOIS, b. c. 1952
 1061 ii Robert Ellsworth DuBOIS, b. c. 1955
 1062 iv Brandon DuBOIS, b. c. 1959

790. HELEN MIDDLETON DuBOIS[7] (Anna Bertha Dehon[6], Helen Middleton[5], Arthur Middleton[4], Margaret Emma Izard[3], Emma Philadelphia Middleton[2], Arthur Middleton[1]) child of Anna Bertha Dehon and Wilbur C. Dubois was born on 1 Aug 1926. She married Alton D. SEARS in say 1947. Children:

+   1063   i   John Chapman SEARS, b. c. 1950
+   1064   ii   Richard Allen SEARS, b. c. 1953
+   1065   iii Susan Carroll SEARS, b. c. 1956

793 CHARLES B. ARBOGAST, Jr.[7] (Eva Russell Dehon[6], Helen Middleton[5], Arthur Middleton[4], Margaret Emma Izard[3], Emma Philadelphia Middleton[2], Arthur Middleton[1]) child of Eva Russell Dehon and Charles B. Arbogast was born about 1925. He married -- (--) in say 1947. Children:

    1066   i   D. B. ARBOGAST, b. c. 1950
    1067   ii   Erica Anne ARBOGAST, b. c. 1954

798. MARY MAULDIN[7] (Mary Dehon[6], Helen Middleton[5], Arthur Middleton[4], Margaret Emma Izard[3], Emma Philadelphia Middleton[2], Arthur Middleton[1]) child of Mary Dehon and Wilbur Hamilton Mauldin was born about 1934. She married Benjamin Charlton GRINER in say 1956. Children:

+   1068   i   Julia GRINER, b. c. 1959
+   1069   ii   Benjamin Charlton GRINER, Jr., b. c. 1961
+   1070   iii Sara GRINER, b. c. 1962
+   1071   iv   Agnes GRINER, b. c. 1965

799. HARRIET MAULDIN[7] (Mary Dehon[6], Helen Middleton[5], Arthur Middleton[4], Margaret Emma Izard[3], Emma Philadelphia Middleton[2], Arthur Middleton[1]) child of Mary Dehon and Wilbur Hamilton Mauldin was born about 1937. She married James Kenneth MORRIS, Jr. in say 1959. Children:

    1072   i   James Kenneth MORRIS, III, b, c, 1961
    1073   ii   Charles Wilder MORRIS, b. c. 1964

801. ANN MAULDIN[7] (Mary Dehon[6], Helen Middleton[5], Arthur Middleton[4], Margaret Emma Izard[3], Emma Philadelphia Middleton[2], Arthur Middleton[1]) child of Mary Dehon and Wilbur Hamilton Mauldin was born about 1942. She married John Andrew CARSON in say 1965. Children:

+   1074   i   John Andrew CARSON, Jr., b. c. 1968
+   1075   ii   Deborah CARSON, b. c. 1970
    1076   iii Michael Wilder CARSON, b. c. 1973
    1077   iv   Aimee CARSON, b. c. 1977

802. MIRIAM MIDDLETON HALLMAN[7] (Miriam Bridge Middleton[6], Walter Izard Middleton[5], Arthur Middleton[4], Margaret Emma Izard[3], Emma Philadelphia Middleton[2], Arthur Middleton[1]) child of Miriam Bridge Middleton and Harry Hightower Hallman was born on 23 Sep 1926. She married Allen Shannon JACKSON on 6 Aug 1947. He was born 0n 11 Jul 1922. Children:

    1078   i   Allen Shannon JACKSON, Jr., b. 29 May 1949

    1079   ii   Mary Ellen JACKSON, b. 30 Apr 1952

    1080   iii   Arthur Middleton JACKSON, b. 15 Sep 1955

804. ROBERT BLAKE CALDCLEUGH[7] (Willie Maxine Hoffman[6], Florence Vernon Blake[5], Arthur Middleton Blake[4], Daniel Blake[3], Anna Louisa Middleton[2], Arthur Middleton[1]) child of Willie Maxine Hoffman and Clarence Milton Caldcleugh was born in Colorado Springs, CO on 16 Jun 1945. He married Connie Ione LOWREY in Abilene, TX on 19 Jan 1968. She was born in Big Spring, TX on 25 Jan 1950. Child:

    1081   i   Bobette CALDCLEUGH, b. 17 Sep 1971

807. OLIVIA CALDWELL HOLT[7] (Eleanor Oliver Rutledge[6], Benjamin Huger Rutledge[5], Emma Craig Blake[4], Daniel Izard[3], Anna Louisa Middleton[2], Arthur Middleton[1]) child of Eleanor Oliver Rutledge and Arnold Rich Holt was born in 1954. She married Michael BARTONE in 1978. Child:

    1082   i   Alexandra Townsend BARTONE, b. 1980

817. FRANCIS P. RHETT[7] (Frances Cheshire[6], Frances Bayley Blake Rutledge[5], Helen Bayley Blake[4], Daniel Izard[3], Anna Louisa Middleton[2], Arthur Middleton[1]) child of Frances Cheshire and Francis Rhett was born in 1951. He married Ann JERVEY in say 1976. Children:

    1083   i   Ann Jervey RHETT, b. c. 1978

    1084   ii   Francis Rutledge RHETT, b. c. 1981

818. JOSEPH CHESHIRE RHETT[7] (Frances Cheshire[6], Frances Bayley Blake Rutledge[5], Helen Bayley Blake[4], Daniel Izard[3], Anna Louisa Middleton[2], Arthur Middleton[1]) child of Frances Cheshire and Francis Rhett was born in 1953. He married Toni AUSTEL in say 1980. Children:

    1085   i   Ann Legare RHETT, b. 1987

    1086   ii   Katherine Cheshire RHETT, b. 1989

823. FRANCES PARKER[7] (Katherine Blount Cheshire[6], Frances Bayley Blake Rutledge[5], Helen Bayley Blake[4], Daniel Izard[3], Anna Louisa Middleton[2], Arthur Middleton[1]) child of Katherine Blount Cheshire and Amory Parker was born in 1955. She married Herbert de LACVIVIER in say 1979. Children:

    1087   i   Claire de LACVIVIER, b. 1985

    1088   ii   Caroline de LACVIVIER, b. 1988

824. OLIVER AMES PARKER[7] (Katherine Blount Cheshire[6], Frances Bayley Blake Rutledge[5], Helen Bayley Blake[4], Daniel Izard[3], Anna Louisa Middleton[2], Arthur Middleton[1]) child of Katherine Blount Cheshire and Amory Parker was born in 1956. He married Barbara ZENKER in say 1980. Children:

    1089   i   Sarah Elizabeth PARKER, b. c. 1984
    1090   ii   William Amory PARKER, b. c. 1986
    1091   iii   Anna Rutledge PARKER, b. c. 1990

827. OLIVER RUTLEDGE EDWARDS[7] (Clementina Rutledge[6], Oliver Middleton Rutledge[5], Helen Bayley Blake[4], Daniel Izard[3], Anna Louisa Middleton[2], Arthur Middleton[1]) child of Clementina Rutledge and Howard Edwards was born about 1961. He married Julie Anne BIRMINGHAM in say 1983. Children:

    1092   i   Christopher EDWARDS, b. 1985
    1093   ii   Dana EDWARDS, b. 1987

828. JOHN LEE MERRILL, III[7] (Helen Blake Rutledge Swan[6], Elise Rutledge[5], Helen Bayley Blake[4], Daniel Izard[3], Anna Louisa Middleton[2], Arthur Middleton[1]) child of Helen Blake Rutledge Swan and John Lee Merrill, Jr. was born in 1950. He married Erica THORMANN in say 1985. Children:

    1094   i   Laura Coleman MERRILL, b. c. 1988
    1095   ii   Samuel Hill MERRILL, b. c. 1991

829. ELIZABETH RUTLEDGE MERRILL[7] (Helen Blake Rutledge Swan[6], Elise Rutledge[5], Helen Bayley Blake[4], Daniel Izard[3], Anna Louisa Middleton[2], Arthur Middleton[1]) child of Helen Blake Rutledge Swan and John Lee Merrill, Jr. was born in 1952. She married David Tominson PRATT in say 1975. Children:

    1096   i   Nicholas Rutledge PRATT, b. 1978
    1097   ii   Thomas Langdon PRATT, b. 1981

830. TIMOTHY WHITNEY BLAGDEN[7] (Josephine Cutter Swan[6], Elise Rutledge[5], Helen Bayley Blake[4], Daniel Izard[3], Anna Louisa Middleton[2], Arthur Middleton[1]) child of Josephine Cutter Swan and George Blagden was born about 1952. He married Beverly BRINE in say 1976. Child:

    1098   i   Tucker Whitney BLAGDEN, b. c. 1980

839. ARTHUR MANIGAULT WILCOX[7] (Caroline Manigault[6], Arthur Middleton Manigault[5], Mary Proctor Huger[4], Daniel Elliott Huger[3], Isabella

Johannes Middleton[2], Arthur Middleton[1]) child of Caroline Manigault and John Walter Wilcox was born on 2 May 1922. He married Katharine MOORE on 25 Nov 1944. She was born on 1 Oct 1922. Children:

1099　i　Margaret WILCOX, b. c. 1947
1100　ii　Arthur WILCOX, b. c. 1950
1101　iii　John WILCOX, b. c. 1952
1102　iv　Priscilla WILCOX, b. c. 1955
1103　v　Robert WILCOX, b. c. 1960

840. MARY HUGER MANIGAULT WILCOX[7] (Caroline Manigault[6], Arthur Middleton Manigault[5], Mary Proctor Huger[4], Daniel Elliott Huger[3], Isabella Johannes Middleton[2], Arthur Middleton[1]) child of Caroline Manigault and John Walter Wilcox was born on 5 Jul 1930. She married John Miles HORLBECK on 2 May 1953. He was born on 29 Jan 1925. Children:

1104　i　John Wilcox HORLBECK, b. c. 1955
1105　ii　Peter Miles HORLBECK, b. c. 1957
1106　iii　Frederick Henry HORLBECK, b. c.1960
1107　iv　Caroline Manigault Wilcox HORLBECK, b. c. 1964

843. FRANCES PELZER HUGER[7] (Daniel Elliott Huger, Jr.[6], Daniel Elliott Huger[5], William Elliott Huger[4], Daniel Elliott Huger[3], Isabella Johannes Middleton[2], Arthur Middleton[1]) child of Daniel Elliott Huger, Jr. and Frances Pelzer was born about 1930. She married Edward Harleston de SAUSSURE, Jr. in say 1951. Children:

+　1108　i　Frances Huger de SAUSSURE, b. c. 1954
+　1109　ii　Eleanor Charlton de SAUSSURE, b. c. 1957
+　1110　iii　Anita de SAUSSURE, b. c. 1960
　1111　iv　Edward Harleston de SAUSSURE, III, b. c. 1961
+　1112　v　Margaret de SAUSSURE, b. c. 1963

846. ELIZABETH PELZER HUGER[7] (Daniel Elliott Huger, Jr.[6], Daniel Elliott Huger[5], William Elliott Huger[4], Daniel Elliott Huger[3], Isabella Johannes Middleton[2], Arthur Middleton[1]) child of Daniel Elliott Huger, Jr. and Frances Pelzer was born about 1940. She married John Maxwell STERLING, Jr. in say 1960. Children:

+　1113　i　John Maxwell STERLING, III, b. c. 1962
+　1114　ii　Elizabeth Huger STERLING, b. c. 1965
　1115　iii　Daniel Elliott STERLING, b. c. 1969

847. CAROLINE HAMPTON LADUE[7] (Caroline Hampton Mullally[6], Caroline Hampton Lowndes[5], Rawlins Lowndes[4], Sabina Elliott Huger[3],

Isabella Johannes Middleton[2], Arthur Middleton[1]) child of Caroline Hampton Mullally and Lawrence Knight Ladue was born in Hendersonville, NC on 22 Aug 1930. She married Gordon Hossley MANN in Charleston, SC on 29 Sep 1953. He was born in Charleston, SC on 28 May 1928. Children:

    1116   i   Caroline Hampton MANN, b. 25 Aug 1954
    1117   ii   Sarah Spencer MANN, b. c. 1959
    1118   iii   Susan Adger MANN, b. 7 Apr 1964

849. MIDDLETON POPE BARROW, Jr.[7] (Middleton Pope Barrow[6], Emma Middleton Izard Huger[5], Joseph Alston Huger, Jr.[4], Joseph Alston Huger[3], Isabella Johannes Middleton[2], Arthur Middleton[1]) child of Middleton Pope Barrow and Katherine Winchester Forsythe was born in Savannah, GA on 26 Dec 1942. He married Giulia Pat MAINIERI in Waretown, Ocean County, NJ on 23 Oct 1976. She was born in Ft. Worth, TX on 26 Oct 1950. Children:

    1119   i   Isabel Angelina BARROW, b. 9 Dec 1977
    1120   ii   Middleton Pope BARROW, III, b. c. 1980
    1121   iii   Rebecca Anne BARROW, b. c. 1983

850. ALICE LOWNDES LEE[7] (Lawrence Lee, Jr.[6], Cleland Kinloch Huger[5], Joseph Alston Huger, Jr.[4], Joseph Alston Huger[3], Isabella Johannes Middleton[2], Arthur Middleton[1]) child of Lawrence Lee, Jr. and Elizabeth Middleton Andrews was born in Savannah, GA on 12 May 1951. She married Joseph Bacon FRASER, III in Savannah, GA on 23 Jun 1973. He was born in Savannah, GA on 28 Jan 1951. Child:

    1122   i   Elizabeth Middleton FRASER, b. 29 Sep 1978

853. ALETTA WOOD JERVEY[7] (James Wilkinson Jervey, Jr.[6], James Wilkinson Jervey[5], Isabella Middleton Wilkinson[4], Sarah Elliott Huger[3], Isabella Johannes Middleton[2], Arthur Middleton[1]) child of James Wilkinson Jervey, Jr. and Laura Aletta Wood was born on 13 Apr 1930. She married R. W. HUDGENS in say 1955. Children:

    1123   i   Peter Halstead HUDGENS, b. 22 Sep 1958
    1124   ii   Mary Eleanor HUDGENS, b. 18 May 1962

855. EDWARD DARRELL JERVEY[7] (James Wilkinson Jervey, Jr.[6], James Wilkinson Jervey[5], Isabella Middleton Wilkinson[4], Sarah Elliott Huger[3], Isabella Johannes Middleton[2], Arthur Middleton[1]) child of James Wilkinson Jervey, Jr. and Laura Aletta Wood was born on 23 Aug 1936. He married -- (--) in say 1958. Child:

    1125   i   Kathrin Gage JERVEY, b. 3 Apr 1960

857. LOUISE BARNWELL ELLIOTT[7] (Marguerite Barnwell King[6], Maria Louisa Wilkinson Barnwell[5], Maria Louisa Wilkinson[4], Sarah Elliott Huger[3], Isabella Johannes Middleton[2], Arthur Middleton[1]) child of Marguerite Barnwell King and William W. Elliott was born in 1928. She married Charles Henry SACKETT in 1953. Children:
- 1126   i   Margaret Elliott SACKETT, b. 1955
- 1127   ii   Sally Elliott SACKETT, b. 1957

858. WILLIAM W. ELLIOTT[7] (Marguerite Barnwell King[6], Maria Louisa Wilkinson Barnwell[5], Maria Louisa Wilkinson[4], Sarah Elliott Huger[3], Isabella Johannes Middleton[2], Arthur Middleton[1]) child of Marguerite Barnwell King and William W. Elliott was born in 1932. He married Erin DOWLING in 1953. Children:
- 1128   i   Isabel Barnwell ELLIOTT, b. 1954
- 1129   ii   William W. ELLIOTT, IV, b. 1957

865. KATHERINE SABINA STEVENSON[7] (Horace Lee Stevenson[6], Sabina Swope Forney[5], Septima Sexta Middleton Rutledge[4], Henry Adolphus Rutledge[3], Septima Sexta Middleton[2], Arthur Middleton[1]) child of Horace Lee Stevenson and Sara Katherine Segrest was born in Jacksonville, AL on 27 Oct 1935. She married William Powell PANNELL on 10 Jun 1956. He was born in Mobile, AL on 7 Aug 1934. Children:
- 1130   i   Katherine Suzanne PANNELL, b. 11 May 1957
- 1131   ii   William Powell PANNELL, Jr., b. 11 Jan 1960
- 1132   iii   John Lee PANNELL, b. 10 Nov 1961

866. MARY CAROLINE POLING[7] (Mary Abernathy Stevenson[6], Sabina Swope Forney[5], Septima Sexta Middleton Rutledge[4], Henry Adolphus Rutledge[3], Septima Sexta Middleton[2], Arthur Middleton[1]) child of Mary Abernathy Stevenson and Arnold A. Poling was born in Jacksonville, AL on 15 Aug 1928. She married Harry Alfred JOHNSON on 1 Dec 1945. He was born in Cambridge, MA on 2 Jul 1923. Child:
- 1133   i   Forney Rutledge JOHNSON, b. 14 Mar 1948

868. ALBURTA MARTIN DAUGETTE[7] (Clarence William Daugette, Jr.[6], Annie Rowan Forney[5], Septima Sexta Middleton Rutledge[4], Henry Adolphus Rutledge[3], Septima Sexta Middleton[2], Arthur Middleton[1]) child of Clarence William Daugette, Jr. and Florence Earle Throckmorton was born in Birmingham, AL on 25 Jun 1948. She married Marvin Lynn LOWE in Gadsden, AL on 2 Aug 1975. He was born in Bruceton, TN on 30 Dec 1947. Child:
- 1134   i   Mary Kinney LOWE, b. 10 Jul 1981

869. FLORENCE ANNE DAUGETTE[7] (Clarence William Daugette, Jr.[6], Annie Rowan Forney[5], Septima Sexta Middleton Rutledge[4], Henry Adolphus Rutledge[3], Septima Sexta Middleton[2], Arthur Middleton[1]) child of Clarence William Daugette, Jr. and Florence Earle Throckmorton was born in Birmingham, AL on 14 Oct 1949. She married Raymond R. RENFROW, Jr. in say 1972. Child:

    1135   i   Anne Clare RENFROW, b. 15 Apr 1974

871. FORNEY RUTLEDGE DAUGETTE, Jr.[7] (Forney Rutledge Daugette[6], Annie Rowan Forney[5], Septima Sexta Middleton Rutledge[4], Henry Adolphus Rutledge[3], Septima Sexta Middleton[2], Arthur Middleton[1]) child of Forney Rutledge Daugette and Mary Elizabeth Moody was born in Anniston, AL on 13 Nov 1932. He married Mary Reed SIMPSON in Eagle Pass, TX on 6 Aug 1955. She was born in Eagle Pass, TX on 7 May 1934. Children:

    1136   i   Forney Rutledge DAUGETTE, III, b. 1 Sep 1956
    1137   ii   William Reed DAUGETTE, b. 27 Dec 1957
    1138   iii   Mary Elizabeth DAUGETTE, b. 18 Oct 1959

875. HARRISON SHELBY MERRITT[7] (Henrietta Middleton Rutledge[6], Thomas Pinckney Rutledge[5], Henry Middleton Rutledge[4], Henrietta Middleton Rutledge[3], Septima Sexta Middleton[2], Arthur Middleton[1]) child of Henrietta Middleton Rutledge and Franklyn Clement Merritt was born in 1942. He married Anne Trapier DRAYTON in say 1968. She was born in 1945. Children:

    1139   i   Harrison Shelby MERRITT, b. 1971
    1140   ii   Elizabeth Heyward MERRITT, b. 1974

877. DONALD THROPP RUTLEDGE[7] (Henry Middleton Rutledge[6], Archibald Hamilton Rutledge[5], Henry Middleton Rutledge[4], Henrietta Middleton Rutledge[3], Septima Sexta Middleton[2], Arthur Middleton[1]) child of Henry Middleton Rutledge and Flora McDonald was born in Lumberton, NC on 27 Dec 1939. He married Leslie Townsend DOTTERER in Yonge's Island, SC on 6 Jun 1964. She was born in Charleston, SC on 1 Aug 1940. Children:

+   1141   i   Leslie Townsend RUTLEDGE, b. 3 Jul 1969
    1142   ii   Henry Middleton RUTLEDGE, b. 15 Oct 1970

878. ELISE PINCKNEY RUTLEDGE[7] (Henry Middleton Rutledge[6], Archibald Hamilton Rutledge[5], Henry Middleton Rutledge[4], Henrietta Middleton Rutledge[3], Septima Sexta Middleton[2], Arthur Middleton[1]) child of

Henry Middleton Rutledge and Flora McDonald was born about 1941. She married William Stewart BRADFORD in say 1963. Children:

+ 1143   i   Robert Morris BRADFORD, b. c. 1967
    1144   ii   William Stewart BRADFORD, b. 1970
    1145   iii   Rutledge McDonald BRADFORD, b. c. 1975

879. HENRY MIDDLETON RUTLEDGE[7] (Irving Hart Rutledge[6], Archibald Hamilton Rutledge[5], Henry Middleton Rutledge[4], Henrietta Middleton Rutledge[3], Septima Sexta Middleton[2], Arthur Middleton[1]) child of Irving Hart Rutledge and Eleanor White was born about 1936. He married -- (--) in say 1960. Children:

    1146   i   Donald RUTLEDGE, b. c. 1963
    1147   ii   Macon RUTLEDGE, b. c. 1966

883. BURWELL MARSHALL HARDY[7] (Elise Rutledge Smith[6], Mary Middleton Rutledge Reese[5], Emma Fredricka Rutledge[4], Henrietta Middleton Rutledge[3], Septima Sexta Middleton[2], Arthur Middleton[1]) child of Elise Rutledge Smith and Ewing Lloyd Hardy was born in Anchorage, KY on 4 Feb 1930, and died on 8 Feb 1989. He married Maria Jisela JANDI in 1954. Children:

    1148   i   Viviana HARDY, b. 9 Feb 1969
    1149   ii   Laura HARDY, b. 24 May 1970
    1150   iii   Jose HARDY, b. 19 Sep 1972

885. ANN COBBS SMITH[7] (Carol Castleman Smith[6], Mary Middleton Rutledge Reese[5], Emma Fredricka Rutledge[4], Henrietta Middleton Rutledge[3], Septima Sexta Middleton[2], Arthur Middleton[1]) child of Carol Castleman Smith and Edith Stollenwerk born in Montgomery, AL on 6 Feb 1929. She married Willis Duke WEATHERFORD, Jr. in Greensboro, AL on 28 Aug 1954. He was born in Asheville, NC on 24 Jun 1916, and died in Black Mountain, NC on 22 May 1996. Children:

+ 1151   i   Edith Cobbs WEATHERFORD, b. 1 Jan 1957
+ 1152   ii   Julia McCrory WEATHERFORD, b. 24 Jun 1958
+ 1153   iii   Willis Duke WEATHERFORD, III, b. 12 Apr 1960
    1154   iv   Susan Parker WEATHERFORD, b. 9 Jan 1962 [twin]
+ 1155   v   Alice Rutledge WEATHERFORD, b. 9 Jan 1962 [twin]

886. CAROL CASTLEMAN SMITH, Jr.[7] (Carol Castleman Smith[6], Mary Middleton Rutledge Reese[5], Emma Fredricka Rutledge[4], Henrietta Middleton Rutledge[3], Septima Sexta Middleton[2], Arthur Middleton[1]) child of Carol Castleman Smith and Edith Stollenwerk born in Montgomery, AL on 7 Sep

1930, and died in Norfolk, VA on 15 Oct 1983. He married Sara Jane CLYDE in Pensacola, FL on 4 May 1957. She was born in Pensacola, FL on 21 Aug 1933. Children:

    1156   i   Paul Rutledge SMITH, b. 14 Dec 1958
    1157   ii Carol Castelman SMITH, III, b. 7 Dec 1960
+ 1158 iii Arthur Middleton SMITH, b. 2 Mar 1964
    1159 iv Laura Manson SMITH, b. 18 Nov 1969

887. ALICE RUTLEDGE SMITH[7] (Carol Castleman Smith[6], Mary Middleton Rutledge Reese[5], Emma Fredricka Rutledge[4], Henrietta Middleton Rutledge[3], Septima Sexta Middleton[2],Arthur Middleton[1]) child of Carol Castleman Smith and Edith Stollenwerk born in Montgomery, AL on 9 Mar 1932. She married Richard Johnson RAMSEY in Tuscaloosa, AL on 3 Aug 1957. He was born in Atlanta, GA on 7 Feb 1932. Children:

+ 1160   i   Richard Johnson RAMSEY, Jr. b. 18 Nov 1958
+ 1161   ii David Rutledge RAMSEY, b. 5 Apr 1960
+ 1162 iii John Walden RAMSEY, b. 16 Feb 1964

888. CHARLES STOLLENWERK SMITH[7] (Carol Castleman Smith[6], Mary Middleton Rutledge Reese[5], Emma Fredricka Rutledge[4], Henrietta Middleton Rutledge[3], Septima Sexta Middleton[2], Arthur Middleton[1]) child of Carol Castleman Smith and Edith Stollenwerk born in Montgomery, AL on 9 Jan 1936. He married Caroline Pauline BACKER in Zurich, SWITZER-LAND on 18 Apr 1961. She was born in NYC on 13 Jul 1938. Children:

+ 1163   i   Jennifer Backer SMITH, b. 12 Mar 1962
    1164   ii Elise Avery SMITH, b. 8 Aug 1964; unm
    1165 iii Charles Whelan Stollenwerk SMITH, b. 11 Dec 1970

890. MARY BURTON SMITH[7] (Frederick Rutledge Smith[6], Mary Middleton Rutledge Reese[5], Emma Fredricka Rutledge[4], Henrietta Middleton Rutledge[3], Septima Sexta Middleton[2], Arthur Middleton[1]) child of Frederick Rutledge Smith and Mary Burton Matthews was born in Montgomery, AL on 13 Aug 1926. She married Henry Ewing HARRIS in Tuscaloosa, AL on 23 Sep 1949. He was born in Atlanta, GA on 9 Apr 1921. Children:

+ 1166   i   Mary Burton HARRIS, b. 30 Jun 1950
+ 1167   ii Henry Ewing HARRIS, Jr., b. 13 Sep 1951
+ 1168 iii Lucy Fairbanks HARRIS, b. 25 Jan 1953
+ 1169 iv Frederick Rutledge HARRIS, b. 23 May 1957
    1170   v John Bowen HARRIS, b. 22 Nov 1960; unm

891. BENJAMIN BOSWORTH SMITH[7] (Frederick Rutledge Smith[6], Mary Middleton Rutledge Reese[5], Emma Fredricka Rutledge[4], Henrietta Middleton Rutledge[3], Septima Sexta Middleton[2], Arthur Middleton[1]) child of Frederick Rutledge Smith and Mary Burton Matthews was born in Montgomery, AL on 6 Dec 1929. He married Barbara Jane HAHN, daughter of Hebert Louis and Sara [sic] Elizabeth (Ransom) Hahn in Birmingham, AL on 26 Oct 1954. She was born in Birmingham, AL on 28 Jun 1929. Children:

+ 1171   i   Elizabeth Ransom SMITH, b. 20 Feb 1956
+ 1172   ii   Mary Middleton SMITH, b. 29 Jan 1959
+ 1173   iii   Benjamin Bosworth SMITH, Jr., b. 16 Jun 1960
+ 1174   iv   Barbara Beene SMITH, b. 18 Jul 1962

893. EDMUND BELLINGER STEWART[7] (Katherine Felder[6], Alice Sophia Reese[5], Emma Fredricka Rutledge[4], Henrietta Middleton Rutledge[3], Septima Sexta Middleton[2], Arthur Middleton[1]) child of Katherine Felder and her 2nd husband Francis Barretto Stewart was born on 30 Dec 1933. He married Anita Maria Carolina WARING in say 1956. She was born in 1936. Children:

+ 1175   i   Edmund Bellinger STEWART, Jr., b. 18 Jul 1958
   1176   ii   Laura Katherine Coster STEWART, b. 13 Apr 1961

894. FRANCIS BARRETTO STEWART, Jr.[7] (Katherine Felder[6], Alice Sophia Reese[5], Emma Fredricka Rutledge[4], Henrietta Middleton Rutledge[3], Septima Sexta Middleton[2], Arthur Middleton[1]) child of Katherine Felder and her 2nd husband Francis Barretto Stewart was born in 1933, and died in 1976. He married Susan SMITH in say 1958. Children:

   1177   i   Francis Barretto STEWART, III, b. 1961
   1178   ii   Geraldine Wilson STEWART, b. 1962
+ 1179   iii   Sarah Rutledge STEWART, b. 1964

897. CHARLES HALLIWELL PRINGLE DUELL[7] (Josephine Scott Smith[6], John Julius Pringle Smith[5], Emma Blake Rutledge[4], Arthur Middleton Rutledge[3], Septima Sexta Middleton[2], Arthur Middleton[1]) child of Josephine Scott Smith and Charles Duell was born on 10 Jun 1938. He married Caroline Nichols WOOD on 31 Aug 1963. Children:

   1180   i   Josephine Clark DUELL, b. 17 Jun 1966
   1181   ii   June Heningham DUELL, b. 1968
   1182   iii   Charles Holland DUELL, b. 1971
   1183   iv   Caroline Middleton DUELL, b. 1974

EIGHTH GENERATION

904. BENJAMIN CHAPIN CHAPMAN[8] (Anne Mangum[7], Eliza Baker Read[6], Oliver Middleton Read[5], Mary Julia Middleton[4], Oliver Hering Middleton[3], Henry Middleton[2], Arthur Middleton[1]) child of Anne Mangum and William McKissick Chapman was born about 1940. He married Ann GREEN in say 1975. Children:

    1184　　i　Katharine CHAPMAN, b. c. 1978
    1185　　ii　Ann CHAPMAN, b. c. 1980

905. JOHN HARLESTON CHAPMAN[8] (Anne Mangum[7], Eliza Baker Read[6], Oliver Middleton Read[5], Mary Julia Middleton[4], Oliver Hering Middleton[3], Henry Middleton[2], Arthur Middleton[1]) child of Anne Mangum and William McKissick Chapman was born about 1943. He married -- (--) in say 1972. Children:

    1186　　i　Elizabeth CHAPMAN, b. c. 1978
    1187　　ii　Christina CHAPMAN, b. c. 1981

906. ALEXANDER GREGORIE CHAPMAN[8] (Anne Mangum[7], Eliza Baker Read[6], Oliver Middleton Read[5], Mary Julia Middleton[4], Oliver Hering Middleton[3], Henry Middleton[2], Arthur Middleton[1]) child of Anne Mangum and William McKissick Chapman was born about 1948. He married -- (--) in say 1973. Children:

    1188　　i　Eliza CHAPMAN, b. c. 1977
    1189　　ii　Christian CHAPMAN, b. c. 1980
    1190　　iii　Rebekah CHAPMAN, b. c. 1984

907. RICHARD ALBERT TILGHMAN, Jr.[8] (Richard Albert Tilghman[7], Eliza Middleton Fox[6], Emily Anne Read[5], Mary Julia Middleton[4], Oliver Hering Middleton[3], Henry Middleton[2], Arthur Middleton[1]) child of Richard Albert Tilghman and Diana Disston was born in Philadelphia, PA on 6 Jan 1945. He married Blanche Joan NUSBAUM in NYC on 23 Jun 1973. She was born in NYC on 27 Feb 1948. Child:

    1191　　i　Richard Albert TILGHMAN, III, b. 29 Apr 1975

908. HARLEY ALLEN CASE[8] (Eleanor Mumford[7], Ayliffe B. Blake[6], Edmund Molyneux Blake[5], Olivia Middleton[4], Oliver Hering Middleton[3], Henry Middleton[2], Arthur Middleton[1]) child of Eleanor Mumford and Harley Allen Case was born on 13 Nov 1944, and died in Jan 1996. He married Cheryl (--) in 1967. Children:

1192   i   Heather Christine CASE, b. 1969
1193   ii   Jeffery CASE, b. 1973

909. MARSHALL CASE[8] (Eleanor Mumford[7], Ayliffe B. Blake[6], Edmund Molyneux Blake[5], Olivia Middleton[4], Oliver Hering Middleton[3], Henry Middleton[2], Arthur Middleton[1]) child of Eleanor Mumford and Harley Allen Case was born in 1947. He married Martha CUNNINGHAM in say 1971. Children:

1194   i   Brian CASE, b. 1975
1195   ii   Andrew CASE, b. 1980

910. NICHOLAS Van SLYCK MUMFORD, III[8] (Nicholas Van Slyck Mumford, Jr.[7], Ayliffe B. Blake[6], Edmund Molyneux Blake[5], Olivia Middleton[4], Oliver Hering Middleton[3], Henry Middleton[2], Arthur Middleton[1]) child of Nicholas Van Slyck Mumford, Jr. and Rosemary Davis was born in 1948. He married Catherine (--) in say 1973. Children:

1196   i   Gregory MUMFORD, b. 1976
1197   ii   Jennifer MUMFORD, b. 1979
1198   iii   Abigail MUMFORD, b. 1981

913. ELIZABETH DAVIS MUMFORD[8] (Nicholas Van Slyck Mumford, Jr.[7], Ayliffe B. Blake[6], Edmund Molyneux Blake[5], Olivia Middleton[4], Oliver Hering Middleton[3], Henry Middleton[2], Arthur Middleton[1]) child of Nicholas Van Slyck Mumford, Jr. and Rosemary Davis was born in 1953. She married Christopher BEEKMAN in say 1977. Children:

1199   i   Emma BEEKMAN, b. 1981
1200   ii   Eleanora BEEKMAN, b. 1984
1201   iii   Adam BEEKMAN, b. 1988
1202   iv   Melissa BEEKMAN, b. 1991

914. ELEANOR PHILLIPS[8] (Harriet Stuart Blake[7], Olivia Middleton Blake[6], Edmund Molyneux Blake[5], Olivia Middleton[4], Oliver Hering Middleton[3], Henry Middleton[2], Arthur Middleton[1]) child of Harriet Stuart Blake and J. Ormsby Phillips was born in 1948. She married Charles BRACKBILL in 1974. He was born in 1948. Child:

1203   i   Elizabeth Blake BRACKBILL, b. 1986

917. KATHARINE BLAKE JOHNSON[8] (Katharine Shannon Blake[7], Daniel Blake[6], Daniel Blake[5], Olivia Middleton[4], Oliver Hering Middleton[3], Henry Middleton[2], Arthur Middleton[1]) child of Katharine Shannon Blake and

Harvey Wilson Johnson was born in 1953. She married Thomas A. BLANTON in say 1976. He was born in 1948. Children:

1204   i   Katharine Johnson BLANTON, b. 1981
1205   ii   Frances McKinley BLANTON, b. 1985

918. ANNA WHITE JOHNSON[8] (Katharine Shannon Blake[7], Daniel Blake[6], Daniel Blake[5], Olivia Middleton[4], Oliver Hering Middleton[3], Henry Middleton[2], Arthur Middleton[1]) child of Katharine Shannon Blake and Harvey Wilson Johnson was born in 1955. She married Steven Dunham SMITH in say 1977. He was born in 1950. Children:

1206   i   Elizabeth Walters SMITH, b. 1980
1207   ii   Anna Miles SMITH, b. 1984
1208   iii Steven Dunham SMITH, Jr., b. 1985

919. JANE SHANNON JOHNSON[8] (Katharine Shannon Blake[7], Daniel Blake[6], Daniel Blake[5], Olivia Middleton[4], Oliver Hering Middleton[3], Henry Middleton[2], Arthur Middleton[1]) child of Katharine Shannon Blake and Harvey Wilson Johnson was born in 1956. She married Raymond Daniel BRADY in say 1982. He was born in 1953. Child:

1209   i   Katharine Shannon BRADY, b. 1989

984. MARIA LOUISA HOYT[8] (Mary Pierrepont Hazard[7], Anne Francis Cope[6], Eliza Middleton Kane[5], Elizabeth Francis Fisher[4], Elizabeth Izard Middleton[3], Henry Middleton[2], Arthur Middleton[1]) child of Mary Pierrepont Hazard and her 1st husband Edwin Hoyt was born about 1952. She married Stephen Douglas CASHIN in say 1983. Children:

1210   i   Oliver Selden CASHIN, b. 15 Nov 1988
1211   ii   Madeline Hoyt CASHIN, b. 20 Nov 1990
1212   iii Benjamin Pierrepont CASHIN, b. 25 Mar 1996

994. ELIZA MIDDLETON COPE[8] (Robert deNormandie Cope[7], Oliver Cope[6], Eliza Middleton Kane[5], Elizabeth Francis Fisher[4], Elizabeth Izard Middleton[3], Henry Middleton[2], Arthur Middleton[1]) child of Robert de Normandie Cope and Margaret Gruenwald was born about 1960. She married Jonathan NOLAN in say 1989. Child:

1213   i   Oliver Cope NOLAN, b. Dec 1995

1015. NANCY THERESA WADE[8] (Rita Izard Hunter[7], Rita Izard[6], Ralph Izard[5], Walter Izard[4], Walter Izard[3], Emma Philadelphia Middleton[2], Arthur Middleton[1]) child of Rita Izard Hunter and Lyle Vincent Wade was born in Fayetteville, NC on 4 Sep 1954. She married Steven Darron McCONNELL in Boca Raton, FL on 2 May 1987. He was born in Highland Park, MI on 14 Apr 1954. Children:

    1214   i   Michael Steven McCONNELL, b. 20 Oct 1990

    1215   ii Daniel Vincent McCONNELL, b. 18 Nov 1998

1016. ANNE BERRY WADE[8] (Rita Izard Hunter[7], Rita Izard[6], Ralph Izard[5], Walter Izard[4], Walter Izard[3], Emma Philadelphia Middleton[2], Arthur Middleton[1]) child of Rita Izard Hunter and Lyle Vincent Wade was born in Fayetteville, NC on 29 Oct 1955. She married (1st) James Allen EDWARDS, Jr. in Greensboro, NC on 5 Apr 1986. He was born in Fort Monroe, VA on 17 Oct 1956. Child:

    1216   i   Hunter Anderson EDWARDS, b. 29 Aug 1988

1022. ROBERT McLAIN HAWKRIDGE, Jr.[8] (Sally Horton Middleton[7], Arthur Middleton[6], William Dehon Middleton[5], Arthur Middleton[4], Emma Izard[3], Emma Philadelphia Middleton[2], Arthur Middleton[1]) child of Sally Horton Middleton and Robert McLain Hawkridge was born in West Chester, PA on 12 May 1958. He married Arlene Frances LEE in Washington, DC on 26 May 1984. She was born in Cherry Point, NC on 2 Oct 1960. Children:

    1217   i   Ian Mclain HAWKRIDGE, b. 9 Oct 1987

    1218   ii Jennings Lee HAWKRIDGE, b. 20 Jun 1990

1023. SALLY HORTON HAWKRIDGE[8] (Sally Horton Middleton[7], Arthur Middleton[6], William Dehon Middleton[5], Arthur Middleton[4], Emma Izard[3], Emma Philadelphia Middleton[2], Arthur Middleton[1]) child of Sally Horton Middleton and Robert McLain Hawkridge was born in West Chester, PA on 20 Aug 1961. She married Munir Nurettin BEKEN in Washington, DC on 26 May 1984. He was born in Istanbul, TURKEY on 12 Apr 1964. Child:

    1219   i   Timur Middleton BEKEN, b. 21 Jul 1995

1024. SAMUEL MACK RAMSEY, III[8] (Annely Blake Middleton[7], Arthur Middleton[6], William Dehon Middleton[5], Arthur Middleton[4], Emma Izard[3], Emma Philadelphia Middleton[2], Arthur Middleton[1]) child of Annely Blake Middleton and her 1st husband Samuel Mack Ramsey, Jr. was born on 30 Mar 1948. He married (1st) Karen Adele LEWIS on 16 Apr 1967. She was born on 28 Dec 1948. Child:

    1220   i   Samuel Clayton RAMSEY, b. 24 Jul 1969

1025. ARTHUR MIDDLETON RAMSEY[8] (Annely Blake Middleton[7], Arthur Middleton[6], William Dehon Middleton[5], Arthur Middleton[4], Emma

Izard³, Emma Philadelphia Middleton², Arthur Middleton¹) child of Annely Blake Middleton and her 1ˢᵗ husband Samuel Mack Ramsey, Jr. was born in Augusta, GA on 1 Dec 1950. He married Katherine Johnson FOLWELL in Augusta, GA on 29 Dec 1973. She was born in Birmingham, AL on 29 Nov 1951. Children:

1221   i   Katherine Campbell RAMSEY, b. 26 Mar 1979
1222   ii Mary Blake RAMSEY, b. 26 Jan 1981

1026. ANNELY BLAKE RAMSEY[8] (Annely Blake Middleton⁷, Arthur Middleton⁶, William Dehon Middleton⁵, Arthur Middleton⁴, Emma Izard³, Emma Philadelphia Middleton², Arthur Middleton¹) child of Annely Blake Middleton and her 1ˢᵗ husband Samuel Mack Ramsey, Jr. was born on 20 Feb 1952. She married Leonard Timothy HILL on 21 May 1983. She was born on 4 Jun 1945. Children:

1223   i   Julia Blake HILL, b. 5 Jun 1984
1224   ii Andrew Middleton HILL, b. 20 Apr 1987

1027. HOPE GARDNER HAYES[8] (Annely Blake Middleton⁷, Arthur Middleton⁶, William Dehon Middleton⁵, Arthur Middleton⁴, Emma Izard³, Emma Philadelphia Middleton², Arthur Middleton¹) child of Annely Blake Middleton and her 2nd husband Richard Burton Hayes, Jr. was born on 8 Nov 1956. She married Kenneth Allan MAXWELL on 26 May 1978. He was born on 12 Feb 1954. Children:

1225   i   Thomas Allan MAXWELL, Jr., b. 14 Nov 1980
1226   ii William Middleton MAXWELL, b. 27 Mar 1984

1029. RICHARD BURTON HAYES, III[8] (Annely Blake Middleton⁷, Arthur Middleton⁶, William Dehon Middleton⁵, Arthur Middleton⁴, Emma Izard³, Emma Philadelphia Middleton², Arthur Middleton¹) child of Annely Blake Middleton and her 2nd husband Richard Burton Hayes, Jr. was born on 20 May 1959. He married Patricia DAILEY on 17 Sep 1988. She was born on 12 Aug 1962. Children:

1227   i   Kathleen Campbell HAYES, b. 4 Jun 1994
1228   ii Richard Burton HAYES, IV, b. 17 Oct 1995
1229 iii Margaret Riely [sic] Heath HAYES, b. 17 Sep 1998

1030. GAY MIDDLETON MASON[8] (Gay Van Assendelft Middleton⁷, Arthur Middleton⁶, William Dehon Middleton⁵, Arthur Middleton⁴, Emma Izard³, Emma Philadelphia Middleton², Arthur Middleton¹) child of Gay Van Assendelft Middleton and Frank Nichols Mason was born in Augusta, GA on

26 Jul 1954. She married James Daniel CORR in West Chester, PA on 7 Mar 1976. He was born in Germantown, PA on 7 Sep 1952. Children:

    1230   i   Anna Mason CORR, b. 27 May 1983 [twin]

    1231   ii Elizabeth Middleton CORR, b. 27 May 1983 [twin]

1031. LEMUEL WYATT MASON[8] (Gay Van Assendelft Middleton[7], Arthur Middleton[6], William Dehon Middleton[5], Arthur Middleton[4], Emma Izard[3], Emma Philadelphia Middleton[2], Arthur Middleton[1]) child of Gay Van Assendelft Middleton and Frank Nichols Mason was born in West Chester, PA on 31 Mar 1959. He married Barbara Anne HAYES in West Chester, PA on 19 Nov 1983. She was born in Philadelphia, PA on 19 Jun 1954. Child:

    1232   i   Colin Hayes MASON, b. 2 Oct 1985

1032. FRANK NICHOLS MASON, Jr.[8] (Gay Van Assendelft Middleton[7], Arthur Middleton[6], William Dehon Middleton[5], Arthur Middleton[4], Emma Izard[3], Emma Philadelphia Middleton[2], Arthur Middleton[1]) child of Gay Van Assendelft Middleton and Frank Nichols Mason was born in West Chester, PA on 19 Mar 1961. He married Sherrell Hollingsworth JOHNSON in High Point, NC on 30 Mar 1991. She was born in High Point, NC on 25 Feb 1962. Children:

    1233   i   Hadley Hollingsworth MASON, b. 27 Dec 1995

    1234   ii Ross Nichols MASON, b. 27 Feb 1997

1047. EUGENIA KIRKLAND PRENTISS[8] (Charles Brewster Prentiss, III[7], Julia Porcher Middleton[6], William Dehon Middleton[5], Arthur Middleton[4], Emma Izard[3], Emma Philadelphia Middleton[2], Arthur Middleton[1]) child of Charels Brewster Prentiss, III and Margaret Naomi Ortmann was born on 14 Jul 1955. She married William Thomas MURRAY on 11 May 1975. He was born on 29 Dec 1954. Child:

    1235   i   William Prentiss MURRAY, b. 29 Sep 1979

1048. JULIE ANN HAGEN[8] (Julia Blake Prentiss[7], Julia Porcher Middleton[6], William Dehon Middleton[5], Arthur Middleton[4], Emma Izard[3], Emma Philadelphia Middleton[2], Arthur Middleton[1]) child of Julia Blake Prentiss and Paul Amberg Hagen, Jr. was born on 16 Mar 1955. She married Frederick Henry VESEL on 25 Aug 1979. He was born on 23 Sep 1949. Children:

    1236   i   Travis Prentiss VESEL, b. 12 Sep 1981

    1237   ii Lindsay Ann VESEL, b. 12 Feb 1983

1049. LARS ROMOREN HAGEN[8] (Julia Blake Prentiss[7], Julia Porcher Middleton[6], William Dehon Middleton[5], Arthur Middleton[4], Emma Izard[3], Emma Philadelphia Middleton[2], Arthur Middleton[1]) child of Julia Blake Prentiss and Paul Amberg Hagen, Jr. was born in Charleston, SC on 10 Mar 1957. He married Catherine Gayle MULLIS in Pineville, NC on 11 Jun 1977. She was born in Ft. Mill, SC on 26 May 1957. Children:

    1238   i   Lars Romoren HAGEN, Jr., b. 1 9 Aug 1979

    1239   ii   Philip Anders HAGEN, b. 13 Apr 1981

1055. FRANK CARTER, III[8] (Jane Morris Munnerlyn[7], Benjamin Munnerlyn[6], Lucy Izard Middleton[5], Arthur Middleton[4], Emma Izard[3], Emma Philadelphia Middleton[2], Arthur Middleton[1]) child of Jane Morris Munnerlyn and Frank Carter, Jr. was born on 16 Sep 1950. He married Anne Marie SIMMS in 1976. Children:

    1240   i   Frank CARTER, IV, b. 11 Apr 1981

    1241   ii   Anne Marie CARTER, b. 2 Aug 1984

    1242   iii Daniel Spring CARTER, b. 22 Jun 1988

1056. BENJAMIN MUNNERLYN CARTER[8] (Jane Morris Munnerlyn[7], Benjamin Munnerlyn[6], Lucy Izard Middleton[5], Arthur Middleton[4], Emma Izard[3], Emma Philadelphia Middleton[2], Arthur Middleton[1]) child of Jane Morris Munnerlyn and Frank Carter, Jr. was born on 26 Dec 1953. He married Patricia Marie REED in 1977. Children:

    1243   i   Palmer Marie CARTER, b. 12 Aug 1979

    1244   ii   Benjamin Munnerlyn CARTER, Jr., b. 10 Feb 1962

1063. JOHN CHAPMAN SEARS[8] (Helen Middleton DuBois[7], Anna Bertha Dehon[6], Helen Middleton[5], Arthur Middleton[4], Margaret Emma Izard[3], Emma Philadelphia Middleton[2], Arthur Middleton[1]) child of Helen Middleton DuBois and Alton D. Sears. was born about 1950. He married Sara ROSENQUIST in say 1974. Child:

    1245   i   Emily Middleton SEARS, b. c. 1978

1064. RICHARD ALLEN SEARS[8] (Helen Middleton DuBois[7], Anna Bertha Dehon[6], Helen Middleton[5], Arthur Middleton[4], Margaret Emma Izard[3], Emma Philadelphia Middleton[2], Arthur Middleton[1]) child of Helen Middleton DuBois and Alton D. Sears. was born about 1953. He married Jenny JAQUE in say 1976. Children:

    1246   i   Eric SEARS, b. c. 1979

    1247   ii   Courtney SEARS, b. c. 1982

    1248   iii Holly SEARS, b. c. 1986

1065. SUSAN CARROLL SEARS[8] (Helen Middleton DuBois[7], Anna Bertha Dehon[6], Helen Middleton[5], Arthur Middleton[4], Margaret Emma Izard[3], Emma Philadelphia Middleton[2], Arthur Middleton[1]) child of Helen Middleton DuBois and Alton D. Sears. was born about 1956. She married Gatewood GALBRAITH in say 1977. Children:

    1249   i   Summer Sears GALBRAITH, b. c. 1980
    1250   ii   Abigail Sears GALBRAITH, b. c. 1984
    1251 iii   Molly Middleton GALBRAITH, b. c. 1989

1068. JULIA GRINER[8] (Mary Mauldin[7], Mary Dehon[6], Helen Middleton[5], Arthur Middleton[4], Margaret Emma Izard[3], Emma Philadelphia Middleton[2], Arthur Middleton[1]) child of Mary Mauldin and Benjamin Charlton Griner was born about 1959. She married Robert Erving POWERS in say 1982. Children:

    1252   i   Heath Hamilton POWERS, b. c. 1985
    1253   ii   Lance Middleton POWERS, b. c. 1989

1069. BENJAMIN CHARLTON GRINER, Jr.[8] (Mary Mauldin[7], Mary Dehon[6], Helen Middleton[5], Arthur Middleton[4], Margaret Emma Izard[3], Emma Philadelphia Middleton[2], Arthur Middleton[1]) child of Mary Mauldin and Benjamin Charlton Griner was born about 1961. He married Sheila KENNY in say 1985. Child:

    1254   i   Benjamin Patrick GRINER, b. c. 1988

1070. SARA GRINER[8] (Mary Mauldin[7], Mary Dehon[6], Helen Middleton[5], Arthur Middleton[4], Margaret Emma Izard[3], Emma Philadelphia Middleton[2], Arthur Middleton[1]) child of Mary Mauldin and Benjamin Charlton Griner was born about 1962. She married Joseph Anthony RAYMOND, Jr. in say 1983. Children:

    1255   i   Tobin Marie RAYMOND, b. c. 1985
    1256   ii   Julian Thomas RAYMOND, b. c. 1988

1071. AGNES GRINER[8] (Mary Mauldin[7], Mary Dehon[6], Helen Middleton[5], Arthur Middleton[4], Margaret Emma Izard[3], Emma Philadelphia Middleton[2], Arthur Middleton[1]) child of Mary Mauldin and Benjamin Charlton Griner was born about 1965. She married Samuel Lee DOWDY, Jr. in say 1984. Children:

    1257   i   Samuel Charlton DOWDY, b. c. 1986
    1258   ii   Megan Dehon DOWDY, b. c. 1989

1074. JOHN ANDREW CARSON, Jr.[8] (Ann Mauldin[7], Mary Dehon[6], Helen Middleton[5], Arthur Middleton[4], Margaret Emma Izard[3], Emma Philadelphia Middleton[2], Arthur Middleton[1]) child of Ann Mauldin and John Andrew Carson was born about 1968. He married Louise (--) in say 1992. Children:

    1259   i   Coleen CARSON, b. c. 1995
    1260 ii Jennifer CARSON, b. c. 1998

1075. DEBORAH CARSON[8] (Ann Mauldin[7], Mary Dehon[6], Helen Middleton[5], Arthur Middleton[4], Margaret Emma Izard[3], Emma Philadelphia Middleton[2], Arthur Middleton[1]) child of Ann Mauldin and John Andrew Carson was born about 1970. She married Terry G. MILLS in say 1991. Children:

    1261   i   Aimee MILLS, b. c. 1993
    1262 ii Jacklyn [sic] MILLS, b. c. 1995
    1263 iii Terry G. MILLS, Jr., b. c. 1998

1108. FRANCES HUGER deSAUSSURE[8] (Frances Pelzer Huger[7], Daniel Elliott Huger, Jr.[6], Daniel Elliott Huger[5], William Elliott Huger[4], Daniel Elliott Huger[3], Isabella Johannes Middleton[2], Arthur Middleton[1]) child of Frances Pelzer Huger and Edward Harleston deSaussure was born about 1954. She married David Custis MEAD in say 1976. Children:

    1264   i   David Custis MEAD, Jr., b. c. 1979
    1265 ii Mary Frances deSaussure MEAD, b. c. 1983
    1266 iii Edward Harleston deSaussure MEAD, b. c. 1986

1109. ELEANOR CHARLTON deSAUSSURE[8] (Frances Pelzer Huger[7], Daniel Elliott Huger, Jr.[6], Daniel Elliott Huger[5], William Elliott Huger[4], Daniel Elliott Huger[3], Isabella Johannes Middleton[2], Arthur Middleton[1]) child of Frances Pelzer Huger and Edward Harleston deSaussure was born about 1957. She married Kendall Gibson BRYAN in say 1977. Children:

    1267   i   Josephine deSaussure BRYAN, b. c. 1979
    1268 ii Kendall Gibson BRYAN, Jr., b. c. 1981
    1269 iii Eleanor Charlton BRYAN, b. c. 1984
    1270 iv Sarah Huger BRYAN, b. c. 1987

1110. ANITA deSAUSSURE[8] (Frances Pelzer Huger[7], Daniel Elliott Huger, Jr.[6], Daniel Elliott Huger[5], William Elliott Huger[4], Daniel Elliott Huger[3], Isabella Johannes Middleton[2], Arthur Middleton[1]) child of Frances Pelzer Huger and Edward Harleston deSaussure was born about 1960. She married Charles TOMM in say 1983. Child:

    1271   i   Daniel Edward Harleston TOMM, b. c. 1989

1112. MARGARET PELZER deSAUSSURE[8] (Frances Pelzer Huger[7], Daniel Elliott Huger, Jr.[6], Daniel Elliott Huger[5], William Elliott Huger[4], Daniel Elliott Huger[3], Isabella Johannes Middleton[2], Arthur Middleton[1]) child of Frances Pelzer Huger and Edward Harleston deSaussure was born about 1963. She married Thomas Roy PRINCE in say 1986. Child:

    1272   i   Thomas Harrison PRINCE, b. c. 1990

1113. JOHN MAXWELL STERLING, III[8] (Elizabeth Pelzer Huger[7], Daniel Elliott Huger, Jr.[6], Daniel Elliott Huger[5], William Elliott Huger[4], Daniel Elliott Huger[3], Isabella Johannes Middleton[2], Arthur Middleton[1]) child of Elizabeth Pelzer Huger and John Maxwell Sterling, Jr. was born about 1962. He married Jennifer Lee TAYLOR in say 1988. Children:

    1273   i   John Maxwell STERLING, IV, b. c. 1990
    1274   ii   Charles Taylor STERLING, b. c. 1993

1114. ELIZABETH HUGER STERLING[8] (Elizabeth Pelzer Huger[7], Daniel Elliott Huger, Jr.[6], Daniel Elliott Huger[5], William Elliott Huger[4], Daniel Elliott Huger[3], Isabella Johannes Middleton[2], Arthur Middleton[1]) child of Elizabeth Pelzer Huger and John Maxwell Sterling, Jr. was born about 1963. She married William Blakely JARRETT in say 1986. Child:

    1275   i   William Blakely JARRETT, Jr., b. c. 1989

1141. LESLIE TOWNSEND RUTLRDGE[8] (Donald Thropp Rutledge[7], Henry Middleton Rutledge[6], Archibald Hamilton Rutledge[5], Henry Middleton Rutledge[4], Henrietta Middleton Rutledge[3], Septima Sexta Middleton[2], Arthur Middleton[1]) child of Donald Thropp Rutledge and Leslie Townsend Dotterer was born in Charleston, SC on 3 Jul 1968. She married Thomas Morrison DICKINSON in "Hampton Plantation:, SC on 6 Nov 1993. Child:

    1276   i   Cole Rutledge DICKINSON, b. 10 Apr 1998

1143. ROBERT MORRIS BRADFORD[8] (Elise Pinckney Rutledge[7], Henry Middleton Rutledge[6], Archibald Hamilton Rutledge[5], Henry Middleton Rutledge[4], Henrietta Middleton Rutledge[3], Septima Sexta Middleton[2], Arthur Middleton[1]) child of Elise Pinckney Rutledge and William Stewart Bradford was born about 1967. He married Carolyn JOYE in say 1992. Children:

    1277   i   Elise BRADFORD, b. c. 1994
    1278   ii   Robert Bennett BRADFORD, b. c. 1996
    1279   iii   Sarah Rutledge BRADFORD, b. c. 1999

1151. EDITH COBBS WEATHERFORD[8] (Ann Cobbs Smith[7], Carol Castleman Smith[6], Mary Middleton Rutledge Reese[5], Emma Fredricka

Rutledge[4], Henrietta Middleton Rutledge[3], Septime Sexta Middleton[2], Arthur Middleton[1]) child of Ann Cobbs Smith and Willis Duke Weatherford, Jr. was born in Bryn Mawr, PA on 1 Jan 1957. She married Meredith Eugene HUNT in Berea, KY on 10 Jul 1982. He was born on 26 Nov 1952. Children:

1280   i   Priscilla Dear HUNT, b. 16 Apr 1983
1281   ii   Arthur Samuel HUNT, b. 1 Dec 1985
1282   iii   Anna Mary HUNT, b. 27 Jul 1987
1283   iv   Jeffery Barnabas HUNT, b. 27 Feb 1989
1284   v   Peter Malcolm HUNT, b. 18 Apr 1992
1285   vi   Christopher Guard HUNT, b. 213 Jan 1995

1152. JULIA McCRORY WEATHERFORD[8] (Ann Cobbs Smith[7], Carol Castleman Smith[6], Mary Middleton Rutledge Reese[5], Emma Fredricka Rutledge[4], Henrietta Middleton Rutledge[3], Septima Sexta Middleton[2], Arthur Middleton[1]) child of Ann Cobbs Smith and Willis Duke Weatherford, Jr. was born in Bryn Mawr, PA on 24 Jun 1958. She married Mark MUELLER on 22 Mar 1980. Children:

1286   i   Pearl Angeline MUELLER, b. 2 Nov 1980
1287   ii   Vergil Christopher MUELLER, b. 27 Sep 1982

1153. WILLIS DUKE WEATHERFORD, III[8] (Ann Cobbs Smith[7], Carol Castleman Smith[6], Mary Middleton Rutledge Reese[5], Emma Fredricka Rutledge[4], Henrietta Middleton Rutledge[3], Septima Sexta Middleton[2], Arthur Middleton[1]) child of Ann Cobbs Smith and Willis Duke Weatherford, Jr. was born in Kuala Lumpur, MALAYSIA on 12 Apr 1960. He married Jane Elizabeth TURNBULL in Berea, KY on 22 Sep 1984. She was born on 18 Aug 1961. Children:

1288   i   Frank Taylor WEATHERFORD, b. 2 Feb 1988
1289   ii   Willis Duke WEATHERFORD, IV, b. 25 Apr 1990
1290   iii   Susanna Grace WEATHERFORD, b. 31 Jul 1994

1155. ALICE RUTLEDGE WEATHERFORD[8] (Ann Cobbs Smith[7], Carol Castleman Smith[6], Mary Middleton Rutledge Reese[5], Emma Fredricka Rutledge[4], Henrietta Middleton Rutledge[3], Septima Sexta Middleton[2], Arthur Middleton[1]) child of Ann Cobbs Smith and Willis Duke Weatherford, Jr. was born on 9 Jan 1962. She married Jeffrey DOWNS in Black Mountain, NC on 12 Aug 1984. He was born on 27 Apr 1952. Children:

1291   i   Avery Anne DOWNS, b. 28 Oct 1986
1292   ii   Rachel Justis DOWNS, b. 3 Feb 1988
1293   iii   Gretta Joy DOWNS, b. 3 Jan 1994
1294   iv   Luke Daniel DOWNS, b. 9 Nov 1995

1158. ARTHUR MIDDLETON SMITH[8] (Carol Castelman Smith, Jr.[7], Carol Castleman Smith[6], Mary Middleton Rutledge Reese[5], Emma Fredricka Rutledge[4], Henrietta Middleton Rutledge[3], Septima Sexta Middleton[2], Arthur Middleton[1]) child of Carol Castelman Smith, Jr. and Sara Jane Clyde was born on 2 Mar 1964. He married -- (--). Children:

1295   i   Krystle SMITH, b.
1296   ii   Lindsi SMITH, b.
1297   iii   Arthur Middleton SMITH, II, b.

1160. RICHARD JOHNSON RAMSEY, Jr.[8] (Alice Rutledge Smith[7], Carol Castleman Smith[6], Mary Middleton Rutledge Reese[5], Emma Fredricka Rutledge[4], Henrietta Middleton Rutledge[3], Septima Sexta Middleton[2], Arthur Middleton[1]) child of Alice Rutledge Smith and Richard Johnson Ramsey was born in Chattanooga, TN on 18 Nov 1958. He married Gretchen VAN DUSEN in Isleford, ME on 7 Sep 1991. She was born in Boston, MA on 24 Mar 1961. Children:

1298   i   Eliza Cobbs Van Dusen RAMSEY, b. 20 Oct 1994
1299   ii   Ian Lane RAMSEY, b. 2 Apr 1998

1161. DAVID RUTLEDGE RAMSEY[8] (Alice Rutledge Smith[7], Carol Castleman Smith[6], Mary Middleton Rutledge Reese[5], Emma Fredricka Rutledge[4], Henrietta Middleton Rutledge[3], Septima Sexta Middleton[2], Arthur Middleton[1]) child of Alice Rutledge Smith and Richard Johnson Ramsey was born in Chattanooga, TN on 5 Apr 1960. He married Nanette Starr PATTERSON in New Bloomfield, Perry County, PA on 11 May 1985. She was born in New Bloomfield, PA on 18 Feb 1958. Children:

1300   i   Julia Alison RAMSEY, b. 18 Jun 1987
1301   ii   Christopher Rutledge RAMSEY, b. 17 Mar 1990

1162. JOHN WALDEN RAMSEY[8] (Alice Rutledge Smith[7], Carol Castleman Smith[6], Mary Middleton Rutledge Reese[5], Emma Fredricka Rutledge[4], Henrietta Middleton Rutledge[3], Septima Sexta Middleton[2], Arthur Middleton[1]) child of Alice Rutledge Smith and Richard Johnson Ramsey was born in Chattanooga, TN on 16 Feb 1964. He married Birgit Elisabeth Marlies HASSE in Black Mountain, NC on 30 Mar 1991. She was born in Paderborn, GERMANY on 18 Oct 1966. Children:

1302   i   Jeremiah Engels RAMSEY, b. 21 Apr 1994
1303   ii   John Middleton RAMSEY, b. 21 Jan 1996

1163. JENNIFER BACKER SMITH[8] (Charles Stollenwerk Smith[7], Carol Castleman Smith[6], Mary Middleton Rutledge Reese[5], Emma Fredricka

Rutledge[4], Henrietta Middleton Rutledge[3], Septima Sexta Middleton[2], Arthur Middleton[1]) child of Charles Stollenwerk Smith and Caroline Pauline Backer was born on 12 Mar 1962. She married Scott Charles GRIFFITH in Greensboro, AL on 15 Jul 1992. He was born on 30 Apr 1963. Children:

    1304   i   Benjamin Charles Raymond GRIFFITH, b. 21 Jul 1994

    1305   ii Samuel Bosworth GRIFFITH, b. 13 Apr 1996

1166. MARY BURTON HARRIS[8] (Mary Burton Smith[7], Frederick Rutledge Smith[6], Mary Middleton Rutledge Reese[5], Emma Fredricka Rutledge[4], Henrietta Middleton Rutledge[3], Septima Sexta Middleton[2], Arthur Middleton[1]) child of Mary Burton Smith and Henry Ewing Harris was born in Louisville, KY on 30 Jun 1950. She married -- NASH in say 1978. Child:

    1306   i   Lena Kai NASH, b. c. 1982

1167. HENRY EWING HARRIS, Jr.[8] (Mary Burton Smith[7], Frederick Rutledge Smith[6], Mary Middleton Rutledge Reese[5], Emma Fredricka Rutledge[4], Henrietta Middleton Rutledge[3], Septima Sexta Middleton[2], Arthur Middleton[1]) child of Mary Burton Smith and Henry Ewing Harris was born in Louisville, KY on 13 Sep 1951. He married Paula JOHNSON in say 1977. Child:

    1307   i   Ruby Carol HARRIS, b. 10 Dec 1979

1168. LUCY FAIRBANKS HARRIS[8] (Mary Burton Smith[7], Frederick Rutledge Smith[6], Mary Middleton Rutledge Reese[5], Emma Fredricka Rutledge[4], Henrietta Middleton Rutledge[3], Septima Sexta Middleton[2], Arthur Middleton[1]) child of Mary Burton Smith and Henry Ewing Harris was born in Louisville, KY on 25 Jan 1953. She married Philip MERTZ in say 1976. Child:

    1308   i   Luke Henry MERTZ, b. 9 Feb 1980

1169. FREDERICK RUTLEDGE HARRIS[8] (Mary Burton Smith[7], Frederick Rutledge Smith[6], Mary Middleton Rutledge Reese[5], Emma Fredricka Rutledge[4], Henrietta Middleton Rutledge[3], Septima Sexta Middleton[2], Arthur Middleton[1]) child of Mary Burton Smith and Henry Ewing Harris was born in Louisville, KY on 23 May 1957. He married Faye GRIFFIN in say 1984. Children:

    1309   i   Evan Matthews HARRIS, b. 15 Feb 1987

    1310   ii Emily Meredith HARRIS, b. 10 Feb 1988

    1311 iii Abigail Victoria HARRIS, b. 10 Apr 1989

1171. ELIZABETH RANSOM SMITH[8] (Benjamin Bosworth Smith[7], Frederick Rutledge Smith[6], Mary Middleton Rutledge Reese[5], Emma Fredricka Rutledge[4], Henrietta Middleton Rutledge[3], Septima Sexta Middleton[2], Arthur Middleton[1]) child of Benjamin Bosworth Smith and Barbara Jane Hahn was born in Birmingham, AL on 20 Feb 1956. She married (2nd) Kurt Hans RITTERS, son of Vernon E. and Margie (Gosch) Ritters in say 1993. He was born in Randall, MN on 16 Nov 1954. Child:

    1312   i   Elizabeth Rutledge RITTERS, b. 27 Dec 1995

1172. MARY MIDDLETON SMITH[8] (Benjamin Bosworth Smith[7], Frederick Rutledge Smith[6], Mary Middleton Rutledge Reese[5], Emma Fredricka Rutledge[4], Henrietta Middleton Rutledge[3], Septima Sexta Middleton[2], Arthur Middleton[1]) child of Benjamin Bosworth Smith and Barbara Jane Hahn was born in Mobile, AL on 29 Jan 1959. She married William Thompson JONES, Jr., son of William Thompson and Betty Lou (Rath) Jones in Charleston, SC on 21 Apr 1990. He was born in Ft. Lauderdale, FL on 11 Jul 1959. Children:

    1313   i   William Middleton JONES, b. 23 Jan 1992
    1314   ii   Benjamin Thompson JONES, b. 6 Mar 1995

1173. BENJAMIN BOSWORTH SMITH, Jr.[8] (Benjamin Bosworth Smith[7], Frederick Rutledge Smith[6], Mary Middleton Rutledge Reese[5], Emma Fredricka Rutledge[4], Henrietta Middleton Rutledge[3], Septima Sexta Middleton[2], Arthur Middleton[1]) child of Benjamin Bosworth Smith and Barbara Jane Hahn was born in Mobile, AL on 16 Jun 1960. He married Kimberly Susan MIXON in Charleston, SC in Oct 1983. She was born on 17 Mar 1960. Children:

    1315   i   Kelly Elizabeth SMITH, b. 25 Feb 1989
    1316   ii   Emily Jane SMITH, b. 20 Jan 1992
    1317 iii   William Reese SMITH, b. 17 Nov 1995

1174. BARBARA BEENE SMITH[8] (Benjamin Bosworth Smith[7], Frederick Rutledge Smith[6], Mary Middleton Rutledge Reese[5], Emma Fredricka Rutledge[4], Henrietta Middleton Rutledge[3], Septima Sexta Middleton[2], Arthur Middleton[1]) child of Benjamin Bosworth Smith and Barbara Jane Hahn was born in Mobile, AL on 18 Jul 1962. She married David Byron RICE, son of the Rev. Richard Jordan and Nancy Lou (Booth) Rice in Charleston, SC on 19 Sep 1987. He was born in Riverhead, NY on 23 Apr 1959. Children:

    1318   i   Richard Byron RICE, b. 8 Jun 1996
    1319   ii   Samuel Bosworth RICE, b. 26 Feb 2000

1175. EDMUND BELLINGER STEWART, Jr.[8] (Edmund Bellinger Stewart[7], Katherine Felder[6], Alice Sophia Reese[5], Emma Fredricka Rutledge[4], Henrietta Middleton Rutledge[3], Setima Sexta Middleton[2], Arthur Middleton[1]) child of Edmund Bellinger Stewart and Anita Maria Carolina Waring was born on 18 Jul 1958. He married Mary Louanne BERK in say 1986. She was born in 1957. Child:

    1320   i   Emma Katherine STEWART, b. 28 Mar 1992

1179. SARAH RUTLEDGE STEWART[8] (Francis Barretto Stewart, Jr.[7], Katherine Felder[6], Alice Sophia Reese[5], Emma Fredricka Rutledge[4], Henrietta Middleton Rutledge[3], Septima Sexta Middleton[2], Arthur Middleton[1]) child of Francis Barretto Stewart, Jr. and Susan Smith was born in 1964. She married John William Peter DYKSTRA in say 1993. He was born in 1964. Child:

    1321   i   Matthew DYKSTRA, b. 1997

GEORGIA

A part of the territory now within the State of Georgia was included as a part of the proprietary charter granted to the Lords Proprietors of Carolina in 1663 by King Charles II of England. A new charter was granted by King George II on 20 Jun 1732 to James Edward Oglethorpe to found a Colony between South Carolina and the area controlled by Spain. The area included in this Charter was "all those lands ... between the Savannah River and the Altamaha River..."[2]. By 1763 the territory between the Alatamaha River and the St. Mary's River was added by Royal Proclamation, and these lands extended to the Mississippi River. In 1802 Georgia ceded her lands west of the present boundaries to the Federal Government, from which areas were created the States of Alabama and Mississippi.

Although originally chartered as a Trustee Colony, under proprietary rule, by 4 July 1752 control was passed to the crown, and Georgia became a Royal Colony. During Olgethorpe's period of control, he was successful in establishing peaceful relationships with the interior tribes of Indians; including the Creeks, Cherokee, and Chickasaw. This became important for the colony during the War of Jenkins Ear [1739-1742] when he invaded Spanish held Florida, while his western flank was protected by these tribes. In later decades, however, with ever encroaching settlement and disruption of their hunting grounds by hordes of newer settlers, these same Indian tribes became a menace to Georgia's western frontier.

As confrontation with the mother country increased because of Acts of Parliament and politically foolish abrasiveness, Georgia aligned herself with the Continental Association by adopting a modified version of other colonial models of non-importation on 23 Jan 1775. By the time of the second Continental Congress, Georgia elected five delegates on 2 Feb 1776: Archibald Bulloch, Button Gwinnett, Lyman Hall, John Houstoun, and George Walton[3], although Bulloch and Houstoun never attended.

---

[2] Franklin Van Zandt, *Boundaries of the United States and the Several States*, (Geological Survey Bulletin # 1212, United States Government Printing Office, Washington, DC, 1966), p. 159.

[3] *Letters of Delegates to Congress, May 16 - August 15, 1776*, (Library of Congress, Washington, DC, 1979), p. xvi.

Button Gwinnett

54: BUTTON GWINNETT

"Vastness! And Age! And memories of old!"

Edgar Allen Poe

Button Gwinnett signed the Declaration at the top of the left hand most column in a rather neat school hand spelling out his full name.

He was the second son, third child of seven children (five sons, two daughters) of The Rev. Samuel Gwinnett and Anne Emes [or Eames]. His father was of Welsh ancestry [Gwynedd] and the mother of English ancestry. No specifics are known about the lads education, but as the son of an Anglican Vicar he was surely tutored in the essentials and is believed learned something of finance and mercantile trade from his Uncle William Gwinnett, a Bristol merchant. By 1757 he had moved to Staffordshire, England and joined his Father-in-law as a partner in a grocery business in Wolverhampton. Two years later Gwinnett entered the export shipping business and built up an extensive trade with the American colonies.

Before September 1765 he emigrated with his family to Savannah, Georgia. He purchased a store, and the following month St. Catherine's Island, a coastal island of 36 square miles near Sunbury.[1] Gwinnett, although deeply in debt, also purchased some lands on credit and received grants of land from the colony. He bought large numbers of slaves to work his holdings, but the combination of overextended land purchase, the cost of buying and keeping his slaves, the problems of raiding by poachers of his live stock, and the care and maintenance of a family and home, soon put him so deeply in financial trouble that all was gobbled up by creditors in 1773. He had become a local Justice of the Peace by 1767 and in 1769 he was a member of the Georgia Colonial Assembly. He voted for and signed the Declaration, returned to Georgia, and in March of 1777 became "President" [Governor] of the State and Commander-in-Chief of its army. Opposed by a political rival, Gwinnett died of wounds from a duel.

---

[1] Robert C. Ferris and Richard E. Morris, *The Signers of the Declaration of Independence*, (Interpretive Publications, Inc., Arlington, VA, 1982), p. 63.

FIRST GENERATION

1. BUTTON GWINNETT was born in Down Hatherly, Gloucestershire, ENGLAND in late March-early April 1735 and was baptized there on 10 Apr 1735 [o.s.].[1] He married Ann BOURNE, daughter of Aaron Bourne in Wolverhampton, Staffordshire, ENGLAND on 19 Apr 1757.[2] Her date and place of birth and death are not known. He died in Savannah, GA on 19 May 1777.[3] Children:

2	i	Amelia GWINNETT, bp. 27 Feb 1758, dy c. 1776
3	ii	Ann GWINNETT, bp. 14 May 1759, dy c. 1761
+ 4	iii	Elizabeth Ann GWINNET, bp. 4 Jan 1762
5	iv	Ann GWINNETT, b. 1764 [Again], dy c. 1778

References:

[1] Charles Francis Jenkins, *Button Gwinnett, Signer of the Declaration of Independence*, (1926, The Reprint Company, Spartanburg, SC, 1974) a rather complete biography with references, but no formal bibliography is useful. So is a work by Burnette Vanstory, *Button Gwinnett*, (FHL Book # 921.73A1). See also Kenneth H. Thomas, Jr., *Georgia's Signers and the Declaration of Independence*, (Cherokee Publishing Company, Atlanta, GA, 1981), Chapter VII, *Genealogies of the Signers*, pp.85-89; and *Dictionary of Georgia Biography*, (University of Georgia Press, Athens, GA, 1983), Vol 1, pp. 374-376. His baptism is reported in the Church Register of St. Catherine's in Down Hatherly, Gloucestershire. See also Della Gray Bartherlmas, *The Signers of the Declaration of Independence, A Biographical and Genealogical Reference*, (Mcfarland & Company, Inc., Jefferson, NC, 1977), pp. 86-88. The Leach MSS material for Button Gwinnett is found in FHL microfilm # 0001756, and the hard copy is in Vol. # 20, pp. 6399-6400. The DAB Article on Button Gwinnett is in Vol. VIII, pp. 65-66. [2] The Marriage Records of the Colligate Church of Wolverhampton, Staffordshire. See also DAB, Vol. VIII, p. 65. [3] His death of death is given in Charles Francis Jenkins, *Button Gwinnett,* p. 152.

SECOND GENERATION

4. ELIZABETH ANN GWINNETT was baptized in Wolverhampton, Staffordshire, ENGLAND on 4 Jan 1762, and died about 1786.[1] She married Peter BELIN, son of Allard and Margaret (Robert) Belin on 26 Mar 1779.[1] His date and place of birth and death are not known. Children:
   None!

References:

[1] The Baptismal Records of the Colligate Church of Wolverhampton, Staffordshire. See Kenneth H. Thomas, Jr. also *Georgia's Signers and the Declaration of Independence*, (Cherokee Publishing Company, Atlanta, GA, 1981), Chapter VII, *Genealogies of the Signers*, p.87.

Button Gwinnett fought a duel with Lachlan McIntosh on 16 May 1777. Both men were wounded, but Gwinnett died of his wounded leg from gangrene. McIntosh survived his wound, and was later acquitted in a trial. The actual location of Gwinnett's gravesite is unknown, although patriotic societies had erected a memorial to him in 1964 in Colony Park Cemetery, Savannah, GA.

His wife is reported by several writers to have died within a few years of Button, surely before 1785. The only surviving child, Elizabeth Ann ("Betsy") Gwinnett, married on 26 Mar 1779, perhaps as his 2nd wife, Peter BELIN [or Beline], a physician, and was reported to be living in Georgia in early 1785. She must have died within a year or so, however, since her husband received land grants, and head rights shortly thereafter, without notation of spouse or children. Any children born of this marriage died young, although none are known.

They had no surviving issue. She died soon after 1785, date and place unknown. Thus, it can be seen the Gwinnett line is extinct. There can be no descendants of Signer Button Gwinnett. His signature is very valuable because there are so few of them.

Lyman Hall

55: LYMAN HALL

"I rejoice that America has resisted."

Wiliam Pitt, Earl of Chatham

The signature of Lyman Hall on the Declaration of Independence is in the middle of the three Georgia signers in the left-most column of the document. He signed his full name in a very neat, classical school hand.

He was the fifth child, third son of John Hall and Mary Street, whose ancestry goes back to the Puritan emigrant, John Hall.[1] The family had settled in New Haven, and then in Wallingford, CT. Young Lyman was tutored and prepared for collegiate work by his uncle, the Rev. Samuel Hall, and entered Yale College, from which he graduated in 1747. He studied for the ministry and was ordained into the Congregational Church in 1749. But Hall soon found that this was not a calling for him, and left the ministry to study medicine with a local physician. He hung out his shingle, but by 1757 he emigrated to Dorchester, South Carolina to a settlement of New England Puritans and a few months later went further down the coast into Georgia in St. John's Parish (the present Liberty County).

In this new environment Hall kept busy providing medical treatment and managing his estate at "Halls Knoll", just north of the present town of Midway. Perhaps because this area was steeped in the New England tradition of independence, it became known as the Southern Cradle of Liberty. When the troubles with Britain erupted in the 1760's, St. John's Parish stood apart in its opposition from most of the rest of the colony of Georgia. He attended Revolutionary conventions in Savannah in the summer of 1774 and by January of 1775 was disturbed at their failure to send delegates to the Continental Congress. The Parish of St. John's elected him in March of 1775 for this purpose, although Georgia as a whole was not represented at this First Continental Congress. Georgia's Provincial
Congress finally voted to join the other colonies in the cause of liberty, Lyman Hall voted for and signed the Declaration in Philadelphia.

---

[1] Robert Charles Anderson, *The Great Migration Begins*, (New England Historic Genealogical Society, Boston, MA, 1995), Vol II., pp. 840-844.

FIRST GENERATION

1. LYMAN HALL was born in Wallingford, CT on 12 Apr 1724.[1] He married (1st) Abigail BURR, daughter of Thaddeus and Abigail (Sturges) Burr in Fairfield, CT on 20 May 1752.[2] She was born in Fairfield, CT on 24 Mar 1729, and died in Fairfield, CT on 8 Jul 1753.[3] He married (2nd) Mary OSBORN, daughter of Samuel and Hannah (Couch) Osborn on 24 Jul 1759.[4] She was born in Fairfield, CT on 8 Aug 1736, and died in Burke County, GA on 18 Nov 1793.[5] He died in "Shell Bluff Plantation", Burke County, GA on 19 Oct 1790.[6] No children by first marriage.

Child by second marriage:

    2   i   John HALL, b. 4 Dec 1765, d. 20 Jan 1792; unm

References:

[1] F. B. Dexter, *Biographical Sketches of the Graduates of Yale College*, (1896), Vol. II has a short piece on Lyman Hall, who was a graduate of the Class of 1747. No full length, quality biography of Signer Lyman Hall has been located. See also Della Gray Bartherlmas, *The Signers of the Declaration of Independence, A Biographical and Genealogical Reference*, (Mcfarland & Company, Inc., Jefferson, NC, 1977), pp. 90-92. The Leach MSS material for Lyman Hall is found in FHL microfilm # 0001756, and the hard copy is in Vol. # 20, pp. 6401-6403. The DAB Article on Lyman Hall is in Vol. VIII, pp. 139-140. His date and place of birth are given in Leach MSS, p. 6401, and in the Vital Records of Wallingford, Births. [2] His first marriage is reported in Leach MSS, p. 6401; See also DAB, Vol. VIII, p. 65. [3] Leach MSS, p. 6401. [4] Lyman Hall's second marriage is reported in Bartherlmas, p. 91. [5] Her date of birth is reported in Donald Lines Jacobus, *History and Genealogy of Old Fairfield*, (Genealogical Publishing Company Reprint, 1991), Vol. I, p. 459; and her date of making a Will and its Probate is found in Leach MSS, p. 6401, meaning she died between 10 Oct 1793 and 22 Nov 1793, the exact date being reported in Kenneth H. Thomas, Jr., *Georgia's Signers and the Declaration of Independence*, (Cherokee Publishing Company, Atlanta, GA, 1981), Chapter VII, *Genealogies of the Signers*, p. 84. [6] His date of death is given in Leach MSS, p. 6401.

This first marriage of Lyman Hall to Abigail Burr lasted exactly one year, one month, and 18 days until her early death on 8 Jul 1753. There were no children born of that marriage. By his second marriage to Mary Osborn, Lyman Hall had only one child, a son, John Hall, who died shortly before his mother, in Burke County, GA on 20 Jan 1792. The lad had never married, and had no issue whatsoever. Thus, it can be seen that Signer Lyman Hall has no descendants!

Geo Walton

56: GEORGE WALTON

"England's on the anvil - hear the hammers ring... "

Rudyard Kipling

George Walton signed the Declaration at the bottom of the Georgia grouping of three signers located on the left most column on the document. He abbreviated his first name as "Geo" and put a period at the end of his name which was written in a moderately large, clear hand.

He was the son of Robert Walton and Mary Hughes. His grandfather, a George Walton, had emigrated from England in 1682, via Barbados, to Virginia. Both his parents died while the boy was very young and he was brought up by an Uncle, and, when old enough, was apprenticed to a carpenter. He attended a local school but was largely self-taught. At age 28, in 1769, he removed to Savannah, Georgia to read law under a local attorney, and five years later, in 1774, was admitted to the Bar. In that same year of 1774, Walton plunged into politics. He helped to organize and played a key part in meetings at Savannah in July and August of 1774 and at the First Provincial Congress the next January[2].

George Walton was chosen as Secretary of the Georgia Provincial Congress, and also served as a member of the Committee on Resolutions and the important Committee of Correspondence. He was elected as a delegate to the Second Continental Congress in Feb 1776, where he both voted for Independence on 2 July 1776, and signed the embossed document on 2 August 1776. He was commissioned Colonel of Georgia Militia in 1778 and served in the siege of Savannah where he was wounded and captured, being finally exchanged in September 1779. He served as Chief Justice of Georgia from 1783 to 1789 and was a Presidential Elector in the latter year. He was also elected to be Governor of the State of Georgia in 1789, during which administration he assisted in the establishment of a State Constitution and the location of the Capitol at Augusta.

---

[2] John and Katherine Bakeless, *Signers of the Declaration*, (Houghton Mifflin Company, Boston, MA, 1969), pp. 296-297.

FIRST GENERATION

1. GEORGE WALTON was born in Farmville, Amelia [Prince Edward in 1752] County, VA in Apr 1741.[1] He married Dorothy CAMBER, daughter of Thomas and Dorothy (Butler) Camber in Savannah, GA in Sep 1778.[2] She was born about 1763, and died in Pensacola, FL on 12 Sep 1832.[3] He died in Augusta, GA on 2 Feb 1804.[4] Children:

    2   i   Thomas Camber WALTON, b. c. 1782, d. 13 Dec 1803; unm

+ 3   ii   George WALTON, Jr., b. 1787

References:

[1] John Sanderson, *Biographies of the Signers of the Declaration of Independence*, (1823), Vol. IV is a very flowery, not documented attempt at biographical history. There is no quality, referenced biography of George Walton. See however, Della Gray Bartherlmas, *The Signers of the Declaration of Independence, A Biographical and Genealogical Reference*, (Mcfarland & Company, Inc., Jefferson, NC, 1977), pp. 272-273; and Edwin C. Bridges, *George Walton: A Political Biography*, (PhD. Dissertation, University of Chicago, 1981). In the period just before the sesquicentennial [150 years] celebration of the Declaration in 1926, the National Society of the Daughters of the American Revolution had become concerned about the quality of the documentation (or lack of it) in some of their lineage papers; and supported the research of Luella Bell (Merrill) Draper, Registrar of the Society in preparing some supporting material for use of application reviewers. This work is housed in the DAR Library in Washington, DC, and is known as the Bell Draper MSS. It contains several pages on the descendants of George Walton. The Leach MSS material for George Walton is found in FHL microfilm # 0001756, and the hard copy is in Vol. # 20, pp. 6405-6421. The DAB Article on George Walton is in Vol. XIX, pp. 403-405. His birth is reported in Bartherlmas, p. 273. [2] The marriage is reported in *Dictionary of Georgia Biography*, (University of Georgia Press, Athens, GA, 1983), Vol 1, p. 1030. [3] Her year of birth is assumed from the year of her parents marriage and of her own marriage to be about 1763, her date and place of death is reported in Kenneth H. Thomas, Jr., *Georgia's Signers and the Declaration of Independence*, (Cherokee Publishing Company, Atlanta, GA, 1981), Chapter VII, *Genealogies of the Signers*, p.90. [4] His date of death is given in DAB, Vol. XIX, p. 403.

SECOND GENERATION

3. GEORGE WALTON, Jr.[2] (George Walton[1]) son of George Walton and Dorothy Camber was born in Savannah, GA in 1787, and died in Petersburg, VA on 3 Jan 1863.[1] He married Sarah Minge WALKER, daughter of

George and Eliza (Talbot) Walker in "Bellevue", Augusta, GA on 10 Jan 1809.[1] She was born in Washington, GA on 19 Jul 1792, and died in Mobile, AL on 14 Jan 1861.[1] Children:

+ 4   i   Octavia Celeste Valentine WALTON, b. 10 Aug 1811
   5   ii   Robert Watkins WALTON, b. 26 Mar 1813, d. 27 Mar 1849; unm

References:

[1] Kenneth H. Thomas, Jr., *Georgia's Signers and the Declaration of Independence*, (Cherokee Publishing Company, Atlanta, GA, 1981), Chapter VII, *Genealogies of the Signers*, pp. 90-91; Leach MSS, p. 6405; see also the Bell Draper MSS in the DAR Library, Addenda, p. 72 for descendants of this couple.

THIRD GENERATION

4. OCTAVIA CELESTE VALENTINE WALTON[3] (George Walton, Jr.[2], George Walton[1]) child of George Walton, Jr. and Sarah Minge Walker was born in "Bellevue", Augusta, GA on 10 Aug 1811, and died in Augusta, GA on 13 Mar 1877.[1] She married Henry Strachey LeVERT, son of Dr. Claude and Ann Lee (Metcalf) LeVert in Mobile, AL on 14 Feb 1836.[2] He was born in King William County, VA on 25 Dec 1804, and died in Mobile, AL on 16 Mar 1864.[1] Children:

   6   i   Octavia Walton LeVERT, b. 20 Nov 1836, d. 1889; unm
   7   ii   Claudia Anne Eugenia LeVERT, b. 22 May 1838, dy 8 May 1849
   8   iii   Sarah Walker LeVERT, b. 6 Apr 1841, dy 3 May 1849
   9   iv   Son LeVERT, b. c. 1843, dy 1843
+ 10   v   Caroline Henrietta LeVERT, b. 6 Dec 1846

References:

[1] Leach MSS, p. 6406, see also Thomas, p. 93 for the children of this marriage. [2] National Intelligencer of 7 Mar 1836.

FOURTH GENERATION

10. CAROLINE HENRIETTA LeVERT[4](Octavia Celeste Walton[3], George Walton, Jr.[2], George Walton[1]) child of Octavia Celeste Walton and Henry Strachey LeVert was born in Mobile, AL on 6 Dec 1846, and died in Augusta, GA on 13 Dec 1876.[1] She married Lawrence Augustus Regail REAB, son of George Brown and Emma Regail (Walker) Reab on 16 Dec

1868.[1] He was born in Augusta, GA on 16 Dec 1844[1], and died on 3 Jul 1909. Children:

    11   i   Regail LeVert REAB, b. 31 Aug 1870, dy 13 May 1871
    12   ii   Child REAB, b. c. 1871, dy 1871
    13   iii   George Walton REAB, b. 4 Jun 1872, d. 6 Mar 1925; unm
References:
[1] Kenneth H. Thomas, Jr., *Georgia's Signers and the Declaration of Independence*, (Cherokee Publishing Company, Atlanta, GA, 1981), Chapter VII, *Genealogies of the Signers*, p. 93; Leach MSS, p. 6407.

The reader can see from this genealogical register presentation of the four generations of Georgia Signer George Walton, that there are **no surviving descendants** of the body of the signer! He had only one child, a son, who had issue, George Walton, Jr. That son died leaving only one child having issue, Octavia Celeste Valentine Walton. While she had five children, it is readily seen that only one of them, Caroline Henrietta LeVert, survived and had issue.

Caroline Henrietta LeVert married and had three children, two of whom died young, leaving only George Walton Reab as a survivor. He died in Augusta, GA on 6 Mar 1925, and is buried in the Walker Cemetery, now located on the campus of Augusta College. George Walton Reab had never married, had no issue, and thus, with his death, the direct line of descent from the signer came to an end.

This author has had several comments from persons, claiming (a few with some vigor) that they are descendants of Signer George Walton. That cannot be! Perhaps they might be a descendant of a relative of the signer, but that is collateral, not direct descent. Sorry, but **no one can be descended** from George Walton, the signer of the Declaration of Independence!

The Rev. and Mrs. Frederick W. Pyne

ABOUT the AUTHOR

The lengthy effort invested to inspire the Board of Governors of the Descendants of the Signers of the Declaration of Independence to proceed with such a massive project as this Register, to fund at least a small part of the out-of-pocket expenses, to contact and seek assistance from many, many contributors, to visit and research at a great many resource centers, and to stick the nose to the grindstone so as to produce these seven volumes, would not have been possible without the aid, comfort, encouragement, and support of my wife, Ann Rammes Pyne.

Her presence, therefore, in the photograph, is a requirement in honoring her greatly appreciated help, without which this work would not exist! Many other persons have assisted in some form; contributors to a particular chapter, proof-readers of a portion of a volume, computer assistance to others, aid in finding a reference, reviewers of text; and most have been noted in the preface to individual volumes.

But none has been as consistently helpful and supportive as Ann R. Pyne. Always there to encourage, offering her time and talents, even though she might prefer to be doing something else. Typing letters, reviewing whole chapters, checking the number system, giving that other eye, without which no work can be polished; going with me to Genealogical Libraries, taking notes, copying documents. Mostly just being there to encourage when I was discouraged, to uplift when nothing was going right, to comfort when I saw no end. She was my right arm in all this long process - thank you so very much, dear wife!

Frederick Wallace Pyne, the eldest son of Frederick Cruger Pyne and Helen Louise Wallace, was born in the William Beaumont Hospital at Fort Bliss, in El Paso, TX on 19 August 1926. His father was a graduate of the USMA [Class of 1924][1], and his mother was a graduate of Goucher College [Class of 1924].

---

[1] USMA Graduate # 7457. See *Register of Graduates and Former Cadets of the United States Military Academy*, (Association of Graduates, West Point, NY, 1990), p. 381.

Through his paternal line he is a descendant of Signer William Floyd, General Philip Schuyler, Governor DeWitt Clinton, all of New York, and of Captain John Underhill of Connecticut. Through his maternal line he is a descendant of Mayflower passenger John Howland, the Rev. James Fitch, Captain Ebenezer ("Swamp") Shaw, and Captain Nathaniel Merriman.

He attended public primary and secondary schools in Elizabeth, NJ, Pittsburgh, PA, and Highland Falls, NY. He served in both the Regular Army during WWII and the Indiana National Guard after WWII for a total of seven years [1944-1951]. He took a degree in Civil Engineering (B.S.C.E.) from Tri-State College (now University) in 1951, and a Masters Degree (M.S.E.) from The John Hopkins University in 1966. He studied for Holy Orders through the Moore Theological College in Syndey, Australia for three years [1989-1992], and was ordained in the United Episcopal Church of North America (UECNA) in 1993.

Pyne married Jo Ann Rammes in Birmingham, MI on 18 July 1952. She is a 1951 graduate of Oberlin College (BA), and a 1968 graduate of Western Maryland College (M Ed). They have four children, and three grandchildren.

Having put in a lifetime career as an Engineer and a Professor of Mathematics during a period of more than 40 years, Pyne entered upon a long delayed call to the Priesthood. He now serves as the Rector of St. Andrew's Episcopal Church (Traditional) in Frederick, MD. Believing strongly in sound families, he had also developed a very serious interest in genealogy, and has made its scholarly pursuit and study a life avocation.

During his earlier career he was a Professional Engineer (P.E.), a Fellow of the American Society of Civil Engineers (F.A.S.C.E.), and a Diplomate of the American Academy of Environmental Engineers. In his more current life work as a Genealogist he is a Certified Genealogical Records Specialist (CGRS), and has been recognized as a Fellow of the American College of Genealogists (FACG). Pyne is listed in recent editions of Who's Who.[2, 3]

---

[2] *Marquis Who's Who in the East*, 1999-2000, 27th Edition, [Reed Reference Publishing Company, New Providence, NJ, [1998], p. 790.

[3] *Marquis Who's Who in America*, 1999, 54st Edition, [Reed Reference Publishing Company, New Providence, NJ, 1999], Vol. II, p. 3957.

He is a Life Member and Past President-General (1975-1978) of the Descendants of the Signers of the Declaration of Independence, a Life member of the Sons of the American Revolution, a Life Member of the Society of Mayflower Descendants. He is a member of a number of Genealogical and Historical Societies, including: The New England Historic Genealogical Society, The New York Genealogical and Biographical Society, The Genealogical Society of Pennsylvania, the Virginia Genealogical Society, and the Society of Genealogists [London, England], and the Association of Professional Genealogists (APG); The Historical Society of Pennsylvania, and The New York State Historical Association [Cooperstown, NY]. He is also a member of Family Associations, such as the Pilgrim John Howland Society, and the Van Voorhees Association.

Pyne is installed on the NEHGS Heraldry Committee's Roll of Arms [Registration #513], his line will be found in Matthew's American Armoury and Blue Book, 1903 [p. 267]. He is the author of a comprehensive Family History[4], and a Genealogical Family Study[5].

He had been a member of the sub-committee to review possibilities for doing "something" with the Leach Manuscript Papers since its inception by the DSDI in 1978. After nearly a decade had gone by without evidence of much movement, he prepared a few preliminary sketches for review between 1988 - 1991. However, it was not until 1993 that he undertook serious efforts toward creating this massive work on The Register. After several delays and various attempts at format, the first volume was finally ready for the publisher by June 1997, and came out in October of that year. With considerable help from many other supporters, each successive volume seemed to be easier. Finally, here in the year 2000, the seventh and last volume was finished, and the series is now complete!

---

[4] *The John Pyne Family in America, being the Comprehensive Genealogical Record of the Descendants of John Pyne (1766-1813) of Charleston, South Carolina,* (Gateway, Baltimore, MD, 1992), xx, 204pp., 67 illus.

[5] *A Bennett - Faville Genealogy, a Study in Family History of the connected lines of Michael Lockwood Bennett and John Faville of Herkimer County, NY,* (Self-published, 2000).

EVERY NAME INDEX

The following Every Name Index compiled by Picton Press contains a total of 10,894 entries. Women are indexed whenever possible under both their maiden and married name(s). Maiden names are given in parenthesis thus: Mary (Smith) Jones. As always, readers are cautioned to check under all conceivable spellings. We have grouped the most popular spellings together and in such cases have added a cross-reference to other spellings, as an aid to your search.

Picton Press   11 April 2000

387

ALTMAN (continued)
Jack Elquit Jr, 159,
187, 224-225
John Heyward, 224
Margaret Lee (Bryson),
224
Nancy Desbouillions,
187, 224
Sally Ann, 187, 225
ALVES
-- McDowal, 5
ANCHER
Emma Cruger (Irving),
152
Frederick Cornelius
Brower, 152
Frederick Lindsay, 152
George Dummer
Brower, 152
Georgine Lindsay
(Dummer), 152
John Beaufaine, 152
ANDERSON
Dorothy Fraser, 170,
206
Dorothy Heyward
(Wilson), 170, 206-207
Lucy Winston, 170,
207
Pelham Hansard Jr,
170, 206-207
ANDREWS
Adella, 18
Anne, 52
Elizabeth Middleton,
322, 346
Ronnie, 41
Thomas Wayne, 41
APPEL
Betty Sue (Wills), 37
Kenneth Chester, 37
Kenni Alicia, 37
ARBOGAST
-- (--), 342
Charles B, 318, 342
Charles B Jr, 318, 342
D B, 342
Erica Anne, 342
Eva Russell (Dehon),
342
Middleton Dehon, 318
ARCHER
Colin Edward, 331
Jeffrey Russell, 331
Joanne Barbara (Rutter),
331
Katelyn Elizabeth, 331
Kirk Russell, 331

Stephanie Ann, 331
ARMAS
Honor Heyward
(Bulkley), 194
Juan Emanuel, 194
Wynanda Heyward
Bulkley, 194
ARMISTEAD
Jean Sinclair, 149
ARMSTRONG
Criss Ann, 238
ASHBY
Agnes (Taylor), 54
Fanny, 54
John Taylor, 54
John Washington, 54
Lucy (Cooke), 54
Marion Gordon, 54
Marshall, 54
Nancy Anne, 266, 287
Tallula, 54
ASHE
Hannah Cochran, 119
ASPINWALL
Lea Thom, 313, 336
ATWOOD
Jane Camp, 143, 164
AUB
Elizabeth Francis, 312,
334
Elizabeth Francis Pym
(Cope), 312, 334
Frances, 312, 334
Joseph C, 312, 334
Nancy Cope, 312, 334
AUSTEL
Toni, 343
AUSTIN
Donna Marie (Nieman),
229
Elizabeth Gail, 229
Elizabeth Huger, 192,
229
Elizabeth Huger
(Harrison), 192, 229
Helen Elizabeth
(Miner), 192
James Keighly, 192
John Hogg, 192
Lawrence Miner, 192,
229
Lawrence Miner Jr,
192, 229
Margaret Elliott, 229
BACHMAN
Rita Marie, 31
BACKAT
Joan Mildred, 201, 233

BACKER
Caroline Pauline, 102,
108, 350, 364
BACKUS
Ellison, 199
BACON
Caroline Castleman, 92,
305
BAGBY
George William, 61
Lucy Parke
(Chamberlayne), 61
Virginia, 61, 69
BAILEY/ BAYLEY
Amelia Kirk (Newton),
275
Emily Keese, 275, 299
Floyd, 275
Helen, 257
BAIRD
Alice, 319
Alice (Tillman), 319
George, 319
Laura, 319
BAKER
Audra, 38
Kaleb, 38
Mary, 246
Mitchell, 37-38
Sarah, 38
BALL
Sophia, xxvi
BANKER
Henrietta Maria, 266
BARBARE
Sarah Kathryn, 239
BARKSDALE
Elise Florence
(Warwick), 63
Elise Warwick, 63,
70-71
George Annesley, 63
Patricia Ann
(Thompson), 220
William, 220
William Jason, 220
BARNETTE
Elaine McKellar
(Heyward), 205
Katherine Heyward,
205
William Augustus III,
205
William Augustus IV,
205
BARNWELL
Annie Bull, 131
Arthur, 277, 300

BARNWELL (continued)
Arthur Jr, 277
Charlotte Bull, 275
Emma, 268
Louis, 277
Margaret Manigault, 277
Maria Louisa (Wilkinson), 277, 300
Maria Louisa Wilkinson, 277, 300, 323
Marie Louise, 277, 300, 323
BARON
Elizabeth Jane (Cadwalader), 336
Eugene Stanley, 336
Owen David Cadwalader, 336
BARRINGER
Beaumont, 162
Elizabeth W, 312, 334
Frances, 335
Paul, 335
Philip, 334
Sophia (Hazard), 334
Thomas, 335
BARROW
Arthur E, 298
David Crenshaw, 298, 322
Emma Middleton Izard (Hùger), 298, 322
Frida, 319
Giulia Pat (Mainieri), 346
Isabel Angelina, 346
Katherine Winchester (Forsythe), 322, 346
Mary, 298
Middleton Pope, 298, 322, 346
Middleton Pope III, 346
Middleton Pope Jr, 322, 346
Rebecca Anne, 346
BARTELS
Jeanette, 193
BARTLETT
--, 285
Elizabeth, 285
Kalyn Rose, 330
Kelly Jeanne (Duncan), 330
Maud Muriel (Middleton), 285

Philip Thomas, 330
Trevor Keegan, 330
William, 285
BARTONE
Alexandra Townsend, 343
Michael, 343
Olivia Caldwell (Holt), 343
BATES
Doreen, 311
BATSON
Avis Irene, 167, 201
BATTEY
Alfred, 186
Allison Paula, 186, 223
Caroline Jordan, 223
Colden Rhind III, 186, 223
Colden Rhind Jr, 186, 223
Kathryn (White), 223
Paula Wood (Lengnick), 223
Rebecca Wood, 223
Susan Ella, 186
BAYLEY
[See Bailey],
BEAM
Jesse, 240
Joshua Scott, 240
Kelly Lynn (Wilkins), 240
Scott E, 240
BEATTY
Charles Francis, 23
Evan William, 23
Joel Christian, 23
Jonathan Lawton, 23
Joseph E, 23
Margaret Susanne (Mellichampe), 23
Pauline (Mieb), 23
BEAVERS
Emily, 89, 302
BECKWITH
Carrie (Kitchell), 142
Elizabeth Eugenia, 142, 161
George, 142
BEDON
Julia (Davis), 268
Julia Davis, 268, 291
Richard Stobo, 268
BEEKMAN
Adam, 111, 353
Catherine A, 276
Christopher, 111, 353

Eleanora, 111, 353
Elizabeth Davis (Mumford), 111, 353
Emma, 111, 353
Melissa, 111, 353
BEIRNE
Andrew, 264
Ellen (Grey), 264
Mary Grey, 264
BEKEN
Munir Nurettin, 355
Sally Horton (Hawkridge), 355
Timur Middleton, 355
BELIN
Allard, 370
Elizabeth Ann "Betsy" (Gwinnett), 371
Elizabeth Ann (Gwinnett), 370
Margaret (Robert), 370
Peter, 370-371
BELL
Elizabeth Jernigan, 21, 32
BENNETT
Bette Jo, 214
BENTIVOGLIO
Angela (Sandri), 253
Comenico, 253
Paolina, 253, 263
BERK
Mary Louanne, 110, 366
BERRY
Brett Yeager, 227
Kelsey Claire, 227
Susan Ellen (Yeager), 227
William Franklin, 227
William Franklin (Berry), 227
William Franklin Jr, 227
BERSCH
Rosemary, 211
BETHEA
John, 240
Loren Deneil (Wilkins), 240
Zachary Tristram, 240
BIGELOW
Horatio, 70
Mary (Riese), 70
Mary DeFord, 70, 74
BIJUR
Betty, 73

BOURNE (continued)
Gertrude, 172
Patricia Semple, 162,
193-194
BOYKIN
Catherine Laing, 119,
127
Charlotte Adamson
(Mortimer), 119
John, 119
Margaret Kennedy, 139,
155-156
BOYLE
Laura Louise, 338
Nancy Ware (Hawkins),
338
Playford, 338
BRACK
Roxana, 274
BRACKBILL
Charles, 353
Eleanor (Phillips), 353
Elizabeth Blake, 353
BRADFORD
Alexis Irenee du Pont,
133
Carolyn (Joye), 106,
361
Edward Elliot, 132
Edward Green, 122,
132-133, 149
Eleuthera du Pont, 133,
148
Eleuthera Paulina (du
Pont), 133, 149
Elise, 106, 361
Elise Pinckney
(Rutledge), 101, 106,
361
Elizabeth Elliot, 132
Hannah Hewson, 200,
232
Isabella, 132
Isabella Middleton, 132
Isabella Mitchell
(Elliot), 132
James Heyward, 122,
132
James Heyward Jr, 132
Joanna du Pont, 133
Mary Alicia (Heyward),
132-133
Mary Alicia Heyward,
133
Mary Cornelia, 122
Mary Eugenia, 132
Moses, 122
Phoebe (George), 122

Robert, 106
Robert Bennett, 106,
361
Robert Morris, 101,
349, 361
Rutledge McDonald,
101, 349
Sarah Rutledge, 106,
361
William Shubrick, 132
William Stewart, 101,
106, 349, 361
William Stewart Jr,
101
BRADY
Jane Shannon (Johnson),
354
Katharine Shannon,
112, 354
Raymond Daniel, 112,
354
BRAGG
Mary, 66
BRANDON
Gary Wayne, 189
Matthew Wayne, 189
BRANDT
A Frankland, 208
David Lawrence
Adams, 208
Ellen Jael (Walker),
208
John Edward Barnwell,
208
Zoe Elizabeth Rea, 208
BRANFORD
Mary Alicia, 118
BREWER
Mary Susan, 40
BRICE
Charles Strong, 11
Susan Annette, 11
Susan Taylor (Hooper),
11
William Robert, 11
BRIDGES/ BRIDGE
Diana M, 207
Joseph W, 207
Maria (--), 207
Mary Brown, 294, 318
BRIGDON
Barbara (Cribbs), 225
Emily Lucille, 225
Harry David, 225
Harry David Jr, 225
Hunter Moore, 225
Sally Ann (Altman),
225

Sarah Elizabeth, 225
BRINE
Beverly, 344
BRINLEY
Deborah, 82, 261
BRINTON
Ann Maria, 267
BROACH
Amy Laura (Trybalski),
236
James, 236
Savanah, 236
Stoney, 236
BRONSON
Susan Francez, 28, 40
BROOKS
Allan Arthur, 170
Lorraine (Wilmoth),
170
Merrily, 170
BROWN
Isabell Delores, 317
Melinda Sue, 35
Sheri Frances, 226
Stephanie Virginia, 226
William Reuben, 226
William Robert, 226
BROWNING
Sarah Eusebia, 62
BRUMBY
Anne (Wallis), 291
Arnoldus Vander Horst,
291
Susan Gruning, 291
BRUNDIGE
Ann, 122
BRUSH
Susan Lewis, 29
BRYAN
Eleanor Charlton, 360
Eleanor Charlton
(deSaussure), 360
Josephine deSaussure,
360
Kendall Gibson, 360
Kendall Gibson Jr, 360
Sarah Huger, 360
Virginia, 239
BRYSON
Margaret Lee, 224
BUCHANAN
Mary Gittings
Simmons, 71
BUFFIN
Catherine, 136
BULKLEY
Anne Cuthbert
(Palmer), 163, 194

BULKLEY (continued)
Derrick Middleton, 163
Honor Heyward, 163, 194
Jonathan Duncan, 163, 194
Peter, 163
BULLOCH
Archibald, 367
BURBAGE
H Dewar, 312
Lee Patrick, 312
Scott Middleton, 312
Susan Ellen (Myers), 312
BURGESS
Cathy (Short), 41
Donnie, 35, 41
Doris Marie, 25, 35
Doris Marie (--), 41
Dustin, 41
Haley, 41
Lawrence, 41
Lisa Kay, 40
Lonny Hubert, 25, 35
Lonny Hubert Jr, 25
Margie Louise, 25
Marvin L, 25, 35, 41
May Elizabeth, 25, 35
Teresa (Gladden), 35, 41
Thelma Rhett (Wills), 35
BURKE
Arthur Michael, 177
Arthur Michael Jr, 177
Katherine Anne (Howard), 177
Kathleen Michaela, 177
Timothy Joseph, 177
BURNET
Alice Marie (Musgrove), 213, 239
Catherine Margaret (North), 175, 213
Elizabeth Howard, 134, 149, 174-175
Emma, 134
Emma Heyward, 150, 176, 213-214
Emma Heyward (Howard), 134, 149-150
Henry DeSaussure, 134, 149-150
Henry Heyward, 134, 150, 175-176, 213
Henry Heyward III,

175, 213, 239
Henry Heyward IV, 239
Henry Heyward Jr, 150, 175, 213
Henry Heyward V, 239
Julie Rutledge, 213
Katherine Emory, 150
Nella, 134, 149
Valeria (North), 150, 175-176
Valeria North, 150, 175, 212-213
Virginia (Bryan), 239
BURR
Abigail, 374
Abigail (Sturges), 374
Thaddeus, 374
BURROUGHS
Mary, 123-124
BURTON
Clara Winston, 97, 327
BUSCH
Deborah Anne, 215
Linda Jean, 215, 239
Richard Ferris, 215, 240
Richard Howard, 215
Virginia Carolyn (Harwood), 215, 240
BUTLER
Ann (Street), 183, 220
Ann Lucille, 158, 185, 222(2)
Anne Warren, 141
Carol (Tolle), 185, 222
Carol McTeer, 158, 185, 223
Catherine, 157, 184, 221
Christopher James, 222
Cindy June (Dewey), 220
Deborah Anne, 183
Debra Wallring, 184
Dorothy, 378
Evie Ryan, 158
Florence Exley, 158, 184, 221-222
Frances Louise, 157, 183
Gerald Leroy, 183
Iona C (McPhail), 184
James Byron, 157, 183, 220
James Leroy, 157, 183-185
James Leroy III, 185,

222
James Leroy Jr, 158, 185, 222
Jeffrey Byron, 220
John Edward, 183
Laura Elizabeth, 222
Margaret McTeer, 157, 183, 220-221
Margaret Williamson (McTeer), 157, 183-185
Michael Robert, 220
Richard Clark, 183
Robert Byron, 183, 220
Robert Henry, 157, 184
Vicki Lee, 222
Vicki Lee (Butler), 222
Vicki Lynn, 185
CADWALADER
Ann Cleland, 288, 314, 337
Beatrice d'Este (Penrose), 313, 336
Benjamin Read, 288
David, 313
Deborah Dean (Richards), 336
Elizabeth Jane, 313, 336
Elizabeth Middleton (Read), 288, 307, 313-314
Gardner Aspinwall, 313, 336
Gardner Owen, 336
Genevive Aspinwall, 336
George, 313, 336
George Jr, 336
Henrietta Maria (Banker), 266
John, 266, 288, 307, 313(2), 336
Kathryn Louise (Kaersher), 336
Lea Thom (Aspinwall), 313, 336
Margaret (Nicoll), 288, 313
Mary Helen, 266, 288
Mary Helen (Fisher), 266, 288, 307
Phyllis Jane (Clegg), 313, 336-337
Sandra Lea, 313
Sophia, 266
Sophia Francis, 313,

CADWALADER
(continued)
   Sophia Francis
   (continued)
   336
  Susannah, 336
  Thomas, 336
  Thomas Francis, 266,
   288, 307, 313-314
  Thomas Francis Jr, 288,
   313, 336
  Yara (Telles), 336
CAHILL
  Marguerite, 226
CAIN
  Ruth Artley, 163,
   195-196
CALDCLEUGH
  Bobette, 105, 343
  Clarence Milton, 99,
   105, 319, 343
  Connie Ione (Lowrey),
   105, 343
  Robert Blake, 99, 105,
   319, 343
  Willie Maxine
   (Hoffman), 99, 105,
   343
CALHOUN
  John C, 77
  Molly Miller, 212
CALLAHAN
  Anne Denise, 33
  Christina Lynn, 231
  Martha Ann (Phenicie),
   231
  Randall, 231
CALLOWAY
  Patricia, 13
CALVERT
  Annie Rowan (Forney),
   95
  Clarence William, 95
  John, xxiv, xxviii
  Palmer (Daugette), 324
  Palmer Daugette, 95
  William Jonathan III,
   95, 324
  William Jonathan Jr,
   95, 324
CAMBER
  Dorothy, 378
  Dorothy (Butler), 378
  Thomas, 378
CAMERON
  Eva, 285, 308
CAMP
  Joseph Pinckney, 22

Juanita (Steel), 22
Julia Victoria, 22
CAMPBELL
  Anne Rebecca, 290
  Annie Caroline, 135
  Debra, 241
  Donald, 241
  Donald Jr, 241
  Joshua, 241
  Kina Marie (Rainey),
   241
  Laura, 241
  Rebecca, 241
  Susannah, 260
CAPORINI
  Isabella Hewson, 232
  Margaret (Heyward),
   232
  Mark, 232
CARD
  Carolynne Renshaw,
   76
  Daniel Parker II, 76
  Henrietta Gittings
   (Renshaw), 75
  Marianne Egerton, 76
  Samuel Parran, 75
CARLTON
  Catherine, 231
CARPENTER
  Charles Kendrick, 88,
   301
  Grace, 170
  Jane Emeline (Miller),
   88, 301
  Jane Scales, 88, 301
CARR
  Jean Heyward
   (Ferguson), 226
  Julie Cahill, 226
  Leo John, 226
  Margaret Ferguson,
   226
  Marguerite (Cahill),
   226
  Sarah Hollinshead, 122
  Stephen Leo, 226
CARSON
  Aimee, 342
  Ann (Mauldin), 342,
   360
  Coleen, 360
  Deborah, 319, 342,
   360
  Jennifer, 360
  John Andrew, 342, 360
  John Andrew Jr, 342,
   360

Louise (--), 360
Michael Wilder, 342
CARSTON
  Christine, 27
CARTER
  Anne, 55
  Anne Hill, 57
  Anne Marie, 358
  Anne Marie (Simms),
   358
  Benjamin Munnerlyn,
   341, 358
  Benjamin Munnerlyn Jr,
   358
  Catherine, 19
  Daniel Spring, 358
  Florence Ida, 56, 64
  Frank III, 341, 358
  Frank IV, 358
  Frank Jr, 341, 358
  George Monroe, 56
  Jane Morris
   (Munnerlyn), 341, 358
  Jane Stewart, 341
  Mary Ann, 168, 203
  Mary Tayloe (Rice), 56
  Palmer Marie, 358
  Patricia Marie (Reed),
   358
  Wilson Munnerlyn,
   341
CASE
  Andrew, 110, 353
  Brian, 110, 353
  Cheryl (--), 110, 352
  Eleanor (Mumford),
   104, 110, 352-353
  Harley Allen, 104, 110,
   329, 352-353
  Harley Allen Jr, 104,
   329
  Heather Christine, 110,
   353
  Jeffery, 110, 353
  Marshall, 104, 110,
   329, 353
  Martha (Cunningham),
   110, 353
CASHIN
  Benjamin Pierrepont,
   354
  Madeline Hoyt, 354
  Maria Louisa (Hoyt),
   354
  Oliver Selden, 354
  Stephen Douglas, 354
CASSIDY
  Elizabeth Heyward,

DUELL (continued)
Charles (continued)
351
Charles Halliwell
Pringle, 99, 105, 327,
351
Charles Holland, 105,
351
Heningham Ann, 99,
327
J Holland, 99, 327
Josephine Clark, 105,
351
Josephine Scott, 99,
327
Josephine Scott (Smith),
99, 105, 327, 351
June Heningham, 105,
351
Mabel (Halliwell), 99,
327
DUFFY
Aileen Archer, 35
Barclay Patrick, 35
Claudia Carol (Smith),
35
Erin Brydges, 35
Michael Gordon, 35
DUKE
Lillian, 25
DUMMER
Georgine Lindsay, 152
DUNBAR
Bessie Lee, 138
DUNCAN
Carmen Lucretia, 27,
40
Christine (Carston), 27
Ellen Barbara, 309,
330
Garret Davies, 27
Gregory Keith, 309
Janet Elizabeth, 309,
330
John Randolph, 277
Keith Joseph, 309, 330
Kelly Jeanne, 309, 330
Marion Barbara
Dorothy (Cousens),
309, 330
Mary Jane, 277
Mary Jane (Duncan),
277
Mary Mildred, 277
Maureen Patricia, 309,
330
DURANT
Margaret Esther, 237

DURRELL
Katherine Grace, 32
DYER
Alexander Heyward,
200
Elizabeth Stuart, 200
Jonathan, 199
Josephine de Rosset
(Heyward), 199
DYKSTRA
John William Peter,
110, 366
Matthew, 110, 366
Sarah Rutledge
(Stewart), 110, 366
EARLE
Akemi (Ogawa), 337
Alexander Jackson, 337
Ann Cleland
(Cadwalader), 314, 337
Cleland Kinloch, 314,
337
Eliza Middleton, 337
Elizabeth C (Weldon),
337
Katherine Cadwalader,
337
Kinloch Mason, 337
Lieko, 337
Miriam Elizabeth
(Nelson), 337
Richard Blair, 314, 337
Richard Blair Jr, 314
Sarah Elizabeth, 337
Sayako, 337
Stephen Jackson, 314,
337
Thomas Cadwalader,
314, 337
EATON
Mary Alice, 140
EBY
David, 37
Deborah Fay (Wills),
37
Kristin, 37
Lauren, 37
ECCLES
Mary Jones, 7
EDGAR
Carolyn Jean, 20, 30
EDINGS
Mary Elizabeth, 254
EDWARDS
Anne Berry (Wade),
355
Beatrice Clyde, 96, 325
Christopher, 344

Clementina (Rutledge),
320, 344
Dana, 344
Howard, 320, 344
Howard Jr, 320
Hunter Andreson, 355
James Allen Jr, 355
Julie Anne
(Birmingham), 344
Laura Lee (Wills), 39
Matthew David, 39
Michael Wayne, 39
Oliver Rutledge, 320,
344
Russell Elliott, 39
Tina, 320
EIKER
Dorris Lyman (Drew),
69
Marion, 69
Walter Moulden, 69
ELBERRS
Brent Colin, 332
Dianne Bernadette
(Cousens), 332
Jason Matthew, 332
Morris Peter, 332
Ryan James, 332
ELEK
Daphne Drinker, 314
Frances Wharton, 314
Henry Drinker, 314
Mary Elwyn (Drinker),
314
Peter S, 314
Susanna Middleton,
314
ELLETT
Heningham, 94, 99,
306, 327
Josephine Lyons (Scott),
306
Tazewell, 94, 306
ELLIOTT/ ELLIOT
Carolina Phoebe, 85,
279
Charlotte Barnwell,
276
Charlotte Bull
(Barnwell), 275
Douglas F, 299
Erin (Dowling), 347
Esther Huger, 276
Harriet Lucas Pinckney
(Huger), 275, 299
Isabel Barnwell, 347
Isabella Mitchell, 132
James, 132

GIGNILLIAT (continued)
Charles Olmstead
(continued)
211
Darrell White, 211
Edward Harris, 174,
211
Elizabeth Ann, 211
Harris McKenzie, 211
Hattie (Heyward), 132
Jean Frances, 148, 174,
211
Laura (Lieberman),
211
Marguerite Montford
(McKenzie), 211
Maria (Olmstead), 148,
173-174
Mary Caroline
(Heyward), 132, 148
Meighan Rebecca, 211
Nora Linda (White),
211
Rosemary (Bersch),
211
William LeSerurier,
132, 148
William Robert, 132,
148, 173-174, 211
William Robert III, 174,
211
William Robert Jr, 148,
174, 211
William Stuart, 211
GILBERTH
Edward Manigault, 178
Frank, 178
Mary (Manigault), 178
Rebecca Motte, 178
GILES
Louise, 155
William, 155
William Jr, 155
GILLAM
Elizabeth Ann, 137
GILLIAM
-- (--), 67
Catharine Elizabeth
(Thornton), 58
Elizabeth Moore
(Taylor), 58, 67
John, 58, 67
Randolph Moore, 67
Richard James, 58, 67
GITTINGS
Harriet (Tenant), 264
Harriet Sterrett, 264,
284

Lambert, 264
GLADDEN
Teresa, 35, 41
GLEASON
Alice Hamilton, 334
David Hollis, 334
Herbert P, 334
Nancy Cope (Aub),
334
GLOVER
Edith Matthew, 282
Eliza, 127
Ruth Anne, 230
GOETHE
Caroline Screven
(Heyward), 160, 189
Patricia Ann, 160, 189
Wallace, 160, 189
GOFREY
Charlene, 312
GOING
Betty Sue (Wills), 37,
41
Jamie (Holder), 41
LaTasha Sheri, 37
Michael Dylan, 41
Michael Todd, 37, 41
Michael Todd Jr, 37,
41
Rebecca Lynn, 41
GOODE
Ann (Leftwitch), 267
John, 267
Sallie, 267, 289-290
GOODRUM
Caroline Elizabeth
(Townsend), 66
Ella Marion, 66
Mildred, 160, 190-191
William, 66
GOODWYN
Margaret Lane, 316,
339
GORDON
Agnes Armistead, 53,
59
Battaile Fitzhugh, 53
Bazil, 53, 59
Candice, 40
Graham, 53
John Taylor, 53
Lucy Penn (Taylor), 53,
59
Lucy Woodford, 53, 59,
68
Margaret McKim, 53
Marion, 51, 54
Mary Helen (Rich), 40

Mary Wallace, 53
Samuel, 51, 53
Susan Fitzhugh (Knox),
51, 53
Thomas Daniel, 40
William Penn, 53
GORMAN
Marguerite Boykin
(Heyward), 155
Ralph Wesley, 155
Ralph Wesley Jr, 155
GOSCH
Margie, 109, 365
GOULDMAN
Elizabeth Moore
(Taylor), 64
George, 64
Ida (Stainback), 64
Robert Henry, 64
Robert Nelson, 64
GOURDIN
Rebecca, 87, 280
GRAVELY
Anne Carter, 72
Anne Carter
(Wickham), 72
Julian Pruden, 72
Robert (Treadway), 72
Roberta Treadway, 72
Wallace Landon, 72
Wallace Landon
(Gravely), 72
Wallace Landon Jr, 72
Willis, 72
GRAVES
Emma (Taylor), 10
Ernest, 10, 14
Ernest Jr, 14
Julia Charlotte
(Hooper), 10, 14
Louis, 10
Lucy Birnie (Horgan),
14
Mary DeBerniere, 10,
14, 19
Ralph Henry, 10, 14
Ralph Henry II, 10
Ralph Henry III, 10
GRAY
Alexander Thomas, 54
Anne Augusta
(Stevens), 54
Elizabeth Coultas, 52
Susan Murray, 54; 61
GREEN
Allen Jones, 256
Ann, 352
Brenda, 35

GREEN (continued)
  Larry, 35
  Larry Jr, 35
  Linda, 35
  Lucia, 28
  Lucy Pride (Jones),
    256
  Mary Cadwallader, 256,
    267-268
  May Elizabeth
    (Burgess), 35
  Virginia, 73
GREGORIE
  Mary Louise, 282, 307
GREY
  Ellen, 264
GRIFFIN
  --, 290
  Anna (Evans), 168
  Faye, 109, 364
  Lila, 168, 203-204
  Wigfall, 168
GRIFFITH
  Benjamin Charles
    Raymond, 108, 364
  Jennifer Backer (Smith),
    108
  Jessica Marie, 23
  Samuel Bosworth, 108,
    364
  Scott Charles, 108, 364
GRILTON
  Louise, 208
GRIMBALL
  Edward Barnwell, 31
  Edward Barnwell Jr,
    31
GRIMKE
  Julia Evelyn, 94, 306
GRINER
  Agnes, 342, 359
  Benjamin Charlton,
    342, 359
  Benjamin Charlton Jr,
    342, 359
  Benjamin Patrick, 359
  Julia, 342, 359
  Mary (Mauldin), 342,
    359
  Sara, 342, 359
  Sheila (Kenny), 359
GRISWOLD
  Martha, 54
GRUENWALD
  Margaret, 335, 354
GUERARD
  Alice (Cuthbert), 126
  Alice (Screven), 121

Elizabeth Martha, 121,
  129-132
George Henry, 126
Jacob Deveaux, 121
Louisa Chisolm, 126,
  139-141
GUERRANT
  Catherine Randolph
    (Lee), 67
  Elizabeth Moore, 67
  John Reevely, 67
  Marie L'Orange, 67
  Peter, 67
  Sarah (Saunders), 67
GUNBY
  Debra Lynn, 332
GUNN
  Heyward Elizabeth,
    188
  Matthew Robert, 188
  Robert D, 188
GUYER
  Margaret Elizabeth,
    235
GWINNETT
  Amelia, 370
  Ann, 370
  Ann (Bourne), 370
  Anne (Emes/ Eames),
    369
  Button, 367, 369-371
  Elizabeth Ann, 370
  Elizabeth Ann "Betsy",
    371
  Samuel, 369
  William, 369
HAAG
  Christian, 236
  Dorothy May
    (Heyward), 204, 236
  Henry Robert, 204
  Lee Ray, 204, 236
  Robert Ray, 204, 236
  Sarah Christine
    (McLeod), 236
  Sarah Lee, 236
HACKETT
  Maria Louisa, 135
HAFFEY
  Helen, 219
HAGEN
  Catherine Gayle
    (Mullis), 358
  Julia Blake (Prentiss),
    340, 357-358
  Julie Ann, 340, 357
  Lars Romoren, 340,
    358

Lars Romoren Jr, 358
Lynn Prentiss, 340
Paul Amberg Jr, 340,
  357-358
Philip Anders, 358
HAHN
  Barbara Jane, 103,
    109-110, 351, 365
  Hebert Louis, 103, 351
  Sara Elizabeth
    (Ransom), 351
  Sarah Elizabeth
    (Ransom), 103
HAIR
  Margaret, 169,
    205-206
HALDEMAN
  Ann Chinn (Howkins),
    232
  Benjamin, 232
  Christen, 232
  Ronald, 232
HALL
  Abigail (Burr), 374
  Eugene Evey, 237
  John, 373-374
  Lyman, 367, 373-374
  Margaret Esther
    (Durant), 237
  Mary (Osborn), 374
  Mary (Street), 373
  Mary Willard, 297
  Samuel, 373
  Sara Welsh, 237
HALLIWELL
  Mabel, 99, 327
HALLMAN
  Harriett, 318
  Harry Hightower, 318,
    342
  Miriam Bridge
    (Middleton), 318, 342
  Miriam Middleton, 318,
    342
HAMILTON
  Adgate, 153
  Ann Hollister, 177,
    216
  Annette Carolina, 125,
    138
  Arthur St Clair, 119,
    124, 137
  Bessie Lee (Dunbar),
    138
  Caroline, 124
  Charlotte Marshall
    (Smith), 137
  Daniel, 153

HAMILTON (continued)
Daniel H, 246
Daniel Heyward, 119,
  123, 135-137, 153,
  177-178
Daniel Heyward III,
  136, 152, 177, 215
Daniel Heyward IV,
  153
Daniel Heyward Jr,
  136, 153-154, 177,
  216
Daniel Howard Jr, 123
Elizabeth, 216
Elizabeth "Bessie", 124
Elizabeth (Lynch), 119,
  246
Elizabeth Heyward,
  119, 123-124, 136,
  138, 153
Elizabeth Matthews
  (Heyward), 123-125
Elizabeth Roulhac, 136
Emma (Levy), 124,
  138
Fanny, 125
Frances, 153
Frances (Ouer), 153
Frances Gray
  (Roulhac), 136, 153
Frances Motte, 123,
  136
Francisca, 137
Gabriella Ravenal, 137
George Elliott, 124
Henrietta, 125
Henry Cruger, 119
Herman Prioleau, 138
James, 119, 123-125,
  137-138, 153
James Jr, 138
Jane Stewart Evans
  (Nicholson), 177, 216
Joanne (Nastasi), 216
Joel, 216
John Heth, 124
John Middleton, 123,
  136
John Randolph, 119,
  125
John Randolph Jr, 125
Joseph Gregorie, 153
Joseph Gregorie
  Roulhac, 136
Katherine Roulhac, 136
Lewis Trevezant, 119
Margaret (Munsell),
  153, 177-178

Margaret Helen (Heth),
  124
Margot, 154, 178, 216
Margot Heyward, 177,
  216
Mary (Thompson), 153
Mary Heyward, 125
Mary Louisa (Whaley),
  125
Mary Middleton, 123,
  135, 151-152
Mary Pringle, 137, 154,
  178, 322
Mary Ravenal (Pringle),
  137, 153-154
Miles Brewton, 124,
  137, 153-154
Motte, 137
Oliver Perry, 119
Rebecca Motte, 124,
  137, 154
Rebecca Motte
  (Middleton), 123,
  135-137
Roulhac, 153
Samuel Prioleau, 119,
  124, 138
Thomas Heyward
  Motte, 177
Thomas Lynch, 119,
  124
Virginia, 124
William Lowndes, 119,
  125
HAMMER
Anne, 341
HAMMES
Abram Glover, 230
Andrew Burchart, 230
Anne Walsh, 197
Claire Elizabeth, 230
Daisy Vincent (Martin),
  164, 196
Dayne Martin, 230
Drayton Marshall, 230
Elmore, 164
Francis Rutledge, 230
Jane Marie, 197
Jane Wynne (Touchey),
  196, 229
John, 164
John Martin, 197
Louise Vincent, 197
Michael L, 197
Michel, 230
R Burke, 164, 196
R Burke Jr, 164, 196,
  229

Robert Touchey, 197
Roman Burchart, 197,
  229
Roman Vincent, 230
Ruth Anne (Glover),
  230
Yvonne (Michel), 229
HANAHAN
Frances Gaillard, 316,
  340
HANCKEL
Pauline Hasell, 20,
  30-31
HANCOCK
Dianne Allee, 30
John, 3, 49
HARDWICK
Jane Elizabeth, 268
HARDY
Benjamin Bosworth, 97,
  326
Burwell Marshall, 97,
  101, 326, 349
Elise, 97, 326
Elise Rutledge (Smith),
  97, 101, 326, 349
Ewing Lloyd, 97, 101,
  326, 349
Ewing Marshall, 97,
  326
Jose, 101, 349
Laura, 101, 349
Maria Jisela (Jandi),
  101, 349
Viviana, 101, 349
HARJES
Emily Nicole, 241
Georgianne (Rainey),
  241
Shane Michael, 241
Shannon, 241
Taylor Jordon, 241
Zachary Paul, 241
HARRINGTON
Benjamin T, 189
Donovan James, 189
Jackson Stewart, 189
Norma (McMurrain),
  189
HARRIS
Abigail Victoria, 109,
  364
Alice DeLancey, 338
Ann Josephine, 174,
  211
Eddye, 22
Edward M, 174
Effie (--), 174

HEYWARD (continued)
Mary Hamilton
  (Seabrook), 131, 147
Mary Izard, 291
Mary Katherine, 148,
  173, 210
Mary Memminger
  (Pinckney), 141, 160
Mary Taylor, 129
Matelyn French
  (Landrum), 156, 180
May (Mulligan), 146
Melanie Clare, 204,
  237
Mildred, 161
Mildred (Goodrum),
  160, 190-191
Minnie Louise
  (Perryclaire), 140
Nathaniel, 257
Nathaniel William, 117,
  121
Ned Watkins, 139, 156,
  180
Ned Watkins Jr, 156,
  180
Nellie Boykin, 139
Nora Lena, 148, 173
Pauline, 129
Pauline (de Caradeux),
  129, 143-144
Pauline Keith, 126
Pauline Virginia, 165
Preston Watkins, 180
Ralph Clarence, 145
Rebecca Matelyn, 180
Rives Boykin, 139, 156,
  179-180
Robert Brian, 156, 179
Robert Chisolm, 121,
  130, 145
Robert Clarence, 130,
  145, 167-168
Robert Clarence III,
  168
Robert Clarence Jr,
  145, 168
Robert Edmund, 164,
  196
Robert Jon, 196
Roberta Guerard, 167,
  200
Roger Joseph, 181
Roland Steiner, 130,
  144, 165-166
Roland Steiner Jr, 144
Rosa Cantey, 174, 212
Rosa Catherine, 119

Rose, 129
Sallie Othello (Long),
  145, 167-168
Sarah Connelly
  (Taylor), 129, 144
Sarah Elizabeth (Howe),
  144, 166
Sarah Gertrude, 148,
  173
Sarah Gertude, 209
Selina, 131, 146, 170
Shubrick, 122, 133,
  149, 174
Stephen Doar, 130, 145
Stephen Doar Jr, 145
Stuart, 144
Sue (Trapnell), 190
Susan Claudia, 166
Susan Gruning
  (Brumby), 291
Susannah Chapman
  (Herbert), 179
Susanne Elise
  (McKellar), 169,
  204-205
Susanne McKellar, 169,
  204
Teri Lynne, 179
Terri Lynne, 202
Theo Belle (Farrar),
  144, 165-166
Thomas, 77, 116-117,
  119-121, 125
Thomas Andrew, 161
Thomas Bentley, 200
Thomas Cuthbert, 140
Thomas Daniel, 121,
  131, 146
Thomas Fleming, 132,
  148, 173
Thomas Fleming Jr,
  148, 173
Thomas Gaillard, 169,
  204, 237
Thomas Gaillard III,
  237
Thomas Gaillard Jr,
  204, 236
Thomas Gailliard, xii
Thomas Jr, 115-118
Thomas Savage, 117,
  119, 121, 125-127,
  131, 139, 145, 147,
  155, 167, 178-179,
  202
Thomas Savage III,
  179, 202, 235
Thomas Savage IV,

235
Thomas Savage Jr, 119,
  125, 138-139, 156,
  168, 202, 235
Travis Paul, 235
Trudy Aliene (Davis),
  201
Virginia (Kreichbaum),
  144, 165
Virginia Eaton, 140
Virginia Hughes, 160,
  189, 226
Virginia Lynn, 159,
  188
Virginia Randolph
  Chapin, 167
Virginia Rutledge, 140,
  159, 188-189
Walter Blake, 257
Walter Izard, 268, 291
Walter Screven, 129
Wayne Marshall, 167
William Burroughs,
  160
William Burroughs
  Smith, 126, 141
William Guerard, 132,
  148, 173
William Henry, 143,
  164, 196
William Landrum, 156,
  180
William Marion, 121
William Nathaniel, 119,
  125, 139-141
William Nathaniel Jr,
  126, 140
William Prestman, 149
William Smith, 141,
  160, 189
William Thomas, 179
Wilmot Holmes, 125,
  139, 155-156
Wilmot Holmes Jr, 139
Wilson Prestman, 122,
  133
HICKS
  Charles Stalford, 25
  Stephen Robin, 25
HIGGENBOTTOM
  David, 163, 195
  David Wallace, 163
  Mary Howard (Lynah),
  163, 195
  Nancy Savage, 163
  Samuel Heyward, 163,
  195
  Susan Eidson

HOOPER (continued)
William M, 13
William Wilberforce,
5-6, 8
HOPKINS
Mary Postell, 15, 20
Susan, 68
HORGAN
Lucy Birnie, 14
HORLBECK
Caroline Manigault
Wilcox, 345
Frederick Henry, 345
John Miles, 345
John Wilcox, 345
Mary Huger Manigault
(Wilcox), 345
Peter Miles, 345
HORNE
Eleanor Beverly, 166
HORRY
Edward, 128
Edward Shubrick, 128
Elias, 128
Elias Edward, 128
Elizabeth Heyward,
128
Harriet Pinckney, 82,
262
Heyward Howard, 128
John Webb, 128
Martha Caroline
(Webb), 128
Martha Webb, 128
Mary (Shubrick), 128
Mary Shubrick, 128
Paul Trapler, 128
William Webb, 128
HORTON
Gloria, 193
HOUSTOUN
John, 367
HOVIS
Kenneth Paul, 235
Mary Elizabeth (Johns),
235
Megan Elizabeth, 235
HOWARD
Adam Hubley, 134
Alton, 35
Annie Heyward
(Webb), 127, 134, 143
Augusta Clayatt, 142,
163-164
Doris Marie (Burgess),
35
Elizabeth, 128, 151
Elizabeth Savage

(Parker), 122, 127, 134
Ellen Fordney, 134
Emma Burnet, 134
Emma Heyward, 122,
134, 149-150
Florence Percy
(Heyward), 159
Henrietta Parker, 134,
150, 176
Henry Parker, 122, 128,
134, 150-151
Henry Parker Jr, 151
John, 122
John Webb, 127
Josephine Silverius,
150, 176, 215
Katherine Anne, 150,
177
Lawrence, 35
Lillian Jenkins, 134,
151, 177
Lisa Kay, 35
Maragaret "Madge"
Glover, 134
Martha Horry, 128,
143, 164
Mary Craig, 134
Mary Huberly Glover
(Jenkins), 134, 150-151
Mary Josephine
(Watters), 150,
176-177
Mary Louise Folliard,
150, 176, 214
May Elizabeth
(Burgess), 35
Norma (Lubs), 151
Patsy, 35
Robert Emmett, 150
Robert Emmett Jenkins,
134, 150, 176-177
Sarah Elizabeth, 122
Thomas Heyward, 122,
127, 134, 143
Thomas Heyward Jr,
128
William, 35
William Carr, 122, 127,
134
William Henry, 122
HOWE
--, xiv
Sarah Elizabeth, 144,
166
HOWKINS
Agnes (Devine), 198
Alice Keller (Huger),
165, 198

Ann (Lord), 198
Ann Chinn, 198, 232
Anthony Chinn, 165
Catherine (Alley), 232
Catherine Alexander,
232
Elise (Heyward), 143
Elizabeth Heyward,
165, 198, 232
Elizabeth Heyward
(Cassidy), 165, 198
Elizabeth Lyons, 198,
231
Elsie (Heyward), 165
Guerard Heyward, 143,
165, 198
Guerard Heyward Jr,
165, 198
John Henry Francis,
165, 198, 232
John Heyward, 198
John Huger, 165, 198,
232
John Huger III, 232
John Huger Jr, 198,
231
John Smallbrook, 143,
165
John Smallbrook III,
165, 197, 231
John Smallbrook Jr,
143, 165, 198
Mary Alice, 198
Mary Anne, 198
Mary Ball, 165
Mary Louise (Key),
198, 232
Phyllis (Dana), 198,
232
Reyna, 198
Thomas Heyward, 165
Virginia Ruth (Lyons),
198, 231
William Beekman, 165
HOWLAND
John, 384-385
HOYT
Edwin, 335, 354
Emily, 335
Maria Louisa, 335, 354
Mary Pierrepont
(Hazard), 335, 354
William, 335
HUBARD/ HUBBARD
Edmund Bolling, 57
Edmund Wilcox, 57
Elizabeth, 238
Ellen Marion, 172

HUBARD/ HUBBARD
(continued)
Henry Taylor, 57
Julia Leiper (Taylor),
57
Julia Taylor, 57
Robert Thruston, 57
Susan Pocahontas
(Bolling), 57
HUDGENS
Aletta Wood (Jervey),
346
Mary Eleanor, 346
Peter Halstead, 346
R W, 346
HUGER
Alfred Huger, 260
Alice Kellar, 276
Alice Keller, 165, 198
Allen, 273
Allen Deas, 259
Alwera, 272, 296
Arthur Middleton, 252,
259-260, 274
Beatrice Kress, 299
Caroline (Proctor), 258,
271-273, 276
Caroline Pinckney, 275
Caroline Proctor, 258,
272-273, 276
Catherine A (Beekman),
276
Charles Lowndes, 258,
260, 274
Charles Lowndes Jr,
274
Clermont Kinloch, 275,
298, 322
Daniel, 252
Daniel Elliott, 252,
258-260, 271-273,
275-276, 296-297,
299, 322
Daniel Elliott Jr, 296,
299, 322, 345
Deas Nott, 273
Edmund Dargan, 274
Eliza Alwera, 272, 297
Eliza Alwera (Noble),
272, 296-297
Eliza Caroline
Middleton, 252, 260,
277-278
Eliza Mackay, 275,
298
Elizabeth (Kress), 299
Elizabeth Allen (Deas),
258, 273-274

Elizabeth Devereux
(Polk), 274
Elizabeth Pelzer, 322,
345, 361
Elizabeth Pringle
(Smith), 272, 296
Elizabeth Smith, 272
Eloise, 273
Elosie, 297
Emily Ann, 263
Emily Hamilton, 274
Emily Keese (Bailey),
275, 299
Emma Middleton, 252,
259
Emma Middleton Izard,
275, 298, 322
Florine (Douglas), 296
Florine Douglas, 296
Floyd Bailey, 275
Frances (Pelzer), 322,
345
Frances Devereux, 274
Frances Kinloch, 276
Frances Pelzer, 322,
345, 360-361
Francis Kinloch, 259
Harriet (Withers), 273,
297
Harriet Horry, 259
Harriet Lucas
(Pinckney), 259
Harriet Lucas Pinckney,
259, 275, 299
Isabella Izard, 258
Isabella Johannes
(Middleton), 252,
258-260
Isabella Johannes
Middleton, 258, 273,
297
Isabella Middleton, 272
James Sutherland, 258
John Izard, 252, 258,
273-274
John Middleton, 274
John Noble, 272
John Wells, 259, 276
Joseph Alston, 252,
259, 275-276
Joseph Alston Jr, 259,
275, 298
Joseph Proctor, 258,
272, 296
Katharine Mackay, 259
Kirkwood King, 260
Leonide Polk, 274
Louisa C, 322

Louisa S (Chisolm),
296, 322
Lucia Polk, 274
Lynch Prioleau, 259,
275, 299
Margaret Campbell,
260
Margaret Campbell
(King), 260
Margaret Deas, 258
Mary Cornelia (Alston),
272
Mary Esther, 259
Mary Esther (--),
275-276
Mary Esther (Huger),
259
Mary Middleton, 252,
258
Mary Proctor, 258,
271, 296
Mary Randolph, 322
Mary Stiles (Elliott),
275, 298
Mary Willard (Hall),
297
Mary Williams Alston,
272
Meta Deas, 274
Mitchell King, 260
Percival Elliott, 275
Richard Proctor, 258,
272, 296-297
Richard Proctor Jr, 272
Ruth (Dargan), 274
Ruth Dargan, 274
Ruth Noble, 296
Sabina (Elliott), 252
Sabina Elliott, 252, 259,
274
Sarah Elliott, 252, 260,
273, 276-277
Stella Noble, 272
Stephen Proctor, 258,
272, 297
Thomas Pinckney, 259
William Beekman, 276
William Elliott, 252,
258, 272, 274, 296
HUGGINS
Cynthia, 210
HUGHES
Ann Elizabeth, 310,
333
Blackburn, 98, 327
Blackburn Jr, 98, 327
Katherine (Felder), 98,
327

HUGHES (continued)
Mary, 377
HUGO
Bernard Jeudy, 331
Chad Gavin, 331
Diane Elaine (Rutter),
331
Kent Derek, 331
HULL
Elizabeth, 59
HUNNICUT
Mary Cobb, 192
HUNT
Anna Mary, 106, 362
Arthur Samuel, 106,
362
Christopher Guard, 106,
362
Edith Cobbs
(Weatherford), 106
Jeffery Barnabas, 106,
362
Meredith Eugene, 106,
362
Peter Malcolm, 106,
362
Priscilla Dear, 106,
362
HUNTER
Alice Stuart, 144,
166-167
Anna Colquitt, 163,
194-195
Rita (Izard), 315, 338
Rita Izard, 315, 338,
354-355
William Blair, 315,
338
HURD
Patience Campbell, 316,
338-339
HUTCHINSON
Ashley Kay, 188, 225
Holly, 188, 225
Kay Heyward
(Sconyers), 188, 225
Morris Eugene, 188,
225
Sheryl Malvina, 212
INGLEHART
Mary, 66
INGLIS
Mary, 251
INGRAM
James Frederick, 192
Jane (McConnell), 192
Mary Lou, 192,
228-229

INMAN
Carol, 190, 227
Laura R (--), 190
Richard M, 190
IRVING
Alfred Hawkins, 136
Anna, 151
Anna Josephine (Day),
151
Arthur Cruger, 135
Emma Cruger, 135,
152
Emma Maria (Cruger),
135
Florence, 151
Helen (Keiley), 152
Henry Cruger, 136
Heyward Hamilton,
135, 151
James Hamilton, 135
Jane Wentworth, 151
John, 151
John Beaufaine, 135(2),
151-152
Lillian Middleton, 152
Mary Elizabeth, 135,
152
Mary Hamilton, 151
Mary Middleton
(Hamilton), 135,
151-152
Rebecca Middleton,
135, 152
William Aemilius, 135,
151
William John, 151
IVESTER
Katherine, 205
IZARD
Alice, 251
Alice (DeLancey), 251
Alice De Lancy, 290
Alice Heyward, 269
Allen Cadwallader, 256,
268, 291
Allen Cadwallader Jr,
269
Ann, 252
Anna Stead, 85, 271,
279
Annie Laura, 268
Annie Wharton (Sale),
290
Eliza Caroline, 251
Elizabeth (Gibbes), 250
Emma A (Dantzler),
290
Emma Philadelphia

(Middleton), 251, 256
George Dantzler, 290
George Lipscomb, 268,
290
Henry, 251, 256, 268,
290
Irene Middleton, 268
James Johnston, 290
John, 268, 290
Josephine Bedon, 269
Julia Davis, 269, 291
Julia Davis (Bedon),
268, 291
Laura (Lipscomb), 268,
290
Laura Elizabeth, 290,
315, 338
Lucy, 256, 268,
290-291
Margaret Emma, 251,
256, 269
Martha, 251
Martha Perry, 269
Mary, 81, 250-253
Mary Cadwallader
(Green), 256, 267-268
Mary Elizabeth, 268
Mary Fowler, 290
Mary Green, 269
Mary Rutherford, 269,
291
Nannie Theresa
(Lyons), 290, 315
Ralph, 251, 268, 290,
315
Ralph De Lancey, 269
Rita, 290, 315, 338
Roberta Pearis
(Johnston), 290
Sallie (Goode), 267,
289-290
Sarah Lyons, 290, 315
Tallulah, 268
Walter, 250-251, 256,
267-268, 289-290
William Lowndes, 268
JACKSON
Allen Shannon, 343
Allen Shannon Jr, 343
Andrew, 81
Arthur Middleton, 343
Charles Klair, 235
Frances Ann, 235
Mary (Evans), 235
Mary Ellen, 193, 343
Miriam Middleton
(Hallman), 342
Sarah French, 272

LABRUCE (continued)
Selina Johnstone
(continued)
172, 208
LACHIOCOTTE
Elizabeth Ingram, 317,
341
LADSON
Eliza, 120
LADUE
Caroline Hampton, 322,
345
Caroline Hampton
(Mullally), 322, 346
Lawrence Knight, 322,
346
Lawrence Knight Jr,
322
LAHMANN
Karen Diane, 74
LAIGHT
Julia, 278
LAMAR
Abner Whatley, 128
Abner Whatley Jr, 128
Edward Horry, 128
Elizabeth B (Webb),
128
Elizabeth Heyward,
128
Hamilton Hickman,
128
Martha Meriwether, 13,
17
Mary (Whatley), 128
Mary Whatley, 128
May (Hooper), 17
Oralie, 128
Thomas C, 13, 17
Thomas C Jr, 13
Thomas Gresham, 128
William Bandrum, 128
LAMB
Frances Motte
(Hamilton), 136
George Buist, 136
George Buist Jr, 136
LAMBERTSON
Elizabeth LaBruce
(Rowe), 208
Katherine Flowers, 208
Michael Daniel, 208
LAMONT
Rosemary, 209
LANDRUM
Herbert Otto, 156
Matelyn French, 156,
180

Willie Clyde (French),
156
LANGHORNE
Agnes McClanahan
(White), 60
Anne Montgomery, 60
Anne Montgomery
(Taylor), 60
George Charles, 60
James Callaway, 60
Lewis Ward, 60
LARKIN
Betty, 216
LEACH
Denny Lynn, 234
Frank Willing, xii,
xxiii-xxvi
J Granville, xxvi
Joseph Smallidge, xxvi
Rebecca M, 129
Sophia (Ball), xxvi
LEADBETTER
Elsie, 164, 197
LEAKE
Andrew Kean, 68
Louis Knight, 68
Susan Morris (Preston),
68
LEBLOND
Mathieu Lucien, 330
Maureen Patricia
(Duncan), 330
Patrick Real, 330
Real Gerhard, 330
Simon Mathieu, 330
LEE
Alice, 67
Alice (Wilkinson), 67
Alice Lowndes, 322,
346
Anne Hill (Carter), 57
Arlene Frances, 355
Catherine Randolph, 57,
67
Charles Carter, 57,
66-67
Cindy Lynn, 173
Clermont, 299
Clermont Kinloch
(Huger), 298, 322
Eliza Lucilla (Haskell),
291
Elizabeth Middleton
(Andrews), 322, 346
Ella Marion (Goodrum),
66
George Taylor, 57, 66
Henry, 57, 66

Huston, 291
James Moultrie, 299
John Penn, 57
Lawrence, 298, 322
Lawrence E, 323
Lawrence Jr, 299, 322,
346
Lillian Elizabeth
(Woollen), 66
Lucy Penn (Taylor), 57,
66-67
Lucy Randolph, 66
Mildred, 57, 67
Pauline, 291
Robert Henry, 66
Robert Mackay, 323
Robert Randolph, 57,
67
Virginia Lillian, 66
Williams Carter, 57,
67
LEFTWITCH
Ann, 267
LEGENDRE
Londine, 178
LEIGH
Anne Carter, 63
LEIPER
Elizabeth Coultas
(Gray), 52
Jean DuVal, 266
Julia Dunlap, 52, 55-57
Thomas, 52
LELAND
Emeline, 255
LENGNICK
Charles Alfred, 158,
185
Emilie Guerard, 158
Georgianna Hasell
(McTeer), 158, 185
Paula Wood, 158, 185,
223
Susan, 158
LEONARD
Buchanan Renshaw, 75
Mary Buchanan
(Renshaw), 75
Maurcie Bixler, 75
Robert Bixler, 75
LEPLEY
Justin Grant, 236
Rhonda Susan
(Trybalski), 236
Robert, 236
LEVERT
--, 379
Ann Lee (Metcalf), 379

MIDDLETON (continued)
  Septima Sexta, 81-83,
    250, 252-253, 257,
    261-262
  Shirley, 285, 308, 330
  Susan, 118
  Susan Matilda, 254
  Susan Matilda
    (Chisholm), 86, 269
  Susan Matilda Harriet
    (Chisolm), 254,
    263-264
  Susan Pringle (Smith),
    255, 265
  Suzanne Romaine
    (Fox), 311, 333
  Thomas Alston, 254,
    264-265
  Virginia, 263, 282, 306
  Walter Izard, 256, 269,
    293-294, 318
  Wesley, 253
  William, 265, 293, 316,
    340
  William Dehon, 269,
    292, 316-317
  William Ian, 285
  William III, 340
  William Jr, 316, 340
  Williams, 251, 255
MIEB
  Pauline, 23
MILES
  Mary, 115
MILLER
  Benjamin Franklin, 62
  Carrie (Colton), 71
  Credilla, 71, 74
  Henry Taylor, 62
  Jane Emeline, 88, 301
  John James, 62
  Lawrence Vernon, 71
  Mary Watson, 62
  Sarah Browning, 62
  Sarah Eusebia
    (Browning), 62
  Susan Watson (Taylor),
    62
MILLIMAN
  Georgianna, 133
MILLS
  Aimee, 360
  Brent Eugene, 236
  Deborah (Carson), 360
  Donald, 236
  Jacklyn, 360
  Kimberly Michelle
    (Rawl), 236

Terry G, 360
Terry G Jr, 360
MILTON
  Carolyn (Tidler), 206
  Isabel, 170, 206
  Isabel Heyward
    (Wilson), 170, 206
  Marshall McCormick
    III, 170
  Marshall McCormick
    Jr, 170, 206
  William Byrd, 206
  William Byrd Lee, 170
  William Byrd Lee Jr,
    206
MINER
  Helen Elizabeth, 192
MINGLEDORFF
  Anne Heyward, 166,
    199
  Carol Jan (Simon), 199
  Colton Everett, 199
  Elizabeth Percival, 166
  Ellison (Backus), 199
  George Heyward, 166,
    199
  Marjory (Heyward),
    166, 199
  Ralston Everett, 166,
    199
  Ralston Everett Jr, 166,
    199
MITCHELL
  Sarah Jordan, 132
MIXON
  Kimberly Susan, 109,
    365
MOBLEY
  Dana (Kendrick), 199
  James B, 199
  James Tyler, 199
  Lauren, 199
MOFFETT
  Caroline Griffin
    (Heyward), 204
  Teresa Lynn, 204
  Thomas Bentley Jr, 204
MONFORT
  Erma, 73
MONGIN
  Mary Lavinia, 136
MOODY
  Mary Elizabeth, 95,
    100, 325, 348
MOONEY
  Benjamin Reed, 222
  Nicholas Judah, 222
  Sean Bernard, 222

MOORE
  --, 180
  Adele, 295
  Albert, 295, 319
  Ann Hollister
    (Hamilton), 216
  Anne, 75
  Anne Blake (Rutledge),
    295, 319
  Barbara, 192
  Benjamin Allston, 295,
    319
  Benjamin Allston Jr,
    295, 319
  Carter Wickham
    (Renshaw), 75
  Cornelia Robinson, 216
  Eleanor, 319
  Emma, 295, 319
  Frida, 319
  Frida (Barrow), 319
  Glenda, 217, 240
  Katharine, 345
  Martha Harvie, 75
  Patricia Josephine
    (Johnston), 180
  Samantha Grosvenor,
    216
  Sumner Kittelle Jr, 216
  Susan Middleton
    (Rutledge), 295, 319
  Thomas, 180
  W Scott, 75
MOREHOUSE
  Joel David, 34
  Johanna Elizabeth, 34
  Nathan Isaiah, 34
  Sarah Ann, 34
  William Raymond, 34
MORGAN
  Ann Desbouillions, 187,
    224-225
  Betty Kay, 318
  Charles Franklin, 187
  Louise (Desbouillions),
    187
MORRIS
  Charles Wilder, 342
  Harriet (Mauldin), 342
  Imogen Maury, 62, 70
  James Kenneth III, 342
  James Kenneth Jr, 342
  James Maury, 62
  Maury, 69
  Susan Dabney, 55
  Victoria Eulalia
    (Phillips), 62

MORTIMER
Charlotte Adamson,
119
MOSELEY
Elizabeth, 11
MUCHMORE
Adam Peter, 331
Alyssa Ann, 331
Pamela Ann (Rutter),
331
Peter Neil, 331
MUELLER
Julia McCrory
(Weatherford), 106,
362
Mark, 106, 362
Pearl Angeline, 106,
362
Vergil Christopher,
106, 362
MULLALLY
Caroline Hampton, 297,
322, 346
Caroline Hampton
(Lowndes), 297, 322
Charles Lowndes, 297
Lane, 297, 322
MULLIGAN
Mary, 146, 168-169
MULLIS
Catherine Gayle, 358
MUMFORD
Abigail, 111, 353
Ayliffe B (Blake), 98,
104, 308, 328-329
Ayliffe Blake, 104, 329
Catherine (--), 111,
353
Eleanor, 98, 104, 110,
308, 328, 352-353
Elizabeth Davis, 104,
111, 329, 353
Gregory, 111, 353
Jennifer, 111, 353
Nicholas Van Slyck, 98,
308, 328-329
Nicholas Van Slyck III,
111, 329, 353
Nicholas Van Slyck Jr,
98, 104, 308, 329,
353
Nicholas Van Slylee,
104
Nicholas Van Slylee III,
104
Nicholas Van Slylee Jr,
111
Robert Blake, 104, 329

Rosemary (Davis), 104,
111, 329, 353
MUNCH
Emily Kathleen, 173
Lonnie Brooks, 173
Nora Lena (Heyward),
173
MUNNERLYN
Benjamin, 293, 317,
341
Elizabeth (Spring), 341
Jane Morris, 317, 341,
358
Lucy Izard (Middleton),
293, 317
Lucy Middleton, 293
Margaret Elizabeth
(Spring), 317
Margaret Middleton,
317
William Wilson, 293,
317
MUNRO
Annette Carolina
(Hamilton), 138
Annette Eleanor, 138
Margaret (Steele), 138
Robert, 138
Theodore, 138
Theodore Hamilton,
138
MUNSELL
Margaret, 153,
177-178
MURPHY
Bena Mae, 224
Brandon Taylor, 223
Megan Catherine, 223
Richard, 223
Terry Catherine
(Shirley), 223
MURRAY
Barbara, 4
Eugenia Kirkland
(Prentiss), 357
William Prentiss, 357
William Thomas, 357
MUSE
Sallie Deborah, 72
MUSGROVE
Alice Marie, 213, 239
MYERS
Catherine Allison, 312
Charlene (Gofrey), 312
Christopher Middleton,
287
David Saxton, 287, 312
Meagan Leigh, 312

Nancy Reeves
(Middleton), 287, 312
Susan Ellen, 287, 312
William Saxton, 287,
312
NASH
--, 364
Lena Kai, 108, 364
Lucretia, 67
Mary Burton (Harris),
108, 364
NASTASI
Joanne, 216
NATALE
Diane Marie, 194
NAULT
Emelia Bernadette, 310,
332
NEBRBAS
Frances Marian, 34
Frances Marian
"Dolly" (Sheffield), 34
Frederick III, 34
NEELEY
Wendy Gale, 236
NEIDLINGER
Mary Arden, 215
NELSON
Gary Allen, 32
Gwen, 209
Julie Anne, 32
Kathryn Diane
(Robison), 32
Laura Alene, 32
Lucy Armistead, 56-57
Melissa, 209-210
Miriam Elizabeth, 337
NEWELL
Harriett, 127
NEWSOME
Jonathan Michael, 231
Martha Ann (Phenicie),
231
Michael Laurence, 231
Robert W, 220
Suzanne Elizabeth
(Thompson), 220
Thomas Eugene, 220
NEWTON
Amelia Kirk, 275
NICHOLSON
Caroline Belle, 82, 84,
261, 278-279
Jane Stewart Evans,
177, 216
NICKERSON
Allison Lynn, 219
Arline McTeer

PARROTT (continued)
Samuel Price, 239
Sarah Bray, 239
Sarah Kathryn
(Barbare), 239
Shirleen, 26, 37-38
Stephen Price, 213,
239
PATRICK
Edward Bell, 147
Edward Bell Jr, 147
Heyward, 147
Mary Hamilton
(Heyward), 147
PATTERSON
Nanette Starr, 107, 363
PATTON
Maria Louisa (Hackett),
135
Mary Montraville, 135
Montraville, 135
PAYSON
Payne Whitney, 307
PEELE
Georgeanna Hasell
(Palmer), 217
Janna Patrice, 217
Joseph Herbert III, 217
Joseph Herbert Jr, 217
PELL
Sally, 335
PELZER
Frances, 322, 345
PENDLETON
Ann Madison (Turner),
52
Edmund, 49
Henrietta, 52
Philip Henry, 52
PENN
--, 50
Catherine (Taylor), 49
John, 49-50
Lucy, 50-52
Moses, 49
Susannah (Lyme), 50
William, 50
PENROSE
Beatrice d'Este, 313,
336
PERKINS
Hannah Marie McAlpin,
200
Katherine Randolph,
200
Roberta Guerard
(Heyward), 200
Sarah Heyward, 200

Stephen Barry, 200
PERRY
Mary Scott, 93, 98,
284, 308
PERRYCLAIRE
Mary Alice (Eaton),
140
Minnie Louise, 140
William Ellis, 140
PETERSON
Heidi, 228
PETIGRU
Susan, 138
PHARRINGTON
Linda, 234
PHENICIE
Ann Cuthbert (Martin),
197, 230-231
James Middleton, 197
Jennifer Marie, 230
John Christopher, 230
John Vincent, 197, 230,
241
John Wilbur, 230-231
John Wilbur Jr, 197
Joshua Vincent, 230
Kaitlyn Nicole, 242
Kelly Michelle, 230
Martha Ann, 197, 231
Melissa Marie
(Richards), 242
Michael Vincent, 230,
242
Pamela Ann (Garrison),
230, 242
Sara Ann (Ragsdale),
230
Tamera Leigh
(Juergens), 230, 241
Thomas Heyward, 197,
230
Thomas Heyward Jr,
230
Tiffany Kathleen, 230,
241
William Martin, 197,
230, 242
PHILLIPS
Charles, 104, 329
Eleanor, 104, 329, 353
Harriet Stuart (Blake),
329, 353
J Ormsby, 104, 329,
353
Victoria Eulalia, 62
Virginia, 104, 329
PICKETT
Christina Eleanor

(Charles), 16
Frances Marion, 16,
22-23
Francis Marion, 16
Margaret, 124
PINCKNEY
Carolina Phoebe
(Elliott), 85, 279
Caroline Phoebe, 85,
279
Charles C, 141
Charles Cotesworth, 85,
91, 279, 303
Edward Rutledge, 85,
90, 279, 303
Elise Rutledge, 303
Elizabeth Rutledge, 91
Harriet Lucas, 259
Louise (Cleveland), 91,
303
Lucy (Memminger),
141
Mary Memminger, 141,
160
Sara Henrietta
(Rutledge), 303
Sarah, 303
Sarah Cleveland, 91
Sarah Donon, 147, 172
Sarah Henrietta
(Rutledge), 85, 91, 279
Stephen Elliott, 85, 279
Thomas, 85, 279
PLAXICO
Barbara Marie
(Johnston), 179
Kelly Ann, 179
Robert, 179
Robert Jeff, 179
POLING
Arnold A, 95, 100, 324,
347
Mary Abernathy
(Stevenson), 95, 100,
324, 347
Mary Caroline, 95, 99,
324, 347
POLK
Elizabeth Devereux,
274
Frances Ann
(Devereaux), 86
Frances Ann
(Devereux), 270, 274
Leonidas, 86, 270, 274
Sarah Hawkins, 86,
270

RUMSEY (continued)
Daniel Walters, 191
Diana (Sweet), 191
Elizabeth Barron, 191
Elizabeth Beckwith
(Lynah), 161, 191
Georgiana Beckwith,
191
Heidi (Peterson), 228
James Lynah, 191
Martha Anne (Osborne),
191, 228
Martha Elizabeth, 191,
228
Rebecca Brown, 192
Robert More, 192
Sarah Louise, 228
Shirley (Walters), 191,
228
Suzanne Beckwith, 192
RUNDLE
Helen (Toulmin), 297
Helen Elmore, 297
Samuel Elmore, 297
RUSSELL
Alicia Hopton, 256
Ann (Westmoreland),
34
Annette, 34
Walley, 34
RUTLEDGE
--, 80, 85, 249, 280
-- (--), 101, 349
Alice, 270, 294, 319
Alice Ann (Weston),
263
Alice Izard, 83, 262
Alice Weston, 263
Amelia Van Cortlandt,
271, 294, 319
Anna Marie (Blake),
85, 91, 279, 303
Anna Wells, 284, 301
Anne Blake, 271, 295,
319
Anne E, 96, 325
Archibald Hamilton, 85,
92, 96, 280, 304,
325-326
Archibald Hamilton Jr,
92, 304
Arthur Middleton, 81,
83-84, 87-88, 253,
262, 281
Arthur Middlton, 280
Beatrice Clyde
(Edwards), 96, 325
Benjamin Huger, 263,

270-271, 283-284,
294-295, 319
Caroline Bell
(Nicholson), 261, 278
Caroline Belle
(Nicholson), 82, 84,
279
Caroline Phoebe, 85,
280
Clementina, 295, 320,
344
Clementina (Kohn),
295, 320
Cotesworth Pinckney,
81, 253
Donald, 101, 349
Donald Thropp, 96,
101, 105, 326, 348,
361
Dorothea Barclay, 271,
295, 321
Edward, 77, 79-83, 88,
252-253, 262, 264,
281, 284, 300
Edward Augustus, 81,
253
Eleanor, 97, 263, 326
Eleanor (Oliver), 294,
319
Eleanor (White), 96,
101, 326, 349
Eleanor Maria
(Middleton), 263,
270-271, 283-284
Eleanor Middleton, 270
Eleanor Oliver, 294,
319, 343
Elise, 271, 295,
320-321
Elise Pinckney, 96, 101,
106, 326, 348, 361
Eliza (Underwood), 83,
87-88, 262, 280-281
Eliza Huger, 284, 301
Eliza Huger (Wells),
284, 300
Elizabeth Pinckney, 83,
262
Elizabeth Underwood,
83, 87, 93-94, 262,
280, 305-306
Ella Middleton, 284,
301
Emma, 270
Emma Blake, 83, 87,
94, 262, 281, 306
Emma Craig (Blake),
270, 283, 294-295

Emma Fredrika, 83, 86,
92, 262, 280, 305
Emma Philadelphia
Middleton, 81-84,
88-89, 253, 257,
261-262, 264,
269-270, 278,
301-302
Ethel Gary (Parrott),
91, 96, 304, 325
Flora (McDonald), 96,
101, 325, 348-349
Florence Louise (Hart),
92, 96, 304,
325-326
Frances Bayley Blake,
271, 295, 320
Franklyn Clement
Merritt, 100
Frederick, 82-83,
85-86, 91, 96, 262,
279-280, 303, 325
Frederick Reeves, 91,
95, 304, 325
Frederick Reeves Jr,
96, 325
Harriet Pinckney
(Horry), 82, 262
Harriott Horry, 85, 91,
280, 304
Helen, 81, 253
Helen Bayley, 271
Helen Bayley (Blake),
271, 283, 295
Henrietta (Middleton),
80-81, 86, 252
Henrietta Middleton,
81-82, 85, 91, 96,
100, 253, 261, 304,
325, 348
Henrietta Middleton
(--), 279-280
Henrietta Middleton
(Rutledge), 82, 85
Henry Adolphus, 81-82,
84, 253, 261,
278-279
Henry Middleton,
80-83, 85, 91-92,
96-97, 101, 252-253,
257, 261-262,
279-280, 303-304,
325-326, 348-349
Hugh, 264
Irving, 92, 304
Irving Hart, 96, 101,
326, 349
John, 77, 79, 91, 304

SMITH (continued)
Mary Burton
(continued)
364
Mary Burton
(Matthews), 97, 103,
327, 350-351
Mary Middleton, 92,
103, 109, 305, 351,
365
Mary Middleton
Rutledge (Reese), 92,
97, 305, 326-327
Norman Griffith, 23,
35
Norman Griffith Jr, 23
Olivia, 323
Paul Rutledge, 102,
350
Randolph Hooper, 23,
35
Robert, 255, 260
Robert Tilghman, 261
Robert Weston, 31
Rosemary (McDurmon),
222
Roy Walter, 31
Samuel, 92
Samuel Bosworth, 305
Sara Jane (Clyde), 102,
107, 350, 363
Sarah Izard, 315
Sarah Lyons (Izard),
315
Stephanie, 222
Steven Dunham, 111,
354
Steven Dunham Jr, 111,
354
Susan, 104, 110, 351,
366
Susan Pringle, 255,
265
Timothy Asher, 35
Walter Roy, 31
William Burroughs,
126
William Mason,
260-261, 277-278,
300, 323
William Mason III, 300,
323
William Reese, 109,
365
SPAAR/ SPAHR
Diana, 237
Jason, 216
Kenneth, 216

Margot Heyward
(Hamilton), 216
SPARKS
Caroline Heyward, 174
Caroline Heyward
(Gignilliat), 210
Jean Marie, 174, 210,
237
Lois Virginia, 174
W Chester, 174, 210
SPAULDING
Barbara Jean, 185
SPEER
Marian, 141, 160-161
SPENCE
Constanza (Middleton),
281
Edgar, 281
George Bentivoglio
Middleton, 281
John Bowring, 281
SPRATT
Elizabeth K, 205
SPRING
Elizabeth, 341
Margaret Elizabeth,
317
SPURLOCK
Brenda Jean, 38, 42
ST PIERRE
Catherine, 233
STAINBACK
Ida, 64
STALL
Eleanor Johnstone, 171,
207
Helen Heyward
(Wilson), 171, 207
Robert Jennings III,
171
Robert Jennings Jr, 171,
207
Walter Heard, 171
STALLINGS
Eva (Driver), 201
Hulda Truit, 18
James Noah, 201
Linnie Mae, 201, 234
STANFIELD
Christopher Heyward,
210
Jean Marie (Sparks),
210, 237
Jean Rebecca, 210, 237
Joseph William, 237
Joseph William III, 210
Joseph William Jr, 210

STARBUCK
Ella, 15
STEBBING
Claire Hunter, 194
Jonathan Heyward, 194
Nancy Colquitt (Lynah),
194
Nowell, 194
Zoe Elizabeth, 194
STEEDLEY
Charles Joseph, 239
Elizabeth Heyward
(Owens), 239
Heyward Rebecca, 239
Laura Laci, 239
STEEL/ STEELE
Juanita, 22
Margaret, 138
STERLING
Charles Taylor, 361
Daniel Elliott, 345
Elizabeth Huger, 345,
361
Elizabeth Pelzer
(Huger), 345, 361
Hazel Howard, 151,
215
Jennifer Lee (Taylor),
361
John Maxwell III, 345,
361
John Maxwell IV, 361
John Maxwell Jr, 345,
361
Lillian Jenkins
(Howard), 151, 177
Martin, 151, 177
Virginia Dare, 151,
177
STEVENS
Anne Augusta, 54
Florence Heyward, 159,
187
Florence Percy
(McTeer), 187
Frances Herlong, 159
William Turner, 159,
187
William Turner Jr, 159
STEVENSON
--, 90, 303
Alice Amy, 170, 207
Belle Herndon, 54
Carter Littlepage, 54
Eleanor, 303
Eleanor Forney, 90
Horace Lee, 90, 94, 99,
303, 324, 347

TALIAFERIO
Mary Turner, 51
TAPAO
Frances Louise (Butler), 183
Papu, 183
Robert Francis, 183
TATE
Charles Lowndes, 298
Joseph Brackin, 298
May Sabina Lowndes (Scott), 298
TAYLOR
--, 57
A Merrit, 174
Agatha Bernard, 54, 61, 69
Agnes, 51, 54
Alice, 69
Alice Marshall, 69
Ann, 51
Ann Gray, 57
Anna C (Young), 65
Anne "Nannie" Isabella, 56, 64, 72
Anne Heyward, 174
Anne Montgomery, 53, 60
Anne Randolph, 52, 58
Bazil Gordon, 51, 54
Belle Herndon (Stevenson), 54
Bernard Moore, 51, 55
Bernard Pendleton, 57, 65
Blair, 53, 59
Caroline May, 54
Caroline Stevenson (Roberts), 60
Carolyn Glenn (Wills), 39, 42
Carter Stevenson, 55
Catherine, 49
Catherine (Randolph), 52, 57-58
Catherine Randolph, 53
Charles E, 39, 42
Charles Rushman, 133
Charles Shoemaker III, 174
Charles Shoemaker Jr, 174
Charlotte, 56
Constance California, 65, 73, 76
David Watson, 55, 62, 69-70, 74
David Watson III, 70, 74
David Watson Jr, 62, 70, 74
Decima Shubrick (Heyward), 133
Donald Allen, 59
Donna, 74
Dorothy Watson, 62, 69
Edmund, 51, 53, 59-61
Edmund Pendleton, 51-52, 55-56
Elizabeth, 51-52
Elizabeth Lewis, 53, 60, 68
Elizabeth Moore, 52, 55-56, 58, 64, 67
Elizabeth Parker, 66
Emily Winifred Whitby (Allen), 65
Emma, 10
Fanny (Ashby), 54
Florence (Wharton), 65
Florence Ida (Carter), 56, 64
George, 51-52, 57-58
George Carter, 56
George Gray Leiper, 52
George Henry, 53
George William Bagby, 69
Georgianna (Milliman), 133
Georgie May, 133
Gwendolyn Hungerford, 65
Henrietta, 57, 65, 73
Henrietta (Pendleton), 52
Henry, 51-52, 55-57, 61-62, 69
Henry Leiper, 56, 64
Imogen Maury (Morris), 62, 70
Imogen Morris, 62, 70
Ira Hamilton, 129
Isabel DeLeon (Williams), 69
Isabella Nelson (Locke), 56, 63-64
James, 51, 54, 61
James Gray, 55
James Heyward, 133
James Watson, 55
Jean (Geary), 74
Jean Sinclair (Heyward), 174
Jennifer Anne, 39, 42
Jennifer Lee, 361
Joan, 66
John, 50-54, 56-57, 63-64, 66
John Monroe, 56
John Penn, 52
John Thomas, 56
Julia Dunlap (Leiper), 52, 55-57
Julia Kay, 39
Julia Leiper, 52, 57(2)
Julia Watson, 55, 62
Julia Wickham, 57
Leslie Milton, 65
Lucy, 50
Lucy (Penn), 50-52
Lucy (Woodford), 51, 53
Lucy Ashby, 54
Lucy Nelson, 56, 63, 72
Lucy Parke Chamberlayne, 61
Lucy Penn, 51-53, 55, 57, 59, 62-63, 66-67
Lucy Woodford, 53, 59, 68
Margaret Deborah (Parker), 66
Margaret Locke, 56, 64, 73
Marguerite Locke, 66
Maria Heyward, 133
Maria Tallula, 54
Marion (Gordon), 51, 54
Marion Gordon, 55, 61, 69
Mary Blair, 59
Mary Coleman, 62, 70
Mary Deborah (Digges), 66
Mary DeFord, 70
Mary DeFord (Bigelow), 70, 74
Mary Elizabeth (Allen), 59
Mary Gordon, 66
Mary Inglehart, 66
Mary Minor (Watson), 55, 61-62
Mary Minor Watson, 61
Mary Street (Connelly), 129
Mary Watson, 55
Mary Woodford, 51

TOMM (continued)
Anita (deSaussure)
(continued)
360
Charles, 360
Daniel Edward
Harleston, 360
TOONE
Lula, 190
TOUCHEY
Jane Wynne, 196, 229
TOULMIN
Helen, 297
TOWLES
Elizabeth Lewis, 53
TOWNSEND
Caroline Elizabeth, 66
TRACY
Annie Caroline
(Williams), 135
Carlos, 123
Carlos Chandos, 123,
135
Clemm Carlos, 135
Clemm Chandos, 123,
135
Elizabeth Parker, 123
Emma Capers, 135
Emma Heyward
(Parker), 123, 135
Jane Dollar (McLean),
123
Jean McLean, 123
TRAPNELL
Sue, 190
TREADWAY
Robert, 72
TREZEVANT
Ann Sarah, 117-118
Catherine (Crouch),
117
Theodore, 117
TROSDAL
Anne Cuthbert (Lynah),
143, 164
Karen, 164
Lynah, 164
Reider, 143, 164
Reider Arnold, 143,
164
TROTTER
Eliza, 83, 262
TRUMBULL
John, xx
TRYBALSKI
Amy Laura, 204, 236
Ann Cuthbert
(Heyward), 203, 236

Karen Lorraine, 204
Rhonda Susan, 204,
236
Thomas E, 203, 236
TUCKER
Doris Jeanne, 201,
233-234
John Alexander, 198
Karen Evelyn
(Thomas), 198
Kelly Rebecca, 198
Susan, 176, 214
TURNBULL
Jane Elizabeth, 106,
362
TURNER
Alexander Pendleton,
68, 74
Alice Lake (Alexander),
68, 73-74
Ann Madison, 52
Anne Pendleton, 58
Augustine Fitzhugh, 58,
68
Caroline (Smith), 64
David Richard, 73
Eddie Caroline, 89,
302
Edwin Chiledes, 84,
88-89, 278, 301-302
Edwin Chiledes Jr, 84,
89, 278, 301
Elizabeth Robinette, 73,
76
Emily (Beavers), 89,
302
Emma Caroline, 84, 88,
278, 301
Emma Philadelphia
Middleton, 88, 301
Emma Philadelphia
Middleton
(Rutledge), 84, 88-89,
278, 301-302
Harry Vivian, 64, 73
Henrietta, 88, 301
Henry, 64
Henry Adolphus, 84,
89, 278, 302
Isabel Foster (DePass),
204
James Jr, 204
James Turner, 204
Jane Scales (Carpenter),
88, 301
Jannie Belle, 88, 301
John Alexander, 74
Karen Diane

(Lahmann), 74
Margaret Locke
(Taylor), 64, 73
Mary Anne Eliza, 84,
89, 278, 302
Mary Anne Eliza
(Thomas), 84, 278
Mary Elizabeth (Slater),
73, 76
Matthew, 84, 88, 278,
301
Michael Lee, 74
Richard Nelson, 64
Richard Vivian, 64, 73
Sallie Penn (Taylor),
58, 68
Taylor Fitzhugh, 58,
68, 73-74, 76
Taylor Fitzhugh Jr, 68,
73
Virginia (Green), 73
TYLER
John, 77
UNDERHILL
John, 384
UNDERWOOD
Eliza, 83, 87-88, 262,
280-281
Eliza (Trotter), 83, 262
Joseph Rogers, 83, 262
VAN DUSEN
Gretchen, 107, 363
VANCE
Eleanor, 161
VASS
Christine Lynah
(Sherrill), 228
John Sharp, 228
John Sharp Jr, 228
VAUGHAN/ VAUGHN
Marietta, 16
Mary Theodosia, 12
VEETCH
Claire, 311
VENABLE
Jean Sinclair, 149, 174
Jean Sinclair
(Armistead), 149
Samuel Woodson, 149
VEREEN
Geneva, 28
VESEL
Frederick Henry, 357
Julie Ann (Hagen), 357
Lindsay Ann, 357
Travis Prentiss, 357
VINCENT
Josephine Macon, 166,

VINCENT (continued)
Josephine Macon
(continued)
199-200
VON HERZEN
Alexander, 73, 76
Alexander Taylor, 73,
76
Constance California
(Taylor), 73, 76
Elizabeth, 76
Helen (Zoty), 73
Jeannette Elizabeth, 73,
76
Stephanie J (Sarno), 76
Virginia Ellen, 73, 76
VON WEISE
Nancy, 24
VOSS
Joan Carol, 215
WADE
Anne Berry, 338, 355
Lyle Vincent, 338,
354-355
Nancy Theresa, 338,
354
Rita Izard (Hunter),
338, 354-355
WAGONER
Tammy, 38
WAINER
David Samuel, 176,
213-214
David Samuel III, 213
David Samuel Jr, 176,
213
Emma Heyward
(Burnet), 176, 213-214
John Benjamin, 213
Joseph Asher, 213
Katherine Amory, 176,
214, 239
Michael Judah, 213
Nancy Rutledge, 176,
213, 239
Patricia (McCormick),
213
Selah Jean, 213
WALKER
--, 131
Agatha Bernard
(Taylor), 61, 69
Agatha Lewis, 61
Anne Barnwell, 131
Anne Simons (Sinkler),
160
Annie Bull (Barnwell),
131

Annie Sinkler, 160,
189
B Wilson, 160
Carrie Heyward, 131
Clare Frances, 204,
237
Daniel Heyward, 131
David, 61, 69
David Alexander, 209
David Pinckney, 172,
209
David Stewart, 61
Dean Barnwell, 172
Edward Barnwell, 131,
147-148
Edward Barnwell III,
147, 172, 209
Edward Barnwell Jr,
131, 147, 172
Edward Tabb, 131
Edward Thomas, 209
Eliza (Talbot), 379
Elizabeth Guerard
(Heyward), 131,
147-148
Elizabeth Heyward,
148
Ellen (West), 148
Ellen Jael, 172, 208
Ellen Marion
(Jennings), 172,
208-209
Emma Regail, 379
George, 379
George Heyward, 131,
148
John Otey, 61
John Stewart, 61
Joseph Rogers, 131,
147, 172
Joseph Rogers Jr, 172
June (Lomme), 172
Lucy Wilhelmina, 61,
69, 74
Lucy Wilhelmina
(Otey), 61
Mary Margarite (Daily),
209
Michelle Heyward, 172,
209
Norma Stewart, 61
Pinckney Heyward,
147, 172, 208-209
Rhett Barnwell, 172
Rosemary (Lamont),
209
Sarah Donon
(Pinckney), 147, 172

Sarah Elizabeth, 172,
209
Sarah Minge, 378-379
Shirley (Sasso), 172,
209
Susan Dabney, 61
Thomas Heyward, 172,
209
WALLACE/ WALLIS
Anne, 291
Helen Louise, 383
Martha, 65
WALPOLE
Ashley Addison Butler,
194
John William Edings,
194
Patricia Bourne
(Palmer), 194
William, 194
WALSH
Alice, 70
Jean Laverne, 210
Julia, 152
WALTERS
Sharon, 238
Shirley, 191, 228
WALTON
Charles Martin, 197
Dorothy (Camber), 378
Ella Nora, 148, 173
Elsie Leadbetter
(Martin), 197, 231
George, 367, 377-378,
380
George Jr, 378-380
Mary (Hughes), 377
Mary Jean (Wilson),
231
Octavia Celeste, 379
Octavia Celeste
Valentine, 379-380
Richard B, 197, 231
Robert, 377
Robert Davenport, 197
Robert Watkins, 379
Ryan Matthew, 231
Sarah Minge (Walker),
378-379
Thomas Camber, 378
William Howard, 197,
231
William Reid, 231
WARING
Anita Maria Carolina,
103, 110, 351, 366
WARLEY
Alexander Fraser, 273,

WICKHAM (continued)
 Margaret Halsey
  (Gearing)
  (continued)
  (Gearing), 75
 Margaret Johnston
  (Stewart), 72
 Margaret Wallis, 75
 Marjorie Jean, 74
 Marjorie Jean
  (Heidinger), 74
 Virginia (Chesterman),
  75
 Virginia Catherine
  (Chesterman), 71
 Virginia Chesterman,
  71
 William Carter, 55, 62
 William Carter Jr, 71
 William Fanning, 55
 William Fanning II, 63,
  72
 William II, 56
 Williams Carter, 63,
  70, 74
WIDMAN
 Barbara Lee, 35
WIESE
 Leigh Ann, 33
WILCOX
 Arthur, 345
 Arthur Manigault, 321,
  344
 Caroline (Manigault),
  321, 345
 John, 345
 John Walter, 321, 345
 Katharine (Moore), 345
 Margaret, 345
 Mary Huger Manigault,
  321, 345
 Priscilla, 345
 Robert, 345
WILKINS
 Edward, 25
 John Deneil, 218, 240
 Judy (Oltmann), 218,
  240
 Kelly Lynn, 218, 240
 Lillian (Duke), 25
 Loren Deneil, 218, 240
 Pauline, 25
WILKINSON
 Alice, 67
 Arthur Manigault, 273
 Caroline Proctor
  (Huger), 273, 276
 Daniel Elliott Huger,

 260, 277
 Eleonora (Withers),
  260
 Frances, 67
 Frances (Wilkinson),
  67
 Isabella Middleton, 260,
  276, 299
 James Withers, 260,
  273, 276-277
 John Cacique, 277
 Louella, 277
 Maria Louisa, 260, 277,
  300
 Mary Mildred
  (Duncan), 277
 Sarah Elliott (Huger),
  260, 273, 276-277
 Sarah Mildred, 277
 William Withers, 67,
  260, 273, 276
 Willis, 260, 273, 277
WILLARD
 Loretta, 26
WILLIAMS
 Alice (Taylor), 69
 Allen Izard, 291
 Amelia Sarah
  (Richards), 291
 Anne Heyward
  (Mingledorff), 199
 Annie Caroline, 135
 Annie Caroline
  (Campbell), 135
 Arthur Middleton, 292
 Chastine Gillespie, 63,
  72
 David Ramsey, 292
 Edith, 291
 Elizabeth Cleneay, 68
 Helen, 169
 Henrietta Ruby, 291
 Henry Reuben, 291
 Isabel DeLeon, 69
 Jemille Reid, 180
 Julia Davis (Izard), 291
 Julia Emma
  (Middleton), 292
 Julian Rhett, 292
 Lucy Middleton, 292
 Lucy Nelson, 64, 72
 Lucy Nelson (Taylor),
  63, 72
 Margaret Annette, 212,
  238
 Margaret Langley, 189
 Margaret Middleton,
  292

 Marion, 292
 Mark, 199
 Mary, 80, 249
 Mary Anne
  (Whitesides), 292
 Nikki, 39
 Norma Stewart
  (Cleneay), 68
 Oliver Perry, 135
 Ralston McAlpin, 199
 Robert White, 68
 Robert Willoughby, 68
 Sallie Frances (Watts),
  64
 Thomas Hall, 292
 Thomas Hall Jervey,
  292
 William, 69
 William Arthur, 63
 William Taylor, 291
WILLING
 Thomas, xx
WILLIS
 Christopher Robert,
  211
 Kimberly Anne, 211
 Patricia Anne
  (Cockrell), 211
 Sallie Elizabeth, 211
 William Earl, 211
WILLS
 Betty Mae (Long), 25,
  35, 37
 Betty Sue, 25, 37, 41
 Beverly Karen, 26, 37
 Brenda Jean (Spurlock),
  38, 42
 Carolyn Glenn, 26, 39,
  42
 Ceclia Mae (Strowd),
  18, 24-26
 Charles Battle, 13, 18
 Charles Battle Jr, 18
 Cheryl Anne, 26, 38,
  41
 Clarence Lucas, 13, 18,
  26-27
 Clarence Lucas Jr, 18,
  26, 38
 Cordelia (Weaver), 25
 Deborah Fay, 26, 37
 Deborah Leigh, 35
 Donald Thomas, 25
 Dwight DeBerniere, 25
 George Blount, 9
 George DeBerniere, 18,
  26, 37
 Harold Bryant, 18, 25,